PHYSICAL VIOLENCE IN
AMERICAN FAMILIES

PHYSICAL VIOLENCE IN AMERICAN FAMILIES

Risk Factors and Adaptations to Violence in 8,145 Families

Murray A. Straus and Richard J. Gelles

Edited with the Assistance of
Christine Smith

Transaction Publishers
New Brunswick (U.S.A.) and London (U.K.)

First paperback edition 1995
Copyright © 1990 by Transaction Publishers
New Brunswick, New Jersey 08903

This book is printed on acid-free paper that meets the American National Standard for Permanence of Paper for Printed Library Materials.

Library of Congress Catalog Number: 88-27549
ISBN: 0-88738-263-0 (cloth); 1-56000-828-8 (paper)
Printed in the United States of America

Library of Congress Cataloging-in-Publication Data

Straus, Murray Arnold, 1926–
    Physical violence in American families: risk factors and adaptations to violence in 8,145 families/Murray A. Straus and Richard J. Gelles.
    p.   cm.
    Includes index.
    ISBN 0-88738-263-0
    1. Family violence–United States.   I. Gelles, Richard J.   II. Title.
HQ809.3.U5S873   1989
362.8′2—dc19   88-27549
                                                                        CIP

Chapters co-authored by

Noel A. Cazenave
Diane H. Coleman
Ursula G. Dibble
Scott L. Feld
Eileen F. Hargreaves
Gerald T. Hotaling
Debra S. Kalmuss
Glenda Kaufman Kantor
Alan Jay Lincoln
Karl Pillemer
Christine Smith
Jan E. Stets
J. Jill Suitor
Barbara A. Wauchope
Kersti A. Yllo

Contents

Part II. Incidence and Trends

Part III. The Social Psychology of Family Violence

Part V. Violence and the Structure of Society

Part VI. The Aftermath of Family Violence: Coping and
Consequences of Violence

Part VII. Stopping Family Violence

Methodological Appendixes

Preface

The two previous books on the National Family Violence surveys, *Behind Closed Doors: Violence in the American Family* (Straus, Gelles, and Steinmetz, 1980) and *Intimate Violence* (Gelles and Straus, 1988), were written for the general public rather than a scholarly audience. These books in addition to presenting some of the main findings of the research reflected our personal commitment to contributing to reducing family violence. They were intended to reinforce public consciousness of the huge incidence of physical abuse of children and spouses, to make the public more aware of the consequences for physical and mental health of this violence, to show that the major cause of these tragedies is to be found in the nature of the American family and American society, and to make clear that it is within our power to change child abuse and spouse abuse.

These publications have reached a wide audience and continue to do so. The findings have been reported in every major newspaper and on every major TV network. Both of us appear on television several times a year because our research has provided the best data available on the high rate of assaults on spouses and children. The book on the first survey is still in print nine years after publication. It seems reasonable to surmise that our two books have contributed to public awareness of and concern about family violence. The book on the 1975 survey is also widely used as a text. Nevertheless, both books leave a void because neither was intended to meet the needs of the research community. Since they were written for the general public, we could not adequately describe the analytical methods used to arrive at the findings; nor was it possible to present the qualifications and alternative theories and interpretations that are critical for the progress of research on family violence.

We attempted to address the needs of the scholarly community through papers in journals and through unpublished articles. These papers are a rich storehouse of knowledge on family violence and methods of studying family violence. However, they have appeared in many different journals, some of which are not easily obtainable, and others are unpublished. This book therefore brings together some of the most widely relevant of the published articles and 13 new chapters. It makes the storehouse of research findings and research methods accumulated during 13 years of intensive effort more readily accessible. It also makes that material more readable because the repetitive sections on the sample and other methodological details have been edited out of each chapter. In addition, presenting these papers in juxtaposition to each other and in a framework that highlights their underlying methodological and theoretical structure may help to clarify what has and has not been accomplished.

Acknowledgments

This books owes much to a marvelously stimulating and productive research environment—the Family Research Laboratory at the University of New Hampshire.

The contribution of David Finkelhor, the codirector of the Family Research Laboratory, needs special mention. David is one of those scholars who can read a paper, almost invariably identify critical problems, and then suggest such insightful and creative solutions to the problems that you are almost glad the problem existed. Actually, there does not need to be a problem to elicit the workings of David Finkelhor's subtle and creative mind. It is irrepressible. In addition to the contributions this has made to the book, David has been one of the key factors setting the tone of the Family Research Laboratory. In intellectual life, the great spectator sport is observing a fine mind at work. Each meeting of the Family Research Laboratory seminar at which David is present is a big-league event.

A key feature of the Laboratory is a weekly seminar in which we discuss drafts of each others' papers and grant applications. That seminar is a demanding but continuously enriching experience. Most of the chapters in this book were read in draft form by members of the seminar, who then regaled us with an hour and a half of insightful and critical comments. Since the members of the seminar include all but one of the co-authors of the chapters, the co-authors also contributed to other chapters of the book. In addition, we also wish to express our appreciation to the following other members of the seminar: Sharon K. Araji, Saundra G. Atwell, Susan E. Ault, Larry Baron, K. Ann Blessing, Bruce W. Brown, Richard A. Bulcroft, John K. Byrne, Scott F. Brown, Dianne Cyr Carmody, Joseph C. Carroll, Barbara A. Carson, Gregg I. Churchill, Susan E. Craig, Ursula G. Dibble, Colleen M. Donlon, Jean E. Ellison, M. Keith Farrington, Scott L. Feld, Joyce Foss, Jean Giles-Sims, Cathy Stein Greenblat, Linda

M. Harris, Campbell Harvey, Susan C. Herrick, John A. Humphrey, Valerie E. Hurst, David Jaffee, Margaret Kieschnick, David F. King, Geraldine L. King, Dean D. Knudsen, Ralph LaRossa, Robert E. Larzelere, Roger W. Libby, Daniel Lobovits, Bruce K. MacMurray, David W. Moore, Patricia A. Murphy, Amy E. Oppenheimer, Karl Pillemer, Margaret S. Plass, Anne M. Platt, Jason Sachs, Daniel G. Saunders, Richard J. Sebastian, Albert A. Shigo, John A. Shwed, Jane G. Stapleton, Gloria G. Straughn, David B. Sugarman, Linda Meyer Williams, and Kersti A. Yllo.

The primary financial support for the research reported in this book was from three National Institute of Mental Health grants. The first National Family Violence Survey was made possible by grant number MH27557. The second survey was funded by grant MH40027. The work of most of the chapter co-authors was funded by predoctoral and postdoctoral fellowships made possible by NIMH "training grant" T32MH15161. The follow-up of the second survey was funded by National Science Foundation grant SES85202232 to Kirk R. Williams and Murray A. Straus.

The work of the Family Research Laboratory has also been supported by the Graduate School of the University of New Hampshire and by grants for a number of other projects. These grants, although not directly supporting this research, contributed importantly. The presence of the scholars funded by the these grants enabled the Family Research Laboratory to create a true community of scholars. Their support and suggestions have helped produce not only the research described in this book, but also 19 other books and many articles. (A bibliography is available on request.) The granting agencies, in addition to those listed above, include the National Institute of Justice, National Center on Child Abuse and Neglect, Centers for Disease Control, Conrad Hilton Foundation, Eden Hall Foundation, and University of New Hampshire. It is a pleasure to acknowledge the support of these organizations.

Sources of Reprinted Articles

The chapters listed below are reprints or modifications of articles originally published elsewhere. They are reprinted here with the permission of the publishers listed.

Chapter 3 is reprinted from Murray A. Straus, "Measuring Intrafamily Conflict and Violence: The Conflict Tactics (CT) Scales," *Journal of Marriage and the Family*, Vol. 41, No. 1, 1979, pp.75–88.

Chapter 6 is reprinted from Murray A. Straus and Richard J. Gelles, "How Violent Are American Families? Estimates from the National

Family Violence Resurvey and Other Studies," in *New Directions in Family Violence Research,* edited by G. T. Hotaling et al. (Newbury Park, CA: Sage Publications, 1988).

Chapter 7 is reprinted from Murray A. Straus and Richard J. Gelles, "Societal Change and Change in Family Violence from 1975 to 1985 As Revealed by Two National Surveys," *Journal of Marriage and the Family,* Vol. 48, (August), 1986, pp. 465–479.

Chapter 10 is reprinted from Ursula Dibble and Murray A. Straus, "Some Social Structure Determinants of Inconsistency Between Attitudes and Behavior: The Case of Family Violence," *Journal of Marriage and the Family,* Vol. 42, No. 1, 1980, pp. 71–80.

Chapter 11 is reprinted from Murray A. Straus, "Social Stress and Marital Violence in a National Sample of American Families," *Forensic Psychology and Psychiatry,* edited by Fred Wright, Charles Bahn, and Robert W. Rieber.

Chapter 12 is reprinted with permission from Glenda Kaufman Kantor and Murray A. Straus, "The 'Drunken Bum' Theory of Wife Beating," *Social Problems,* Vol. 34, No. 3, 1987, pp. 213–230.

Chapter 13 is reprinted from Jan E. Stets and Murray A. Straus, "The Marriage License as a Hitting License: A Comparison of Dating, Cohabiting, and Married Couples," *Journal of Family Violence,* Vol. 4, 1989.

Chapter 15 is reprinted from Richard J. Gelles and Eileen F. Hargreaves, "Maternal Employment and Violence Toward Children," *Journal of Family Issues,* Vol. 2, No. 4, 1981, pp. 509–530.

Chapter 16 is reprinted from Richard J. Gelles, "Violence and Pregnancy: Are Pregnant Women at Greater Risk of Abuse?" *Journal of Marriage and the Family,* Vol. 50, No. 3, 1988, pp. 841–847.

Chapter 17 is reprinted from Diane H. Coleman and Murray A. Straus, "Marital Power, Conflict, and Violence in a Nationally Representative Sample of American Couples," *Violence and Victims,* Vol. 1, No. 2, 1986, pp. 141–157.

Chapter 19 is reprinted from Noel A. Cazenave and Murray A. Straus, "Race, Class, Network Embeddedness, and Family Violence: A Search for Potent Support Systems," *Journal of Comparative Family Studies,* Vol. 10, No. 3 (Autumn 1979), pp. 280–299.

Chapter 21 is reprinted from Debra S. Kalmuss and Murray A. Straus, "Wife's Marital Dependency and Wife Abuse," *Journal of Marriage and the Family,* Vol. 44, No. 2 (May 1982), pp. 277–286.

Chapter 22 is reprinted from Kersti A. Yllo and Murray A. Straus, "Patriarchy and Violence Against Wives: The Impact of Structural and Normative Factors," *International Journal of Comparative Social Welfare,* Vol. 1, No. 1 (Fall 1984). The version published in that journal is an abridgement of the chapter appearing in this book.

Chapter 23 is reprinted from Murray A. Straus, "Ordinary Violence, Child Abuse, and Wife Beating: What do They Have in Common?" *The Dark Side of Families: Current Family Violence Research,* edited by D. Finkelhor, R. J. Gelles, G. T. Hotaling, and M. A. Straus (Newbury Park, CA: Sage, 1983).

Chapter 24 is reprinted from Richard J. Gelles and Murray A. Straus, "The Costs of Family Violence, Preliminary Results from a National Survey," *Public Health Reports,* November–December 1987.

Chapter 25 is reprinted from Gerald T. Hotaling and Murray A. Straus with Alan J. Lincoln, "Violence in the Family and Violence and Other Crime and Violence Outside the Family," *Crime and Justice, An Annual Review of Research,* edited by M. Tonry and L. Ohlin (Chicago: University of Chicago Press, 1989).

Chapter 27 is reprinted from Scott L. Feld and Murray A. Straus, "Escalation and Desistance of Violence In Marriage," *Criminology,* Vol. 27, 1989, pp. 141–161.

Part I
RESEARCHING FAMILY VIOLENCE

1

The National Family Violence Surveys

Murray A. Straus

This book brings together the methods and findings of two landmark studies: the National Family Violence Survey conducted in 1975 and the National Family Violence Resurvey of 1985. These two studies are landmarks in the field of family violence in several senses. First, the 1975 study represents the earliest attempt to measure the incidence of violence in a large and representative sample of American families. Second, the availability of data on a representative sample enabled researchers to move beyond the "individual pathology" model of family violence (Gelles, 1974; Gelles and Straus, 1979) to investigate underlying social causes. Finally, use of the same measures of violence in the two surveys allowed us to examine national trends in the incidence of family violence over that ten-year period.

The Samples

The National Family Violence Surveys are the only nationally representative studies of family violence.[1] Before 1975 the empirical research was based on an insufficient number of cases or samples that represent special populations, such as students or women who have gotten help from a shelter for battered women. There are obvious limitations to how far one can generalize on the basis of samples of university students about their families—the method we first used to gather data on intrafamily violence (Straus, 1971, 1973).

There are also limits on what is possible with studies of families that have come to public attention (e.g., police intervention), or clients of battered women's shelters, or of men in treatment programs for batterers. Data on those groups are extremely important because police departments and shelters need information about the people they will actually deal with and such studies provide that information. However, studies based on "clinical" samples run the risk of what has been called the "clinical fallacy" because the information may not apply to families where the wife has been assaulted but the husband was not arrested or the wife did not seek help from a shelter for battered women. These are the overwhelming majority of cases. The police intervene or the wife goes to a shelter in only a tiny proportion of cases of wife beating. For example, the 1985 survey found that an arrest was made in only 1% of the cases involving assaults on wives (see Chapter 25). So research based on samples from police records or clients of safe houses, such as Dobash and Dobash (1979), leaves out 99% of all assaulted wives. At the same time, the fact that clinical populations tend to be different from populations who seem to exhibit the same problem but are not receiving treatment suggests that it may be dangerous to base treatment methods on findings from epidemiological surveys such as the two National Family Violence Surveys. In Chapter 5, I call this the "representative sample fallacy."

The importance of a large as well as a representative sample also needs to be emphasized. The 2,143 families in the first survey, together with the 6,002 in the second survey, may be more than the combined number of cases in all other research on family violence so far. The decision to interview six thousand couples for the second survey was particularly difficult because, with a limited budget, this meant a shorter interview and therefore not obtaining much important information that we obtained on the families in the first survey. However, one of the purposes of the 1985 survey was to determine if there had been a change in the rates of child abuse and spouse abuse between 1975 and 1985 (see Chapter 7). Even the large differences we found would not have been statistically reliable had we done the 1985 survey with the same number of cases as were studied in 1975. This is because the behavior being studied has a low "base rate." For example, "only" about 4% of American wives report being severely assaulted in 1985. In addition, there are groups in the population such as unmarried cohabiting couples who, although a small percentage of the total, are theoretically important. If such couples have the same incidence of assault on a partner as married couples, the number of violent cohabiting couples in a sample of 6,002 is : (6002 * .04 * .04) = 9.6. Thus, even starting with a sample of six thousand, only about ten cases of violent cohabiting couples would be available for analysis. Thus a large number of families must be surveyed in order to have sufficient numbers of violent families to carry out statistical analyses.

Appendix 1 describes how the samples were selected and other information about how the two surveys were conducted. One point to note on the terminology used in this book concerns the fact that unmarried cohabiting couples were included in both surveys. For some purposes the cohabiting couples were analyzed separately from the married couples (e.g., Chapter 13). Unless stated otherwise, we treated cohabitation as simply one of many variations in the family, in which case terms such as *marital, spouse, wife,* and *husband* are used to refer to all couples, regardless of whether they are married or nonmarried cohabiting persons.[2]

The Conflict Tactics Scales

The second way in which these two surveys are landmarks lies in the method of gathering the data that made them possible—the Conflict Tactics Scales (CTS). Before the 1975 survey few people believed it would be possible to knock on the door of a random sample of households and be able to obtain data on the incidence and extent of violent acts between members of that household. Gelles's pioneer study of *The Violent Home* (1974) demonstrated that one could obtain such information by personal interviews. However, the great advantage of that study—its use of in-depth qualitative interviews—made it unsuitable for large epidemiological surveys. The insights gained from exploratory interviews conducted by Straus in 1971 and from Gelles's 1974 study provided the basis for an instrument to measure family violence that is suitable for use in large-scale surveys: the Conflict Tactics Scales.

As its name implies, the CTS is designed to measure a variety of behaviors used in conflicts between family members. The tactics fall into three general modes: rational discussion, termed Reasoning; verbal or nonverbal acts that symbolically hurt the other, termed Verbal Aggression; and the use of physical aggression, termed Violence. The CTS is now the most widely used method of obtaining data about physical violence in families. It is the means of measuring family violence in over 200 papers and 5 books.

Since almost all the chapters in this book are based on data obtained through the use of the CTS, it is desirable to gain an understanding of this instrument by reading Chapter 3—the basic methodological and theoretical source on the CTS. However, by way of summary, a brief description of the CTS is given below.

As indicated above, the CTS measures behaviors or tactics used in response to a conflict or anger situation during the previous 12 months, rather than the substantive issue giving rise to the anger or conflict. Indeed, there may have been conflicts over a number of issues. The CTS asks respondents to recall the times "in the past year" when they and their partner "disagree on major decisions, get annoyed about something the other person does, or just have spats or fights because they're in a bad mood or tired or for some other reason."

The instructions go on to say: "I'm going to read a list of some things that you and your partner might have done when you had a dispute and would like you to tell me for each one how often you did it in the past year." The list begins with the items from the Reasoning scale, such as "Discussed the issue calmly," goes on to the items in the Verbal Aggression scale, such as "Insulted or swore at the other," and ends with the Physical Aggression or "Violence" or "Assault" items, such as "Threw something at [the child or partner]."

The Violence items are further subdivided into "Minor" and "Severe" Violence. The Minor Violence items are threw something at the other family member; pushed, grabbed, or shoved; and slapped or spanked. The Severe Violence items are kicked, bit, or punched; hit or tried to hit with an object; beat up; choked, or for parent-to-child violence burned or scalded; threatened with a knife or gun; and used a knife or gun. These items have been used to create a number of measures. The following are the most frequently used of these (others are described in the chapters where they are used and in Appendix B):

Overall Violence: the use of any of the above acts.

Minor Violence: use of the minor violence acts, but not any of the acts in the severe violence list.

Severe Violence: use of any of the acts in the severe violence list. Almost all such persons have also engaged in minor assaults. The severe violence index is the way in which we usually measured "child abuse" and "wife beating."

Very Severe Violence: This measure was created because hitting a child with certain objects, such as hairbrush or belt, is often considered part of traditional physical punishment, rather than "abuse." Omitting the "hit with object" item leaves a list of acts that are indubitably abusive and therefore come closer to the popular conception of child abuse. In some chapters this is identified as the "Child Abuse-1" rate and the Severe Violence Index is called the "Child Abuse-2" rate.

The Social Causes of Family Violence

A third way in which the two National Family Violence Surveys are landmark studies is that they provide a large body of evidence suggesting that the major causes of physical violence in the family are to be found in certain basic characteristics of the American family and American society. Among these characteristics are male dominance in the family and the society and millions of people living in poverty in one of the wealthiest societies in human history.

This is not to say that the two surveys were the first manifestation of the theoretical perspective that looks to characteristics of the society (rather than the characteristics of individual persons) as the causes of violence. There is a long tradition of such research in sociology (see for example Curtis, 1974; Gil, 1970; Loftin and Hill, 1974; Wolfgang and Ferracuti, 1967). It has been the theoretical core of our research since 1970, as illustrated by articles on the social causes of both ordinary physical punishment (Straus, 1971) and child abuse (Gelles, 1973), male dominance, and wife beating (Straus, 1973) and an entire book devoted to *The Social Causes of Husband-Wife Violence* (Straus and Hotaling, 1980). However, these studies either were theoretical analysis or used inadequate empirical data. The National Family Violence Surveys changed that radically. Analyses of these large and nationally representative samples of families reported in Parts III, IV, and V reveal that a large proportion of the variance in wife beating and child abuse is linked to the social characteristics of the families and their position in society.

A More Comprehensive Analysis of Violence

Still another way in which these surveys broke new ground is that they breached the pattern of basing research on interviews with battered women. It is critically important that assailants also be studied. In both 1975 and 1985 about half of the respondents were husbands and half were wives. It would have been even better to study husbands and wives in the same household. But just the fact that we were able to obtain data from aggressors as well as victims resulted in unique and controversial findings.

Until the 1975 study, research on family violence was focused on either child abuse *or* spouse abuse. There do not seem to have been studies that gathered data on both, despite the obvious theoretical links (Gelles and Straus, 1979). The 1975 survey broke new ground by obtaining data on both child abuse and spouse abuse and also data on sibling abuse and physical abuse of parents by children. This enabled us to investigate the links between different types of family violence.

Trend and Panel Studies

The two National Family Violence Surveys are unique in still another respect. The same method of measuring violence was used in both studies.

This made it possible to provide information on the much-debated question of whether child abuse and wife beating have been increasing. No other data exist that can provide information on changes in the rate of child abuse and spouse abuse during the 10-year period between the two surveys.

The annual tabulations of child abuse cases known to Child Protective Services in each of the states seem to provide information on change in the incidence of child abuse. These figures have been increasing at a compound annual rate of about 10% per year since the statistics were first gathered in 1976 (American Association for Protecting Children, 1986). However, it is almost certain that child abuse did not increase at this rate (if at all) between 1975 and 1985.

As explained in Chapter 7, the increase in "officially reported" cases of child abuse represents an increase in the number of "interventions" or "treatments" for child abuse, not an increase in the number of abused children. The real rate could have remained the same or been decreasing or increasing. Only a comparison of rates derived from "epidemiological surveys" such as the 1975 and 1985 surveys could even begin to provide data on this issue.

Finally, both the 1975 and the 1985 surveys provide the basis for future studies that can and should be extended into the future. If the basic procedure is replicated again in 1995 and 2005 it will provide the nation with a unique time series on this important social indicator. We have not made plans for such work, but it seems highly likely that there will be resurveys in the future.

On the other hand, we have already used the 1985 survey as the baseline year for a three-wave panel study (see Chapter 27). The families interviewed in 1985 were reinterviewed in 1986 and 1987, and we may try to locate them again after five years in 1992. Thus the trend studies using 1975 as the base year and the panel studies using 1985 as the base year mean that the work described in this book will be the basis for important research continuing into the next century.

Differences and Similarities between the Two Surveys

Since the 1985 survey provides the most current data and is based on a larger and therefore more dependable sample, why does this book include analyses based on both surveys? Mainly because some issues require data that are only available in the 1975 study and others require data that are only available in the 1985 study. The 1975 and 1985 surveys have certain things in common but are distinctive in other ways.

Among the common elements are the use of the CTS and certain demographic information. However, the measurement of violence in the 1985 survey went beyond the 1975 survey by adding supplemental questions to deal with some important issues that the CTS was not designed to answer. These include which marital partner hit first and whether the violence resulted in an injury.

Despite these similarities, the main objectives of the 1975 and 1985 surveys differ in fundamental ways. The main objective of the 1975 survey was to gather information that could be used to test causal theories. For example, the 1975 survey included a measure of "decision power" in the family to test the theory that the more male-dominant the family, the higher the rate of wife beating.

As much as we would have liked to include measures such as the "decision power" questions in the 1985 study, that was not possible for two reasons. First, the 1985 interviews were shorter (30 versus 60 minutes in 1975). Second, the primary objective of the 1985 survey was to obtain information on how families cope with violence and information on the consequences of the violence on physical and mental health. These questions required every minute of interview time that was not allocated to measuring violence and to the minimum set of family demographic characteristics.

Critics of the National Surveys

Although the research reported in this book probably constitutes the most widely cited and widely respected body of research on physical violence in families (see for example Morash, 1986), some reviewers of our research have been skeptical and others consider the results erroneous. In addition to the inevitable limitations and problems of all real research, there are also a number of reasons for the criticisms that arise because we investigated issues that are the focus of strong value commitments. We ourselves had to overcome some of these value-based problems.

Conceptual Blinders

There are powerful social and psychological forces that interfere with even perceiving the fact that there is a great deal of violence in families (see Steinmetz and Straus, 1974: Chapter 1). I had been studying families for 20 years before a variety of circumstances led me to "discover" family violence in 1970. This omission is particularly glaring because my research was then focused on how families solve problems and the effect of a frustrating problem on family relationships. That research had been in progress for several years and had produced a book (Aldous, Condon,

Hill, Straus, and Tallman, 1971) and many articles, including a focus on power and gender differences (see for example Straus, 1968; Straus and Straus, 1968). There is not a word in any of these publications about the use of physical violence to deal with family problems, yet over 90% of all parents of three year olds use spanking or slapping to deal with problems with their children (see Chapter 8, Figure 1 and Chapter 23, Figure 4).

Sociological Critics

In addition to the perceptual blocks, scholars engaged in research on a "sensitive" issue like family violence must overcome strong barriers to this type of research in the institutional and political structure of social science.

The criticisms and doubts about the research reported in this book began long before these surveys. Our first preliminary efforts in the early 1970's were regarded with skepticism by those who believed it was not possible to obtain data on intrafamily violence through survey research methods. These skeptics argued that almost no one would disclose such information and that those who did would be unrepresentative. They thus defined the possibilities so that it was heads you lose and tails I win.

When our initial studies started to reveal extremely high rates of intra-family violence, there was again wide skepticism, but this time it was charges of exaggeration and sensationalism. A family therapist also told me that the findings were implausible. He said he deals with couples in conflict every day yet almost never encounters physical violence. How-ever, when asked if a question about hitting was a standard part of his intake questions, the answer was "no." I then suggested he try asking the next 10 new couples if any hitting had occurred. It turned out that one or more violent incidents had occurred in seven of these ten cases. Thus even a simple question can reveal the "hidden" world of family violence and also show that it is hidden mainly because we close our eyes to it. At the same time, more refined techniques are needed like the CTS described in Chapters 3, 4, and 5.

There were also political obstacles to conducting research on intrafamily violence. First, there is the politics of science. For example, one paper and a grant application were rejected, at least in part because some reviewers regarded the topic as "trendy" and therefore, by definition, not theoretically important. The irony of this obstacle is that the issue of family violence gets at some of the core theoretical issues concerning the nature of the family (Goode, 1971; Gelles and Straus, 1979; Steinmetz and Straus, 1974: Chapter 1). The effort to formulate and test theories of family violence is at least as fundamental as the effort to explain such aspects of the family as gender role differentiation and power. Indeed, one cannot be understood without the other. Yet because violence is also a "social problem," even efforts to formulate and test theories of family violence are regarded as "applied" research and thereby denigrated in the value hierarchy of science.

Feminist Critics

Research on wife beating was stimulated and aided by the women's movement (Straus, 1974). At the same time the fact that wife beating became a feminist issue also created problems because it embroiled us in the politics of the women's movement. These problems were precipitated by an unfortunate combination of two factors. First, the findings reported in Chapter 6 revealed that in contrast to their behavior outside the family, within the family women are about as violent as men. Second, our research tended to use quantitative methods. This is contrary to a school of feminist scholarship which holds that quantitative methods are inherently male oriented and distort the reality of women's lives. Our research no doubt seemed to be a glaring example of what these critics saw as the inherent defects and biases of quantitative research. As a result, some of us became the object of bitter scholarly and personal attacks, including threats and attempts at intimidation. Chapters 4 and 5 discuss the substance of this feminist critique.

In the late 1970's and early 1980's my public presentations were sometimes obstructed by booing and shouting and in one case picketing. In elections for office in scientific societies I was labeled an antifeminist despite being a pioneer feminist researcher on wife beating (see for example Straus, 1973, 1976).

Ironically, coincidental with attacks from some feminists, I was also denounced by political and religious conservatives such as Jerry Falwell as being antifamily for arguing that eliminating the concept of the husband as the "head of the household" would help reduce wife beating. In addition to the protest letters that I received (two of which were accompanied by Bibles), letters were also sent to members of congress and to the National Institute of Mental Health demanding that the grant for this research be terminated.

Suzanne K. Steinmetz, a coinvestigator in the first National Family Violence Survey, was the victim of more severe attacks. There was a letter-writing campaign at the time she was considered for promotion urging that it be denied. There were phone calls threatening her and her family and a bomb threat at a conference where she spoke.

As suggested earlier, the intensity of the feminist attack was an outgrowth of a double transgression—the sin of reporting evidence that women assault their spouses and children and the sin of using quantitative methods. The first of these sins, in the view of the critics, is an outgrowth of the second.

Our own methodological assumption is that a full understanding of family violence (or any other aspect of human behavior) depends on the use of a multifaceted approach. Within the scope of a single research *project* it is desirable to use both qualitative and quantitative methods, but for practical reasons this is often not possible. However, within the scope of a research *field* or research issue, it is essential that this type of triangulation occur because each approach brings into focus aspects of a phenomenon that are hidden to other approaches. This perspective is the opposite of that taken by the critics of our research who state or imply that *only* qualitative methods can provide an adequate understanding of the phenomenon.

In the field of family violence research, this type of methodological monism has been vigorously asserted by a number of authors, such as Dobash and Dobash (1979, 1983, 1984), Breines and Gordon (1983), and Stark and Flitcraft (1983). Breines and Gordon, for example, after asserting that they are "committed to empirical research" (which they correctly hold need not be quantitative), go on to deny the validity of quantitative empirical research by equating it with what they call "empiricist" research. The problem is that their definition of "empiricist" is a caricature of quantitative research, but they nonetheless imply that quantitative equals empiricist.

Breines and Gordon define empiricist research as studies that ask only questions answerable by yes or no and that do not involve questions of social and cultural meaning (Breines and Gordon, 1983:492–493). However, *all* quantitative research (regardless of whether the study goes beyond yes or no questions and regardless of whether it takes into account cultural factors, gender, etc.) is labeled as "empiricist" and, by implication, invalid. For example, they condemn Kalmuss and Straus's study of the impact of the women's movement on services for battered women (1983) and Yllo and Straus's study of state-to-state differences in gender inequality (Chapter 22) because "Even [this] more overtly feminist work to have emerged from this school of family violence sociology is empiricist" (Breines and Gordon, 1983:509). Since both of these studies are investigations in which gender, cultural norms, structured inequality, etc., are among the fundamental issues of the research and since neither use yes or no questions, it seems that any quantitative research is "empiricist" in the eyes of Breines and Gordon.

However, as noted previously, the feminist criticism of our research is not simply a reflection of methodological absolutism. It also seems to reflect a belief on the part of some feminists that women can do no wrong and anyone who discloses wrongdoing by women must be using incorrect methods, be a misogynist, or both. This can be seen by comparing Breines and Gordon's evaluation of David Finkelhor's research with their evaluation of the research reported in this book. They condemn this research because it is quantitative but praise the research of David Finkelhor, which also used quantitative methods. It is not implausible to suggest that the reason for the differential evaluation of David Finkelhor's research on sexual abuse of children, even though it is quantitative, is that, at least up to the time Breines and Gordon's article was written, Finkelhor had not yet published studies showing sexual abuse by women.

Other feminist critics seem to be so eager to discredit the findings of the National Family Violence Surveys (and other research done using the Conflict Tactics Scales that shows high rates of intrafamily violence by women) that they ascribe theoretical assumptions to us that were never stated or implied and are often opposite to what we have clearly stated. For example, Stark and Flitcraft (1983:342) make a number of assertions that even the most casual reading of our work would show to be false. Stark and Flitcraft claim that we "see violence prone families as a deviant subtype" whereas a central tenet of our research is that intrafamily violence is normative (Gelles and Straus, 1979; Straus, 1974, 1976). They also assert that we "set aside the . . . distinction between conflict and violence," whereas a central point in the conceptual underpinning of the CTS (see Chapter 3) is that there are many modes of trying to resolve a conflict, including the three (reasoning, verbal aggression, and violence) measured by the CTS. Stark and Flitcraft claim that we attribute violence in families to "social heredity" whereas in almost every publication we stressed the multiplicity of causes of intrafamily violence, including cultural norms tolerating violence, male dominance in the family and society, the stresses created by poverty and racism, etc. (see Straus, 1976, 1977a, b, 1980; Straus, Gelles, and Steinmetz, 1980: Chapters 10, 18, 19, and 21). Finally, Stark and Flitcraft claim we argue that violence can be prevented only if conflict is suppressed. The ridiculousness of attributing this view to us can be gauged by the opening sentence of the article on the CTS (reprinted as Chapter 3): "Conflict theorists present a convincing case showing that conflict is an inevitable part of all human association." The article goes on to point out that while conflict may be inevitable, the use of violence to resolve conflict is not.

The dissatisfaction of certain feminists with our research is perhaps best illustrated by the history of the Conflict Tactics Scales (CTS)—the instrument that made it possible to conduct two national surveys on intrafamily violence, which has been widely used by other investigators and which is increasingly used for clinical diagnosis and evaluation of treatment. The incidence rates made possible by the development of this instrument and its use in epidemiological surveys were at first welcomed by feminists. The high rate of wife beating was used to press the case for funding shelters and other services for battered women.

Despite these major contributions to the campaign against wife beating, the CTS became anathema to many feminist scholars. This was not always the case. As noted above, the criticism began when use of the CTS revealed that within the family women have approximately the same rate of physical assault against partners as men. Some feminist scholars were unwilling to accept the empirical evidence, now confirmed by at least a dozen studies (see Chapter 6). One of the ways they attempted to reconcile their denial of female violence with the empirical data was by attacking the integrity of the instrument and those who use it, even to the point of implying deliberate distortion of the data (see Pleck, Pleck, Grossman, and Bart, 1977, and the reply by Steinmetz, 1978). Chapters 4 and 5 were written partly in response to these critics of the Conflict Tactics Scales, but mainly as a guide for the growing number of researchers who use this instrument.

The Issues

Each of these two national surveys has its advantages and limitations. Together we believe that they have enabled us to deal with some of the major issues concerning physical violence within American families. The specific questions addressed in each of the seven parts of the book include

Part I. Researching Family Violence

- Is it possible to obtain reliable and valid information on physical abuse of children and of spouses in a form that is useful for researchers and clinicians?

Part II. Incidence and Trends

- How often does violence occur in American families, including assaults by parents, spouses, and children?
- Is child abuse and spouse abuse increasing, and if so how fast?
- To what extent do physical punishment and physical abuse of children differ according to the age and gender of the child and the gender and socioeconomic status of the parent?

Part III. The Social Psychology of Family Violence

- How does gender affect:
  —Reporting of family violence in surveys
  —Who hits first
  —How much physical injury occurs
  —Psychological problems of victims
- What is the relationship between attitudes about violence and behavior, and what influences that relationship?
- Is there really a relationship between stress and wife beating, or does it take some other variable in combination with stress?
- Is there any truth to the popular image of wife beaters as "drunken bums"?

Part IV. Family Organization and Family Violence

- Does getting married increase the risk of violence compared to what happens among dating and cohabiting couples?
- Do women in the paid labor force have the same rate of child abuse as housewives?
- Are pregnant women at greater risk of being assaulted than other women?
- Male-dominant marriages are more violent. But is this true if both husband and wife agree that he should have the final say?
- Why are older people less likely to hit a family member? Is it due to cohort effects, social factors, or some independent effect of age?

Part V. Violence and the Structure of Society

- What difference is there in rates of child abuse and spouse abuse between Black, Hispanic, and non-Hispanic White families?
- To what extent are the differences "spurious" due to social factors?
- Do battered women stay because they are economically dependent on their partner?
- Is inequality between men and women outside the family related to wife beating?

Part VI. The Aftermath of Family Violence: Coping and Consequences of Violence

- Do physical punishment and physical abuse increase the risk of child abuse and spouse abuse in the next generation?
- Is there a relationship between violence in the family and violence and other crime outside the family?

- Do battered women have more medical and psychological problems than other women?

Part VII. Stopping Family Violence

- Once it starts, does wife beating usually continue and escalate?
- To what extent do the police intervene in wife beating?
- Is "primary prevention" of family violence (as compared to treatment of existing cases) possible, and what are some of the steps needed to prevent family violence?

Notes

1. We do not consider the National Crime Survey to be a survey of family violence because most respondents did not perceive assaults by a spouse as a "crime." Therefore, few such assaults were reported, and those which were reported are unrepresentative of the typical assault by a spouse (see Chapter 27, Note 1 for further explanation).
2. See Smith and Straus (1988), Yllo (1978), and Yllo and Straus (1981) for analysis of differences and similarities between married and cohabiting couples in the two surveys.

2

Methodological Issues in the Study of Family Violence

Richard J. Gelles

A review of the table of contents of social science journals published prior to 1970 would uncover virtually no articles on family violence. Readers would be left convinced that family violence was not a significant social problem. The reports of child abuse or occasional wife abuse that were tucked away in the middle pages of newspapers, emblazoned on the front pages of the *National Enquirer,* or presented as clinical case studies in social service and medical journals appeared to be rare aberrations that most certainly were the product of the mental illness of the offenders.

Today we know that violence in the home is a significant social problem with an estimated incidence far greater than the risk of experiencing violence on the streets (Straus, Gelles, and Steinmetz, 1980:49). Research points to a problem that is not confined to a few mentally ill or emotionally disturbed individuals. Battered wives are not the cause of their victimization, nor are those who remain in violent homes masochists.

With the vision of hindsight we now assemble historical records and uncover centuries of violence and abuse between family members (see for example Bakan, 1971; DeMause, 1974, 1975; Radbill, 1980; and Shorter, 1975). Additional research reveals that the pattern of violent family relationships cuts across cultures (Gelles and Cornell, 1983; Korbin, 1981; Taylor and Newberger, 1979). Finally, research finds violence in virtually all family relations—victims not only include children and women, but young and elderly parents, siblings, and dating partners.

That there has been an explosion of research on all facets of family violence is obvious even to a casual consumer of the professional literature. Although there is an abundance of research, the collected body of knowledge is diverse, often contradictory; and frequently the data collected, and even published, fail to meet stringent standards of empirical evidence. The uninformed conventional wisdoms of the 1960's and 1970's have been replaced with semi-informal and ill-informed conventional wisdoms of the 1980's.

This chapter reviews methodological issues in the study of family violence. Our review covers the standard issues of research design—conceptual issues, sources of data, sampling, and measurement. Although the issues are the same as those that confront any social scientist, the context of research is unique. The family is a private and intimate social institution. As a unique social group, the family presents special challenges and constraints for social scientists. Add to this the fact that violence, like mental illness, suicide, and sexuality, is a taboo topic that is infrequently discussed in private, let alone with strangers. Finally, and perhaps an equally salient methodological issue, the study of family violence is often governed more by the heart than the head. Emotions run high among those who have responsibility for serving, treating, protecting, or understanding victims of violence and abuse. There is so much tragedy, anger, frustration, and ultimately cynicism involved in working with violent families that rational thought and logic—the very foundation of research design—are often left behind.

Major Questions in the Study of Family Violence

In the first decade of research on domestic violence, questions about the extent of the problem dominated the research and policy agenda. Answering the questions with scientific data was aimed at exploding the myth that violence in the home is rare. Another goal was to convince policymakers, opinion leaders, and the public that the various forms of domestic violence were extensive enough to be considered legitimate social problems—especially since one part of the definition of a social problem is that a behavior is found harmful to a *significant* number of people (Merton and Nisbet, 1976). Finally, social scientists required data on the incidence of family violence in order to plan more theoretical research.

A second question focused on identifying the correlates of family violence. Here too, answers were needed to deflate the conventional wisdom that violent family members and abusers suffered from some form of personality disorder or psychopathology. A third dominant question concerned the causes of violence in the home.

In the second decade of research on family violence two additional questions have been added to the list of research concerns. One question focuses on the consequences of experiencing and observing domestic violence. The statement that abused children grow up to be abusers is reported so often in the professional and lay literature that it is considered by many to be a deterministic truism. Yet precious little prospective evidence has actually been collected on the relationship between experiencing violence as a child and later violent behavior as an adult. Similarly, many researchers, clinicians, and the public in general presume that experiencing violence produces lifelong psychic and social scars. Yet, again, although this seems to be a reasonable assumption, there is very little scientific evidence to indicate what proportion of victims experience such effects and why some victims do not.

Finally, a recent concern has turned to the effectiveness of various forms of intervention and treatment. Researchers and clinicians alike are interested in the effectiveness and impact of the various intervention and treatment strategies that were developed once family violence was placed on the public agenda as a major social problem.

This chapter will not attempt to answer these questions. The central concern of this chapter is not with *what* we know about family violence, but with *how we know it.* We will, however, review some of the research on family violence as a means of illustrating some of the methodological issues in the field.

Issues of Definition

Thus far we have used the terms *violence, abuse, domestic violence, intimate violence,* and *family violence* interchangeably, without defining any of these concepts. One of the major problems that confronts investigators who attempt to study domestic violence has been the quagmire of conceptual dilemmas encountered. The terms *violence* and *abuse* are often used interchangeably by those who study domestic violence. These concepts, however, are not conceptually equivalent. Moreover, there is considerable variation in how each concept is nominally defined.

Defining Abuse

The first form of family violence that was uncovered and recognized as a problem was child abuse or the battered child syndrome. The first widely disseminated article defined the battered child syndrome as a clinical condition (with diagnosable physical and medical symptoms) having to do with those children who have been injured deliberately by physical assault by a parent or caretaker (Kempe et al., 1962). The term *battered child syndrome* quickly gave way to terms such as *child abuse, child abuse and neglect,* and *child maltreatment.* The term *abuse* was not only applied to physical assault, but also to malnutrition, failure to thrive, sexual exploitation, educational neglect, medical neglect, and emotional abuse. The official federal definition of child abuse, stated in the Child Abuse Prevention and Treatment Act of 1974 (PL 93-237) was

> . . . the physical or mental injury, negligent treatment, or maltreatment of a child under the age of eighteen by a person who is responsible for the child's welfare under circumstances which would indicate that the child's health or welfare is harmed or threatened thereby.

This definition has consequences for research methodology because it became the model for state definitions, which are in turn the basis for state statutes that require the reporting of suspected cases of child abuse and neglect. This in turn is consequential (as we shall see below) because the vast majority of investigations of child abuse begin by operationally defining child abuse as those cases that are reported to official agencies and are determined to be valid cases of abuse. Also, the federally financed compilations of officially reported child abuse and neglect (American Humane Association, 1983) employ this as the nominal definition of abuse. Thus most official report data, which are the data used in the majority of studies of child abuse, are influenced, to one degree or another, by the federal definition.

It would be a mistake, however, to assume that since there is a federal definition, there is uniformity in how child abuse is norminally defined by researchers. In point of fact, most studies of child abuse and violence toward children cannot be compared to one another because of the wide variation of nominal definitions employed by investigators. While some researchers study violence toward children (see for example Gelles, 1978), others examine the full range of acts of commission and omission (see for example Newberger et al., 1977). As a result, reports of incidence, correlations, causes, and consequences vary from study to study for many reasons, one being that researchers define child abuse differently and are therefore investigating different phenomena.

To a lesser extent, the same definitional problems that have plagued the study of child abuse and violence toward children have been part of the development of research on violence toward women. Initial definitions of wife abuse focused on acts of damaging physical violence directed toward women by their spouses or partners (see for example Gelles, 1974; Martin, 1976). As wife abuse became recognized as a social problem, the definition of abuse was broadened to include sexual abuse, marital rape, and even pornography (London, 1978).

Defining Violence

Violence has also proven to be a concept that is not easily defined. First, *violence* has frequently been used interchangeably with the term *aggression*. While *violence* refers to a physical act, *aggression* refers to any malevolent act that is intended to hurt another person. The hurt may not be only physical, but may be emotional injury or material deprivation. Second, because of the negative connotation of the term *violence,* some investigators have tried to differentiate between hurtful violence and more legitimate acts. Thus Goode (1971) tried to distinguish between legitimate acts of force and illegitimate acts of violence. Spanking a child who runs into the street might be considered force, while beating the same child would be violence. Attempts to clarify the concept of violence have demonstrated the difficulty of distinguishing between legitimate and illegitimate acts. Offenders, victims, bystanders, and agents of social control often accept and tolerate many acts between family members that would be considered illegitimate if committed by strangers (Gelles. 1974; Gelles and Straus, 1979; Straus and Lincoln, 1985).

Additional theoretical and ideological concerns influence the ways in which the concept of violence is defined. Violence is frequently a political concept used to attract attention to undesirable behaviors or situations. Thus some members of the political left define various federal programs, such as Aid to Families with Dependent Children, as violent. The far left defines the entire capitalistic system as violent. Members cf the political right likewise claim that abortion is a violent act.

One frequently used nominal definition of violence, proposed by Gelles and Straus (1979), defines violence as "an act carried out with the intention or perceived intention of physically hurting another person." The "hurt" can range from the slight pain caused by a slap or a spanking to harm that results in severe injury or even death.

Defining Family

Weis (1989) notes another conceptual concern in the study of family violence. Not only are there difficulties in defining abuse and violence, but as Weis notes, there is a need for conceptual clarity in determining who are the participants in acts referred to as family violence (see also Straus and Lincoln, 1985). Weis identified three possible relationships that could come under the heading of family or domestic violence. First, there are instances when victims and offenders share *kin relationships*—they are related through birth or marriage. Kin relationship violence refers to the classic forms of violence toward wives or children, sibling violence, and violence toward parents. A second category is *intimate relationships*. These include relationships where the participants know each other in a close and personal way—such as dating partners. Finally, violence can occur between those who share a *domestic relationship* by virtue of sharing the same household.

Random Sample Surveys:
Questionnaires, In-Person Interviews, and Telephone Interviews

Random sample surveys offer the advantages of large sample size, efficiency of data collection, standardization of measurement instruments, and generalizability to a general or specific population. However, as with all forms of data collection, fielding a random sample survey on the topic of family violence involves a series of logical decisions and compromises. The first is the choice between sample size and instrument length. The choice arises because investigators with a limit on funding must choose between how many subjects or families will be included and how much data will be collected from them.

Sample Size

We note again that the low base rate of family violence impinges on the collection of data using a random sample survey. The results of the first National Family Violence Survey (Straus, Gelles, and Steinmetz, 1980) are an example. When that survey was designed in 1974, estimates of the incidence of physical child abuse ranged from .5% to perhaps 3 or 4%. There were no estimates of the extent of wife abuse available other than from our own exploratory sample surveys. We opted for a sample size of some two thousand households. Children under the age of 18 years old live in about half of the households in the United States.[1] Thus a national sample of houses would yield about 1,000 containing children under 18 years of age. If 40 children in 1,000 are victims of severe physical violence at the hands of their parents each year, then we would expect to find 40 victims of physical abuse in our national sample. That is barely enough cases to conduct simple cross-tabular and correlational analysis. However, if one wants to control for the impact of income on the relationship between race and abuse (for example), 40 would be an insufficient number of cases for such an analysis.

Thus even a sample of 2,143 homes proved to be too small for some forms of multivariate analysis. The obvious solution would be to expand the sample size. This was done in our second National Family Violence Survey; the sample for that survey was 6,002 households. However, by increasing the sample size we placed constraints on how much data we could collect.

Instrument Length

Our First National Family Violence Survey collected data by in-person interview. Interviewers traveled to the homes of the 2,143 subjects and conducted interviews that lasted, on average, 60 minutes. However, by expanding our sample size to six thousand households for the second survey, it would have been extremely expensive to conduct one-hour in-person interviews. Our estimate was that the interviewing alone would cost in excess of one million dollars in 1985. Thus by opting for more subjects, we needed to choose a more cost-efficient data collection method. We chose to collect data by using telephone interviews. We shall compare the advantages and disadvantages of in-person vs. telephone interviewing in the following section. A major disadvantage of telephone interviewing is that telephone interviews cannot reasonably expect to keep subjects on the telephone for much more than 35 minutes. Interviews that last longer than 35 minutes tend to produce lower completion rates and data that are inferior in reliability and validity to data collected from shorter interviews.

In summary, investigators of low base rate behavior, such as child abuse, wife abuse, elder abuse, and marital rape, face tradeoffs of larger sample sizes and smaller amounts of data collected vs. smaller sample sizes and the ability to collect richer and more detailed information.

Measurement Issues

A number of scholars are wary of applying survey research to the study of abuse and violence because they assume that subjects will not provide either reliable or valid answers (Pelton, 1979). While the number of random sample surveys of domestic violence in addition to our own is small (see for example Harris, 1979; Steinmetz, 1977), efforts to study domestic violence using this method have been successful.

Self-report research on deviant or taboo behavior has always been subject to criticism. The basic criticism offered is the question "Assuming they can remember, why would people tell the truth about deviant, illegal, or embarrassing behavior?" Thus the major threats to validity in self-report research on family violence are inaccurate recall, conscious or unconscious distortion, and differential interpretation of the questions and terms (Weis, 1987). For example, suppose the question is "Have you ever abused your child?" The subject's definition of the term *abuse* may well be quite different from the investigator's definition. Other threats to validity include whether or not another family member is present during the interview. Choosing to interview one member of a family can also product distortion. Szinovacz (1983) used the Conflict Tactics Scales with couples as respondents. She found that husbands tended to under-report both their own offenses and their own victimization.

Our approach to the problem of measuring family violence is the Conflict Tactics Scales (CTS). The CTS, rather than using ambiguous concepts such as abuse and violence, uses a series of specific acts (e.g., "slapped," "hit with an object") to assess the ways in which families deal with conflict among themselves. The following three chapters fully discuss the measurement methods and issues of the CTS.

Research Designs: Cross-Sectional and Longitudinal Designs

The non-experimental, cross-sectional design has been the most frequently employed research design in the study of family violence. In part, this is true because clinical data or official report data have been the most common sources for research on family violence. There are a number of inherent weaknesses in the non-experimental, cross-sectional design. These weaknesses are often exacerbated by the sampling and data collection techniques employed by many students of family violence.

Cross-sectional designs such as those of the 1975 and 1985 national surveys limit the investigator's ability to determine the time order of the variables studied. For example, in our most recent survey of family violence, we asked respondents to list the kinds of trouble and difficulty that their children had encountered in the previous year. We found substantial associations between experiencing violence and various forms of delinquent behavior, including vandalism, drug abuse, stealing, alcohol abuse, and getting arrested. Further, children who experienced violence were also reported as having more school problems as well as problems with violent behaviors in and out of the home (Chapter 24). While it was tempting to conclude that violence had led to the troublesome behaviors, it is just as plausible that the children had gotten into trouble and had been physically punished as a result. Even if we had asked the respondents to identify time order, our ability to infer time order would have been limited by the reliability and validity of the respondent's recall. Long-term memory can be faulty, and there is always the threat to validity of the respondents "telescoping" behaviors from the past into the present.

Longitudinal design, especially a panel design, is a means of resolving the issues of temporal ordering and change of behavior. However, longitudinal research on domestic violence is limited by the low base rate of domestic violence and the need to follow subjects over a long period of time. Take for example the question about the intergeneraticnal transmission of violence. The hypothesis of the intergenerational transmission of violence cannot be tested adequately using a cross-sectional design. Yet there are significant limits on fielding an appropriate longitudinal study that would test the hypothesis. To begin with, the study ought to start with children as subjects. The first measures would be aimed at assessing how much violence the children experience. The children ought to be followed until they are adults with children of their own. Given that the estimated incidence of severe violence toward children is about 4% (see Chapter 6) and assuming that a quarter of abused children grow up to be abusive, the initial sample size to be followed might well need to be more than twenty thousand. The expense and complexity of such a survey would be overwhelming. A second approach might be to retrospectively assess violence experience among young adults and follow these subjects through the birth and rearing of their own children. This would limit the time needed to follow subjects. The sample size would still need to be substantial, however, and the study design would not control for the threat to validity of faulty recall.

A third approach would be to follow a population that has been defined as high risk for family violence. This "prospective" approach has been used by Egeland and his colleagues (see for example Egeland, Breitenbucher, and Rosenberg, 1980; Egeland and Sroufe, 1981; and Egeland, Jacobvitz, and Papatola, 1987). Starting in 1975, Egeland and his research group began enrolling a sample of 267 mothers who were in their last trimester of pregnancy. The mothers were patients at the Minnesota public health clinics and were considered at high risk for caretaking problems due to their low socioeconomic status and a number of other factors, such as young age (mean 20 years). Sixty-two percent of the mothers were unwed at the time of the birth, and 86% of the pregnancies were unplanned. Many of the mothers encountered a high number of other life stress events and lacked support from a husband/boyfriend, family, or friends.

Within the high risk group there were 44 cases of child maltreatment, which included 24 cases of physical abuse, 24 cases of neglect, and 19 cases of hostile/rejecting behavior. Egeland and his group have followed these mothers for over 12 years. Among the mothers who had been abused as children, 70% have mistreated their own children. Egeland and his colleagues have not only examined the pattern of continuity of abuse across generations, but also have looked at discontinuity—instances where abused mothers did not maltreat their children. While one can generalize from Egeland's sample only with considerable caution, his study is an example of a cost-efficient use of a longitudinal design to study a fundamental question in the field of family violence.

Weis (1989) notes that the few prospective longitudinal studies of family violence that have been conducted have focused almost exclusively on examining the notion of the cycle or intergenerational transmission of violence or the likelihood of early abuse leading to later juvenile delinquency. The majority of these studies begin by defining child abuse as those cases that have been officially reported to public or private agencies. Many of these studies fail to employ any kind of control or comparison group, thus threatening the external validity of the study. If a control group is used, the typical one is a group made up of children from similar social backgrounds but who have not been reported for abuse. These longitudinal studies are typically flawed from the outset. The investigators who choose to operationalize child abuse as those cases reported to official agencies fail to obtain an adequate baseline measure of violence and/or maltreatment experienced by the child. The design presumes that the control children have not been abused, yet virtually all students of family violence recognize that abuse is under-reported to official agencies. Thus the study design inevitably includes children in the control group who may well have been abused, but who have not been officially recognized. If the number of abused-but-not-reported children is substantial (even a small number would be substantial if the overall sample size is low), the investigation runs the serious risk of falsely accepting the null hypothesis.

Other methodological issues threaten the validity of prospective longitudinal studies. Investigators frequently fail to select measures with adequate reliability. Thus what changes they report may well be due to measurement error. The typical prospective study collects data at but two points in time. As a result, the investigator is often unable to rule out regression artifacts as a threat to the validity of the survey. A number of prospective studies collect data from samples that are too small to allow the investigator to statistically rule out major plausible rival explanations to the findings reported.

In the end, the cost and effort of conducting prospective longitudinal research on an issue with a base rate as low as family violence poses a major obstacle to fielding such research. The issues of funding and management are so overwhelming that many investigators conclude that cross-sectional research, even with its inherent limitations, produces a greater yield for the time and energy expended than would longitudinal research.

A Note on Experimental Designs

This section on research design has not mentioned experimental design. Most of the experimental research on domestic violence has focused on the relationship between child abuse and aggressive behavior of the children (from Weis, 1989; see Kinard, 1980; Bousha and Twentyman, 1984; Herrenkohl, Herrenkohl, Toedter, and Yanushefski, 1984). Given the sensitive and dangerous nature of family violence, many forms of experimental research would be considered unethical. This would include designs where abuse was the dependent variable, as well as evaluation studies where victims and/or offenders would be randomly assigned to treatments. One exception is the Minneapolis police experiment (Sherman and Berk, 1984). The design of this study involved the random assignment of an intervention strategy to cases of misdemeanor domestic violence. Police officers in Minneapolis were randomly assigned one of three strategies prior to arriving at the scene of the violence. The strategies included arrest, offering advice or mediation, and ordering the offender from the home. The investigators report that arrest produced significantly less violence than the other two forms of intervention.

On the surface, the Minneapolis police experiment is an impressive example of a field experiment. Beneath the surface are some troubling threats to valdity. The investigators admit they had no way of monitoring whether the officers actually followed the randomly assigned instructions. Second, a majority of the cases in the study were contributed by a handful of police officers. Finally, a significant amount of missing data forced the investigators to statistically substitute for missing data, thus raising the possibility that the significant findings were a statistical artifact. The Minneapolis police experiment is now being replicated in a number of cities. Methodological problems notwithstanding, it remains an example of a creative and ingenious approach to the ethical and practical constraints of applying experimental methods to the study of domestic violence. We do not, however, expect to see a widespread application of the method. Randomly assigning police intervention is possible, but many researchers and even more policymakers and social service personnel resist designs that would withhold services from a control group, including the establishment of "wait list controls" for overcrowded services such as battered wife shelters.

Toward Improved Research on Family Violence

While the opening chapters of this book review the many benefits of the survey designs of our two national studies, there is no question that many research issues and problems remain. First and foremost, the field of family violence must continue to improve upon the definitions of *abuse, violence,* and *the family.* Until such time as the majority of investigators are employing similar definitions for the central concepts in the field, confusion and contradiction will dominate the study of family violence.

Although the problems of fielding adequate longitudinal designs are many, there is a need to employ more of these designs. Change and time order should not be inferred exclusively from cross-sectional data. Panel and cohort studies are a necessity if knowledge of family violence is to be advanced.

Students of family violence need to attend to the major measurement issues in the study of violence and aggression. The field has been well served by the CTS, but a single scale is not a solution to measurement problems. Weis (1989) points out that there is not one validation study of family violence yet published. An experimental design that compares measures on the same sample is imperative.

The field must move beyond accepting conventional wisdoms and post hoc conclusions as theory. For the study of family violence to be truly advanced, programs of research must begin to test the various notions, hypotheses, and propositions that have been developed over the past 25 years.

Notes

1. The sample of households that contained children in the first National Family Violence Survey was limited to those homes where there was at least one child aged 3 to 17 years of age. This was done because one of the goals of the First National Family Violence Survey was to measure violence between siblings. It was assumed that violence initiated by a child under the age of three years old would not be meaningful in the same sense as violence initiated by a child 3 years of age or older.

3

Measuring Intrafamily Conflict and Violence: The Conflict Tactics (CT) Scales

Murray A. Straus

Conflict theorists present a convincing case showing that conflict is an inevitable part of all human association (Adams, 1965; Coser, 1956; Dahrendorf, 1959; Scanzoni, 1972; Simmel, 1955; Sprey, 1969). They further hold that without the changes brought about by conflict, a social unit—be it a nation, an academic department, or a family—runs a high risk of collapse. If conflict is suppressed, it can result in stagnation and failure to adapt to changed circumstances and/or erode the bond of group solidarity because of an accumulation of hostility.

Despite the above, most people fear conflict and try to avoid it. Professionals concerned with the family also tend to take an almost opposite view to that of conflict theorists. They treat conflict as something to be avoided. Sociologists and psychologists do research to find out why conflict occurs, implicitly to be able to provide information which will enable people to avoid conflict. Marriage counselors, with a few exceptions such as Bach and Wyden (1968) and Shostrom and Kavanaugh (1971), focus much of their efforts on helping families avoid conflict.

There are a number of factors involved in creating this hiatus between the truths revealed to us by sociological conflict theorists and those revealed by our daily experience and emotional reactions to conflict. However, since this paper is concerned with methods of measuring conflict tactics rather than with the important theoretical questions raised by this hiatus, the available space permits only a discussion of one of the factors. This is the conceptual confusion which characterizes analyses of conflict.

Some Conceptual Distinctions

It is essential to distinguish between a series of closely related yet clearly different phenomena, all of which are called conflict. For purposes of this paper, even this list must be confined to only three of these: "conflict of interest," "conflict," and "hostility" (further conceptual distinctions are discussed in Foss, 1980; Gelles and Straus, 1979).

Conflict of Interest

When conflict theorists talk about the ubiquity of conflict, they are referring to what is here called "conflict of interest"; that is, to the fact that members of a social group, no matter how small and intimate, are each seeking to live out their lives in accordance with personal agenda that inevitably differ. These differences range in importance. Which TV show will be watched at eight? Should money be saved or spent on a vacation? Which is more important to control: inflation or unemployment? There is no way to avoid such conflicts without running the risks to which conflict theorists have alerted us. However, there is a tendency among those writing from a conflict theory perspective to imply that "the more conflict the better," or at least not to discuss the question of how much conflict is necessary or desirable.

The question of how much conflict is desirable is also beyond the scope of a methodological paper such as this. But I would like to suggest that it is an important question for empirical research, and to further suggest the hypothesis that there is a curvilinear relationship between the amount of conflict and group well-being. That is, the absence of conflict (in the sense of conflict of interest) is theoretically impossible and (as noted in the introductory paragraph) even if it could be brought about, would be fatal for group well-being. But at the same time, very high levels of conflict can create such a high level of stress and/or such rapid change that group welfare is adversely affected.

Conflict

The second phenomenon which must be distinguished if we are to have any hope of doing sound theoretical or empirical research on intrafamilial conflict is the method used to advance one's own interest; that is, the means or the tactics used to resolve conflict. Two families can have the same level of conflict over the types of interests mentioned in the previous section. But even though conflict in that sense is identical, the two may differ vastly—and with profound consequences—in respect to how they deal with these conflicts. One family might resolve the issue of which TV program to watch by rotation, another by a "first there" strategy, and another by a threat of force by the physically strongest.

Some conflict theorists have attempted to deal with the conceptual confusion by using the term "conflict" to refer to conflict of interest, and a different term to refer to the means of resolving such conflict. Dahrendorf (1959), for example, uses "conflict" to refer to conflict of interest, and "conflict management" to refer to the means of advancing one's interests. However, the situation remains confused because other theorists follow the opposite strategy. Coser (1956) uses "conflict" to refer to the means or behavior used to pursue one's interest rather than conflict of interest itself. So, when Coser and Dahrendorf use the term "conflict," they are often referring to quite different phenomena. There is no resolution in sight for this confusing state of affairs. The best that can be done is to make clear which usage one is following. Therefore, in the context of the present paper, Coser's usage will be followed: *i.e.,* "conflict" will refer to "conflict tactics" in the sense of the overt actions used by persons in response to a conflict of interest.

Hostility

When, for whatever reason, members of a group have a feeling of dislike or antipathy for each other, this fact is also often referred to as conflict. But, paradoxically, as conflict theorists have pointed out, hostility is likely to be extremely high when the existence of conflict (in the sense of conflict of interest) is denied. This is true because such a situation prevents the actors from achieving ends which are important to them. Hostility develops out of this frustration. Of course, hostility can arise from other sources as well. However, that only highlights the need to keep distinct the phenomena of conflict of interest, conflict, and hostility. Therefore, in this chapter, hostility will be restricted to refer to the level of negative cathexis between members of the family groups.

It follows from the previous discussion that further theoretical work on conflict in the family requires as a minimum first step that we avoid the all too common confusion of "conflict of interest," "conflict," and "hostility." Similarly, clear empirical work on intrafamily factors also depend on having separate measures of these three variables. This chapter is, therefore, devoted to describing a technique for measuring one of these: intrafamily conflict in the sense of the means used to resolve conflicts of interest.[1]

The Conflict Tactics Scales (CTS)

There is an almost infinite variety of techniques which members of a family can employ in a conflict. In principle, only open-ended free response methods can tap all of these. But, in practice, the way people deal with conflict is so much a part of the unrealized, "taken for granted," ongoing pattern of life that much will be missed unless the respondent is specifically asked. Other omissions occur because certain tactics, such as the use of physical force—although extremely common—may be pushed out of memory because they are unacceptable presentations of the self. Consequently, for any but the most lengthy and in-depth interviews carried out by a highly sensitive investigator, structured methods are needed. This means that some choice of conflict tactics must inevitably be made because one cannot include every possible act in such an instrument.

In the case of the Conflict Tactics Scales (CTS) shown in Figure 3.1, the choice of the tactics to be measured was based on the fact that the following three modes of dealing with conflict are particularly important for testing the "catharsis theory" of violence control (Straus, 1974a):

1. The use of rational discussion, argument, and reasoning—an intellectual approach to the dispute, which for purposes of this instrument is called the "Reasoning" scale.[2]
2. The use of verbal and nonverbal acts which symbolically hurt the other, or the use of threats to hurt the other, which, for purposes of this instrument, is called the "Verbal Aggression" scale.[3]
3. The use of physical force against another person as a means of resolving the conflict, which is called the "Physical Aggression" or "Violence" scale (see Gelles and Straus, 1979, for a more extended definition of violence as used in this statement).

It is also possible to obtain measures of Child Abuse, Wife beating, and Husband beating by summing items for violent acts that carry a risk of serious injury (items n through s), as explained in Appendix B.

As previously noted, the three tactics measured by the CT Scales are theoretically based, but still arbitrary, selections from a much larger (but as yet undefined) set. Even though Reasoning, Verbal Aggression, and Violence were chosen with a specific theoretical issue in mind, these three are so important that they are likely to be found useful in a wide range of investigations. But, of course, there will be research issues which require data on other conflict tactics. Even in such cases, the general strategy of measurement outlined in this paper might still be applicable.

Another aspect of the CT Scales which needs to be made clear is that

FIGURE 3.1

The Conflict Tactics Scales, Couple Form R*[1]

ASK IN SEQUENCE Q35a Q36a AND (IF NEVER ON BOTH Q35a AND Q36a) ASK Q37a. THEN ASK Q35b, Q36B AND (IF NEVER ON BOTH Q35b AND Q36b) ASK Q37b, ETC.

Q35. No matter how well a couple get along, there are times when they disagree, get annoyed with the other person, or just have spats or fights because they're in a bad mood or tired or for some other reason. They also use many different ways of trying to settle their differences. I'm going to read some things that you and your (spouse/partner) might do when you have an argument. I would like to tell me how many times (Once, Twice, 3-5 times, 6-10 times, 11-20 times, or more than 20 times) in the past 12 months you (READ ITEM)

Q36. Thinking back over the last 12 months you've been together, was there ever an occasion when (your spouse/partner) (READ ITEM)? Tell me how often (he/she)...

Q37. (IF EITHER "NEVER" OR "DON'T KNOW" ON ITEM FOR BOTH Q35 AND Q36, ASK Q37 FOR THAT ITEM) Has it ever happened?

	Q35. Respondent In Past Year 1 = Once 2 = Twice 3 = 3-5 Times 4 = 6-10 Times 5 = 11-20 Times 6 = More than 20 0 = Never(con't read)	Q36. Spouse In Past Year 1 = Once 2 = Twice 3 = 3-5 Times 4 = 6-10 Times 5 = 11-20 Times 6 = More than 20 0 = Never(don't read)	Q37.For items marked "Never" on both Q35 and Q36: Has it Ever happened? 1 = Yes 0 = No
A. Discussed an issue calmly	1 2 3 4 5 6 0	1 2 3 4 5 6 0	1 0
B. Got information to back up your/his/her side of things	1 2 3 4 5 6 0	1 2 3 4 5 6 0	1 0
C. Brought in, or tried to bring in, someone to help settle things	1 2 3 4 5 6 0	1 2 3 4 5 6 0	1 0
D. Insulted or swore at him/her/you	1 2 3 4 5 6 0	1 2 3 4 5 6 0	1 0
E. Sulked or refused to talk about an issue	1 2 3 4 5 6 0	1 2 3 4 5 6 0	1 0
F. Stomped out of the room or house or yard	1 2 3 4 5 6 0	1 2 3 4 5 6 0	1 0
G. Cried	1 2 3 4 5 6 0	1 2 3 4 5 6 0	1 0
H. Did or said something to spite him/her/you	1 2 3 4 5 6 0	1 2 3 4 5 6 0	1 0
I. Threatened to hit or throw something at him/her/you	1 2 3 4 5 6 0	1 2 3 4 5 6 0	1 0
J. Threw or smashed or hit or kicked something	1 2 3 4 5 6 0	1 2 3 4 5 6 0	1 0
K. Threw something at him /her/you	1 2 3 4 5 6 0	1 2 3 4 5 6 0	1 0
L. Pushed, Grabbed, or shoved him/her/you	1 2 3 4 5 6 0	1 2 3 4 5 6 0	1 0
M. Slapped him/her/you	1 2 3 4 5 6 0	1 2 3 4 5 6 0	1 0
N. Kicked, bit, or hit him/her /you with a fist	1 2 3 4 5 6 0	1 2 3 4 5 6 0	1 0
O. Hit or tried to hit him/her /you with something	1 2 3 4 5 6 0	1 2 3 4 5 6 0	1 0
P. Beat him/her/you up	1 2 3 4 5 6 0	1 2 3 4 5 6 0	1 0
Q. Choked him/her/you	1 2 3 4 5 6 0	1 2 3 4 5 6 0	1 0
R. Threatened him/her/you with a knife or gun	1 2 3 4 5 6 0	1 2 3 4 5 6 0	1 0
S. Used a knife or fired a gun	1 2 3 4 5 6 0	1 2 3 4 5 6 0	1 0

1. The question numbers are from the 1985 National Family Violence Resurvey interview schedule as given in the appendix to Gelles and Straus, 1988. The CTS is not copyrighted. Anyone may therefore use or modify it without permission. However, if you are thinking of using the instrument, write for papers which might apply to your proposed use. In addition, I would appreciate copies of any reports using the CTS so that the bibliography can be updated for the benefit of other scholars.

this instrument does not provide information on the extent to which conflicts get resolved. In fact, as conflict theorists such as Dahrendorf (1959) and Sprey (1969) note, some conflicts are never resolved; they may be regulated, but they remain part of the system.

Factorial Design

The CT Scales was developed through the use of a model analogous to a 3 by 8 factorial design experiment (Straus, 1964:350–351). The three levels of the first factor are the conflict tactics: Reasoning, Verbal Aggression, and Violence. The 8-level factor corresponds to the nuclear family role structure: husband-to-wife, wife-to-husband, father-to-child, child-to-father, mother-to-child, child-to-mother, child-to-sibling, and sibling-to-child. There are therefore a total of 3 × 8 = 24 different CTS scores. In addition, one can combine the pairs of role scores to get four "role-relationship" scores; one each for the conjugal, father-child, mother-child, and sibling relationships. Finally, all the role scores can be summed to obtain total family scores for Reasoning, Verbal Aggression, and Violence. However, not every investigation will need the full 3 by 8 matrix of questions. For example, a study focusing on the husband-wife relationship would only need to obtain data on the husband-to-wife and the wife-to-husband roles.

The Component Items

The CTS consists of a list of actions which a family member might take in a conflict with another member. The items start with those low in coerciveness (such as discussing the issue with the other) and become gradually more coercive and aggressive toward the end of the list (such as using slapping and hitting). The response categories ask for the number of times each action occurred during the past year, ranging from "Never" to "More than 20 times."

The CTS items are usually presented with pairs of response categories. Thus, if the husband-wife relationship is the focus, respondents are asked to indicate how often they did each act in relation to their spouse in the past year, and how often the spouse carried out each action. Similar pairs can be presented for other "role-relationships" in the family, such as parent-child and the sibling-sibling roles.

There have been three versions of the CTS. Form A, which is reprinted at the end of this chapter, was used for Bulcroft and Straus (1975) and Straus (1973, 1974a, 1974b). Form N was used in the 1975 National Family Violence survey, and form R in the 1985 National Survey. Forms N and R differ from Form A as follows: (1) There is a greater focus on the Verbal Aggression and Violence modalities, brought about by dropping one Reasoning item and adding two Verbal Aggression and three Violence items. If one wishes to use the CTS in the context of a study in which it is important to measure Reasoning with the same depth and reliability as Violence, then the Reasoning items cut from Form A can be restored. (2) The response category range was increased from 0 to 5 to 0 to 6. (3) Use of a "response card" has been added. (4) Wording changes have been made in some items. (5) A place to record if the act ever happened was added. (6) In Form R, as shown in Figure 3.1, the response categories were changed to require subjects to volunteer "never" as a response, rather than presenting "never" as the first response category (see Appendix B for discussion of this change). A second change was the addition of two violent acts as item Q. For the spouse-to-spouse iterations item Q is "Choked him/her/you, and for the parent-to-child iteration item Q is "Burned or scalded him/her."

Acceptability to Respondents

The husband-wife Verbal Aggression scales and, even more, the husband-wife Violence scales ask about highly sensitive and normatively deviant types of behavior. There is, therefore, a corresponding risk of high refusal rates, arousal of antagonism in respondents, and self-defensively distorted responses. All of these can result in invalid data. The question of validity is discussed in a later section. However, before one can even consider validity, the data must be obtained. Experience with the CTS indicates low refusal and antagonism rates. For example, in the 1975 national survey, a "completion rate" only slightly lower than is currently typical of such mass surveys was obtained (65 percent as compared to the then typical 70–75 percent). The 1985 national survey achieved an 84% completion rate. Four factors seem to account for the acceptability of the CTS.

First, the instrument is presented in the context of disagreements and conflicts between members of the family and the ways in which such conflicts are resolved. Since almost everyone recognizes that families have conflicts and disagreements this serves as the first step in legitimizing response.

Second, as previously explained, the items start with conflict tactics which most respondents positively value and then gradually increase in coerciveness and social disapproval. The respondent is, therefore, given a chance to first present the "correct" things which he or she has done to resolve the conflict. In the context of a society in which there is widespread acceptance of violence "if all else fails," this serves to legitimize reporting the use of violence.

A third factor is the sequence in which the data on behavior in different family roles are obtained. The CTS begins with the items concerning parent-to-child relationships. This sequence was deliberately selected because the use of physical force between family members is most legitimate in the parental role, especially if everything else has been tried. Next, the CTS items are presented for conflicts between children in the family. Since fighting between children is also widely considered as normal, respondents are again being asked about behavior which, although not liked, is also not threatening to their self-esteem. The fact that they are describing the behavior of someone other than themselves also makes this cycle of the CTS more acceptable.

A final factor which seems to account for the willingness of respondents to provide data on acts of physical violence between themselves and their spouses is that, by the time the husband-wife cycle of items is reached, they are familiar with the questions which will be asked. Having responded to these questions previously, the strangeness of responding to a question about throwing things or hitting someone else has sharply diminished.

Although this practice effect seems, on the face of it, to be important, the evidence from the Bulcroft and Straus (1975) study shows that it is far from essential. In that study, mail questionnaire versions of only the spousal role section of the CTS were used. These were completed and returned by 72 percent of the parents of a sample of university students to whom questionnaires were sent.

Scoring

There are several methods of scoring the CTS. The four original methods are given below. Further details and additional scoring methods are in Appendix B.

1. The simplest method is to add the response category code values for the items making up each CT Scale. Thus, the Reasoning score can range from 0 to 18 because it consists of the sum of items a, b, c, each of which is scored 0 to 6.
2. The items can be weighted in accordance with the frequencies indicated by the response categories presented to the respondent. To do this, substitute for the 0 to 6 scale, 0, 1, 2, 4, 8, 15, and 25.
3. Each of the scales can be standardized on a 0 to 100 scale indicating the percentage of the possible total score. This is done by simply dividing the score for each respondent by the maximum possible score,

multiplying by 100, and rounding to an integer. Thus, for the Reasoning scale, a respondent with a raw score (by method 1) of 9 would have a percentage score of 50, and a respondent with a raw score of 12 would have a percentage score of 67. The advantage of the percentage standardization is that it expresses all scales in the same units and uses units that have meaning to the general public: *i.e.*, percentage of the maximum possible score (see Straus and Kumagai, 1977). However, there is no statistical advantage.[4]

4. Because this instrument has been administered to a nationally representative sample of couples, a final method of expressing CTS scores is available for Forms N and R: percentiles of the norming population. Tables giving these norms, for form N and the 1975 sample, are at the end of this article; and for form R and the 1985 sample in Appendix B. The raw scores used to determine the percentile scores are those described as method 1 above.

The scores for Verbal Aggression and Violence are obtained in a similar way. For Verbal Aggression add items d, e, f, h, i, and j. *Note that item g is omitted.* This was included in the list of actions because pre-test interviewing showed it to be a frequent response and because respondents became uneasy if there was no place to record this. The Violence score consists of the sum of items k through s.[5] See Appendix B for information on scoring "child abuse" and "wife-beating."

The list of violent acts is longer than the list for the other two modalities in the CTS for two reasons. First, items q, r, and s were included, even though they are relatively rare occurrences, because it was felt that inclusion of these two acts of extreme violence might make respondents more willing to describe the less extreme acts on the list. In practice, however, many instances of using a knife or gun were uncovered (Straus, 1977; Straus et al., 1979). The second reason for the longer list of acts of physical violence is that the study for which this version of the CTS was developed had intrafamily physical violence as its primary focus.

Analysis of Violence Scores

With the exception of the child-to-child violence score, the violence indexes produce extremely skewed distributions. Consequently, even "robust" statistics such as correlation may produce incorrect results. The most satisfactory procedure is to dichotomize the Violence indexes into violent and nonviolent categories, scored 0 and 1. This produces violence rates, as in Table 3.5, which can be analyzed using nonparametric statistics. Logistic regression may be particularly useful (see Chapter 20 for an example).

Factor Structure of the CTS

The three conflict tactics which served as the basis for selecting the items to be included in the CTS, and which form the basis for the scoring described in a previous section, are theoretical constructs. But to what extent do the CTS items actually group themselves into these three modalities? One method of providing empirical data on this issue is a factor analysis. Factor analyses were, therefore, computed for the spousal role, using Form A and the sample described in Straus, 1974a (N = 385) and replicated using Form N and the First Family Violence Survey (N = 2143). The method used for these analyses is "Principal Factoring with Iteration" using a Varimax rotation, as computed by SPSS option PA2 (Nie et al., 1975).

Husband-to-Wife Data

The results of these factor analyses correspond fairly closely with the theoretical grouping of the items explained previously. Specifically, the analysis of Form A produced three factors, each of which identifies one of the three CT Scales. Factor I clearly corresponds to the Violence scale (see factor loadings in Table 3.1), Factor II to the Verbal Aggression scale, and Factor III to the Reasoning scale.

Turning to Form N, Table 3.1 reveals the three factors postulated in the design of the CTS: Factor I is the Violence scale, Factor II is the Verbal Aggression scale, and Factor IV is the Reasoning scale. What then is Factor III? Inspection of the factor loadings shows that the core of this factor is the last two items. These items were added when Form N was designed and refer to the use of a knife or a gun. The fact that they refer to potentially lethal acts, and the fact that the loadings on this factor decrease rapidly as the seriousness of the violence diminishes, suggests that Factor III represents the Wife-beating subscore described earlier. The finding of a separate factor for "serious" violence also supports the notion of the marriage license as a hitting license (Straus, 1974a, 1974b, Chapter 13), provided the violence is not "excessive." Even those who accept the legitimacy of violence in marriage (typically without realizing that they do) differentiate between a beating and the "ordinary" or "normal" violence (such as slapping and plate throwing), and it is the former which manifests itself as Factor III.

Wife-to-Husband Data

The factor analysis of the conflict tactics used by wives produced very similar results to those just reported for the husbands. The most important

TABLE 3.1

Factor Loadings for Form A (N = 385) and Form N (N = 2143) for

Husbands and Wives

CT Item	Form A Factors			CT Item	Form N Factors			
	I	II	III		I	II	III	IV
				A. Husband-to-Wife Data				
a	-0.23127	-0.16161	0.83564	a	-0.06890	0.01893	-0.00307	0.53285
b	-0.18984	-0.29661	0.81986	b	0.00382	0.14771	-0.03133	0.70899
c	-0.07601	0.00055	0.59017	c	0.11212	0.20555	0.05830	0.26763
d	0.07920	0.12769	0.32877	d	0.15238	0.70421	0.03234	0.12480
e	0.10979	0.57488	0.19269	e	0.02572	0.55026	-0.00934	0.11673
f	0.19427	0.81668	-0.10098	f	0.13787	0.65913	-0.00774	0.06222
g	0.07886	0.61290	-0.07980	h	0.13075	0.72242	0.03044	0.12513
h	0.19864	0.63951	-0.11681	i	0.55660	0.49279	0.03155	-0.08034
i	0.71975	0.22022	-0.14915	j	0.40762	0.54265	0.05440	-0.00654
j	0.77915	0.25702	-0.13520	k	0.51970	0.25804	0.24833	-0.02459
k	0.92868	0.06955	-0.02819	l	0.71076	0.39624	-0.00907	0.00411
l	0.84875	0.17066	-0.12079	m	0.82132	0.16751	0.07995	0.00943
m	0.91708	0.13842	-0.05816	n	0.71760	0.06333	0.26939	0.04118
n	0.77411	0.04637	0.04205	o	0.65134	0.14028	0.31346	0.00192
				p	0.71374	-0.02460	0.41558	0.04791
				q	0.33765	0.02195	0.94048	0.00142
				r	0.29721	0.00532	0.90618	0.00924
				B. Wife-to-Husband Data				
a	-0.06239	0.00694	0.88926	a	-0.05474	0.06215	-0.02890	0.44539
b	-0.08368	-0.18301	0.83287	b	0.03579	0.18549	0.04396	0.82394
c	-0.03935	0.20978	0.47796	c	0.16236	0.25549	0.02094	0.25851
d	0.05196	0.33520	0.17867	d	0.24794	0.65880	0.03580	0.14247
e	-0.01144	0.66145	0.12001	e	0.06504	0.55217	0.05199	0.10711
f	0.17023	0.76283	-0.11870	f	0.13298	0.71357	0.01530	0.03668
g	0.11717	0.58157	-0.03507	h	0.17225	0.67467	0.03792	0.15517
h	0.28972	0.63807	-0.07019	i	0.62976	0.43413	0.00662	0.00708
i	0.76279	0.19718	-0.03624	j	0.56102	0.44523	-0.06085	0.02812
j	0.76845	0.24701	-0.15485	k	0.73059	0.23559	0.04521	0.02580
k	0.91023	0.03394	0.00592	l	0.71399	0.24018	0.08635	0.01505
l	0.88562	0.13876	-0.01849	m	0.67712	0.13799	0.14229	-0.00261
m	0.90080	0.12058	-0.04682	n	0.82331	0.06968	0.18356	0.03150
n	0.85132	0.02678	-0.00676	o	0.77995	0.09681	0.14347	0.01605
				p	0.37491	0.03487	0.35559	0.00334
				q	0.32082	0.04788	0.38534	0.01858
				r	0.04023	0.03165	0.81766	-0.01388

difference is the last item of Factor I in the Form N data. Although Factor I is clearly a general violence factor (as it was for the husband-to-wife data), the item on using a knife or gun has almost zero loading. It seems as though, for wives, the use of a knife or a gun is even more a separate phenomenon, distinct from the "ordinary" violence of marriage, than it is for husbands.

The only other difference between factor analysis of the wife-to-husband and the husband-to-wife data is in Form A, item d. This refers to bringing in another person to help settle a conflict. For husbands, this loads most heavily on the Reasoning factor, as originally planned. But, for wives, the largest factor loading is on the Verbal Aggression factor. Perhaps when a wife seeks help in this way this is an aggressive act, but that does not seem likely. Instead, our speculation is that, given the privacy norms of the contemporary American nuclear family, it takes a conflict involving violent acts to make the partners desperate enough to be willing to (or to be forced to) breach this privacy by bringing in an outsider to help mediate the conflict.[6]

The results of several other factor analyses are given in Chapter 4.

Reliability

The internal consistency reliability of the CTS was examined by two techniques. For Form A, an item analysis was computed to determine the correlation of the items making up the CTS with the total score. The resulting correlations are summarized in Table 3.2 and indicate that Form A has an adequate level of reliability.

For Form N, the *Alpha* coefficient of reliability (Cronbach, 1970:160) was computed. These coefficients are given in Table 3.3. The reliability of coefficients are high for the Verbal Aggression and Violence scales and low for the Reasoning scale. This difference is largely a function of the small number of items (only three) making up the Reasoning scale. This emphasizes the point made earlier: that for research in which measurement

TABLE 3.2

Internal Consistency Reliability of Husband-Wife Conflict Tactics Scales,

Form A (N = 385)

| | Item-Total Correlations (r) | | | |
| | Range | | Mean | |
Conflict Tactics Scale	Husband	Wife	Husband	Wife
Reasoning	.53 - .82	.52 - .78	.74	.70
Verbal Aggression	.47 - .85	.44 - .81	.73	.70
Violence	.79 - .91	.84 - .91	.87	.88

TABLE 3.3

Coefficient of Reliability (Alpha) for Conflict Tactics Scales, Form N (N = 2143)

| | Conflict Tactics Scale | | |
Family Role	Reasoning	Verbal Aggression	Violence
Child to Child	.56	.79	.82
Parent to Child	.69	.77	.62
Child to Parent	.64	.77	.78
Husband to Wife	.50	.80	.83
Wife to Husband	.51	.79	.82
Couple Scores	.76	.88	.88

of Reasoning is an important focus, the complete set of Form A items should be used. (See Chapter 4 for additional data on reliability.)

Validity

Concurrent Validity

Evidence of "concurrent validity" (Cronbach, 1970:122; Straus, 1964:365) is reported in a study by Bulcroft and Straus (1975). The CTS was completed by students in two sociology courses. The students responded for a referent period consisting of the last year they lived at home while in high school. They were asked to indicate, to the best of their knowledge, how often during that year their father and mother had done each of the items in the CTS.

Each student was also asked to fill in a separate form with the names and addresses of their parents so that a similar questionnaire could be sent to them. Participation was voluntary and students were assured that they would not be mentioned in the letter to the parents, and that as soon as the mailing was completed the names and addresses would be destroyed and all documents identified by a number only from then on. Of the 110 students present in these classes, 105 completed the questionnaire. Of the 168 questionnaires sent to the mothers and fathers (each was sent separately with its own return envelope) 121 or 72 percent returned the questionnaire. A comparison of parent reports with student reports in this study, and also with student reports from a previous study (Straus, 1974a), is given in Table 3.4.

The correlations shown in Table 3.4 are difficult to interpret. First, the pattern is varied. The correlations are low for the Reasoning scale and high (relative to typical concurrent validity results for most social psychological tests and scales) for the Verbal Aggression and Violence scales. An analysis by Bulcroft and Straus (1975) suggests that the higher correlations

TABLE 3.4

Correlation of Spouse Report CTS Scores with Student Report CTS Scores

Conflict Tactics Scale	Correlation (r) for:	
	Husbands (N = 57)	Wives (N = 60)
Reasoning	.19	−.12
Verbal Aggression	.51	.43
Violence	.64	.33

for the two aggressive modes of conflict are due to such acts being more dramatic and emotionally charged and, therefore, better remembered.

Another way of examining the concurrent validity of the CTS is to compare incidence rates for violence as reported by each spouse, and also as reported by students for their parents. The rates are shown in Table 3.5. For the Bulcroft and Straus (1975) study, the first two rows of the table show a tendency for the students to report somewhat more violence by husbands than the husbands themselves reported, but to report less violence by wives than the wives themselves reported. One does not know which data (the student report or the reports of the spouses themselves) are more accurate since each has its own potential source of bias. The last two rows of Table 3.5, however, suggest that these discrepancies might be the result of the small size or other characteristics of the sample used in that study, since the results obtained by student report for the larger sample in the Straus (1974a) study (third row) are almost identical with the violence rates reported by the nationally representative sample of spouses shown in the last row of Table 3.5.

Content Validity

Fortunately, it is not necessary to evaluate the validity of the CT Scales solely on the basis of the data just presented. First, the Violence items have a degree of "face" or content validity since they all describe acts of actual physical force being used by one family member on another.

Construct Validity

The results of a number of analyses using the CTS measure of violence may be taken as providing at least some evidence of "construct validity."

TABLE 3.5

Percentage of Respondents Reporting One or More Acts of Physical Violence

	% Violent in Last Year	
Source of Data	Husbands	Wives
Spouses*	9.1	17.9
Students*	16.7	9.5
Students**	11.3	11.4

*From Bulcroft and Straus, 1975 (Husband N = 57, Wife N = 60).
**From Straus, 1974a (N = 385).

The following are examples of the meaningful results obtained with CTS data:

1. There is a consistency between findings using the CT Scales and the large body of evidence concerning the "catharsis" theory of aggression control (Straus, 1974a).
2. The CTS is succussful in obtaining high rates of occurrence for socially undesirable acts of verbal and physical aggression. These high rates are consistent with previous in-depth interview studies (Gelles, 1974).
3. The CTS data on the extent to which patterns of violence are correlated from one generation to the next (Steinmetz, 1977a, 1977b; Straus *et al.*, 1980) are consistent with previous empirical findings and theory on familial transmission of violent behavior (Carroll, 1977).
4. Numerous correlations exist between CTS scores and other variables in five independent studies (Bulcroft and Straus, 1975; Jorgensen, 1977; Mulligan, 1977; Steinmetz, 1977b; Straus *et al.*, 1980). Although these are not replications of previous empirical findings, they are consistent with relevant theory. Examples include the repeated findings (using the CTS with different samples) of a negative correlation between socioeconomic status and violence (Straus, 1974a; Straus *et al.*, 1980); high violence when the conjugal power structure is either extremely husband-dominant or (especially) extremely wife-dominant (Straus, 1973; Straus *et al.*, 1980); and the finding that the lower a husband's economic and prestige resources relative to his wife, the greater his tendency to use physical violence to maintain a male-dominant power position (Allen and Straus, 1980).

Additional validity evidence is given in Chapter 4.

Norms

Percentile norms are given in Table 3.6, based on data obtained from the 1975 survey. Appendix B gives norms based on the 1985 national survey. Actually, it provides two sets of norms. The first set are incidence rates which enable one to compare the rate characterizing a specific group with a representative sample of the U.S. population. The second set of norms provide information on what in Chapter 8 is called the "chronicity" of violence. These norms can be used to evaluate individuals.

Summary and Conclusions

The importance of the Conflict Tactics Scales (CTS) stems from the assumption that conflict is an inevitable part of all human association,

TABLE 3.6

Percentile Equivalents of Conflict Tactics Scale Raw Scores

Raw Scores for:

Centile	Husband-Wife			Wife-Husband			Couple			Child-Child			Father-Child			Mother-Child		
	RS	VB	VL	RS	VB	VL	RS	VB	VL	RS	VB	VL	RS	VB	VL	RS	VB	VL
1	1	—	—	1	—	—	1	—	—	—	—	—	—	—	—	—	—	—
5	2	—	—	2	—	—	—	—	—	—	—	—	1	—	—	2	—	—
10	3	—	—	3	—	—	4	—	—	1	1	—	3	—	—	4	—	—
15	—	—	—	—	—	—	6	—	—	2	3	—	—	—	—	5	—	—
20	—	—	—	—	—	—	—	1	—	4	5	—	4	—	—	6	—	—
25	4	—	—	4	—	—	7	2	—	5	6	1	5	—	—	—	—	—
30	—	1	—	—	1	—	8	3	—	6	8	3	—	—	—	—	—	1
35	5	2	—	5	2	—	9	4	—	—	10	4	6	—	—	7	1	2
40	—	3	—	—	3	—	10	5	—	7	11	5	—	—	1	8	2	3
45	6	—	—	6	4	—	11	7	—	8	12	6	—	1	2	9	3	—
50	—	4	—	—	—	—	12	8	—	9	13	7	7	2	—	—	4	4
55	—	5	—	7	5	—	—	10	—	10	14	8	8	3	3	10	5	—
60	—	6	—	—	6	—	13	12	—	11	16	9	—	4	4	11	6	5
65	7	7	—	8	7	—	14	14	—	11	18	10	9	5	—	12	—	6
70	8	8	—	—	8	—	15	16	—	12	19	12	10	6	5	—	7	—
75	9	9	—	9	9	—	16	18	—	—	21	14	11	—	—	—	8	7
80	10	11	—	10	11	—	18	21	—	13	23	16	12	7	6	13	9	8
85	11	13	1	11	13	1	20	25	1	14	25	19	13	9	8	15	12	9
90	12	15	2	12	15	2	22	30	2	16	27	22	14	11	10	16	14	12
95	13	19	4	13	20	4	24	36	5	17	30	26	16	14	12	18	18	14
99	15	30	14	15	28	15	29	53	19	18	36	36	18	22	19	18	26	22

RS = Reasoning, VB = Verbal Aggression, VL = Violence. These distributions are based on the following N's: Husband-Wife = 2105, Wife-Husband = 2114, Couple = 2088, Child-Child = 899, Father-Child = 521, Mother-Child = 620.

including that of the family. A key factor differentiating what the public and many professionals regard as "high conflict families" is not the existence of conflict *per se,* but rather, inadequate or unsatisfactory modes of managing and resolving the conflicts which are inherent in the family. Therefore, research and professional services concerned with intrafamily conflict requires techniques for measuring the way in which families attempt to deal with conflicts. The CTS is a step in this direction. The evidence presented in this chapter shows that the technique can be used under a variety of conditions, including personal interview and mail surveys. The CT Scales has moderate to high reliabilities, and there is evidence of concurrent and construct validity. It is hoped that the availability of this technique will encourage empirical research on one of the most central, yet neglected, aspects of the family.

Notes

This chapter is slightly revised from the original version. The revisions reflect the fact that Form N of the Conflict Tactics Scales has been replaced by Form R. Consequently scoring procedures which previously refered to Form N now refer to Form R.

1. Measures of "hostility" and "conflict of interest" are not presented in this paper for the following reasons: (1) there are space limitations; (2) some measures for these variables are already available in the form of family problem

Figure 3.A.1

Conflict Tactics Scales, Husand Form A, As Used in Straus, 1974a and Bulcroft and Straus, 1975

Here is a list of things you might have done when you had a conflict or disagreement with your wife. We would like you to try and remember what went on during the last year your son or daughter was in high school. Please circle a number for each of the things listed below to show how often you did it that year:

0 = Never
1 = Once that year
2 = Two or three times
3 = Often, but less than once a month
4 = About once a month
5 = More than once a month

a.	I *tried* to discuss the issue relatively calmly	0	1	2	3	4	5
b.	*Did* discuss the issue relatively calmly	0	1	2	3	4	5
c.	Got information to back up my side of things	0	1	2	3	4	5
d.	Brought in someone else to help settle things (or tried to)	0	1	2	3	4	5
e.	Argued heatedly but short of yelling	0	1	2	3	4	5
f.	Yelled and/or insulted	0	1	2	3	4	5
g.	Sulked and/or refused to talk about it	0	1	2	3	4	5
h.	Stomped out of the room	0	1	2	3	4	5
i.	Threw something (but not at my wife) or smashed something	0	1	2	3	4	5
j.	Threatened to hit or throw something at her	0	1	2	3	4	5
k.	Threw something *at my wife*	0	1	2	3	4	5
l.	Pushed, grabbed, or shoved her	0	1	2	3	4	5
m.	Hit (or tried to hit) her but *not* with anything	0	1	2	3	4	5
n.	Hit (or tried to hit) her with something hard	0	1	2	3	4	5

checklists and measures of family disagreement (Straus and Brown, 1978; Straus, Gelles and Steinmetz, 1980; Appendix B), whereas there are almost no existing measures of "conflict" in the specific sense of the means of resolving conflicts of interest.

2. In the first published data using these scales (Straus, 1974a), the Reasoning scale was called "Intellectualization." This was true because the article was, in part, a criticism of certain anti-intellectual tendencies of the "encounter group" movement. I wanted to show that opposing the intellect and the affect is a false dichotomy, and that the use of the intellect in family disputes is associated with a low level of physical violence (which is what the findings indicated). However, among therapists, "intellectualization" also has another meaning: a mechanism for *avoiding* dealing with a problem, of *hiding* behind intellectual issues. That use of intellectualization is almost exactly the opposite of what was intended! Instead of avoiding the issue, my use of "intellectualization" was meant to signify an active and assertive, but also a "civil" and nonaggressive (in the sense of non-malevolent) approach to conflicts in the family. For obvious reasons, then, "intellectualization" is not a satisfactory way of designating the first of the CT Scales. "Reasoning" was substituted even though there are also certain problems associated with its use. The main problem is that it does not adequately denote the active, problem-solving, getting-the-issues-on-the-table appproach which is so crucial for conflict management.

3. The concept of "aggression" is beset by even more conceptual confusion than is conflict. Space does not permit the kind of explication given in Gelles and Straus (1979). However, it is necessary to at least state the way the concept is used here: an act carried out with the intention of, or perceived as having the intention of, hurting another person. The injury can be either symbolic, material, or physical.

4. There may also be situations in which it might be desirable to weight the items in accordance with factor loadings or factor scores. However, a recent methodological study of weighting and other aspects of index construction (Straus and Kumagai, 1977) suggests that little or nothing is likely to be gained by such weighting, since the CTS items were selected to represent acts of increasing degrees of coerciveness. Guttman scaling is also an appropriate technique to apply to the CTS. This can be done as a means of determining the extent to which the items form a single hierarchical order. But Guttman scale scores are not recommended because the required dichotomization of the items results in an unnecessary loss of measurement precision (Straus and Kumagai, 1977).

5. Item j (threatening physical violence) was included in the *Form A* Physical Aggression index because it was felt that since the other physical aggression items would not always be visible to the child, they would understate the amount of violence between husband and wife. It was assumed that if the child observed the parents threatening each other with physical violence, then some violence is likely to have occurred. This reasoning was supported by the results of an item analysis of the Physical Aggression indexes. The correlation of the threat item (j) with the Index is .86 for the husband and .87 for the wife. But since item-total correlations with only five items are inflated by the part-whole correlation problem, the correlation of item j with each of the other four physical aggression items was also computed. For the husband, these coefficients (of item j with items k, l, m, and n, respectively) were found to be .69, .71, .68, and .57. For the wife, the parallel correlations are .68, .70, .71, and .60. See also the factor loadings for item j given later in this paper.

6. It may not intuitively be clear why the high loadings of item d on the Violence factor does *not* warrant rescoring the Violence scale to include them. The reason is that factor analysis, like all correlation techniques, indicates the amount of association, not the reason for the association. The two reasons for an association which concern us here are (a) that the items being correlated are casually related, or (b) that they are manifestations of the same variable. In most instances, an index should be restricted to items which are taken as measures of the same variable.

4

The Conflict Tactics Scales and Its Critics: An Evaluation and New Data on Validity and Reliability

Murray A. Straus

The first study reporting data on intrafamily physical violence obtained by means of the Conflict Tactics Scales (CTS) was published in 1973 (Straus, 1973). By January 1989 this instrument had been employed in more than two hundred papers and five books. It is also being used for assessment in clinical work. As might be expected, the largest number of publications are by scholars associated with the Family Research Laboratory at the University of New Hampshire, where the instrument was developed. However, almost 100 empirical studies by other investigators have been located. There is also a substantial literature criticizing the CTS, including at least nine books and articles that devote major sections to the CTS. Feminists have been particularly critical of the instrument for allegedly understating victimization of women and overstating violence by women.[1]

Despite these long-standing criticisms, the CTS continues to be the most widely used instrument for research on intrafamily violence, including use by some feminist critics such as Okun (1986), who employ the CTS for want of a better alternative. Thus, for better or for worse, much of the "knowledge" generated by the large volume of research on "partner violence" is based on (or critics would say, "biased by") use of the CTS.

Objectives of the Chapter

In view of both the wide use and the criticism of the CTS, it is important to have a comprehensive assessment of this instrument. Researchers need to know how to make the most effective use of the CTS, which is not always obvious, and they need to know the limitations of the data generated by the CTS.[2] To achieve this, the chapter

1. Brings together and evaluates criticisms of the CTS as a measure of violence between couples so that users are alerted to problems and limitations of the instrument. Some of these criticisms will be shown to be correct, and others are erroneous.
2. Describes revisions and supplementary questions that were introduced in the 1985 National Family Violence Resurvey to deal with some of the criticisms.
3. Presents new data on factor structure, reliability, and validity based on the 1985 National Family Violence Resurvey and on data reported by a number of other investigators who have used the CTS.

Appendix B is an extension of this chapter for readers who use the CTS in their own research or clinical practice. It describes and evaluates alternative methods of scoring the violence items of the CTS that have been developed since the original publication of Chapter 3 in 1979. Appendix B also presents comprehensive normative tables for tactics used in the parent-to-child and spouse-to-spouse roles.

Two important issues are not covered in this chapter because they are so important that they warrant separate treatment. One of these is whether wife beating and child abuse should be measured by the occurrence of assaults, by whether injuries result, or by both. This is covered in Chapter 5. Another issue not covered in this chapter is use of the CTS to measure child abuse. Although much of this chapter is also relevant for measuring child abuse, there are enough unique issues that a separate paper was written specifically about child abuse (Straus, 1988).

Description of the CTS

Readers unfamiliar with the CTS should first read Chapter 3, which is the basic methodological and theoretical source on the CTS. A very brief summary is given in Chapter 1.

There have been three versions of the CTS: The first *(Form A)* was developed as a self-administered questionnaire and was used with a sample of college students in 1971–1972 (Straus, 1973, 1974). *Form N* expanded the list of violent acts and was used in face-to-face interviews with the 1975 Family Violence Survey. *Form R* was used in the 1985 Family Violence Resurvey, with additional items for choking and burning or scalding and slightly different response categories (see Appendix B).

The CTS questions are designed to be replicated for any family role-relationship. For the first National Family Violence Survey (Straus, Gelles, and Steinmetz, 1980) the CTS questions began with the tactics used by one randomly selected child in conflicts with siblings. They were then repeated for tactics used by the respondent toward that child, by the child toward the parent, by the respondent toward his or her spouse, and by the spouse toward the respondent, for a total of five family role-relationships. Some other studies have used fewer replications of the CTS question (e.g., Gelles and Straus, 1988) and some have used more.[3]

Criticisms of the CTS Violence Measures[4]

Every method for obtaining data on the family has its limitations, and the CTS is no exception. Many of these limitations arise because when designing an instrument, it is often necessary to choose between incompatible approaches.[5] For example, both open-ended and fixed response categories are valid under different circumstances and for different purposes. It is therefore important to be aware of the explicit and implicit choices that underlie each instrument in choosing which is most appropriate for a given purpose. Alternative procedures will be mentioned where possible, including some newly developed methods of using the CTS items to construct measures of intrafamily violence. These criticisms described below informed the design of the 1985 survey. Chapter 9 on gender and violence presents findings that address many of these criticisms empirically.

Restricted to Conflict-Related Violence

There were two reasons for presenting the CTS items as responses to conflict and disagreement. First, the CTS also measures the use of reasoning as a tactic for dealing with intrafamily conflicts. Consequently, an introduction putting the questions within a conflict framework is essential. Second, the focus on conflicts and disagreement was one of several methods built into the CTS to enhance its acceptability to respondents. "Since almost everyone recognizes that families have conflicts and disagreements, this serves as the first step in legitimizing responses" (Straus, 1979:78–79). Of course, as in many instrument design decisions, there is a price to be paid. In this case the price was the possible loss of data on purely malevolent acts.

Informal discussion with some respondents, however, revealed that the danger of missing violence that was not conflict-related was small. A number of respondents ignored the literal instructions and reported acts of expressive violence, for example: "I still can't figure out what was bothering him. He just walked in the door, slammed me against the wall and kicked me and sat down to watch TV."

Although the introductory statement specifically includes expressive violence in the phrase "or just have spats or fights because they're in a bad mood or tired or for some other reasons," it continues to emphasize behavior in response to specific conflicts. The possibility therefore remains that the CTS underestimates violence in the form of relatively pure acts of hostility and malevolence, but there is no evidence that it does so to a greater extent than alternative methods.

Limited Set of Violent Acts

The use of a fixed response category may force respondents to deal with concepts that are alien to their thinking and lack personal meaning. Although this is always a possibility, it does not seem to be applicable to the CTS. The acts in the CTS have been determined to be almost universally meaningful in in-depth interviews. Moreover, other investigators, including strident critics of the CTS such as Dobash and Dobash (1984:274), have produced an almost identical set of violent acts. One reason these pre-determined questions are so broadly meaningful is that they refer to overt acts, rather than to opinions, attitudes, or beliefs. In the case of overt acts, although it may also be important to determine the subjective meaning of the acts, the primary problem is completeness and accuracy of recall. A checklist of acts, such as the CTS, tends to remind respondents of things that might otherwise be forgotten and therefore results in a higher incidence of violence than open-ended questions (Smith, 1987).

There must be hundreds of ways to be physically violent to another family member. Yet the violence scale of Form R lists a total of only 14 violent acts. For example, pushing a spouse down the stairs is a highly dangerous act that is not included in the CTS. The CTS was restricted to relatively few acts of violence because it was developed for use in survey research. Interview time must also be allocated for the Reasoning and Verbal Aggression scales, as well as to the other variables whose relationship to the violence measures are to be tested, such as data on possible causes or consequences of family violence. Further, the list of CTS items must be repeated for each of the family role-relationships of interest. In the 1975 survey, for example, conflict tactics in five separate roles were measured: child-to-child, parent-to-child, child-to-parent, husband-to-wife, and wife-to-husband. That makes a total of $8 \times 5 = 40$ violent items, which was believed to be the limit of many respondents' patience.

There might also be objections to the specific acts included in the CTS and to the omission of other acts. The acts were selected to enable the same items to be used to measure violence in each of the five role-relationships listed above. They therefore needed to be sufficiently general to be appropriate for each role-relationship. Thus placing someone on a hot radiator, although relevant for measuring child abuse, was not felt to be appropriate to measure violence between siblings or spouses. Time constraints are also the reason why several violent behaviors are combined in two of the CTS items (e.g., "Kicked, bit, or hit with fist" comprise item N). Kicking and biting are not necessarily equivalent acts, especially in regard to potential outcomes. However, even if separate items were given for each violent act, equivalence would still be problematic. Kicking a man in the shins, for instance, is not the same as kicking a man in the groin, and both of these instances are distinct from kicking a pregnant woman in the abdomen. Further, lack of exact equivalence applies to all the CTS items. "Throwing something" may refer to a pillow or a brick; "stabbing with a knife" may refer to a stab in the arm or in the chest. Questions that obtain data at this level of specificity are rarely possible in survey research; this is one of the many reasons why in-depth qualitative research is also needed.

The CTS was revised for the 1985 Resurvey to include "choked" for spouses and "burned or scalded" for violence by parents. Table 4.1 shows that the additional items resulted in increased rates, especially for severe violence. The one additional severe violence item increases the rate of severe assaults by 4 to 9%.

Threats Are Counted as Violence

Several critics of the CTS have mistakenly assumed that the item "Threatened to hit or throw something" is counted as one of the violent acts (see for example Dobash and Dobash, 1983:271; Stark and Flitcraft, 1983:343) despite the scoring instructions to the contrary (see Chapter 3). The threat item is part of the *Verbal* Aggression scale. It was deliberately placed right before the first of the Physical Aggression items because pretesting showed that it helped respondents distinguish between threats and overt acts. It gives respondents an opportunity to first describe threats. Having done that makes more clear the distinction between threats

TABLE 4.1

Effect of Additional Severe Assault Items in Form R on Child Abuse and
Spouse Abuse Rates

| Type of Violence | Rate per 100 | | Increase |
	Form N	Form R*	
Very Severe Violence Against Child	2.1	2.3	9.5%
Severe Violence Against Child	10.8	11.0	1.9%
Any Husband-to-Wife Violence	11.6	11.6	0.0
Severe Husband-to-Wife Violence	3.2	3.4	6.3%
Any Wife-to-Husband Violence	12.4	12.4	0.0
Severe Wife-to-Husband Violence	4.6	4.8	4.3%
Any Violence Between the Couple	16.0	16.1	0.6%
Severe Violence Between the Couple	6.0	6.3	5.0%

* The violent acts in form R are identical to those in Form N, except
that "burned or scalded" is added to the list for parental violence and
"chocked" is added to the list for couple violence.

and overt acts, and in the subsequent items, which are focused on overt
acts, they are less likely to report threats when the question asks for actual
acts of overt violence. Ironically, still others have criticized the CTS
precisely because it does *not* take into account threats (c.f., Breines and
Gordon, 1983).

Self-Reports Are Inaccurate Using a One-Year Period

Response distortion. All self-report measures are subject to memory
errors and also to a variety of conscious and unconscious distortions of
what is reported. The CTS attempts to minimize the distortions by
presenting the violence items in a context that has meaning and legitimacy
to respondents (see Chapter 3). The high rate of participation for both
interview and mail surveys using the CTS is indirect evidence that this is
effective.

Response distortion was investigated in the 1975 sample by asking each
respondent about his reactions to the instrument, including whether he
had exaggerated to make it ". . . seem like there was more physical fighting
than there really was" or played down the fights ". . . so that the interview
makes it seem like there was less physical fighting than there really was."
Of course, one cannot tell whether the respondents answered *these* ques-

tions accurately. But for what it is worth, only eight tenths of one percent (0.8%) said that they had exaggerated and only 1.1% said that they had understated the amount of violence. Still, one can be fairly sure that not all respondents told all. Cross-tabulating the question just described by the self-reported violence rates shows that the percent who said they played down the amount of violence is about 0.5% of those who reported no violence toward their child or spouse, but about 7% of those who reported frequent severe assaults to a child or spouse. For these and other reasons given in Straus, Gelles, and Steinmetz (1980: 35–36, 64–65) the CTS violence rates—high as they are—probably underestimate the true rates by a considerable amount.

Referent period. The CTS asks respondents to indicate whether any of the violent acts occurred during the preceding twelve months. This is too long a period for accurate recall. The problem is particularly acute for the items in the Reasoning and Verbal Aggression scales and for the minor acts of violence by parent toward children such as slapping. Some of these occur so often that parents would have to keep a diary to provide accurate data. On the other hand, marital violence is relatively rare—a rate of about 16% during a one-year period. This is such a highly skewed distribution that if a shorter referent period were to be used, the distribution would be even more skewed (since fewer events would have occurred in a shorter period). Consequently, investigations of marital violence are faced with a difficult choice. If a one-year referent period is used, the recall error problem is exacerbated. If a shorter time period is used, recall errors will be less, but the resulting data would be extremely skewed. (The distribution might be 1% versus 99% if a one-month referent period is used).

A one-year referent period was chosen for the CTS because that seemed to be the lesser of the two evils just discussed. However, if the research is concerned with violence between siblings or violence by parents to children, a shorter referent period might be a better choice. Violence in these roles occurs with such frequency that an impossibly skewed distribution would not result from a three- or six-month, or perhaps even a one-month, referent period.

Equates Acts That Differ Greatly in Seriousness

The violence scale items start with relatively minor acts, such as pushing and slapping, and end with assaults using a knife or gun. The desirability of distinguishing the more severe acts of violence from the others was mentioned in the first publication on the CTS (Chapter 3), but its importance was not emphasized. Moreover, the only normative data presented in that publication combine all forms of violence in a simple sum index.

Consequently, two slaps are counted the same as two knife attacks. Subsequently, this omission was partly rectified by giving separate rates for "severe violence." However, even the Severe Violence index may not be satisfactory, because it also includes acts that differ greatly in their seriousness. A "Severity Weighted" scale has also been developed that weights each item by its relative severity and the frequency with which it occurred. The specific method of computing this index is given in Appendix B.

Context Is Ignored

One of the most frequent criticisms of the CTS as a measure of spouse abuse is that it counts acts of violence in isolation from the circumstances under which those acts occur. Who initiates the violence, the relative size and strength of the persons involved, and the nature of their relationship affect the meaning and consequences of the act. Hitting someone with a stove poker in self-defense is different than the same physical act as an unprovoked assault. A punch by a 120 pound woman will, on the average, have different consequences than a punch by a 175 pound man.

These criticisms are based on a misunderstanding of (or disagreement with) the approach to research design that underlies the CTS. Our approach assumes that "context" *is* extremely important but that it is usually desirable to measure the context variables separately from the violence variable. That is why verbal aggression is kept separate from physical aggression in the CTS. Indeed, each of the three scales is context for the other (see Straus, 1974; Steinmetz, 1977 for examples). The view that research using the CTS ignores context is also based on the assumption that quantitative research does not and cannot take context variables into account. In actuality, quantitative measures of context are highly developed and widely used under such labels as "interaction effects" and "specification" (for examples see the chapters in Part III and Linsky and Straus, 1987).

Why context should be assessed separately. There are several reasons for separating the measurement of the acts of violence and other tactics from the measurement of the context of those acts. One reason is that there are so many context variables that including all would make an impossibly long and cumbersome instrument. More important, combining the CTS acts with the context variables assumes a relationship, rather than testing whether such a relationship exists. For example, if injury were part of the CTS violence measure, it would preclude investigating the extent to which the assaults that are measured by the present version of the CTS result in injuries. Chapter 5 presents a number of other reasons why it is usually desirable to measure injury separately from the assaults that cause the injury.

Methods of combining context measures with the CTS. Although the CTS deliberately measures the occurrence of so-called context variables separately from the occurrence of the violent acts, as mentioned above, the CTS is intended to provide the framework for obtaining information on whatever context measures are needed for a specific study or clinical purpose. Almost any context issue can be investigated by adding questions that provide the needed information on the circumstances surrounding the violent incidents. If, for example, one wants to investigate the extent to which alcohol is involved in assaults on a spouse, the interview can ask if the respondent and his or her partner had been drinking at the time, how much they had drunk, etc., when the violence occurred as was done in the study reported in Chapter 12. The interview can ask the context questions in relation to each violent act or just the most recent occurrence of the most severe type of assault that was reported in response to the CTS Violence items. Chapters 9 and 12 are examples of such analyses using the 1985 Resurvey data.

Ignores Who Initiates Violence

Analyses of the 1972 and 1975 studies using the CTS (Straus, 1973, 1974; Straus, Gelles and Steinmetz, 1980) and an independent study of a Delaware sample by Steinmetz (1977) revealed the surprisingly high rate of wife-to-partner violence that has since been confirmed by many studies (see Chapter 6). Straus (1980) attempted to determine how much of this was self-defense from assaults initiated by men. Among those couples reporting one or more violent incidents, about half of them reported both partners had engaged in assaultive behavior, about one quarter of them the husband had committed the only violent acts, and in the remaining 25% the wife had committed the only violent acts. Data from the 1985 Resurvey (reported in Chapter 9) suggest that about half of all marital violence is initiated by wives.

"Minor" Versus "Severe" Classification Has
No Empirical Basis and Distorts Gender Differences

As indicated in Chapters 1 and 3 (also Appendix B), the Physical Violence items in the CTS are classified into two levels of severity on the basis of their presumed risk of injury. The occurrence of items classified as "Severe Violence," such as kicking, punching, and attacks with objects, is used to estimate the extent of "child abuse" and "wife beating" in the United States and to identify such cases for further analysis.

The need to distinguish between minor and severe violence is clearest in the case of child abuse. The criterion for child abuse is not simply hitting a child; rather it requires a level of assault that is likely to physically injure the child, and this is what the Severe Violence items are intended to represent. In the case of violence between spouses, the public still seems to make the distinction between "only" slapping or shoving a wife and "wife beating." Consequently, the distinction between minor and severe violence is also useful in identifying cases that approximate the concept of wife beating.

The distinction between minor and severe assaults is roughly parallel to the legal distinction between "simple assault" and "aggravated assault." An aggravated assault is an attack that is likely to cause grave bodily harm, such as an attack with a knife or gun, regardless of whether the object of the attack was actually injured.

Although the distinction between minor violence and severe violence is important and probably necessary, it is not without problems. One problem is that the classification of some acts as "minor" and some as "severe" was based on the *assumption* that the latter entail a greater risk of injury and this has never been demonstrated by empirical data. Egley (1988), however, found that the Severe Violence items characterized men in a treatment program and concluded that "most men don't enter treatment until violence has reached the severity of Straus' Wife Beating Index."

Another problem occurs because of gender differences in relative size and strength. Men, on average, are 3 inches taller, weigh 28 pounds more, and have better developed muscles than women. Therefore, the distinction between minor and severe violence may serve to understate male "minor" violence and overstate female "severe" violence. A frequent scenario in marital violence is that the husband is "only" slapping or shoving his wife. Then the wife, out of fear or anger, attempts to even the odds by kicking, punching, or using an object. In the CTS classification of violent acts, the husband is counted as having engaged in minor violence, whereas the wife is counted as having engaged in a severe assault. Critics of the CTS argue that this artificially overstates violence by women.

A related problem is that a slap or a punch by a 190 pound man is likely to be much more damaging than a slap or a punch by a 125 pound woman, yet the CTS counts them as though they were the same. Moreover, being repeatedly slapped is highly abusive and dangerous, but the standard scoring of the CTS counts that as minor violence. In principle it is possible to score the CTS in ways that correct the underestimation of minor violence by males. For example, to correct for differences in the height and weight of each spouse, CTS scores could be increased by the percent to which the height and weight of the respondent exceeded that of his or her spouse. To correct for repeated slapping, a respondent who exceeds a certain level could be classified as having engaged in severe violence, even though he or she may not have committed one of the acts in the Severe Violence list. The latter procedure was used, for example, in Chapter 25 in an attempt to refine the identification of child abuse cases. The results, however, were almost identical to those obtained by simply classifying any occurrence of one of the Severe Violence acts as "child abuse." It seems unlikely that much is to be gained from such weighting systems. Moreover, as argued in Chapter 5, kicking, punching, and hitting with objects are abusive acts regardless of whether an injury occurs.

Does Not Measure Process and Sequence

The CTS is basically intended to measure the extent to which each of the three tactics were used during a given time period, such as the preceding year or month, and therefore does not provide information on the specific interaction sequence that was involved in the use of any of the tactics in the scale. There are, however, ways in which the CTS can be used to investigate processes and sequences, such as what leads to escalation into violence. One method is to readminister the CTS at specified intervals, such as months, quarters, or years, and then use standard methods of panel analysis. Another method is to supplement the standard CTS items with questions on the sequence of events. For example, after completing the CTS, respondents can be asked about the sequence of events that led up to the most coercive act that was reported to have occurred and to provide further information about the nature of the conflict and how it was ultimately resolved.

Alternative Measures

Although the evidence to be presented below shows that the CTS is a reasonably reliable and valid means of determining the nature and extent of intrafamily violence, a number of modifications as well as completely different methods may be used to measure family violence.

Single Questions, Short Forms, and Modifications

Different studies have added and subtracted items, and the results seem to be roughly consistent with the results from use of the CTS. Illustrative of this is the study by Scanzoni (1978), who asked a sample of 321 women: "How often does his refusal to listen, or do what you want him to do, make you so angry that you: Swear at him; Try to hit him; Ignore him or give him the cold shoulder, stamp your feet or hit something like a table or a wall; Do something to spite him." Fourteen percent of the women indicated that they had tried to hit the husband. Since this figure refers to the entire period of the marriage, not to the immediately preceding 12 months, it cannot be compared directly to the 12% of women in the National Family Violence Resurvey who reported having hit their husband in the past year. However, it does indicate that even relatively simple techniques can be used to obtain data on marital violence.

The CTS has been administered in the form of a questionnaire (Form A, Straus, 1973, 1974), personal interview (Form N, Straus, Gelles, and Steinmetz, 1980), and telephone interview (Straus and Gelles, 1986). The identity of the respondent has also varied, including children describing their own behavior and that of their parents and husbands, wives, and dating partners describing the tactics used by themselves and by their partner. Alford (1982) used a modification of the CTS to obtain information on conflict tactics used in 26 different role-relationships, both within and outside the family.

It is clear that the CTS can be modified and used in a wide variety of ways. However, if the intent is to measure conflict tactics as defined in Chapter 3 and as summarized in the introduction to this chapter, two principles need to be followed: (1) Include only acts of overt behavior. Beliefs and attitudes about violence are extremely important, but Chapter 10 shows they are far from the same thing as actual violence. Therefore, they should be measured by a separate scale, such as the one developed by Saunders et al. (1987). (2) Do not mix tactics, either in the phrasing of an item or in combining items to compute a scale. Alford's measure of "dispute styles," for example, combines "yell, scream, push, shove, hit, throw things, and make extremely insulting references" (Alford, 1982). Such a measure cannot differentiate between parents or spouses who "only" use verbal aggression from those who are both verbally and physically aggressive.

Alternative Abuse Measures

The CTS has been most widely used and most widely criticized as an instrument to measure violence between spouses. However, no satisfactory alternative has as yet been developed. The CTS has been less often used to measure child abuse, in part because more alternative child abuse measures are available.

The Index of Spouse Abuse (Hudson and McIntosh, 1981). This was developed with commendable use of appropriate statistical techniques, such as factor analysis, and each of the two sub-scales (Physical Abuse and Non-Physical Abuse) has high reliabilities. However, this instrument suffers from the same fundamental problem as Alford's measure of dispute styles: it confounds physical aggression with other variables. Only four of the eleven items in the Physical Aggression scale (as given in the footnote to Appendix 1 in Hudson and McIntosh) are actual acts of physical aggression. The remaining items may be abusive in a broader sense (e.g., "My partner becomes surly and angry if I tell him he is drinking too much"), but are not physical acts of violence.

National crime survey. This is a carefully conducted survey that provides the most extensive data available on assaults between members of the same household because it is based on a sample of approximately sixty thousand households and is repeated annually. Nevertheless, the National Crime Survey (NCS) spouse abuse rate is only 0.2% (Gaquin, 1977–1978), compared to the rate of 16.1% found in the 1985 Resurvey using the CTS. The most likely reason for this tremendous discrepancy lies in differences between the context of the NCS vs. the Family Violence surveys. The NCS is presented to respondents as a study of crime, whereas our surveys are presented as studies of family problems. Only a minute proportion of assaults by spouses may be reported in the National Crime Survey, because most people think of being kicked by their spouse as wrong, but not a "crime" in the legal sense. See Chapter 27, footnote 1 for additional information on use of the NCS to measure wife abuse.

National incidence study of child abuse and official reports. Child abuse cases that come to the attention of Child Protective Service (CPS) agencies under mandatory reporting laws form the basis for widely known and widely accepted statistics on child abuse in the United States (American Association for Protecting Children, 1986). However, many cases of child abuse may never be reported to CPS (Hampton and Newberger, 1985). The National Incidence Study (NIS) attempts to find unreported cases of child abuse, interviewing community professionals directly about abused children they are aware of. While the physical child abuse rate from the NIS was 26% higher than the rate indicated by CPS reports, the NIS rate is still much lower than the rate from surveys using the CTS. This is true because the CPS and NIS rates are best thought of as *intervention* rates, rather than true incidence rates, because the respondents were entirely service providers or law enforcement personnel (see Chapter 7 for other explanations for the discrepancies in these rates).

Emergency room protocols. While some victims of family violence do present to hospital emergency rooms for treatment, the intentional origin of the injury is usually not divulged (Stark et al., 1981). Protocols have therefore been developed to identify abuse victims so that more appropriate treatment and referral can be provided (McGrath, et al., 1980; Pleck et al., 1987). The efficacy of such protocols was demonstrated in a study of hospital records that identified about 20% of female trauma cases as victims of intentional injury (Stark, et al., 1981).

However, for research purposes such protocols must be used with caution, since only a small fraction of abuse victims receive medical attention for injuries (see discussion of injury earlier in the chapter). Nevertheless, emergency room data can be extremely useful if one is careful to define the subjects under study as "abuse victims who are beaten seriously enough to require medical treatment" and to make clear that this level of injury is rare even among severely assaulted victims.

Randomized response technique. This technique has been highly touted for use in surveys on sensitive subjects (Kolata, 1987; Warner, 1965). In its most commonly used format, respondents are given some randomizing device (like flipping a coin) for selecting one of two unrelated questions, one sensitive and the other not, to answer. Respondents are thought to be more likely to give honest answers to the sensitive question because the researcher does not know which of the two questions was randomly selected. (Detailed guidelines for use of this technique are in Fox and Tracy, 1986). In theory, the technique is attractive because the researcher can promise the respondent complete anonymity of response.

The technique has been used at least twice in regard to child abuse. Zdep and Rhodes (1976) estimated that 15% of a national probability sample of two thousand responded "yes" to the question "Have you or your spouse ever *intentionally* used physical force on any of your children in an effort specifically meant to hurt or cause injury to that child?" Finkelhor and Lewis (1987) asked "Have you ever sexually abused a child at any time in your life?" and obtained estimates of 17% and 4% in split samples of 1,313 in a national probability survey. The divergence of their two estimates and the absence of associations with any other expected characteristics of sexual abusers led Finkelhor and Lewis to conclude that the estimates probably were not valid. Randomized response technique does offer some intriguing possibilities for family violence researchers, but more testing is required before concluding that it can produce valid and reliable results.

Reliability and Validity

Reliability

Six studies assessing the internal consistency reliability of the CTS have been located and are summarized in Table 4.2. Comparison of the columns for the scales measuring the three tactics shows that the *Alpha* coefficients are low for the Reasoning scale, higher for Verbal Aggression, and highest for the Violence scale. The differences are largely a function of the number of items in each scale. The reasoning scale in Forms N and R have only three items. Consequently, as suggested in Chapter 3, for research in which measurement of reasoning is an important focus, the reasoning items dropped from Form A (because of the interview length limitations of the studies using Forms N and R) should be restored to the version used in any such studies. In fact, still other items can be added to both the Reasoning and the Verbal Aggression scales to the extent that they figure importantly in the study for which the CTS is used.

Factor Structure of the CTS

At the time the CTS was developed, the three tactics that served as the basis for designing items to be included were hypothesized dimensions. Several investigators have since confirmed the existence of these dimensions though the use of factor analysis. To the extent that factor analysis identifies these dimensions, it supports the original conceptualization. In addition, the identification of orthogonal factors provides evidence of the "discriminant validity" (Campbell and Fisk, 1959) of the three tactics.

Straus analyses.   Chapter 3 reports the results of a factor analysis of data using Form A, completed by a sample of 385 college students with reference to the tactics used by their parents during the last year they lived at home. The results reveal three factors that correspond to the three hypothesized dimensions: reasoning, verbal aggression, and physical aggression (violence). The factor loadings for each item are given in Table 1 of that chapter.

Chapter 3 also reports the results of a factor analysis of Form N for the 1975 national sample of 2,143 families. This analysis yielded the same three factors and an additional factor. The items with the highest loadings on this factor are the use of a knife or gun. The factor loadings for the other violence items go down as the severity of the violence decreases. This additional factor is represented by the Severe Violence index and suggests that the "minor violence" within the family is a somewhat distinct phenomenon from the repeated and severe assaults that characterize child abuse and wife beating.

Replications by others.   Five studies have been located that report factor analyses on the CTS items. Although there are some differences in the findings, these analyses all found a factor structure that approximates the three originally postulated tactics of reasoning, verbal aggression, and physical violence.

TABLE 4.2

Alpha Reliability Coefficients for the Conflict Tactics Scales

Study	Perpetrator - Victim Relationship	Reason- ing	Verbal Aggr.	Physical Aggr.
Barling et al. 1987	Husband-to-Wife	.50	.62	.88
Mitchell & Hodon, 1983[*] (sample of battered women)	Husband-to-Wife	--	--	.69
Schumm et al. 1982	Rural Husband/Father[**]	--	.80	.96
	Wife/Mother	--	.78	.93
	Urban Husband/Father	--	.76	.95
	Wife/Mother	--	.85	.95
Straus, 1979	Child-to-Child	.56	.79	.82
	Parent-to-Child	.69	.77	.62
	Child-to-Parent	.64	.77	.78
	Husband-to-Wife	.50	.80	.83
	Wife-to-Husband	.51	.79	.82
	Couple	.76	.88	.88
Straus, 1987	Parent-to-Child	.59	.62	.42
	Husband-to-Wife	.42	.77	.86
	Wife-to-Husband	.43	.76	.79
	Couple	.48	.83	.82
Winkler & Doherty, 1983	Couple	.61	.81	.83

-- Indicates that a reliability coefficient was not reported.

[*] The reliability data for this sample is not really comparable to the other studies because the entire sample experienced violence. Under these circumstances, the CTS is a measure of how much violence occurs, whereas for non-clinical samples the highly skewed distribution (i.e. the fact that most couples are not violent) makes the violence index primarily a measure of whether violence occurred at all.

[**] Husband/Father means acts of aggression by the husband toward his wife or toward the child who completed the questionnaire. The same procedure was used for the Wife/Mother data. See Schumm et al. footnote 2.

Three of these studies analyze the CTS as a measure of marital violence. Two of them (Barling et al., 1987; Jorgensen, 1977) derived three component factors: reasoning, verbal aggression, and a single physical aggression factor. Hornung et al. (1981) derived four: the same reasoning and verbal aggression factors, one for physical aggression, and a separate factor for life-threatening violence (the threat or use of a weapon). The differentiation of the Violence items into minor and severe violence factors is parallel to the findings from the analysis presented in Chapter 3 (summarized above).

The other two studies examine the CTS as a measure of parent-to-child or child-to-parent violence. Schumm et al. (1982) found the three basic factors (physical violence, verbal aggression, and reasoning) in the self-reported behavior of 181 adolescents toward their parents. Eblen (1987) found that Verbal Aggression items mixed with Severe or Minor Violence items in parental behavior as reported by children from grades 5 through 8. The factor structure in Eblen's study also varied slightly by sex of parent. For fathers, it combined *"threatened* to hit or throw something" with the Severe Violence items; for mothers, Severe Violence combined with two acts of verbal aggression and "Threw you out of the house." The second factor for both parents combined other acts of verbal aggression with minor violence, plus "Sent you to your room" and "Grounded you." The third factor consisted solely of Reasoning items for fathers, but also included "cried" and two other items of negative affect among mothers.

Concurrent Validity

Validity is the most important and the most difficult aspect of an instrument to ascertain. In part this is true because of inherent difficulties in obtaining data that are appropriate for measuring concurrent validity. Concurrent validity is estimated by the degree to which the new instrument is related to other presumably valid instruments. This association cannot be determined if the new measure is the only measure of the phenomenon or if (rightly or wrongly) other measures are thought to be inaccurate or invalid.

Another difficulty in evaluating validity is that despite a huge literature, the criteria for judging the validity of an instrument are far from precise. Remarkable as it may seem, there are no established standards for judging concurrent validity coefficients. Inspection of several psychometrics texts revealed that almost none give numerical figures, nor does the Standards for Educational and Psychological Tests and Manuals published by the American Psychological Association. Perhaps the reason is that the assessment of validity is a complex issue that is best approached multidimensionally (see for example Brindberg and Kidder, 1982; Campbell and Fisk, 1959). Nevertheless, some numerical frame of reference can be helpful. Cronbach (1970) is one of the few authors who provides this. His Table 5.3 "Illustrative Validity Coefficients" includes 18 coefficients for widely used tests and subtests. My tabulation of these coefficients shows that the mean is .37. Cronbach comments: "It is unusual for a validity coefficient to rise above 0.60. . . ."

Standards for judging concurrent validity are even more elusive in sociology. Sociological research reports rarely include any validity evidence at all (Straus, 1964; Straus and Brown, 1978). Sociologists place great importance on the representativeness of the sample and seem to implicitly assume that if the sample is representative, the measures used in studying that sample are valid.[6]

Studies of agreement between family members.[7]   One approach taken to investigate the concurrent validity of the CTS has been to examine the level of agreement between CTS scores as reported by more than one family member. The importance of viewing couple agreement as an indication of the validity of the CTS as a measure of spouse abuse is stressed by Edelson and Brygger (1986) and Szinovacz (1983).

Treatment samples.   Two of the studies examine spousal agreement in clinical samples of men who were in treatment for having assaulted their wives (Browning and Dutton, 1986; Edelson and Brygger, 1986). Edelson and Brygger (1986) urge caution in the use of the CTS as a diagnostic and evaluation tool in treatment programs for assaultive men, since these men's self-reports may be inaccurate (page 377). At the time of intake, they found women reported higher rates of all 13 violent acts in their version of the CTS, including 4 that were statistically significant. In a six-month follow-up administration of the CTS, violence had greatly decreased and the gender difference in reporting was no longer present except for the "pushed, grabbed, or shoved" item.

Browning and Dutton (1986) found that each partner tended to under-report his or her own violence in his or her treatment sample. The mean violence index for the husbands was 9.3 as reported by the husband, but almost twice as high (17.3) as reported by the wives; the mean index score for violence by wives was 6.7 as reported by the husbands, but only 3.9 as reported by the wives. The correlation between spouses for husband's violence was .65, but only .26 for violence by the wife.

Community samples.   The first study reporting concurrent validity for the CTS compared college students' reports of family violence with reports by their parents (Bulcroft and Straus, 1975). The results, summarized in Chapter 3, indicated a moderate level of concurrent validity as measured by correlation coefficients, and rates of family violence as reported by students and their parents.

Jouriles and O'Leary (1985) present their findings as an indication of "interspousal reliability," seeming to implicitly assume the validity of the CTS violence measure. They compare husbands' and wives' responses on the CTS Violence items among 65 couples beginning marital therapy and

37 couples in a "community sample." For spouses in the therapy sample, they found 72% agreement with regard to both the husband's violence and the wife's violence. The percentage of agreement was only slightly higher in the community sample (77% for husband's violence and 80% for wife's violence). However, these high agreement scores largely reflect consensus on the nonoccurrence of violence in an extremely skewed distribution. Consequently, they also reported a better measure of agreement—the kappa coefficient. The coefficients for husband's violence were .43 for the therapy sample and .40 for the community sample and for wife's violence .40 for the therapy sample and .41 for the community sample.

Szinovacz's (1983) analysis of data from 103 couples is the most detailed and thorough analysis of agreement between spouses in response to the CTS. At the aggregate level, Szinovacz, like other investigators, found almost identical violence index rates regardless of the sex of respondent. However, when comparing the report of one spouse with the report of the other spouse, she found only 40% agreement for use of violence by the wife and 27% agreement on the use of violence by the husband. The lack of agreement on the wife's violence was mainly due to "a considerable number of women [who] report at least one incidence of violence against the husband that is not acknowledged by their spouse" (page 638). Szinovacz also found that when the Violence index is based on events reported by either or both spouses, the rate is about 50% higher than rates based on the report of only one spouse alone.

Social Desirability as a Threat to Validity

Since the first paper describing the CTS, the fact that not every respondent will be willing to describe instances in which he or she kicked or punched a child or a spouse has been emphasized. This has typically been followed by statements that the true rate is probably much higher than the measured rate (Straus, Gelles, and Steinmetz, 1980:33). The degree to which the true rates are greater than the rate obtained by using the CTS is not known. Consequently, the best that can be said about the accuracy of the CTS is that it is probably closer to the true incidence rate than other methods because it produces a higher incidence rate than any other method.

For research on family violence (as compared to clinical use), a more serious problem than underestimating the amount of violence is the possibility that the degree of underestimate varies from subject to subject and that this is correlated with other characteristics of the subject. This problem, which is referred to as "correlated error" rather than random error, can produce erroneous findings. For example, the correlation between having been the victim of violence by a spouse and depression (Chapters 9 and 24) might be spurious if both reflect person-to-person differences in willingness to tell an interviewer about such socially stigmatized behavior. This possibility has been investigated using measures of "social desirability response set."

Treatment samples.   In an analysis of a clinical sample of 52 battered women, Saunders (1986) found little evidence that social desirability response set is related to the CTS scores reported by these women. The only husband-to-wife violence item found to be related to social desirability ($r = -.28$) was slapping, and this correlation was not statistically significant in view of the experiment-wise error rate. The only wife-to-husband item related to social desirability was wife's severe violence in response to husband's severe assaults ($r = .36$), and this relationship was in the opposite direction than expected.

Saunders and Hanusa (1986) also utilized the Marlowe-Crown Social Desirability scale in a pre-test–post-test study of treatment outcomes in a sample of 90 abusive men. They found that after social desirability was partialed out, the measured outcome effects of the treatment program remained significant.

Community samples.   Newberger (1987) examined the relationship of the social desirability response set to both the marital and parent-to-child CTS scores in a community sample of 34 mothers. The CTS scores were not found to be correlated with the Marlowe-Crown Social Desirability scale scores of these women. However, Arias and Beach (1987) did find social desirability to be correlated with the CTS scores reported by a community sample of 90 couples. The correlations of the MCSD to the CTS violence index were $-.23$ for violence by husbands and $-.32$ for violence by wives. Both correlations are statistically significant, but in the light of the stigmatizing behavior measured by the CTS Violence index, are much lower than might be expected. In addition, among subjects who reported engaging in violence, social desirability was not related to their reports of frequency and/or severity of the violence; and no relationship was found between reports of being a *victim* and tendency to respond in a socially desirable manner. Arias and Beach's most important finding was similar to that of Resick and Reese (1986): controlling for social desirability does not eliminate the relationship between the CTS and other demographic, personality, and marital relationships variables.

Summary of Concurrent Validity and Social Desirability Effects

While the research indicates that social desirability presents little threat to the validity of the CTS, most of the agreement studies reviewed found large discrepancies between the reports of violence given by husbands and by wives. These often take the form of under-reporting by the perpetrator. It is therefore important to obtain data from both spouses, particularly if CTS scores are used for treatment decisions or program evaluation. In particular, if the severity of violence is of interest to the researcher, separate analyses by gender of respondent are called for, since results given in Chapter 9 indicate that women are more likely to report severe assaults than are men.

However, when the CTS is used for basic research where the issue is not the absolute level of violence but the relationships between variables, obtaining data from both spouses becomes less crucial. This can be seen in the similarity in the overall (i.e., aggregate) rates based on male and female subjects and the way relationships between variables are parallel regardless of the gender of the respondent. Figure 1 in Szinovacz (1983) illustrates the relationships of demographic measures (e.g., education or income) to husband's or wife's violence, plotting the reports of husbands and wives separately. The figure shows essentially the same curves regardless of which spouse's reports are plotted. Further, in data gathered from one spouse only (e.g., the two National Family Violence Surveys), Chapter 9 reveals that findings are typically replicated when female and male respondents are considered separately.

Construct Validity

Construct validity refers to the association between the measure in question and other variables. The extent that these associations are consistent with theoretical or empirical knowledge is used to evaluate construct validity (Cronbach, 1970; Nunnally, 1978; Straus, 1964). Thus a measure of the caloric intake should be correlated with feeling hungry, based on the theory that the subjective experience of hunger is caused by lack of food intake. Of course, the correlation will be less than 1.00, because there are other factors that also influence subjective feelings of hunger.

There is even more ambiguity as to the size of the coefficient that will be taken as evidence of construct validity than there is for concurrent validity. This is inherent in the process. If the theory being tested with the new measure specifies a close linkage between the independent and dependent variable, then a large correlation is needed; if (as in most theories) only a weak bivariate relation is posited because of the numerous other factors that are involved, then low but statistically significant correlations support the construct validity of the measures used to test that theory.

It follows from the above that the construct validity of the CTS can be assessed by the degree to which the CTS measures produce findings that are consistent with theoretical or empirical propositions about the variable that the instrument purports to measure. Chapter 3 gives a summary of the construct validity evidence that was available ten years ago. Since then, a large number of studies using the CTS have been published and they provide much more evidence. In fact, the number is so great that only some can be mentioned and even those only briefly.

- The CTS data on the extent to which patterns of violence are correlated from one generation to the next (see Chapter 3 and Carroll, 1977; Straus, Gelles, and Steinmetz, 1980) are consistent with many other empirical findings and social learning theory and have also been confirmed by many other investigators (see meta-analysis by Hotaling and Sugarman, 1986).
- Use of the CTS in the two National Family Violence Surveys has confirmed the existence of many hypothesized "risk factors" for family violence (Straus, Gelles, and Steinmetz, 1980), including
    Inequality between spouses and especially male dominance
    Poverty and unemployment
    Stress and lack of community ties
    Youthfulness
    Heavy drinking
- Comparisons in Chapter 9 of women who experienced relatively minor violence and women who experienced severe violence in 1985 with women who had not been attacked by their husbands show that the more severe the assault, the greater the probability of physical and mental health problems.
- Gelles and Straus (Chapter 24) also compared children who had been severely assaulted by a parent with the other children in the sample and found that the abused children consistently experienced more behavior problems. For example, the child victims of severe violence had two to four times higher rates of:
    Temper tantrums and troublemaking friends
    Failing grades in school
    Disciplinary problems in school and at home
    Physically assaultive behavior at home and elsewhere
    Vandalism, theft, and arrest
    Drinking and drug abuse

Many relationships indicative of the construct validity of the CTS Violence scores have been found by other investigators, for example:

- The less affection between the parents of a respondent, the higher the incidence of violence against a marital partner (Szinovacz, 1983).

- Violent couples identified with the CTS, compared to non-violent couples matched on the Marlowe-Crown Social Desirability scale, are characterized by asymmetry in power, high conflict, lack of organization, and low sharing of pleasurable activities (Resick and Reese, 1986).
- Physically abusive men identified by the CTS have lower self-esteem (Neidig, Friedman, and Collins, 1986).

Summary and Conclusions

Every instrument has its limitations, and the CTS is no exception. This chapter alerts readers to as many of the possible limitations I or critics of the CTS have been able to identify. In some cases the concerns are groundless or erroneous; in other cases they point to *possible* but not empirically demonstrated problems. In still other cases, real problems and limitations that are inherent in the instrument as it is currently structured are identified and must therefore be kept in mind when interpreting the results of research using CTS data.

The chapter also reviews the evidence on factor structure, reliability, and validity. The factor structure is remarkably consistent across studies using widely varying populations and conducted by different investigators. The internal consistency reliability is at best moderate, due to the small number of items in each scale. Selection of these few items was necessary for the CTS to be sufficiently brief so as to be suitable for survey research. The concurrent validity measures of agreement between family members are within the range of validity coefficients typically reported. The strongest evidence concerns the construct validity of the CTS. It has been used in a large number of studies producing findings that tend to be consistent with previous research (when available), consistent regardless of gender of respondent, and theoretically meaningful.

Ironically, the weakest aspect of the CTS is the scales that have received the least criticism: Reasoning and Verbal aggression. The number of items used to measure Reasoning scale is clearly inadequate, and neither scale has been used sufficiently to be able to reach conclusions about validity. The low usage of the Reasoning and Verbal Aggression scales reflects the fact that the major attraction of the CTS has been the measure of physical violence. However, on both theoretical and methodological grounds it is almost certain that more will be learned about violence if it is studied in the context of other tactics for resolving conflicts, as was done by Straus (1974) and Steinmetz (1978).[8]

Although far from a perfect instrument, the comparison presented in this chapter of the CTS with the available alternatives, together with the evidence on stable factor structure, moderate reliability and concurrent validity, and the strong evidence of construct validity, suggests that the CTS is the best available instrument to measure intrafamily violence.

Notes

It is a pleasure to express appreciation to Michael Martin, David M. Klein, and Maximiliane Szinovacz for comments and suggestions that aided in the revision of this chapter.

1. It is ironic that the main criticism of the CTS has come from feminists. There are actually three ironies. First, I consider myself a feminist and published the first empirical research showing the relation of male dominance to violence (Straus, 1973). A year earlier I presented a paper on sexual inequality, cultural norms, and wife beating (Straus, 1976). That paper was widely distributed by women's groups until I became persona non grata for publishing data on violence by women. The second irony is that the CTS has provided and continues to provide the most powerful "hard data" on the extent of wife beating. These data have been used in countless communities to help build the case for shelters and other services needed by battered women and have also figured in state and national legislative hearings. Third, the two most specific feminist criticisms of the CTS (not indicating who originates the violence and the extent to which women are physically injured) are "defects" that strengthen the case for women because when this information is obtained, it turns out that women initiate as often as men and the injury rate is actually very low. See the sections on initiation in Chapter 6 and on injury in Chapters 5 and 9.

2. This is an appropriate place to clear up a misunderstanding about who may use the CTS. Although the article that serves as a manual for the CTS (Straus, 1979) is copyrighted, the instrument itself is not. Anyone may therefore use the CTS in its original form or modify it without permission of either the author or the journal in which the CTS was published. However, I would appreciate copies of any reports using the CTS so that the bibliography can be updated for the benefit of other scholars.

3. For convenience and economy of wording, the terms *spouse, partner, husband, wife, couple, marital*, etc., are used to refer to couples, irrespective of whether they are a married or a non-married cohabiting couple. For an analysis of differences and similarities between married and cohabiting couples see Chapter 13, Yllo 1978, and Yllo and Straus, 1981.

4. The analysis in this section focuses mainly on criticisms of the CTS as a measure of spouse abuse. However, many points apply regardless of whether the application is to spouse abuse or child abuse.

5. By "incompatible" I am referring to what is possible within the scope of a particular *instrument*. However, within the scope of a research *project* more than one approach can be and, where possible, should be used. Within the scope of a *field* or research issue, it is essential that this type of triangulation occur, because each approach brings into focus aspects of a phenomenon that are hidden to other approaches. This perspective is the opposite of that taken by extreme partisans of a particular method who state or imply that *only* their method can provide an adequate understanding of the phenomenon.

6. The situation is almost the opposite in psychology. Relative to sociologists,

psychologists pay much more attention to the validity of the measures and seem to implicitly assume that if the measure is valid, the sample is not crucial.

7. In reviewing these studies, the focus will be on the Violence *index* scores as computed from the responses of husbands and wives, not on differences between spouses in respect to the individual *items* that are combined to create the index. This was done because the space to present results at the item level is not justifiable in the context of this chapter and, more important, because the key question is the validity of the composite scores or indexes, not the separate items making up the instrument. The reliability and validity of separate items is always lower than that of the overall instrument, which of course is the reason for using multi-item tests rather than single items.

8. To take this suggestion seriously, one needs to go beyond the CTS and also use an instrument that measures a broader range of non-punitive methods of resolving conflicts than can be accomplished with even an expanded set of reasoning items.

5

Injury and Frequency of Assault and the "Representative Sample Fallacy" in Measuring Wife Beating and Child Abuse

Murray A. Straus

A number of difficulties in defining and measuring "child abuse" and "wife beating" have been identified in the previous chapters. This chapter examines some of those difficulties in more detail, with particular emphasis on the role of injuries and of frequency of assault as criteria for identification of cases of child abuse and wife beating. The discussion of injury focuses on whether injury should be included as part of the operationalization of abuse, and the discussion of frequency of assault focuses on a sampling rather than a measurement question. Although these are somewhat different issues, they are brought together in this chapter because both bear on a more general question: under what circumstances is it appropriate to generalize from a sample of all families characterized by violence to those families or persons who seek or receive services as victims of violence or as offenders?

Violence, Abuse, and Assault

There is no doubt that husband-wife, parent-child, and other intimate relationships are the locus of much noxious and harmful behavior as well as much loving and supportive behavior. Research on "family violence" has come to include not only studies of physical abuse but also of psychological abuse of children, spouses, and the elderly; child sexual abuse; marital rape; physical, emotional, and educational neglect of children; and other forms of interpersonal maltreatment. (See Chapters 2 and 25 for discussion of the expansion of the concept of family violence and Straus and Lincoln, 1985 for a theoretical analysis of the implications of involving the criminal justice system in these phenomena.) All of these behaviors are harmful and are in need of careful research, but subsuming them under the general heading of "abuse" or "family violence" may create conceptual confusion and inhibit theory development and theoretically based research.

The research reported in this book focuses exclusively on physical attacks for both theoretical and practical methodological reasons. The theoretical reason is the assumption that the antecedents and consequences of one form of maltreatment are likely to be different from the antecedents and consequences of others, despite the fact that there may be some common elements. The methodological reason for focusing exclusively on physical attacks was to concentrate the limited interview time with each family on this phenomenon in order to obtain data in sufficient depth. This decision was entirely a matter of research strategy. It does not imply that physical abuse is more important or more damaging than other types of maltreatment, such as psychological or sexual abuse.

Even when the focus is narrowed to *physical* attacks, conceptual confusion is more the rule than the exception. As noted in Chapter 2, there is no consensus on the criteria required for an act to be considered "abuse." Since there is such wide variation in use of the term *abuse* and no consensus on the degree of severity, it is important to make clear the way the terms *violence* and *abuse* are defined and operationalized by the Conflict Tactics Scales (CTS) in this book and the relation of these concepts to the legal concept of *assault* and the psychological concept of *aggression*.

Violence is defined as an act carried out with the intention, or perceived intention, of causing physical pain or injury to another person. See Gelles and Straus (1979) for an explication of this definition and an analysis of alternative definitions.

Violence as defined here is synonymous with the term *physical aggression* used in social psychology (Bandura, 1973; Berkowitz, 1962). The legal concept of "assault" is somewhat different. *Assault* is the "unlawful intentional inflicting, or attempted or threatened inflicting of injury upon another" (U.S. Department of Justice, 1976). The difference hinges on the word *unlawful*. Not all violence is unlawful. Some violent acts, in fact, are permissible or required by law—corporal punishment of children and capital punishment of certain offenders, for example. Since the focus of this chapter is on child abuse and wife beating, both of which are illegal

types of violence, we will use the terms *violence* and *assault* interchangeably.

Although the CTS provides information on whether there has been an
act intended to cause physical pain or injury, this is not sufficient for
understanding violence. Gelles and Straus (1979) identify several other
dimensions that also need to be considered, for example:

- The severity of the assault, by which is meant the potential for producing
  an injury that requires medical treatment. This can range from a slap to
  stabbing and shooting.
- The level of physical injury actually inflicted, which can range from none
  to death.
- The motivation for the violence. Two broad categories are whether the
  violence is "instrumental" to some other purpose or "expressive," i.e.,
  an end in itself. Examples of instrumental violence include spanking a
  child for going into the street or slapping a spouse "who just won't shut
  up otherwise." Expressive violence, on the other hand, involves inflicting pain as an end itself, as in the case of an attack carried out under
  extreme anger and hostility.
- Whether the motivation is to cause physical pain or to cause injury or
  death. In most cases of intrafamily violence, the intent is to cause
  physical pain but not to cause an injury that requires medical treatment.
- The normative legitimacy of the violent act. For many purposes it is
  crucial to know if the act of violence is normatively legitimate, as in the
  case of slapping a child, or illegitimate, as in the case of slapping a
  spouse. However, this presumes a knowledge of which norms are applicable and what the relevant norms are. Slapping a spouse may be illegal,
  but in the actual operation of the criminal justice system, "an occasional
  slap" is much less likely to be prosecuted than an occasional slap by a
  colleague in a sociology department. Moreover, even if prosecuted, it is
  not necessarily a violation of the norms of a particular ethnic, social
  class, or family group.

Although the dimensions listed above are extremely important for
understanding any particular act of violence or for understanding a pattern
of violence characterizing a certain population, it is important to measure
each of them separately from the assaultive acts identified as "violence."
This makes it possible to investigate such issues as whether "expressive"
violence has a different etiology and a different set of consequences from
"instrumental" violence and whether injuries occur more frequently in
husband-to-wife assaults than in wife-to-husband assaults. Since the question of whether injury is a necessary part of the definition and measure-

ment of abuse is particularly important, a major section of this chapter is devoted to that issue.

Abuse.   The difference between violence and abuse is a matter of social norms: These can be informal, administrative, legal, or some combination of the three. Further, the difference depends on both the severity of the act and the relationship between victim and offender. Thus slapping a child for "talking back" is not considered abuse by the general population and is not an assault in the legal system, but slapping a store clerk for "talking back" is.

As indicated above, the severity of the act (defined as the potential for causing physical injury) is also important in labeling an act abuse: parents have the right to hit children, but it becomes an assault in the legal sense if they bite, kick, or choke a child. An important source of ambiguity in the conceptualization and measurement of "abuse" is which acts are severe enough to be classified as abuse and whether the criterion for abuse should be whether a child or a spouse is injured. Another source of ambiguity arises from the fact that acts that are normatively legitimate, even expected, such as spanking or slapping a child, can be regarded, after the fact, as abuse if a child is injured. These issues are discussed in the following section.

Acts and Injury as Criteria for Abuse

The conceptualization and operationalization of "abuse" by the Conflict Tactics Scales (CTS) is based on the identification of certain *acts* as being inherently "abusive," regardless of whether an injury occurs.[1] Thus the CTS measures of abuse use normative criteria concerning inappropriate behavior by parents and spouses. This section of the chapter will explain the reasoning underlying the focus on acts to measure abuse. At the same time, there are strong arguments for taking injury into account, and these will also be discussed.

Abusive Acts

In the case of children, the parental behaviors used in the CTS to measure abuse, such as kicking, punching, or hitting a child with an object, are acts that go beyond ordinary physical punishment. However, as explained in previous chapters, there have been objections to including hitting a child with an object such as a belt or paddle in the abuse category. We therefore created two child abuse measures: one that is restricted to acts that are indubitably abusive, such as kicking and punching, and one that adds hitting with an object to the list of abusive acts.

In the case of spouses, there is a similar difficulty. We consider any hitting of a spouse "abuse." However, the popular conception of "wife beating" tends to involve repeated and severe attacks. Consequently, we operationalized wife beating as the occurrence of any of the Severe Violence acts (see Chapters 1 and 3 and Appendix B for the list of these items). Nevertheless, since one of the bases for differentiating "severe" from "minor" acts of violence was a judgment that the latter involved a greater risk of injury, even a measure based on acts takes potential for injury into account.

Acts Versus Injuries

Although a number of reasons will be given for the importance of measuring intrafamily violence by acts, this does not contradict the idea that it is also important to measure injuries. Without data on injuries, CTS scores, which show that women engage in as many *assaults* as men, can be misinterpreted as indicating that these assaults result in as much *injury*. This is contrary to our repeated cautions (Straus, 1977–78, 1980; Straus, Gelles, and Steinmetz, 1980), to the similar warnings by others (e.g., Breines and Gordon, 1983; Dobash and Dobash, 1983, 1984, 1988), and to the injury rates presented in Chapters 9 and 24. However, it will be argued that injuries must be measured separately from the acts that produce those injuries.

A similar problem occurs in regard to physical abuse of children. The definition of child abuse in both federal and state laws, although mentioning acts that put a child at risk of injury, emphasizes injury. Since the CTS measures physical abuse of children by assaultive acts of parents rather than by injury, there is a discrepancy between child abuse as measured by the CTS and child abuse legislation and child welfare practice, both of which give primary attention to injury.[2]

Reasons for Measuring Violence as Acts

In view of the fact that injury data are extremely important, why does the CTS measure wife beating and child abuse using acts rather than injuries? There are a number of reasons:

Consistent with legal usage. The first reason for measuring child abuse and wife beating as acts regardless of whether injuries occurred is that this makes the measure consistent with the legal definition of assault given above and therefore permits integration of family violence research and theory with the work of criminologists and legal scholars.

In explaining the concept of assault, an article in the *Encyclopedia Of*

Crime and Justice states that "Physical contact is not an element of the crime . . ." (Marcus, 1983). The Uniform Crime Reports state that "Attempts are included [in the tabulation of aggravated assault] because it is not necessary that an injury result . . ." (U.S. Department of Justice, FBI, 1985:21). However, it is widely but mistakenly believed that the legal criterion for assault is injury.[3]

There are several reasons why assaults can occur without injury. First, assailants often intend only to produce pain, not injury. Second, the attempted assault may not be successful. A husband may swing at a wife and she ducks out of the way. I once interviewed a woman whose husband attacked her with a knife, but she was successful in getting out of the house. I also interviewed a parent who unsuccessfully chased a child with a broomstick. Second, not all potentially injurious blows produce an injury. Had this parent caught her child and hit him with the broomstick, it would not necessarily have resulted in an injury. In fact, the evidence given below indicates that relatively few severe assaults result in an injury that needs medical attention. Finally, as will be explained below, the occurrence of injury depends to a great extent on characteristics of the victim. Some victims are more easily injured, such as infants compared to older children, women as compared to men. Therefore, if injury were the criterion, it would make the crime as much dependent on the characteristics of the victim as on the behavior and motivation of the aggressor.

Reflects humane values.   Consistency with legal usage, while having certain advantages, need not be a deciding factor. There are additional reasons for focusing on acts, despite the great importance of injuries. One of these reasons is the moral and humane value of non-violence. I take the view that it should not be necessary for a spouse or child to be injured to classify behavior as abusive. From the perspective of this value orientation, punching a spouse or a child is *inherently* wrong, even if no injury occurs. This is widely accepted for adult sexual acts toward children (Finkelhor, 1984, Chapter 2), and I suggest that the same principle should apply to physically assaultive acts. Similarly, an *attempt* to hit a spouse with a stick is a crime in the legal sense, not only because of the danger of physical injury, but also because, by current public standards, it is morally wrong regardless of whether the attempt is successful.[4]

Injury and assault loosely linked.   A third reason for making acts the primary measure of intrafamily violence is that the connection between assaults and injury is far from direct. A husband who "only" slapped his wife may seriously injure or kill her if she falls and hits her head on a protruding object, and a husband who intends to kill and goes after his wife with a knife in most instances will fail to achieve that objective. One of the reasons the legal system defines assault on the basis of acts carried out, rather than on whether that act resulted in injury, is probably this somewhat random pattern of outcomes. Moreover, as will be shown below, the actual rate of injuries that require medical attention is low, even for severely assaulted children and spouses.

In contrast to the above, some critics of the CTS apparently assume that domestic violence and injury are almost synonymous, particularly when the agressor is male, and that this fact is covered up by the focus of the CTS on assaultive acts. However, the opposite is the case: rather than hiding the relationship between assaults and injuries, measuring assaults and injury separately enables one to provide evidence on the degree to which this assumption is correct, as we do in Chapters 9 and 23.

A more realistic measure of incidence rates. Most assaults, even severe assaults, do *not* result in an injury that requires medical attention. Data on confirmed cases of physical child abuse show that over 95% of children who are being seriously assaulted do *not* have injuries that need medical attention (Garbarino, 1986; Runyon, 1986). In the case of battered spouses, the 1985 National Family Violence Resurvey found that 3% of women victims of spouse assaults reported needing medical attention for any resulting injuries (see Chapter 9). Most victims, whether children or spouses, evidently do not incur serious injuries as a result of severe assaults. The relatively few instances of medically treated injuries indicate that statistics based solely on injury as the criterion for abuse would underestimate the extent of spouse assault or child abuse by a huge amount.[5]

Psychological injury. Another reason for using acts as the primary criterion of child abuse and spouse abuse is that, as Sullivan (1988) shows, psychological injury occurs even when there is no physical injury. Thus operationalizing child abuse and wife beating on the basis of physical injury also fails to take into account psychological injury. In principle, one can correct this by including measures of psychological problems, as we did in the 1985 survey (see Chapters 9, 24, and 25). However, psychological injury is difficult to clearly identify and even more difficult to attribute to the physical assaults. Moreover, since a typical investigation can include measures of only a few of the many possible psychological injuries, the typical pattern will be to underestimate the extent of victimization.

More useful for planning prevention programs. The underestimate of child abuse and wife beating that occurs when the criterion is injury (either physical or psychological) is a practical as well as a scientific problem. The practical problem is that it denies to those who formulate and implement public policy the true extent of the problem and therefore impedes planning and implementing programs of primary prevention and treatment.

Risk of Injury and Actual Injury

Despite the reasons just given for the CTS definition and measurement of "child abuse" and "spouse abuse" as assaults rather than as injuries, it is questionable whether abuse can be defined without reference to harm or injury. In fact, the CTS operational definition of abuse does include injury as a criterion by distinguishing between "minor" and "severe" acts of violence. This distinction is based on the presumption that the severe violence acts entail a higher *risk* or injury; for example, that the *risk* of injury is greater if a child or a wife is kicked than if slapped.[6]

Although the CTS operationalization of child abuse and spouse abuse takes the risk of injury into account, risk is not an entirely satisfactory approach. The question is whether actual injury must also be measured. In my opinion, it makes a difference to most people whether a child or a wife who is hit with a stick is actually injured. In the legal system, judges and juries are also likely to take that into account.

One reason for requiring a demonstration of actual injury before labeling a behavior as abuse is based on the pluralistic nature of American society. In a multicultural society, there is a danger in judging parents (and possibly removing their children) for parental practices that those in the dominant group regard as deviant. On the other hand, if these practices result in demonstrable harm, the value of protecting children takes precedence over the value of protecting cultural and family autonomy.

Another reason for requiring actual injury as a criterion for abuse is that there is a tremendous variation in the harmfulness of behaviors labeled as a certain type of act. For example, throwing an object at a spouse is classified as an act of minor violence, whereas hitting with an object is classified as severe violence. But what if the object thrown is a brick?

Finally, injury is relevant because, as noted above, characteristics of the victim and the assailant influence the dangerousness of the act and hence influence judgments concerning whether an act is "abuse." Shaking a six year old is unlikely to cause an injury, but shaking a six month old can be fatal. Similarly, a punch by a 175 pound man is more likely to produce an injury that requires medical treatment than a punch by a 120 pound woman.

Choice of Measure Depends on the Purpose

In principle there should be no need to choose between measuring assaults and measuring injuries. Every study should obtain both assault data and injury data. However, given limited interview time or other resources, one or the other must sometimes be omitted. In those situations it is necessary to decide which is the more crucial measure. The answer depends on the purpose.

There are a number of purposes (such as estimating the need for emergency medical services by abused children or wives) for which the most appropriate measure is data on injuries. In addition, it is important to recognize that the use of assaultive acts rather than injuries as the criterion for measuring violence poses a problem for communication of research results with the general public. The public tends to think of child abuse and wife beating as indicating an injured child or spouse. Researchers who use the CTS with a view to providing information relevant for public policy formation need to keep this problem in mind to avoid serious misunderstandings.

Assaults with Injury May Have a Different Etiology

An important potential problem with measuring child abuse and wife beating on the basis of assaults, regardless of whether an injury resulted, is the possibility that the cases with injury may differ in other ways from cases where there were assaults but no injuries. Indeed, assaults with and without injury may be different phenomena, even though closely related. The etiology of hitting someone and of hitting to the point of injury may be different. Even if the occurrence of injury owes as much to chance circumstances as was suggested above, assailants in injury cases may intend to injure, not only to cause pain. There may be other subtle but important differences. Assailants in injury cases may be more calloused and therefore, even though intending only to cause pain, may have less concern for the safety of the victim than parents or spouses who carry out an equally serious assault that does not result in injury. To the extent that this is the case, one must be cautious in applying the findings based on a representative sample of severely assaulted children and wives to the minority who are injured. This issue will be discussed later under "The Representative Sample Fallacy."

Frequency of Assault

The 1985 National Family Violence Survey revealed that about 12% of the women interviewed were assaulted by their husband or partner during the year of the survey and that these 644 women were assaulted an average of 6 times during the year. Thus when an assault by a husband occurs it is not unusually an isolated instance. In fact, it tends to be a recurrent feature of the relationship. These were truly startling figures.

Since the average number of assaults was so high, it seemed as though the survey had been successful in identifying a group of "battered women" and that an analysis of the experiences of these women could provide clues to prevention and treatment of wife beating. On the other hand, there are a number of discrepancies between the findings of our surveys and the findings of studies of shelter populations. These discrepancies raise questions about the validity of generalizing from the experiences of assaulted women in the survey to battered women in shelters.

These questions about the equivalence of battered women in our survey and battered women in shelters suggested the need for a direct comparison of the two groups. Two studies that used the CTS with women in shelters were located. The first is a study by Giles-Sims (1983) of 31 women at a shelter in Portland, Maine. These women reported an average of 68.7 assaults during the year preceding their shelter stay (p. 53). A second study by Okun (1986) is based on 300 women in a shelter in the Ann Arbor, Michigan, area. These women reported an annualized frequency of 65 assaults. 65 to 68 assaults per year is about 11 times greater than the 6 assaults per year experienced by the women in our survey.[7] It also means that the women in these two shelters averaged more than one assault per week. It seems plausible that, despite what seemed to be a very high average number of assaults experienced by the women in the national survey, the women in these two shelters, who were beaten more than once a week, had suffered a qualitatively as well as a quantitatively different experience.

The data analysis for the 1985 study was designed to deal with this discrepancy by focusing on the women in the sample who had used the services of a shelter. However, only 13 of the 622 assaulted women had done so. The average number of assaults experienced by this subgroup of women (15.3) was 3 times greater than the number of assaults experienced by the women who had not used the services of a shelter, but still fell far short of the average of 65 to 68 assaults experienced by the 2 shelter samples.

The discrepancy between the assaulted women in the National Family Violence Survey and the shelter samples studied by Giles-Sims and Okun is brought out even more dramatically by the frequency distribution of assaults in the national survey. This shows that of the 622 assaulted women, 440 or 71% experienced "only" minor assaults (pushing, shoving, slapping, throwing things). Of the 182 who were severely assaulted, only 4 were assaulted as many as 65 times during the year. Thus the national survey includes only four women who experienced assaults at a rate that is comparable to the average experience of battered women in shelters. This poses an important dilemma. On the one hand, these four cases are not sufficient for statistical analysis. On the other hand, if women who were assaulted so much less frequently are included, their experiences were so different that they may not apply to women who were assaulted more than once a week.

These differences raise serious questions about the applicability of survey findings to clinical populations. Perhaps the incidence rate for such high levels of violence is extremely low and therefore too few such cases are identified even by a sample as large as 6,002. A more plausible explanation is that cases of extremely high violence are underrepresented because high levels of violence are associated with other family problems (Straus, Gelles, and Steinmetz, 1980). Regardless of the topic of the survey, individuals from multiproblem families living in poverty are difficult to interview. Even more important, couples experiencing frequent severe assaults probably have the highest rate of refusal. Many women who have been assaulted an average of more than once a week are probably afraid to talk to an interviewer for fear of possible repercussions, and men who are this violent no doubt know that they are engaging in more than just "family fights." It is true that the overall refusal rate in the 1985 survey was only 16%. If, however, half of these 16% experienced high levels of violence, then the survey will have omitted more high violence couples than were included and perhaps the only couples for whom the frequency of assault matched that experienced by women in a shelter.

Whatever the reason for the 11 times higher rate of assault on shelter clients than on assaulted women in the National Family Violence Surveys, this difference probably explains some of the discrepancies in research findings based on the two populations. One of the most controversial differences is the finding that women in the two national surveys had a high rate of assault on their spouses and indeed often hit first (see section on wife-to-husband violence in Chapters 6 and 9), whereas studies of women in shelters show that they almost never assault their partner (Saunders, 1986). Perhaps this is true because the shelter women were assaulted so frequently—an average of more than once a week—that they did not dare even hit back.

It can be concluded that the discrepancies described above result from difference in the experience of the populations studied, rather than (as charged by those who object to our findings on violence by wives) from the use of the CTS. Studies of representative samples using other instruments (such as the study by Scanzoni cited in Chapter 6) also find high rates of assault by wives. Indeed, it was only by applying the CTS to clinical samples, as in the research of Giles-Sims (1983) and Okun (1986), that it has been possible to resolve the contradictions between different studies and the contradictions between the facts as known to shelter workers and the findings of the many studies reviewed in Chapter 6.

The Representative Sample Fallacy

Sociologists sometimes use the term *clinical fallacy* to call attention to the fact that research based on "clinical" samples (i.e., samples of persons or families receiving assistance or treatment for a problem) may have limited applicability because those who seek or receive "treatment" are often not representative of the entire population manifesting the problem. An extreme example of this problem is the frequent statement that "Once abuse starts, it gets worse and more frequent over time" (leaflet published by the Domestic Violence Project, Ann Arbor, Michigan, 1988) or, as Pagelow (1981:45) puts it: "One of the few things about which almost all researchers agree is that batterings escalate in frequency and intensity over time."

These statements are based on the experience of thousands of battered women who have received help from shelters. Ironically, the very fact that they are based on the experience of such "real cases" makes their applicability to the general population questionable, because women whose partners stopped assaulting them are unlikely to seek help from a shelter. Of course, it *could* apply to all assaulted women, but the analysis reported in Chapter 27 shows that this is probably not the case.

The other side of the coin poses a similar problem, and I therefore call it the *representative sample fallacy*. This refers to the danger inherent in attempting to generalize from the characteristics and experiences of the total population who manifest a certain problem (such as assaults on wives) to populations receiving assistance for the problem (such as clients of a battered women's shelter).

The representative sample fallacy refers to the assumption, implicit in most survey research, that a representative sample of the population is always superior to clinical samples. This assumption is unwarranted if persons in the general population who manifest the problem are different from a "clinical" population manifesting the problem. The preceding section on frequency of assault provides an example. Women in shelters experienced a frequency of assault that is so much greater than that experienced by assaulted women in the general population that it is reasonable to assume a qualitatively different experience for these two groups of women. This difference could explain why studies based on women in shelters show that very few report assaulting their partner, whereas survey findings reveal that women tend to assault their spouses at about the same rate as husbands assault their wives and indeed often hit first. The survey findings are the basis for the recommendation in Chapters 6 and 7 that part of the effort to prevent wife battering should stress the importance of non-violence by women. However, for women who are assaulted more than once a week, while this may be appropriate advice on other grounds, it is not likely to be helpful in alleviating their immediate situation.

A similar situation exists in research on elder abuse and on other types of deviant behavior. In regard to abuse of old people, the characteristics associated with abuse among a representative sample of persons 65 and over in the Boston metropolitan area studied by Pillemer and Finkelhor (1987) differ in important ways from the characteristics associated with the abuse cases known to the Adult Protective Services departments of the states as reported by Steinmetz (1988). Pillemer and Finkelhor find that the victims tend to be men in their seventies who are assaulted by their wives, whereas Steinmetz finds that the victims tend to be older, widowed women. She suggests that the difference arises because the minor assaults of elderly women on their husbands rarely produce the type of injury that will bring a case to the attention of Adult Protective Services.

Criminologists point out that research on criminal behavior using samples of incarcerated persons is analogous to research on business using samples of businesses that have failed. In both cases, one learns about what produces failure, and that is important. But it is also important to realize that the findings may not apply to the majority of criminals who are not apprehended and incarcerated, nor to the majority of businesses that do not fail. Similarly, findings based on samples of successful criminals and successful business may not be useful in working with failed criminals and failed businesses because such studies do not provide evidence on the causes of the failure.

In mental health research, discrepancies have been found between alcoholics identified among the general population and alcoholism in treatment samples and between depression identified in the general population and in clinical samples.[8] As in the case of assaulted women, the population classified as "alcoholic" or "depressed" in the surveys is much greater than the population being treated for these problems. Moreover, many of the social and psychological characteristics of persons in treatment for alcoholism and depression are quite different from the characteristics of the populations identified as alcoholic or depressed in community surveys (Room, 1980). For example, alcoholics in the general population tend to be young, whereas alcoholics in treatment tend to be middle-aged or older.

Why Do Community and Treatment Groups Differ?

We need to know more about the characteristics of women in shelters and men in treatment programs because an understanding of those differences can aid in understanding and working with the different circumstances that characterize each group. If the reason alcoholics in a representative sample of alcoholics are much younger than alcoholics in a treatment population is that it takes a certain number of years to reach the point where one is desperate enough to take action or is forced into action by family, friends, or loss of job, this can suggest a different approach to the two groups.

In regard to violence, the evidence presented in this chapter indicates that women in shelters were the victims of many times more assaults than were assaulted women in the general population. This means that they are also more likely to have suffered an injury. But other factors than frequency of assault and injury no doubt also play a part in determining who is likely to be in a treatment population. Giles-Sims (1983), for example, found that the most usual precipitant for seeking help from a shelter was not the severity of the attack which preceded going to a shelter, but the advice and encouragement of another person or an attack on one of the victim's children.

There are a number of reasons for the discrepancies between findings based on representative community surveys and findings based on treatment samples. This chapter mentions only two of these—the selection process by which someone decides to get help (or comes to the attention of authorities and is forced into treatment) and the fact that the typical treatment population may represent the extreme tail of a distribution. Other factors that could produce differences between representative community samples and clinical samples include

- Community epidemiological surveys are usually limited in the amount of data that can be obtained from each subject, as compared to the extensive data that are gathered on a clinical population.
- Persons in service or treatment programs or criminals in prison have a different relationship to the investigator, and this may affect what is presented. The difference is not simply a matter of whether the treatment group divulges more or less than persons interviewed anonymously in their own homes; it may also involve qualitative differences in how persons in different circumstances reconstruct their life histories.
- A clinical population provides more opportunities to check on the accuracy of information. This can produce more accurate data, both directly and indirectly. The indirect effect could occur if the possibility of cross-checking affects the information volunteered by subjects.

These and other factors that could account for differences between clinical and community samples need careful investigation.

Appropriate Generalization from Clinical and Representative Samples

The analysis presented above does not mean that one type of sample is superior to another. It also does not necessarily mean that the findings from a clinical sample are not applicable to a community sample or visa versa. Rather, it means that without a specific investigation, there is no way of knowing if the experiences of a representative sample of families in which there is child abuse or wife beating apply to a treatment population of child abuse or wife beating cases.

In the absence of such cross-validation, the appropriateness of the sample depends on the purpose for which the information is used. On the one hand, findings based on a random sample of assaulted women may be misleading if the goal is to uncover relationships that can be the basis for assisting battered women in shelters. As will be noted in the conclusion to Chapter 9, this requires knowledge based on the experiences of the population being assisted, regardless of whether their experience is representative of the total population. The experience of other populations may or may not be relevant.

On the other hand, findings based on a "treatment sample" do not necessarily apply to the community at large. The experience of women who have sought assistance from battered women's shelters may not be relevant for designing intervention in the larger community to *prevent* martial violence because, unless the program is based on information obtained from the experiences of a representative sample of the community, one cannot know if it fits their life circumstances. Community survey samples, such as the two National Family Violence Surveys, provide information about that population. This information indicates that there are a large number of women and children who are being abused, but not to the point that brings the child to the attention of child welfare authorities or to the point that drives a woman to a shelter. Their needs may be less acute, but they are real. The assaulted women in the 1985 national survey, for example, were attacked an average of six times during the year. Six assaults a year may be one-eleventh of the 68 assaults per year experienced by women in shelters, but it indicates an urgent need for steps to end these assaults. Moreover, the fact that a representative sample was studied enables us to estimate that there are over six million such women in the United States and thus makes clear the magnitude of the task.

Notes

I am indebted to Scott Feld, David Finkelhor, and Suzanne Steinmetz for particularly helpful comments and suggestions on an earlier draft of this chapter; to Christine Smith for statistical analysis and editorial assistance; and to Amy Oppenheimer, whose comparison of couples characterized by increasing levels of frequency and severity of violence (Oppenheimer, 1988) helped me crystallize some of the ideas in this chapter.

1. See Chapters 3 and 4 for conceptualization and Appendix B for the operationalization of abuse.
2. In fact, under some circumstances, state law and child welfare practice tend to define a child as having been abused even it it is clear that the parent did not intend to injure. An example is the case (described to me in a 1988 personal communication by Walter Baily) of ". . . a lawyer who was trying to assault his wife, and in running across the room to hit her, stepped on his infant's chest and broke numerous ribs. He didn't mean to do it but it was abuse." Identification of this case as abuse is not consistent with either the definition of violence or that of assault given above. My interpretation is that it is defined as abuse by the child protective system for a least two reasons: First, the primary concern of the child welfare system is maltreatment of children, and theoretical and definitional issues are secondary. If a child needs help, the tendency of the system is to apply whatever label is needed to deliver the needed services. Second, this is an example of what can be appropriately (or more appropriately) considered "neglect" and the two forms of maltreatment tend to overlap in fact and in the thinking of child protective service personnel.
3. Although the legal definition of assault given in the previous section does not require actual injury, other aspects of the legal system do take into account injury. At the extreme, the crime of homicide is the same as that of assault, except that in the latter case the victim died. In less extreme cases, judges and juries are almost certain to take into account whether the assault resulted in an injury. In general, it seems reasonable to assume that if there were no injuries, neither the legal system nor the social service system would continue to deal with violent acts.
4. It is surprising to me that some feminist writers such as Dobash and Dobash (1988:59) object to including attempted assaults with objects and weapons in the CTS. One would think that even if they did not find it morally objectionable, they would be the first to recognize such acts as parts of the process of intimidation used to maintain male superiority in the family.
5. Such analyses would underestimate the level of violence regardless of whether the data were obtained from the victim or the offender or from a male or female respondent. Although victims of spouse abuse do report more injuries than offenders, particularly female victims of male violence, the injury rate reported by female victims of severe assaults is still only 7.3%. This means that if the criterion for abuse were injuries, even those based on female victims' own accounts, 92.7% of severe assaults would not be counted as abuse, nor would 98.4% of minor assaults against women.
6. The research of Egley (1988) described in Chapter 4 provides empirical evidence that the assumptions used to differentiate between minor and severely violent acts corresponds to differences in attitudes and behavior.
7. Although these figures are useful for comparing groups, they cannot be taken as literal descriptions of the actual number of assaults. First, it is unlikely that any of the assaulted spouses kept the necessary records, for example in a diary, that would be needed for descriptively accurate statistics. Second, as noted in Chapter 4, a few respondents interpreted the CTS frequency categories to mean number of blows rather than number of occasions.

8. Other examples include the differences found between persons who attempt suicide versus those who actually commit suicide, and the repressed emotions of certain types of patients in therapy versus the opposite problem—inadequate control of "emotional outbursts"—in the population at large (Straus, 1974).

Part II
INCIDENCE AND TRENDS

6

How Violent Are American Families?
Estimates from the National Family Violence
Resurvey and Other Studies

Murray A. Straus and Richard J. Gelles

Eighteen years after statistics on the incidence of child abuse cases started being collected (Gil, 1970) and fifteen years after such data were first reported for spouse abuse (Straus, 1973), the question of how much violence occurs in American families remains controversial. However, a considerable body of evidence is now available from a variety of studies, but this evidence has not been brought together. The purpose of this chapter is to present the rates of spousal, parent-to-child, and sibling violence from the 1985 national survey and to compare these rates to the rates from other epidemiological research on family violence.

In addition to the violence rates presented in this chapter, there are other rates in a number of chapters. These refer to specific groups. Many of these are in Appendix B, which has normative data by gender and age of the spouses (for marital violence) and by age of child (for violence involving children). Other chapters that include violence rates for important groups are Chapter 9, which provides more detailed gender-specific rates; Chapter 13, which gives rates for dating and cohabiting couples; Chapter 18, which gives age-specific rates over the life course; and Chapters 19 and 20, which give rates for Black and Hispanic families.

The methods used to compute the violence rates in this chapter are summarized in the section on the CTS in Chapter 1 and presented in detail in Chapters 3 and 4 and Appendix B.

Violence between Spouses

1985 National Survey Rates[1]

Couple violence. The rate of 161 in the first row of Table 6.1 indicates that just over 16% or one out of six American couples experienced an incident involving a physical assault during 1985.[2] Applying this rate to the approximately 54 million couples in the United States that year results in an estimate of about 8.7 million couples who experienced at least 1 assault during the year.

Most of those assaults were relatively minor—pushing, slapping, shoving, or throwing things. However, the Severe Violence rate of 61 (see second row of Table 6.1) indicates that a substantial part were serious assaults such as kicking, punching, biting, or choking. Thus the figure in the column headed "Number Assaulted" indicates that, of the 8.7 million households where such violence occurred, 3.4 million were instances in which the violence had a relatively high risk of causing injury.

Husband-to-wife violence.[3]   The middle two rows of Part A of Table 6.1 focus on assaults by husbands. The rate of 116 per 1,000 couples shows that almost 1 out of 8 husbands carried out 1 or more violent acts during the year of this study. The most important statistic, however, is in the row labeled "SEVERE violence by the HUSBAND." This is the measure we use as the indicator of "wife beating." It shows that more than three out of every hundred women were severely assaulted by their partner in 1985. If this rate is correct, it means that about 1.8 million women were beaten by their partner that year. However, the rate of 34 per 1,000 wives, along with all the other rates shown in Table 6.1, must be regarded as a "lower bound" estimate. There are a number of reasons for this (see Straus, Gelles, and Steinmetz, 1980:35), including the virtual certainty that not every respondent was completely frank in describing violent incidents. The true rates could be as much as double those shown in Table 6.1.

Wife-to-husband violence.   The last two rows of Part A show the rates for assaults *by* wives. Comparison of these two rows with the rates for husband-to-wife assaults in the previous two rows shows that the rates for violence by wives are remarkably similar to the rates for violence by husbands. The fact that women are so violent within the family is inconsistent with the extremely low rate of assault by women outside the family, but consistent with our 1975 national survey (Straus, Gelles, and Steinmetz, 1980) and with a number of other studies, such as Lane and Gwartney-Gibbs (1985), Laner and Thompson (1982), and Steinmetz (1977–1978).

Although the studies cited above and the studies to be reviewed later

TABLE 6.1

Annual Incidence Rates for Family Violence and Estimated Number of Cases Based on These Rates. Data from the 1985 National Family Violence Resurvey

Type of Intra-Family Violence[1]	Rate per 1,000 Couples or Children	Number Assaulted[2]
A. VIOLENCE BETWEEN HUSBAND AND WIFE		
ANY violence during the yr (slap, push, etc)	161	3,700,000
SEVERE violence (kick, punch, stab, etc)	63	3,400,000
ANY violence by the HUSBAND	116	5,250,000
SEVERE violence by the HUSBAND ("wife beating")	34	1,800,000
ANY violence by the WIFE	124	6,800,000
SEVERE violence by the WIFE	48	2,600,000
B. VIOLENCE BY PARENTS - CHILD AGE 0-17		
ANY hitting of child during the year	Near 100% for young child[3]	
VERY SEVERE violence ("Child Abuse-1")[4]	23	1,500,000
SEVERE violence ("Child Abuse-2")	110	6,900,000
C VIOLENCE BY PARENTS - CHILD AGE 15-17		
ANY violence against 15-17 year olds	340	3,800,000
SEVERE violence against 15-17 year olds	70	800,000
VERY SEVERE violence against 15-17 year olds	21	235,000
D. VIOLENCE BY CHILDREN AGE 3-17 (1975-76 sample)		
ANY violence against a BROTHER OR SISTER	800	50,400,000
SEVERE violence against a BROTHER OR SISTER	530	33,300,000
ANY violence against a PARENT	180	9,700,000
SEVERE violence against a PARENT	90	4,800,000
E. VIOLENCE BY CHILDREN AGE 15-17 (1975-76 sample)		
ANY violence against a BROTHER OR SISTER	640	7,200,000
SEVERE violence against a BROTHER OR SISTER	360	4,000,000
ANY violence against a PARENT	100	1,100,000
SEVERE violence against a PARENT	35	400,000

Footnotes for Table 1

1. Section A rates are based on the entire sample of 6,002 currently married or cohabiting couples interviewed in 1985. Note The rates in Section A differ from those in Chapter 7 because the rates in that chapter are computed in a way which enabled the 1985 rates to be compared with the

more restricted sample and more restricted version of the Conflict Tactics Scale used in the 1975 study.

Section B rates are based on the 1985 sample of 3,232 households with a child age 17 and under. Note: The rates shown in section B differ from those in Straus and Gelles (1986) for the reasons given in footnote 1.

Section C and D rates are based on the 1975-76 study because data on violence by children was not collected in the 1985 survey.

2. The column giving the "Number Assaulted" was computed by multiplying the rates in this table by the 1984 population figures as given in the 1986 Statistical Abstract of the United States. The population figures (rounded to millions) are 54 million couples, and 63 million children age 0-17. The number of children 15-17 was estimated as 11.23 million. This was done by taking .75 of the number age 14-17, as given in Statistical Abstract Table 29.

3. The rate for 3 year old children in the 1975 survey was 97%. See Chapter 22, Figure 4, for age-specific rates from age 3 through 17.

4. See "Definition and measurement" section for an explanation of the difference between Child Abuse-1 and Child "Abuse 2.

leave little doubt about the high frequency of wife-to-husband assault, the meaning and consequences of that violence are easily misunderstood. For one thing, as pointed out elsewhere (Straus, 1977; Straus, Gelles, and Steinmetz, 1980:43), the greater average size and strength of men and their greater aggressiveness mean that the same act (for example, a punch) is likely to be very different in the amount of pain or injury inflicted (see also Greenblatt, 1983). Chapter 9 shows the extent to which women suffer greater physical and psychological injury.

To understand the high rate of intrafamily violence by women, it is also important to realize that many of the assaults by women against their husbands are acts of retaliation or self-defense (Straus, 1980). One of the most fundamental reasons why women are violent within the family (but rarely outside the family) is that for a typical American women, her home is the location where there is the most serious risk of assault. The rates of husband-to-wife assault just presented are many times the female assault victimization rate outside the family. The high risk of being assaulted at home relative to outside the home is also shown by statistics on homicide. The homicide victimization rates in Plass and Straus (1987: Table 6.2) show that women are seldom murder victims outside the family: 21% of stranger homicide victims but 76% of spouse murder victims. Since women are so often the victims of murderous assault within the family, it is not surprising that women, who commit only about a tenth of the non-spouse murders in the United States, commit nearly half (48%) of the murders of spouses (see Plass and Straus, 1987; Straus, 1986, for the rates and Browne, 1987, for case examples).

Couple Violence Rates from Studies Using Other Methods

Although we believe that the rates just presented provide the best estimate currently available of the incidence of physical violence in American families, there is always the possibility of some unknown error or bias. It is therefore important to also have information from other sources. Most of these studies also used the CTS to measure violence. However, before turning to those studies, this section presents incidence rates from three studies that used other techniques.

National crime survey.   This survey provides the most extensive data available because it is based on a sample of approximately sixty thousand households and is repeated annually. It is also an extremely carefully conducted survey. Nevertheless, the National Crime Survey rate is drastically lower than the rate of spouse abuse found by the National Family Violence Resurvey: 2.2 per thousand (Gaquin, 1977–1978). By comparison, the National Family Violence Resurvey rate of 161 is more than 73 times higher.

The huge discrepancy between the National Crime Survey (NCS) rate of 2.1 and the National Family Violence Survey rate of 161 (and also the rates to be presented in the next section) raises the question of why the NCS rate is so low. The most likely reason for the tremendous discrepancy lies in differences between the context of the NCS versus the other studies. The NCS is presented to respondents as a study of crime, whereas the others are presented as studies of family problems. The difficulty with a "crime survey" as the context for determining incidence rates of intrafamily violence is that most people think of being kicked by their spouse as wrong, but not a "crime" in the legal sense. Thus only a minute proportion of assaults by spouses are reported in the National Crime Survey.

Scanzoni (1978) studied a sample of 321 women. Violence was measured by response to a question that asked what they did in cases of persistent conflict. Sixteen percent (160 per 1,000) reported trying to hit the husband—a figure that is well with the range of rates obtained by studies using the CTS (see Table 6.2).

Fergusson et al. (1986:409) interviewed 960 mothers of a birth cohort of New Zealand children, for a six-year period starting in the first year of the child's life. "The mothers were asked if their husband (legal or de facto) had assaulted them during the previous year." The rate for the first year was 34, and the cumulative rate for the 6 year period was 85. The U.S. rate of 116 per 1,000 shown in Table 6.1 is almost three and a half

TABLE 6.2

Marital Violence Rates from CTS Studies by Other Investigators

Study	Sample	Comments*	Rate per Thousand
A. Any violence between husband and wife			
Henton, Cate, Koval, Lloyd, & Christopher (1983)	volunteer (N = 644)	1, 2b, 3b	121
Legg, Olday, Wesley (1984)	volunteer (N = 1,465)	1, 2a, 3a	134
Brutz & Allen (1986)	volunteer (N = 289)	3c	149
Kennedy & Dutton (1987)	probability (N = 708)		151
Hornung, McCullough, & Sugimoto (1981)	probability (N = 1,553)		157
Straus & Gelles	probability (N = 6,002)		161
Murphy (1984)	probability (N = 485)	1, 3a	191
Cate, Henton, Koval, Christopher, & Lloyd (1982)	volunteer (N = 355)	1, 2b	223
Sack, Keller, & Howard (1982)	volunteer (N = 211)	3a	240
Meredith, Abbott, & Adams (1986)	probability (N = 304)		250
Margolin (1984)	volunteer (N = 45)		290
Gully, Dengerink, Pepping, & Bergstrom (1981)	volunteer (N = 335)		322
Szinovacz (1983)	volunteer (N = 103)	1	360
Roscoe & Benaske (1985)	volunteer (N = 82)	1, 2b, 3d	510
B. Severe violence between husband and wife			
Hornung, McCullough & Sugimoto (1981)	probability (N = 1,553)		29
Kennedy & Dutton (1987)	probability (N = 708)		55
Straus & Gelles	probability (N = 6,002)		63

(continued)

TABLE   2 Continued

Study	Sample	Comments*	Rate per Thousand
C. Any violence by the husband			
Rouse (1984)	probability (N = 120)	3m	108
Kennedy & Dutton (1987)	probability (N = 708)		112
Straus & Gelles	probability (N = 6,002)		<u>116</u>
Makepeace (1983)	volunteer (N = 244)	1, 2a, 3a	137
Brutz & Ingoldsby (1984)	volunteer (N = 288)	3c	146
Dutton (1986)	volunteer (N = 75)	3e	183
Makepeace (1981)	probability (N = 2,338)	1, 2b, 3a	206
Smith (1986)	probability (N = 315)	2b	206
Meredith, Abbott, & Adams (1986)	probability (N = 304)		220
O'Leary, Barling, Arias, Rosenbaum, Malone, & Tyree (1987)	volunteer (N = 393)		240
Szinovacz (1983)	volunteer (N = 103)		260
O'Leary, Barling, Arias, Rosenbaum, Malone, & Tyree (1987)	volunteer (N = 393)		270
Clarke (1987)	volunteer (N = 318)	3k	274
O'Leary, Barling, Arias, Rosenbaum, Malone, & Tyree (1987)	volunteer (N = 393)	1	340
Lockhart (1987)	volunteer (N = 307)	3f	355
Barling, O'Leary, Jouriles, Vivian, & MacEven (1987)	therapy (N = 187)	2a	740

(continued)

TABLE   2 Continued

Study	Sample	Comments*	Rate per Thousand
D. Severe violence by husband			
Brutz & Ingoldsby (1984)	volunteer (N = 288)	3c	8
Kennedy & Dutton (1987)	probability (N = 708)		23
Straus & Gelles	probability (N = 6,002)		<u>34</u>
Meredith, Abbott, & Adams (1986)	probability (N = 304)		60
Schulman (1979)	probability (N = 1,793)		87
Makepeace (1983)	volunteer (N = 244)	1, 2a, 3c	93
Clarke (1987)	Probability (N = 318)	1, 2a, 3k	102
E. Any violence by the wife			
Makepeace (1983)	volunteer (N = 244)	1, 2a, 3a	93
Makepeace (1981)	probability (N = 2,338)	1, 2b, 3a	120
Straus & Gelles	probability (N = 6,002		<u>124</u>
Brutz & Ingoldsby (1984)	volunteer (N = 288)	3c	152
Meredith, Abbott, & Adams (1986)	probability (N = 304)		180
Szinovacz (1983)	volunteer (N = 103)		300
O'Leary, Barling, Arias, Rosenbaum, Malone, & Tyree (1987)	volunteer (N = 393)		310
O'Leary, Barling, Arias, Rosenbaum, Malone, & Tyree (1987)	volunteer (N = 393)		330
O'Leary, Barling, Arias, Rosenbaum, Malone, & Tyree (1987)	volunteer (N = 393)	1	420
Barling, O'Leary, Jouriles, Vivian, & MacEven (1987)	therapy (N = 187)	2a	730

(continued)

TABLE 2 Continued

Study	Sample	Comments*	Rate per Thousand
F. Severe violence by the wife			
Brutz & Ingoldsby (1984)	volunteer (N = 288)	3c	25
Straus & Gelles	probability (N = 6,002)		<u>48</u>
Meredith, Abbott, & Adams (1986)	probability (N = 304)		50
Makepeace (1981)	volunteer (N = 244)	1, 2a, 3c	59

*Key to comments:

1. = Dating couples

2. = CTS rates are for acts that occur over the previous year unless noted below:
   a. study did not report whether rates were for previous year or for "ever"
   b. study reports rates for acts occurring "ever"

3. = additional sample information
   a. college students
   b. high school students
   c. Quakers
   d. battered women
   e. batterers
   f. half-black/half-white
   g. urban mothers
   h. rural mothers
   i. urban fathers
   j. rural fathers
   k. women
   m. men
   n. mothers
   p. fathers
   q. delinquents

4. = rates reported as a range
   a. low end
   b. high end

times greater. This is not surprising considering the much higher rates of other types of violence in the United States. For example. in 1980 the U.S. homicide mortality rate was 105, which is 8 times greater than the New Zealand rate for that year.

Couple Violence Rates from Other Studies Using the CTS

Over 40 different investigators have used the CTS in addition to the studies done with data from the two National Family Violence Surveys. A number of these studies present incidence rates that were computed by roughly the same method as the rates from the National Family Violence Resurvey in Table 6.1. Table 6.2 lists the rates that have been located so far in ascending order. The underlined rate in each row is the rate from the National Family Violence Resurvey.

Couple violence.   The first row of Part A gives the rates for 12 studies. The range is from 121 per 1,000 couples to 510 per 1,000 couples. The National Family Violence Resurvey rate of 161 is close to the median of 159. The rate of 820 is for assaults experienced by a sample of battered wives when they were dating.

There are too few studies in the second row to generalize about the pattern for severe violence for couples.

Husband-to-wife violence.   The largest number of rates are for assaults by husbands, regardless of the severity of the assault (third row of Part A). The studies with high rates use populations at high risk of violence, such as Blacks, and couples in therapy for marital conflict.

When severe assaults are considered, the fourth row shows a large range, especially because the lowest rate (8 per 1,000) is only one-third as high as the next lowest rate. For this type of violence, as for the others discussed so far, there are special characteristics of the populations that account for outliers at the low and high ends. The rate of 8 per 1,000 might suggest that the other rates are erroneously too high. Rather, it probably reflects the fact that the sample for this study were Quakers, a pacifist denomination. Similarly, the scores at the high end are based on samples of students describing dating relationships. This fits the fact that youth tend to be the most violent age group and dating and cohabiting couples tend to have much higher violence rates than married couples (Chapter 13; Yllo and Straus, 1981).

Wife-to-husband violence.   The most important aspect of this row of Part A is the extent to which the rates parallel those in Row 3 for husband-to-wife assault. The repeated finding that the rate of assault by women is similar to the rate by their male partners is an important and distressing aspect of violence in American families. It contrasts markedly to the behavior of women outside the family. It shows that within the family or in dating and cohabiting relationships, women are about as violent as men. This highly controversial finding of the 1975 study is confirmed by the 1985 study and also by the rates found by other investigators listed in Table 6.2.

The importance of intrafamily violence by women should not be dismissed because men are larger and heavier and can inflict more serious injury. Nor should it be dismissed on the grounds that it is in self-defense or in retaliation, as is true of a substantial part of wife-to-husband violence (Straus, 1980). In the 1985 survey, we asked who hit first. According to the husbands, they struck the first blow in 44% of the cases, the wives in 45% of the cases, and the husband could not remember or disentangle it in the remaining 11% of the cases. According to the wives, husbands struck the first blow in 53% of the cases, wives in 42% of the cases, and the remaining 5% of wives could not disentangle who hit first.

Violence by women is a critically important issue for the safety and well-being *of women*. Let us assume that most of the assaults by women are the "slap the cad" genre and are not intended to and do not physically injure the husband (Greenblatt, 1983). The results of a longitudinal study in Chapter 27 show that danger to a woman of such behavior is that it sets the stage for the husband to assault her. Sometimes this is immediate and severe retaliation. But regardless of whether that occurs, the fact that she slapped him provides a precedent and justification for him to hit her when *she* is being obstinate, "bitchy," or "not listening to reason" as he sees it. Unless women also forsake violence in their relationships with male partners and children, they cannot expect to be free of assault. Women must insist as much on non-violence by their sisters as they rightfully insist on it by men. That is beginning to happen. After years of denial, shelters for battered women are confronting this problem. Almost all shelters now have policies designed to deal with the high rate of child abuse, and some are also facing up to the problem of wife-to-husband violence.[4]

Violence against Children and by Children

National Survey Rates

Overall violence rate.   No rates or numbers are shown in the first row of Part B of Table 6.1 because statistics on whether *any* violence is used are almost meaningless unless one takes into account the age of the child. For children age three and under, the true figure is close to 100%. For example, 97% and 90% of the parents of three-year-olds in the 1975 and 1985 surveys reported one or more times during the year when they had hit the child (Chapter 8, Figure 1; Straus, 1983, Figure 4), i.e., a rate of 997 or 990 per 1,000. For children age 15 and over, the rate of 340 per 1,000 in the first row of Part C of Table 6.1 shows that the rate is much lower, but it nonetheless means that about a third of 15–17-year-olds were hit by a parent during the year of the study.

The most important data in Part B are the statistics on "very severe" and "severe" violence. These are alternative measures of child abuse. The first (as noted in Chapters 1 and 7) omits hitting the child with an object such as a stick or belt and will be called "Child Abuse 1." The second, which will be called the "Child Abuse 2" rate, adds hitting with an object, on the grounds that hitting with an object carries a relatively greater risk of injury than spanking or slapping with the hand. For this reason we think that the more inclusive measure (Child Abuse 2) is the best indicator of the extent of physical abuse of children.

Child abuse 1.   The rate of such indubitably abusive violence was 23 per 1,000 children in 1985. If this rate is correct, it means a minimum of 1.5 million children are seriously assaulted each year. As in the case of the estimated number of beaten wives, the actual rate and the actual number are almost certainly greater because not all parents were willing to tell us about instances in which they kicked or punched a child.

Child abuse 2.   The third row of Part B shows that in 1985 11 out of every 100 children were assaulted by a parent in a way that we regard as "abuse." When this rate is applied to the 63 million children living in the U.S. in 1985, it results in an estimate of 6.9 million abused children per year.

Abuse of children age 15–17.   Teenagers are by no means immune. About 1 out of 3 parents of a child age 15 through 17 reported having physically assaulted the child at least once during 1985. This was usually one of the acts of "minor violence" such as slapping. However, serious assaults were far from absent. In fact, part C of Table 6.1 shows that seventy out of every one thousand children this age were victims of a serious assault by one of their parents, including 21 per 1,000 who were victims of very serious assaults.

Violence by Children

Children 3 through 17.   The first row of Section D in Table 6.1 reveals that children are the most violent people of all in American families. The rates are extremely high for violence against a sibling—eight hundred out of one thousand had hit a brother or sister, and more than half had engaged in one of the acts in the CTS "Severe Violence" list. This came as a surprise, even though it should not have. Had we analyzed the issue theoretically beforehand, it would have been an obvious prediction because of the well-known tendency for children to imitate and exaggerate the behavioral patterns of parents and because there are implicit norms that permit violence between siblings, exemplified by phrases such as "kids will fight."

The rate of assault against parents is much lower, perhaps because of the strong norms against hitting one's father or mother. However, this rate is still substantial and is not confined to minor violence: 90 per 1,000 children severely assaulted a parent during the year of this survey.

Children 15 through 17.   There is a vast difference between being punched by a five-year-old and being punched by a fifteen-year-old—at least in respect to the pain or injury that can result. Consequently, we computed separate rates for assaults by 15–17-year-olds. The first row in Part E of Table 6.1 shows that even in their late teens, two-thirds of American children assault a sibling at least once during the course of a year and in over a third of these cases the assault involved an act with a relatively high probability of causing injury (kicking, punching, biting, choking, attacks with a knife or gun, etc.). These incredible rates of intrafamily violence by teenagers make the high rates of violence by their parents seem modest by comparison.

Finally, the last two rows in Table 6.1 show that teenagers attack their parents about as often as the parents attack each other. The overall violence rate is slightly lower (100 per 1,000 children this age versus 113 per 1,000 husbands and 121 per 1,000 wives), and the rate of severe violence against a parent (35 per thousand children) is midway between the rate of severe husband-to-wife violence (32) and severe wife-to-husband violence (45).

Parent-Child Violence Rates from Studies Using Other Methods

There are two major sources of data on physical child abuse in addition to the rates produced by studies using the CTS. However, both of these are measures of *intervention* or treatment rather than *incidence* rates (see Chapter 7 for further explanation). They are presented here because they are probably the most widely known and cited statistics on intrafamily violence in the United States and therefore need to be evaluated in relation to other measures of child abuse.

CPS rate. Annual statistics are compiled on the number of child abuse cases reported to the Child Protective Services (CPS) under the mandatory reporting laws that are in effect in all the states. The 1984 rate was 27.3 per 1,000 children (American Association for Protecting Children, 1986). However, the CPS rate covers not only physical abuse, but also sexual abuse, and neglect. Other information in the report indicates that about one-quarter of these cases involved physical abuse. If this interpretation is correct, the incidence rate is approximately 6.8 per 1,000. By contrast, the National Family Violence Resurvey rates in Table 6.1 are 23 per 1,000 for "Child Abuse 1" and 110 per 1,000 for the "Child Abuse 2" measure. Thus the survey rate for the more severe assaults on children is 3.4 times greater than the CPS rate, and the survey rate for the more inclusive measure of physical abuse is 16 times greater than the CPS. We think that the best way to interpret these differences is to say that comparison of the CPS rate with the rate obtained in the National Family Violence Resurvey shows that there are from 3.4 to 16 times more physically abused children in the United States than receive help.

National incidence study. This study attempted to find out about all known cases of child abuse in a sample of 26 counties surveyed in 1980 (National Center on Child Abuse and Neglect, 1981). The procedure went beyond the official reporting system described above by also collecting data on cases known to personnel in community institutions (schools, hospitals, police, courts), regardless of whether the cases had been reported officially. It produced a physical abuse rate of 3.4 per 1,000 children. This is about 26% higher than the rate of officially reported cases of physical abuse in *1980* (the CPS rate has gone up tremendously since then because the new attention to sexual abuse has produced an influx of cases), but is still much lower than the rate from either the 1975 or the 1985 National Family Violence Survey.

Parental Violence Rates from Other Studies Using The CTS

Part B of Table 6.2 summarizes the incidence rates for physical child abuse from studies that used approximately the same method of computing the rate as was used in the National Family Violence Resurvey.

Any violence. It is difficult to interpret the distribution of rates shown in the first row of Part B of Table 6.2. Part of the problem stems from the fact that the "any violence" measure includes ordinary physical punishment and the fact that the rate at which physical punishment is used declines sharply with each year after age six (Chapters 8 and 23). Thus the rates at the low end are for studies of adolescents. A second problem is that some of the studies combined rates for violence by the father and by the mother and some used only the rate of hitting by one or the other parent. Finally, as in the case of the other rows in the table, the nature of the sample affects the rate.This is shown by the fact that the rate of 908 per 1,000 is for the children of a sample of battered women.

Severe violence. We have so far not located any other study using the Child Abuse 1 measure, which focuses on the most severe and dangerous assaults on children. However, the second row of Part B of Table 6.3 allows comparison of the National Survey rate with several other studies that used the Child Abuse 2 measure. At first it seems as though the National Survey rate is unusually low. However, the difference is not that great, because the three highest rates included only cases from high violence populations—battered women and delinquent children.

Summary and Conclusions

This chapter presented the rates of spouse abuse and child abuse from the 1985 National Family Violence Resurvey and compared those rates with estimates from other studies. We found that:

TABLE 6.3

Parent-to-Child Violence Rates from CTS Studies by Other Investigators

Study	Sample	Comments*	Rate per Thousand
A. Any hitting of child			
Schumm, Martin, Bollman, & Jurich (1982)	probability (N = 98)	3i	322
Schumm, Martin, Bollman, & Jurich (1982)	probability (N = 83)	3h	338
Schumm, Martin, Bollman, & Jurich (1982)	probability (N = 98)	3j	352
Schumm, Martin, Bollman, & Jurich (1982)	probability (N = 83)	3z	390
Meredith, Abbott, & Adams (1986)	probability (N = 304)	3n	500
Meredith, Abbott, & Adams (1986)	probability (N = 304)	3p	580
Gelles & Straus	probability (N = 3,232)		620
Brutz & Ingoldsby (1984)	volunteer (N = 288)	3p	689
Brutz & Ingoldsby (1984)	volunteer (N = 288)	3n	742
Giles-Sims (1985)	volunteer (N = 27)	3d	908
B. Severe violence—"child abuse-2" (ages vary)			
Brutz & Ingoldsby (1984)	volunteer (N = 288)	3p	88
Gelles & Straus	probability (N = 3,232)		110
Brutz & Ingoldsby (1984)	volunteer (N = 288)	3n	113
Meredith, Abbott, & Adams (1986)	probability (N = 304)	3n	170
Meredith, Abbott, & Adams (1986)	probability (N = 304)	3p	211

(continued)

TABLE   3 Continued

Study	Sample	Comments*	Rate per Thousand
Dembo, Bertke, LaVoie, Borders, Washburn, & Schneidler (1987)	volunteer (N = 145)	2a, eq, 4a	460
Giles-Sims (1985)	volunteer (N = 27)	3d	593
Dembo, Bertke, LaVoie, Borders, Washburn & Schneidler (1987)	volunteer (N = 145)	2a, e1, 4b	680

*See key to comments in Table 1.2.

- One hundred sixty-one out of every thousand couples experienced one or more physical assaults on a partner during the year of the study.
- Attacks by husbands on wives that were serious enough to warrant the term "wife beating" (because they involved dangerous forms of assault such as punching, biting, kicking, choking, etc.) were experienced by 34 per 1,000 American wives. If this rate is correct, it means that about 1.8 million women were severely assaulted by their partner in 1985.
- Assaults by women on their male partners occur at about the same rate as assaults by men on their female partners, and women initiate such violence about as often as men.
- Two estimates of child abuse were computed. The first is based on whether the child was kicked, bitten, punched, beaten up, burned, or scalded or was threatened or attacked with a knife or gun. Using this measure, we found an abuse rate of 24 per 1,000 children. If this rate is correct, it means that about 1.5 million children are physically abused each year.
- The second child abuse measure adds hitting the child with an object to the above list. This measure results in a rate of 110 per 1,000 children, which if it is correct means that about 6.9 million children are severely assaulted each year.
- Children are the most violent persons in American families. Almost all young children hit a sibling, and more than one out of five hit a parent. The intrafamily violence rate for children in their late teens (15–17) is much lower, but still substantial: about two-thirds hit a sibling, and 10% hit a parent.

We also compared these rates with data from other studies, both studies using similar survey methodology and studies using different methods.

- The rate of assault between spouses from the National Family Violence Survey is more than 70 times greater than the rate based on the National Crime Survey, the only other national survey. The difference probably results from the fact that most people consider hitting a spouse wrong, but not a crime in the legal sense.
- Comparison of the National Family Violence Resurvey rates for child abuse with the rates for child abuse cases known to the Child Protective Services (CPS) of each state shows that the incidence rate found by this survey is about three and a half times greater than the rate of physical abuse cases known to CPS. If child abuse is defined to include hitting a child with an object, then the survey rate is about 16 times greater than the number of cases reported to protective service agencies in 1985.
- A number of other studies have used the CTS to measure intrafamily violence. Some of these studies resulted in rates that are much higher and some much lower than those reported in this chapter. However, these differences seem to be due to differences in the composition of the samples used in those studies and differences in certain other factors such as the age of the children in studies of child abuse.

In Chapter 7, we compare the rates found in the two national family violence surveys and suggest that there were substantial reductions between 1975 and 1985 in the rates of child abuse and wife beating. Despite these reductions, it is obvious from the rates reported in this chapter that the incidence of intrafamily violence remains extremely high. In 1985 the FBI reported 723,250 "aggravated assaults." The approximate equivalent from the 1985 survey is an estimated 3,400,000 severe assaults on a spouse.[5] The national Family Violence Survey assault rate is therefore more than five times the FBI rate. American society still has a long way to go before a typical citizen is as safe in his or her own home as on the streets or in a workplace.

Notes

We are pleased to acknowledge the help of Diane Cyr Carmody and Barbara A. Wauchope in locating and summarizing the many studies that have used the CTS.

1. The rates to be reported here are higher than those in Chapter 7 comparing violence rates in 1985 with those found in 1975–1976 (Straus and Gelles, 1986) because the need for comparability meant that the analysis could not use the 1985 additions to the CTS list of violent acts (described earlier), and also could

not use the 1985 additions to the sample (children under three, single parents, and information about marriages that had recently been terminated).

2. The term *couple violence* in this context refers to whether *either* partner was violent and both were not necessarily violent. Of the couples where either was violent, in about half the cases both were violent, about one quarter were cases in which the husband was violent but not the wife, and in the remaining one quarter the wife was violent but not the husband.

3. For convenience and economy of wording, terms such as *marital, spouse, wife,* and *husband* are used to refer to couples, irrespective of whether they are a married or a non-married cohabiting couple. For an analysis of differences and similarities between married and cohabiting couples, see Chapter 13 and Yllo 1978; Yllo and Straus, 1981.

4. This will not be easy to accomplish, in part because, as we noted in Chapter 7, the cost of giving publicity to violence by wives is that it will be used to defend male violence. Our 1975 data, for example, have been used against battered women in court cases and also to minimize the need for shelters for battered women. However, the cost of failing to attend to this problem will ultimately block the goal of being free from violence by men. There may be costs associated with acknowledging the fact of female domestic violence, but the cost of denial and suppression is even greater. Rather than attempting to deny the existence of such violence (see Pleck, et al., 1977, for an example and the reply by Steinmetz, 1978), a more productive solution is to confront the issue and work toward eliminating violence by women. The achievements of the twenty-year effort to reduce child abuse and the ten-year effort to reduce wife beating (see Straus and Gelles, 1986) suggest this is a realistic goal.

5. Comparison between the two figures is problematic and must be interpreted with caution for a number of reasons. First, both figures are underestimates, but not necessarily by the same amount. Second, the severity of an assault and the other circumstances that lead to an assault being recorded by the police as an "aggravated assault" differ from the severity and circumstances that led to a case being included in the survey statistics, but again the specific differences are not known. Third, the FBI rate includes some intrafamily assaults. For the survey, we know that about 1 out of 14 severe assaults were reported to the police. However, there are no FBI statistics on the percent of assaults that were between family members.

7

Societal Change and Change in Family Violence from 1975 to 1985 As Revealed by Two National Surveys

Murray A. Straus and Richard J. Gelles

Child Abuse and Wife Beating in Previous Historical Periods

Although our purpose is to compare the rates for physical violence against children and spouses in 1985 with the rates found in a 1975 study, we begin with a brief historical overview because that information is helpful for evaluating the results to be reported for 1975–85.

Wife Beating

The subordinate status of women in American society, and in most of the world's societies, is well documented (Blumberg, 1978; Chafetz, 1984). Since physical force is the ultimate recourse to keep subordinate groups in their place, women in the history of Euro-American society have often been the victims of physical assault (Straus, 1976).

Blackstone's codification of the common law in 1768 asserted that a husband had the right to "physically chastise" an errant wife, provided the stick was no bigger than his thumb. As recently as 1867 this rule was upheld by an appellate court in North Carolina. It would be bad enough if the violence against women had been limited to this "rule of thumb." However, more severe beatings were common. In the Middle Ages women were burned alive "for threatening their husbands, for talking back to or refusing a priest, for stealing, for prostitution, for adultery, for bearing a child out of wedlock, for permitting sodomy (even though the priest or husband who committed it was forgiven), for masturbating, for Lesbianism, for child neglect, for scolding and nagging, and for miscarrying, even though the miscarriage was caused by a kick or a blow from the husband'' (Davis, 1971).

Burning at the stake is now part of the dim historical past. The *right* to physically chastise has long since disappeared from the common law. However, what actually takes place in American marriages is a different matter. In 1975–76 we carried out a study of a nationally representative sample of 2,143 American couples. That study revealed that at least one violent incident occurred in 16% of American families during the year of study (1975–76). If the referent period is since the marriage began, the figure is 28% (Straus, Gelles, and Steinmetz, 1980). Although about two-thirds of the violent incidents were minor assaults such as slapping and throwing things, the other third of the incidents were serious assaults such as punching, biting, kicking, hitting with an object, beating up, or assaults with a knife or gun.

Child Abuse

The history of Western society reveals that children have also been subject to unspeakable cruelties, including the abandonment of infants to die of exposure (Radbill, 1980). Although every American state now seeks to protect children through child abuse laws, the task which remains is huge. Even prisoners in jail cannot legally be hit or verbally abused, but physical punishment of children is legal in every state. Anyone who spends an afternoon at a supermarket or shopping mall is likely to observe instances of children being hit or verbally abused. And that is but the tip of the iceberg. Most of the physical and mental cruelty that children experience every day goes on behind the closed doors of millions of American homes.

The rate of physical child abuse revealed by the 1975 study is astounding. Interviews with parents indicate that 36 out of every thousand American children from 3 through 17 years old (i.e., almost 4%) experienced an assault that is serious enough to be included in our "Very Severe Violence index." A rate of 36 per thousand means that of the 46 million children of this age group in the United States who were living with both parents in 1975, approximately 1.7 million were "abused" that year.[1]

It may be that these data overstated the amount of child abuse because a family is included if even one isolated incident of abusive violence occurred during the year. This was not the case. We found that if one assault occurred, several were likely. In fact, in only 6% of the child abuse cases was there a single incident. The mean number of assaults per year was 10.5 and the median 4.5.

Is There an Epidemic of Child Abuse and Spouse Abuse?

Child Abuse

Given the fact that millions of American children were physically abused by their parents in 1975 and that the number of cases of child abuse reported to social service agencies has been rising at a rate of about 10% per year since the mid-seventies (American Humane Association, 1983), one is tempted to take this as evidence that child abuse is rapidly escalating. Certainly, the statistics gathered by the American Humane Association show a rising trend. However, neither the high incidence rate nor the increase in the officially reported rate necessarily mean that child abuse is increasing. In fact, those concerned with America's children might be pleased that each year's "official statistics" on child abuse tops the previous year's figures. This is true because the figures might indicate something quite different from a real increase in the rate of child abuse. The true incidence of child abuse may actually be *declining*, even though the number of cases is increasing. What then do the reports from the 50 states indicate? There are at least two factors that might produce an increase in cases reported, even though the actual rate is declining.

The first factor is that all states now have compulsory child abuse reporting laws. As a result, a larger and larger proportion of the millions of previously unreported cases come to the attention of child welfare services. A dramatic example of this occurred in Florida. The year before the introduction of a statewide "hot-line" for reporting suspected cases of child abuse, only a few hundred cases of child abuse were known to state authorities. However, in the year following the introduction of the hot-line, several thousand cases were reported (Nagi, 1976).

The second factor is much more fundamental. Without it, the reporting system would not work even to the extent that it now operates. This is the fact that new standards are evolving in respect to how much violence parents can use in childrearing. American society is now undergoing a "moral passage" (Gusfield, 1963) in which the definition of child abuse is being gradually enlarged to include acts that were not previously thought of as child abuse. This can create the misleading impression of an epidemic of child abuse. Changed standards are also the real force behind the child abuse reporting laws. Were it not for these changing standards, the reporting laws would not have been enacted; or if enacted, they would tend to be ignored.

Wife Beating

Until recently, there were no statistics on wife-beating cases known to the police or social service agencies (Lerman, 1981). Consequently, even the data for the three states that now record such cases cannot tell us about trends. However, the number of cases reported in newspapers and the number of magazine articles and television documentaries on wife beating increased dramaticaly during the 1970s and '80s. Although most of these articles described an "epidemic" of wife beating, the apparent increase may reflect a growing awareness and recognition of an already existing high incidence of wife beating, combined with an inability or unwillingness to believe that this much violence could previously have been characteristic of an institution as sacred as the family.

Comparing the Two National Surveys

Family violence may, in fact, be increasing; or it may be declining. An earlier paper argued that both wife and child abuse are probably decreasing (Straus, 1981b), but no empirical evidence was available at that time. The purpose of this chapter is to compare the rates of physical abuse of children and spouses at two distinct points in time as found in the two national surveys.

As explained in Chapter 1, the 1975 study surveyed currently married or cohabiting couples, while the 1985 study also included separated or divorced individuals as well as single parents. In order to make rates from the two studies comparable, data from the 1985 survey had to be adjusted in the following ways. First, only the national cross-section portion of the 1985 sample was used (N = 4, 032), omitting cases from the state, Black and Hispanic oversamples. Second, cases were also omitted from the 1985 study (for purposes of this chapter) if the respondent was not currently coupled. Third, the additional items in the 1985 versions of the Severe Violence Index (scalding in the case of parent-to-child violence and choking in the case of husband-wife violence) were also excluded in this analysis. Omitting those cases and the new violence items (which are the major distinctions between the two national surveys) allows for direct comparisons of the violence rates.

Violence Against Children in 1975 and 1985[2]

Table 7.1 enables one to compare the 1975 and 1985 rates per thousand children for each violent act as well as three summary indexes of violence.[3] The data in Parts A and B show that, with the exception of the most unusual and severe forms of violence (Items 7 and 8: threatening and using guns and knives), *the occurrence of each form of violence toward children declined in the last 10 years.* However, only two of these differences are statistically significant. The more important and reliable results are those for the summary indexes shown in Part C and discussed below.

Overall Violence Rate

The Overall Violence row of Part C indicates whether a parent used *any* of the eight forms of violence at least once during the 12-month period covered by the survey. It shows that there was essentially no change in the rate of violence between 1975 and 1985. The decrease from 630 per thousand children in 1975 to 620 per thousand children in 1985 is equivalent to saying that in 1975 almost two-thirds of the parents in the sample (63%) reported hitting the "referent child" (the child selected as the focus of the interview) during the survey year, and that in 1985 the figure was 62%. However, these high rates are somewhat misleading because they do not take into account the age of the child. For 3-year-olds, the 1975 figure was much higher: 97%. For children aged 15 and over, the rate was much lower: "only" about a third of 15-to-17-year-olds were hit by a parent during the year of the study.

Severe Violence

The second row of Table 7.1, Part C, shows that the rate of Severe Violence (kicking, biting, punching, hitting or trying to hit with an object, beating, threatening with a gun or knife, or using a gun or knife) declined from 140 per thousand children in 1975 to 107 in 1985.

Child Abuse Rate

The difficulty with the Severe Violence Index as a measure of physical child abuse is that many parents do not consider Item 5 (hitting with an object such as a stick, hairbrush, or belt) to be abuse. Consequently, as explained earlier, we used the Very Severe Violence Index, shown in the third row of Part C, as the measure of child abuse for this paper. This is the same as the Severe Violence Index, except that it omits hitting with an object and is therefore the index that comes closest to the public concep-tion of child abuse. The rate of such indubitably abusive violence declined from 36 per thousand children to 19. This is *a decline of 47% in the rate of physical child abuse since 1975.*

TABLE 7.1

Parent-to-Child Violence: Comparison of Rates in 1975 and 1985

Type of Violence	Rate per 1,000 Children Aged 3 through 17[a]		t for 1975–1985 Difference
	1975 $n = 1,146$[b]	1985 $n = 1,428$[c]	
A. Minor Violence Acts			
1. Threw something	54	27	3.52***
2. Pushed/grabbed/shoved	318	307	0.54
3. Slapped or spanked	582	549	1.68
B. Severe Violence Acts			
4. Kicked/bit/hit with fist	32	13	3.31**
5. Hit, tried to hit with something	134	97	2.91**
6. Beat up	13	6	1.86
7. Threatened with gun or knife	1	2	0.69
8. Used gun or knife	1	2	0.69
C. Violence Indexes			
Overall Violence (1–8)	630	620	0.52
Severe Violence (4–8)	140	107	2.56**
Very Severe Violence (5–8) ("child abuse" for this article)	36	19	2.67***

[a]For two-caretaker households with at least one child 3 to 17 years of age at home.
[b]A few respondents were omitted because of missing data on some items, but the n is never less than 1,140.
[c]A few respondents were omitted because of missing data on some items, but the n is never less than 1,418.
*$p < .05$; **$p < .01$; ***$p < .001$ (two-tailed tests).

TABLE 7.2

Marital Violence Indexes: Comparison of 1975 and 1985

Violence Index	Rate per 1,000 Couples		t for 1975–1985 Difference
	1975	1985	
A. Husband-to-Wife			
Overall Violence (1–6)	121	113	0.91
Severe Violence (4–8) ("wife beating")	38	30	1.60
B. Wife-to-Husband			
Overall Violence (1–6)	116	121	0.57
Severe Violence (4–8)	46	44	0.35
C. Couple			
Overall Violence (1–6)	160	158	0.20
Severe Violence (4–8)	61	58	0.46
Number of cases[a]	2,143	3,520	

[a]A few respondents were omitted because of missing data on some items, but the n is never decreased by more than 10.

Violence between Spouses in 1975 and 1985

Table 7.2 summarizes the findings on violence between married or cohabiting couples in the form of three indexes (data on each violent act separately is presented in Table 7.3).[4] These indexes differentiate between "minor violence" (pushing, slapping, and throwing things) and "severe violence" (kicking, biting, punching, etc.). All but one of the nine comparisons in Table 7.2 show that the rate of violence was lower in 1985 than in

1975. However, as compared to the changes in parental violence, the decreases from 1975 to 1985 are much smaller.

Husband-to-Wife Violence

The first row of Table 7.2, Part A, shows that the Overall Violence rate of violence by husbands declined from 121 to 113. Thus, the husband-to-wife violence rate declined by 6.6%, which is not statistically significant.

The second row of Part A reports the rate of Severe Violence by husbands—our measure of "wife beating." It shows that the rate declined from 38 per thousand couples to 30 per thousand couples in 1985. A decrease of 8 per thousand may not seem large, and it is not statistically significant ($p < .10$). However, it is worth interpreting because, relative to the 1975 rate, it represents a 21.8% decrease in the rate of wife beating, and the difference comes close to being significant. In addition, a decrease of 8 per thousand in the rate of wife beating is worth noting because, if correct, it represents a large number of couples. Specifically, if the 1975 rate for husband-to-wife severe violence had remained in effect, the application of this rate to the 54 million couples in the U.S. in 1985 results in an estimate of at least 2,052,000 severely assaulted wives each year. However, if there has been a 27% decrease in the rate, that translates to 1,620,000 beaten wives, which is 432,000 fewer than would have been the case if the 1975 rate prevailed. That would be an extremely important reduction. On the other hand, the 1985 estimate of 1.6 million beaten wives is hardly an indicator of domestic tranquility.[5]

Wife-to-Husband Violence

Although the trend for husband-to-wife violence is encouraging, the situation for wife-to-husband violence is at best mixed. Part B of Table 2 shows that the Overall Violence rate actually increased slightly. The rate for Severe Violence against a husband decreased, but only slightly. Neither of these changes is statistically significant.

In addition to the trends, the violence rates in Part B reveal an important and distressing finding about violence in American families—that, in marked contrast to the behavior of women outside the family, women are about as violent within the family as men. This highly controversial finding of the 1975 study is confirmed by the 1985 study and also by findings on other samples and by other investigators (Brutz and Ingoldsby, 1984; Gelles, 1974; Giles-Sims, 1983; Laner and Thompson, 1982; Lane and Gwartney-Gibbs, 1985; Jouriles and O'Leary, 1985; Makepeace, 1983;

Sack, Keller, and Howard, 1982; Saunders, 1986; Scanzoni, 1978; Steinmetz, 1977, 1977–78; Szinovacz, 1983).

Although the two national surveys and the ten studies just cited leave little doubt about the high frequency of wife-to-husband violence, the meaning and consequences of that violence are easily misunderstood. For one thing, as pointed out elsewhere (Straus, 1977; Straus, Gelles, and Steinmetz, 1980:43), the greater average size and strength of men, and their greater aggressiveness (Maccoby and Jacklin, 1974; Tavris and Offir, 1977), mean that the same act (for example, a punch) is likely to be very different in the amount of pain or injury inflicted (see also Greenblat, 1983). Even more important, a great deal of violence by women against their husbands is retaliation or self-defense (Straus, 1980; Saunders, 1986). One of the most fundamental reasons why some women are violent within the family, but not outside the family, is that the risk of assault for a typical American woman is greatest in her own home (Straus, Gelles, and Steinmetz, 1980: chapters 1 and 2). Nonetheless, violence by women against their husbands is not something to be dismissed because of the even greater violence by husbands.

On the other hand, the cost of drawing attention to violence by wives is that the information will be used to defend male violence. Our 1975 data, for example, have been used against battered women in court cases, and also to minimize the need for shelters for battered women. However, in the long run, the results of the present study suggest that the cost of denial and suppression is even greater because, as shown in Chapter 27, even minor violence by wives greatly increases the risk of subsequent severe assault by the husband. Rather than attempting to deny the existence of such violence (see Pleck, Pleck, Grossman, and Bart, 1977, for an example and the reply by Steinmetz, 1978), a more productive solution is to confront the issue and attempt to eliminate violence by women. This is beginning to happen. Almost all shelters for battered women now have policies designed to deal with the high rate of child abuse, and some are also facing up to the problem of wife-to-husband violence.

Couple Violence and Specific Violent Acts

Couple violence.   Part C of Table 7.2 combines the data on violence by husbands and wives. The first row shows that in 1975, a violent act occurred in 160 out of every thousand families, and that the 1985 rate was almost as high. Similarly, the second row reveals only a small decrease in the rate of *severe* assaults on a spouse—from 61 to 58 per thousand couples. This is a 5% reduction, which is not statistically significant.

Specific violent acts.   Table 7.3 presents the rates for each of the violent

TABLE 7.3

Marital Violence: Comparison of Specific Acts, 1975–1985

Type of Violence	Husband-to-Wife		Wife-to-Husband	
	1975	1985	1975	1985
A. Minor Violence Acts				
1. Threw something	28	28	52	43
2. Pushed/grabbed/shoved	107	93	83	89
3. Slapped	51	29**	46	41
B. Severe Violence Acts				
4. Kicked/bit/hit with fist	24	15*	31	24
5. Hit, tried to hit with something	22	17	30	30
6. Beat up	11	8	6	4
7. Threatened with gun or knife	4	4	6	6
8. Used gun or knife	3	2	2	2
Number of cases[a]	2,143	3,520	2,143	3,520

[a]A few respondents were omitted because of missing data on some items, but the n is never decreased by more than 10.

*$p < .05$; **$p < .01$ (two-tailed t tests for 1975–85 differences).

acts making up the 1975 and 1985 versions of the CTS. These rates are presented for the record and to show what went into the summary indexes discussed above.

Prevention and Treatment Programs and Change in Family Violence

This section considers the extent to which change in different forms of intrafamily violence parallels the extent of the intensity of prevention and treatment programs.

Child Abuse

This form of physical violence entered the public agenda as a major social problem with the classic paper by Kempe, Silverman, Steele, Droegemueller, and Silver (1962). Since 1971, every state has adopted compulsory reporting laws, and an extensive educational effort has developed across the country. In comparison to other forms of domestic violence, the largest share of financial resources has been allocated to child abuse. There are now thousands of social workers assigned to child abuse work who were not available a decade or more ago. The fact that we found a larger decrease for child abuse than for any other aspect of family violence may reflect the fact that it has been the object of the longest and most intensive campaign.

Wife Beating

The campaign against wife beating, by contrast, began a decade or more later and has been less intensive, and far fewer resources have been invested. Providing shelters has mostly been a private endeavor of the women's movement. Even the feeble effort of the federal government in the form of an information clearinghouse was abolished early in the Reagan administration. Many bills to provide funds for shelters have been introduced and defeated. When a bill appropriating a modest sum was finally passed in 1985, the administration refused to spend the funds. Nevertheless, by 1985 the women's movement succeeded in creating a national consciousness and in establishing hundreds of shelters for battered women (Back, Blum, Nakhnikian, and Stark, 1980; Warrior, 1982); and by 1985 our study found a substantial reduction in the rate of wife beating.

Violence by Wives

Violence by wives has not been an object of public concern. There has been no publicity, and no funds have been invested in ameliorating this problem because it has not been defined as a problem. in fact, our 1975 study was criticized for presenting statistics on violence by wives.[6] Our 1985 finding of little change in the rate of assaults by women on their male partners is consistent with the absence of ameliorative programs.

Physical Punishment of Children

Not only has physical punishment of children not been a focus of a public effort, but most Americans consider it morally correct to hit a child who misbehaves (Straus, Gelles, and Steinmetz, 1980). Consistent with this, we found only small and nonsignificant differences between 1975 and 1985 in the overall rate of parent-to-child violence.

Overall, the findings of this study are consistent with the idea that the longer an aspect of violence has been the object of public condemnation, and the more resources that are put into the effort to change that aspect of violence, the greater the reduction in the objectionable behavior.

Alternative Interpretations of the Findings

We have presented some startling and controversial findings. When the *Christian Science Monitor* interviewed criminologist Richard Berk concerning the results of this study ("2 researchers say," 18 November 1985, pp. 3–4), he commented, "Given all we know about the pattern of crime statistics, a 47% drop is so unprecedented as to be unbelievable. Never before has there been a drop of that magnitude, that rapidly." But, contrary to Berk's assertion, other crime rates *have* changed that much and that fast. The homicide rate, for example, increased by over 100%

between 1963 and 1973; and in the four years from 1980 to 1984 homicide dropped by 29%—a rate which, if continued for another 6 years, will produce a 10-year decrease that is greater than the 47% decrease we found for child abuse (Straus, 1986).

The homicide statistics indicate that there is a precedent for changes in crime rates of the magnitude we found for physical child abuse and wife beating. In fact, our statistics on the decrease in child abuse and wife beating parallel the recent decreases in homicide, including intrafamily homicide (Straus, in press). Nevertheless, it is important to regard these results with caution because, with the data available, one can only speculate about the processes that produced the decreases. We will discuss three possible explanations for the findings.

Methodological Differences between the Two Surveys

Data for the 1975 survey were collected by in-person interview, while the 1985 survey was conducted over the telephone. Research on differences between telephone and in-person interviews has shown no major differences in results (Groves and Kahn, 1979; Marcus and Crane, 1986; Smith, in press), and telephone interviewing is now the most widely used method of conducting surveys, including the National Crime Survey. To the extent that there is a difference, we believe, the anonymity offered by the telephone leads to more truthfulness and, therefore, increased reporting of violence. The difference in interview method should have produced *higher,* not lower, rates of reported violence in 1985.

However, a characteristic of telephone surveys that is usually an advantage—the higher rate of completed interviews—might have affected the difference between the 1975 and 1985 rates. The 1985 survey had an 85% completion rate, versus 65% for the 1976–76 survey. Assuming that a higher completion rate means a more representative sample, the question is whether this makes for a lower or a higher rate of reported violence. That depends on whether those who refused to participate are more or less likely to be violent. If those who refused are less likely to be violent, then the fact that there were fewer refusals in 1985 would tend to reduce the violence rate.However, we think it more likely that the violence rate is higher among those who refuse to participate. If so, a reduction in refusals would tend to produce a higher rate of violence, whereas we found a lower rate of violence in 1985 despite the much lower number of refusals.

Another methodological difference is that, in the 1975–76 survey, respondents were handed a card listing the response categories for the Conflict Tactics Scales. All possible answers, including "never," were on the card. For the 1985 telephone survey, interviewers read the response categories, beginning with "once" and continuing to "more than 20 times." Respondents had to volunteer "never" or "don't know" responses. Experience has shown that rates of reported sensitive or deviant behavior are higher if the subject has to volunteer the "no" or "never" response (see, for example, Kinsey, Pomeroy, and Martin, 1948).

These differences in methodology between the two studies should have led to higher, not lower, rates of reported violence. Since the rates of child abuse and wife beating decreased, it seems unlikely that the change is due to the different methods of data collection.

Reluctance to Report

A second plausible explanation for the decline in the rate of child abuse and wife beating is that respondents may have been more reluctant to report severe violence in 1985 than in 1975. As indicated above, the last 10 years have seen a tremendous increase in public attention to the problem of child abuse and wife beating. National media campaigns, new child abuse and neglect laws, hot-lines, and almost daily media attention have transformed behaviors that were ignored for centuries into major social problems. The decrease in child abuse and wife beating may reflect a "moral passage" (Gusfield, 1963), as family violence becomes less acceptable and consequently fewer parents and fewer husbands are willing to admit to participating in violence. The implications of such a change in American culture are discussed at the conclusion of this article.

Change in Behavior

The third explanation is that there has indeed been a decline in child abuse and wife beating. This explanation is consistent with changes in the family and other developments during the last 10 years that might have served to reduce the rate of family violence. These fall into five broad categories: changes in the family and the economy that are associated with less violence, more alternatives for abused women, treatment programs, and deterrence.

Change in family structure.   There have been changes in a number of aspects of the family that are associated with violence, including: a rise in the average age at first marriage, an increase in the average age for having a first child, a decline in the number of children per family, and therefore, a corresponding decrease in the number of unwanted children (Statistical Abstract, 1985: Tables 120, 92, 63, 97). Parents in 1985 are among the first generation to be able to choose a full range of planned parenthood options (including abortion) to plan family size. All these factors are related to lower rates of child abuse and may have an indirect effect on spouse abuse by lowering the level of stress.[7] In addition, later marriage and the greater acceptability of divorce tend to equalize the balance of power between husband and wife.

The fact that, bit by bit, American marriages are becoming more equalitarian (Thornton, Alwin, and Camburn, 1983) has important implications for family violence because previous research shows that male-dominant marriages have the highest, and equalitarian marriages the lowest, rate of violence (Coleman and Straus, 1986; Straus, 1973; Straus, Gelles, and Steinmetz, 1980). There are many reasons for the increasing equality between husbands and wives in addition to the two mentioned above. For the decade in question, two of the most important factors are the diffusion of feminist ideology to a broader population base, and the increase in the percentage of women with paid jobs. Moreover, we found that full-time housewives experience a higher rate of wife beating (Straus, Gelles, and Steinmetz, 1980); thus the rapid increase in paid employment (Statistical Abstract, 1985; Tables 669–672) might also be associated with a lower rate of wife beating.

Economic change.   Both child abuse and wife beating are associated with unemployment and economic stress. The economic climate of the country is better in 1985 than in 1975 (at least for the population we are examining—intact families). The rate of employment and inflation is down compared to 10 years ago (Statistical Abstract, 1985; Table 777). The one-year referent period used for the 1985 survey coincided with one of the more prosperous years in the past decade. Thus, the lower level of economic stress in 1985 may have contributed to the decline in severe violence.

Alternatives for battered women.   As noted earlier, there were only a handful of "safe houses" or "shelters" for battered women in 1975, as contrasted with about 700 in 1985 (Back et al., 1980; Warrior, 1982). The existence of shelters provides an alternative that did not exist in 1975. In addition, the fact that shelters provide an alternative may have emboldened more women to tell their partner that his violence is unacceptable, and to make this more than an idle threat. Similarly, the tremendous growth in paid employment of married women in the 1975–85 period not only helped rectify the imbalance of power between spouses, but also provided the economic resources that enable more women to terminate a violent marriage (Kalmuss and Straus, 1982). Finally, the increased acceptance of divorce probably also helped more women to terminate violent marriages.

Treatment programs.   New and innovative prevention and treatment programs for child abuse and wife beating proliferated during or immediately before the 1975–85 decade. All 50 states enacted compulsory reporting laws for child abuse and neglect, and public and private social services have been developed to treat and prevent child abuse. Despite the underfunding and understaffing of these programs, the presence of thousands of new workers in child protective services is likely to have had an impact.[8] Only a small percentage of the cases they deal with are the gory (and difficult to treat) cases that make the newspaper headlines. Most are parents at their wits' end who can and do benefit from the help and the additional resources that state social service departments provide.

In respect to wife beating, whereas no treatment programs for men who assault their wives existed in the early 1970s, many such programs were available by 1985 (Pirog-Good and Stets-Kely, 1985), including a number of court-mandated programs; and there is some evidence of their effectiveness (Lerman, 1981). Finally, family therapy of all types has grown tremendously. It was probably the fastest-growing human service profession in the 1975–85 decade.[9] The increased use of family counseling and the increasing proportion of therapists who directly raise the issue of violence may have had a part in reducing intrafamily violence.

Deterrence.   Deterrence of a crime depends on the perception of potential offenders that the act is wrong and that there is a high probability of being apprehended and punished (Williams and Hawkins, in press). The decade in question has been characterized by activities that were intended to change both internalized norms and objective sanctions about family violence. Extensive efforts have been made to alert the public to the problem of child abuse and wife beating. In addition, shelters for battered women may have an indirect effect. The process of publicizing the availability of a shelter can contribute to a husband's redefining "I just slapped her a few times" to "I was violent." Each of these activities probably contributed to a changed perception of the legitimacy of violence against children and wives and therefore plays a preventative or deterrent role. Public opinion poll data suggest that those programs seem to have been effective. A 1976 study found that only about 10% of Americans considered child abuse a serious problem (Magnuson, 1983), whereas a 1982 poll conducted by Louis Harris and Associates found that 90% felt that child abuse was a serious national problem. This is a huge increase in public awareness. The problem of wife beating, although emphasized less than child abuse, has also received a major amount of publicity. It is not implausible to suggest that the advertising campaigns and media attention have had some effect in making parents more cautious about assaulting children and husbands more cautious about severely assaulting wives.

Another important change affects the certainty and severity of legal sanctions for wife beating. The police are gradually changing methods of dealing with wife beating. At the time of the 1975 study, the training manual for police officers prepared by the International Association of Chiefs of Police recommended separating the warring parties and leaving the scene of the marital violence. That manual now recommends dealing with all assaults on the same bases, irrespective of whether they are in the home or elsewhere (International Association of Chiefs of Police, 1976). A growing number of police departments are doing that. To the extent that this change in police policy was known to potential offenders, it is not implausible to think that it has had an effect. Indeed, a study comparing three different methods used by the police to deal with domestic violence suggests that there is a lower recidivism rate when wife beating is treated as a criminal act rather than a private problem (Sherman and Berk, 1984).

Summary and Conclusions

This article compares the rates of physical violence against children and spouses from a 1975–76 survey with the rates from a 1985 study that used the same instrument to measure violence. The most important findings are as follows: (a) Physical child abuse (as measured by the number of children who were kicked, punched, bitten, beaten up, or attacked with a knife or gun) decreased by 47% from 1975 to 1985. (b) Wife beating (measured by the occurence of these same acts, plus hitting with an object) decreased by 27%, but similarly severe assaults by wives on husbands decreased only 4.3%. (c) Even with these reductions, the rates of child abuse and wife beating remain extremely high.

Factors Underlying the Findings

The lower rates of severe violence in the 1985 study could have been produced by a number of factors, including: (a) differences in the methodology used in the two surveys, (b) a greater reluctance on the part of the respondents to report violence, or (c) a decrease in the amount of child abuse and wife beating. Our interpretation is that the decrease is probably not due to differences in the methods used in the two surveys because those differences would tend to increase rather than decrease the 1985 rate. This leaves two plausible explanations—the decrease could reflect a change in reporting behavior or a change in violent behavior.

From the perspective of the welfare of children and families, the most desirable interpretation is that the differences between 1975 and 1985 represents fewer physically abused children and fewer beaten wives. However, even if the reduction is entirely due to a greater reluctance to report violence, that is also important. It suggests that the effort to change public attitudes and standards concerning family violence have achieved a certain measure of success. In view of the fact that this decrease refers to changes in a relatively short period of 10 years, perhaps it could even be considered a remarkable degree of success. Moreover, a change in attitudes and cultural norms is an important part of the process leading to change in overt behavior. If all that has been accomplished in the last 10 years is to instill new standards for parents and husbands about the inappropriateness of violence, that is a key element in the process of reducing the actual rate of child abuse and wife beating.

Most likely the findings represent a combination of changed attitudes and norms along with changes in overt behavior. This interpretation is based on a number of changes in American society that took place during or immediately before the decade of this study, including: changes in the family, in the economy, in the social acceptability of family violence, in alternatives available to women, in social control processes, and in the availability of treatment and prevention services.

Policy Implications

If nationwide availability of child abuse treatment programs is one of the factors bringing about a decline in the child abuse rate, it helps explain the seeming contradictions between the decrease reported in this article and the even greater *increase* in cases known to child protective services (American Humane Association, 1983). To understand this, it is necessary to abandon the terminology used earlier in this article, which identifies the cases known to protective service workers as the "official" or "reported" rate, and the rate from our survey as the "real" rate of child abuse. Both are reported rates and both are real rates. The difference is not that one is right and the other wrong, but that they measure different phenomena. The rate based on cases known to child protective services in the various states can be thought of as a measure of services provided, or as a *treatment* rate, whereas the rate produced by our surveys is closer to an *incidence* rate.[10] The increase in the former (which is a proxy for the number of cases treated) is one of the factors that made possible the decrease in the number of child abuse incidents reported in this article.

The interpretations of the findings presented here have important policy implications that contrast sharply with the interpretation given in *Child Protection Report* under the headline "Gelles Study Strikes Discordant Note" (22 November 1985, p. 3), which reports that child protection advocates were angered at our findings because they fear the sharp decrease in rates of child abuse might undercut support for child abuse programs. But what if we had found no change? Critics could then argue that 10 years and millions of dollars of public and private funds had been wasted. We believe that the findings should be regarded in the same way as the findings on the sharp decrease in smoking by men, and the parallel finding that lung cancer rates for white males have turned down (*New York Times,* "Lung cancer," 3 December 1985, p. A1). Those findings supported rather than hindered increased efforts to reduce smoking.

As in the case of research on smoking, our findings provide a basis for believing that when a national effort is made about some aspect of intrafamily violence, a national accomplishment can be achieved. Moreover, the findings also show that an intensified effort is needed. Even if all the reductions from 1975 to 1985 were in actual assaults (i.e.. none of it a reduction in reporting of assaults), and even disregarding the underestimate resulting from the omission of the "high risk" categories of single-parent families and children under three, a reduction in child abuse of 47% still leaves a minimum estimate of over a million abused children aged 3 through 17 in two-parent households. Similarly, a reduction of 27% in wife beating still leaves over a million and a half beaten wives each year in the United States.

Notes

We are indebted to John Harrop for coding to compute many complicated indexes and for getting a large, complicated data set to run; to members of the 1985–86 Family Violence Research Program Seminar (Angela Browne, Jean Ellison, David Finkelhor, Gerry King, Christine Smith, Jill Suitor, and Barbara Wauchope); and to Suzanne K. Steinmetz for comments and suggestions on an earlier draft.

1. See Chapters 1, 2, and 3 for definitions of the terms *abuse* and *violence* as they are used in this report.
2. This section is relatively brief because violence against children is covered in detail in a companion paper focused entirely on that aspect of family violence (Gelles and Straus, 1985).
3. Previous reports on the 1975 study expressed the violence rate as a *percentage* of husbands, wives, or children, whereas, in this chapter, we use a rate per thousand couples or children. There are three reasons for this. (a) *Rate per thousand is comparable with other crime and child abuse rates.* The National Crime Survey (U.S. Department of Justice, 1985), which has become the de facto standard for survey research on the incidence of crime and victimization, and the annual rates of child abuse cases reported to child protective services in the United States both use rate per thousand. Adopting that standard facilitates comparison of rates from this survey with the rates for reported cases of child abuse and with National Crime Survey rates for assault and other crimes. Another alternative is the Uniform Crime Reports system of rates per hundred thousand. However, such a rate is not appropriate, because our survey samples were in the thousands, not hundred thousands. (b) *Results are presented as integers.* It is customary in demography, criminology, and medical sociology to use a rate that enables the data to be presented in integers. For

example, the 1981 cancer death rate is given in the *Vital Statistics* as 184 per 100,000 population rather than 0.00184 per capita or 0.184% because most people find it easier to conceptualize integers. Thus, the difference between the cancer rate and the suicide rate is more easily perceived when presented as 184 versus 12 per 100,000, rather than as 0.184% versus 0.012%. (c) *Rate per thousand avoids confusion with percentage change.* In the context of this article, using "X per thousand" instead of "X%" avoids confusion with "X% change" or the awkwardness in spelling out the latter as "X% change in the percentage violent."

4. For convenience and economy of wording, terms such as *marital, spouse, wife,* and *husband* are used to refer to couples, irrespective of whether they are married or nonmarried cohabiting persons. For an analysis of differences and similarities between married and cohabiting couples in the 1975–76 study, see Yllo (1978); Yllo and Straus (1981).

5. In addition, the 1985 rate presented in this chapter is restricted to the comparable part of the sample and the comparable list of violent acts. The figures to be presented in a later paper using all couples and the enlarged CTS list of violent acts yields a somewhat higher rate.

6. For a few years, the advocacy of karate on the part of some in the women's movement put women on record as favoring violence as a means of ending violence. The futility of such an approach is indicated by the fact that the willingness of men to use force does not protect them from assault. Three times as many men are murdered as women (Riedel and Zahn, 1985: Table 7.3–2), and three times as many men are victims of assault (Bureau of Justice Statistics, 1985: Table 7.3). Readiness to use force, in our opinion, is no more likely to provide security for women than it does for men.

7. Although this section focuses on changes in the family that are associated with a reduction in violence, there have also been changes in aspects of the family that are plausibly associated with an increase in violence (see Straus, 1981b, for a listing and discussion).

8. Calls to several federal and private organizations concerned with child abuse revealed that no national statistics are available on the number of child protective service (CPS) workers. However, some indication of the magnitude of the change can be gleaned from data on the New England states. I am grateful to the directors or associate directors of the relevant departments for providing the following statistics in response to my telephone requests: *Connecticut:* The number of case workers assigned to children's services increased from 244.5 full-time equivalent workers in 1976 to 308 in 1985, an increase of 63.5, or 26%. *Maine:* The number of CPS workers increased from 163 in 1977 to 238 in 1985, an increase of 75, or 46%. *Massachusetts:* The budget for child protective services increased from $120 million in 1980 (the earliest date for which comparable figures are available) to $293 million in 1985, a 144% increase in the last five years of the 1975–85 decade. *New Hampshire:* Separate figures are not kept on CPS workers. The number of state-employed social workers increased from 95 in 1972 to 136 in 1985, an increase of 41, or a 43% increase. *Rhode Island:* The number of CPS workers increased from 12 in 1974 to 125 in 1985, a 792% increase. *Vermont:* Separate figures were not kept for CPS. The total number of state-employed social workers was essentially unchanged from 1975 to 1985 (from 105 to 110). However, a larger proportion of this staff was probably engaged in CPS work in 1985 than in 1975. Allowing for a few states

such as Vermont, it is not unreasonable to assume that even small states added at least 50 CPS workers during the decade under review, and larger states many more. If each state added an average of only 50 CPS workers during this decade, that would result in 2,500 CPS workers providing services in 1985 who were not engaged in child abuse intervention in the early 1970s.

9. For example, membership in the American Association of Marriage and Family Therapists tripled from 3,373 in 1975 to 12,302 in 1985 (information provided by telephone to Straus, 11 March 1986).

10. Of course, both rates are confounded with other factors. The rate of cases known to protective services is confounded with the resources available to conduct investigations and provide treatment. consequently, it is much higher than the number of families actually receiving assistance. Similarly, the survey rate is confounded with willingness to self-report violence and is therefore much lower than the "true" incidence rate. Nevertheless, we regard the former as a reasonable indicator of trends in treatment and the latter as a reasonable indicator of trends in incidence.

8

Physical Punishment and Physical Abuse of American Children: Incidence Rates by Age, Gender, and Occupational Class

Barbara A. Wauchope and Murray A. Straus

This chapter examines the extent to which age, gender, and class are related to the incidence and chronicity of physical punishment and physical abuse of children.

Previous Research on the Incidence of Physical Punishment and Physical Abuse

Age of Child

We have found only two studies that systematically compare the percentage of parents who use physical punishment on children of different ages (Chapter 23 and Anderson, 1936/1972). Physical punishment is frequent for young children and decreases as the child matures. For example, Figure 4 in Chapter 23 shows that 97% of three-year-olds were physically punished and the rate declined steadily as age increased. Nevertheless, almost a third of the parents of children in their late teens (15–17) reported using physical punishment.

To our knowledge, rates of physical punishment of children under three have not been reported, although studies of beliefs about its use for this age group are available. The majority of parents believe that physical punishment, particularly spanking, is acceptable for very young children

(Newson and Newson, 1963; Stolz, 1967), while some parents feel it is less appropriate for older children (Stolz, 1967).

Physical Abuse. There is some evidence that physical *abuse* (i.e., violence against a child that, in the judgment of the person classifying the behavior, goes beyond permissible physical punishment) is also highest in early childhood. In studies of officially reported cases of abuse, children are most at risk during the ages of three months to three to five years (American Association for Protecting Children, 1986; Gelles, 1973/1974; Gil, 1970). However, studies using other types of data do not show a clear decrease with age.

Straus et al.'s (1980) study of the 1975 sample of children ages 3–17 found a bimodal pattern: children under 5 and older teenage children were the most likely to experience violence that was serious enough to be considered child abuse. Incidents of physical abuse reported by professionals in a representative sample of U.S. counties (Office of Human Development Services, 1981) was highest for the youngest boys, peaking at ages three to five, although rates increased with age for girls. Others also suggest a heightened rate of physical abuse among adolescents, particularly adolescent girls (Garbarino and Gilliam, 1980; Olsen and Holmes, 1986).[1]

Gender of Child

Physical Punishment. Maccoby and Jacklin's comprehensive review of gender differences (1974) concluded that parents more often use physical punishment on boys than girls. Our previous research also led to this conclusion. In addition, we found an interaction with age: the older the child the more the rate for boys exceeded that for girls (Straus, 1971; Straus, Gelles and Steinmetz, 1980). These could reflect differences in the extent to which boys and girls may provoke parental anger (de Lissovoy, 1980), with boys more resistant to directions than girls (Maccoby and Jacklin, 1974), resulting in more punishment. In addition, culturally patterned child-rearing methods are gender-differentiated: sons must be "toughened up" through physical punishment (Henry, 1963/1974; Miller, 1983; Straus et al., 1980), while girls are believed to be less able to take care of themselves and are more easily hurt (Maccoby and Jacklin, 1974).

Physical Abuse. Although most studies find that boys are at higher risk of physical abuse than girls (American Humane Association, 1986; Bryan and Freed, 1982; Gil, 1970, Straus et al., 1980), the differences are often small (e.g. Gil, 1970). Moreover, there seems to be a gender by age interaction, but in the opposite direction than the interaction reported above: the incidence is higher for boys than girls in age groups below age

12, while girls outnumber boys among teenage victims (Gil, 1970; Office of Human Development Services, 1981; Olsen and Holmes, 1986). The rate for teenage girls may be greater than for boys because of greater demands for conformity, especially in respect to the emotionally charged issue of sex, and because parents may be less likely to fear physical retaliation by girls.

Gender of Parent

For physical *abuse,* the rate is higher for mothers than for fathers (American Association for Protecting Children, 1986; Straus et al., 1980). Straus et al. found an abuse rate of 17.7% for mothers and 10.1% for fathers. This difference may reflect mothers' primary responsibilities for children (Gecas, 1976; Pleck, 1977), placing them at risk of committing more violence. Also, social service agencies tend to list the mother as the client, even when the father is the abusing parent (Stark, 1986).

However, other studies report higher rates of abuse by fathers (Bryan and Freed, 1982; Gil, 1970). Gil found that fathers were the perpetrators in nearly two-thirds of the abuse incidents while mothers were involved in slightly fewer than one-half. These findings may be related to studies showing that men are more aggressive than women (Maccoby, 1980) and are also allowed greater license to use physical violence in society (Toby, 1966/1974; Young, Beier, Beier, and Barton, 1975).

Socioeconomic Class of Parent

Physical Punishment. Several researchers have found higher rates of physical punishment by lower socioeconomic status parents (e.g., Bronfenbrenner, 1958/1979; Kohn, 1969; Kohn and Schooler, 1983). However, in a national survey, Stark and McEvoy (1970) reported higher rates for middle-class parents. Moreover, Erlanger (1974) concluded from a review of the available studies that there is at best only a weak relation between socioeconomic status and physical punishment.

Physical Abuse. Researchers using officially reported cases of child abuse (Garbarino and Gilliam, 1980; Gil, 1970; Olsen and Holmes, 1986) consistently report higher rates of physical abuse among blue collar families than among white collar families and the highest rates of all among the poor. Rates in all of these studies are based on cases known to child welfare workers. Consequently, the higher rate of abuse among low socioeconomic status (SES) families might be due to a greater tendency for abuse to come to public attention when the family is receiving welfare aid (Hampton and Newberger, 1985). However, Straus et al. (1980) found a similar set of SES differences in a study that used self-report interview data.

One interpretation of these differences is that blue collar parents tend to be more authoritarian, emphasize conformity more (Bronfenbrenner, 1958/ 1979; Kohn, 1969; Kohn and Schooler, 1983), and be less permissive. Such parents see physical punishment as a more effective means of control than reason and isolation (Bronfenbrenner, 1958/1979; Kohn, 1969).

Evidence that stress is associated with higher rates of violence (Chapter 11 in this volume; Linsky and Straus, 1986; Straus and Kaufman Kantor, 1987) could also help explain higher rates of abuse in blue collar families. Low SES families experience more life stresses, (e.g., unemployment, serious illness, disruption, overcrowding, etc.) and have fewer means than more affluent families of coping with them (Pearlin and Schooler, 1978/ 1982). Additional stress arises out of the disparity between the aspirations of low SES people to rise to the top and the limited opportunities that actually exist (Rubin, 1976).

Chronicity of Physical Punishment and Abuse

The epidemiological work on violence against children described above has been directed at obtaining incidence rates that indicate how widespread the problem is. In addition, it is important to know how often the violence occurs or what we will refer to as the "chronicity" of violence. There is an important difference in the potential for physical and psychological injury between an act of violence that occurs once a year and one that occurs daily.

Very few studies of this type are available. Sears, Maccoby, and Levin (1957) found that parents who spank young children infrequently continue that pattern as the children grow older. Officially reported cases of physical abuse suggest that when children are assaulted, the attacks are not isolated incidents (Herrenkohl, Herrenkohl, Egolf, and Seech, 1980). However, this may not apply to a non-clinical sample of abusing parents such as those in the present study.

Method

Given the inadequacies and inconsistencies between studies of violence against children, the purpose of this chapter is to present the incidence rate and chronicity of physical punishment and physical abuse of children at different age levels. In addition, we will compare male and female children, fathers and mothers, and blue collar and white collar parents.

Although the discussion will raise certain theoretical questions, the purpose of the paper is descriptive rather than theory testing.

Sample

The data are from the National Family Violence Resurvey conducted in 1985. Since the present analysis is concerned only with parents, the sample consists of the 3,229 respondents with a child under 18 living at home. Approximately two-fifths of the respondents are fathers ($n = 1,269$) and three-fifths are mothers ($n = 1,960$).

Definitions of Physical Punishment and Physical Abuse

There appears to be no national or scientific consensus on what constitutes violence and physical "abuse." An example of one of the many aspects on which there are sharp disagreements is whether to define a child as abused on the basis of having been injured or on the basis of the severity of the assault, regardless of whether an injury occurs (see Chapter 5 for a discussion of this controversy). In this study, we focus on the nature of parental acts, regardless of whether there is an injury.

Physical punishment and *physical abuse* differ in at least two respects: (1) the severity of the assault; and (2) the cultural "legitimacy" of the act. Thus slapping a child is categorized as physical punishment because it is a relatively minor act of violence in the sense of having low potential for causing injury. In addition, there are cultural norms (including statutes) that give parents the right to do this. If, however, a Little League baseball coach were to slap the child, the same "minor" violence could be considered abuse. Therefore, *physical punishment* is defined as a legally permissible violent act (or acts) carried out as part of the parental role and *physical abuse* is defined as a violent act (or acts) by a parent that, in our judgment, exceeds the level of severity permitted by law and custom and exposes the child to a greater risk of injury.

Measures of Physical Punishment and Physical Abuse

The procedures used to operationalize the concepts of physical punishment and abuse are the violence indexes of the CTS (described briefly in Chapter 1 and in more detail in Chapters 3 and 4).

Physical Punishment. The violent acts comprising the minor violence index are, in our opinion, typically categorized as physical punishment. Children are often pushed, grabbed, or shoved away from or toward objects and people, either because they have been told not to go near them (e.g., hot stove or street) or because they are supposed to move toward them, (e.g., to clean up their room or help a sibling). Slaps or spanks are common negative sanctions.

Physical Abuse. Two CTS indexes were used to measure physical abuse. The *Very Severe Violence index* includes items that are almost universally regarded as indicators of "abuse," namely: "Kicked/bit/hit with fist," "Beat up," "Burned or scalded," and "Used gun or knife." This index includes all incidents of this type of violence, regardless of whether there was also physical punishment. The *Severe Violence Index* adds an item that is intermediate in severity and whose categorization as abuse or punishment is controversial. In particular, the item for hitting with an object is ambiguous because it could be a paddle (an object commonly associated with physical punishment), or a frying pan that would commonly be seen as an object for abuse.

Chronicity. We also present data on the *chronicity* of violence within the subgroup of parents who reported one or more instances of physical punishment or physical abuse. To obtain this data, we asked the parents to estimate the number of times they used each of the acts in the CTS during the previous 12 months. This measure must be treated with caution because of the difficulty in recalling behavior that is as frequent or common as physical punishment. In addition, some of the more severe acts are likely to be unreported. For these reasons, the chronicity measure is more appropriate for comparisons between groups than as a description of the actual numbers of occurrences.

Measure of Socioeconomic Status

Each respondent was classified as "blue collar" or "white collar" using the Bureau of Labor Statistics revised Occupational Classification System following a procedure developed by Rice, as given in Robinson, Athanasiou, and Head (1969). The occupation of the respondent was used because the interview focused on the child-rearing practices of the respondent and it seemed appropriate to use the occupational status of the parent whose behavior was actually measured, particularly with single parents included in the sample.

Statistical Procedure

Analysis of variance was used to test for differences in the rate and chronicity of physical punishment and physical abuse by age of child, gender of child, gender of parent, and occupational class of parent.

Incidence and Chronicity by Age of Child

Incidence Rates

The lower part of Figure 8.1[4] shows the rate for physical punishment, and the shaded upper part adds incidents of more severe violence. Thus the top line shows the cumulative rate for *any* physical violence (Physical Punishment index added to the Severe Violence index) experienced by age. For infants, 209 per 1,000 (21%) experienced at least one act of physical violence over a year's time. This rate peaks at 905 per 1,000 3–4-year-olds and declines with increasing age to 180 per 1,000 17-year-olds, $F(17, 3199) = 67.503, p < .001$.

The curvilinear pattern for any violence is largely accounted for by parents who use physical punishment only (lower part of Figure 1). In infancy, 177 per 1,000 parents used at least 1 act of physical punishment on their children over a year's time, reaching a peak of 789 per 1,000 3-year-olds. The rate steadily declines with age, although almost half (47.3%) of the parents reported using punishment on children as old as age 12; 23% at age 16, $F(17, 3199) = 43.93, p < .001$.

The lower line in Figure 8.2 shows the rate for the most extreme acts of physical abuse (Very Severe Violence index).[5] In contrast to the age-

FIGURE 8.1
Incidence of Physical Punishment and More Severe Assaults: Annual Rates per 1,000 by Age of Child

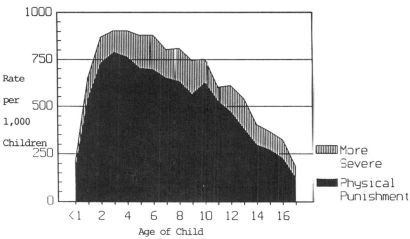

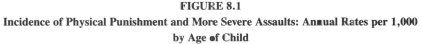

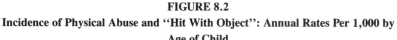

FIGURE 8.2

Incidence of Physical Abuse and "Hit With Object": Annual Rates Per 1,000 by Age of Child

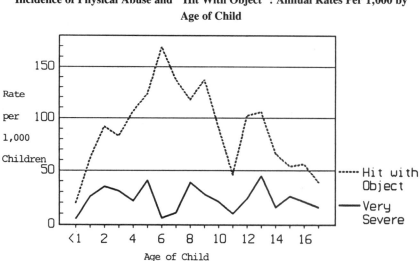

related patterns of physical punishment and hitting with an object, the physical abuse rates in Figure 8.2 show no significant relationship to age.

The upper line in Figure 8.2 was included to examine the ambiguous item "Hit or tried to hit with something" (see "Method" section). This line (which is *not* cumulative) displays the curvilinear pattern of physical punishment, although it peaks at a slightly older age, $F(17, 3207) = 3.497$, $p < .001$. Thus hitting with an object is, in one respect, more similar to physical punishment than to physical abuse.

Chronicity of Violence

The upper line of Figure 8.3 shows the average number of times that severely assaulted children were attacked. During the year covered by this survey, the average for infants was 19.49 assaults, rising to 32.35 for 3-year-olds and declining to 5.98 for 17-year-olds.

Physical punishment follows a similar pattern. Parents who used physical punishment with infants reported using this technique an average of 6.81 times. The mean peaks at 14.8 acts for 2-year-olds and steadily declines to a mean of 1.81 for 17-year-olds, $F(17, 1968) = 3.48, p < .001$.

No age trend was found for the chronicity of "Very Severe Violence" (data not shown). The means varied widely (from 6.32 to 46.58), are based on very small n's (from 1 to 9 cases per age group), and are not significant.

FIGURE 8.3

Chronicity of Physical Punishment and More Severe Assaults: Mean Acts per Year by Age of Child

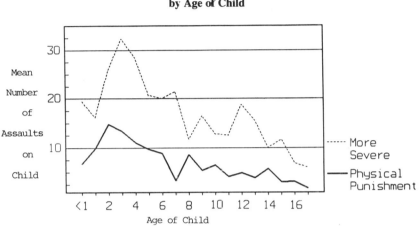

Incidence and Chronicity by Age, Gender, and Class

Incidence Rates

The top two panels of Table 8.1 show no significant differences in physical punishment or physical abuse by gender of child or gender of parent. The lower panel of Table 8.1 shows a significant difference by occupational class for physical abuse, but not for physical punishment. The rate of physical abuse among blue collar parents was almost twice that of white collar parents, $F(1, 3042) = 7.95$, $p < .01$. This class difference remained even when the other variables were included in the analysis.

The incidence of physical *punishment* across age groups when graphed (graph not shown) is similar to Figure 8.1 for both parents. However, mothers are more likely to punish than fathers for 13 of the age groups and there is a slight tendency for fathers to punish very young children (ages 1, 2, 4, 8, and 13), $F(17, 3181) = 1.853$, $p < .02$.

For physical *abuse,* the age by gender of parent interaction was significant. However, this interaction contained a number of empty cells, leaving interpretation open to question.

Interactions without age, between gender of child, gender of parent, and occupational class of parent, were not significant for either physical punishment or physical abuse.

TABLE 8.1

Incidence of Physical Violence: Annual Rates by Gender of Child, Gender of Parent, and Occupational Class

| Independent Variables | Rate Per 1,000 Children | | | |
| | Physical Punishment | | Physical Abuse | |
	Rate	(n)	Rate	(n)
Gender of Child				
Boy	512	(828)	28	(45)
Girl	488	(782)	19	(31)
Gender of Parent				
Father	485	(613)	22	(28)
Mother	511	(998)	25	(48)
Occupational Class				
Blue Collar	512	(645)	31*	(39)
White Collar	504	(895)	16	(28)

* F for occupational class comparison of physical abuse $(1, 3042) = 7.95$, $p < .01$.

Chronicity of Violence

Table 8.2 displays the number of times physical punishment and physical abuse occurred (among those who used these behaviors). We found no significant difference for gender of child, gender of parent, or occupational class. This table is presented for descriptive purposes only.

When the age of the child is specified (Table 8.3), there are significant interaction effects for chronicity of physical punishment by age and gender of child, age and gender of parent, and age and occupational class of parent. However, the differences are small (even though statistically significant), occur sporadically in age groups, and do not change the overall age pattern shown in Figure 1.

We found one similar but weak interaction for chronicity of physical *abuse,* age and gender of child, $F(13, 287) = 1.84$, $p < .05$. However, because abuse occurs much less frequently than physical punishment, cases are missing in several age groups, making interpretation of consistent differences across age groups difficult (table not shown).

Both fathers and mothers used physical punishment more often against sons than daughters, $F(1, 1996) = 4.38$, $p < .05$ (table not shown). Fathers

TABLE 8.2

Chronicity of Physical Violence: Mean Acts per Year by Gender of Child, Gender of Parent, and Occupational Class

Independent Variables	Physical Punishment			Physical Abuse		
	M	SD	(n)	M	SD	(n)
Gender of Child						
Boy	8.99	9.40	(828)	14.97	11.92	(45)
Girl	8.10	9.07	(782)	20.80	25.32	(31)
Gender of Parent						
Father	9.24	10.27	(613)	17.41	24.43	(28)
Mother	8.13	8.54	(998)	17.27	14.57	(48)
Occupational Class						
Blue Collar	8.52	8.67	(645)	16.17	14.71	(39)
White Collar	8.56	9.68	(895)	19.67	24.43	(28)

Note. Differences are not significant.

punished both sons ($M = 10.00$) and daughters ($M = 8.42$) more than mothers (M incidents for sons $= 8.36$; M incidents for daughters $= 7.91$).

When occupational class is included in this interaction, sons of blue collar fathers experienced punishment more frequently than any other group, while daughters of blue collar mothers experienced physical punishment the least often (Table 8.4). Daughters of white collar parents were punished more often than those of blue collar parents, while sons were more frequently physically punished by blue collar parents. Fathers punished more frequently than mothers in all groups, and boys were the targets of physical punishment more than girls, except from white collar mothers, $F(1, 1893) = 11.53$, $p < .01$. The similar interaction for physical abuse was not significant.

Social Norms, Physical Punishment, and Physical Abuse

We have presented data on the incidence and frequency of physical punishment and physical abuse and how this varies according to the age and gender of the child and the occupational class and gender of the parent. Since the objective was to describe these patterns rather than to test a theory, this discussion simply presents our interpretations of some of the findings and makes suggestions for research to test these and other interpretations.

TABLE 8.3

Chronicity of Physical Punishment: Mean Acts per Year by Age by Gender of Child, Gender of Parent, and Occupational Class

Age of Child	Gender of Child		Gender of Parent		Class of Parent	
	Boys	Girls	Fathers	Mothers	Blue	White
<1	6.07[a]	7.32	7.96[b]	6.04	7.13[c]	7.69
1	9.97	9.85	10.37	9.54	9.97	9.81
2	16.34	13.43	14.98	14.61	14.01	15.22
3	13.29	13.44	14.01	12.97	13.35	13.74
4	13.50	9.18	11.03	11.17	11.12	11.57
5	8.35	10.97	8.97	10.22	8.99	10.25
6	10.03	7.88	9.56	8.50	9.56	8.58
7	9.47	6.72	8.96	8.00	9.57	6.61
8	9.49	7.78	8.98	8.33	6.29	9.79
9	5.42	5.46	4.50	5.91	5.77	4.64
10	7.52	4.83	7.02	6.32	5.80	6.90
11	4.39	3.98	3.87	4.34	4.88	3.36
12	5.95	3.40	4.95	4.89	4.99	4.72
13	4.18	3.59	3.57	4.21	3.90	3.96
14	5.73	5.89	7.87	4.58	7.41	3.74
15	3.99	2.12	3.47	3.00	3.36	2.78
16	2.36	3.72	2.21	3.33	3.66	2.87
17	1.88	1.73	2.28	1.55	2.21	1.62

[a] F for gender of child comparison (17, 1932) = 2.55, $p < .001$
[b] F for gender of parent comparison (17, 1932) = 3.38, $p < .001$
[c] F for occupational class comparison (17, 1837) = 2.01, $p < .01$

Age

We found that physical *punishment* is highly related to the age of the child. Both the incidence rate and the chronicity are lowest for infants, rise sharply to a peak at ages three and four, and decline thereafter. On the other hand, no relationship to the age of the child was found for either the incidence or the chronicity of physical *abuse*.

The reasons for the age relatedness of physical punishment and the lack of the relationship for physical abuse are far from clear. Parents may withhold the use of physical punishment until a child is old enough to understand why he or she is being punished, because a baby is, as a mother in Stolz's study (1967) said, "too young to understand force" (p. 142). However, other parents use the opposite reasoning. One of our respondents said, "What should I do? Give him a lecture on the germ

TABLE 8.4

Chronicity of Physical Violence: Mean Acts per Year by Gender of Child, Gender of
Parent, and Occupational Class

Gender of Child	Father				Mother			
	Blue Collar		White Collar		Blue Collar		White Collar	
	M	SD	M	SD	M	SD	M	SD
Physical Punishment *								
Boy	10.15	9.92	9.67	11.24	8.61	8.31	8.16	8.63
(n)	(141)		(163)		(178)		(310)	
Girl	8.57	9.08	8.74	10.73	7.21	7.53	8.26	9.22
(n)	(133)		(149)		(193)		(271)	
Physical Abuse								
Boy	18.17	16.58	7.48	4.24	15.64	9.66	14.71	10.13
(n)	(14)		(5)		(13)		(9)	
Girl	3.22	1.16	38.36	51.86	18.75	19.38	21.82	20.88
(n)	(3)		(4)		(8)		(10)	

* F for 3-way interaction $(1,1893) = 11.53$, $p < .01$

theory?'' Research is needed on this and other possible reasons for the
age patterns reported in this paper. For example, the increase with age in
the size and strength of children may be influential. Some parents we
interviewed volunteered views such as ''I wish I could still take him over
my knee,'' but systematic data were not collected on this issue. Another
possibility is that the decrease in the frequency and chronicity of physical
punishment is related to the increasing experience and maturity of parents.
As will be suggested below, cultural norms concerning appropriate types
of discipline play a part, and this also needs investigation.

Both the legal and the informal norms of the United States give parents
the right to use physical violence in controlling and training children.
Parents are expected or obligated to use physical punishment ''when
necessary.'' The existence of this normative expectation to use physical
punishment is rarely perceived until it is called into question by a parent
who fails to conform (see Garfinkel, 1964, for examples of this process).
Carson (1986) found that non-spanking parents tend to be the objects of
social control efforts by friends and relatives in the form of polite but
pointedly expressed doubts about consequences for the child. Carson
found that non-spanking parents, like other ''deviants,'' tend to develop
socially acceptable accounts to justify their unwillingness to use physical
punishment to themselves and others. We suggest that these norms are

closely tied to the age of the child and that this is an important factor explaining the close relationship between the age of the child and physical punishment. Acts of physical abuse (such as punching or kicking a child), however, are not part of the normative prescription for physical punishment at any age. If it is true that age-specific norms influence whether physical punishment is used by parents and if there is an absence of normative support for physical abuse at any age, this can help explain our finding of a relationship to age for physical punishment and an absence of such as relationship for physical abuse. However, the physical abuse findings are based on a small number of cases ($n = 76$). A larger sample might reveal age patterns in abuse.

Gender and Class

Introducing gender of child, gender of parent, and occupational class into the analyses had no important effect on the patterns found for age. We did not find the higher rates of abuse of teenage girls than boys reported by other studies (Garbarino and Gilliam, 1980; Gil, 1970; Olsen and Holmes, 1986). This may be due to small numbers of cases, or it may reflect a difference in methodology. Our findings are based on a community sample, whereas the studies cited use clinical samples (cases known to child welfare agencies). The higher rate for girls in official cases may be due to assaults against teenage girls being more likely to come to official attention, rather than a greater tendency to hit girls. On the other hand, the higher rate for boys in our study may be due to a greater willingness of parents to tell our interviewers about violence against boys, rather than a greater tendency to hit boys.

The 1975 Family Violence Survey (Straus et al., 1980) found higher rates of both physical punishment and physical abuse by mothers than fathers. Ten years later, we found no differences between mothers and fathers in the incidence rates. Perhaps this reflects the changing roles of men and women in families. Fathers are reported to participate more in child care when their wives are also working outside the home (Crouter, Perry-Jenkins, Huston, and McHale, 1987; Pleck, 1979). Fathers' involvement in control and discipline of children may increase the risk of abuse by fathers. In addition, mothers' greater reliance on day care and other child care alternatives may remove them from continuous involvement with their children, reducing their risk of abusive behavior.

We found that the physical abuse rate of blue collar parents is almost double that of white collar parents. This difference corresponds to that found in the 1975 study (Straus et al., 1980) and other studies showing a strong relationship between incidence and severity of child abuse and neglect and poverty (Pelton, 1981).

Measurement Issues

We measured physical punishment and physical abuse in a manner we believe is appropriate. Nevertheless, it is very likely that the more severe acts were under-reported. Moreover, the sample did not include parents under 18. This eliminates one of the populations that might be at highest risk for abuse. In addition, questions can be raised about whether the rates and chronicity describe punishment and abuse. Almost 21% of the parents reported pushing, grabbing, shoving, slapping, or spanking an infant, with an average chronicity of almost nine times over a year. These same acts were used by 73% of the parents of 2-year-olds, with an average chronicity of 17 times. These numbers do not reflect how hard the children were slapped or how many slaps occurred in a given incident. It seems reasonable to assume that among the children we classified as experiencing "only" physical punishment, some received physical punishment that many people would call abusive.

Links between Physical Punishment and Physical Abuse

The incidence and chronicity of normatively approved physical punishment against children may have important implications for understanding and preventing physical abuse i.e., violence that exceeds the culturally permissive level. Although most physical punishment does not turn into physical abuse, most physical abuse begins as ordinary physical punishment (Kadushin and Martin, 1981). Moreover, being the subject of physical punishment trains future parents in use of violence. In Chapter 23 (also Straus et al. 1980) we show that the more physical punishment a parent experienced as a child, the higher the proportion who engaged in abusive violence toward their own children and their own spouses. Frude and Goss (1979) found that the more parents used ordinary physical punishment, the greater the percentage who were worried that they might get carried away to the point of child abuse. Moore and Straus (1987) found that parents who approved of slapping a child who talked back to them had a much higher rate of *severe* violence than other parents. These and other studies suggest that the nearly universal use of physical punishment documented in this paper is part of the explanation for the high rate of physical abuse of American children.

Notes

It is a pleasure to express appreciation for their comments and suggestions to Peggy Kieschnick, Gerri King, Dan Lobovits, Peggy Plass, and Linda Williams. In addition, we gratefully acknowledge the helpful comments provided by three anonymous reviewers on a draft of this chapter.
1. Officially reported rates of abuse may be higher for infants and toddlers because even minor acts of violence (such as slapping and shaking) that would only cause pain or a bruise to a 12-year-old may cause serious injury or death to an infant. Since officially reported cases of child abuse are highly influenced by the presence of injury and by perceptions of how permissible the assault is relative to the age of the child, studies based on officially reported cases will give a different picture of the relative numbers of infants and toddlers who are abused than studies that are based on whether a serious assault (such as a punch or kick) occurred. Finally, adolescent abuse may go unreported because abuse of older children is "often hidden within such other problems as parent-child conflict, running away, and delinquency" (Olsen and Holmes, 1986, p. 16).
2. The rates reported using the CTS measures should not be confused with or compared directly with "official" or "reported" rates of child abuse, those based on cases known to child protective services (American Association for Protecting Children, 1986). While both are reported rates of child abuse, they measure different phenomena. The "official" rate can be thought of as an *intervention* rate, whereas the self-reported rate from our survey is closer to an *incidence* rate. Discussion of important distinctions between these rates are given in Chapters 4 and 7.
3. The limitation of such an approach lies in the assumption within ANOVA of normality of the residuals, which is violated here by the skewed distributions of the dependent measures (particularly of physical abuse). While the rates shown in the ANOVA tables are unbiased estimates, the F tests of significance may be inaccurate (Iversen and Norpoth, 1976:23). These significance tests should therefore be interpreted with caution.
4. In Figures 8.1 and 8.3, the number of cases for physical punishment for each age group, > 1-year-olds to 17-year-olds, respectively, is: 36, 86, 150, 158, 156, 122, 111, 109, 86, 78, 107, 81, 77, 76, 48, 54, 48, 26. For severe violence, > 1-year-olds to 17-year-olds, respectively, n = 6, 18, 29, 23, 28, 30, 30, 25, 24, 25, 21, 12, 22, 31, 17, 19, 20, 12.
5. In Figure 8.2, the number of cases for Very Severe Violence for each age group, > 1-year-olds to 17-year-olds, respectively, is: 1, 4, 7, 6, 5, 7, 1, 2, 5, 4, 4, 1, 4, 9, 3, 5, 4, 3. For "Hit with something" for > 1-year-olds to 17-year-olds, respectively, n = 4, 10, 19, 17, 22, 21, 27, 23, 16, 19, 16, 7, 17, 21, 11, 11, 12, 8.

Part III
THE SOCIAL PSYCHOLOGY OF FAMILY VIOLENCE

9

Gender Differences in Reporting Marital Violence and Its Medical and Psychological Consequences

Jan E. Stets and Murray A. Straus

One of the most controversial findings of the 1975 National Family Violence Survey was the high rate of violence *by wives* (Straus, 1980c; Straus et al., 1980).[1] In that study, wives had as high a rate of physical assault as husbands. Specifically, among violent couples, in about half of the cases both partners were violent, in about one-quarter of the cases the husband was the only partner who was violent, and in about one-quarter of the cases the wife was the only one who was violent (Straus, 1980; Straus et al., 1980). The finding that women assault their partners about as often as men assault their partners has been documented in other studies (see Chapter 6; Nisonoff and Bitman, 1979). However, some studies reveal that most offenders are men (Dobash and Dobash, 1979; Pagelow, 1981). The inconsistent findings may be due to different samples. Studies that find gender differences are generally based on clinical samples, while studies that find no gender differences are based on nonclinical samples.

As discussed in Chapters 4 and 5, the finding from the first National Family Violence Survey that wives assault husbands about as often as husbands assault wives has been criticized on the grounds that the Conflict Tactics Scales (CTS) fails to take into account two key elements: the *context* of the violence and the degree of *injury* that is sustained (Ferraro and Johnson, 1983; Breines and Gordon, 1983). When researchers neglect the context, specifically whether the wife's violence was in self-defense, it can lead to blaming women for their own victimization. When sheer

151

number of assaults is counted without taking into account the degree of injury, it can lead to assuming that women are victimized to the same extent as men, whereas given the greater average size and strength of men, women will probably experience greater injury than men. Chapters 4 and 5 offer several reasons for why context and injury should be measured separately from the acts of violence that make up the CTS. This paper uses that methodology to provide some of the needed empirical evidence on the relationship between violence, its context, and injury by gender.

We investigate the context of violence by examining 1) whether the high rate of assaults by women are largely retaliatory as claimed by Saunders (1986) and Straus (1980c), and 2) how individuals respond when their partners initiate violence (enabling us to examine whether violence begets violence). We also investigate physical and psychological injury sustained by men and women victims. Our primary concern is whether violence by men has more negative consequences than violence by women.

Finally, we investigate gender differences in reporting violence. We examine whether men underreport their violence when compared to women's reports of men's violence as revealed in previous research (Sinovacz, 1983; Jouriles and O'Leary, 1985; Edleson and Brygger, 1986). It has been suggested that men who batter may deny their use of violence (Coleman, 1980; Pagelow, 1981; Walker, 1979) more than women. The gender difference in reporting violence may be another example of the "his/her marriage" (Bernard, 1982) or Rashomon effect (Condran and Bode, 1982) where wives have different perceptions of their marriage than husbands.

Types of Victims

The data are from the 1985 National Family Violence Resurvey. A total of 6,002 persons were interviewed. However, the analyses to be reported used subsets of the total number of cases. Each of the following numbered rows is a subset of the previous numbered row.

1. Respondents for whom data were obtained	6,002
Women	3,522
Men	2,480
2. Currently coupled with complete data	5,248
Women	2,947
Men	2,301
3. Respondents who experienced one or more assaults	825
Women	476
Men	349

4. Women victims	349
Of minor assaults by spouse	204
Of severe assaults by spouse	145
5. Men victims	281
Of minor assaults by spouse	172
Of severe assaults by spouse	109
6. Women whose spouse initiated the assault	182
Men whose spouse initiated the assault	131

Measures of Context and Injury

Violence Measures

The CTS (described briefly in Chapter 1 and fully in Chapters 3 and 4) was used to measure the incidence of husband-to-wife and wife-to-husband violence. Spouses who had used minor violence "only" were examined apart from those who had used more severe forms of violence.

Context Measure

To measure who initiated the violence, respondents were asked, "Let's talk about the last time you and your partner got into a physical fight and [MOST VIOLENT ACT]. In that particular instance, who started the physical conflict, you or your partner?"

To examine how individuals responded when their partners initiated violence, respondents were asked, "Which of the following describes what you did as a result: 1) hit back or threw something, 2) cried, 3) yelled or cursed him [her], 4) ran to another room, 5) ran out of the house, 6) called a friend or relative, 7) called the police, or 8) other."

Physical Injury Measures

Three measures were used to operationalize physical injury. First, respondents who had been assaulted were asked whether in the last 12 months they had been hurt badly enough as a result of violence that they needed to see a doctor. Second, assaulted respondents were asked whether they took time off from work because of violent incidents. Finally, all respondents were asked how many days they spent in bed due to illness in the last month. This last measure enables us to compare the illness rate of respondents who are physically assaulted with those who are not assaulted. Responses were collapsed into two categories: zero and one or more days in bed.

Psychological Injury Measures

The interview also included measures of depression, stress, and psychosomatic symptoms. The following six items were combined to form the Depression index: 1) been bothered by feelings of sadness or depresssion, 2) felt very bad or worthless, 3) had times when you couldn't help wondering if anything was worthwhile anymore, 4) felt completely hopeless about everything, 5) thought about taking your own life, and 6) actually tried to take your own life (Dohrenwend et al., 1980). The alpha reliability is .78.

The following three items from the "Measures of Perceived Stress" (Cohen et al., 1983) were combined to form the Stress index: 1) felt nervous or stressed, 2) felt difficulties were piling up so high that you could not overcome them, and 3) found that you could not cope with all of the things that you had to do. The alpha reliability is .73.

The following two items were combined to form the Psychosomatic Symptoms index: 1) had headaches or pains in the head, and 2) had been bothered by cold sweats (Dohrenwend et al., 1980). The correlation between these two items is .60 ($p < .01$).

For each of the items, respondents were to indicate whether they "never," "almost never," "sometimes," "fairly often," or "very often" experienced these feelings or symptoms. We operationalized having "high" depression, stress, and psychosomatic symptoms as the fourth quartile, that is, a score that exceeds the score of 75% of the respondents in the survey. The appropriateness of this procedure was confirmed by an analysis comparing the effect of using the 25th, 50th, and 75th percentiles. It revealed that the largest and most consistent gender differences occurred using the percentage of respondents in the highest quartile.

Context

Initiation of Violence

Of the 825 respondents who experienced one or more assaults, both parties engaged in violence in 49% of the cases, violence by men occurred in 23% of the cases, and violence by women occurred in 28% of the cases. No significant differences were found by gender of respondent ($X^2 = 4.36$, n.s., df = 2). These results are similar to those found in the first National Family Violence Survey (Straus, 1980c).

Of the 297 men and 428 women who responded to the question regarding who initiated the physical conflict, the men said that they struck the first blow in 43.7% of the cases, their partner hit first in 44.1% of the cases, and the men could not remember or disentangle who hit first in the remaining 12.2% of the cases. According to the women, their partners struck the first blow in 42.6% of the cases, they hit first in 52.7% of the cases, and the women could not remember or disentangle who hit first in the remaining 4.7% of the cases ($X^2 = 16.13$, p <.01, df = 3). Although slightly more women than men reported that they initiated violence, the main conclusion to be drawn from these findings is that women not only engage in physical violence as often as men, but they also initiate violence about as often as men.

Since women initiate violence at least as often as men, we might conclude that violence by women is not primarily self-defensive. However, caution is needed regarding this conclusion for at least two reasons. First, some respondents may have answered the question in terms of who began *the argument,* not who began *hitting.* Interviewers were instructed to rephrase the question in such cases. However, there were probably instances in which the misunderstanding of the question went unnoticed. Second, obtaining information on who initiated the violence deals with only part of the context. We do not know whether women initiated violence because they perceived that their partner was going to hit them and, in response, hit first. It should be pointed out, however, that though this seems plausible, Saunder's (1986) results reveal that this is not likely to happen.

Response to Violence

To obtain more detailed information on the context surrounding violent incidents, we examined how individuals responded to violence. The results are presented in Table 9.1. Of the 131 men and 182 women whose spouse initiated an assault, women were more likely than men to report having hit

TABLE 9.1
Response to Assaults Initiated by Partner*

| Type of Response | Percent of | | X^2 | P | df |
	Women	Men			
Hit back	24.4%	15.0%	3.62	.05	1
Cried	54.6%	5.8%	78.51	.01	1
Yelled or cursed him/her	42.0%	28.7%	5.28	.05	1
Ran to another room	28.6%	13.9%	8.58	.01	1
Called a friend/relative	11.4%	2.2%	8.05	.01	1
Called the police	8.5%	0.9%	7.39	.01	1
Run out of the house	14.0%	18.0%	0.67	n.s.	1
Other	7.3%	32.2%	30.61	.01	1

* N = 182 women and 131 men

back, cried, yelled or cursed, run to another room, called a friend or relative, and called the police.

Our findings suggest that violence begets violence since respondents, particularly women, return violence with violence. Although men were *less* likely to respond violently, the large percentage of men in the "other" category suggests the need for research to identify how else they respond.

Gender Differences in Reporting Violence

As mentioned earlier, women are about as likely as men to report initiating violence. In this section, we explore whether this seeming equality in violence occurs because of a tendency by men to under-report their own violence. The results are presented in Table 9.2.

The first two percentages in the column labeled "Minor Only" show the opposite of a male bias in reporting their own violence. The rate of minor-only violence by men reported by men (9.2%) is *greater* than minor-only violence by men as reported by women (6.9%). The bottom two rows in the "Minor Only" column show that the rate of violence by women is about the same, regardless of whether the data are obtained from men or women.

The column headed "Severe" shows the expected pattern of men under-reporting their own assaults. The rate of severe violence by men is almost four times greater when the respondents are women than when they are men. Finally, the bottom two rows in the "Severe" column show no significant difference by gender of respondent in the rate of severe assaults by women.

The data on severe violence rates by men indicate a "reporting effect" and suggest that men "understate" their violence. Consequently, data on violence by men obtained from men needs to be treated with skepticism. We therefore reexamined Table 9.2, disregarding data obtained from men.

TABLE 9.2
Violence Rates by Gender of Perpetrator and Gender of Respondent

Perpetrator	Gender of Respondent	Level Of Violence Minor Only	Severe	None	N	x^2	P	df
Men	Men	9.2%	1.3%	89.5%	2299			
	Women	6.9%	4.9%	88.1%	2945	60.75	.001	2
Women	Men	7.5%	4.7%	87.8%	2301			
	Women	7.7%	4.4%	87.9%	2947	0.32	n.s.	2

Ironically, Table 9.2 still indicates that, within the family, women are about as violent as men. For example, on the bases of interviews with women, Table 9.2 shows that the estimated rates are 6.9% for minor-only violence by men and 7.7% for minor-only violence by women. Similarly, the rows for women in the "Severe" column show a violence rate by men of 4.9% and a violence rate by women that is almost as high (4.4%).

Physical Injury

Though women may be as violent as men within the home, it has been argued that the consequences are more serious for women victims than for men victims (Straus, 1980c; Straus et al, 1980). We examined this by comparing the physical and psychological injury sustained by women and men victims.

Medical Care

Three percent of the 336 women victims and 0.4% of the 264 men victims responding reported needing to see a doctor for a violent incident ($X^2 = 5.54$, p <.05, df = 1). When we examined the subgroups experiencing minor and severe assaults, of those sustaining minor assaults, none of the 199 women and less than .1% of the 169 men needed to see a doctor ($X^2 = 1.13$, n.s., df = 1). However, of those who were severely assaulted, 7.3% of the 137 women and 1.0% of the 95 men needed medical attention ($X^2 = 4.85$, p <.05, df = 1). Thus women who sustain severe assaults are much more likely to need medical care.

Time off From Work

Of the 205 women and 226 men victims who were employed, 9.3% of the victimized women took time off from their job compared to 5.8% of the victimized men ($X^2 = 1.93$, n.s., df = 1). Of the 133 women and 142 men sustaining minor assaults, 4.0% of the women and 4.0% of the men took time off from work ($X^2 = .01$, n.s., df = 1). Of the 72 women and 84 men severely assaulted, there is a tendency for more women (19%) than men (10%) to take time off from work ($X^2 = 3.15$, p <.10, df = 1). Although this difference is not quite significant, it suggests that severe assaults by men have a greater effect on women's absenteeism than vice versa.

Days in Bed Due to Illness

There is a tendency for more women than men to be sick enough to stay in bed. Of the 349 women victims, 13.3% lost one or more days due to illness compared to 13.2% of the 281 men victims ($X^2 = 3.09$, p $<.10$, df $= 1$). We also compared men and women by severity of the assault. Of the 204 women victims sustaining minor assaults, 15.2% were bedridden for one or more days compared to 12.8% of the 172 men victims ($X^2 = 0.45$, n.s., df $= 1$). Comparing the 145 women and 109 men sustaining severe violence, we found a tendency for more women (22.8%) than men (13.8%) victims to be bedridden for one or more days ($X^2 = 3.29$, p $<.10$, df $= 1$). Although this difference is not quite significant, it is consistent with the view that severe violence has a greater effect on women's health than men's health.

Previous research reveals that, on average, more women than men make visits to physicians and spend time in bed due to illness (Marcus and Siegel, 1982; Verbrugge, 1985). We could not examine whether needing medical attention was more likely to occur when one was a victim than not a victim because the question was asked only in terms of whether medical care was needed as a result of an assault. However, we did examine whether being bedridden was more likely to occur when an individual was abused as opposed to not abused. When men and women are abused, they are more likely to spend time in bed due to illness than those who are not abused (men: $X^2 = 9.90$, p $<.01$, df $= 2$; women: $X^2 = 13.67$, p $<.01$, df $= 2$). Though the results in Figure 9.1 show that women victims spend more days in bed due to sickness than men victims, especially when we examine the "Severe Violence" level, the difference is not significant ($X^2 = 1.84$, n.s., df $= 2$).

In general, the differences between women and men victims in terms of the rate of needing to see a doctor, taking time off from work, and being bedridden are not particularly strong or large. For severe assaults, there is some tendency for women to experience more negative effects than men. Consequently, women victims may be more likely than men victims to experience negative effects on their health.

Psychological Injury

Psychosomatic Symptoms

Figure 9.2[2] provides information on whether being a victim of physical assault is associated with a high level of psychosomatic symptoms and whether this relationship is more pronounced for women than men victims. The plot lines for both women and men show that as one moves from the no-violence category to those who are victims of severe assaults, the percent who report a high level of psychosomatic symptoms goes up (men: $X^2 = 28.43$, p $<.01$, df $= 6$; women: $X^2 = 25.77$, p $<.01$, df $= 6$). Though it

FIGURE 9.1

Percent Reporting Days in Bed Due to Illness by Violence Level and Gender

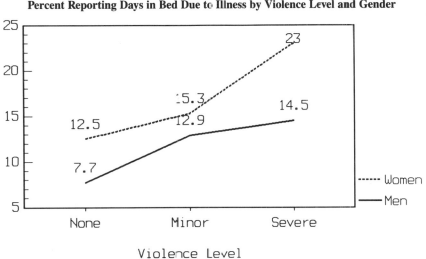

FIGURE 9.2

**Percent Reporting High Level of Psychosomatic Symptoms by
Violence Level and Gender**

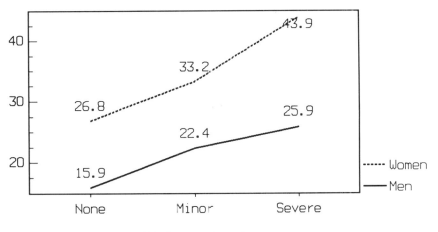

appears that the increase for women is more dramatic than for men, the results reveal no significant gender difference ($X^2 = 1.17$, n.s., df $= 2$).

Stress.

Figure 9.3 shows the percent of women and men in the high-stress category for those who were not assaulted and those who experienced minor and severe assaults. For both women and men, the percent in the high-stress category increases significantly with the level of violence (men: $X^2 = 56.54$, p $<.01$, df $= 6$; women: $X^2 = 108.12$, p $<.01$, df $= 6$). A comparison of the two plot lines in Figure 9.3 shows that the increase in stress has a tendency to be greater for women than men victims ($X^2 = 4.63$, p $<.10$, df $= 2$).

Depression

Finally, Figure 9.4 shows that a high rate of depression is associated with being a victim of assault by a spouse (men: $X^2 = 62.13$; p $<.01$, df $= 6$; women: $X^2 = 134.38$, p $<.01$, df $= 6$). The negative effect of assaults by a spouse is greater for women than men victims ($X^2 = 6.26$, p $<.05$, df $= 2$).

In summary, the results reveal that those who are assaulted are more likely to experience psychosomatic symptoms, stress, and depression than those who are not assaulted. The results also suggest that women victims suffer more psychological injury than men victims. However, these are cross-sectional data and do not prove assaults *cause* psychological injury.

FIGURE 9.3

Percent Reporting High Level of Stress by Violence Level and Gender

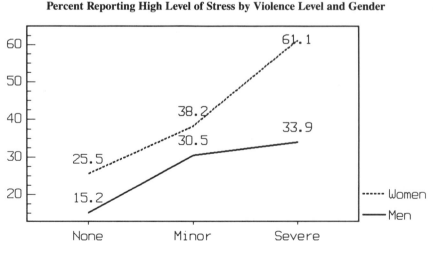

FIGURE 9.4

Percent Reporting High Level of Depression by Violence Level and Gender

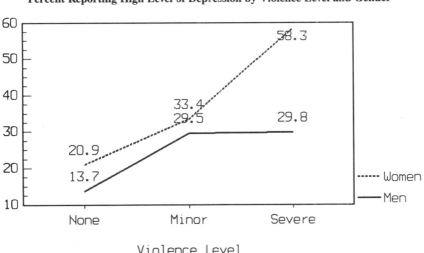

Are Women as Violent as Men?

This study was undertaken to provide empirical data on a controversial finding of the First National Family Violence Survey (Straus et al., 1980): that wives assault husbands at about the same rate as husbands assault wives. Some critics believe that the statistics are misleading because violent acts by wives are almost always acts of self-defense (Berk et al., 1983; Saunders, 1986). Other critics believe that physical assaults by a wife have fewer physical, economic, and psychological consequences than physical assaults by husbands (Breines and Gordon, 1983; Greenblat, 1983; Saunders, 1986). We used data from the second National Family Violence Survey to investigate these issues.

We found that among couples where violence occurred, both partners are violent in about half of the cases, violence by only the male partner occurs one-quarter of the time, and violence by only the female partner occurs one-quarter of the time. These results are similar to those of the first National Family Violence Survey. Turning to the question of whether the rates are misleading because violence by women is largely self-defensive, we find that women initiate violence about as often as men. These results cast doubt on the notion that assaults by women on their partners primarily are acts of self-defense or retaliation.

When we examined how men and women responded to violence, we found that women are more likely than men to respond with verbal and physical assaults. However, a large portion of men responded in the category "other." Consequently, it is unclear how men respond and future research needs to examine this. Men may merely view violence by women as amusing or, at most, annoying (Adler, 1981). They may interpret it as nonthreatening because they may perceive the potential damage that their partner cannot match the damage they can do. Thus they may be less inclined to respond with verbal and physical assaults.

The findings on gender differences in reporting violence show that, for "minor only" violence such as slapping and throwing things, the gender of the respondent makes no difference in either the victimization rate or the offense rate. However, when more severe types of violence are measured, such as punching, choking, and attacks with weapons, the rate of violence by men is much higher when based on interviews with women than when based on interviews with men. It is possible that some women make false allegations of violence by men, but we think it is unlikely that this occurs very often in anonymous interviews. Moreover, the lower rate of severe violence as reported by men is consistent with research comparing members of the same couple. These studies (Szinovacz, 1983; Jouriles and O'Leary, 1985; Edleson and Brygger, 1986) found that men report less violence than their partners. We suggest that the difference occurs because of men under-reporting severe assaults against their partner. Consequently, incidence rates for severe assaults on women based on interviews with men should be treated with skepticism.

Given these results, it seems advisable to base analyses of violence by men on data provided by women. However, even when this is done, the analysis indicates that women assault their partners at about the same rate as men assault their partners. This applies to both minor and severe assaults. Moreover, these findings are consistent with earlier studies, starting with Gelles (1974) and Steinmetz (1977–1978), and more recently with research on dating violence, which also finds that women are about as violent as men (Deal and Wampler, 1986; Arias et al., 1987; Stets and Pirog-Good, 1987). These findings are so consistent that they leave little doubt about the high rate of assaults by women.

Why might women be as violent as men? Straus (1980c) offers some suggestions: (1) Women who are assaulted by their partners may incorporate violence in their own behavioral repertoire. (2) Women may follow the norm of reciprocating violence ("if hit, hit back"). (3) The use of violence in one sphere, for example, child care, may carry over to other spheres, specifically, interaction with one's mate. Longitudinal data are needed to test these ideas. In addition, there seems to be an implicit norm that a woman should use minor violence on certain occasions. Probably millions of girls have been told by their mother, "If he gets fresh, slap him." There is hardly a day in which such ritualized "slap the cad" type of behavior is not presented as an implicit model to millions of women in a television show, movie, or novel.

The Cost of Violence to Women

Though women may be as violent as men within the home, we found that there is a tendency for women victims to sustain more physical injury than men victims. Specifically, for severe assaults, more women than men victims require medical care, and there is a tendency for more women than men victims to lose more time from work and spend more days in bed due to illness.

There may be several interpretations for why women experience more physical injury than men. First, it may be a direct result of abuse. Given the greater average size and strength of men, men can do more injury than women. This would lead women to have a greater propensity than men to need medical care, take time off from work, and be bedridden. However, when we compared men and women victims of abuse to non-victims in terms of days in bed due to illness, while both men and women victims are more likely to spend time in bed due to illness, women victims are no more likely than men victims to be bedridden. Future research needs to examine whether women's greater need for medical care and time off from work is a direct result of abuse.

Second, adoption of the sick role may be easier for women than men because many have fewer work or time constraints than men (Marcus and Siegel, 1982). On the other hand, there are large numbers of women whose occupational and familial roles impose greater time constraints than those under which men operate. Given this, some have argued that it is not objective time constraints but flexibility or discretion in time schedules that is important (Verbrugge, 1985). Since women have more flexible schedules than men, they are more likely to care for themselves when they are sick.

Third, women's socialization may lend itself to women being more sensitive to body discomforts and seeking help for them. On the other hand, men's socialization of self-reliance and toleration of pain may predispose them to avoid help from others or neglect care for themselves (Marcus and Siegel, 1982; Verbrugge, 1985). These different socialization experiences will influence women to attend to their illness and for men to decline help.

The differences between victims and non-victims in the incidence of such psychological problems as psychosomatic symptoms, stress, and depression reveal that assaults do increase the propensity to experience psychological injury. Previous research has examined battered and non-battered women on these dimensions and has found similar results (Stark et al., 1981). In this research, we find that these findings hold for men as well.

We found that while there is a tendency for women victims to experience more stress than men victims, women victims are significantly more likely to experience depression than men victims. These findings cast doubt on the fact that the higher rate is due to women experiencing these psychological problems in general (Radloff, 1975; Weissman and Klerman, 1977; Weissman and Klerman, 1985; Verbrugge, 1985) because our findings compare assaulted women with other women.

Resolving the Contradictions in Research on Violence by Wives

An important problem is the need to reconcile the findings reported here with the findings of the studies cited by Saunders (1986), which show that battered women assault their spouse much *less* frequently than they are assaulted and rarely or never initiate such assaults. We suggest that the discrepancy may occur because the studies cited by Saunders are based on self-selected "treatment group" samples or police records, whereas the studies showing little or no gender difference are based on random or non-clinical samples. This is consistent with research on many other social problems (such as alcoholism, depression, and burglary) that shows that treatment populations differ in important ways from non-treatment populations evidencing the same behavior (Room, 1980b).

Our suggestion that the differences may reflect the fact that one group of studies is based on clinical samples and the other group is based on general population samples should not be taken to imply that the random sample findings are correct and the clinical sample studies are incorrect. Each is correct, but each applies to a different population and has different implications. This issue is discussed more fully in Chapter 5.

For purposes of understanding and assisting clients of shelters for battered women and their partners, the experience of a random sample is not necessarily an appropriate knowledge base. Such intervention requires knowledge based on the experiences *of the population being assisted,* regardless of whether their experience is representative. The experience of other populations may or may not be relevant. If the women in this group are rarely violent and rarely initiate violence, then the focus needs to be gender-specific, i.e., on violence by men.

Similarly, knowledge based on a "treatment sample" does not necessarily apply to the community at large. The experience of women who have sought assistance from a battered women's shelter may not be relevant for designing intervention in the larger community to *prevent* marital violence. The results of this study illustrate that point. They suggest that "primary prevention" of marital violence, rather than concentraing on male violence, needs to pay as much attention to assaults by women on their partners as it does to assaults by husbands on their wives.

There is no simple answer to the question of whether violence should be defined in terms of assaultive *acts* or *injuries*. When violence is measured by acts, women are as violent as men; when violence is measured by injuries, men are more violent. Which type of measure to use depends on whether the purpose is to provide information relevant for acute care services or relevant for primary prevention.

If the purpose is to provide estimates of acute care needs, such as shelters and medical services, an injury-based measure is necessary. If, however, the purpose is to provide information on primary prevention needs, the number of assaulted spouses, regardless of injury, is important for at least two reasons. First, as shown in this paper, only a small percentage of abused women are injured seriously enough to require medical attention. Consequently, as noted in Chapter 5, an act-based measure shows that the population at risk is much larger than would be estimated on the basis of an injury-based measure. Perhaps even more important, an act-based measure is consistent with non-violence as a moral principle. According to this standard, it is not necessary for a woman to be injured to classify the event as abusive because hitting a spouse is wrong, regardless of whether it is "just a slap" and regardless of whether an injury occurs.

Notes

1. For purposes of this paper, the term *violence* refers to physical violence. Therefore, the terms *violence* and *assault* will be used interchangeably.
2. The chi-squares and the percentages shown in Figures 9.2, 9.3, and 9.4 are based on the following N's: No violence = 2,011 men and 2,583 women, minor violence victims = 172 men and 204 women, and severe violence victims = 109 men and 145 women.

10

Some Social Structure Determinants of Inconsistency between Attitudes and Behavior: The Case of Family Violence

Ursula Dibble and Murray A. Straus

Many investigators of family violence explain the presence or absence of domestic violence in terms of individual beliefs or personality dispositions (see, for example, Walker, 1977–1978). According to this approach, violent behavior should be a consequence of violent attitudes. Rather than concentrating on attitudes as determinants or family violence, or on violent behavior as a determinant of violent attitudes, this study is concerned with the degree to which attitudes and behavior are mutually consistent. In particular, the paper focuses on the social structural determinants of attitude-behavior consistency.

Social structure in this context refers to a system of patterned social interactions. For example, families are social structures which consist of various role relationships. Each role relationship involves mutual expectations and obligations between members, as, for example, those between husband and wife, or between mother and son. One of the characteristics of primary group interaction is that the role expectations and obligations of members of primary groups (such as the members of a family) are diffuse rather than segmental, exposing us to conflicting demands and expectations (Goode, 1960). The likelihood that one member is unwilling or unable to live up to another member's expectations is, therefore, increased, enhancing the possibility of family conflict.

In short, from a theoretical perspective, this study tries to avoid the false dichotomy between individual dispositions and social structural variables as determinants of family violence. Instead, the theoretical focus is on the ways in which variations in patterns of family interaction are related to the extend to which behavior and attitude are consistent.

The empirical literature to date shows little association between attitude and behavior with respect to domestic violence. Ball-Rokeach (1973) reports a weak association between attitudes which favor violence and violent behavior. Straus (1977) found only a low positive relationship between approval of marital violence and violent behavior.[1] What accounts for this lack of consistency?

According to Ball-Rokeach, the reason for the lack of association between attitudes which favor violence and violent behavior is that violence and norms about violence are primarily interpersonal rather than intrapersonal. One, therefore, should not expect a causal connection between attitudes and behavior when the attitudes and behavior of only one interacting party are taken into account. For example, in order to study the attitude-behavior consistency of wives with respect to domestic violence, it is necessary to take the attitudes and behavior of the husband into consideration.

In the family, as in any other social structure, there are forces which help to maintain the status quo as well as forces which produce change (Straus and Hotaling. 1979: Chapter 1). For some, the contingencies of everyday life work toward what "should be" in terms of the normative system of the traditional family. For many, however, the contingencies of everyday life work against the realization of what "should be." For example, we may prefer having a job to hitting other people. However, a person may end up without a job and find himself hitting his wife. What we actually end up doing is always influenced by a host of factors, such as what a spouse does, how much money we have, or what our friends think of us.

The specific questions considered in this paper include what are some of the patterns of interaction inside the family which affect domestic violence; how are variations in the norms concerning the sex-linked division of labor in a marriage related to consistency of attitudes and behavior with respect to family violence; are the patterns of interaction inside the family related to the family's position in the larger society (using total family income as an indicator of the family's economic position)? The theory which the paper is designed to explore underlies each of these questions. The theory asserts that the extent to which a person's attitudes and behavior with respect to domestic violence are consistent is related, not only to patterns of interaction within the family, but also to the extent to which larger social forces enable husbands and wives to live up to their mutual role obligations as socially defined or inhibit them from doing so.

Sample and Method

The findings are based on the 1975 survey. The forms of family violence under study are both spousal and parental violence.

The survey contains information on the violent or nonviolent *behaviors* of both the respondent and of the respondent's spouse. As regards *attitudes* with respect to violence, it contains data only on respondents. It will, therefore, not be possible to examine how spouse's attitude affects the consistency of respondent's attitude and behavior. However, it will be possible to investigate whether spouse's *behavior* is related to respondent's attitude and behavior. Spouse's behavior may affect respondent's behavior independently of respondent's attitude. Or spouse's behavior may affect the attitude-behavior consistency of the respondent because it affects the relationship between respondent's attitude and respondent's behavior.

The survey contains two semantic differential items (Osgood *et al.*, 1957). One asks about parents' attitudes towards slapping or spanking a 12-year-old. The other item refers to respondent's attitude towards couples slapping each other. For each of these, respondents indicate the degree to which they consider this kind of behavior "necessary," "normal," and "good" on scales with a range from 1 to 7. Each rating was dichotomized to read 1 versus 2–7; for example, "unnecessary" versus "necessary." The scales were dichotomized in this way so that people can be classified unambiguously into "nonviolent" versus "all other." A clearly nonviolent attitude should be related to nonviolent behavior and vice versa.

Two dependent variables were any minor violence by respondent or spouse.

In this case, the respondents acted as informants about their spouses' behavior (see footnote 7). Twelve percent of the respondents (N = 2,122) pushed, shoved, slapped, or threw something at their spouse during the 12 months preceding the interview.

A third dependent variable was any minor violence by the respondent against the referrent child. Sixty-three percent of the parents (N = 1,146) reported they had pushed, shoved, or slapped their child during the 12 months preceding the interview.

Yule's Q will be used as a measure of the consistency between attitude and behavior for two reasons. First, the skewed distribution of one of the dependent vairables (respondent's violence against spouse) precludes the use of parametric statistics. Second, Yule's Q is an appropriate measure of consistency because it does not make any assumptions about the direction of causality. Our theoretical approach, as stated earlier, and the limitations of cross-sectional data, led to the focus on the consistency between attitude and behavior, as distinguished from the question of whether attitude causes behavior or behavior causes attitude.

Attitudes and Behavior

The findings show, first, that slapping a 12-year-old is normatively more acceptable than slapping one's spouse. Almost all parents (81.5 percent) expressed at least some approval of one or more of the three parental violence items (belief that slapping a 12-year-old is necessary, normal, or good), and 65 percent indicated approval along all three dimensions (N = 1,098). In contrast, only 27.6 percent of the respondents indicated that slapping a *spouse* was either necessary, normal, or good; and only five percent answered positively on all three dimensions (N = 2,048).

Second, our data show that such attitudes do have at least some relation to actual slapping, especially in relation to parental violence. Of the parents who believe that slapping a 12-year-old is necessary, normal, and good (N = 714), 72 percent actually used violence against their children during the survey year. But, of the respondents who believe that slapping one's *spouse* is necessary, normal, and good (N = 96), only 33 percent reported an actual act of violence against their spouses. Thus, among those with pro-violence attitudes, the consistency is greater in the parent-child relationship than in the husband-wife relationship.

However, among those with nonviolent attitudes, inconsistent behavior is also greater in the parent-child relationship than in the husband-wife relationship.[2] Of the respondents who believe that slapping one's spouse is not necessary, not normal, and bad (N = 1,479), only 8 percent engaged in minor violence against their spouses. In contrast, of the parents who think that slapping a 12-year-old is unnecessary, not normal, and bad (N = 199), over one-third, 37 percent, engaged in violence against their children.[3]

In analyzing these data further, we explored several alternatives: using a typology of attitudes, treating each of the three attitudes in question separately, and creating an index of violent attitudes.[4] It turns out, however, that the findings remain essentially unchanged, whether an index or the single attitude, "normal versus not normal," is used. This is the case because there are very few respondents who believe that slapping a member of one's family is not normal, but who believe at the same time that it is necessary and/or good. Believing that slapping another member of one's family is "not normal" is, therefore, an adequate measure of the most antiviolent attitudes. Hence, for simplicity of presentation, we will report only those findings that deal with the "normal-not normal" attitude.

Control for Sex

Parental violence.   The findings in the left panel of Table 10.1 show that, among both mothers and fathers, a pro-violent attitude is related to parent's minor violence. The table also shows that mothers are more likely to slap their children than are fathers (see also Gelles, 1978). However, in relation to the objectives of this paper, the most interesting finding in Table 10.1 is the fact that there is an inconsistency between attitudes and behavior for a larger proportion of the mothers than the fathers. Among the 117 mothers who believe that slapping a 12-year-old is not normal, 42 percent did actually hit the child and were therefore inconsistent, as opposed to 32 percent of the 116 fathers who engaged in minor violence against their children despite their beliefs to the contrary.

Spousal violence.   The findings in the right panel of Table 10.1 show that, among both husbands and wives, a pro-violent attitude is related to minor violence against one's spouse. Those who believe that slapping one's spouse is normal are more likely to have pushed, slapped, or thrown something at their spouse than those with an antivolent attitude. In contrast to the data on fathers and mothers, there is no difference between husbands and wives in the rate of minor violence against their spouse, nor in the percentage who are inconsistent.

TABLE 10.1
Percentage of Respondents Who Were Violent by Sex and Belief in the Normality of Violence

A. Parent-Child Violence		
Belief that Slapping a 12-Year-Old is Normal	Percentage of Parents with Minor Violence Against Their Child	
	Fathers	Mothers
Not Normal	32% (116)	42% (117)
Normal	65% (390)	74% (477)
B. Spousal Violence		
Belief that Slapping a Spouse is Normal	Percentage of Respondents with Minor Violence Against their Spouse	
	Husbands	Wives
Not Normal	8% (653)	8% (867)
Normal	24% (259)	22% (264)

Structural Factors and Parental Violence

Role Differentiation

Why do more mothers than fathers tend to be inconsistent in slapping their children when they don't believe in it? This greater inconsistency among mothers is probably due to the fact that full-time mothers tend to spend more time with their children than do fathers. They are more often "at risk" of behaving in a way which is inconsistent with their beliefs.

To test this explanation, we need a measure of the sex-linked division of labor in the family. Although there is no direct measure in the survey of sex-linked division of labor with the family as the unit of analysis, there are six items on segregated decision norms as seen by the husband, and the same six for the wife.[5] The total number of segregated decision norm items is therefore 12. The index has a range of 0–12.

The findings in Table 10.2 show that the attitude-behavior inconsistency among mothers increases with an increase in the number of segregated decision norms. For mothers who believe that child slapping is not normal, the greater the number of segregated decision norms in the family, the more likely they are to have a minor violence count against their children. For mothers in families with the highest number of segregated decision norms, Yule's Q is smallest (.35), confirming the relatively low consistency between attitude and behavior. In contrast, for fathers in families with the highest number of segregated decision norms, Q = .52, which shows a higher consistency between their attitudes and their behavior.

More detailed analysis produced further data that support the idea that the greater inconsistency of mothers is due to their being the ones responsible for the children most of the time. These mothers tend to be

TABLE 10.2

Percentage of Fathers and Mothers Who Were Violent to Their Children by Belief Regarding the Normality of Slapping a 12-Year-Old and by Number of Segregated Decision Norms

Number of Segregated Decision Norms	Percentage Violent Among *Fathers* Who Believe Slapping is:			Percentage Violent Among *Mothers* Who Believe Slapping is:		
	Not Normal	Normal	Q	Not Normal	Normal	Q
0-4	34% (32)	63% (73)	.53	29% (35)	66% (124)	.66
5-7	30% (33)	72% (151)	.70	43% (40)	82% (195)	.71
8-12	36% (42)	64% (135)	.52	61% (36)	77% (133)	.35

full-time housewives. It is among full-time housewives that number of segregated decision norms increases the inconsistency between attitude and behavior. In families with a low number of segregated decision norms (0–4), 37 percent of the full-time housewives slap their children when they don't believe in it (N = 27). In contrast, in families with a high number of segregated decision norms (8–12), 69 percent of the full-time housewives slap their children when they don't believe in it (N = 29). The number of segregated decision norms seems to have no such effect among mothers who have a full-time job, whether they believe in child slapping or not.

Partner's Violence

One might assume that wives who physically punish their children do the job for their husbands so that the latter do not have to do it themselves. But this is not what the data show. On the contrary, as seen in Table 10.3, controlling for attitude, both fathers and mothers are much more likely to be violent to their children when their partners have used physical punishment against their children than when they have not.

Table 10.3 shows that attitude-behavior consistency is greatest among fathers whose wives physically punish their children, while among mothers whose husbands use physical punishment attitude makes little difference. They are uniformly high on minor violence against their children. A Q of .25 confirms the relatively low consistency of the behavior of those mothers with nonviolent attitudes whose husbands have also physically punished their children. In contrast, among mothers whose husbands do not use physical punishment the attitude-behavior consistency is increased (Q = .53).

In short, parent's behavior tends to be in agreement with spouse's behavior even if it is in disagreement with respondent's own attitude. The findings suggest that the partner's behavior serves as legitimation or has a

TABLE 10.3

Percentage of Fathers and Mothers Who Were Violent to Their Children by Belief Regarding the Normality of Slapping a 12-Year-Old and by Actual Physical Punishment of Child by Partner

Partner Physically Punished Child	Percentage Violent Among *Fathers* Who Believe Slapping is:			Percentage Violent Among *Mothers* Who Believe Slapping is:		
	Not Normal	Normal	Q	Not Normal	Normal	Q
No	18% (77)	34% (143)	.40	26% (81)	53% (184)	.53
Yes	61% (36)	83% (234)	.52	81% (32)	88% (286)	.25

reinforcing influence on the parent's own behavior with respect to child punishment.[6] Among mothers, their partners' behavior tends also to legitimize the respondents' violent behavior towards their children when they appear to have internalized the opposite norm.

Other Social Relationships

What if a third party enters the picture in the form of a relative or friend with whom the respondent has talked about domestic problems? Table 10.4 shows that talking to relatives and friends about a domestic problem decreases the consistency between attitude and behavior among parents who do not believe in slapping a 12-year-old, but whose spouses have used physical punishment (as shown by the drop in the value of Q from .50 to .20). Also, consulting with relatives and friends increases the consistency between attitude and behavior among parents who believe in slapping a 12-year-old, but whose spouses do not do it (Q = .57). However, among parents whose own attitudes with respect to child punishment are in agreement with their spouses' behavior, consulting with relatives and friends makes little difference with regard to their violent behavior. For example, among parents with a pro-violent attitude whose partner physically punished their child, 88 percent of those who consulted with relatives and friends and 85 percent of those who did not consult engaged in minor violence.

These findings show that, among those with a nonviolent spouse and a violent attitude or violent spouse and a nonviolent attitude, consultation with relatives and friends is related to higher rates of violence. If there is a domestic problem and disagreement over the use of violence, consultation with relatives and friends may be a last-ditch attempt for those who

TABLE 10.4

Percentage of Parents Who Were Violent to Their Children by Actual Physical Punishment of Child by Partner, by Belief Regarding the Normality of Slapping a 12-Year-Old, and by Discussion of Problems with Relatives and Friends

Talked About Domestic Problems with Relatives, Friends	Percentage Violent Among Those Whose Partner Hit Child and Who Believe Slapping a 12-Year-Old is:			Percentage Violent Among Those Whose Partner Did *Not* Hit Child and Who Believe Slapping a 12-Year-Old is:		
	Not Normal	Normal	Q	Not Normal	Normal	Q
Yes	83% (23)	88% (260)	.20	26% (43)	56% (142)	.57
No	65% (43)	85% (244)	.50	20% (95)	38% (161)	.42

have a violent spouse and a nonviolent attitude (or vice versa) to resolve the problem. In this case, third parties may sanction the use of violence.

To recapitulate, the data show that the partner's behavior vis-a-vis the child lends further sanctioning to the parent's own behavior Do these findings also apply to spousal violence? It can be argued that the partner's behavior should make an even greater difference for respondent's own behavior than in the case of physical punishment of children.[7]

Structural Factors and Marital Violence

Partner's Violence

The findings in Table 10.5 are in line with the above reasoning. The data show that for both men and women who believe that slapping one's spouse is normal, violence by their partner increases attitude-behavior consistency.[8] A possible reason for the increase in consistency is that being hit by one's spouse is not just an act of provocation. It also seems to provide moral sanctioning or justification of one's own violent behavior. Spousal violence is most frequent in those families in which the respondent's own violent attitude is accompanied by the violent behavior of the spouse. This pattern continues despite a control for talking to third parties, such as relatives and friends, about a domestic problem. Whether they have consulted with relatives and friends or not, the majority of these respondents tend to have engaged in minor violence against their spouses.

These findings suggest that, with respect to domestic violence, involvement in a personal network of friends and relatives can support not only acts which are normative, but also acts which are clearly deviant as far as the "standard" norms of the society are concerned. The following section will attempt to show why this should be the case.

TABLE 10.5

Percentage of Respondents Who Were Violent to Their Spouses by Belief Regarding the Normality of Slapping a Spouse and by Marital Partner's Violence

Was Marital Partner Violent?	Percentage of *Husbands* Who Hit Spouse Among Husbands Who Believe Slapping a Spouse is:			Percentage of *Wives* Who Hit Spouse Among Wives Who Believe Slapping a Spouse is:		
	Not Normal	Normal	Q	Not Normal	Normal	Q
No	5% (607)	9% (196)	.31	4% (794)	6% (202)	.23
Yes	57% (42)	76% (58)	.40	52% (62)	74% (61)	.45

Family Position in the Economic System

Data not reported here show that parents' minor violence against their children declines only in the highest income group ($20,000 or more). In contrast, minor violence against spouses decreases as income goes up. The lower the total family income, the greater the probability of violence (see O'Brien, 1971; Straus *et al.*, 1979). The two-variable relationships are significant, even though they are not very strong. On the other hand, *belief* that for a husband or wife to slap the other is normal, is not related to income. These findings suggest that the family's position in the economic system affects the role relationship inside the family, but not attitudes about violence.

The findings in Table 10.6 show that, when the marital partner has not engaged in violence, there is a low rate of spousal violence, irrespective of attitude or income. However, among those who have marital partners who have hit them, being in the lower income groups sharply decreases the consistency between attitudes and behavior (as shown by the decrease in Q from .56 to .11).

Other analyses of the data show that the above findings tend to hold for women rather than for men. That is, lower-income women who consider slapping "not normal" but whose husbands have hit them, are highly inconsistent. Very likely these are the women who hit in self-defense or just "hit back." But, among women in the higher income groups who have been hit by their husbands, being nonviolent increases the consistency between attitude and behavior.[9]

Among husbands who have been hit by their wives, those who have a pro-violent attitude are more likely to have been violent than those who do not. This is especially pronounced in the lower income groups though

TABLE 10.6
Percentage of Respondents Who Were Violent to Their Spouses by Belief Regarding the Normality of Slapping a Spouse, by Marital Partner's Violence and by Total Family Income

Total Family Income	Percentage Violent Among Those Whose Partner is Nonviolent and Who Believe Couple Slapping is:			Percentage Violent Among Those Whose Partner is Violent and Who Believe Couple Slapping is:		
	Not Normal	Normal	Q	Not Normal	Normal	Q
0-$11,999	5% (414)	10% (122)	.34	67% (39)	71% (63)	.11
$12,000 or more	4% (854)	7% (254)	.24	49% (59)	78% (49)	.56

the Ns are too small to draw any definite conclusions. However, the data are in line with another finding. Among men, the lower the total family income, the greater the consistency of those respondents who believe that slapping one's spouse is normal. Of the husbands who have a total family income under $6,000, 52 percent of those who believe that slapping one's spouse is normal (N = 23) engaged in minor violence against their spouse as against 13 percent of those who have the nonviolent attitude (n = 64). In contrast, among the husbands with a total family income of $20,000 or more, only 11 percent of those who believe that slapping one's spouse is normal (N = 74) and 7 percent of those with the nonviolent attitude (N = 185) were actually violent.

We think that these findings reflect the fact that lower-income husbands are less able to fulfill the provider role and are, therefore, less able to live up to the expectations of other family members than are husbands with higher incomes (Rodman, 1968). In contrast to the higher social classes, in which husbands have more prestige, money, and power, lower-income men have no such resources to fall back on to control their wives. Physical violence can be used as a resource by lower-class men to control their wives when other resources are lacking (Allen and Straus, 1979; Steinmetz and Straus, 1974). In the higher income groups, men are able to control their wives in other than violent ways. "Money belongs to him who earns it, not her who spends it, since he who earns it may withhold it" (Hill and Becker, 1955:790). Violence is, therefore, used as a means to obtain a socially approved goal, namely the leadership role in the family, when society withholds legitimate means to obtain that goal (Merton, 1938).

Another reason why marital violence is somewhat less frequent in higher income families than in lower income families may be that middle-class women have internalized a social-emotional, expressive, supportive role to a greater extent than have working-class women. This is, in part, because of different socialization patterns and, in part, because they are compensated in other ways, namely through the prestige, power, and income of their husbands' positions (Goode, 1971). For these reasons, middle-class wives with nonviolent attitudes are less likely to retaliate when they are hit by their spouses than are their lower-class counterparts.

Conclusion

It is now possible to answer the questions posed at the beginning of this paper: to what extent are social structural variables, such as patterns of interaction inside the family and the family's position in the economic system, related to domestic violence and to the consistency or inconsistency between attitudes and behavior?

The findings show that attitudes and behavior are indeed related. However, they also show that *violent behavior by the spouse has a much greater impact on the respondent's violence than the respondent's own attitudes about violence*. This applies to both hitting one's child and hitting one's spouse. With respect to spousal violence, the consistency between attitude and behavior is greatest among those respondents who have pro-violence attitudes and a violent partner.

More generally, the findings suggest that consistency between attitude and behavior depends, not simply on a person's attitude, but also on social structural factors which reinforce or inhibit violent behavior. Whether one's behavior is consistent with one's beliefs about violence (*e.g.,* slapping a spouse when one believes this is permissible under certain circumstances, or not slapping a spouse when one believes this is never permissible), depends on being in roles and life circumstances which bring forth behavior that is consistent. Consistency can also occur by being in life circumstances which make it unnecessary to engage in the behavior believed to be wrong.

For example, low-income husbands are less in a position to live up to their role obligations as providers than are middle-class husbands. Their wives are, therefore, less likely to recognize the males as the head of the house than are their middle-class counterparts. When such recognition and other resources are lacking, husbands may, in turn, use force to control their wives. Thus, lack of resources increases the consistency between attitude and behavior among those husbands who have a pro-violent attitude.

In contrast, among high-income husbands, attitude about spousal violence shows little relation to behavior. They may approve of slapping a wife under certain circumstances, but they are uniformly low in actual slapping. We suggest that this is true because high-income husbands have economic and prestige resources which let them control their wives without the need to use force.

Turning now to wives, the higher the total family income, the greater the consistency between their attitudes and behavior with respect to spousal violence even when they have been hit by their husbands. Middle-class wives less often have paid employment and are economically more dependent on their husbands than are wives from lower-income families. They are, therefore, more likely than their lower-class counterparts to practice what they have been taught to believe in, namely to refrain from hitting their husbands. The risks and costs involved in doing otherwise are great.

Lower-class wives are more likely to be hit than their middle-class counterparts. Furthermore, the data show that being hit by one's spouse has a greater impact on respondent's violent behavior than respondent's own attitude. These findings, plus the lack of access to resources, might account for the fact that lower-class wives who have been hit by their husbands tend to have a relatively high rate of spousal violence, irrespective of attitude.

In short, the results of this research show that the consistency between attitude and behavior cannot be taken for granted in the study of family violence. Patterns of interaction with spouse and kin are at least as important in the study of domestic violence as are respondents' attitudes. These patterns of interaction, in turn, are related to the extent to which the environment facilities or inhibits the performance of various roles in the family, such as that of parent, provider, or spouse.

Notes

The authors are grateful to Noel Cazenave, Gerald Hotaling, and Roger Libby for discussions of drafts of this manuscript.
1. These findings are consistent with some of the studies reviewed by Liska (1974, 1975) which show an inconsistency between attitude and behavior. The classic study indicating a lack of association between attitude and behavior is that by LaPiere (1934). LaPiere discovered that there was little relationship between hotel managers' verbally expressed attitudes concerning the accommodation of a Chinese couple and their actual behavior. For a review of the literature on the consistency between attitude and behavior, see Schuman and Johnson (1976).
2. When we discuss those with a *violent* attitude, the percentages in the tables indicate the degree of *consistency* between the respondent's attitude and violent behavior. When we discuss those with a *nonviolent* attitude, the percentages in the tables indicate the degree of *inconsistency* between the respondent's attitude and violent behavior.
3. The relationship between parental attitudes and parental behavior has a Q of .59, while the relationship between spousal attitudes and behavior has a Q of .56.
4. The index in question assigns a code of 0 to all respondents who believe that slapping a member of one's family is unnecessary, not normal, and bad; and it assigns a code of 1 to everyone else.
5. These involve normative expectations on who should have the final say on "Buying a car; Having children; What house or apartment to take; What job your (husband/partner) should take; Whether you should go to work or quit work; How much money to spend on food per week" (answers: wife only or mostly; or husband only or mostly). In about half of the cases, husbands were interviewed. They also acted as informants concerning their wives' beliefs. In about half of the cases, wives were interviewed who also acted as informants about their husbands' beliefs.
6. This implicit legitimation by the spouse seems to be important also in families with a high number of segregated decision norms. For example, in families with a high number of segregated decision norms (8–12) in which the spouse also uses physical punishment, 100 percent of the mothers who do not believe in

slapping (N = 14), and 92 percent of the mothers who think slapping a 12-year-old is normal (N = 73) were violent.

7. It will be remembered that the respondent was the wife in a random half of the sample, and the husband in the other half of the cases. The reader may wonder to what extent we can depend on the husband to accurately report the frequency of the wife's violence and vice versa. A detailed analysis of the accuracy of respondent's reports when respondent is used as an informant (Bulcroft and Straus, 1975) suggests that the latter depends on the type of information gathered. Fortunately, the data show that the incidence rates obtained for husband's violence using the husband as the respondent (12.8 per hundred) are almost identical to the incidence rates obtained when asking the wives about the husband's violence (12.9). Similarly, the incidence of violence per hundred wives is 11.2 when the data are based on interviewing husbands, and 11.5 when they are based on interviewing wives. Of course, this similarity could come about in a number of ways; for example, the spouses might be reporting only incidents in which both were violent. That this was not the case can be seen from the fact that violence was reported for only one of the two spouses in about half the couples among whom there was a violent incident during the survey year.

8. There might appear to be an interaction effect in Table 10.5, but the relationships are additive. In this as in most other tables, we used hierarchical models as developed by Goodman (1970, 1971, 1972) and exposited by Davis (1973–1974) to test for interaction effects. The final hierarchical model for the data in Table 10.6 is additive. It consists of four two-variable relationships: Sex, Attitude; Attitude, Respondent's Minor Violence Count; Attitude, Partner's Minor Violence Count; Partner's Minor Violence Count, Respondent's Minor Violence Count. The final model has a *Chi*-Square Likelihood Ratio of 2.5556 with 7 D.F. The Probability of *Chi*-Square = 0.9226.

9. Among wives whose husbands have hit them and who are in the 0–11.999 income group, 67 percent of those with the nonviolent attitude (N = 24) and 62 percent of those with the pro-violent attitude (N = 29) were actually violent. In contrast, among women who have been hit by their spouses and who are in the $12,000 or more income group, 45 percent of the antiviolent (N = 33) as opposed to 86 percent of the pro-violent (N = 28) were actually violent to their spouse.

11

Social Stress and Marital Violence in a National Sample of American Families

Murray A. Straus

The National Family Violence Surveys suggest that the family is the most violent institution, group, or setting that a typical citizen is likely to encounter. There are of course exceptions, such as the police or the army in time of war. But the typical citizen has a high probability of being violently assaulted only in his or her own home.

The Paradox of Family Violence and Family Stress

Family Violence

These data point to the first of many ironies or paradoxes about the family. In this case, the paradox is that the family is also the group to which people look for love, support, and gentleness. The hallmark of family life is *both* love and violence.

Much of the work of the Family Research Laboratory at the University of New Hampshire has been designed to unravel this paradox. We are a long way from a complete explanation. However, some progress has been made. This paper examines one of the several factors that contribute to the explanation: the link between stress and violence.

Stress in Families

Another irony of family life is that, although the family is often seen as a place where one can find respite from the tensions of the world, the family tends to be a group with an inherently high level of conflict and stress.

The theoretical case for this view is presented in detail elsewhere (Farrington, 1980; and Gelles and Straus, 1979). In this paper, there is space to illustrate only two of the stress-producing factors of the family.

First, in addition to the normal differences and conflicts between two or more people, the family has built into its basic structure the "battle of the sexes" and the so-called generation gap.

A second source of stress is inherent in what is expected of families. For example, families are expected to provide adequate food, clothing, and shelter in a society that does not always provide the necessary resources to do this. Another example is the expectation that families bring up healthy, well-adjusted, law-abiding, and intelligent children who can get ahead in the world. The stress occurs because these traits and the opportunity to get ahead are factors beyond the control of any given family to a greater or lesser extent.

The basic argument of the paper is that the second of these stress-producing factors is part of the explanation for the first. Specifically, a major cause of the high rate of violence in families is the high level of stress and conflict characteristic of families. Of course, this is only a plausible argument. Brenner, for example, has shown a clear relationship between stress as indexed by unemployment rate and the rate of assault and homicide in the United States, Canada, and Great Britain (Brenner, 1976). But is it other members of their own families who are assaulted or murdered by the unemployed? This needs to be demonstrated with empirical data. Consequently, a major part of this paper is devoted to such an empirical study.

The Theoretical Model

Although the empirical findings will start with the relationship between the levels of stress and violence in families, it is not argued that stress *directly* causes violence. Violence is only one of many possible responses to stress. Among the alternatives are passivity, resignation, or just leaving. University departments, for example, are also stressful environments, but the rate of physical violence within such departments is close to zero.

The absence of a *necessary* link between stress and violence is shown in Brenner's data on the correlates of unemployment (Brenner, 1976). Unemployment is highly correlated with assault and homicide. But it is also correlated with hypertension, deaths from heart attacks, mental hospital admissions, and alcoholism. Similarly, Brown and Harris (1978) studied a random sample of women in London, using highly reliable and valid data on life stresses. They demonstrated a clear tendency for these women to respond to stress by *depression* rather than violence.

Mediating Variables

Figure 11.1 suggests that other factors must be present for stress to result in violence. The center box of Figure 11.1 illustrates some of the other variables that must also be present to produce a correlation between stress and violence. For example, people are unlikely to respond to stress by violence unless this is part of the socially scripted method of dealing

FIGURE 11.1

Partial Model of Relationship Between Stress and Family Violence. This diagram is labeled as a partial model for two main reasons: The most obvious reason is that it includes only a sampling of the intervening variables that could be included in the center box. Second, the model omits negative feedback loops (i.e., deviation dampening processes) which must be present. Without them the violence would escalate to the point where the system would self-destruct—as it sometimes, but not typically, does. See Reference 27 for a systems model of family violence which includes negative feedback processes and other elements of a cybernetic system.

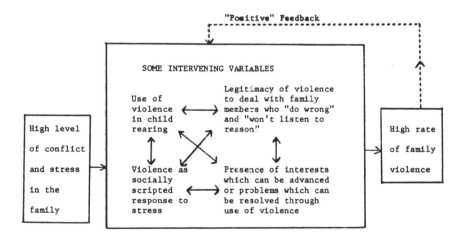

with stress and frustration—as it is in our society. Therefore, an important part of the model is the existence of norms or images of behavior that depict striking out at others when under stress as part of human nature.

However, these are very general behavioral scripts. They cannot explain *family* violence because they are part of the society's image of basic nature in *all* types of situations. These general scripts may be part of the explanation, but they are not sufficient. To find the additional variables that will lead to a sufficient explanation, one has to look at the nature of the family itself.

Normative Legitimacy of Family Violence

One very simple, but nonetheless important, factor is that the family has different rules about violence than do other groups. In an academic department, an office, or a factory, the basic rule is that no one can hit anyone else, no matter what they do wrong. A person can be a pest, an intolerable bore, negligent, incompetent, selfish, or unwilling to listen to reason. But that still does not give anyone the right to hit such a person. In the family the situation is different. There, the basic rule is that if someone does wrong and won't listen to reason, violence is permissible and sometimes even required.

This is clearly the case in respect to the rights and obligations of parents; but it also applies to spouses. As one husband said about an incident in which his wife threw a coffee pot at him: "I was running around with other women—I deserved it." Statements like that are made by many husbands and wives. In fact, the evidence suggests that a marriage license is also a hitting license (Straus, 1976; 1979). Still, that does not explain why or how such a norm arose or why it persists. Here again, there are a number of factors, one of which is the use of violence in child rearing, that is, physical punishment (Figure 11.1).

Family Socialization in Violence

Physical punishment provides the society's basic training in violence but, of course, training that applies most directly to behavior in the family. At least some use of physical punishment is just about universal in American society, typically beginning in infancy (Steinmetz and Straus, 1974). What are the reasons for saying that learning about violence starts with physical punishment?

When physical punishment is used, several things can be expected to occur. Most obviously, the infant or child learns to do or not to do whatever the punishment is intended to teach; for example, to not pick up things from the ground and put them in his or her mouth. Less obvious, but equally or more important, are four other lessons, which are so deeply learned that they become an integral part of one's personality and world view.

The first of these unintended consequences is the association of love with violence. Parents are the first and usually the only ones to hit an infant. For most children this continues throughout childhood (Straus, 1971). The child therefore learns that his or her primary love objects are also those who hit.

Second, since physical punishment is used to train the child or to teach about which dangerous things are to be avoided, it establishes the moral rightness of hitting other family members.

The third unintended consequence is the "Johnny I've told you ten times" principle—that when something is really important, it justifies the use of physical force.

Fourth is the idea that when one is under stress, tense, or angry, hitting—although wrong—is "understandable," i.e., to a certain extent legitimate.

Involuntary Nature of Family Membership

The last of the mediating variables for which there is space to discuss is the simple fact that the family is only a semivoluntary institution. This is most obvious in the case of children. They cannot leave, nor can parents throw them out, until a legally set age. So leaving—which is probably the most widely used and effective method of avoiding violence—is not available as an alternative in the parent-child aspect of the family.

To a considerable extent the same is true for the marital relationship. Ninety-four percent of the population marries, and anything done by this large percent of the population is not likely to be voluntary. No system of socialization is that effective. In fact, we all know the tremendous informal social pressures that are put on people to get married and stay married. Although divorces are now easier to get, the economic, social, and emotional barriers to breaking up a marital relationship are still extremely strong. Even couples who are living together without a formal marriage find it difficult to end the relationship. In cities like Boston and New York, there is a booming business in marriage counseling for the unmarried.

There are a number of other factors that should be included in Figure 11.1 and in this discussion. Those that have been discussed, however, should be sufficient to illustrate the theory that guided the analysis reported in this paper.[1]

By way of summary, the theory underlying this paper rejects the idea that people have an innate drive toward aggression, or an innate tendency to respond to stress by aggression. Rather, a link between stress and aggression occurs only if (a) the individual has learned an "aggressive" response to stress; (b) if such a response is a culturally recognized script for behavior under stress; and (c) if the situation seems to be one that will produce rewards for aggression. The data from the 1975 survey were used to examine this theory.

Definitions and Measures of Stress

There has been a vast debate on the concept of stress (Lazarus, 1966; Levine and Scotch, 1967; McGrath, 1970; Mechanic, 1962; Scot and Howard, 1970; and Selye, 1966). For example, one issue is whether stress is a property of the situation (such as illness, unemployment, family conflict, getting married, or getting promoted to a new job) or whether it is a subjective experience. For some people a new set of job responsibilities is experienced as stress, whereas for others *lack* of such new responsibility is a stress.

The definition of stress used here treats stress as a function of the interaction of the subjectively defined demands of a situation and the capabilities of an individual or group to respond to these demands. Stress exists when the subjectively experienced demands are inconsistent with response capabilities. This inconsistency can be demands in excess of capabilities or a low level of demand relative to response capabilities.[2]

In fact, there is a gap between the definition of stress given above and data I will actually report. This is true because the methodology of this paper *assumes* (a) that some life event, such as moving or the illness of a child, produces a certain but unknown degree of demand on parents; (b) that on the average this is subjectively experienced as a demand; (c) that the capabilities of parents to respond to these demands will not always be sufficient; and (d) that the result is a certain level of stress. On the basis of these assumptions, it is then possible to investigate the relationship between such stressful life events and the level of violence in the family. Obviously, that leaves a large agenda for other investigators to develop a more adequate measure of stress.

As indicated in Tables 11.1 and 11.2, the aspect of stress that is measured in this study is limited to what are called "stressor stimuli." The data were obtained by a modified version of the Holmes and Rahe stressful life events scale (Holmes and Rahe, 1967). Because of limited interview time, the scale was restricted to the 18 items listed in Table 11.1 (See Appendix, Section I.) The scores on this scale ranged from 0 to 18, with a mean of 2.4 and a standard deviation of 2.1. In addition to the overall stress score,

TABLE 11.1

Percent Experiencing 18 Life Stresses During Previous Year

Life Event	Male (N = 960)	Female (N = 1,183)	Total (N = 2,143)
1. Troubles with the boss	25.8	9.9	17.0
2. Troubles with other people at work	31.4	11.2	20.3
3. Got laid off or fired from work	10.0	5.9	7.7
4. Got arrested or convicted of something serious	1.9	0.9	1.3
5. Death of someone close	41.5	38.8	40.0
6. Foreclosure of a mortgage or loan	1.5	1.6	1.6
7. Being pregnant or having a child born	8.1	15.8	12.4
8. Serious sickness or injury	18.9	16.7	17.6
9. Serious problem with health or behavior of a family member	23.0	29.0	26.3
10. Sexual difficulties	9.0	13.1	11.6
11. In-law troubles	10.9	12.0	11.5
12. A lot worse off financially	15.8	12.1	13.7
13. Separated or divorced	3.6	2.6	3.0
14. Big increase in arguments with spouse/partner	8.1	9.4	8.8
15. Big increase in hours worked or job responsibilities	28.9	16.3	21.9
16. Moved to different neighborhood or town	17.2	16.4	16.8
17. Child kicked out of school or suspended	1.6	1.6	1.6
18. Child got caught doing something illegal	2.7	3.0	2.8

TABLE 11.2

Mean Scores on Stress Indexes

Index	Items	Mean Score* Male (N = 960)	Female (N = 1,183)	Total (N = 2,143)
Overall stress index	1 to 18	14.9	12.4	13.5
Occupational stress	1, 2, 15	28.7	12.4	19.7
Economic stress	3, 6, 12	9.0	6.5	7.6
Occupational and economic stress	Occ. + Econ.			27.3
Interpersonal stress	5, 9, 11, 16	23.1	24.1	23.6
Health stress	7, 8	13.3	16.2	14.9
Spousal stress	10, 13, 14	7.1	8.2	7.7
Parental stress	17, 18	2.7	3.1	2.9
Nuclear family stress	Spousal + Parental	14.3	14.2	14.2

* The scores are in percentage form in order to make the scores on each index somewhat comparable. Each is a percentage of the maximum possible raw score. Thus, a mean of 14.9 on the overall stress index means that this group averaged 14.9% of the 18 points that are possible; a mean of 28.7 on the occupational stress index means that this group averaged 28.7% of the three points that are possible on this index. See Reference 35, Chapter 2 for further explanation of percentage standardization.

we also considered different subgroupings of items. The subscores and their means are given in Table 11.2.

Sex Differences

The first thing to notice in Table 11.1 is that the experiences reported by the men and women respondents are quite similar. The exceptions are events for which men and women have different exposure. Thus, fewer women have paid employment, so it is not surprising that two to three times as many men as women experienced an occupationally related stress, such as troubles with a boss or losing a job.[3] There are a few other interesting sex differences.

Item 4 shows that twice as many men were arrested or convicted of a serious crime. An interesting sidelight is that to a noncriminologist, an annual arrest or conviction rate of 2 per 100 men seems quite high.

The only other item with a nontrivial difference is item 10, having had some type of sexual problem in the previous year. The rate for women is half again higher than the rate for men (13.1 versus 9.0).

Frequency of Different Stressors

The most frequently occurring stress among the 18 items is the death of someone close to the respondent (item 5). This happened to 40% of our respondents during the year we asked about. The next most frequent stress is closely related—a serious problem with the health or behavior of someone in the family (item 9). This occurred in the lives of about one out of four. For men, however, occupational stresses occurred more frequently. Item 2 shows that about 30% had a difficulty with their boss, and at the positive end about the same percentage had a large increase in their work responsibilities (item 15).

Definition and Measures of Violence

As in the case of the measurement of stress, there is a gap between what this set of definitions demands and what is available for analysis. The descriptions of violent acts given in the Conflict Tactics Scales were designed to permit a measure of the severity as well as the frequency of family violence. The list starts out with pushing, slapping, shoving, and throwing things. These are what can be called the "ordinary" or "normal" violence of family life. It then goes on to kicking, biting, punching, hitting with an object, beating up, and using a knife or gun. This latter group of items was used to compute a measure of "severe violence," which is comparable to what social workers call child abuse, feminists would call wife beating, and criminologists would call assaults. The Conflict Tactics Scales is described briefly in Chapter 1, and fully in Chapters 3 and 4.

Spouse Violence Rates

The first row of Table 11.3 shows that violence by a husband against his wife that was serious enough to be classified as wife beating occurred at a rate of 3.8 per 100 couples. Violence by a wife serious enough to be classified as husband beating occurred at an even higher rate—4.6 per 100 couples. However, it is important to remember that these data are based on attacks, rather than on injuries produced. If one uses injuries as the criterion, then wife beating would far outdistance husband beating. (See Appendix II.)

What proportion of these attacks were isolated incidents? Our data suggest that this was rarely the case. For those who experienced an assault, the medians in the last colume of Table 11.3 show that assaults happened about three times during the year. If the means are used as the measure of the frequency of occurrence, the figure is much higher—about eight or nine times. But this is true because of a relatively few couples at the extreme for whom such violence was just about a weekly event.

Stressful Life Events and Assault between Spouses

For purposes of this analysis, the Stress Index was transferred to Z scores and grouped into categories of half a Z score. Therefore, in Figure

TABLE 11.3

Incidence Rates for Severe Violence Index, Overall Violence Index, and Items Making up These Indexes

Conflict Tactics Scale Violence Indexes and Items	Rate Per 100 for Violence By:		Frequency*			
			Mean		Median	
	H	W	H	W	H	W
Wife Beating and Husband Beating (N to R)	3.8	4.6	8.0	8.9	2.4	3.0
Overall Violence Index (K to R)	12.1	11.6	8.8	10.1	2.5	3.0
K. Threw something at spouse	2.8	5.2	5.5	4.5	2.2	2.0
L. Pushed, grabbed, shoved spouse	10.7	8.3	4.2	4.6	2.0	2.1
M. Slapped spouse	5.1	4.6	4.2	3.5	1.6	1.9
N. Kicked, bit, or hit with fist	2.4	3.1	4.8	4.6	1.9	2.3
O. Hit or tried to hit with something	2.2	3.0	4.5	7.4	2.0	3.8
P. Beat up spouse	1.1	0.6	5.5	3.9	1.7	1.4
Q. Threatened with a knife or gun	0.4	0.6	4.6	3.1	1.8	2.0
R. Used a knife or gun	0.3	0.2	5.3	1.8	1.5	1.5

* For those who engaged in each act, i.e., omits those with scores of zero.

11.2, each horizontal axis category indicates the families who fall within a band that is half a standard deviation wide.

The data plotted in Figure 11.2 clearly show that the higher the stress score, the higher the rate of assault between husband and wife. For the wives, the curve approximately fits a power function. For the husbands the relationship shows a general upward trend, but is irregular.[4]

Both the smooth shape of the curve and the fact that the line plotted for the women is above the line for the men at the high stress end of the graph suggest that stress has more effect on violence by wives than on violence by husbands. At the low end of the scale, women in the −1.0 to −1.4

FIGURE 11.2

Marital Assault Rate by Stress Index Score.

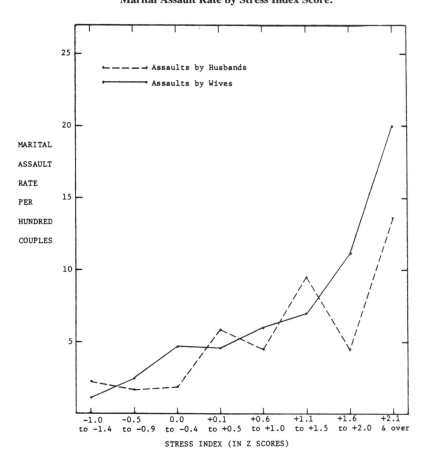

stress group have an assault rate about half that of the men in this group (1.1 per 100 versus 2.2 for the men). But at the high stress end of the scale, women in the +1.6 to +2.0 and +2.1 and over categories have assault rates that are, respectively, 150% and 50% greater than the rates for the husbands who experienced this much stress. It seems that in the absence of stress, women are less violent to their spouse than are men, but under stressful conditions women are more violent.

An analysis identical to that in Figure 11.2 was done, except that the dependent variable was not limited to the types of severely violent acts used in Figure 11.2. That is, the measure included pushing, slapping, shoving, and throwing things. Except for the fact that the rates are much higher—they start at 5 per 100 and range up to 48 per 100—the results are very similar.

The importance of this similarity is that it helps establish a connection that is extremely important for understanding serious assaults. Again and again in our research, we find a clear connection between the "ordinary" violence of family life, such as spanking children or pushing or slapping a spouse, and serious violence, such as child abuse and wife beating. Actually, the connection goes further. *Verbal* aggression is also part of this pattern of relationships. People who hurt another family member verbally are also the ones most likely to hurt them physically (Straus, 1977). Moreover, the same set of causal factors applies to both the milder forms of violence and acts of violence that are serious enough to be considered child abuse or an assault on a spouse. The similarity of the relationship between stress and the overall violence index and the relationship between stress and serious assaults is but one of many such examples found for this sample (Straus, Gelles, and Steinmetz, 1980).

Types of Stressors and Assaults

The analyses just reported were also carried out using each of the stress subscores listed in Table 11.2 as the independent variable. In each case, as the amount of stress increased, so did the assault rate. These relationships were strongest for the "spousal stress' and the "economic plus occupational stress" subscores.

The fact that a very strong relationship was found between stress in the spousal relationship and assault on a spouse is what might be expected, because in such cases, the assaulter is lashing out at what he or she may believe is the cause of the stress. The relationship between economic and occupational stress and assault is therefore better evidence that stress per se is associated with violence. This relationship is shown in Figure 11.3.[5]

FIGURE 11.3

Marital Assault Rate by Economic Plus Occupational Stress Index.

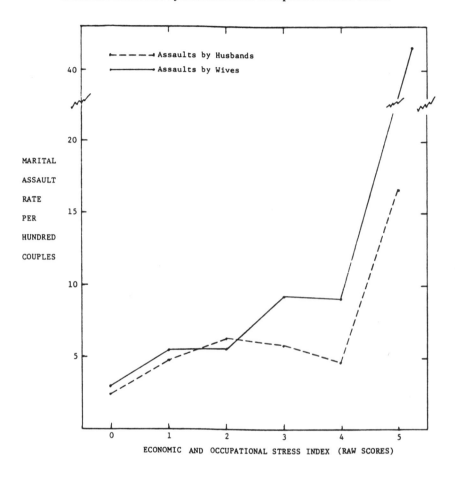

ECONOMIC AND OCCUPATIONAL STRESS INDEX (RAW SCORES)

Factors Linking Stress and Wife Beating

Interesting as are the findings presented so far, they do not reflect the theoretical model sketched at the beginning of this paper (Figure 11.1). One might even say that the data just presented distort the situation because the graphs tend to draw attention away from a very important fact: most of the couples in this sample who were subject to a high degree of stress were not violent.

A critical question is raised by this fact. What accounts for the fact that some people respond to stress by violence whereas others do not? Part of the answer to that question was suggested in the center box of Figure 11.1. The variables included there were selected to illustrate the theory. They were not intended to be a complete list, either of what is theoretically important or of the variables available for this sample. The available data actually cover three of the four variables listed in Figure 11.1 plus a number of other variables.

An analysis was carried out to take into account these intervening variables. This analysis focuses on assaults by husbands on their wives. It is restricted to this aspect of intrafamily assault because, along with child abuse, it is the most serious problem of intrafamily violence, and because of limitations imposed by the length of the paper.

The analysis started by distinguishing husbands in the sample who experienced none of the stressful events in the past year ($N = 139$) from those in the high quartile of the index ($N = 258$). Each of these groups was further divided into those who were in the high quartile of each mediating variable versus those in the low quartile. This enables us to see if the presumed mediating variable was, as specified in the theoretical model, necessary for life stresses to result in violence.

If the theory outlined in Figure 11.1 is correct, the men who had the combination of high stress and the presence of a mediating variable will have a high rate of violence, whereas the men who experienced a similar high amount of stress but without the presence of mediating variable will *not* be more violent than the sample as a whole, despite the fact that they were under as much stress during the year as the others.

Socialization for Violence

The first row of Table 11.4 runs directly contrary to the theory being examined. It shows that the men who were physically punished the most by their mother when they were teenagers were slightly *less* violent under stress than the men who were not or only rarely hit at this age by their mother. On the other hand, having been physically punished on more than just a rare occasion by a *father* does relate to assaulting a wife. Husbands whose father hit them the most have an assault rate against their wives that is slightly higher than do husbands who were under equally high stress that year but who did not experience this much violence directed against them as a teenager. The difference between the effect of having been hit by one's mother versus by one's father suggests that violence by the father against a teenage boy is a more influential role model for violent behavior that the son will later display under stress.

The next two rows of Table 11.4 refer to violence *between the parents*

TABLE 11.4

Effect on Intervening Variables on the Incidence of Assault by Husbands
Experiencing High Stress

Intervening Variable	Assault Rate per 100 Husbands when Intervening Variable Was:		$N*$	
	Low	High	Low	High
A. Childhood Experience With Violence				
Physical punishment after age 12 by mother (0 vs. 4 + per yr)	7.1	6.7	85	89
Physical punishment after age 12 by father (0 vs. 4 + per yr)	7.4	8.4	81	83
Husband's father hit his mother (0 vs. 1 + per yr)	5.4	17.1	167	41
Husband's mother hit his father (0 vs. 1 + per yr)	4.6	23.5	176	34
B. Legitimacy of Family Violence				
Approval of parents slapping a 12-year-old (0 vs. high ¼)	5.9	9.9	34	71
Approval of slapping a spouse (0 vs. any approval)	2.7	15.0	150	100
C. Marital Satisfaction and Importance				
Marital satisfaction index (low vs. high quartile)	12.3	4.9	73	61
Marriage less important to husband than to wife = high	5.9	11.7	17	34
D. Socioeconomic Status				
Education (high vs. low quartile)	6.1	5.4	49	56
Husband a blue collar worker = low	9.2	5.4	284	202*
Income (low ≤ $9,000, high ≥ $22,500)	16.4	3.5	122	113*
E. Marital Power				
Power norm index (high = husband should have final say)	4.2	16.3	71	55
Decision power index (high = husband has final say)	5.2	16.1	58	62
F. Social Integration				
Organizational participation index (0 vs. 11 +)	10.5	1.7	86	60
Religious service attendance (0–1/yr vs. weekly)	8.9	5.4	79	56
Relatives living near (0–2 vs. 13 +)	5.7	11.9	124	118*

* The Ns vary because, even though the intent was for the high and low groups to be the upper and lower quartiles, this was not always possible. In the case of occupational class, for example, the comparison is between a dichotomous nominal variable. In the case of continuous variables, we sometimes wanted to preserve the intrinsic meaning of a score category, such as those with a score of zero, even though this might be more or less than 25% of the sample. Another factor causing the Ns to vary is that the division into quartiles was based on the distribution for the entire sample of 2,143 rather than just the high stress subgroup analyzed in this table. Finally, there are three variables for which the data were obtained from the wife as well as the husband (husband's occupation, family income, and relatives living nearby). The Ns for these variables are roughly double those for the other variables because they are based on the entire sample, rather than only on those families where the husband was the respondent.

of the husbands in this sample. These two rows show large differences between husbands who are the sons of parents who engaged in physical fights and those who are sons of parents who did not. The assault rate by husbands whose own father had hit their mother was 216% higher than the rate for the men whose father never hit their mother (17.1 per 100 vs. 5.4). Surprisingly, the largest difference of all is in the much greater assault rate by husbands who had grown up in families where their *mother* had hit their father. This contradicts the idea of the same-sex parent being a more influential role model. Whatever the intervening process, however, Section A of Table 11.4 shows that the men who assaulted their wives were exposed to more family violence as teenagers than were the men who were not violent despite an equally high level of stress.

Legitimacy of Family Violence

Section B of Table 11.4 reports "semantic differential" scores (Osgood, Suci, and Tannenbaum, 1957) in response to questions about slapping a child and slapping one's husband or wife. Each score is made up by combining the ratings for how "necessary," "normal," and "good" the respondent rated slapping.

The first row of Section B shows that husbands who approved of slapping a child had a 68% greater rate of assaulting their wives than did the husbands with a score of zero on this index. When it comes to approval of slapping a *spouse,* there is a 456% difference in the predicted direction. These findings are consistent with the theoretical model asserting that the relation between stress and violence is a process that is mediated by social norms, rather than a direct biologically determined relationship. However, since these are cross-sectional data, the findings do not prove the correctness of the model. It is also quite plausible to interpret the greater assault rate by men who approved of violence as an after-the-fact justification. Except for a few variables that clearly occurred at a previous time, such as violence experienced as a child, this caution applies to most of the findings to be reported.

Marital Satisfaction and Importance

The first row of Section C compares men who were low in marital satisfaction with men in the high quartile. The low quartile men had a 151% higher assault rate. A similar difference is shown by comparing men who rated their marriages as a less important part of their lives than the marriage played in the lives of their wives. Of course, these differences, like a number of others reported in this paper, could reflect the effect of marital violence rather than the cause. Only a longitudinal study can adequately sort out this critical issue.The findings of this study are not inconsistent with the idea that men under stress are more likely to be violent if they do not find the marriage a rewarding and important part of their lives.

Socioeconomic Status

Three aspects of socioeconomic status are examined in Section D of Table 11.4. The first of these, the educational level of the couple, shows findings that many will find surprising. The husbands in the high quartile of education were only slightly less violent than those in the low quartile. This is inconsistent with the widely held view that less educated people are more violent. Actually, a careful review of the available studies fails to support this widespread idea (Straus, 1979). A number of studies (including an analysis of this reported in the Finkelhor (1977) sample) suggest there is little or no difference in aggression and violence according to education.

On the other hand, when it comes to indicators of present socioeconomic position, the low groups are, as expected, more violent. The second row of Section D, for example, shows that the assault rate of blue collar husbands is 70% greater than the assault rate of the white collar employed husbands. If the combined income of the couple was $9,000 or less, the rate of assault by husbands on their wives was 368% higher than in families with a more adequate income (16.4 per 100 versus 3.5 per 100).

What could account for the sharply different findings for education as compared to occupation and income? One fairly straightforward possibility is that low income and low status occupations are indirect indicators of even more stress than is measured by the stress index. Low or high education, on the other hand, does not necessarily mean that the couple is currently in an economically bad position, such as is indicated by a total family income of $9,000 and under.

Marital Power

One of the most important factors accounting for the high rate of marital violence is the use of force by men as the "ultimate resource" to back up their position as "head" of the family (Allen and Straus, 1980; Goode, 1971; Straus, 1976; 1977). Section E provides evidence that this may be part of the explanation for why some men assault their wives when under stress and others do not.

The first row of Section E shows that the assault rate of husbands who feel that husbands *should have* the final say in most family decisions is

288% higher than it is for husbands who are not committed to such male-dominance norms. The second row suggests that when this is translated into actual decision power, the differences are almost as great. The husbands who actually did have the final say in most family decisions had an assault rate of 16.1 per 100 as compared to 5.2 for the husbands who were also under high stress but shared decisions with their wives.

Social Integration and Isolation

The last set of mediating factors included in this paper explores the theory that violence will be higher in the absence of a network of personal ties. Such ties can provide help in dealing with the stresses of life and perhaps intervene when disputes within the family become violent.

The first row of Section F shows that men who belonged to no organizations (such as clubs, lodges, business or professional organizations, or unions) had a higher rate of assault than did the men who participated in many such organizations. The same applies to men who attended religious services as compared to men who rarely or never attended services.

The third row of Section F, however, shows opposite results. Couples who had many relatives living within an hour's travel time had a *higher* rate of assault than did couples with few relatives nearby. This finding is not necessarily inconsistent with social network theory. The usual formulation of that theory *assumes* that the network will be prosocial. That is usually a reasonable assumption. However, a social network can also support antisocial behavior. This is the essence of the differential association theory of criminal behavior. A juvenile gang is an example.

In respect to the family, Bott (1971) and others have shown that involvement in a closed network helps maintain sexually segregated family roles, whereas couples not tied into such networks tend to have a more equal and shared-task type of family organization and to be less traditional (Straus, 1969). In the present case, the assumption that the kin network will be opposed to violence is not necessarily correct. For example, a number of women indicated that when they left their husband because of a violent attack, their mothers responded with urgings for the wife to deal with the situation by being a better housekeeper, by being a better sex partner, or by just avoiding him, etc. In some cases, the advice was "you just have to put up with it for the sake of the kids—that's what I did."

Summary and Conclusions

This study was designed to determine the extent to which stressful life experiences are associated with assault between husbands and wives, and to explore the reasons for such an association. The data used to answer these questions come from the 1975 survey. Stress was measured by an instrument patterned after the Holmes and Rahe scale. It consisted of a list of 18 stressful events that could have occurred during the year covered by the survey. Assault was measured by the severe violence index of the family Conflict Tactics Scales.

The findings show that respondents who experienced none of the 18 stresses in the index had the lowest rate of assault. The assault rate increased as the number of stresses experienced during the year increased. This applies to assaults by wives as well as by husbands but is most clear in the case of the wives. Wives with a stress score of zero had a lower rate of assault as compared to the assaults by husbands with a stress score of zero. But the assault rate of wives climbed steadily with each increment of stress and gradually became greater than the assault rate of the husbands. Thus, although wives were less assaultive under normal conditions, under stress they were more assaultive than the husbands.

The second part of the analysis was based on the theory that stress by itself does not necessarily lead to violence. Rather, it was assumed that other factors must be present. Several such factors were examined by focusing on men who were in the top quartile in stresses experienced during the year. These men were divided into low and high groups on the basis of variables that might account for the correlation between stress and violence. If the theory is correct, the men who were in the high group of the presumed intervening or mediating variable should have a high assault rate, whereas the men in the low group on these variables should not be more assaultive than the sample as a whole, despite the fact that they were under as much stress during the year as were the other high-stress subgroup of men.

The results were generally consistent with this theory. They suggest the following conclusions:

1. Physical punishment by fathers and parents who hit each other train men to respond to stress by violence.
2. Men who assault their wives believe that physical punishment of children and slapping a spouse are appropriate behavior. Their early experience with violence therefore seems to have carried over into their present normative stance. However, a longitudinal study is needed to establish whether this is actually the causal direction.
3. Men under stress are more likely to assault their wives if the marriage is not an important and rewarding part of their life.
4. Education does not affect the link between stress and violence. However, low income and a low-status occupation do, perhaps because these are indicators of additional stresses.

5. Men who believe that husbands should be the dominant person in a marriage, and especially husbands who have actually achieved such a power position, had assault rates from one and a half to three times higher than the men in more equalitarian marriages who were also under stress.
6. Men who were socially isolated (in the sense of not participating in unions, clubs, or other organizations) had higher rates of assault on their wives, whereas men who were involved in supportive networks only rarely assaulted their wives despite being under extremely high stress.

Of course, these conclusions, although consistent with the findings reported in this paper, are not proved by the findings. Many of the findings are open to other equally plausible interpretations, particularly as to causal direction. The question of causal direction can only be adequately dealt with by a longitudinal study. In the absence of such prospective data, the following conclusions must be regarded as only what the study suggests about the etiology of intrafamily violence.

We assume that human beings have an inherent capacity for violence, just as they have an inherent capacity for doing algebra. This capacity is translated into actually solving an equation, or actually assaulting a spouse, *if* one has learned to respond to scientific or technical problems by using mathematics, or if one has learned to respond to stress and family problems by using violence. Even with such training, violence is not an automatic response to stress, nor algebra to a scientific problem. One also has to believe that the problem is amenable to a mathematical solution or to a violent solution. The findings presented in this paper show that violence tends to be high when certain conditions are present; for example, where people are taught the use of violence through childhood experiences and where the need of an individual to dominate a marriage provides a situation that is likely to yield to violence. If conditions such as these are present, stress is related to violence. If these conditions are not present, the relation between stress and violence is absent or minimal.

Appendix

1. Stress Index Modifications

The stress index used in this study departs from the Holmes and Rahe scale in ways other than length. One of the criteria used to select items from the larger original set was the elimination of stresses that have a positive cathexis. Methodological studies show that the negative items account for most of the relationship between scores on the stress index and other variables (Gersten, Langner, Eisenberg and Orzek, 1974; and Paykel, 1974). We modified some items and added some that are not in the Holmes and Rahe scale to secure a set of stressors best suited for this research. The Holmes and Rahe weights were not used in computing the index score for each respondent. This decision was based on research that found the weighting makes little difference in the validity of scales of this type (Straus and Kumagai, 1979) and of the Holmes and Rahe scale specifically (Hotaling, Atwell, and Linsky, 1979).

An important limitation that this stress index shares with the Holmes and Rahe index is that one does not know the time distribution of the stressful events. At one extreme, a person who experienced four of the stressors during the year could have had them spread out over the year, or at the other extreme, all four could have occurred at roughly the same time.

II. Wives As Victims

Although these findings show high rates of violence *by wives,* this should not divert attention from the need to give primary attention to wives *as victims* as the immediate focus of social policy. There are a number of reasons for this.

a. A validity study carried out in preparation for this resarch (Bulcroft and Straus, 1975) shows that under-reporting of violence is greater for violence by husbands than it is for violence by wives. This is true probably because an act of violence, so much a part of the male way of life, is typically not the dramatic and often traumatic event that it is for a woman. Physical violence is not unmasculine. But it *is* unfeminine according to contemporary American standards. Consequently, if it was possible to allow for this difference in reporting rates, even in simple numerical terms, wife beating would probably be the more severe problem.

b. Even if one does not take into account this difference in under-reporting, the data in Table 11.3 show that husbands have higher rates in the most dangerous and injurious forms of violence (beating up and using a knife or gun).

c. Table 11.1 also shows that when violent acts are committed by a husband, they are repeated more often than is the case for wives.

d. These data do not tell us what proportion of the violent acts by wives were in response to blows initiated by husbands. Wolfgang's data on husband-wife homicides (Levine and Scotch, 1967) suggest that this is an important factor.

e. The greater physical strength of men makes it more likely that a woman will be seriously injured when beaten up by her husband than the reverse.

f. A disproportionately large number of attacks by husbands seem to occur when the wife is pregnant (Gelles, 1975), thus posing a danger to the unborn child.

g. Women are locked into marriage to a much greater extent than are men. Because of a variety of economic and social constraints, they often have no alternative but to endure beatings by their husbands (Gelles, 1976; Martin, 1976; Straus, 1976; 1977).

Notes

It is a pleasure to acknowledge the many helpful criticisms and suggestions by the members of the Family Violence Research Program seminar: Joanne Benn, Diane Coleman, Ursula Dibble, David Finkelhor, Jean Giles-Sims, Cathy Greenblatt, Suzanne Smart, and Kersti Yllo; the computer analysis of Shari Hagar; and the typing of this paper by Sieglinde Fizz.

1. Figure 11.1 illustrates the general nature of the theory, without listing all of the variables that need to be taken into account. There are two aspects of the model that are included simply to alert readers to their importance, but that are not analyzed. First, this paper will not deal with feedback processes. Second, in the center box the arrows show that each intervening variable is related to the others. They are a mutually supporting system, and interaction effects are no doubt also present. However, in this paper, these and other intervening variables will be deal with singly.

2. A more adequate formulation of stress includes a number of other elements. Farrington has identified six components used in research on stress: the stressor stimulus, objective demands, subjective demands, response capabilities, choice of response, and stress level. Important as these six components are, there is no way to investigate them with the data from the sample.

3. The sex difference in item 7 (being pregnant or having a child) is probably due to men misunderstanding the question. It was meant to apply to the men as well as the women in the sample, in the sense of whether the wife was pregnant or had a child in the last year.

4. The number of husbands and wives, on which each of the rates in Figure 11.2 is based, are $-1.0 = 361$ and 365; $-0.5 = 459$ and 460; $0.0 = 414$ and 415; $+0.1 = 304$ and 303; $+0.6 = 224$ and 218; $+1.1 = 128$ and 129; $+1.6 = 45$ and 45; $+2.1 = 103$ and 105.

5. The numbers of husbands and wives, on which each of the rates in Figure 11.3 is based, are $0 = 1,053$ and $1,058$; $1 = 544$ and 548; $2 = 258$ and 256; $3 = 135$ and 130; $4 = 43$ and 44; $5 = 12$ and 12.

12

The "Drunken Bum" Theory of Wife Beating

Glenda Kaufman Kantor and Murray A. Straus

The belief that male drunkenness is a major cause of wife beating has been part of American consciousness at least since the Temperance movement (Bordin, 1981; Pleck, 1987). American cultural images of the association between alcohol and violence are also evident in films depicting wild-west barroom brawls and in Tennessee Williams's notable characterization of the drunken, boorish Stanley Kowalski striking his pregnant wife, Stella. These images link alcohol and aggression and suggest, first, that excess drinking is the principal cause of violence; and second, that drunkenness and wife beating are culturally scripted masculine behaviors. A third part of this cultural script portrays wife beating as a phenomenon of the underclass. Together, these images identify the "drunken bum" as the prototypical wife beater.

In this analysis we consider both aspects of this folk theory of the causes of intra-family violence. First we examine alcohol and class explanations of intra-family violence, and their convergence in the "drunken bum" theory of violence. Then we use data from a nationally representative sample of American families to test these ideas empirically. The three major questions we address are: (1) Do men who drink heavily have a higher rate of wife beating than others? (2) To what extent does drinking occur at the time of the violent incident? (3) Are such linkages between drinking and wife beating found primarily among working class men?

Explanations of the Drinking-Violence Relationship

Disinhibition Theory

Central to suppositions of a direct alcohol-violence linkage are centuries-old and widely held beliefs that alcohol releases inhibitions and alters judgment. This belief has persisted for the greater part of this century as well. It has been bolstered by the medical, biological, and psychoanalytic opinion that alcohol's effects on the central nervous system release inhibitions by depressing brain function or suppressing super-ego function, thereby allowing the expression of rage. However, disinhibition theory has recently fallen into disrepute as researchers develop a growing awareness of the complexity of the alcohol-violence syndrome. Mayfield (1983:142) points out that the location of the inhibition center of the brain is unknown and "disinhibition is no more than a tautological expression for drunkenness." Contemporary alcohol researchers now regard disinhibition as a complex process resulting from alcohol's pharmacologically induced "cognitive disruption" (Leonard, 1984:79) and mood-altering effects (Blum, 1981) interacting with varying individual expectancies about alcohol's powers (Marlatt and Rohsenow, 1980; Sher, 1985).

Social Learning and Deviance Disavowal Theory

MacAndrew and Edgerton's (1969) classic cross-cultural analysis provides an alternative explanation of the alcohol-violence linkage. These authors argue that drunken comportment is learned and may take the form of "time-out behavior" (1969:90). When individuals take time out by drinking, they are exempted from the usual behavioral constraints associated with sobriety. Similar doubts about disinhibition theory are expressed by other researchers (Coleman and Straus, 1983; Gelles, 1974; Gottheil et al., 1983; Pernanen, 1976; Taylor and Leonard, 1983). Coleman and Straus's (1983) analysis of data for 2,143 families suggests that social learning and deviance disavowal theories provide a better accounting of the alcohol-violence relationship within families. They argue that people learn a "script" for violence by observing that individuals are excused and forgiven for violent behavior which occurs while drinking ("It was the booze made me do it"). Gelles's study (1974) of 80 families led him to conclude that "individuals who wish to carry out a violent act become intoxicated in order to carry out the violent act" (1974:117). Moreover, McClelland and his associates (1972) found that men drink to heighten their sense of power—a finding consistent with the attributions of intentionality implicit in deviance disavowal views. Furthermore, Room (1980:8) argues that alcohol is "an instrument of intimate domination" used to excuse the exercise of illegitimate force against subordinates.

Integrated Theoretical Models

Pernanen's comprehensive theoretical reviews (1976, 1981) demonstrate the complexity of the association between alcohol and violence. Pernanen notes, as do other researchers (Blum, 1981; Boyatzis, 1983; Brown et al., 1980; Levinson, 1983; Powers and Kutash, 1982) that many factors may intervene to determine alcohol-violence outcomes. These include, but are not limited to, the symbolic meaning attached to alcohol use and expectancies about alcohol's effects; contextual factors present in the setting or the interaction of individuals; and perceptual and cognitive changes produced by alcohol. Disentangling these relationships can constitute a major difficulty for researchers.

Theoretical understanding is also hampered by narrow empirical tests of single cause-effect relationships and by implying that association equals causality. Instead of reflecting a causal relationship, the link between alcohol abuse and family violence may be "spurious" in the sense that both the drinking and the violence may reflect an underlying third factor or factors. The underlying factors may be at the individual, structural, or cultural level. At the structural level, the high degree of conflict inherent in American family structure may lead to marital discord and violence (Hotaling and Straus, 1980) as well as to alcohol abuse as a response to this stress (Linsky et al., 1985). This would produce a correlation between alcohol abuse and violence even though there is no causal relationship. At the cultural level, norms that legitimate violence as a masculine form of power assertion may co-exist with norms regarding the husband as the "head" of the household and excess drinking as acceptable masculine behavior.

Finally, these and other factors may interact with family socioeconomic status. First, while there has been considerable debate over the existence of a subculture of violence (Baron and Straus, 1987; Loftin and Hill, 1974), there do seem to be regional and social class differences in actual violence (Straus et al., 1980). Second, there is some consensus that alcohol abuse problems are most prevalent among lower-class men (Cahalan, 1970; Cahalan et al., 1969). Third, Brown and her associates (1980) found that heavy drinkers are more likely than others to believe that drinking increases sexual and aggressive behavior. In addition, some researchers (Cahalan, 1970; Cahalan and Room, 1974) have found that lower-class men more often express aggressive feelings while drinking. Fourth, lower blue collar families have been described as the last bastion of patriarchy (Komarovsky, 1967) where wife beating, although infrequent, occurs more often than within higher socioeconomic status families (Allen and Straus,

1980; Straus et al., 1980). These presumed characteristics of low socioeconomic status individuals and families seem to provide the basis for the drunken bum theory.

Empirical Research on Alcohol Abuse and Intrafamily Violence

A substantial body of literature exists on alcohol and violent interpersonal crimes.[1] However, there are many methodological problems with this research (see Greenberg, 1981; Pernanen, 1976, 1981). The major criticisms include sample biases, nonuniform measures of alcohol use and crime, and failure to specify antecedent conditions under which alcohol use and crimes occur. There are a number of general reviews of the relationship between alcohol abuse and family violence (Critchlow, 1983; Klein, 1981; Morgan, 1982, 1983; Room and Collins, 1983). Therefore, we limit our review of the literature to the link between alcohol and spouse abuse which is our empirical focus. (See Appendix for a more detailed review.)

Association of Alcohol with Intrafamily Violence

To a great extent, there is little consensus in the literature even on the elementary question of whether there is a *correlation* between drinking and intra-family violence. Take for example two of the most frequently cited works. Bard and Zacker's study (1974) of domestic assaults reported to police found little association between alcohol and family violence; whereas Wolfgang (1958) found that victims of family violence were frequently drinking. One difference between these studies is that Wolfgang studied the most extreme end of the family violence continuum—spousal homicide—while Bard and Zacker focused on assault.

Our systematic examination of 15 empirical studies produced a wide range of estimates of alcohol involvement in spousal violence—from 6 to 85 percent.[2] However, this is not surprising given the limitations of these studies. Most used descriptive or bivariate statistics and therefore lack controls for confounding variables. Some are based on clinical samples and others on more-or-less representative community samples. Some use self-reports, whereas others use the report of the spouse, and still others use the report of a police officer. Finally, the 15 studies employed a variety of measures of both alcohol use and wife abuse.

Six of the 15 studies (Byles, 1978; Caesar, 1985; Coleman and Straus, 1983; Gelles, 1974; Rosenbaum and O'Leary, 1981; Van Hasselt et al., 1985) used a violent vs. non-violent research design, and two (Coleman and Straus, 1983; Eberle, 1980) compared drinking with non-drinking couples. All seven of these comparative design studies found an associa-tion between drinking and marital violence. This is consistent with Hotal-ing and Sugarman's (1986) comprehensive analysis of case-controlled studies of husband-to-wife violence. They found that alcohol abuse was one of the risk factors which met their criteria for consistency across two-thirds or more of the studies they reviewed. Thus, alcohol seems to be an important correlate of wife abuse.

Even if one grants that the evidence supports a *correlation* between alcohol use and wife abuse, there are many inconsistencies and shortcom-ings in existing studies. For example, only one study (Van Hasselt et al., 1985) used a Quantity-Frequency Index to measure alcohol consumption, but the study was limited to a clinical population. Moreover, because the previous research is almost entirely descriptive or bivariate, it does not provide information appropriate to testing the complex interrelation of factors specified by the theories we reviewed earlier. In our analysis below, we use a modified Quantity-Frequency Index measure of alcohol use in the 1985 resurvey. We also use multivariate techniques that allow us to take into account the complex factors which figure prominently in existing theories—alcohol, occupational status, and norms concerning violence.

Method

Alcohol Abuse Measures

Drinking index.   The first of our two measures of alcohol abuse is the Drinking Index. It combines data from two survey questions:

1. In general, how often do you consume alcoholic beverages—that is, beer, wine, or liquor? never, less than 1 day a month, 1–3 days a month, 1–2 days a week, 3–4 days a week, 5–6 days a week, daily? (The median frequency of drinking was 1–3 times a month.)
2. On a day when you do drink alcoholic beverages, on the average, how many drinks do you have? By a "drink" we mean a drink with a shot of 1½ ounces of hard liquor, 12 ounces of beer, or 5 ounces of wine. (The median number of drinks per day was two.)

We used the frequency and amount data from these questions to develop six categories of drinking:

0 = Abstinent: Never drinks (30.6 percent).
1 = Low: Drinks on infrequent occasions, ranging from less than once a month up to 1–2 times a week; never more than 1 drink at a time.

Drinks less than once a month and no more than 2 drinks at a time (26.8 percent).

2 = Low Moderate: Drinks from 1 to 3 times a month up to daily; never more than 2 drinks (22.1 percent).

3 = High Moderate: Drinks less than once a month up to 1 to 2 times a week; 3–4 drinks a day (10.5 percent).

4 = High: Drinks 3–4 times a week up to daily; 3 or more drinks a day (4.9 percent).

5 = Binge: Drinks on infrequent occasions—once a month up to 1 to 2 times a week; 5 or more drinks a day (4.6 percent).

The distribution for the drinking index reveals that over half the sample were abstinent or low drinkers, and for the individuals who did drink, moderate patterns predominated. Significant sex differences in drinking patterns were also present. Two thirds of women were abstinent or infrequent drinkers, and less than 5 percent of women were high or binge drinkers. These findings are comparable to previous national surveys that investigate drinking patterns (ADAMHA, 1980; Cahalan, 1970; Gallup, 1978).

Although the distribution of drinking types is roughly consistent with previous drinking survey data, there are some possible limitations of this measure. First, it measures the average drinking pattern of each respondent and does not provide information on days when an individual departs from his/her typical drinking pattern. Thus the index may miss those who are normally moderate drinkers but binge on occasion. Second, the Drinking Index differs from the traditional Quantity-Frequency measure developed by Cahalan and associates (1969) because it does not estimate absolute alcohol content. However, this measure is comparable to those used by other researchers (e.g., Neff and Husaini, 1985) and does differentiate patterns and levels of drinking. The drinking index is also sensitive to binge patterns of drinking, a pattern important for our analysis, but not identified by typical quantity-frequency indexes.

Drinking at Time of Violence measure (DTV). For purposes of this study, the most serious limitation of the Drinking Index is that it does not provide information about whether drinking was one of the immediate antecedents of violence. Therefore, we included a third question in the survey to provide a "Drinking at the Time of Violence"(DTV) measure. We asked this question of all respondents who reported incidents of physical violence. The most recent and most severe act of violence (see below) was used as the reference, and the respondents were asked (in reference to the most recent and most violent act): "Were either or both of you drinking right before the conflict started?" However, this measure does not indicate the amount of alcohol consumed at that time. Although this measure may be further limited by its reliance on self and spousal reports of drinking at the time of violence, a substantial literature exists validating both self and spousal reports of drunkenness (e.g., Hesselbrock et al., 1983; Maisto et al., 1979; Polich, 1982; Sobell and Sobell, 1978; Van Hasselt et al., 1985; Vernis, 1983).

Approval of Violence

To measure norms tolerating wife abuse, we replicated the measure first employed in a 1968 survey conducted for the President's Commission on the Causes and Prevention of Violence: "Are there situations that you can imagine in which you would approve of a husband slapping his wife?" (Owens and Straus, 1975; Stark and McEvoy, 1970).

Violence Measure

While we consider both husband-to-wife and wife-to-husband violence to be important, we believe that they cannot be equated. Assaults on women are a far more serious problem given men's greater size and strength. Men, in fact, may laugh at their wife's attempts to slap or punch them, and much of the violence by wives is in self-defense (Saunders, 1986; Straus, 1980). Consistent with this, our data on the effects of violence show that women are three times more likely to require medical care for injuries sustained in family assaults. Therefore, we chose to focus this paper on husband-to-wife acts of physical violence. For brevity and convenience, this will be referred to as "wife abuse" for the balance of the paper. Wife abuse existed if the husband engaged in one or more of the violent acts listed above during the one-year referent period of the survey.

Occupational Status Measure

Each respondent was asked: What kind of work do you do? What kind of work does your spouse/partner do? This information was coded using the Bureau of Labor Statistics revised Occupational Classification System. Then, each Bureau of Labor Statistics occupation code was classified as either "blue-collar" or "white-collar" using the list of occupations falling into these categories by Rice (see Robinson et al., 1969).

Drinking Patterns and Wife Abuse

As a first approach to the question of the link between drinking and family violence, we computed the wife abuse rates for each of the six types of drinkers identified by the Drinking Index. The results in Figure 12.1 provide strong evidence of a linear association between drinking and wife abuse. The percentage of violent husbands rises monotonically from 6.8 percent for abstainers to a three times higher rate of violence (19.2 percent) for the binge drinkers. It appears that the more potentially problematic the drinking level, the higher the rate of violence between

FIGURE 12.1

Husband-to-Wife Violence Rate by Drinking Index

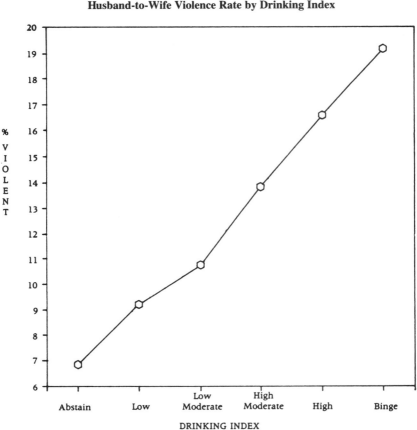

spouses. However, it is extremely important not to overlook the substantial amount of wife abuse by abstainers and moderate drinkers.

Drinking at the Time of the Violent Incident

As indicated earlier, an important limitation of the Drinking Index is that it refers to the respondents' *usual* pattern of drinking and does not provide information on whether there was drinking at the time of the violence. However, the DTV (Drinking at Time of Violence) measure provides this information and permits us to test the hypothesis that drinking is one of the immediate antecedents of family violence. Our data clearly demonstrate that alcohol was *not* used immediately prior to the conflict in the majority (76 percent) of cases. On the other hand, it is also important that in a substantial number of couples (24 percent) one or both partners *were* drinking at the time of the violent incident. In 14 percent of these couples only the male was drinking, in 2 percent only the female was drinking, while in 8 percent both were drinking.

We also investigated whether there is a link between the respondent's usual pattern of drinking and the drinking that occurred at the time of the violence by cross-tabulating the DTV measure by the Drinking Index. One might expect that the more one usually drinks, the greater the likelihood that drinking will be involved in a specific incident of wife abuse. This expectation finds strong support in these data (chi square = 77.65, p < .001). The percent drinking at the time of violence increased from 19.4 percent for the low drinking categories, to 20.8 percent for the high moderates, 47.5 percent for the highs, and 48.4 percent for the binge drinkers. Thus, there is little or no difference between the abstainers, low drinkers, low moderate drinkers, and high moderate drinkers with respect to the percentage of couples in which one or both of the spouses was drinking at the time of the violence. However, for high drinkers and bingers, the percent with alcohol involvement at the time of the violence more than doubles, to about half of all such couples.

Socioeconomic Status and Violence Norms

The thesis that there is a lower-class "culture of violence" (Wolfgang and Ferracuti, 1967) is widely disputed by both criminologists and sociologists who study social stratification. Steinmetz and Straus (1974) and Ball-Rokeach (1973) are among many who question this theory. Instead they argue that class differences in violence are a product of lower resources and higher economic and occupational frustration, and they note there are large differences in approval of violence *within* classes. Nevertheless, as we pointed out earlier, the belief persists that wife beating is perpetrated largely by drunken, lower-class men. To test this theory, we simultaneously considered three of its key elements—occupational status, norms concerning violence, and alcohol abuse. However, before examining the joint effects, Table 12.1 permits us to look at all three elements of the "drunken bum theory" one by one.

Occupational Status Differences in Drinking, Approval of Violence, and Wife Abuse

The results in Table 12.1 are consistent with those of other national surveys that show greater levels of both abstinence and high consumption patterns for working-class males (Cahalan, 1970). Binge and weekend drinking among the lower classes and conflict with spouses when drinking have been more frequently identified in lower socioeconomic groups (Cahalan, 1970; Cahalan and Room, 1974).

Table 12.1 also shows that tolerance of wife abuse is more prevalent among blue-collar males (18.5 percent) than among white collar males (14.4 percent). However, the great majority of men express disapproval of wife slapping regardless of their occupational status. Finally, the last row of Table 12.1 shows that blue-collar men are more likely to abuse their wives than are white-collar men.

The results of the vibariate analyses presented in Table 12.1 are consistent with previous research on status differences in alcohol abuse and wife abuse, and they provide some support for the "drunken bum theory." However, while all the predicted differences are statistically significant, none are very large.

The Drunken Bum Theory

We used a hierarchical log-linear analysis to examine the adequacy of the drunken bum model and to determine the relative importance of drinking, occupational status, and norms. This is a more appropriate test of the "drunken bum theory" because, unlike the tests in Table 12.1, the log-linear analysis enables us to look at the interaction of the three key elements of the theory: drinking patterns, violence norms, and occupational status.

We used a backward elimination procedure (Benedetti and Brown, 1978) to select the best-fitting theoretical model. This method systematically removes effects that produce the least significant changes in the likelihood-ratio chi squares. The first model tested, a saturated model, examines all main and interaction effects between husband-to-wife violence, the drink-

TABLE 12.1

Occupational Class Differences in Drinking Patterns, Approval of Violence,
and Wife Abuse

Variable	Blue Collar	White Collar
Husband's Drinking Pattern		
Abstinent	29.4%	20.4%
Rare	19.8	24.1
Low Moderate	16.9	31.8
High Moderate	14.1	10.6
High	10.5	7.7
Binge	9.2	5.4
N =	1089	1266
	Chi-square = 98.85, p <.001	
Husband's Approval of		
Slapping a wife	18.5%	14.4%
N =	1079	1253
	Chi-square = 6.74, p <.01	
Violent Husbands	13.4%	10.4%
N =	2462	2568
	Chi-square = 11.17, p <.004	

Note:
a. The N's for Husband's Drinking Pattern and Husband's Approval of Slapping
   are the number of husbands in the sample, whereas the N for the Wife
   Abuse Rate is the number of couples.

ing index, norms, and occupational status. The final, best-fitting model
includes the three-way interaction between drinking levels, occupational
status, and norms, and the two-way interactions between occupational
status and violence, and norms and violence (Likelihood-ratio chi square
= 13.022, df = 17; p = .735). Figure 12.2 presents the percentages in
each cell.[6]

Reading across Figure 12.2 shows that within all four of the sub-groups,
the husbands' drinking pattern is related to the probability of wife abuse.

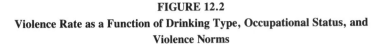

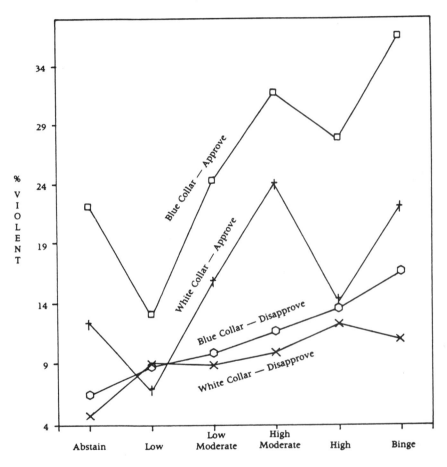

FIGURE 12.2

Violence Rate as a Function of Drinking Type, Occupational Status, and Violence Norms

Even for the group whose violence seems to be least affected by alcohol—white-collar men who do not approve of violence—the percent violent among binge drinkers is more than double the percent for abstainers.[7]

Figure 12.2 also shows that men who believe that there are circumstances under which they "would approve of a husband slapping his wife" have higher percentages of violence than men who disagreed with this statement. The differences between the two groups are large and consistent: 11 of the 12 comparisons possible in Figure 12.2 show that those who agreed with this traditional view had a higher rate of wife abuse than did those who disagreed.

The top two lines of Figure 12.2 show that among men who approve of wife slapping, blue-collar men have a substantially higher rate of wife abuse. The lower two lines of Figure 12.2 show that the blue-collar rate of wife abuse is also higher than the white collar rate among men who disapprove of wife slapping, but the differences are small. In general, Figure 12.2 demonstrates that blue-collar men have a higher rate of wife abuse, even after controlling for norms approving violence and drinking. However, normative effects appear to outweigh those of occupational status.

As a further test of the theoretical model, we computed the partial chi-square values to determine which variables exert the strongest net effects. Table 12.2 shows that there is a significant three-way interaction between

TABLE 12.2

Tests of Partial Associations for Wife Abuse, Drinking Types, Norms, and Occupational Status

Effects	Partial L.R. X^2	df	p Value
D.T.[a] by Occ. by Norms	13.46	5	.019
Wife Abuse by D.T.	18.11	5	.003
Wife Abuse by Occ.	3.95	1	.047
D.T. by Occ.	95.02	5	.000
Wife Abuse by Norms	26.21	1	.000
D.T. by Norms	42.45	5	.000
Occ. by Norms	2.97	1	.080
D.T.	482.20	5	.000
Occ.	15.44	1	.000
Norms	1103.61	1	.000

Note:

a. D.T. = drinking type

drinking type, approval of violence, and occupational status. All of the two-way interactions are also significant. Most marked of all the effects are the main effects for drinking types and norms. However, it is clear from the very large Likelihood-ratio chi-square that the most pronounced relationship is between norms regarding violence and wife abuse.[8]

Summary and Conclusions

In this study, we used survey data based on a nationally representative sample of 5,159 couples to examine three questions: (1) Do men who drink heavily have a higher probability of wife beating than others? (2) To what extent does drinking occur at the time of the violent incident? (3) Are such linkages between drinking and wife beating found primarily among working-class men?

Our findings revealed a strong link between alcohol use and physical abuse of wives. We found that the usual pattern of drinking of the respondent (as measured by a Drinking Index with six categories ranging from abstainers to binge drinkers) was directly related to the percent of wife abuse. Moreover, our analyses of drinking as an immediate antecedent of the violence revealed that alcohol was involved in about one out of four instances of wife abuse. When alcohol was an immediate antecedent, it was drinking by the husband alone, or by both the husband and the wife, and only rarely drinking by the wife alone that preceded the violent incident.

On the other hand, it is important not to overstate the extent of the link between alcohol use and wife abuse. For example, although Figure 12.1 shows that men who were classified as high or binge drinkers had a two-to-three times greater rate of assaulting their wives than did husbands who abstained, we should stress that about 80 percent of the men in both the high and binge drinking groups did *not* hit their wives at all during the year of this survey. Similarly, while we found that alcohol was often an immediate antecedent of wife abuse, most instances of such abuse took place when neither the husband nor the wife had been drinking. Thus, it is evident that alcohol use at the time of violence is far from a necessary or sufficient cause of wife abuse despite the stereotype that all drunks hit their wives or all wife hitting involves drunks.

Although blue-collar husbands tended to have a higher rate of wife abuse than white-collar husbands, Figure 12.2 shows that the *combination* of blue-collar occupational status, drinking, and approval of violence is associated with the highest likelihood of wife abuse. Men with these characteristics have a rate of wife abuse which is 7.8 times greater than the wife-abuse rate of white-collar men who do little drinking and do not approve of slapping a wife under any circumstances. These findings clearly fit the "drunken bum" theory. However, because there are cross-sectional data, the causal order of violence approval is unknown. For some men, normative approval of violence may be an antecedent condition, while for others it may be a rationalization of past wife beating.

Finally, even though we found that the rate of wife abuse is seven times greater among binge-drinking blue-collar men who approve of violence, two-thirds of men with these characteristics did *not* assault their wives during the year of the study. Thus, although the results of this study show that there is more than a "kernel of truth" in the drunken bum theory of wife beating, the findings also provide the basis for demythologizing this stereotype.

Toward an Integrated Theory of the Alcohol-Violence Link

Because some of the results of this study replicate those of a previous study using a large, representative sample (Coleman and Straus, 1983), there are grounds to believe that alcohol use is associated with an increased probability of wife abuse. However, the processes which produce this linkage have yet to be examined empirically, despite a large literature on the subject. For example, Kaufman (1985:79) holds, as do others (Flanzer, 1982; Gelles, 1974), that

> Many arguments are triggered by drinking and drunkenness. Fights start over how much alcohol has been consumed and whether the spouse is drunk or not and may escalate over related sensitive matters. The ensuing verbal fights are intense and use ammunition from a wide range of issues in the relationship.

Although this is a plausible scenario, experimental studies of marital conflict during drinking (Billings et al., 1979; Frankenstein et al., 1985; Gorad, 1971; Leonard, 1984; Steinglass et al., 1977) have yielded conflicting results on the effect of intoxication on verbal aggression, and also varying theoretical interpretations. Similar ambiguities exist in survey research findings. For example, Coleman and Straus (1983) argue that their findings demonstrate a link between drinking and marital violence and reflect processes of social learning and deviance disavowal, but they present no empirical evidence to back up this interpretation.

The evidence is somewhat stronger, but hardly definitive, for certain other causal processes and etiological factors. For example, the motivation or purpose of drinking may account for part of the drinking-marital violence relationship. Several researchers have found an association between power motivation and drinking (Brown et al., 1980; Cahalan, 1970;

McClelland et al., 1972; Room, 1980). Thus, heavy drinking may be a means of asserting power and control in the marital relationship. Men who are concerned about demonstrating their masculinity may try to accomplish this symbolically by drunkenness, by dominance over women, and by the exertion of physical force on others.

The results reported here suggest that, whatever other factors may be operating, norms concerning violence in combination with low socioeconomic status are important. This is most clearly indicated by the finding that when neither of these factors are present—i.e., among white-collar men who reject the legitimacy of hitting a wife—there is a limited relationship between alcohol abuse and wife abuse. Among other men, alcohol abuse may be the only most visible correlate of family violence, or it may be an important facilitating factor.

The facilitating process can be illustrated by considering men who reject the traditional norm permitting a man to slap his wife. For these men, we found that alcohol *is* associated with wife abuse. The process underlying this association may well involve a combination of the factors we discussed above. At the individual level, it probably includes acting on a belief in the disinhibiting power of alcohol—i.e., that drinking enables one to engage in activities that one would otherwise hesitate to engage in, such as extramarital sex, telling off the boss, or slapping the spouse. At the societal level, the underlying process probably includes norms which excuse "drunken comportment," especially in the form of binge drinking (see MacAndrew and Edgerton, 1969). This socially accepted "time out" from normal rules permits men who reject the legitimacy of hitting their wives to disavow responsibility for their otherwise reprehensible behavior.

These speculations suggest some of the interrelationships among the various theories purporting to explain the alcohol-violence link. These different theories are not necessarily at odds but may be complementary. Much work needs to be accomplished before a logically integrated and empirically verified theory can be produced. However, the results of our study call into question the use of alcohol treatment programs as a means of combatting wife abuse. As desirable as alcohol treatment programs may be on other grounds, most intrafamily violence occurs in the absence of alcohol. Moreover, reducing alcohol abuse does not deal with what are probably the basic factors underlying the high rate of wife abuse in the United States. To the extent that this is the case, steps to reduce wife abuse should focus on these underlying factors—especially the high rate of poverty and economic inequality, and the cultural tradition which glorifies violence, assumes male dominance, and tolerates violence by men against women.

Appendix: Review of Literature on Alcohol Abuse and Intrafamily Violence

A substantial body of literature exists on alcohol and violent interpersonal crimes (see for example Amir, 1971; Collins, 1981; Greenberg, 1981; Rada, 1978; Roizen, 1981; Roizen and Schneberk, 1977; Shupe, 1954; Wolfgang, 1958). However, there are many methodological problems with this research (see Greenberg, 1981; Pernanen, 1976, 1981). The major criticisms include sample biases, non-uniform measures of alcohol use and crime, and failure to specify antecedent conditions under which alcohol use and crimes occur. Because there are a number of general reviews and because this paper focuses on the link between alcohol and spouse abuse, our review of the literature will be specific to this area.

Association of Alcohol with Intrafamily Violence

To a great extent, the literature has lacked consensus on even the elementary question of whether there is a *correlation* between drinking and intrafamily violence. This can be illustrated by considering two of the most frequently cited works. Bard and Zacker's study (1974) of domestic assaults reported to police found little association between alcohol and family violence, whereas a study by Wolfgang (1958) found that victims were frequently drinking. Perhaps the difference is that Wolfgang studied the most extreme end of the family violence continuum—spousal homicide.

Table 12.A.1. permits a more systematic examination of previous research because it summarizes the findings of 15 empirical studies. The main conclusion to be drawn from the column headed "Violent Couples" is that these studies produced a wide range of estimates of alcohol's presence in spousal violence—from 6 to 85%. However, this is not surprising given the limitations of the studies summarized in Table 12.A.1. Most used descriptive or bivariate statistics and therefore lack controls for confounding variables. Some are based on clinical samples and others on more or less representative community samples. Some use self-reports, whereas others use the report of the spouse, and still others use the report of a police officer. Finally, the 15 studies employed a variety of measures of both alcohol use and wife abuse.

A Rashomon-like effect (perceptions of the event vary according to the role and identity of the actor) may account for the discrepancies shown in Table 12.A.1 between the reports of police, victims, and offenders. Police, for example, may be more likely to arrest drunken men if they are assaultive toward police as well as their spouses and less likely to arrest if both parties have been drinking. On the other hand, battered women have

TABLE 12.A.1

Incidence of Alcohol Associated with Wife Abuse

Study	Sample	Percent Drinking Among:		Alcohol Measure	Analysis
		Violent Group	Comparison Group		
Bard & Zacker, 1984	Police reports of family disputes N=1388	6% (victim accounts) 21% (police accounts)	None	Police/Victim reports of drunkenness	Descriptive
Byles, 1978	Family court sample N=139	69%	27% (No violence but attending family court)	Alcohol reported as "a problem in the marriage"	Chi Square p<.001
Caesar, 1985	Men in therapy 26 batterers 18 non-batterers	58%	28%	Michigan Alcoholism Screening Test (MAST)	Chi Square p<.05
Coleman & Straus, 1983	National proba- bility sample N=2,143 American couples	Violence rates by frequency of drunkenness: Never drunk = 2.1% Drunk very often = 30.8% Almost always drunk = 17.6%		Alcohol reports by frequency of drunkenness	Descriptive
Dobash & Dobash, 1979	Police reports in Scotland N=3,020 Interviews with battered women N=109	Police report 30% Women report 25%	None	Police report intoxication Women report abusers drunk at time of violence	Descriptive
Eberle, 1980	Battered women N=390	Differences between two groups of batterers: Those using alcohol to excess & those not using for 4 incidents 16% abused alcohol 19% none 65% used inconsistently		Women's reports of abuser's alcohol use during violence	Discriminant 83% correctly classified (none vs. excessitivity)
Gelles, 1974	N=44 social case work families N=36 neighbor- hood comparison group	48% of violent families	Not asked	Spouse reports of drinking related violence	Descriptive
Labell, 1977	Battered women in shelter N=512	72% of men	None	Self reports & reports of mates' drinking problem	Descriptive
Nisonoff & Bitman, 1979	Random phone sur- vey sample of Suffolk County, NY N=297	26.4%	Not asked	"Is alcohol a factor when you hit your husband/wife?"	Descriptive
Okun, 1986	Battered women in shelter, N=278 Batterers in counseling, N=110	68%	27.3*	Self reports, women's reports; counselor reports	t test p=.001

Study	Sample	Percent Drinking Among:		Alcohol Measure	Analysis
		Violent Group	Comparison Group		
Rosenbaum & O'Leary, 1981	52 abuse couples	MASD=12.97 (abused wives) MASD=4.55 (abusive couples)	x=4.30 (nonviolent discord) x=.85 (marital satisfaction)	MAST scores of husband	1 way ANOVA p<.01
	20 Satisfactorily married couples				
	20 Non-violent but maritally discordant				
Roy, 1977	Battered women N=150	85% (alcohol or or drugs)	None	Women's reports of abuser's alcohol or drug use	Descriptive
Van Hasselt, Morrison & Bellock, 1985	Couples in treatment: 26 violent 26 non-violent with marital discord.	x=17.02 x QFI=.95	Marital discord x=3.54 Satisfactory couple x=4.6 M.D.=.61 S.C.=.60	MAST QFI QFI	ANOVA p<.001 n.s.
	15 Satisfactorily married				
Walker, 1979	120 battered women	"Over half" of battered women reported a relationship between drinking & violence	None	Women's reports of spouse's drinking	Descriptive
Walker, 1984	401 battered women. Comparison with their prior non-battering relationships N=220	67% frequent use N=401	43%	Women's reports	Descriptive

*Estimated incidence of male problem drinking in county studied.

commented on their intoxicated spouses' ability to appear sober when police arrive (Reed et al., 1983). Men may use drunkenness to justify violent behavior yet be capable of sober behavior when this serves their needs. Additionally, women may need to attribute the batterer's violence to alcohol as a way of comprehending the irrational, predicting the unpredictable, and excusing the violence (Dobash and Dobash, 1979; Gelles, 1974). Further, some researchers find that alcohol is used inconsistently in separate violent episodes (Eberle, 1980; Walker, 1984).

Clinical vs. Survey Samples

Table 12.A.1 shows higher rates of alcohol abuse among clinical samples such as shelter populations or batterers in therapy (Caesar, 1985; Eberle,

1980; Labell, 1977; Okun, 1986; Roy, 1977; Walker, 1979; 1984) than in random survey groups (Nisonoff and Bitman, 1979; Coleman and Straus, 1983) and in police samples (Bard and Zacker, 1974; Dobash and Dobash, 1979).

Comparative Studies

Research that compares a measure of drinking among violent couples with the same measure applied to a comparison group provides a way of controlling for many of the discrepancies identified in the previous section. Three studies (Caesar, 1985; Rosenbaum and O'Leary, 1981; Van Hasselt, Morrison, and Bellock, 1985) utilize the Michigan Alcoholism Screening Test (MAST). This is a widely used, standardized test assessing alcohol-associated problems (Selzer, 1971). All of these studies found significantly higher MAST scores for violent men versus non-violent.

A standard measure of alcohol consumption is the QFI or Quality Frequency Index (Cahalan, Cisin, and Crossley, 1969; Straus and Bacon, 1953). However, only Van Hasselt and associates (1985) used this measure. Interestingly, these researchers found no significant differences in QFI scores for violent men compared to non-violent men in maritally discordant families or compared to non-violent men in satisfactory marriages. While the authors argue that the non-significant differences are due to the nature of the treatment population, other interpretations are possible. One is that individuals may under-report excess drinking, and a second is that levels of alcohol consumption are not necessarily consistent with problem behaviors (Linsky, Colby, and Straus, 1986).

Six of the 15 studies in Table 12.A.1 used a violent vs. non-violent design, and two (Coleman and Straus, 1983; Eberle, 1980) compared drinking with non-drinking couples. All seven of these comparative design studies found an association between drinking and marital violence. This is consistent with Hotaling and Sugarman's (1986) comprehensive analysis of case-controlled studies of husband-to-wife violence. Alcohol abuse was one of the risk factors that met their criteria for consistency across two-thirds or more of the studies they reviewed. Thus alcohol seems to be an important correlate of wife abuse.

Even if one grants that the evidence supports a *correlation* between alcohol use and wife abuse, there are many inconsistencies and shortcomings in the research to date, such as the fact that only one study used a QFI measure of alcohol consumption and that study described a clinical population. The research described in this paper provides modified QFI data for a large and representative sample of American families. Moreover, because the previous research is almost entirely descriptive or bivariate, it does not provide information that is appropriate to testing the complex interrelation of factors specified by the theories reviewed in a previous section. By contrast, the methods used in the research to be presented below reflects some of the theoretical complexity. It uses a multivariate analysis taking into account all the factors that figure prominently in these theories: alcohol, social class, and norms concerning violence.

Notes

1. For example see Amir (1971), Collins (1981), Greenberg (1981), Rada (1978), Roizen (1981), Roizen and Schneberk (1977), Shupe (1954), and Wolfgang (1958).
2. These 15 studies are Bard and Zacker (1974); Byles (1978); Caesar (1985); Coleman and Straus (1983); Dobash and Dobash (1979); Eberle (1980); Gelles (1974); Labell (1977); Nisonoff and Bitman (1979); Okun (1986); Rosenbaum and O'Leary (1981); Roy (1977); Van Hasselt, Morrison, and Bellock (1985); and Walker (1979, 1984).
3. Experience with studies of family problems including spouse abuse, rape, and parental kidnapping. (Gelles, 1983) shows that telephone interviewing produces higher response rates than face-to-face interviews on sensitive family topics. Not only do the flexibility and anonymity of the telephone lead to a higher response rate, but there is reason to believe that these attributes also yield data which are equivalent in reliability and validity to those gathered by face-to-face interviews. For example, Bradburn et al. (1979) found statistically indistinguishable differences in admitting to a conviction for drunken driving among persons who had in fact been convicted of that offense between face-to-face and phone surveys.
4. For convenience and economy, we use terms such as "marital" and "spouse" and "wife" and "husband" to refer to the respondents, regardless of whether they were married or a non-married cohabiting couple. For an analysis of differences and similarities between married and cohabiting couples with respect to violence and other characteristics, see Yllo (1978) and Yllo and Straus (1981).
5. See Gelles and Straus (1979) for an explication of this definition and an analysis of alternative definitions.
6. We used the SPSSX program, HILOGLINEAR, for these analyses. The cell frequencies used to compute the percentages in Figure 12.2 are from the observed cell frequencies included in the log-linear analysis output.
7. Figure 12.2 also shows that there is considerable fluctuation around each of the four trend lines. This can be interpreted as indicating that the relationship between drinking and wife abuse is not simply "the more drinking, the higher the rate of wife abuse." For example, among white collar men who express approval of slapping a wife, the proportion violent is greatest at the "High Moderate" level of drinking, declines for the "High" category, and rises again for "Binge" drinkers, though not to the same level as among the "High Moderate" drinkers. This is consistent with Coleman and Straus (1983), who also found a similar drop in violence for those with the most serious alcohol abuse. However, as is almost always the case for a multi-dimensional cross-tabulation, there are a number of cells with relatively few cases. In such instances, a shift of one or two cases from the non-violent to the violent category

can produce a large change in the percent violent. Consequently, it is best to concentrate on the two main findings shown in Figure 12.2: the general upward trend in violence as drinking increases, and the higher actual rate of wife abuse among men who believe that there are "situations that you can imagine in which you would approve of a husband slapping his wife." Because the findings are subject to varying interpretations, and especially because others may want to re-analyze the data, it is desirable to document the actual Ns which are the basis for the percentages in Figure 12.1. Reading from left to right for each plot line these Ns are Blue collar-Approve = 36, 23, 37, 22, 36, 30. White collar-Approve = 32, 30, 50, 29, 21, 9. Blue collar-Disapprove = 264, 181, 131, 118, 65, 65. White collar-Disapprove = 213, 261, 329, 99, 64, 54.

8. Given the relatively high rates of husband-to-wife violence that Straus et al. (1980:129) found for unemployed and part-time workers, and the relevance for the drunken bum stereotype, we examined the relationship between unemployment and wife abuse. Consistent with the previous study, we found that a larger percentage of unemployed men assaulted their wives during the year of the survey. When unemployment was added to the log-linear model, it continued to be significant, but the overall model did not meet the goodness-of-fit criterion as well as the model presented in this section. To the extent that the drunken bum stereotype includes unemployment, we think it refers to the *chronically* unemployed, whereas most of the unemployed husbands in this sample are probably not chronically unemployed. We infer this from the fact that most unemployment is transitory. Therefore, if our sample is representative of adult males, most of the unemployed in the sample are also temporarily unemployed.

Part IV
FAMILY ORGANIZATION AND FAMILY VIOLENCE

13

The Marriage License as a Hitting License: A Comparison of Assaults in Dating, Cohabiting, and Married Couples

Jan E. Stets and Murray A. Straus

Gelles and Straus coined the term *the marriage license as a hitting license* in the early 1970's in response to the discovery that the assault rate among married couples was many times greater than the assault rate between strangers. They argued that the common law rule that gave husbands the right to "physically chastise an errant wife," although not formally recognized by the courts since the mid-1800's, lived on in popular culture and in the way the criminal justice system actually operated (Straus, 1975, 1976). Since then, the pervasiveness of violence in intimate relationships has been well documented by the two National Family Violence Surveys and by other investigations. As reported in Chapter 6, more than three million married couples experience one or more severe assaults each year.

Subsequent investigations revealed that violence in cohabiting relationships is also quite common. In fact, physical assaults may be more common and more severe among cohabiting couples than married couples (Yllo and Straus, 1981; Lane and Gwartney-Gibbs, 1985). Given that cohabitation as an alternative living arrangement has steadily increased since 1970 (Glick and Spanier, 1980; Spanier, 1983), more individuals may be at risk not only of minor violence, but severe violence.[1]

The most recent research shows that dating violence is also pervasive and is a hidden serious social problem (Bogal-Allbritten and Allbritten, 1985). About 20% of college students have been physically assaulted by a dating partner (Makepeace, 1981; Cate et al., 1982; Stets and Pirog-Good, 1987).

The findings on violence between cohabiting couples and between dating couples raise questions about the implication that the status of being married is one of the factors accounting for the high rate of violence among married couples. While some research suggests that the overall assault rate in dating may be comparable to or higher than that found in marriage (Bernard et al., 1985; Makepeace, 1986), the comparisons are questionable because the rates are not based on the same measure (e.g., Makepeace, 1981). Even when the same measure is used, researchers do not usually identify which partner is violent, the severity of the assault, or whether this is different from that found in marriage or cohabiting relationships (for example Cate et al., 1982). A similar problem occurs when cohabiting and marital violence are compared because of the neglect in identifying which partner is violent and the severity of the assault. In response to these problems, the present research compares physical assaults across dating, cohabiting, and married relationships using the same measure. Additionally, we examine which partner is violent and the form of abuse used across marital status groups.

There has been a long tradition in sociology of studying group differences in rates to better understand the phenomenon under study. For example, Durkeim (1951) found that suicide was related to social integration only after comparing suicide rates of Catholics vs. Protestants, married vs. single people, men vs. women, and young vs. old people. A comparison of group rates is also used in epidemiology studies. However, the rate of physical assault not only has to be measured in the same way across the different groups, but also other fators that may influence the group rates need to be controlled. We do this in the present study by controlling on key demographic variables, including age, education, occupation, and gender.

Research Questions

The primary objective of this research is to compare the frequency and form of violence among those who date, cohabit, and are married. The following questions will be addressed.

1. *Are there differences in the frequency of assault across marital status groups?* Given prior research, we anticipate that violence will be more common in cohabiting than marital relationships (Yllo and Straus, 1981; Lane and Gwartney-Gibbs, 1985). Researchers have not adequately explained why cohabitors are more violent than married individuals. Later

we discuss why this pattern might arise. We do not know how those who date will compare with the other marital status groups.

2. *Does the severity of the assault vary by marital status?* Based on prior research (Yllo and Straus, 1981), we expect that violence will be more severe in cohabiting than dating or marital relationships. Later we discuss why this might occur.

3. *Does the partner who is violent vary by marital status?* Prior research has not directly examined whether the use of violence by men and women varies across different marital status groups. There is evidence that husbands are victims of marital violence as often as wives (Steinmetz, 1977–1978; Nisonoff and Bitman, 1979; Straus et al., 1980; Straus and Gelles, 1986; see also the summary in Chapter 6 and the findings given in Chapter 9). However, other studies based on clinical samples reveal that most offenders are men (Dobash and Dobash, 1979) and that if women hit, it is usually out of self-defense (Saunders, 1986). The finding that women are more likely to hit out of retaliation or self-defense (Straus, 1980) has not been supported by the findings in Chapter 9, which show that women in the 1985 Resurvey *initiated* violence as often as men. As explained in that chapter, these mixed results may be due to differences between the samples.

Evidence on the frequency of violence used by men and women while dating is also mixed (see the summary in Chapter 6). For example, some researchers have found no difference in the assault rate by sex (Deal and Wampler, 1986; Arias et al., 1987; Stets and Pirog-Good, 1987). Others reveal that men are more likely than women to be the aggressors (Makepeace, 1983), and that if women hit, it is usually out of self-defense (Makepeace, 1986). Still others find that women are more likely than men to be the aggressors (Plass and Gessner, 1983). More research is needed to resolve these contradictory findings.

This paper examines violence by both men and women in dating, cohabiting, and marital relationships. We view violence as a mutual problem of both sexes (Breines and Gordon, 1983), even though when injury occurs it is probably not as grave for men as for women because men, on average, are physically stronger (Chapter 9; Straus et al., 1980; Greenblat, 1983). Indeed, Chapter 9 reveals that women victims of violence are more likely than men victims of violence to experience physical and psychological injury.

This research attempts to answer the above questions and controls for age, education, occupational status, and gender of respondent. These controls are introduced to help rule out spurious relationships. Because many other controls could be introduced, our results are suggestive and not definitive of physical assaults across marital status groups.

Method

Samples

For the dating couples, a survey was administered to a probability sample of students at a large Midwestern university during the Spring of 1987. The response rate was 83%. A total of 526 individuals had complete information on physical violence and were included in our analysis.

The sample of married and cohabiting couples is from the 1985 National Family Violence Resurvey, excluding single-parent families, making a total of 5,005 married and 237 cohabiting couples.

Violence Measures

Conflict tactics scales (CTS). The CTS (described briefly in Chapter 1 and fully in Chapters 3 and 4) was used to measure the incidence of violence in dating, cohabiting, and marital relationships. Both minor and severe categories of violence were analyzed. If any act of minor violence occurred, then a score of one was given for minor violence; otherwise this category was zero. If any act of severe violence occurred, then a score of one was given for severe violence; otherwise this category was zero. When severe violence occurred, there was almost always minor violence. Consequently, the "severe violence" measure does not exclude minor assaults. In other words, a respondent who used acts 4 through 8 also could have used any of acts 1 through 3.

Assault rate and violence type percentages. Three different but overlapping measures of violence are used in this paper because each serves to illuminate a different facet of interpersonal violence. The first measure is the *assault rate* per one hundred couples. This provides information on the incidence of physical violence among married, cohabiting, and dating couples. These data will be shown in the form of graphs.

The second and third measures are typologies. These violence types are used for a more detailed analysis of the sub-set of respondents who experienced one or more violent acts during the year of the survey. These data will be given in tables.

Two violence types are identified: *Physical Violence I* and *Physical Violence II*. Physical Violence I identifies which partner is violent: Male Only, Female Only, or Both. Physical Violence II uses the same categories of violent actors, but also accounts for the severity and mutuality of assaults (see Appendix 2 for computing techniques). There are eight categories:

(1) male used minor violence, and female did not use violence;
(2) male did not use violence, and female used minor violence;
(3) both used minor violence;
(4) male used severe violence, and female did not use violence;
(5) male did not use violence, and female used severe violence;
(6) male used severe violence, and female used minor violence;
(7) male used minor violence, and female used severe violence;
(8) both used severe violence.

Demographic Measures

The married and cohabiting respondents are persons in households containing a currently married or cohabiting heterosexual couple. Households with a single parent or recently terminated marriage were excluded. The dating respondents were based on individuals who had dated during 1986. Married individuals were excluded.

For married and cohabiting respondents, the respondent's age was grouped into four categories: 18–24, 25–34, 35–44, and 45 and over. The dating respondents included only those ages 18–24.

Married and cohabiting respondents' education was grouped into five categories: no education through eighth-grade education, some high school education, high school graduate, some college, and college graduate and post-graduate work.

The occupational status of those who date was not collected because all respondents were attending school full-time. Married and cohabiting respondents were classified as "blue collar" and "white collar" (which are somewhat parallel to "working class" and "middle class") using the Bureau of Labor Statistics revised Occupational Classification system. Each Bureau of Labor Statistics occupation code was classified as either blue collar or white collar using the list of occupations falling into these categories by Rice (see Robinson et al., 1969).

If respondents were currently unemployed or housewives, their occupational code was based on their most recent paid job. If they never held a job for pay, they were coded as missing. To establish the occupational status of the relationship, the respondent's occupational status was used. When we examined the relationship between husbands' and wives' occupations, we found that two-thirds of the cases were concordant. Therefore, respondent's occupational status approximates the occupational status of the relationship.

Assault Rates and Assault Types by Marital Status

Figure 13.1 shows that cohabiting couples are more likely to have experienced violence than those in dating or marital relationships

FIGURE 13.1

Assault Rates by Marital Status (the "Either" category is the sum of the other three)

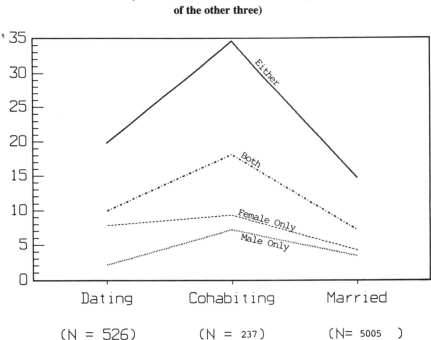

$(X^2 = 84.4, p < .01, df = 6).^2$ The line for "Either" shows that almost 35 out of every 100 cohabiting couples experienced a physical assault during the previous year, compared to 20 per 100 dating couples and 15 per 100 married couples. Moreover, cohabiting couples have the highest rates for each of the three specific types of violence. For example, in 18 out of every 100 cohabiting couples, both were violent, which is about double the rates for dating and married couples.

Two other points worth noting about the rates in Figure 13.1 are that Female Only violence is less common among the married than the other marital status groups and the lowest rate for Male Only violence is among dating couples.

Table 13.1 focuses on the subsample who reported one or more assaults. It shows the distribution of types of violence among those couples who experienced violence. Comparison of the percentages in the first column shows that Female Only violence type is a larger proportion of the violence among dating couples (39.4%) than other marital status groups (28.6% and

TABLE 13.1

Violent Couples: Percent in Physical Violence Type I by Marital Status

| Marital Status | Physical Violence Type I | | | |
	Female Only	Male Only	Both	N
Dating	39.4%	10.5%	50.0%	104
Cohabit	26.9%	20.7%	52.4%	82
Married	28.6%	23.2%	48.2%	736

$X^2 = 10.4$, p <.05, df=4

26.9% for those who are married and cohabit, respectively). Male Only violence is a larger proportion of the violence in cohabiting (20.7%) and marital (23.2%) than dating (10.5%) relationships. There is little difference among marital status groups with respect to the Both Violent category.

In general, these results answer research questions #1 and #3. Figure 13.1 indicates that among all couples there is a tendency for assaults to be most common in cohabiting relationships and slightly more common in dating than marital relationships. Among couples where there is an assault, Table 13.1 shows that Female Only violence most often occurs in dating relationships and Male Only violence mostly occurs in marital and cohabiting relationships. Situations in which both partners are violent occur about equally often in all marital status groups.

Marital Status and Severity of Assault

Figure 13.2 and Table 13.2 extend the analysis by taking into account the *severity* of assault by men and women in marital, cohabiting, and dating relationships. With two exceptions, the plot lines in Figure 13.2 show that cohabiting couples have the highest assault rate ($X^2 = 135.4$, p <.01, df = 16). For minor violence committed by both partners, cohabiting couples have roughly double the rate of the other two groups (8.0 versus 4.2 and 4.2) (#6 in Figure 13.2). For severe violence committed by both partners, cohabiting couples have more than six times the rate of the dating and married couples (#1 in Figure 13.2). Exceptions to the tendency for assault to be greatest among cohabiting couples involve a more severe

FIGURE 13.2
Assault Rates (II) by Marital Status

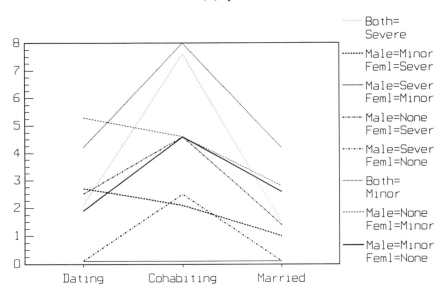

TABLE 13.2
Violent Couples: Percent in Physical Violence Type II by Marital Status

	Physical Violence Type II							
	M-Minor F-None	M-None F-Minor	Both Minor	M-Sev F-None	M-None F-Sev	M-Sev F-Minor	M-Minor F-Sev	Both Sev	N
Dating	9.6%	26.9%	21.2%	.1%	12.5%	4.8%	13.5%	10.6%	104
Cohabit	3.5%	13.4%	23.2%	7.3%	13.4%	1.2%	6.1%	22.0%	82
Married	7.5%	18.9%	28.3%	5.7%	9.6%	2.4%	7.1%	10.5%	736

$X^2 = 33.9$, p < .01, df=14

level of violence by the female partner than the male partner (#2 and #7 in Figure 13.2).

Turning to the subsample of violent couples, Table 13.2 indicates some types of violence in which there is little difference between dating, married, and cohabiting couples and other types in which the difference is large. There is little difference in the percent of violent couples who are in the Both Minor category (both partners engaged in minor assaults).

However, there is a large difference in the Both Severe category (both severely violent). Twenty-two percent of violent cohabiting couples have both partners using severe violence compared to less than 11% of violent dating or marital couples. Furthermore, the high percentage of Female Only violence while dating and Male Only violence while cohabiting and married typically manifests itself in minor violence.

In sum, the results in Figure 13.2 and Table 13.2 answer research question #2. They suggest that not only are cohabiting couples at greatest risk for violence, but in addition the most dangerous forms of violence occur when individuals cohabit. This is true because severe violence that is carried out by both partners is most common in cohabiting relationships.

The above conclusions are the type that might be made across different studies if the dependent variable (physical assault) is measured in the same way. However, these comparisons do not take into account the fact that married, cohabiting, and dating couples vary in other characteristics that might affect their overall violence rates. Unless these other factors are controlled or otherwise standardized, incorrect conclusions may be drawn. To see this, we turn first to age-controlled results.

Controls for Age, Education, and Occupation

Age

It is possible that the relationship between marital status and physical assault is spurious because age exerts an influence on both marital status and violence. Dating and cohabiting couples are likely to be younger. Additionally, studies have found that marital violence and cohabiting violence declines with age (Straus et al., 1980; Yllo and Straus, 1981). Therefore, the relationship between marital status and violence may change or disappear when age is controlled.

To investigate this possibility, we analyzed the relationship between: 1) age and marital status, 2) age and assault, and 3) marital status and assault with age controlled. With respect to age and marital status, younger couples are more likely to cohabit and older couples are more likely to be married ($X^2 = 298.0$; $p < .01$, df = 3). With respect to age and violence, age negatively influences the assault rate ($X^2 = 357.3$; $p < .01$, df = 6). This is not surprising given that criminal violence is most common among the young (U.S. Department of Justice, 1984). These findings indicate the importance of controlling for age in reducing a spurious relationship between marital status and assault.

We then examined the effects of age and marital status on violence through log-linear analysis (Knoke and Burke, 1980). This provides a test of the effect of age (net of marital status), marital status (net of age), and the interaction of age and marital status on violence. The dating category is omitted from the long-linear analysis because individuals are between ages 18 and 24. However, the descriptive statistics for the dating group are shown in Figure 13.3 discussed below.

The results indicate that while age and marital status exert their own influence on violence, the interaction between age and marital status is nonsignificant (X^2 for Age = 3.06, p < .01, df = 9; Marital Status = 10.5, p < .05, df = 3; Age*Marital Status = 11.0, n.s., df = 9). Thus age and marital status each have their own independent effects on violence. The age effects are not contingent upon marital status, and the marital status effects are the same for all age groups.

The rates for each of the cells in the log-linear analysis are displayed in Figure 13.3. All but 3 of the 16 marital status comparisons in Figure 13.3 show a higher rate for cohabiting than married couples, and most of the differences are large.

Table 13.3, like the other tables, is focused on the subsample who report one or more assaults. The table labeled *Age* shows that there is no strong tendency for age to be related to *Physical Violence I* or marital status.

FIGURE 13.3
Assault Rates by Marital Status and Age

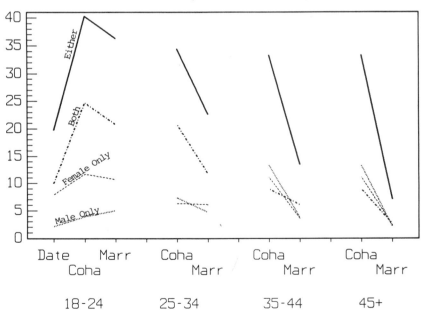

TABLE 13.3

Violent Couples: Percent Physical Violence Type I by Age and Occupational Status

| Control | Marital Status | Physical Violence Type I | | | N |
		Female Only	Male Only	Both	
Age					
18-24	Cohabiting	29.0%	3.7%	61.3%	31
	Married	29.1%	13.6%	56.4%	110
25-34	Cohabiting	18.2%	21.2%	60.6%	33
	Married	26.9%	20.7%	52.4%	309
35-44	Cohabiting	33.3%	40.0%	26.7%	15
	Married	26.9%	28.0%	45.1%	175
45+	Cohabiting	66.7%	33.3%	0%	3
	Married	34.2%	29.4%	36.4%	142

x^2 for Age — 12.3, p <.10, df—6; Marital Status — 0.1, n.s., df—2; Age*Marital Status — 3.6, n.s., df—6

Occupational Status					
Blue C.	Cohabiting	19.0%	31.0%	50.0%	42
	Married	30.8%	24.5%	44.7%	302
White C.	Cohabiting	38.2%	11.8%	50.0%	34
	Married	27.1%	23.5%	49.4%	399

x^2 for Occ. Status — 4.8, p <.10, df—2; Marital Status — 1.0, n.s., df—2; Occ. Status*Marital Status — 6.0, p <.05, df—2

The importance of controlling for age is brought out by comparing the assault rate for those ages 18–24 who are married, cohabiting, and dating. Without the age control, it seems as though dating couples are more violent than married couples (for example, see the line titled "Either" in Figure 13.1). However, comparison of the violence rate for dating couples with the rates for married and cohabiting couples of the same age (18–24) in the left panel of Figure 13.3 shows that violence is most common in cohabiting relationships and more common in marital than dating relationships.

Education

The low rate of violence among dating couples after controlling for age may be due to the fact that they have a higher education than the other marital status groups. Since education negatively influences husband-to-wife violence (Hotaling and Sugarman, 1986), the violence rate in the dating sample may be depressed. We tested this by controlling for education in the age group 18–24 for married and cohabiting couples. We found that education did not significantly influence the rate of violence (X^2 for Marital Status = 0.9, n.s., df = 3; Education = 0.7, n.s., df = 3; Marital Status*Education = 3.4, n.s., df = 3). Consequently, education does not explain the lower rate of violence among dating couples as compared to married and cohabiting couples.

Occupation

The relationship between marital status and assault may also be influenced by occupational status. For example, Straus et al. (1980) found a lower rate of marital violence among white collar than blue collar workers. Similar results were found in this survey; that is, violence is more common in blue collar than white collar relationships (X^2 = 10.2, p < .05, df = 4).

A log-linear analysis of violence by occupational status and marital status reveals significant main effects for marital status, occupational status, and a significant marital status by occupation status interaction (X^2 for Occupational Status = 10.2, p < .05, df = 3; Marital Status = 47.3, p < .001, df = 3; Occupational Status* Marital Status = 7.9, p < .05, df = 3). Figure 13.4 displays the rates.

Figure 13.4 shows an overall tendency for the assault rate to be lower among married couples compared to cohabiting couples and for white collar rates to be lower than blue collar rates, but the difference between married and cohabiting couples is somewhat less pronounced among white collar couples than blue collar couples.

The panel in Table 13.3 headed *Occupational Status* shows that among violent couples, there is no significant main effect for either marital status or occupational status. However, there is a significant interaction effect between these two variables: the proportion of Female Only and Male Only changes from blue to white collar but only for those who cohabit.

In summary, our results reveal that after controlling for age, education, and occupation, the marital status difference in assault rates remains; that is, cohabiting couples have the highest assault rate, followed by dating and married couples. However, it should be pointed out that after controlling for age, dating couples have a lower rate of assault than married couples.

Gender of Respondent

Returning to Figure 13.1, we find that Female Only violence is more common than Male Only violence in every marital status group. These

FIGURE 13.4

Assault Rates by Marital Status and Occupational Class

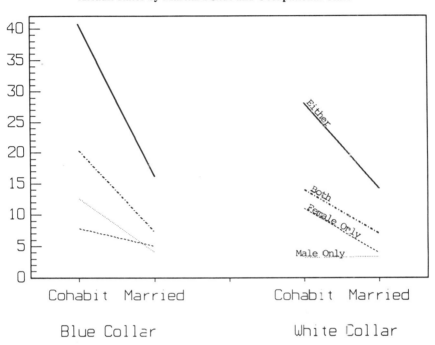

differences may be due to gender differences in *reporting* assaults. In other words, the percent of Female Only violence may be higher than the percent of Male Only violence not because it actually occurs with greater frequency, but because men are less likely than women to report their violence, as revealed in previous research (Szinovacz, 1983; Jouriles and O'Leary, 1985; Edleson and Brygger, 1986). It has been suggested that men who batter may deny their use of violence (Coleman, 1980; Pagelow, 1981; Walker, 1979) more than women. The gender difference in reporting violence may be another example of the "his/her marriage" (Bernard, 1982) or Rashomon effect (Condran and Bode, 1982), where wives have different perceptions of their marriage than husbands.

The analysis to investigate whether violence by gender is due to differences in reporting violence is conducted for respondents aged 18–24 (the only age group for which we have data on all three marital status groups). The results are presented in Figure 13.5.

The left side of Figure 13.5, which displays the violence rates as described by male respondents, is clearly different from the picture based

FIGURE 13.5

Assault Rates by Marital Status and Gender of Respondent

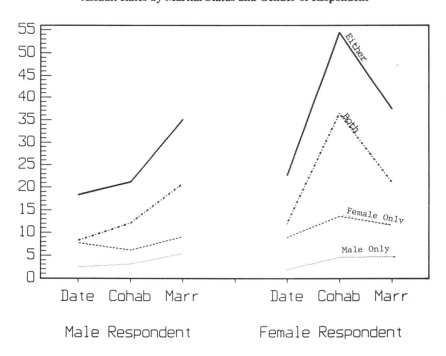

on information provided by female respondents on the right side of the figure. However, in every marital status category, the Female Only assault rate is greater than the Male only assault rate (X^2 for Sex = 10.0, p < .05, df = 3; Marital Status = 27.5, p < .01, df = 6; Sex*Marital Status = 6.6, n.s., df = 6).

We investigated two factors that might explain the high rate of female violence in this study. First, we examined minor and severe violence separately to see if the higher rate of Female Only violence was mainly due to more minor violence by women, but found no support for this (X^2 for Sex = 3.7, n.s., df = 7; Marital Status = 7.9, n.s., df = 14; Sex*Marital Status = 9.6, n.s., df = 14).

Another possibility is that the high rate of Female Only assaults in Figure 13.5 occurs because the data refer to young couples (age 18–24). We therefore replicated the analysis for men and women ages 25 and older who were married and cohabiting. The results showed that, consistent with other research reported in Chapter 9, the Female Only assault rate is similar to the rate of Male Only assaults (X^2 for Sex = 2.6, n.s., df = 3;

Marital Status = 2.5, n.s., df = 3; Age = 8.3, n.s., df = 6; Sex*Marital Status = 1.3, n.s., df = 3; Sex*Age = 2.4, n.s., df = 5; Marital Status*Age = 6.2, n.s., df = 6; Sex*Marital Status*Age = 6.4, n.s., df = 6).

These analyses rule out the possibility that the results are due to confounding with age and gender. However, they leave unresolved the reasons for the high rate of Female Only violence among young couples and indeed the even more fundamental question of the reasons why violence by females primarily occurs within the family (see Straus, 1980, and Chapter 5 for some suggestions).

We examined whether the high rate of Female Only violence is due to gender differences in reporting violence. After controlling for gender of respondent, Female Only violence is still more common than Male Only violence in all three marital status groups. After controlling for age, Female Only violence is similar to Male Only violence.

This may seem like a surprising finding, but similar results have been reported in a number of previous studies (summarized in Chapter 6, see also Chapter 9). The high rate of female assaults in this study is also consistent with the data on homicidal assaults. The rate of homicides committed by females overall is one-fifth the rate of male homicides, but within the family women commit nearly half (48%) of all homicides (Plass and Straus, 1987).

Theories Explaining Marital Status Differences in Violence

Without controlling for age, dating couples have a higher rate of assault than married couples. When age is controlled, dating couples have the lowest assault rate of the three marital status groups. Moreover, controls for age, education, and occupational status do not alter the finding that there is much more violence and more severe violence among cohabiting than married and dating couples. These findings are consistent with an earlier study (Yllo and Straus, 1981). Thus the greater risk of assault typically occurs when individuals live together but are not married.

If age, education, and occupation do not explain the differences in assault rates by marital status, then what does? What is unique about cohabiting couples when compared to dating and married couples that might explain the higher assault rate? We offer some suggestions.

Social Isolation

Cohabiting couples may be more likely to be isolated from their network of kin than dating and married couples. For those who are dating or are married, being tied to one's kin may have the unintended consequence of helping to monitor violent behavior. (See Chapter 19 for a discussion of the influence of kin networks on violence.) Whether cohabiting couples are isolated by choice or because of a lingering stigma on this type of relationship, physical violence may be less likely to be recognized or challenged.

Autonomy and Control

Issues of autonomy and control also may be relevant in explaining why assaults are more common in cohabiting than dating or married relationships. It is possible that some enter cohabitation rather than marriage to keep more of their own independence, only to find that there are frequent arguments over rights, duties, and obligations, which may lead to violence. This suggests that successfully controlling another or being controlled by another may be more problematic in cohabiting than married relationships and thus lead to more incidents of violence. Indeed, research indicates that where the issue of control frequently arises, violence often occurs (Stets and Pirog-Good, 1987; Stets and Pirog-Good, 1988; Stets, 1988).

The issue of control may not be as problematic among dating and married couples as it is among cohabiting couples. Those who date but are not serious with their partner may feel that they do not have the right to control the other. Consequently, conflict over control may be less likely to arise, hence explaining the lower rate of dating assault. On the other hand, those who are married and are more committed to one another may not only feel that they have the right to control the other but also may agree to be controlled. Married individuals may "give in" to their partner's wishes, believing that they need to make sacrifices or compromises for the sake of keeping the relationship intact. In this sense, the marriage license may also be a control license.

It should be pointed out that as dating relationships become more serious, control may take more precedence and violence may become more frequent. Therefore, research that has shown that the more serious or involved the partners, the more likely that violence will occur (Hotaling and Straus, 1980; Cate et al., 1982; Laner and Thompson, 1982; Laner, 1983, Henton et al., 1983; Sigelman et al., 1984; Roscoe and Benaske, 1985; Arias et al., 1987) may, in part, be explained by conflict arising over control (Stets and Pirog-Good, 1987).

Investment in the Relationship

Finally, differences in the investment in the relationship may help explain the high rate of assaults while cohabiting. Cohabiting couples may be more violent than married couples because they tend to share certain features that gives rise to conflict, but they may lack some features of marriage that serve to constrain the conflict from escalating into physical assaults. The feature that cohabiting couples share with married couples is the conflict inherent in a primary group relationship (Straus and Hotaling, 1980; Straus, 1987). To take one example, in a marital or cohabiting relationship, everything about the partner is of concern to the other and hence little or nothing is off-limits for discussion and conflict. Consequently, there is an inherently high level of conflict in marriage and cohabiting.

On the other hand, conflict does not necessarily lead to violence. There are other modes of resolving conflicts, or one party may implicitly decide that the potential costs of violence cannot be risked. These costs may be greater for married than for cohabiting couples to the extent that married couples have a greater material, social, and psychological investment in the relationship and a greater long-term interest in the relationship. Consequently, Straus (1987) argues that they may be more constrained to control assault to avoid the risk of such acts terminating the marriage and to lessen the risk of the partner being injured or even killed (resulting in even greater loss). Thus although the marriage license may be an implicit hitting license in a normative sense (Straus, 1976), the structural realities of marriage also tend to impose a ceiling on the frequency and severity of violence, whereas the similar normative tolerance of violence in cohabiting couples is not subject to the same structural constraints.

Dating couples may be less violent because they are less involved in a relationship and thus the conflict-generating characteristics do not apply as strongly in their case as they do among cohabiting and married couples. In this respect, they are different from cohabiting couples. However, they share with cohabiting couples the low investment in the relationship as compared to married couples. It is possible that as a dating relationship became more serious, the rate of assault would approximate that found in cohabiting relationships, given not only their increased level of conflict and low investment in the relationship, but also as discussed above, the more frequent issue of control.

Our suggestions on the cause for the high rate of assault among cohabiting as compared to dating and married couples are speculative and not definitive. Future research needs to directly examine these factors. Identifying what might explain cohabiting violence may help us obtain a better understanding of why violence occurs at all.

Notes

1. However, it is projected that by 1990 only about 3% of all households and 5% of all couple households will comprise cohabitors (Glick, 1984).

2. Since the X axis variable is not continuous, readers familiar with graphing conventions will wonder why line graphs were used rather than bar charts. Graphs were explored because the tables were difficult to comprehend. However, the bar chart versions were equally or more difficult to comprehend, especially Figures 13.2, 13.3, and 13.5. The line graphs, in our opinion, bring out the main points more clearly than any other mode of presentation.

14

Family Patterns and Child Abuse

Murray A. Straus and Christine Smith

The Social Causes of Child Abuse

What can cause a parent to punch, kick, bite, burn, or stab a child? The causes are complex in at least two ways.

First, there seem to be a multitude of factors, each of which increases the probability of a violent physical attack on a child. At the same time, no one of these factors accounts for a very large proportion of the cases of child abuse. For example, this chapter will show that men who hit their wives are much more likely to abuse a child than are other men. Still, most men who hit their wives do not attack a child violently enough for it to be considered child abuse by contemporary standards.

A second complication making it difficult to pinpoint the causes of child abuse is that these factors do not operate in isolation from each other. Rather, it is likely that certain combinations of factors are much more potent than either of the factors by themselves and also much more potent than one might imagine by just adding together the effects of each of the two factors. For example, living in a low-income family is associated with child abuse, as is having witnessed violence in one's childhood home (Chapter 24; Straus, Gelles, and Steinmetz, 1980). Let us say (hypothetically) that each of these factors increases the chances of a child being abused by 75%. But the combination of poverty and a parent's prior history of witnessing violence during childhood may increase the probability of committing child abuse by 400% rather than 150%. In short, there are likely to be "explosive combinations," or what statisticians call "interaction effects," among the factors contributing to child abuse.

The purpose of this chapter is to present data on several of the factors that have been found to be related to the incidence of child abuse in the two National Family Violence Surveys. To be more specific, the data to be presented relate 25 different variables to child abuse. One might therefore think that the first complication in studying child abuse—the multiplicity of causal factors—has been addressed. But that is not entirely the case because all of the factors to be discussed are, broadly speaking, social variables. That is, they describe the social characteristics and social interactions of parents and children. We do not have data on the psychological characteristics of the parents—their mental health, aggressiveness, anxiety, rigidity, etc.—that may well be part of the explanation for child abuse.

Sample and Method

The findings reported in this chapter are based on data from the 1975 and the 1985 Family Violence Surveys. The 1975 data include 1,146 American families who had a child age 3 through 17 at home. A limitation of the 1975 sample is that it does not include children younger than three years of age—a high-risk age. The 1985 survey includes 3,235 families with children from infancy through age 17. Further details on the sampling methods of the two surveys are given in Appendix 1.

Interviews in both surveys were conducted with the father in a random half of the families and with the mother in the other half of the families. The data on physical violence were obtained for only one child in each family and only concerning violence by the parent who was interviewed. When there was more than one child, the "referent child" for the study was selected by a random number table.

Child abuse was measured using the Conflict Tactics Scales (described briefly in Chapter 1 and fully in Chapters 3, 4, and 5). The measure that pertains to severe violence by the respondent parent toward the referent child included all the items that refer to violence more severe than spanking, pushing, shoving, slapping, and throwing things. Specifically, the list consists of whether, during the 12 months prior to the interview, the parent had ever kicked, bit, or punched the child, hit the child with an object, beaten up the child, or used a knife or gun on the child. The 1985 survey contains an additional item for burning or scalding the child. A parent who did any of these things was counted as having abused the child.

The two surveys covered a great many aspects of family patterns and life circumstances. Data from both of the surveys were used in the analyses for this chapter. If data for both 1985 and 1975 are available, and if the findings for 1985 parallel those for 1975, we report the 1985 data because they are the most comprehensive and most recent data.[1] However, some of the variables are available only for the 1975 sample, in which case findings based on the 1975 study are reported. If findings from the two surveys do not agree, these discrepancies will be presented, along with possible explanations for the differences.

Men, Women, and Jobs

We begin this discussion of the social causes of child abuse with two of the most elementary but also the most important characteristics that are associated with child abuse: gender and socioeconomic status.

It is widely known that women are less violent that men. The rates of assault and murder by women are a fraction of the rates by men. But in the family it is different. Using our index of child abuse, the rate in 1975 for child abuse by fathers was 10.1 per hundred children whereas the rate by mothers was 75% greater: 17.7 per hundred children. In the 1985 sample, the rates are more similar: 10.2 per hundred children by fathers and 11.2 per hundred children by mothers. The rates from both samples indicate that women are at least as violent as men against their own children.

This finding emphasizes the importance of social, rather than psychological, factors in explaining child abuse. These, after all, are the same women who, outside the family, are much less violent than men. So the reasons why they are as violent as men toward their own children is unlikely to be anything in the personality or other mental characteristics of women as compared to men. Rather, the reasons start with the simple fact that husbands and wives do not have equal responsibility for the care of their children. The way our type of society is organized, child care is the responsibility of women. So women are simply exposed more to both the joys and the trials and tribulations of caring for children—they experience more time "at risk." This could also explain the reduction between 1975 and 1985 in the difference in child abuse rates of mothers and fathers. To the extent that fathers are assuming somewhat more responsibility for child care (and some studies, e.g., Thorton, Alwin, and Cambrun, 1983, suggest that this is happening), they share more equally in this "time at risk."

"Time at risk," however, is not the whole story. The factors underlying women's "equality" in violence against children go well beyond that. At least two other factors need to be considered. First, it is the mother who tends to be blamed if the child misbehaves or does not achieve what is expected of children at a given age. Since all children misbehave and since standards of achievement are ambiguous, almost all mothers tend to feel anxiety, frustration, and guilt about their children and their adequacy as mothers. This is true not because women are any more anxiety prone than men, but because our society creates a situation in which a high level of anxiety and frustration is almost inevitable in the maternal role.

A third factor that might account for child abuse by women is that the unequal division of labor and the responsibility for the child's conduct is not a voluntary choice. These are roles assigned to women by long historical tradition and on which most husbands insist. It may be less of a problem for those women who wish to focus their lives on the role of mother and homemaker, but in a society where other opportunities beckon, millions of women feel frustrated by the fact that they—not their husbands—still have the overwhelming responsibility for the children, even when these women work outside the home.

Homemakers

The cultural ideology of women as mothers and homemakers may make it difficult to see the argument just presented. There is neither the space nor the evidence to prove the point. But there is a way of getting at this issue indirectly. We can compare mothers who are full-time homemakers with mothers who are also employed outside the home. Chapter 15 provides a more complete analysis of this issue using the 1975 data.

From one point of view, the higher rate of child abuse should be among women who have paid employment in addition to their work as mothers and housekeepers. This is true because the research shows that such women continue to have the major burden of housekeeping and child care. They therefore carry a double burden. The opposite point of view is also plausible. Women who have jobs outside the home may have a lower rate of child abuse because the hours spent in the workplace (and away from the home) reduce their time at risk, because they can escape the stress and frustration of being occupied in the homemaker role (which may not be of their own choosing), and because being employed for wages gives women more power in the family and control over their own lives.

Neither theory is supported by the findings of the 1975 or the 1985 survey. In 1975 women with full-time paid employment had a child abuse rate of 17.1, as compared to 17.4 for the full-time homemakers. In 1985 women with full-time paid employment had a child abuse rate of 10.3 as compared to 11.1 for the full-time homemakers. Neither of these differences is large enough to be statistically significant. However, the consistency of results between the two surveys suggests that this small difference is statistically dependable. One can therefore interpret the findings of the two surveys as indicating that, although mothers with paid employment have a lower rate of child abuse, the difference is very small. A related conclusion is that the decrease in child abuse from 1975 to 1985 described in Chapter 7 occurred for both mothers with full-time paid employment and mothers who were full-time homemakers.

Socioeconomic Status

Child abuse is found at all social levels, from paupers to royalty. But that is not the same as saying that the rates are equal at all social levels. Officially reported cases of child abuse are much higher among the poor. Studies of professionals' attitudes have shown that physicians, nurses, police, and other officials are more likely to report suspected cases of abuse involving poor or minority families than those from more middle-class backgrounds (Hampton and Newberger, 1985; O'Toole, Turbett, and Nalepka, 1983).

Our data do not depend on official reports. Table 14.1 displays child abuse rates for mothers and fathers from the 1985 Resurvey by various socioeconomic measures. The first row of Table 14.1 reveals that families earning less than twenty thousand dollars a year have the highest rates of child abuse. This seems especially true for mothers, whose child abuse rates in lower-income families is more than a third higher than for mothers in higher-income families (14.6 versus 10.8). Although this is a substantial difference, it is a much smaller difference than is typical when officially reported child abuse rates are used to compare social classes. Thus part of the social class differences in officially reported child abuse does seem to be the result of biases in the system of reporting. At the same time, the data also suggest that there is a considerably higher rate of actual child abuse in lower-income families.

Another measure of social class is, of course, occupational status. Rows 4 and 5 of Table 14.1 show that the incidence of child abuse by either parent is higher in families where the husband is a blue-collar worker. Blue-collar fathers have a rate of abuse that is a third higher than white-collar fathers (11.9 versus 8.9). Interestingly, *wives* of blue-collar workers also have higher child abuse rates (p < .001). Perhaps the higher rates of abuse by wives of blue-collar workers reflects more traditional family roles where these mothers are charged with the full responsibility of raising the children.

Of course, it is not just the absolute level of poverty that matters, important as that is. Also entering the situation is the importance of

TABLE 14.1

Child Abuse Rates by Socioeconomic Measures for Fathers and Mothers in the 1985 Resurvey

Socioeconomic Status Variable	Rate of Child Abuse	
	by Fathers (N=1267)	by Mothers (N=1966)
Family Annual Income		
None - $20,000	12.5	14.6***
$20,000 - $40,000	9.5	9.4
$40,000 and over	9.5	10.8
Husband's Occupational Status		
Blue Collar	11.9	13.9***
White Collar	8.9	8.1
Wife's Occupational Status		
Blue Collar	10.3	12.6
White Collar	10.3	10.7
Husband's Employment		
Full Time	10.5	11.0
Part Time	8.4	12.5
Unemployed	8.8	16.2
Student, retired	6.9	2.6
Wife's Employment		
Full Time	8.9	10.3
Part Time	8.1	12.5
Keeping House	10.7	11.0
Unemployed	10.8	14.2
Student, retired	14.1	17.2

Chi-Square tests: *p < .05, **p < .01, ***p < .001

income as a symbol of personal worth. A measure of this symbolic dimension was included in the 1975 data. Anyone with a family income of under six thousand dollars in the U.S. in 1975 in effect received with each paycheck a reminder that he or she is not worth very much. The child abuse rate for husbands who were dissatisfied with their standard of living was 61% greater than the rate for other husbands (14.4 versus 8.9), and for wives who were not satisfied with their standard of living the rate was 77% greater than for other wives (22.3 versus 12.6).

There is also the frustration imposed by an unstable economic system, which was particularly true at the time of the 1975 survey. Families in which the husband was unemployed in 1975 had a child abuse rate that was 62% greater than that of other families (22.5 versus 13.9). A similar high rate of child abuse was associated with part-time employment of the husband (27.3 versus 14.1). These large differences were, for the most part, not replicated in the 1985 survey. However, the second column in Table 14.1 shows that mothers whose husbands were unemployed in 1985 had a child abuse rate nearly 50% higher than those whose husbands worked full-time (16.2 versus 11.0). This probably reflects the added stress on the family when the father is out of work.

Finally, there are a number of factors on which we do not have data but which are likely to enter the picture. Working-class parents are known to be more authoritarian with their children and to have greater faith in physical punishment as a means of child rearing and a lesser understanding of child psychology (Hess, 1970; Kohn, 1985). In addition, low-income areas of American cities have much higher rates of violence outside the family. Each of these in their own way is a condition making for higher rates of child abuse among lower-income or working-class families.

Family Structure and Child Abuse

Some analysts of child abuse, for example David Gil (1975), write as though the direct and indirect effects of an unjust and unstable economic system and its associated oppression of women and minorities fully explain the paradox of child abuse. Unfortunately, the etiology of child abuse is far more complicated. One can see this from a comparison of child abuse in Black and in White families. Blacks are one of the most economically and socially oppressed groups in American society. Yet up to the time of the 1975 survey both that study and some studies of officially reported child abuse (Billingsley, 1969; Young, 1963) showed that Blacks did not have a significantly higher rate of child abuse than Whites. Blacks in the 1975 sample had a rate of 15.7, which was only 11% greater than the White rate of 14.1. The analysis of race and support networks of the 1975 sample in Chapter 19 suggests one reason why Blacks had a rate of child abuse that was much lower than expected on the basis of their low income, high unemployment, and rejection by the rest of the society: the aid and support, especially in the care of children, provided by Black extended families.

The 1985 study, however, presents quite a different picture. In Chapter 7 we present data showing that the rate of child abuse for Whites decreased substantially between 1975 and 1985. However, for the Black part of the sample there was essentially no change in the rate of child abuse between 1975 and 1985. The decrease in the rate for White children from 14.1 to 10.3, combined with essentially no change in the rate at which Black children are abused, means that Black children in the 1985 sample were abused at a significantly higher rate than White children. It is possible that the changes in family structure and economic circumstances (such as later age at marriage and a lower unemployment rate) that we suggested in Chapter 7 as partly responsible for the decrease in the rate of child abuse have so far had relatively little impact on Black families. These and other possible explanations for the 1985 findings are analyzed in detail in Hampton and Gelles (1988).

Husband-Wife Conflict

An important aspect of the pattern of interaction in the family is the amount of conflict between husband and wife. To measure the extent of such conflict we obtained information on how often the couple disagreed on five issues: money, sex, social activities, housekeeping and maintenance, and children. The first row of Table 14.2 enables us to compare the child abuse rates of fathers in the 1985 survey who reported an above-average level of conflict with the child abuse of fathers in more harmonious marriages and the same for mothers. The column headed Fathers shows that men who reported more than the average amount of conflict have a higher incidence of child abuse (a rate of 13.0 for husbands in high-conflict marriages abused one of their children compared to 7.4 for other men). The columns headed Mothers show more mothers in high-conflict marriages abused a child than other mothers (13.6 versus 8.0).[2]

Verbal Abuse and Physical Abuse

At least as important as the amount of conflict are the tactics used when a couple has a conflict. Some family therapists argue that the best tactic is to release and not to repress one's anger. One advocate of this approach is quoted by Howard (1970:54) as recommending: "Don't be afraid to be a real shrew, a real bitch. Tell them where you're really at. Let it be total, vicious, exaggerated, hyperbole . . ." Venting one's anger in this way is claimed to provide a release from the tension of a dispute and therefore to help avoid physical aggression. The research evidence, however, shows that the more husbands and wives are verbally aggressive to each other,

TABLE 14.2

Child Abuse Rates by Family Characteristics for Fathers and Mothers in the 1985 Resurvey

| Family Characteristic | Rate of Child Abuse By: | | | |
| | Fathers with Characteristic | | Mothers with Characteristic | |
	PRESENT	ABSENT	PRESENT	ABSENT
Parent's Relationship				
High Marital Conflict	13.0	7.4***	13.6	8.0***
Husband-Wife Verbal Aggression	11.2	4.9**	12.7	4.4***
Wife-Husband Verbal Aggression	11.9	4.1**	12.3	5.3**
Husband-Wife Violence	22.3	8.0***	21.7	9.3***
Wife-Husband Violence	20.5	8.2***	22.9	9.2***
Parent-Child Relationship				
Parent-Child Verbal Aggression	14.3	4.2***	16.3	1.8***
Parent's Childhood Family				
Father used physical punishment	13.1	8.1**	17.6	9.3***
Mother used physical punishment	12.4	8.4*	16.7	8.0***
Father hit Mother	12.5	10.0	20.2	10.1***
Mother hit Father	18.5	9.3**	23.1	10.3***

Chi-Square tests: *p < .05, **p < .01, ***p < .001
N for fathers — 1,267; N for mothers — 1,966.

the higher the rate of physical aggression (Straus, 1974). The main reason for this is that verbal aggression, no matter how emotionally satisfying it may be, does not come to grips with the substance of the dispute. Rather, it creates additional animosity, which makes it even more difficult to deal with the original source of the conflict.

Exactly the same results were found in this study for the relation between verbal aggression and child abuse.[3] Parents who were verbally aggressive to the referent child in 1975 had a child abuse rate that is six times that of other parents (21.0 versus 3.6). In 1985, Row 6 of Table 14.2 shows a child abuse rate nearly ten times greater for verbally abusive mothers (16.3 versus 1.8) and three and a half times greater for verbally aggressive fathers.

It could be argued that verbal aggression is a consequence rather than a cause of this high rate of violence. A child has been slapped and then either slaps back or kicks or insults the parent. The parent then verbally assaults the child. No doubt that does happen. But such a sequence does not explain another finding: the rate of child abuse is also higher for parents who are verbally aggressive to each other. Row 2 demonstrates that husbands who were verbally aggressive to their spouses, have a child abuse rate of 11.2, compared to 4.9 for other husbands. Row 3 shows that wives who were verbally aggressive to their husband have a child abuse rate of 12.3, compared to 5.3 for other wives. All of this suggests that verbal aggression is a relatively stable pattern in such families and, as just suggested, is a mode of relating that interferes with dealing with the actual issues, creates additional problems, and often sets in motion an escalating cycle of events that ends in physical violence.

Violence as a Mode of Relating

Marital Violence and Child Abuse

One of the clearest findings to emerge from the two National Family Violence Surveys is that violence in one family relationship is related to violence in other family relationships (see Chapter 23, Baron and Straus, 1987; Straus, 1971; Straus, Gelles, and Steinmetz, 1980). In families where the husband had hit his wife during the year of the 1985 survey, even if the violence was restricted to slaps, pushes, and throwing things, the incidence of child abuse was 150% greater than in other families (22.3 versus 8.0). If it is the wife who hits the husband, this is associated with a 120% greater incidence of child abuse by the mother (22.9 versus 9.2).

Physical Punishment as Training for Child Abuse

Early in life, most of us receive a kind of basic training in violence in the form of physical punishment. Mommy slaps an infant's hand to teach the child not to put dirty things in his or her mouth. But this also teaches the child that love and violence go together. Moreover, it does more than establish the empirical fact that those who love you are those who hit you. Ironically, it also teaches that the use of violence within the family is morally right.

In some families slapping a child is replaced by non-violent forms of punishment and by the use of reasoning and negotiation. If this happens, what is learned in infancy and early childhood can be replaced by non-violent modes of dealing with others—though the earlier patterns may still emerge in extreme conditions. But when the use of physical punishment continues into the early teen years and when children observe their parents being violent to each other (as is the experience of millions of American children), the chances are greater that the use of physical force will become a regular part of the way these children will later interact with others in adulthood (see Chapter 23; Gelles and Straus, 1979; Owens and Straus, 1975).

To what extent are the ideas expressed in the previous two paragraphs supported by the data for these two nationally representative samples of parents? To find out, we asked the parents how much their own parents had used physical punishment when they were about age 13. The first two rows in the section of Table 14.2, labeled "Parent's Childhood Family," demonstrate the relationship between having been physically punished at age 13 and later abusive behavior toward one's own children for the 1985 sample of parents. The first of the two rows shows that parents who were physically punished by their father were more likely to engage in severe violence against their own children. Fathers who had been hit at age 13 by their own fathers exhibited a child abuse rate of 13.1, compared to 8.1 for fathers who had not been hit (p < .01); likewise, mothers who had been hit show a rate of 17.6, compared to 9.3 for mothers who had not been hit (p < .001). Row 8 reveals that parents who were physically punished by their mothers show similarly higher rates of child abuse than parents who were not. Since very similar results were found for the parents interviewed in 1975, both studies indicate a connection between having experienced physical punishment as a child and later committing child abuse as a parent.

Observing Parents Fight as Training for Child Abuse

The data just presented suggest that one of the ways children learn to be violent to others is by being the victims of violence at the hands of their parents. Ironically, the learning effect is probably enhanced because, by and large, parental violence is done out of concern for the child and for other morally desirable ends. Parents also teach violence to their children in a number of other ways, for example, by teaching boys to "stand up and fight like a man" (Stark and McEvoy, 1970), and by example, through violence toward each other.

More than one out of ten of the parents in both the 1975 and the 1985 samples could remember at least one instance when they saw their own parents hitting each other. And in both studies being the child of parents who hit each other was associated with a greater rate of child abuse compared to not having grown up in a household in which the parents assaulted each other. The last two rows of Table 14.2 show that among the fathers interviewed in 1985 those who had witnessed their father hit their mother had a 25% higher rate of physically abusing a child (12.5 versus 10.0) and those who witnessed their mother hit their father had almost double the rate compared to fathers who had not grown up in a family with this type of violence (18.5 versus 9.3). Similarly, mothers who observed their father hit their mother had double the rate of child abuse compared to other mothers in the 1985 sample (20.2 versus 10.1). Mothers who observed their own mother hit their father were also twice as likely to have engaged in child abuse (23.1 versus 10.3).

Isolation from Kin and Community

Chapter 19 refers to the important role played by the extended family in the Black community. Moreover, the results for the entire sample using the 1975 data reveal that when we take into account the length of the marriage and the social class of the parents, important differences emerge. Having lived in a neighborhood only a relative short time (zero to three years) makes only a small difference for those who had been married for less than ten years. Their child abuse rate is high, regardless of whether they had lived in the neighborhood four or more years (18.5) or zero to three years (21.8). But for the older couples, lack of neighborhood ties is associated with much more child abuse. Those who lived in the neighborhood less than four years have a child abuse rate that is 84% higher than the rate for parents who had been in the same neighborhood for four or more years (17.8 versus 9.7).

Similar differences were found for the 1975 sample using an index of participation in organizations such as clubs, lodges, unions, church groups, etc. One point was given for each group belonged to and one point for each meeting of such a group attended in a month. Those who neither belonged to nor attended such meetings have a child abuse rate of 18.5

compared to 12.0 for those with a score of one or more. Since involvement in organizations tends to be associated with being more settled in life, the same comparison was computed for those married less than ten years and for those married ten or more years. For the younger group, their generally high rate of child abuse reduced the effect of organizational involvement. Still, the incidence of child abuse among those with no ties to organized groups is a third higher than the rate for those who have even a minimal organizational involvement (21.4 versus 15.5). For the longer married group, those without organizational ties have a 72% greater rate of child abuse (14.3 versus 8.3). Both these data and the results of other studies (see the review in Maden and Wrench, 1977; Smith, 1975) all point to a strong association between child abuse and social isolation.

A Child Abuse Checklist

Up to this point, each of the factors associated with child abuse has been considered separately from the others. This is clearly inadequate. These factors do not exist in isolation. Some overlap, and the existence of certain combinations may be particularly important. As a first approach to at least partly overcoming these limitations, a child abuse checklist score was computed.

A discriminant analysis of the 1975 data (Nie et al., 1986: Chapter 36) identified 16 variables that distinguished between abusing parents and other parents and that did not significantly overlap with each other. For the 1985 sample, information was available on 14 of the original 16 variables. A new discriminant analysis used these 14 variables and 2 additional variables (family income and whether the respondent reported any instances in which his father hit his mother). Fourteen of these 16 variables were found to differentiate abusing from non-abusing parents. These 14 variables are listed in Table 14.3.

These 14 variables were used to create a "Child Abuse Checklist" score for each parent in the sample. First, the 14 variables identified in the discriminant analysis of the 1985 data were dichotomized at the point where the earlier cross-tabulations had shown the highest rates of child abuse. Second, each parent was given a checklist score by assigning a point for any of the 14 variables on which his or her characteristics matched that of the abusing parents. Since all 14 variables distinguished between abusing and non-abusing mothers, the mothers in the sample could have a score theoretically ranging from zero to 14, but the actual scores ranged from zero to 12. Ten of the variables differentiated between abusing and non-abusing fathers and were used to assign checklist scores

TABLE 14.3

Characteristics Included in Child Abuse Checklist For the 1985 National Family
Violence Resurvey*

A. Significant for Child Abuse by Either Parent

Was verbally aggressive to the child
   (insulted, swore at, etc.)
Husband verbally aggressive to wife
Wife verbally aggressive to husband
Husband physically aggressive to wife
Wife physically aggressive to husband
Marriage high in conflict
More than one child in family
Parent was physically punished as adolescent by father
Parent was physically punished as adolescent by mother
Mother hit father in parent's childhood family

B. Significant for Child Abuse by Mother

Father hit mother in parent's childhood family
Husband is a blue collar worker
Married less than 10 years
Lived in neighborhood five years or less

----
*The three variables which did not replicate for the 1985 sample were:
(1) For abuse by fathers: wife was a full-time homemaker. (2) For abuse by
mothers: wife age 30 or younger, and wife was a manual worker. The
additional variable found in the 1985 sample was mothers who had witnessed
their own father hit their mother.

to the fathers. Thus fathers' scores have a theoretical range from zero to
ten, but the actual range was from zero to eight.

Figure 14.1 clearly shows the powerful relationship between the combination of these factors and the incidence of child abuse. Parents with none
of the factors present were entirely free of child abuse. Parents with scores
of no more than 4 had relatively low rates of child abuse, ranging from 4
to 7%. The incidence of child abuse climbs steadily from there on, reaching
a rate of over 35 per hundred children for fathers with 7 or more (on the
scale of 0–10) of these factors and for mothers with a score of 11 or more
(on a scale of 0–14).

The social factors identified in this research obviously are strongly
associated with child abuse. The incidence for abuse for those unfortunate
enough to be characterized by most of the elements of the syndrome is
staggering. But even among this group of parents, about two thirds did *not*
abuse a child. This fact should serve as a caution against attempting to use

FIGURE 14.1

Incidence Rate of Child Abuse by Checklist Score of Father and Mother

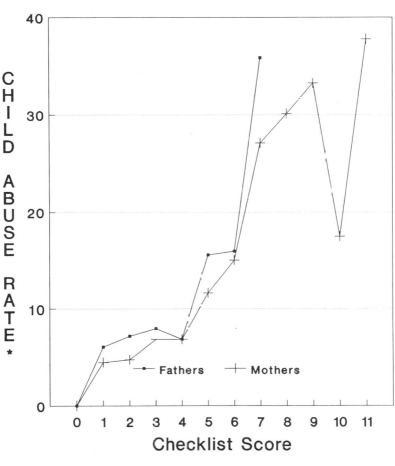

* Per 100 Children

the Child Abuse Checklist as a means of locating high-risk parents in order to provide services that might prevent child abuse. Tempting as is that possibility, it is not worth the harm that is likely to be inflicted on millions of parents who have high scores but who have not and will not abuse a child.

The fact that the child abuse rate for mothers with scores of 12 is "only"

49 per hundred children also indicates that we still have a long way to go in pinpointing the causes of child abuse. As suggested in the introduction, there is an obvious need to include data on the psychological characteristics of the parents and the characteristics of the child (Parke, 1978). If such characteristics were included and if we were to use more adequate methods of measuring the unique combinations of factors, it might be possible to account for even more of the cases of child abuse. But even limiting the study to purely social factors and using a technique as simple as the checklist score, we have been able to isolate many of the factors associated with child abuse.

Summary and Conclusions

The main purpose of this chapter was to examine social factors that might account for the extremely high incidence of child abuse reported in Chapters 6, 7, and 8. The findings suggest that the causes of child abuse can be found in (but are not limited to) the following factors: (1) The structure of the contemporary American family, for example, the practice of placing almost the whole burden of child care on mothers. This is a main reason why women have an equally high rate of child abuse as men, despite lower rates of violence outside the family. (2) The economic and psychological stress created by poverty and an unstable economic system. Illustrative of this is the finding of a higher incidence of child abuse among lower-income families and manual workers. (3) Isolation from the help and social control that occur when a family is embedded in a network of kin and community. This is illustrated by the finding that short-term residents of a neighborhood have a higher incidence of child abuse than longer-established residents. (4) Unintended but powerful training in the use of violence as a means of teaching and resolving conflicts. Parents who had been physically punished abuse their children much more often, as do parents who engage in physical fights with each other. Parents who saw their parents hit each other have a much higher rate of child abuse than other parents.

Overall, the results of this study suggest that a large part of the explanation of child abuse is in the very nature of American society and its family systems. This has profound implications for the prevention of child abuse (see Chapter 28). Although psychotherapy may be appropriate in some cases, a more fundamental approach lies in such things as a more equal sharing of the burdens of child care, replacement of physical punishment with non-violent methods of child care and training, reducing the stresses and insecurity that continue to characterize our economic system for many families, and strengthening the ties of individual families to the extended family and to the community.

Notes

1. Readers interested in the specific statistics for 1975 can find them in Straus, 1979.
2. The effects in 1975 were less pronounced for wives: a 28% greater rate (20.0 versus 15.6 for those low in conflict). For husbands, a high level of conflict with a wife was associated with a 79% greater rate of child abuse (12.7 versus 7.1).
3. As measured by the Verbal Aggression scale of the CTS described in Chapter 3 and Appendix 2. This includes such things as insults, sulking, venting anger by smashing things and slamming doors, and cutting remarks.

15

Maternal Employment and Violence toward Children

Richard J. Gelles and Eileen F. Hargreaves

A number of reports on child abuse have suggested that the risk of child abuse is greater in families where the mother is employed (Mahmood, 1978; Fontana, 1973; Conger, 1978; James, 1975; Delli Quadri, 1978; Galdston, 1965; Justice and Duncan, 1975). Mahmood (1978) captures the essence of the proposal that physical abuse is greater among working mothers by stating that irritation resulting from day-long employment often leads to child abuse. Garbarino (1976) suggests that the demands placed on women by home and work are associated with child abuse and neglect.

Other writers have proposed that nonworking mothers are more likely to be abusive. Korbin (1978), citing from Rohner (1975) and Whiting (1972), notes cross-cultural evidence that indicates that a woman isolated in the child-care role without relief is more likely to treat her child in a negative fashion. Chapa et al. (1978) report on a study of child abuse and neglect that found that abusive mothers were more likely to be unemployed than mothers in the nonabusive comparison group. Steele and Pollock (1968, 1974) imply a ''time at risk'' explanation of the nonworking mother's risk of abusing her child. When explaining that fathers are less abusive than mothers, Steele and Pollock note the low rate of unemployment of the fathers in their sample and state that there were less hours of contact between the fathers and the children. Steele and Pollock go on to hypothesize that in samples where the mothers work and the fathers stay at home, the rate of paternal abuse would be higher. Although they do not explicitly state that ''time at risk'' explains the higher rate of maternal abuse, this proposition is a logical derivation from their line of reasoning.

263

Finally, students of child abuse have also found support for the claim that maternal employment is not related to child abuse and neglect. Starr et al. (1978) found no difference between abusers and nonabusers in terms of the current employment of the mothers. Jameson and Schellenbach (1977) studied a sample of 82 perpetrators and concluded that mother's employment status was not an important factor in the female abuser profile. Martin (1970) also reports no differences in employment status of 50 mothers of burned or scalded children and 41 mothers in a comparison group. Oakland and Kane (1973) similarly note no differences in the employment of mothers of neglected Navajo children and the comparison group.

Research on maternal employment also provides varying evidence as to the possible relationship between mother's employment and violence toward children. Hoffman (1961) reported that working mothers were *less likely* to be coercive with their children and that working mothers with positive attitudes toward their employment were less severe in their discipline. On the other hand, Yarrow et al. (1962) concluded that there were no differences in discipline techniques among employed and unemployed women.

When researchers have assessed the relationship between maternal employment and child abuse there have been numerous methodological problems. One problem has been the frequent combination of abuse and neglect into one dependent variable. Some definitions of neglect imply that a mother who works is neglectful simply by the act of leaving home and going to work. Another problem which arises in much of the child abuse literature is the failure to use control or comparison groups (Gelles, 1979). Investigators will often report what percentage of abusive mothers in their sample were employed, but fail to provide comparison data from nonabusing families which would indicate whether the employment rate is higher among the abusing families. Some researchers will report the percentage of mothers who worked but fail to cross-tabulate that by whether they abused their children or not. Other times, data on maternal employment are presented with no indication of which parent committed the abusive act. Maternal employment status is frequently confounded with other variables. A finding that working mothers are more likely to abuse their children becomes less clear when the data show that many of the employed mothers were also single parents. Perhaps the most important drawback of the current information on maternal employment and child abuse is that the reports (where there are comparison groups) confine their data analysis to two-by-two tabular presentations of employment status and abuse. Few controls, if any, are introduced in the analyses to explain the relationships.

Methods

Sample and Violence Measures

This article examines the relationship between maternal employment and violence toward children. The data for this examination come from interviews with parents in the 1975 study ($N = 1,146$). One of the major limitations of this sample, both for purposes of estimating the national incidence of violence toward children (Gelles, 1978b; Straus, 1979a) and for examining the relationship between maternal employment and violence, is that one and two year olds—a high-risk age group (Fontana, 1975; Galdston, 1965; Kempe et al., 1962)—are omitted. Thus, in this study we have no information on the relationship between employment of the mother and violence toward the high-risk group of the youngest children.

The two CTS measures of violence toward children used in this study are the "Overall Violence Index," which includes all acts of physical violence, and the "Severe Violence Index." The latter is the measure of "Child Abuse." It includes only those items from the Overall Index where there was a high probability of injury to the child.

The dependent variables in this investigation—violence and child abuse—differ from the dependent variables used in other studies which relate child abuse to maternal employment. First, the measure of child abuse is quite different from that used in other investigations. The CTS relies on a self-report of violence which we believe places the child at risk of being injured. We have no direct, or even indirect, measure of whether the "referent child" was actually injured as a consequence of any of these acts. For example, a parent may report using a gun or knife, but we do not know if the child was actually stabbed or shot.

Most studies of child abuse operationalize the term *child abuse* as those cases which have been publicly recognized and labeled as children who have been injured by their parents (Gelles, 1975). This creates a systematic bias which insulates some families from being labeled as abusers and increases the chances that other families—especially low-income and racial and ethnic minority families—will be accurately or inaccurately labelled child abusers. Operational definitions of child abuse which rely on publicly labelled cases have been subject to increasing criticism (Gelles, 1975).

A second difference is that rather than confine our investigation to only acts of abusive violence, we also examined a larger range of violent acts.

Maternal Employment

Subjects were asked if they were employed at the time of the interview. This produces the disadvantage of having a measure of violence for the previous 12 months, but a measure of employment for only one point in time.

Employed women were asked how many hours a week they were employed, to describe the type of job they held, how many people they supervised, and whether they liked their work.

We also asked about which partner had the greatest say in whether the wife worked. This was accomplished by using the responses to the question "Who has the final say on what job you should take?" This question was part of a series of items used to measure family power (derived from Blood and Wolfe, 1960).

Other Variables

As noted before, one problem with attempts to investigate the relationship between maternal employment and child abuse has been the failure to introduce control variables. Since we were testing three possible directions of a single relationship, we wanted to introduce factors into the analysis which could aid in explaining any of the three possible relationships we could find.

Role strain.   Those theorists subscribing to the hypothesis that working mothers are likely perpetrators of child abuse explain the relationship on the basis of stress caused by the work and mother role. We attempted to assess the level of role strain by measuring the disjunction between domestic responsibilities the mother actually had versus the level of responsibilities she desired. The measure, which asked subjects to report on five areas of domestic activity (managing money; cooking, cleaning, or repairing the house; social activities; supervising the children; and disciplining the children), was based on French et al.'s (1964) work on person-environment fit. Subjects were asked how much responsibility they had and how much responsibility they would like to have for each of the five areas. An index was created by subtracting the scores for "responsibility had" from "responsibility desired."

We assessed the level of stress the mothers experienced by administering a modified version of the Holms and Rahe (1967) Stressful Life Events Scale.

Findings

Employment and Violence toward Children

Mothers who did not work and mothers who reported working part-time were the most likely to have used some form of violence toward their children during the previous year.[1]

While there was a relationship between employment and violence for all acts of violence, there was no statistically significant relationship between employment and child abuse. (see Table 15.1).

The rate of child abuse among mothers who held professional, technical, managerial, administrative, sales, clerical, craft, and operative positions was around 15%. The rate for women employed as laborers or in service positions was appreciably higher (27.6%), but not enough to be statistically significant. This difference may, in part, be due to factors such as income, education, and need to work.

Most of the women surveyed reported liking their work. There were an insufficient number of women working full- or part-time who disliked their work to allow for a meaningful analysis of work, work satisfaction, and violence toward children.

TABLE 15.1
Mother to Child Violence by Maternal Employment

	Violence Rate Per 100 Children	
	Overall Violence	Child Abuse
By Mother's Employment		
Full Time (N = 140)	57.6	17.1
Part Time (N = 102)	70.3	19.6
Housewives (N = 373)	71.0	17.4
	$\chi^2 = 8.684$	$\chi^2 = 0.303$
	$p \leq .05$	p NS

Work and Household Responsibility

The finding that working mothers are not more prone to use violence against their children does not rule out the hypothesis that the dual responsibility of work and home combine to produce violence and abuse. It may be that only a portion of working women feel overwhelmed by their work and family responsibilities (see Table 15.2).

The relationship between work and violence was examined, controlling for whether or not the mothers felt they had more responsibility for domestic activities than they desired.

In all but two situations (part-time employed mothers with excess responsibility for money and household matters), mothers who reported excess domestic responsibilities had higher rates of violence and abuse than mothers with the same work status who said they had equal or less responsibility than they desired. Women who were employed part-time and also found that they had more domestic responsibilities than they desired had the highest Overall Violence Index rates—nearly 9 out of 10 mothers with part-time jobs who reported an excess of social responsibilities said they had used violence against their children in the previous year. The abuse rate was highest among mothers with full-time jobs who felt excess responsibility for disciplining their children.

Stress

Since excess responsibility for domestic activities helped explain and specify the relationship between employment and violence, we thought

TABLE 15.2

Mother to Child Violence by Maternal Employment and Domestic Responsibility

Type of Responsibility		N			Violence Rate Per 100 Children					
					Overall Violence			Child Abuse		
		Full Time	Part Time	House- wives	Full Time	Part Time	House- wives	Full Time	Part Time	House- wives
Money:	Excess	41	36	98	72.5	77.1	75.3	17.1	13.9	22.4
	Not Excess	97	48	271	50.5	67.7	69.0	16.5	23.1	15.5
House:	Excess	67	53	164	68.2	75.0	78.7	19.4	18.9	18.3
	Not Excess	72	48	203	47.2	64.6	64.4	13.9	20.8	17.2
Social Activities:	Excess	29	19	85	62.1	89.5	83.5	20.7	21.1	18.8
	Not Excess	109	82	280	56.0	66.7	66.7	14.7	19.5	17.1
Supervising Children:	Excess	47	44	157	71.7	86.0	79.5	21.3	27.3	19.1
	Not Excess	91	58	206	50.5	58.6	64.1	14.3	13.8	16.0
Disciplining of Children:	Excess	51	46	156	72.0	86.7	77.4	25.5	21.7	20.5
	Not Excess	86	56	207	50.0	57.1	66.2	11.6	17.9	15.0

that life stress would also be a relevant variable. Previous analyses of the data from the 1975 national survey showed that the families which had experienced the greatest life stress in the previous year had the highest yearly rates of violence and abuse (Gelles, 1978a).

Controlling for whether the families experienced less or more than the mean number of stressful events (the mean number of stressful events experienced by the entire sample of 2,143 was 2) did not alter, in any major way, the relationship between mother's work status and violence and abuse toward children (see Table 15.3).

Decisions about Maternal Employment

We would have liked to look deeper into the reasons for the mother's decision to work or not. Specifically, it would have been of great value to compare mothers whose decision to work was motivated by a desire to avoid mothering, or to at least minimize the mothering role, to the mothers whose desire to work was a consequence of economic need, desire for a career, and so on. Hoffman's (1974) research supports the claim that

TABLE 15.3
Mother to Child Violence by Employment and Stress

Employment	Stress	Violence Rate Per 100 Children	
		Overall Violence	Child Abuse
Full Time	0-2 Stressful Events (N = 76)	52.6	13.2
	3+ Stressful Events (N = 61)	63.3	21.3
Part Time	0-2 Stressful Events (N = 61)	71.7	21.3
	3+ Stressful Events (N = 35)	71.4	17.1
Housewives	0-2 Stressful Events (N = 255)	70.1	18.0
	3+ Stressful Events (N = 112)	75.9	17.0

maternal employment, when motivated by noneconomic factors, is not bad for the child.

We were able to glean some information about the decision to work from the series of questions used to measure family power. When the wife or husband has more influence over whether the wife should go to work or quit work, the relationship between employment of the mother and the Overall Violence Index is essentially unchanged from the original relationship. But, when the decision is a joint one, the difference between women with full-time jobs and women without employment is reduced. Children of mothers who work full-time are less likely to be struck if their mothers have at least an equal say in whether they should go to work (see Table 15.4).

The rate of abuse is highest among housewives whose husbands had the final say on whether the wife should work. The abuse rate is lowest when housewives have the final say on whether they should work.

Income

Surveys of violence toward children report an inverse relationship between rates of violence (and abuse) and income (Gelles, 1978a, Gil, 1970; Parke and Collmer, 1975; Straus et al., 1980). This study found that although there was not a statistically significant relationship between kind

TABLE 15.4

Mother to Child Violence by Employment and Decision Making about Mother's Work

Employment	Final Say on Mother's Employment		Violence Rate Per 100 Children	
			Overall Violence	Child Abuse
Full Time	Wife More	(N=79)	57.7	16.5
	Equal	(N=49)	55.1	18.4
	Husband More	(N=11)	63.6	18.2
Part Time	Wife More	(N=50)	73.5	20.0
	Equal	(N=33)	63.6	15.2
	Husband More	(N=18)	72.2	22.2
Housewives	Wife More	(N=136)	72.8	9.6
	Equal	(N=124)	65.3	20.2
	Husband More	(N=103)	77.5	26.2

of job and violence or child abuse, the rate of violence and abuse was higher in families when women worked as laborers or in service positions. Based on this we expected to find that the income a woman received from her work would affect the relationship between violence and maternal employment (see Table 15.5).

The relationship between employment and violence was not altered to any important extent when we controlled for the annual income of the woman worker. Housewives still had a higher rate of Overall Violence than women who worked full-time for the least amount of money. In terms of the child abuse rates, women who worked full-time and had incomes in excess of $6,000 had higher rates of abusive violence than housewives.

The total family income did affect the relationship between the rate of Overall Violence and employment. The difference between women with full-time jobs and women who did not work was greater among those in the lower income groups (income under $12,000), compared to the differences in the zero-order relationship between employment and the rate of Overall Violence. In the lowest income group (under $6,000) the rate of Overall Violence among women who did not work was 50% higher than the rate for women with any type of employment.

The difference between employed women and housewives disappeared in the upper income groups (income $12,000 or more). One plausible reason for this could be that nonworking women with greater than average

TABLE 15.5

Mother to Child Violence by Employment and Wife's Annual Income

Employment	Wife's Annual Income	Violence Rate Per 100 Children	
		Overall Violence	Child Abuse
Full Time	less than $6,000 (N=70)	59.4	17.1
	$6,000 or more (N=63)	58.7	19.0
Part Time	less than $6,000 (N=81)	71.6	19.8
	$6,000 or more (N=8)	62.5	12.5
Housewives	less than $6,000 (N=319)	72.0	18.5
	$6,000 or more (N=8)*	75.0	12.5

*It is possible to have cases in this cell because women were asked if they worked *at the time of the interview*. The question on income related to *the previous 12 months*. Thus, 8 women who were not employed when the interviews were conducted, apparently had worked in the previous 12 months.

family incomes can use their financial resources to insulate themselves from the stress and strain of child rearing and the maternal role.

When we controlled for the income of only the husband, we found that, again, women who reported not working and women who worked had the same rates of Overall Violence in the highest income groups ($20,000 or more) (see Table 15.6).

Age of Child

An examination of the age of the "referent child" and the relationship between violence and employment provides some insight into the "time at risk" hypothesis which proposes that the more time mothers and children spend together, the more opportunities there are for violence or abuse. The "time at risk" hypothesis implies that women who do not work, have preschool children, and thus spend the most time with their children would be the most violent and abusive, while women with full-time positions,

TABLE 15.6

Mother to Child Violence by Employment, Family Income, and Husband's Income

Employment	Percent Violent When Income Is:				Percent Abusive When Income Is:			
	less than $6,000	$6,000 to $11,999	$12,000 to $19,999	$20,000 or more	less than $6,000	$6,000 to $11,999	$12,000 to $19,999	$20,000 or more
A. Total Family Income								
Full Time	50.0 (2)	48.3 (29)	72.3 (47)	58.3 (48)	0 (2)	23.3 (30)	19.1 (47)	16.7 (48)
Part Time	50.0 (6)	78.6 (14)	75.0 (44)	64.5 (31)	50.0 (6)	7.1 (14)	20.5 (44)	16.1 (31)
Housewives	76.7 (43)	81.3 (80)	72.1 (129)	60.0 (85)	25.6 (43)	21.3 (80)	17.7 (130)	8.2 (85)
B. Husband's Income								
Full Time	55.6 (18)	66.1 (56)	54.8 (31)	59.1 (22)	22.2 (18)	22.8 (57)	9.7 (31)	18.2 (22)
Part Time	57.1 (7)	76.0 (25)	78.0 (41)	52.9 (17)	28.6 (7)	8.0 (25)	22.0 (41)	23.5 (17)
Housewives	73.3 (45)	81.2 (85)	72.9 (133)	58.7 (75)	24.4 (45)	20.0 (85)	17.2 (134)	9.3 (75)

who have children in their late teens, and spend the least time with their children would have the lowest rates. (This assumption, of course, is speculative and is neither directly nor indirectly testable with the data from the 1975 national survey of family violence.) (See Table 15.7).

The data partially bear out the "time at risk" hypothesis. The highest rate of child abuse is found among the housewives with children 3 to 4 years of age. These women also had the second highest rate of Overall Violence—exceeded only by women with part-time jobs and referent children 5 to 9 years of age. The lowest rate of abuse was for mothers with full-time jobs and preschool children. Full-time employed mothers with teen-age children were expected to have the lowest rates of violence and abuse. We found that they had the second lowest rate of child abuse and Overall Violence.

It is risky to infer that age of the child implies how much time a mother spends with the child, especially in light of the finding that violence toward children is generally inversely related to age of the child (Straus et al., 1980). Mothers may be less likely to hit older children, not because they spend less time with them but because other forms of punishment are viewed as more acceptable and effective for children once they are past preschool age. In addition, mothers may be less likely to hit their children as the children grow older because the danger of getting hit back increases.

TABLE 15.7

Mother to Child Violence by Employment and Age of Child

Employment	Age of Referent Child	Violence Rate Per 100 Children	
		Overall Violence	Child Abuse
Full Time	3-4 (N=13)	69.2	0
	5-9 (N=34)	82.4	38.2
	10-14 (N=45)	61.4	17.8
	15-17 (N=46)	34.8	6.5
Part Time	3-4 (N=14)	85.7	14.3
	5-9 (N=36)	94.4	19.4
	10-14 (N=26)	65.4	30.8
	15-17 (N=25)	29.2	8.0
Housewives	3-4 (N=71)	90.0	25.4
	5-9 (N=129)	83.7	21.7
	10-14 (N=110)	58.2	10.9
	15-17 (N=55)	41.8	9.1

Clearly, though, age of child does make a difference, and we need to know more about the relationship between employment, age of child, and violence.

Father's Employment Status

If a husband works, even part-time, the original difference between the rate of Overall Violence and maternal employment persists. However, if the husband is out of work, the relationship changes. In this instance, it is the working woman who has a higher rate of Overall Violence than the woman at home. This could be a consequence of resentment over the typical situation of still having to meet domestic and work obligations, even though her husband is available to carry out domestic chores. Or, this could be a consequence of a major status inconsistency between the working wife and the nonworking husband.

Mother's Employment and Father's Violence

Mother's employment status is related to use of violence toward children, although whether she works is not related to whether she reports abusing her child. Mother's work is also related to the father's use of violence. Since we asked each respondent only about his or her own violence against his or her children, we had no measure of partner's violence. We did, however, assess the interviews with male subjects in terms of their reports of their wives' employment and their own use of violence.

Fathers who reported that their wives worked had the lowest rates of violence toward children. Even more important, the rate of child abuse among fathers with wives who did not work was 2.5 times greater than the rate for fathers married or living with women who worked full-time. Thus, while maternal employment is not related to the mother's chances of being abusive, it is related to the father's use of abusive violence. It is possible that men whose wives do not work maintain traditional beliefs about the man being the head of the household and believe that it should be the father who takes responsibility for physically punishing the children (e.g., "Wait 'til your father gets home").

Discussion and Conclusions

What do our results say about the claim that maternal employment has negative consequences for the child (Fontana, 1973)? The data on child abuse show that working mothers are not more likely to be abusive. The data from the Overall Violence Index further undermine the claim that employed mothers are more violent. Women who worked full-time had the *lowest rate* of Overall Violence toward their children, while mothers with part-time jobs and mothers who were not working at the time of our interviews reported higher rates.

Research on child abuse and violence toward children has failed to try to empirically explain any proposed or demonstrated relationship between mothers' work and violence toward their children. Our analysis identified: (1) factors that increase the chances that a working mother will hit her child and (2) situations in which mothers at home were less likely to be violent toward their children.

Factors That Increase the Chances of Working Mothers Using Violence

One of the factors that was related to the impact of maternal employment on the rate of Overall Violence toward children was perceived excess domestic responsibility. If a working mother felt that she had too much responsibility for financial matters and child care, then her chances of hitting her children rose to the level of violence reported by the nonworking mothers. Excess domestic responsibility had an even greater impact on mothers with part-time jobs. When a woman works part-time and feels she has excessive domestic responsibility, the chances are quite high that she will hit her children.

The likelihood of a mother working full-time and being violent increased slightly if the decisions about her work were made by her husband.

The tendency for mothers at home and mothers employed part-time to hit their children was *increased* if these mothers had preschool children. Working full-time and caring for young school-aged children also increased the chances that a mother would hit her child.

One of the most disadvantageous situations for a mother, in terms of her likelihood of striking her child, is to work full-time and be married to a man who is unemployed. This is the only situation where we found full-time employed mothers exceeded other mothers in their use of violence toward their children.

Factors That Reduce the Level of Violence of Nonworking Mothers

Mothers who did not work had high rates of violence in nearly all of the situations we analyzed in this study. One factor which lessened the chances of a mother at home being violent was if her husband earned more than $20,000 per year. Another factor which lowered the nonworking mothers' rates of violence toward children was if the decisions about their work (or nonwork) were made jointly by them and their husbands. In addition, nonworking mothers had lower rates of violence toward older children. These findings imply that if mothers can get some relief from the total responsibility of child rearing—either by using financial resources to pay for baby-sitting or day care or by having older children who require less intense supervision—the chances of violence will be reduced. (This interpretation must be read with caution, since we have no direct data on how income was used or whether mothers in these situations actually had less contact with their children.)

Policy Implications

Earlier research on child abuse which found children with unemployed *fathers* the most likely to be abused has been used to argue for child abuse prevention programs designed to increase employment opportunities for men and thus reduce family stress. Our data on maternal employment and child abuse cannot be used to argue that increased employment opportunities for women are necessary to prevent child abuse—although paternal abuse might be lessened if more mothers worked.

The relationships that we found between maternal employment and the rate of Overall Violence toward children is quite complex. Despite the complexity, our data are useful for formulating policy which could reduce the overall level of violence toward children.

First, the issue of excess domestic responsibility must be met. Women must either be released from the gender-linked burdens of child care and domestic duties or they must be provided with adequate assistance to help them cope with their responsibilities. We suggested that financial resources help in reducing the level of violence among women at home. We believe that women with sufficient financial resources either directly or indirectly use them to insulate themselves from the pressure and responsibility of child rearing. It has previously been argued that gender equality in the home and in society can lessen the level of family violence (Gelles, 1978a; Straus, 1977), and the results of this study are consistent with that recommendation.

Women need to have a major role in the decisions affecting their employment either in the paid labor force or as housewives. One of the worst situations for a woman who works full-time is to have little or no input in the decision to work.

Last, our data provide additional evidence that unemployment among men has serious noneconomic, negative consequences for their families. One of the major burdens of the father's unemployment falls on the shoulders of the working wife and then, through her violence, onto the children.

Conclusion

While this investigation has supported one of the three alternative directions of a hypothesis about the relationship between maternal employment status and violence toward children, the data from the national survey of family violence do not provide the final word on this issue. The national survey was planned and carried out to ask and answer broad questions about the incidence, nature, and causes of violence in the home. While many facets of family life were explored, many others had to be omitted or given brief coverage due to the limits of time and financial resources. When one considers the constant and detailed attention paid to the relationship between male employment and violence toward children, then it is obvious that we have failed to pay adequate attention to the role of maternal employment in the case of violence toward children. It is necessary and important for the development of knowledge about child abuse and family violence to continue to pursue this issue and to further refine the empirical evidence and theoretical perspectives on this issue.

Appreciation is expressed to Andrea Carr, John Scanzoni, and Murray Straus for their helpful comments and insightful critiques of earlier drafts of this article.

Notes
1. We had great difficulty in choosing the appropriate label for women who reported that they did not work. "Unemployed" does not capture the true nature of their situation—since many did not choose to work—and using this term would deprecate the occupational functions and value of housework. We finally chose "housewife" because 96.2% of the women who said they were not working at the time of the interview placed themselves into this category (3% said they were unemployed and .8% said they were disabled).

16

Violence and Pregnancy: Are Pregnant Women at Greater Risk of Abuse?

Richard J. Gelles

An unanticipated finding of one of the first exploratory studies of violence toward women was that pregnant women appeared to be at high risk of violence and abuse. Our in-depth interviews with individuals in 80 households uncovered the fact that in 44 homes where violence had occurred during the marriage, 10 women recalled that they were pregnant during a violent incident (Gelles, 1974; 1975). Other investigators have also reported finding a relationship between pregnancy and violence (Carlson, 1977; Eisenberg and Micklow, 1977; Flitcraft, 1977; Flynn, 1977; Gayford, 1975; Giles-Sims, 1983; Hilberman and Munson, 1978; Helton, 1986; Roy, 1977; Sammons, 1981; Stacy and Shupe, 1983; Walker, 1979; 1984).

Despite the frequency with which the association between violence and pregnancy has been reported in the professional literature, there is still a question as to whether pregnant women are at higher risk of being victimized by their husbands or partners. A number of the studies that purport to find a link between violence and pregnancy actually provide no empirical data to support the claim (see for example, Giles-Sims, 1983, Hilberman and Munson, 1978, Roy, 1977, Sammons, 1981). Those studies that provide empirical data find a range of association from 4% to half of all pregnant women experiencing violence (see, for example, Carlson, 1977; Eisenberg and Micklow, 1977. Flynn, 1977; Gelles, 1974; Stacy and Shupe, 1983).

Even in the studies that do provide empirical data, there are significant external and internal validity problems. Since wife abuse and pregnancy are phenomena with relatively low base rates in the general population,[1] most studies that examine a possible link between violence and pregnancy base the findings on relatively small samples. Gelles (1974, 1975) interviewed 80 individuals. Eisenberg and Micklow (1977) based their findings on interviews with 20 victims of wife battering. Helton (1986) interviewed 112 women selected at random during prenatal clinic appointments. Gayford's (1975) findings are based on 100 cases, while Carlson's are based on 101 cases. The largest sample was obtained by Walker (1984), who interviewed 401 battered women in the Rocky Mountain region. None of the empirical investigations that report a link between violence and pregnancy are based on representative samples of a defined larger population. Thus, generalizations from the studies must be made with care.

Each of the empirical investigations has internal validity problems. In the Gelles study, which first reported a possible link between violence and pregnancy, violence was found in 44 out of the 80 households studied. Ten of the women spontaneously mentioned that violence had occurred while they were pregnant. On the one hand, it is possible that more women would have reported violence during pregnancy if we had systematically asked this question. Thus, we may have underestimated the link between pregnancy and violence. On the other hand, the link may have been overestimated. It is possible that women mentioned violence during pregnancy because pregnancy is a memorable and time-related cue to past events. The lack of precision in our in-depth interviews makes if difficult to establish firmly if and what the relationship between violence and pregnancy might be. Eisenberg and Micklow's finding that pregnant women are at risk of abuse is based on victims' volunteered discussions of where (not when) they were hit. Seven women described being hit in the abdominal area during a pregnancy.

Stacy and Shupe (1983) report that 42% of the women calling a hotline indicated that they were physically abused during pregnancy. However, among shelter residents, only 14% noted an association between pregnancy and violence. When Carlson (1977) asked women what they perceived to be the cause of abuse, 4% of the responders cited pregnancy.

Helton's (1986) and Walker's (1984) investigations were somewhat more systematic in the search for a possible link between violence and pregnancy. Helton found that 38% of 112 pregnant women said they had been battered or were at risk of being battered. Twenty-one percent reported actually being battered, while 9% said they had been battered during the current pregnancy. Since Straus and Gelles (1986) report that 4.4% of women in the population are battered each year, Helton's data appear to indicate a substantially greater risk to pregnant women. However, Helton's study does not include an appropriate comparison group that would indicate whether the rate is higher among pregnant women as compared to nonpregnant women.

Walker (1984) finds a much higher risk to pregnant women. Nearly 6 in 10 of the battered women Walker interviewed (59%) said they were beaten during their first pregnancy; 63% reported being beaten during a second pregnancy; 55% said they were beaten during their third pregnancy. The question of recall of events over the course of an entire marriage is a major threat to the internal validity of Walker's study. As with the Gelles report, it is not clear whether women are indeed at risk of being beaten while pregnant or whether they are simply linking together two memorable events. It is also possible that being attacked when pregnant is so outrageous that women who were beaten when pregnant were led to volunteer for Walker's study.

The various methods of measuring violence and assessing the possible link between pregnancy and violence account for the wide variation in reported associations. This variation actually makes it nearly impossible to compare the differing estimates of the hypothesized association between pregnancy and violence.

The present study examines the hypothesis that pregnant women are at increased risk of being victims of violence and battering by their partners. Unlike previous investigations, which are based primarily on small, nonrepresentative samples, this investigation is based on the 1985 Second National Family Violence Survey—a large, nationally representative sample of American households.[2]

Method

Measurement of Violence and Abuse

Violence was nominally defined as "an act carried out with the intention or perceived intention of causing physical pain or injury to another person." The injury could range from slight pain, as in a slap, to murder. The motivation might range from a concern for a person's safety (as when a child is spanked for going into the street) to hostility so intense that the death of the person is desired (Gelles and Straus, 1979). Abuse was defined as those acts of violence that have a high probability of causing injury to the person (an injury does not actually have to occur).

Violence was operationalized through the use of the Conflict Tactics Scales (described briefly in Chapter 1 and fully in Chapters 3, 4, and 5). There are various scoring methods for the Conflict Tactics Scales. This study uses two indices. The first is ''Most severe form of violence experienced in last 12 months.'' This ordinal scoring method has three values:

no violence experienced; minor violence (threw something at other; pushed, grabbed, or shoved other; slapped or spanked other); and severe violence (kicked, bit, or hit with fist; hit or tried to hit other with an object; beat up the other; choked other; threatened with a knife or gun; used a knife or gun). The second index is a measure of overall violence. This dichotomous index indicates whether any form of violence occurred at least once in the previous 12 months.

The items of the Conflict Tactics Scales are presented to subjects, and the subjects are asked how often they used each technique when they had a disagreement or were angry with a family member, both in the previous year and in the course of the relationship with the family member.

The reliability and validity of the Conflict Tactics Scales have been assessed over the 15-year period of their development. A full discussion of their reliability and validity can be found in Chapter 4. There is evidence of adequate internal consistency reliability, concurrent validity, and construct validity.

All subjects, with the exception of single male parents, were asked, "Are you (your wife/partner) currently expecting a child?" For those answering yes, we asked, "How many months are you/is she pregnant?"

Violence Rates by Pregnancy Status

The rates of violence overall, minor, and severe were higher in the households where the wife or female partner was pregnant at the time of the interview. As Table 16.1 shows, a pregnant women's risk of experienc-

TABLE 16.1

Difference in Rate of Husband-to-Wife Violence Experienced by Pregnant and Other Women, by Gender of Respondent

Gender of Respondent	Level of Violence	Rate per 1,000 Couples		% Difference
		Not Pregnant	Pregnant	
Both	Minor	81	104	28.3
	Severe	33	53	60.6
	Overall	115	156	35.6
		(n = 5,138)	(n = 193)	
	χ^2 = 3.52, p = .17			
Female	Minor	72	85	18.1
	Severe	49	82	67.3
	Overall	121	167	38.0
		(n = 2,892)	(n = 96)	
	χ^2 = 2.52, p = .28			
Male	Minor	93	122	31.2
	Severe	13	24	84.6
	Overall	106	145	36.8
		(n = 2,246)	(n = 98)	
	χ^2 = 1.58, p = .43			

ing violence in the previous year was greater than those who were not pregnant at the time of our interviews. Pregnant women's risk of minor violence was 28.3% greater than that of nonpregnant women, Pregnant women's risk of abusive violence was 60.6% greater than that of nonpregnant women, while the overall risk of any form of violence to pregnant women was 35.6% greater than that of nonpregnant women.

Not only did pregnant women report higher rates of violence, but men with pregnant wives or partners reported that they were more violent to their partners than were men married to women who were not pregnant at the time of the interview.

Women are slightly more likely to be hit during the later half of their pregnancies. The rate of overall violence during the first four months of pregnancy was 154 per 1,000, while the rate of violence toward women in the fifth through ninth months was 170 per 1,000.

Although some of the differences between the rates of violence in households where women are pregnant compared to homes where women are not pregnant are large and impressive, the differences are not statistically significant. Only the differences for the overall rate of violence for all 6,002 respondents approaches significance at the .05 level.[3] The problem with achieving statistical significance is, in part, a result of the problems created by studying the relationship of two low-base-rate phenomena.[4]

Age, Pregnancy, and Violence: A Test for Spuriousness

Previous investigations have failed to test for a possible threat to the validity of the conclusion that pregnancy is associated with victimization. This is largely due to the fact that most previous studies are based on small samples without appropriate comparison groups of nonpregnant women.

We know from past research that the rate of violence toward women 30 years of age or younger is roughly double the rate among women 31 years old or older (Straus, Gelles, and Steinmetz, 1980). Pregnancy is also more likely among women under 30 years of age. It is at least plausible that the purported relationship between violence and pregnancy is spurious.

Table 16.2 indicates that the relationship found between overall violence and pregnancy is indeed spurious.[5] An examination of the percentage differences reported in the right-hand column of Table 16.2 indicates that the large differences in rates of violence experienced by pregnant women compared to nonpregnant women are greatly reduced or disappear when we control for age of respondents, age of female respondents, and age of male respondents.[6] The only exception is that males 25 years of age or older report higher rates of violence toward their pregnant wives compared

TABLE 16.2

Difference in Rate of Overall Husband-to-Wife Violence Experienced by Pregnant and Other Women, by Gender of Respondent and Age of Respondent

Gender of Respondent	Age	Rate per 1,000 Couples		% Difference
		Not Pregnant	Pregnant	
Both	Under 25	275 (336)	265 (51)	.03
	$\chi^2 = 0.00, p = 1.0$			
	25 or older	104 (4,784)	117 (142)	.12
	$\chi^2 = 0.14, p = .70$			
Female	Under 25	302 (208)	289 (30)	.04
	$\chi^2 = 0.00, p = 1.0$			
	25 or older	108 (2,670)	112 (66)	.04
	$\chi^2 = 0.00, p = 1.0$			
Male	Under 25	230 (128)	230 (21)	0
	$\chi^2 = 0.00, p = 1.0$			
	25 or older	99 (2,114)	122 (76)	.23
	$\chi^2 = 0.21, p = .64$			

to males 25 years of age or older married to women who were not pregnant at the time of the interviews.

Discussion

We were surprised 13 years ago when we discovered what appeared to be a special vulnerability of pregnant women to being hit and abused by their husbands. We are more surprised in this analysis to find that relationship to be spurious. One might think that the repeated reporting of a relationship between violence and pregnancy is yet another example of the "Woozle Effect" (Gelles, 1980). However, the "Woozle Effect" involves the repeating of a supposed finding without data that meet normal standards of empirical evidence. In the case of the hypothesized relationship between violence and pregnancy, numerous investigators had collected data that appeared to support the association.

There are a number of reasons why investigators have found and may continue to find apparent high rates of violence among pregnant women. First, as we have pointed out, the rates of pregnancy among women under 25 and the rates of victimization are both relatively high. Our finding of an incidence rate of 265 per 1,000 pregnant women under the age of 25 is in the middle of the range of rates of violence toward pregnant women reported by other investigators. As we noted earlier, the fact that few other investigations employed control groups of nonpregnant women, and that no one had previously controlled for age, accounts for the conclusion that pregnant women appear to be a special risk group.

A second plausible explanation for high rates of violence among pregnant women reported by investigators such as Walker (1984) is a methodological artifact. Those women who are asked to report whether they were ever struck when pregnant may over-report their victimization. Women may find violence during pregnancy so outrageous that they were more likely to volunteer for a study of wife abuse. Pregnant women may also feel more vulnerable, and actual violent events during their pregnancy may stand out in their memories when they are asked to report whether they were ever hit when pregnant or to volunteer for a study.

A third possibility is that the nature of the attacks may change while a woman is pregnant. Some investigators (Eisenberg and Micklow, 1977; Gelles, 1974, 1975) have found that the nature of the violent events is different when women are pregnant. Some women report that their partners focused their blows on their abdomens instead of the face or other parts of the body. It is also possible that husbands may increase the frequency and/or severity of their violence toward women during pregnancy. The cross-sectional data from the 1985 survey and the small number of cases do not allow us to examine these possibilities. Additional research is needed to examine whether pregnancy brings about changes in the nature of violent attacks. Of particular value would be longitudinal studies that could determine whether some husbands increase or decrease their violence when their wives become pregnant and the conditions under which such changes occur.

Conclusions

Data from the 1985 Second National Family Violence Survey indicate that the previously reported association between pregnancy and husband-to-wife violence is spurious and is an artifact of the effect of another variable, age. Young women have high rates of pregnancy, and they also experience violence at a relatively high rate.

That pregnant women are not statistically at special risk of violence does not relieve society from the need to provide appropriate intervention and preventive services. Although our data do not confirm the hypothesis that pregnant women are at higher risk of being hit and abused, the sad fact is that pregnant women enjoy no special relief from the threat of violence either. Clinical and descriptive research suggests that the nature of the attacks changes when victims are pregnant and that women are often hit in the abdominal area. The vulnerability of pregnant women and their unborn children is sufficient to confirm the recommendation that health service personnel and agents of social control should be prepared to provide effective treatment and prevention strategies for these women (Helton, 1986).

Notes

I am indebted to John Harrop for his assistance in coding the indices in the data set, organizing the data analysis, and assisting in the statistical analysis. Wayne Velicer also provided valuable consultation on the statistical analysis of the data. My colleague and co-principal investigator, Murray Straus, aided in the organization and analysis of the data for this article.

1. The following rates of violence toward women, on the basis of the 1985 data, are given in Chapter 6. The overall violence rate was 113 per 1,000 households. Severe violence, or what is referred to as wife beating, occurred in 30 households per 1,000. The same survey found that women were pregnant at the time of the interview in 34 households per 1,000.
2. A complete description of the sampling and methodology is given in Appendix 1.
3. When we treated the dependent variable (violence) as interval data and analyzed the data by using a two-way analysis of variance (sex, by pregnancy, by overall violence), the F statistic was 3.351, with 1 degree of freedom, with a statistical significance of .067. When both variables are treated as ordinal, the gamma statistic is .18.
4. The problem of selecting an appropriate measure of association for categorical data when the largest number of cases falls into one call (e.g., no violence, not pregnant) has been reviewed by Goodman and Kruskal (1959), who note that the issue was first raised in 1884 in a discussion of predicting tornadoes (Finley, 1884).
5. There were too few cases of severe or minor violence to analyze the relationship between pregnancy and types of violence while controlling for age.
6. Unfortunately, our survey only recorded the age of the respondent. We have no measure of the age of the respondent's partner. Thus, we can control only for the age of the respondent.

17

Marital Power, Conflict, and Violence in a Nationally Representative Sample of American Couples

Diane H. Coleman and Murray A. Straus

Many theories have been put forth to explain the paradox that the family is both the most loving and supportive of human institutions and the most violent (Gelles & Straus, 1979; Hotaling & Straus, 1980). One of the most prominent of these focuses on the male-dominant balance of power which characterizes the family in most societies (Dobash & Dobash, 1979; Straus, 1973, 1976). However, research on the relationship of the balance of power to violence seems to have a contradictory aspect. The nature of the contradiction can be seen by considering the following three propositions:

1. The higher the level of conflict, the greater the probability of violence (Straus, Gelles & Steinmetz, 1980).[1]
2. Equalitarian marriages in contemporary American society are characterized by a high level of conflict. The presumed reasons include reluctance of males to give up their traditional prerogatives (Whitehurst, 1974); the need to negotiate many issues which are normatively prescribed for couples following the traditional "husband as the head of the household" pattern (Brown, 1980; Kolb & Straus, 1974; Scanzoni, 1970); and the fact that equality leads to greater interpersonal intimacy, which in turn is associated with conflict (Coser, 1956; Foss, 1980; Sprey, 1972).
3. Equalitarian marriages have the lowest incidence of violence (Straus, 1973; Straus, Gelles, & Steinmetz, 1980).

The contradictions between these propositions can be seen by considering their interrelationships: if conflict is associated with violence, and if equalitarian couples have a high level of conflict, a logical deduction is that equalitarian couples have a high rate of violence. However, as indicated in proposition 3, the empirical evidence suggests that equalitarian couples have the *lowest* rate of violence. The research reported in this paper was designed to provide information which might help to resolve this contradiction. It compares the level of conflict and the rate of violence within four marital power types: male-dominant, female-dominant, divided power, and equalitarian.

Of the several possible explanations for the contradictory propositions, the data available permit us to examine three. First, the differences may come about because the studies have used different methods and populations. The present study tests hypotheses derived from the propositions on a single and representative sample. A second explanation for the discrepancies is that there may be less violence in equalitarian relationships because, contrary to proposition 2, there is less conflict. This is quite plausible since, as Alford (1982) notes, the link between intimacy and conflict is virtually untested by empirical data. A third possibility hinges on the degree of *consensus* over how the power is distributed. Weber (1947), for example, emphasizes the importance of legitimated power and uses the concept of authority to identify that type of power. Scanzoni (1975), Sprey (1971), Verhoff and Feld (1970), and Brown (1980) each suggest that consensus over how the power is distributed is an important factor in decreasing the probability of marital conflict.

These issues overlap with the debate between functionalist and conflict theorists. Functionalists such as Parsons and Bales (1955) tend to focus on the degree of consensus because the very existence of society (and families and other subunits) depends on the level of "normative integration." On the other hand, conflict theorists such as Coser (1956) and Dahrendorf (1959) focus on the extent of social inequality because, from that perspective, the existence of society depends on whether there are mechanisms for adjudicating and adapting to the conflicts inherent in social inequality (Sprey, 1969, 1971). Although the findings presented in this paper cannot be considered a "test" of functionalist and conflict theories, the results of testing the following hypotheses provide evidence that bears on both theories:

1. Equalitarian couples have *less* marital conflict.
2. Equalitarian couples have *more* consensus concerning the appropriate power structure.
3. Couples who have consensus concerning power have less conflict, irrespective of whether the marriage is equalitarian or asymmetrical.

4. The higher the level of conflict, the higher the rate of violence, irrespective of the power structure.

Method

Measurement of Marital Power

The balance of power between spouses was measured by questions based on the work of Blood and Wolfe (1960) that asked the respondent to indicate "Who has the final say" in making decisions about the following six issues: buying a car, having children, what house or apartment to take, what job either partner should take, whether a partner should go to work or quit work, and how much money to spend each week on food. The responses for each issue are: husband only, husband more than wife, husband and wife exactly the same, wife more than husband, and wife only.[3]

Marital power types. The pattern of responses to these six questions was used to classify each couple into one of the following four power types: male-dominant, female-dominant, equalitarian, and divided power. The difference between the equalitarian and the divided power types is that the former are equal in the sense of making most decisions jointly, whereas the latter are equal in the sense of dividing responsibility for decisions, with the wife and husband each having the final say for different decisions. The typology is derived from cross-classifying a measure of the extent to which the husband versus the wife tends to have the "final say" in family decisions (the "Decision Power Index") by the degree to which husband and wife share in making decisions (the "Shared Power Index").[4]

Measurement of Power Norm Consensus

For purposes of this study, legitimation of power (in the sense of agreement between the spouses on who has the right to decide) was measured in reference to the same set of six decisions used to classify the couples into four power types. In order to do this, the questions asked who the respondent believed *should have* the final say, in contrast to the question used for the Decision Power Index, which asked who "actually does have the final say." Respondents were asked for their own opinion, and also to indicate their perception of their partner's view about who should have the final say. The Power Norm Consensus Index was computed by first obtaining the difference between spouses for each of the six decisions, and then summing the difference without regard to sign. The resulting index has a theoretical range of 0 to 24, but the actual index ranges from 8, the least amount of consensus, to 24 or complete consensus. There was a high degree of consensus on power norms in this sample, as shown by the mean of 21.8 (standard deviation = 2.3).[5]

Measurement of Marital Conflict

A Marital Conflict Index was constructed from responses to questions which asked how often during the past year there was agreement on each of the following: managing the money, cooking, cleaning, or repairing the house; social activities; affection and sexual relations; and things about the children. The response categories ranged from always agree (scored 1 for conflict) to never agree (scored 5 for conflict). The index was created by summing the scores for the five questions and dividing by 5 (or by 4 if the question on conflict over children was omitted because of no children in the home). The scores ranged from 1 to 4.8, with a mean of 2.0 and a standard deviation of 0.68.

Measurement of Marital Violence

This research uses the "minor violence" index rate for husbands and for wives. The Minor Violence Index includes the following items: threw something, pushed, grabbed, shoved, slapped. There were both theoretical and empirical reasons for focusing on minor violence. The theoretical basis was the importance of *any* act of violence, even relatively minor violence. When such violence occurs, and especially when it is dismissed as "only minor violence," it implies that physical force can and will be used when it is perceived as "necessary." Although it is minor in the sense that there is relatively little chance of physical harm, it is of immense importance in understanding the balance of power between husbands and wives because it carries the message that one is at risk of assault if he or she does not acquiesce to the partner's demands (LaRossa, 1980). There is also no guarantee that minor acts of violence will remain minor. Minor violence is often a prelude to more severe violence.[6]

The empirical basis for focusing on minor violence is the fact that serious assaults (the "severe violence" index of the CTS) are much less common: such assaults occurred between "only" 6% of couples during the year of this survey, compared to almost three times that many couples who experienced minor violence (16%). If the severe violence index had been used, there would often not be sufficient cases in a cell to reach statistically reliable conclusions.

Sample and Data Analysis

Data were derived from the 1975 Family Violence Survey. Cross-tabulation was used for the statistical analysis of these data because the central independent variable—the marital power typology—is a nominal level variable, and the dependent variable is dichotomous and extremely skewed (16 vs. 84%). In addition, the Power Norm Consensus and Marital Conflict indexes were trichotomized into low, middle, and high categories for purposes of the major analyses. These variables were trichotomized because the focus of the research is cn the effects of high levels of conflict and consensus. Trichotomization facilitates focusing on the couples of greatest theoretical interest: those who were in the high third of the distribution in respect to consensus and conflict. The analysis begins by examining bivariate relationships and then goes on to test interaction effects predicted by functionalist and conflict theories.[7]

Marital Power and Conflict

A fundamental issue is whether, as the authors cited in proposition 2 suggest, equalitarian marriages have higher conflict than more traditional marriages. Examination of the "high conflict" column in Table 17.1 shows that, contrary to that view, the equalitarian couples are the type with the *lowest* percentage in the high-conflict category. Male-dominant couples are the type most likely to have experienced a high degree of conflict during the year of this study. In fact, they were almost twice as likely to have high conflict as equalitarian relationships: 39% versus 20% of the

TABLE 17.1
Marital Conflict by Marital Power Structure

Marital power type	*N*	Level of marital conflict (%)		
		Low	Medium	High
Male-dominant	200	25.0	36.0	39.0
Female-dominant	160	23.8	43.1	33.1
Divided power	1146	20.5	45.7	33.8
Equalitarian	616	32.5	47.1	20.5

$\chi^2 = 56.09$, d.f. $= 6, p < .001$.

equalitarian couples. Divided power and female-dominant couples are in between and have about the same frequency of conflict.

These differences in the level of conflict are extremely important because they contradict the fear that equality in marriage will be achieved at the expense of marital harmony. In addition, the high level of conflict among the male-dominant type couples is consistent with one of the basic tenants of conflict theory; namely, that asymmetrical power structures inherently generate conflict because those low in the status hierarchy struggle to alter the structure to their favor. Functionalist theory, on the other hand, suggests that this is *not* necessarily the case, provided the system is integrated or legitimated through normative consensus. In short, if the spouses agree that male-dominance is a legitimate and desirable power structure, male-dominance will not be associated with a high level of conflict. Fortunately, the data on these couples permit that proposition to be tested later in this paper.

Marital Power and Normative Consensus

The importance of a *legitimated* power structure has been emphasized by almost all power theorists as a factor which is critical to understanding the relationships between power and conflict (Blau,1964; Buckley,1967; Weber, 1947). Conflict is less likely to appear in realtionships where the less powerful person accepts the right of the more powerful person to make decisions. Consequently, we need to determine the extent to which couples agree and disagree about the appropriate balance of power in marriage; particularly the extent to which there is normative consensus among couples in the male-dominant type. This is important information for understanding contemporary American marriage. Consensus will also be used later as a covariate or specification variable in the present analyses.

The data in Table 17.2 show that only 22% of the male-dominant couples have high consensus in respect to who should have the final say, compared to 48% of the couples in equalitarian relationships. Thus, as might be expected on the basis of the long-term decline of patriarchal authority, relatively few male-dominant couples exist by consensus between the partners. The low consensus concerning the distribution of power is probably part of the reason for the high conflict over issues such as household chores, social activities, and money, as shown in the previous section. It probably also helps explain the high level of violence in male-dominant relationships found by previous studies (Straus, 1973; Straus, Gelles, & Steinmetz, 1980).

TABLE 17.2

Power Norm Consensus by Marital Power Structure

Marital power type	N	Level of consensus (%)		
		Low	Medium	High
Male-dominant	200	43.5	34.5	22.0
Female-dominant	160	35.6	38.1	26.3
Divided power	1,146	24.9	44.4	30.7
Equalitarian	616	15.3	37.0	47.7

$\chi^2 = 112.70$, d.f. $= 6$, $p < .001$.

Consensus Concerning Marital Power and Its Effect on Conflict

The findings that equalitarian couples have the lowest level of conflict and the highest degree of consensus in respect to power are broadly consistent with hypotheses derived from conflict theory. However, those findings do not necessarily refute functionalist norm-consensus theory. From the functionalist perspective, the crucial group are the male-dominant couples who *do* agree on the legitimacy of such a power structure. Such couples can be expected to have no higher rate of violence than couples in the other power types. By contrast, conflict theory leads to the hypothesis that consensus makes little difference. This is true because conflict theory assumes that it is inherent in the human condition for the powerless to seek to gain control of their lives (Collins, 1975). This being the case, coercion—including physical coercion—will sooner or later be employed by the dominant person or group to maintain the asymmetrical power structure (Goode, 1974). Table 17.3 was designed to provide data on that issue.

Table 17.3 shows the relationship between power and conflict separately for three groups of couples: those who are high in normative consensus concerning marital power, as compared to those who are middle and low. There are three types of "effects" shown in this table: (1) a consensus effect, (2) an equality effect, and (3) an interaction effect.

The consensus effect is revealed by comparing the percentages in the high-conflict column of A, B, and C. This shows that, irrespective of power type, the higher the level of consensus, the lower the level of conflict. For example, when consensus is low (Part A of Table 3), 54 percent of male-

TABLE 17.3

Marital Conflict by Marital Power Structure Controlling for Norm Consensus

Marital power	N^*	Level of marital conflict		
		Low	Medium	High
A. Low power norm consensus				
Male-dominant	81	9.9	35.8	54.3
Female-dominant	55	16.4	43.6	40.0
Divided power	280	21.1	42.1	36.8
Equalitarian	88	28.4	44.3	27.3
		$\chi^2 = 17.1$	d.f. = 6	$p < .009$
B. Medium power norm consensus				
Male-dominant	62	25.8	41.9	32.3
Female-dominant	60	21.7	43.3	35.0
Divided power	497	16.5	46.7	36.8
Equalitarian	194	26.8	50.5	22.7
		$\chi^2 = 19.7$	d.f. = 6	$p < .003$
C. High power norm consensus				
Male-dominant	42	50.0	28.6	21.4
Female-dominant	40	37.5	45.0	17.5
Divided power	342	25.1	48.2	26.6
Equalitarian	282	39.0	44.3	16.7
		$\chi^2 = 24.1$	d.f. = 6	$p < .0005$

*The Ns in this table sum to fewer cases than in Tables 1 and 2 because of missing data on one or the other of the two questions needed to derive the consensus measure.

dominant couples have a high level of conflict. But the percentage of high-conflict couples drops to only 21% when there is a high degree of consensus on the legitimacy of a male-dominant power structure (Part C of Table 17.3). Each of the other three power types also shows decreases in conflict when there is consensus over the power structure. The aspects of Table 17.3 discussed up to this point are consistent with a basic principle of functionalist theory—that normative consensus makes for social intergration and cohesion. Male-dominant power structures are *not* characterized by a high level of conflict in respect to such things as household chores, money, or social activities *if* the couple agree on the legitimacy of a male-dominant marriage. However, that is not all that can be gleaned from Table 17.3. The "equality effect" revealed by Table 17.3 also provides evidence which is consistent with conflict theory. Although the differences in Part C are small, equalitarian relationships have the lowest proportion of high-conflict couples, regardless of the level of consensus. Finally, there is an interaction effect revealed by the fact that the difference between equalitarian and other couples is greatest for the high-consensus group.

Marital Conflict and Violence

The findings presented up to this point show that male-dominant couples have the lowest level of consensus concerning the legitimacy of the power structure and the highest level of conflict over family responsibilities. It was suggested that the high conflict in male-dominant marriages is probably one of the factors which accounts for the high level of violence found in such marriages. As a first step in testing that proposition, Figure 17.1 plots the relationship between the level of conflict and the rate of minor violence for husband-to-wife violence, wife-to-husband violence, and couple violence. Figure 17.1 reveals a significant tendency ($p < .001$) for the rate of minor violence to increase as the level of conflict increases.[8]

The findings shown in Figure 17.1 not only support proposition 1, but also another proposition which is emphasized by conflict theorists: that although conflict is an inherent part of human interaction, violence is not. Conflict produces violence only under certain circumstances. Thus, even among the high-conflict couples, Figure 17.1 shows that 74% were *not* violent. What then accounts for the fact that some of the high-conflict couples experienced violence and others did not? The analyses which follow test two explanations; that normative consensus about power helps to avoid violence, and that equality between the actors helps to avoid violence.

Marital Power Structure and the Conflict-Violence Relationship

The final set of analyses concerns the interrelation of power, conflict, and violence. Essentially, the issue to be addressed is whether, holding constant the level of conflict, the power structure of the family makes a difference in the rate of violence. Figures 2, 3, and 4 do this by showing the relationship between the level of conflict and the rate of violence separately for each of the four marital power types. The difference between the three figures is that Figure 17.2 gives the data on husband-to-wife

FIGURE 17.1
Minor Violence by Level of Conflict

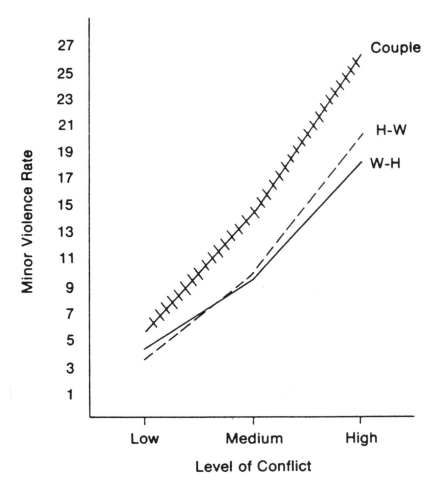

violence, Figure 17.3 on wife-to-husband violence, and Figure 17.4 on couple violence (the sum of the other two). The data in each of the figures demonstrate that the relationship between conflict and violence is strongly influenced by the power structure of the marriage. Or, putting it another way, unless one considers the power structure characterizing a marriage, important differences in the rate of violence experienced at different levels of conflict are hidden.

An important hidden difference is that, when compared to the other

FIGURE 17.2

Husband-to-Wife Minor Violence by Level of Conflict and Marital Power Structure

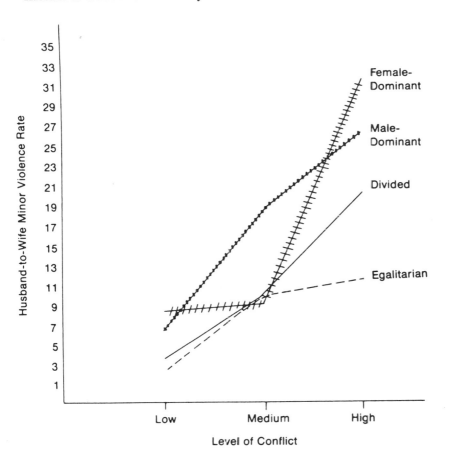

three marital power types, couples with an equalitarian relationship experience relatively *little increase* in the violence rate when conflict increases, and this is especially the case for husband-to-wife violence (Figure 17.2 compared to Figures 17.3 and 17.4).

Figures 17.2, 17.3, and 17.4 also suggest there may be a "breaking point" or a "tolerance level" for how much conflict can be experienced before events escalate into violence. All three figures show that the violence rates for the four marital power types are about the same when conflict is low. They start diverging at the medium level of conflict but are still relatively similar. However, when conflict is high, violence rates

FIGURE 17.3

Wife-to-Husband Minor Violence by Level of Conflict and Marital Power Structure

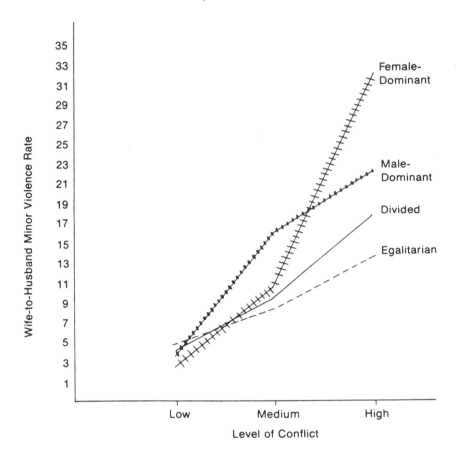

increase substantially, especially for the female-dominant couples; and so do the differences between the four marital power types. For example, husband-to-wife violence in female-dominant relationships increases from about 9% to 30%, and among divided power couples, the increase in violence is from about 9% to 20%. The increases are even higher when couple violence is considered. By contrast, as previously noted, equalitarian couples seem to be able to tolerate high conflict without a correspondingly large increase in the violence rate.

Finally, Figures 17.2, 17.3, and 17.4 are consistent in showing that violence is highest among female-dominant couples who experience a high

FIGURE 17.4

Minor Violence in Couples by Level of Conflict and Marital Power Structure

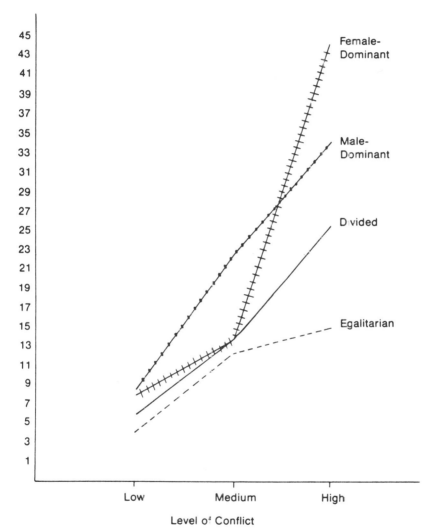

level of conflict over household chores, money, and social activities—higher than the violence rate of the male-dominant couples. A possible explanation is that such couples are characterized by three "risk factors" for violence, as compared to two for the male-dominant couples. Both the male-dominant and the female-dominant couples are at risk of violence because of conflict and inequality, but the female-dominant couples also have the burden of social deviance relative to the still prevalent male-dominant norms of American society.

Summary and Conclusions

This chapter explored the interrelationships of the power structure of marriage, power norm consensus, the level of marital conflict, and the rate of violence among the 1975 national sample of 2,143 couples. Each of the couples was classified into one of four types of marital power structure: equalitarian, male-dominant, female-dominant, or divided power.

Normative Integration and Conflict Theories of Marital Violence

Comparison of the four types of relationships revealed that agreement on the legitimacy of the power structure is an important factor in reducing the level of conflict over family responsibilities. Although male-dominant relationships have the highest amount of conflict of the four marital power types, the difference is sharply reduced if the couple agree on the appropriateness of that arrangement. This finding is consistent with "normative integration" theories of the family, such as proposed by Parsons and Bales (1955).

At the same time, the findings are consistent with certain aspects of conflict theory. Although they show that the higher the level of conflict the greater the rate of violence, the experience of these couples also reveals that the *power structure* of the relationship is strongly and independently related to violence.

Perhaps the most important finding is that there is an interaction effect. The power structure affects the relationship between conflict and violence: When conflict occurs in an asymmetrical power structure (the male-dominant and female-dominant types) there is a much greater risk of violence than when conflict occurs among the equalitarian couples. It appears that equalitarian relationships can tolerate more conflict before violence erupts than other power structures. Thus, although normative consensus reduces conflict, when conflict does take place it is associated with a much higher risk of violence than occurs when similar conflicts occur in equalitarian families. In addition, conflict theory assumes that it is in the nature of the human condition for persons who are low in a status hierarchy to attempt, sooner or later, to achieve a more equitable structure. To the extent that this is the case, regardless of the degree of consensus or legitimacy at a given time point, there is an inherent potential for conflict built into an asymmetrical power structure; and, ironically, this inherently higher conflict potential occurs in the type of power structure in which conflict is most likely to be associated with violence.

These findings also explain the contradictory propositions which led to this research. They show that the problem lies with proposition 2—the idea that equalitarian marriages are characterized by high conflict (presumably because of reluctance on the part of men to grant legitimacy to an equalitarian power structure, and because of conflict over having to negotiate formerly taken-for-granted role relationships). Since, contrary to this proposition, equalitarian marriages were found to have the least amount of conflict over family responsibilities, proposition 3—that equalitarian marriages are low in violence—follows logically from the first two propositions.

Finally, the results provide one more indication of the importance of including the power structure of intimate relationships as part of an analysis of marital violence (for other examples, see Dobash & Dobash, 1980; LaRossa, 1980; Straus, 1973, 1976).

Marital Equality and Marital Quality

The findings also have important policy implications. The theories summarized in proposition 2, and also certain religious and so-called "pro-family" critics of equalitarian social policies, argue that abandonment of the traditional male-dominant power structure leads to chaos and conflict. This research suggest the opposite of these concerns about the effects of gender equality in marriage. The equalitarian couples had the *highest* consensus in respect to power, and the *lowest* rates of both conflict and violence. Moreover, when there is conflict, equalitarian couples display the greatest resiliency to violence.[9] Those findings do not support the fear that the family will be weakened by policies which undermine the traditional pattern of "husband as the head of the family." On the contrary, our findings suggest that, since equality in marriage is associated with low rates of intra-family conflict and violence, laws, administratiave decisions, and services that empower women and encourage men to value an equal partner are likely to be important steps to reduce violence and strengthen the family.[10]

Notes

1. This proposition is not necessarily inconsistent with theorists such as Coser (1956) or Dahrendorf (1959), who highlights the adaptive functions of conflict. This is the idea that, without the adaptations and changes which emerge from the process of reconciling conflicts, a social unit is at risk of stagnation and eventual collapse. Suppression of conflict results in a failure to adapt to changed circumstances, whereas recognition of differences, and accommodation to those differences, is not only adaptive in the instrumental sense just mentioned, but also results in less accumulated hostility and therefore increases group solidarity. The key point is that the positive aspects of conflict take place only to the extent that the conflict is managed in a way which permits such an adaptive response.

2. For convenience and economy of working, we use "wife" to refer to "wives and female cohabiting partner"; and the same applies to "husband" and "marriage." For an analysis of differences and similarities between married and cohabiting couples in this sample, see Chapter 13, Yllo 1978, and Yllo and Straus, 1981.

3. Blood and Wolfe's method of measuring marital power has been strongly criticized on both theoretical and methodological grounds. Every aspect of the measure has been questioned, ranging from the method of weighting items to the overall reliability and validity of the measure (Safilios-Rothschild, 1970; Gillespie, 1971; Cromwell & Olson, 1975). These criticisms cannot be adequately discussed within the space limitations of a journal article. However, they have been examined in a number of empirical studies (e.g., Allen, 1984; Allen & Straus, 1985; Bahr, 1973; Price-Bonham, 1976; Straus, 1977). These studies are reviewed in Coleman (1985). The results of that review lead to the conclusion that as cogent as the criticisms are in principle, when empirical tests have been conducted, almost none of the criticisms have been supported. In addition, no one has developed an alternative which can be used in survey research and which has superior evidence of validity and reliability.

4. This was done using the procedure described by Wolfe (1959). The specific procedures were:
   a. *Compute Decision Power Index* by scoring responses for each decision form 1 ("wife only") to 5 ("husband only") and summing these scores. The resulting index has a range of 6 to 30. The raw score index was then transformed to a 0–100 scale to indicate the percentage of the maximum score. Low scores (for example, a percentage score less than 33) indicates wife dominance in decision making and high scores (for example, scores of 66 and above) indicate husband dominance in the sense that the husband most often had the final say.
   b. *Compute Shared Power Index.* This index is the number of decisions for which the respondent indicated the decision was made by the "husband and wife exactly the same." The resulting index has a range of 0 to 6, which was also transformed to 0–100 percentage scale by dividing by the maximum score of six.
   c. *Cross-Classify Decision Power Index by Shared Power Index.* Couples with a score of 66 or more on the Shared Power Index (i.e., who shared two-thirds or more of the six decisions) were classified as having an equalitarian power structure. Couples who shared fewer decisions *and* had a score of

less than 33 on the Decision Power Index were defined as having a female-dominant relationship. Couples with a score of less than 65 on the Shared Power Index *and* more than 66 on the Decision Power Index were defined as male dominant. Couples with scores of less than 65 on the Shared Power Index *and* between 34–65 on the Decision Power Index were classified as a divided-power relationship. The number of couples in each of these types is shown in Table 17.1.

5. However, that may be true because the partner's beliefs were measured by the respondent's perception of those beliefs rather than by interviewing the partner directly. See Thompson and Walker (1982) for a discussion of these methodological problems.

6. Minor violence is also important for the socialization function of the family. Children learn appropriate behavior by observing the actions of their parents. Seeing parents engaged in the use of even minor violence is a powerful lesson in how one is to behave in intimate relationships.

7. A number of other analyses (reported in Coleman, 1985) were also carried out, in part to deal with possible confounding factors, such as socioeconomic status (SES). Although SES effects which are important in their own right were found, the results reported in this paper do not seem to be a function of SES. Similarly, a set of analyses was computed to test the hypothesis that the underlying factor is whether counter-productive techniques—such as withdrawal and verbal aggression—are used to deal with conflict. Both withdrawal and verbal aggression were found to be related to violence, but that relationship is not what underlies the findings reported in this paper. Asymmetrical power structures were found to have a higher rate of violence irrespective of whether reasoning, withdrawal, or verbal aggression are used to deal with conflicts.

8. The test of significance used for Figures was carried out in the same way as the tests in Table 17.3. That is, chi-square tests were computed for the table giving couple violence by level of conflict, husband-to-wife violence by level of conflict, and wife-to-husband violence by level of conflict. In all cases the p values were less than 0.001. The same procedure was used for Figures 17.2, 17.3, and 17.4, except that each of these figures required four chi-square tests.

9. The reason for the greater ability of the equalitarian couples to avoid violence, even in the face of high conflict, cannot be investigated with the data on this sample. There are at least three possibilities. First, the seeming difference might be the result of selective attrition rather than a real difference in conflict management skills. That is, equalitarian couples with high conflict might be more likely to terminate the marriage than more traditional couples with an equally high level of conflict. If that is the case, then those most at risk of violence would not be in the sample. Second, the shared decision making which characterizes the equalitarian group gives them more practice in negotiation than the other three power types. Thus, when conflict does occur, they have greater conflict management skills. A third possibility is that the causal sequence might be the reverse: those with negotiation skills are able to sustain an equalitarian marriage and also to avoid violence. Further research is needed to investigate these issues.

10. Space limitations prevent a more lengthy discussion of the specific actions that might be taken to bring this about. However, a few examples can be mentioned. (1) A constitutional amendment confirming gender equality as a national principle. (2) Rectifying the huge differential between the earnings of men and

women by policies such as setting wages on the basis of "comparable worth." (3) Changing marriage vows not only to delete the "obey" part of the marriage vows (which is now common), but also to include a statement that explicitly disavows the doctrine of the husband as the "head of the household" and instead affirms the equality of husband and wife. (4) Marriage and family workshops and courses, both for students and adults, which assume equality and conflict and teach negotiation skills. (5) Programs for girls and young women which present the research findings showing that early marriage, marriage to someone older (especially when combined with early marriage), early child rearing, and traditional female occupations are all associated with being subordinate to men, and hence increasing the risk of violence. Such programs are probably not going to sweep the nation, but they are beginning, as exemplified by the program which is being developed by the senior author of this paper in a small New England city.

18

Marital Violence in a Life Course Perspective

J. Jill Suitor, Karl Pillemer, and Murray A. Straus

During the past decade, family scholars have increasingly devoted attention to understanding the causes and consequences of marital violence (cf. Hotaling and Sugarman, 1986; Margolin, Sibner, and Gleberman, 1988, for recent reviews of this literature). One of the most consistent findings of community surveys of this phenomenon is a negative relationship between spousal violence and age of both the husband and wife (cf. Gaquin, 1977; Gelles, 1974; Pillemer and Suitor, 1988; Schulman, 1979; Straus et al., 1980; Stark, Flitcraft, Zuckerman, Gray, Robinson, and Frazier, 1981).

Despite its consistency, there have been no empirical attempts to account for this pattern. This fact is particularly surprising in the light of the substantial attention criminologists have devoted to attempting to explain a similar decline in other forms of violence across the life course (cf. Greenberg, 1979, 1985; Hirschi and Gottfredson, 1983; Rowe and Tittle, 1977). The present paper uses data from the 1975 and 1985 National Family Violence Surveys to attempt to explain the observed decline in marital violence across the life course.[1] Specifically, the paper investigates the extent to which the relationship between marital violence and age can be explained by two alternative hypotheses. First, we examine whether the relationship between marital violence and age can be explained by cohort effects; second, we examine whether the relationship can be explained by life-course variations in the factors that affect marital violence.

Cohort Explanations for the Decline in Marital Violence

The most important question at the outset is whether the observed decline in marital violence across the life course can be accounted for primarily by cohort effects. Disaggregating actual changes in behavior and attitudes across the life course from differences in the experiences of particular age cohorts has been an issue in social science for more than two decades (cf. Bengtson, Cutler, Mangen, and Marshall, 1985; Riley, 1973, 1985, 1987; Ryder, 1965; Schaie and Willis, 1986). The literature on cohort effects suggests that systematic life course variations found in cross-sectional studies may be the result of differences in the experiences of individuals raised in a particular historical period (i.e., those in the same birth cohort), rather than the result of actual changes as individual's age.

This argument can be used to suggest that marital violence does not actually decrease as couples move across the life course. Instead, the level of violence experienced by younger couples may be substantially higher than that experienced by older couples when they were younger. If this were the case, couples born in recent decades would continue to experience relatively violent marriages as they moved through the life course and the relationship between age and violence would weaken substantially.

While it would be best to examine this issue by following the same couples over time, data to conduct such an analysis are not available. It is possible, however, to use the 1975 and 1985 National Family Violence Surveys to compare the behaviors of representative samples of the same age cohorts across time, a methodology that has been employed in other studies of violent behavior across the life course (cf. Greenberg, 1985). If the cohort effect argument is correct, the same age cohort should show no less violence in 1985 than in 1975. If on the other hand, marital violence actually declines across the life course, the same age cohort should have experienced less violence in 1985 than 1975. The cohort argument would also be supported if the negative relationship between age and marital violence was weaker in 1985 than 1975, as older cohorts that reported very low levels of marital violence were replaced by younger cohorts reporting greater violence.

Social Factors Explaining the Decline in Marital Violence

An alternative hypothesis for the relationship between age and marital violence is that age affects violence primarily or exclusively through other social factors. Investigating this possibility requires selecting variables that meet two criteria.

First, only variables whose decline across the life course parallels that of marital violence should be included in the analysis, since only variables that decrease in this manner could account for the age/violence relationship. A review of the domestic violence literature reveals that most of the factors that are associated with marital violence do not meet this criterion, since they cannot vary or are unlikely to vary across the life course (for example, witnessing physical aggression between one's own parents, husband's occupational prestige, and religious incompatability). Several other variables associated with violence vary across the life course, but do not follow the same pattern as marital violence (e.g., marital satisfaction and income are curvilinearly related to age); thus they also cannot contribute to our understanding of the life course dimunition in violence.

Second, only variables that have been found consistently to be associated with marital violence in community surveys should be included in the analysis. Confining the analysis to these variables makes it possible to focus on the way in which they might serve to intervene between age and violence, rather than whether they are in fact related to violence.

A review of the relevant literatures revealed that only three variables met these criteria: (a) marital conflict; (b) husband's alcohol consumption; and (c) verbal aggression. These factors were chosen for inclusion in the analysis presented below and are discussed in detail here.

Marital Conflict

Marital conflict readily meets out two criteria. First, it has been found to decline monotonically across age groups (Straus et al., 1980; Suitor and Pillemer, 1987), even when demographic characteristics, such as educational attainment and income are controlled (Suitor and Pillemer, 1987). Second, it has consistently been found to be positively associated with marital violence (cf. Coleman, Weinman, and Hsi, 1980; Straus et al., 1980). Further, it is possible to make a reasonable argument that conflict affects marital violence, rather than the reverse. If the causal order were from violence to conflict, we would expect to find violence related similarly to all types of conflict (e.g., issues involving household labor, child care, sex, etc.); however, this is not the case. As Straus and his colleagues have shown (Straus et al., 1980), conflict over some issues (e.g., children) is substantially more strongly related to violence than is conflict over other issues (e.g., sex or affection). These findings suggest that the causal direction is more strongly from conflict to violence than the reverse.

Husband's Alcohol Consumption

Husband's alcohol consumption also meets both of our criteria for inclusion in the analysis. First, alcohol consumption has consistently been found to decline across the life course (cf. Berger and Snortum, 1986; Cahalan, 1970; Cahalan et al., 1969) in a manner that parallels the decline in marital violence. Second, alcohol consumption (particularly by husbands) has been found to be associated with marital violence in studies using both community surveys (see Chapter 12) and small matched samples (cf. Hotaling and Sugarman, 1986); in addition, the relationship continues to be found when controlling on variables related to both drinking and violence, such as socioeconomic status and approval of marital aggression (see Chapter 12).

Verbal Aggression

Verbal aggression also meets our two criteria. First, although previous research has not examined the relationship between verbal aggression and age, both cross-tabular and correlational analyses using the 1975 and 1985 National Family Violence Surveys indicate that verbal aggression does decrease monotonically across the life course (see Tables 18.2 and 18.3 for correlation matrices including these variables).

Second, although some psychologists have suggested that ventilating aggression verbally might reduce the likelihood of physical violence between partners (cf. Berkowitz, 1973; Howard, 1970; and Straus, 1974, for discussions of this issue), the empirical evidence has consistently shown that individuals who engage in verbal aggression toward their spouses are *more* likely to engage in physical violence (Straus, 1974; Straus et al., 1980). Further, recent longitudinal research by Murphy (1987) indicates that verbal aggression is a precipitant to physical aggression in marriage.

To summarize, we have provided a model of these relationships in Figure 18.1:

If these variables are related as depicted, the relationship between age and marital violence should become substantially weaker or disappear altogether when the effects of intervening variables are held constant. If instead the relationship between age and violence remains, even when

FIGURE 18.1

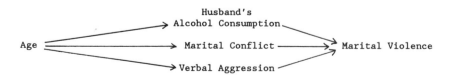

these variables are included in the analysis, it suggests that age has an independent effect on marital violence.

Measurement of the Variables

Marital Violence

Marital violence was measured using the following items from the CTS in both 1975 and 1985: threw something at the other one; kicked, bit, or hit with a fist; hit or tried to hit with something; beat up the other one; threatened with a knife or gun; or used a knife or gun. Each item was coded on a scale from 0 (never during the previous year) to 6 (more than 20 times during the previous year). Scores were summed across the six items. For the present analysis, the total scores were dichotomized into "never" and "one or more times" during the previous year. Given that the variable was dichotomous, we employed logistic rather than OLS regression for the analysis.

The data used for this analysis are the reports of violence experienced by couples during the previous year, combining both husband-to-wife and wife-to-husband violence. This choice was made to maximize variation in the dependent measure; reports of any violence experienced within the relationship are greater than that reported by only one partner toward the other. This procedure was important for the present analysis, given the very low reports of any type of violence in the latter part of the life course. Further, as we have shown elsewhere (Pillemer and Suitor, 1988), the relationship between marital violence and age is unaffected by the gender of the aggressor.

Intervening Variables

Marital conflict.   Marital conflict was measured in both 1975 and 1985 by asking the respondents how often, in the past year, they had agreed with their spouse on issues regarding money management, the division of household labor (including both housework and home repairs), social activities and entertaining, and affection and sex. The response choices were "always agreed" (1), "almost always" (2), "usually" (3), "sometimes" (4), and "never agreed" (5). The four items were combined in a scale that has a Cronbach's Alpha of .76 for the 1975 data and .71 for the 1985 data.

Verbal aggression.   Verbal aggression was measured by using the Verbal Aggression Index of the CTS in both 1975 and 1985. The large majority of the respondents reported very low levels of verbal aggression; thus this variable was logged to meet the distributional requirements of regression analysis.

Husband's alcohol consumption. Husband's alcohol consumption was the only variable that was not measured using the same items in 1975 and 1985. In 1975, respondents were asked how often the husband "gets drunk." The response categories ranged from "never" (1) to "almost always" (6). In 1985, respondents were asked to state how often *during the past year* the husband "got drunk." Responses ranged from 0 to 365. In both cases, the variable was highly skewed. To increase the similarity of the analyses, the responses to both items were collapsed into three categories. The 1975 data were collapsed into "never," "rarely," and "occasionally, often, very often, or almost always." The 1985 data were collapsed into "never," "once or twice," and "three or more times during the past year." The distribution of the two variables was similar following this transformation.

Cohort Effects and the Decline in Marital Violence across the Life Course

Table 18.1 presents cross-tabulations of marital violence by ages of husbands and wives. We have partitioned the data by gender because respondents in the 1985 survey were not asked the age of their spouses. Thus, to make comparisons between the effects of age in the two data sets, it was necessary to analyze husbands' and wives' reports separately. From Table 18.1, it is clear that the direction and strength of the relationship between age and violence are similar in the 1975 and 1985 data and are similar regardless of whether the reports are made by women or men.

Most important are the comparisons of reports by the same cohort across the period. These comparisons demonstrate that the apparent decline in marital violence across the life course cannot be explained by cohort effects. Specifically, the findings show a decline in violence for each cohort across the ten-year period. For example, the violence reported by the cohort of men ages 30 to 39 in 1985 is substantially lower than that reported when the same cohort was 18 to 29 in 1975 (20.8% in 1985, 34.9% in 1975). A similar pattern is revealed when we compare the reports of the cohort of men ages 40–49 in 1985 to the reports of that cohort a decade earlier (when they were 30–39); a decrease from 15.8% in 1975 to 8.5% in 1985. The same pattern was found in the women's reports of marital violence.

It is important to note that this pattern was unaffected by whether the respondents were in first marriages or were remarried; data from individuals in both types of marriages revealed a similar pattern of decline across the life course. These findings not only lend support to the hypothesis that

TABLE 18.1

Rate of Marital Violence per One Hundred Couples Reported by Husbands and
Wives in 1975 and 1985 by Age

Year of Survey	Husband's Age				x^2	p
	18-29	30-39	40-49	50-65		
1976	34.9	15.8	11.0	6.1		
Total N	(195)	(222)	(173)	(314)	79.5	.000
1985	26.6	20.8	8.5	7.4	89.1	.000
Total N	(345)	(677)	(426)	(578)		

	Wife's Age				x^2	p
	18-29	30-39	40-49	50-65		
1976	29.8	15.8	10.0	4.8		
Total N	(252)	(240)	(160)	(248)	63.8	.000
1985	30.3	17.2	11.3	6.5		
Total N	(548)	(844)	(518)	(663)	156.9	.000

the likelihood of violence decreases across the life course, but they call into question Kalmuss and Seltzer's (1986) conclusion that more violence occurs in remarriages than first marriages. While a bivariate analysis indicates that couples in first marriages are less likely to experience violence than are those in remarriages, this difference disappears when controlling on age.[2]

These findings suggest that the observed decline in marital violence across the life course cannot be accounted for by cohort effects; however, there is one additional issue that we need to address before drawing this conclusion. Could the apparent decline be accounted for by cohort differences in response bias due to social desirability, rather than actual variations in violence across the life course? The tendency for individuals to present overly harmonious pictures of their family relations has long been recognized (cf. Edmunds, 1967; Schumm and Bugaighis, 1986; Schumm, Jurich, Bollman, and Bugaighis, 1985). This concern becomes particularly salient in collecting data from older family members, since the elderly generally receive somewhat higher scores on social desirability scales than do their younger counterparts (Campbell, Converse, and Rodgers, 1976; Gove and Gerrken, 1977). Thus it is possible that differences in concern with social desirability could account for some of the changes observed between the youngest and oldest age groups. However, the evidence indicates that there are only small differences in sensitivity to social desirability between adjacent age cohorts (e.g., 20–29 years versus 30–39 years) (Gove and Geerken, 1977). Thus, variations in sensitivity to this issue could not account for the substantial differences between adjacent age cohorts shown in Table 18.1

Explaining the Decline in Violence across the Life Course

Tables 18.2 and 18.3 present correlation matrices of the variables for both men and women in the 1975 and 1985 data sets. As anticipated, the correlations indicate that marital violence was related to marital conflict, verbal aggression, and both husbands' and wives' ages in both 1975 and 1985. In addition, the findings show that marital conflict and verbal aggression decline across the life course, as indicated by the negative correlations between these variables and both husbands' and wives' ages. Thus our assumptions both regarding the relationships among these variables are supported in both data sets. Husband's alcohol consumption was related to age and violence as expected in both husbands' and wives' reports according to the 1975 data. However, husband's alcohol consumption was not related to either violence or age in the expected manner according to the 1985 data.[3]

We examine next whether the relationship between age and marital

TABLE 18.2

Correlation Matrix, Means, and Standard Deviations, 1975 Data (N = 794 Men, 993 Women)[a,b]

	(1)	(2)	(3)	(4)	(5)	Means[c] Men	Women
1. Marital Violence	1.00	-.26**	.26**	.46**	.14**	.16 (.37)	.15 (.36)
2. Age	-.27**	1.00	-.16**	-.38**	-.25**	41.21 (12.61)	38.94 (12.61)
3. Marital Conflict	.24**	-.14**	1.00	.41**	.20**	8.85 (2.96)	8.50 (2.88)
4. Verbal Aggression	.40**	-.28**	.40**	1.00	.30**	2.16 (1.53)	2.31 (1.55)
5. Husband's Drinking	.21**	-.20**	.16**	.29**	1.00	1.44 (.50)	1.38 (.48)

[a] Data on men are presented in the upper half of the matrix; data on women are presented in the bottom half of the matrix.
[b] Fewer cases were used in this analysis than the analysis presented in Table 1. This is due to the smaller number of cases for which data were available on all of the variables.
[c] Standard deviations are presented in parentheses below the means.
*p < .05
**p < .01

TABLE 18.3

Correlation Matrix, Means, and Standard Deviations, 1985 Data (N = 1,750 Men, 2,285 Women)[a,b]

	(1)	(2)	(3)	(4)	(5)	Means[c] Men	Means[c] Women
1. Marital Violence	1.00	-.19**	.24**	.42**	.03	.16 (.36)	.15 (.36)
2. Age	-.21**	1.00	-.14**	-.25**	.03	41.16 (11.96)	40.16 (12.04)
3. Marital Conflict	.20**	-.04*	1.00	.42**	.03	8.28 (2.86)	8.37 (2.97)
4. Verbal Aggression	.38**	-.24**	.42**	1.00	.02	2.02 (1.40)	2.30 (1.41)
5. Husband's Drinking	-.04*	.01	-.03	-.02	1.00	1.47 (.75)	1.49 (.77)

[a] Data on men are presented in the upper half of the matrix; data on women are presented in the bottom half of the matrix.
[b] Fewer cases were used in this analysis than the analysis presented in Table 1. This is due to the smaller number of cases for which data were available on all of the variables.
[c] Standard deviations are presented in parentheses below the means.
*$p < .05$
**$p < .01$

violence can be explained by other factors that vary across the life course. The logit analyses presented in Tables 18.4 and 18.5 demonstrate that age continues to affect marital violence after taking into consideration the effects of marital conflict, husband's drinking, and verbal aggression. The analysis labeled "Step 1" in both tables shows the degree to which marital violence can be explained by marital conflict, husband's alcohol consumption, and verbal aggression. The analysis labeled "Step 2" repeats Step 1, adding age to the equation. This shows the degree to which violence can be explained by age after the effects of conflict, alcohol, and aggression have been taken into consideration. As can be seen in both tables, age was significantly related to marital violence, even after holding the effects of the other three variables constant. Thus it appears that the negative relationship between age and marital violence cannot be accounted for by a concomitant life course decline in marital conflict, husband's drinking, or verbal aggression.

Discussion and Conclusions

The findings presented in this chapter indicate that the observed decline in marital violence cannot be accounted for by either cohort effects or the parallel decline in three other social factors that are associated with both

TABLE 18.4

Logit Analysis of Marital Violence Reported by Husbands and Wives in 1975

	Husbands			
	Step 1		Step 2	
	Unstandardized Regression Coef.	Standard Error	Unstandardized Regression Coef.	Standard Error.
Marital Conflict	.097*	.041	.094*	.042
Husband's Alcohol Consumption	.105	.230	-.040	.237
Verbal Aggression	1.258**	.126	1.179**	.129
Age of Respondent			-.028**	.010
Log Likelihood	-248.182**		-242.663**	
N		794		

	Wives			
	Step 1		Step 2	
	Unstandardized Regression Coef.	Standard Error	Unstandardized Regression Coef.	Standard Error.
Marital Conflict	.073*	.036	.075*	.038
Husband's Alcohol Consumption	.640**	.205	.529**	.212
Verbal Aggression	.993**	.104	.931**	.108
Age of Respondent			-.058**	.011
Log Likelihood	-316.046**		-294.892**	
N		993		

*p<.05
**p<.01

domestic violence and age. Thus these findings suggest that there may be an independent effect of age on marital violence. However, it is important to consider alternative explanations.

In light of the dearth of information on this subject in the family violence literature, we have turned to the literature on age and crime to propose other explanations. Some of the frequently used explanations for the age/crime relationship cannot help to account for the life course decline in marital violence, since they are applicable to only the period during which adolescents move into early adulthood (e.g., the decline in "masculine status anxiety" following adolescence; new opportunities for increased prestige through attainment of adult statuses, such as marriage and employment). However, other explanations discussed in this literature might help to account for the age/marital violence relationship.

TABLE 18.5

Logit Analysis of Marital Violence Reported by Husbands and Wives in 1985

	Husbands			
	Step 1		Step 2	
	Unstandardized Regression Coef.	Standard Error	Unstandardized Regression Coef.	Standard Error
Marital Conflict	.084**	.027	.037**	.028
Husband's Alcohol Consumption	.041	.099	.050	.100
Verbal Aggression	1.029**	.078	.984**	.079
Age of Respondent			-.030**	.007
Log Likelihood	-560-123**		-550.583**	
N		1646		

	Wives			
	Step 1		Step 2	
	Unstandardized Regression Coef.	Standard Error	Unstandardized Regression Coef.	Standard Error
Marital Conflict	.050*	.021	.070**	.022
Husband's Alcohol Consumption	-.119	.085	-.119	.087
Verbal Aggression	1.004**	.066	.938**	.067
Age of Respondent			-.043**	.006
Log Likelihood	-814.448**		-788.105**	
N		2311		

*p<.05
**p<.01

First, criminologists both implicitly and explicitly suggest that variations in physical strength help to account for the relationship between age and violent criminal behavior (cf. Greenberg, 1977; Hirschi and Gottfredson, 1983; Rowe and Tittle, 1977). Thus we might expect that decreases in strength across the life course might account for the negative relationship between age and marital violence. However, an analysis presented elsewhere (Suitor and Pillemer, 1988) showed that individuals in better health—and therefore presumably stronger—where no more likely to engage in marital violence than were their less healthy counterparts; in fact, in some subgroups, less healthy individuals were *more* likely to be perpetrators of domestic violence (see Pillemer, 1985; Finkelhor and Pillemer, 1987; and Suitor and Pillemer, 1988, for discussions of the relationship between health, dependency, and violence). Thus it does not appear that the decline in physical strength from early to late adulthood can account for the decline in marital violence across the life course.

The criminology literature suggests two other related reasons for the decrease in violence across age groups that might help to explain the relationship between age and marital violence: (a) the greater cost of deviance; and (b) the greater "stake in conformity" (Hirschi and Gottfredson, 1983:557). These arguments suggest that as one moves from adolescence through early adulthood, not only do courts deal increasingly harshly with offenders, but greater informal pressure is brought to bear on individuals to conform. Perhaps pressure to conform to norms of nonviolence continues to increase across the life course, contributing to the observed decline in marital violence.

While we do not have direct measures of pressure to conform to norms of non-violence in the present data, we do have an indirect measure—attitudes toward marital violence held by individuals who do not themselves engage in such acts. All of the respondents were asked whether there were any situations in which they would approve of a husband slapping his wife's face and vice versa. An examination of these data showed no relationship between age and attitudes toward violence for either men or women (tables not presented). Thus the data do not demonstrate that older individuals receive more informal pressure from age-peers to conform to norms of non-violence in their marital relationships than do younger couples.

This is not to say that pressure to conform to norms is not important in explaining the decline in violence across the life course. It may be that age-related pressure for conformity to norms of non-violence in the family occurs as part of more general expectations that individuals demonstrate greater adherence to societal norms as part of the maturational process throughout the life course.

In sum, it appears that we cannot adequately explain the observed relationship between age and marital violence with the data currently available on this issue. It is possible that there is a direct relationship between age and marital violence that can only be explained by biological changes that take place across the life course. We are inclined to think, however, that biological aging does not account for the decrease in marital violence—that instead, the age/marital violence relationship can be explained by intervening variables that have not yet been investigated. We hope that the findings presented here will encourage other researchers to undertake further investigations of this issue.

The explanation for the age/violence relationship will have not only important theoretical implications for family violence research, but may provide information that can be used to develop policies that will help reduce the incidence of this phenomenon. If we can discover precisely what it is about age that reduces individuals' likelihood of engaging in violence, it may become possible to use this information to reduce violence in younger age groups.

Notes

1. The concept of "life course" should not be confused with the concept of "family life-cycle." *Family life-cycle* is used to refer to different stages in the family career (e.g., early childrearing years; postparental years, etc.), whereas life course is generally used to refer to movement across the life-span, regardless of the particular family life-cycle stage currently occupied. Separate analyses of the data used in this paper showed that any effects of family life-cycle stage disappeared when controlling on place in the life course (as measured by age).

2. The only notable difference remaining between first-marrieds and remarrieds after controlling for age is in the category of men ages 18 to 29, using the 1976 data. In this subgroup, 31.7% of men in first marriages reported having experienced violence within the past year, while 48.3% of men who were remarried reported experiencing violence.

3. It is interesting to note that the findings regarding the effects of husband's alcohol consumption on marital violence in the 1985 Resurvey differ from those reported in Chapter 12. There are two possible explanations for this inconsistency. First, Kantor and Straus analyzed only husband-to-wife violence, as opposed to any violence occurring between partners. Second, husband's alcohol consumption was measured differently in the analyses for the two chapters. Kantor and Straus's measure combined the frequency of husband's drinking (as opposed to drunkenness) and the number of drinks consumed per day. In contrast, the measure in the present analysis included only the frequency of husband's drunkenness. The decision to employ this measure was to allow comparability across the 1975 and 1985 data sets.

Part V
VIOLENCE AND THE STRUCTURE OF SOCIETY

19

Race, Class, Network Embeddedness, and Family Violence: A Search for Potent Support Systems

Noel A. Cazenave and Murray A. Straus

There is a growing body of literature which suggests that social isolation is a crucial factor associated with severe forms of family violence. In fact, Garbarino (1977) concludes that social isolation is the most important necessary condition for child maltreatment to occur.

Most of these assertions, however, are based on case studies of abusing families. Professionals who work with severe cases of family violence report that many such families are isolated from social contacts who can provide advice and assistance in child rearing and dealing with marital problems, and who can intervene when things get out of hand. However, that is also true of a great many other American families. Although there is much speculation, one does not know from the research published to date if families in which child and spousal abuse occur are any more isolated from a network of a socially supportive community and kin than other families. The data to be reported in this paper should make an important contribution toward answering that question.

At a more practical level we are concerned with the identification of social networks which reduce the level of family violence. If the involvement of a family in potent "support systems" (Caplan, 1974) does reduce family violence, this has important implications for social workers and social policymakers alike.

Race, Class, and Violence

Race and Family Violence

Straus, Gelles, and Steinmetz (1979a) caution that ". . . simply present-ing rates of violence by race could be misleading." They suggest that race differences may be due to income level and employment status, as well as differences in cultural expectations and values concerning violence. A review of the literature on family violence and race under-scores the need for caution.

Most of the existing studies of family violence have dealt with child-abuse, and while some have suggested that Blacks as compared to Whites have higher rates of child-abuse (Gil, 1970), others have found that Blacks have lower rates (Billingsley, 1969; Griswald and Billingsley, 1967), others report no noteworthy differences (Young, 1963), and still others have suggested that some types of family violence are higher for whites and others are higher for Blacks (Straus, Gelles and Steinmetz, 1979a). Straus, *et al,* (1979a) in the 1975 survey report that the rates of Black spousal violence are much higher than it is for other racial and ethnic groups. More specifically they found that wife abuse is twice as high for Black respondents as compared to other racial minorities and 400% higher than the rate for White men. It was also found that the rate of husband abuse was twice as high for Black women as compared to women from other racial and ethnic groups. Staples (1976b) also concludes that marital violence rates are generally higher for Blacks than for Whites. Staples suggests that this is especially true for the Black lower classes. However, there is still insufficient evidence and agreement on the frequency of spousal violence by race, and no adequate causal or explanatory models delineating why such differences exist, if in fact they do. What does this all mean? It suggests that more empirical data are needed before social scientists can make any firm conclusions regarding how family violence is related to race or ethnicity.

Social Class and Family Violence

Generally speaking there tends to be a close relationship between the access that a particular group has to societal resources and the degree and types of problems encountered by its membership. For example, in refer-ence to child-abuse, Gil (1970) found higher rates among parents of low income, low educational attainment, and among those who experienced high rates of unemployment and dependence upon public assistance.

Although Young (1963; 1964), like Gil and others (e.g., Justice and

Justice, 1976), found that the "reported" cases of child abuse were more likely to involve families of the lower class and Levinger (1974) found that lower class divorce applicants were more likely to give physical abuse as legal grounds for divorce, she cautions that there are reporting biases which enable much middle class family violence to go undetected.

Given these and other methodological problems it is easy to lose sight of the fact that violent behavior cuts across all class boundaries. In reference to what they refer to as "the class myth," Steinmetz and Straus (1974) caution that family violence is not limited to the lower classes. However they conclude from their overview of the literature that while family violence is not limited to any one particular social class or group, the lower strata of American society seem (overall) to be more vulnerable to family violence than those who are better off.

Social Networks

According to Fischer (1977:17) a society can be thought of as "a mesh of social networks" and consequently, ". . . to understand the individual in society, we need to understand the fine mesh of social relations between the person and society . . ." Bert Adams (1975) states that perhaps the most important social networks integrating the individual into society are his family-kin networks. Along with neighborhood ties these networks constitute the primary focus of this paper.

Race and Social Networks

There is a continuing debate about the extent to which American nuclear families are "isolated" from their kin (Sussman, 1959). There is also an increasing amount of evidence which shows that the amount of isolation differs by social class, residence, and race (Straus, 1969). In a study of 25 Black and White families Hays and Mendel (1972:11) found that "Black families interacted with extended kin more and perceived them as more significant." They suggested that the Black extended family-kin system was an important support system which served as a buffer from a racially hostile environment. Shimkin, Louie, and Frate (1973) studied a large Black extended family system in the South and found that one of its unique functions is the prevention of child abuse and neglect among the Black lower-classes. Like Hays and Mendel (1972), Shimkin, Louie, and Frate (1973), Stack (1974), Aschenbrenner (1973, 1975), Hill and Shackleford (1978), and Jack (1979) all see the Black extended family-kin system as an important support system for the Black family.

Class and Social Networks

The tendency for Blacks and other ethnic groups (Gans, 1962) to place a heavy emphasis on extended family and kin ties must be accounted for by class as well as ethnic and other cultural characteristics. In fact, Bert Adams (1971:173) concluded that

> In general, research of the 60's has found the working classes to express a stronger kin orientation, live closer to their kin and interact with them more regularly than the middle classes.

One explanation for these differences is suggested by Fischer (1977) who found that members of the higher social classes placed heavier emphasis on occupational as opposed to kin based networks and that their residential mobility reduced both the extent and quality of their involvement in family-kin networks.

In brief, because of ethnic and class considerations we might expect the extended family-kin network to be operative as a support system against family violence for the Black respondents and their families. In fact, McAdoo (1978) found the extended family network to be an important source of social support for Blacks at all socio-economic levels.

Methodology

Data for this analysis are from the 1975 national survey. The data on parent to child violence are based on the 1,146 respondents who had children between the ages of 3 and 17 living at home. The subsample used in the present analysis consisted of the 147 (N = 75 for parents) Black respondents interviewed in the nationwide survey and a randomly selected sub-sample of 427 (N = 232 for parents) white respondents, for a total of 574 respondents.[1]

Measures of Violence

Data were obtained on both normative and behavioral aspects of violence. The normative aspect was measured by "semantic differential" ratings (Osgood, Succi, and Tannenbaum, 1957). The concepts rated were "Slapping or spanking a 12 year old" and "Couples slapping each other." Each of these was rated on three scales of 1 to 7: unnecessary-necessary, not normal-normal, and bad-good. These three ratings were combined to form a Violence Approval Index for parent to child violence and for spousal violence. The Conflict Tactics Scales was used to obtain data on parent to child, sibling, and spousal violence.

Findings

Child Abuse

As Table 19.1 indicates, Black and White respondents are very similar in rates of approval of slapping or spanking a twelve year old. However, Blacks are *less* likely to report having actually slapped or spanked a child within the last year. Black and White respondents report nearly the same rate of severe parental violence against children.

TABLE 19.1
Family Violence Norms and Behavior by Race

Family Violence Norm or Behavior	Race		Percent Diff.*a*
	White	Black	
A. *Parent-Child Violence*			
Approval of Slapping or Spanking a 12 Year Old	81% (407)	83% (137)	2
Parent Slapped or Spanked Child in Last Year	59% (232)	51% (75)	—8
Child-Abuse in Last Year	14% (228)	15% (74)	1
B. *Sibling Abuse in Last Year*	46% (187)	41% (59)	—5
C. *Parent Abuse in Last Year*	11% (220)	3% (69)	—8
D. *Spousal Violence*			
Approval of Couple Slapping	27% (413)	39% (137)	12b
Husband Slapped Wife Last Year	5% (420)	12% (144)	7c
Wife Slapped Husband Last Year	3% (418)	6% (145)	3
Wife-Beating in Last Year	3% (415)	11% (142)	8d
Husband-Beating in Last Year	4% (414)	8% (144)	4

a + Black is greater,—white is greater
b Chi square=6.81, 1 d.f., p ≤ .01
c Chi square=8.34, 1 d.f., p ≤ .01
d Chi square=11.44, 1 d.f., p ≤ .001

Sibling Abuse and Parent Abuse

Blacks are *less* likely to report the occurrence of either sibling abuse or parent abuse within the last year than are white parents.

Spousal violence.   Black respondents express more approval of couple slapping then White respondents and Black husbands are also more likely to have actually slapped their wives and engaged in severe violence against them within the last year. Although the rates are relatively low for both races, the rates for Black husbands are three times greater than the rates for White respondents. Black wives are only slightly more likely to have slapped their husbands within the last year than White wives but are twice as likely to have engaged in severe violence against husbands.

Racial Differences When Income and Husband's Occupation Are Controlled

Figures 19.1 and 19.2 show that Black-White income differences appear to be a major factor contributing to the Black-White differences in family violence norms and behavior. This is dramatically demonstrated when we look at the differences between Black and White respondents within the same family income range.

Blacks in the two highest income groups are *less* likely than whites at these income levels to report having engaged in child abuse within the last year.

A similar trend exists for sibling violence. At every income level above poverty Blacks are *less* likely to report the occurrence of sibling violence within the last year than is the case for whites. Finally, Blacks are much *less* likely to report the occurrence of parent abuse at all income levels.

Figure 19.2 shows that when income is controlled, Black respondents are *less* likely to have slapped their spouses within the last year in all income groups except $6–11,999. However, it must be noted that the $6–11,999 range is the largest income group for Blacks, with 40% of these respondents. In addition to higher family income the labor force participation of women may have an effect on the relative status of women in the home and how they are treated. Our data support this view in that 84% (31) of the Black women and 31% (136) of the white women in the $12–19,999 income range are employed and wife slapping is less common among these middle-income Black women than their white counterparts. This is consistent with the resource theory explanation of family violence. That is, women with more resources (e.g., power and alternatives to leave) are less compelled to tolerate abuse from their husbands. Black and white

FIGURE 19.1

Severe Family Violence by Race and Income

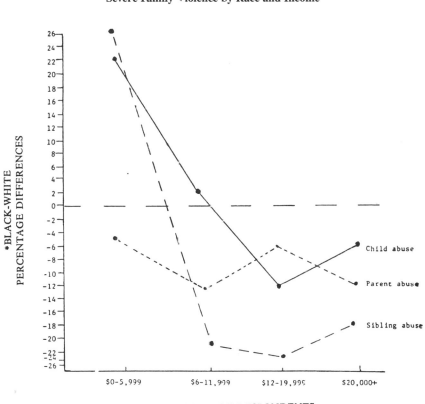

FAMILY INCOME OF RESPONDENTS

* +Black is greater
— White is greater

respondents also have similar rates of severe spousal violence except at
the $6–11,999 income level where the rates are notably higher for Blacks.

A control for the occupational class of the husband is shown in Table
19.2. The husband's occupational class is more highly associated with the
occurrence of child abuse, sibling abuse, and parent abuse for Black
respondents than it is for white respondents. In fact, when we control for
class, white collar Blacks are *less* likely to have slapped or spanked their
children or engaged in any of these forms of severe family violence than
their white counterparts.

However, higher Black rates of hitting a spouse occur within both

FIGURE 19.2

Spousal Violence by Race and Income

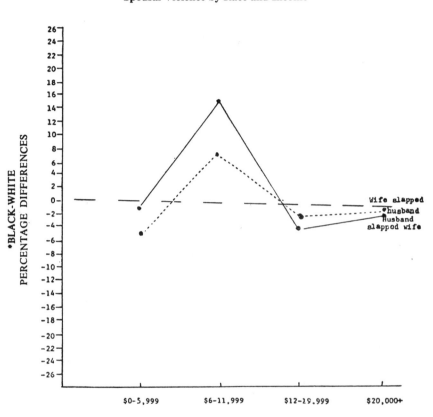

FAMILY INCOME OF RESPONDENTS

* +Black is greater
  —White is greater

occupational class groups. A similar trend is notable in respect to Black rates of severe spousal violence, with the exception that the Black-White differences in severe wife-to-husband violence disappear for white collar respondents. For simplicity and clarity, the remaining analysis of spousal violence will focus exclusively on husbands slapping wives and wives slapping husbands within the last year. Parent to child violence will be limited to severe parental violence, that is, child abuse.

FIGURE 19.3

White Spousal Violence by the Number of Non-Nuclear Family Adults A in the Home

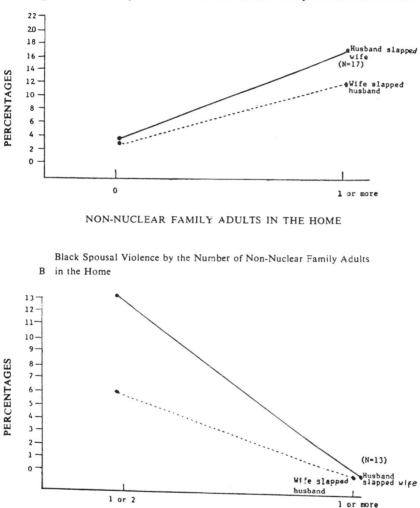

NON-NUCLEAR FAMILY ADULTS IN THE HOME

Black Spousal Violence by the Number of Non-Nuclear Family Adults
B   in the Home

NON-NUCLEAR FAMILY ADULTS IN THE HOME

TABLE 19.2

Racial Differences in Family Violence, Controlling for Occupational Class of Husband

Aspect of Family Violence	Occupational Class of Husband	Race White	Race Black	Percent Diff.ᵃ
A. *Parent-Child Violence*				
Slapped or Spanked Child	Blue-Collar	59% (118)	54% (56)	− 5
	White-Collar	59% (110)	40% (15)	−19
Child Abuse	Blue-Collar	15% (117)	18% (55)	+ 3
	White-Collar	12% (107)	7% (15)	− 5
B. *Sibling Abuse in Last Year*	Blue-Collar	43% (94)	44% (48)	1
	White-Collar	51% (90)	25% (8)	−26
C. *Parent Abuse in Last Year*	Blue-Collar	10% (108)	4% (51)	− 6
	White-Collar	12% (108)	0% (14)	−12
D. *Spousal Violence*				
Husband Slapped Wife	Blue-Collar	6% (206)	14% (108)	+ 8ᵇ
	White-Collar	3% (199)	7% (29)	+ 4
Severe Husband-to-Wife Violence	Blue-Collar	4% (205)	13% (107)	+ 9ᶜ
	White-Collar	3% (195)	7% (28)	+ 4
Wife Slapped Husband	Blue-Collar	4% (204)	6% (108)	+ 2
	White-Collar	3% (199)	7% (30)	+ 4
Severe Wife-to-Husband Violence	Blue-Collar	4% (203)	9% (108)	+ 5
	White-Collar	3% (196)	3% (29)	0

ᵃ+ Black is greater, − white is greater
ᵇChi square=4.12, 1 d.f., p≤.05
ᶜChi square=6.56, 1 d.f.. p≤.02.

Race and Network Embeddedness

Race Comparisons

The five indicators of network embeddedness used in this study are the number of years in the neighborhood, the number of non-nuclear family adults living in the home, the number of husband's relatives living within one hour's travel time, the number of wife's relatives living within one hour's distance, and the total number of children. These indexes measure only the structural aspects of these networks and not interactional aspects like intensity, types, and quality of interactions.[3]

The major areas of differences by race are in the number of non-nuclear family adults in the home and the total number of children. Nine percent (N = 147) of the Black respondents have non-nuclear family adults residing in their homes compared to 4% (N = 427) for white respondents. Thirty percent of the Black respondents have five or more children compared to 12% for white respondents.

Another interesting finding is that fewer Black respondents do not have relatives living within one hour's distance: 28% of the white husbands compared to 21% for the Black husbands. Similarly, 25% of the white wives have no relatives living within one hour compared to 18% of Black wives. Also consistent with this finding is the fact that Black respondents show more neighborhood stability: 26% of the white families lived in their neighborhoods for two or fewer years compared to 17% of Black families.

Family-Kin Embeddedness as a Support System for Violence Control

Table 19.3 shows that the number of years lived in the neighborhood and number of children are the most important social network variables associated with low parent-child and spousal violence. The relationship between network embeddedness and family violence is consistent with observations and research based on clinical populations (e.g., Young, 1963; Newberger and Hyde, 1975) that suggest that families where severe child and/or spousal-abuse takes place are often cut off physically (e.g., with unlisted or no telephones, closed blinds and shutters, and no transportation) and socially (e.g. no organizational memberships or neighborhood ties) from normal social interaction.

The finding on number of children is surprising in that much of the literature dealing with child-abuse (Gil, 1970; Young, 1963, 1964) report that, among the lower classes at least, families with a large number of children tend to have higher rates of family violence. However, Morse, et al. (1977) found that one of the defining characteristics of child-abuse is

TABLE 19.3

Family Violence by Race and Social Networks

			Spousal Violence[b]			
Social Network Variable	Child Abuse[a]		Husband Slapped Wife		Wife Slapped Husband	
	White	Black	White	Black	White	Black
Years in Neighborhood						
0—2	20% (60)	38% (8)	6% (110)	32% (25)	7% (110)	20% (25)
3—9	17% (78)	20% (30)	4% (116)	9% (44)	1% (116)	4% (44)
10—19	6% (49)	6% (16)	3% (86)	9% (32)	2% (13)	0% (33)
20+	8% (30)	5% (20)	4% (107)	5% (43)	3% (108)	2% (43)
Non-Nuclear Adults						
None	14% (221)	13% (70)	4% (403)	13% (131)	3% (401)	6% (132)
1 or more	0% (7)	50% (4)	18% (17)	0% (13)	12% (17)	0% (13)
Husband's Relatives One Hour Away						
None	13% (62)	35% (17)	2% (11)8	16% (31)	2% (118)	6% (31)
1 or 2	13% (46)	5% (20)	5% (91)	14% (35)	6% (90)	6% (35)
3—5	12% (50)	11% (19)	7% (91)	7% (40)	1% (90)	2% (40)
6 or more	16% (70)	11% (18)	5% (120)	10% (38)	5% (120)	8% (39)
Wife's Relatives One Hour Away						
None	13% (62)	20% (10)	2% (106)	11% (26)	3% (106)	11% (26)
1 or 2	11% (44)	11% (19)	2% (96)	17% (36)	2% (95)	6% (36)
3—5	20% (60)	18% (22)	5% (97)	4% (44)	2% (98)	0% (44)
6 or more	10% (62)	13% (23)	8% (121)	16% (38)	6% (119)	8% (39)
Children						
None	— —	— —	6% (53)	16% (19)	7% (53)	10% (19)
1 or 2	17% (84)	19% (32)	4% (177)	15% (58)	3% (176)	9% (58)
3 or 4	13% (108)	13% (16)	6% (140)	4% (25)	3% (139)	0% (25)
5 or more	8% (36)	12% (25)	0% (50)	9% (42)	0% (50)	2% (43)

[a]The number of times respondents reported participation in any of the four most severe categories of parent-child violent behavior within the last year.

[b]The number of times respondents reported that the husband slapped the wife or the wife slapped the husband within the last year.

few children. This finding is further supported by our data which show that sibling violence also decreases sharply for those respondents with 5 or more children (i.e., from 48% Ns = 63 and 92 respectively) for whites with 1 or 2 children compared to 37% (N = 32) for Whites with 5 or more children. This effect is even more dramatic for Black parents (i.e., a drop from 50% (Ns = 20 and 14 respectively) for those with 1 or 2 and 3 or 4 children to 28% (N = 25) for those with five or more children. This suggests the possibility that the number of children living in the home may serve as a social support system against family violence, or at a minimum, more children may reduce much of the privacy and isolation associated with severe abuse. It is also possible that more children facilitate a greater degree of family-kin interaction and may provide more help in child care both inside and outside of the home. Both may serve as additional family violence controls.

Race, Networks, and Family Violence

Child abuse.   The number of years in the neighborhood and the total number of children are the network variables most closely associated with low rates of severe parent to child violence for both Black and White parents. The presence of a non-nuclear adult seems to be associated with lower levels of child abuse for White respondents, but the small N's here make this finding undependable. For Black parents, there is a definite difference in child abuse between those who do and those who do not have relatives living nearby. The highest rates of child abuse occur among Black parents whose husbands have no relatives (35%) or wives have no relatives (20%) living within one hour away. This type of social isolation appears to have adverse consequences for these Black respondents.

Spousal violence.   The only social network associated with lower white spousal violence (i.e., husband and/or wife slapping) is the total number of children. For example Table 19.3 shows that 7% of the White respondents with no children, compared to none for those with five or more children report that the wife slapped the husband within the last year. In addition to the explanation given earlier (i.e., of less isolation and more kin interaction), respondents with more children may place less emphasis and demands on the marital relationship because of the needs of the total family system.

Control for Confounding with Age

Age is, in and of itself, very closely associated with family violence rates. For example, for our total sample, child abuse drops from 25% for those 18 to 29 years of age (N = 59) to none for those 55 and older (N = 14). Whereas 14% of the husbands (N = 140) and 11% (N = 139) of the wives 18 to 29 years old slapped their spouse, 2% and none, respectively, of those 55 and older (N's = 105 in both cases) engaged in such acts.

To control for the confounding with age, we divided the respondents into two age groups (18 to 44, and 45+) and into two groups by the number of years they have lived in the neighborhood (0–9 years, and 10+ years).

Child abuse.   As Table 19.4 indicates, for both races the "high risk" group in terms of high rates of severe child abuse is the low age (18 to 44) and low number of years (0–9 years) in the neighborhood group. *Even when age is controlled, however, the number of years lived in the neighborhood is associated with lower rates of child abuse, especially for Black respondents.*

The number of children appears to have less of an effect overall within the same age group. Again the greatest impact seems to be for Black parents.

Spousal violence.   Embeddedness in primary networks appears to be more closely associated with low spousal slapping for Black couples than for White couples. For Black couples the total number of years in the neighborhood, the number of children, and the number of non-nuclear family members are all associated with low levels of spousal slapping. Whereas for White respondents, controlling for age completely eliminates the effect of number of years in the neighborhood on spousal slapping, for Black respondents there appears to be an additive relationship between those two variables.

However, although number of children does have an effect for Black couples independent of age, age seems to be a better predictor of low levels of husband-to-wife slapping for White couples than the total number of children. For wife-to-husband slapping the number of children does have some effect independent of age, especially for Black respondents. In summary, controlling for age leads to the conclusion that none of the social networks analyzed in the present study have much of an ameliorative effect on *White* spousal slapping.

The most dramatic Black-White difference, however, is in the association between the number of non-nuclear family adults present in the home and spousal violence (See Table 19.4). This difference is therefore worth considering, even though the number of cases is too small to be statistically significant. For white respondents the presence of nonnuclear family adults is associated with a substantial *increase* in spousal slapping. On the other hand, for the Black respondents, having non-nuclear family members in the home is associated with a dramatic *decrease* in this type of spousal violence. White non-nuclear family members tend to be grandparents

TABLE 19.4

Family Violence by Race by Selected Networks by Age

		White		Black	
		18—44	45+	18—44	45+
A.	*Child Abuse*				
	Years in Neighborhood				
	0—9	21% (117)	5% (21)	28% (29)	13% (8)
	10+	12% (43)	2% (46)	5% (22)	7% (14)
	Number of Children				
	0—2	20% (71)	0% (17)	20% (30)	0% (2)
	3+	17% (90)	4% (54)	14% (21)	10% (20)
B.	*Husband Slapped Wife*				
	Years in Neighborhood				
	0—9	7% (76)	0% (49)	20% (49)	11% (19)
	10+	9% (66)	1% (127)	11% (27)	4% (48)
	Number of Children				
	0—2	6% (154)	1% (82)	19% (52)	8% (25)
	3+	8% (95)	0% (94)	13% (24)	5% (42)
C.	*Wife Slapped Husband*				
	Years in Neighborhood				
	0—9	5% (175)	0% (50)	12% (49)	5% (19)
	10+	6% (64)	1% (127)	4% (27)	0% (49)
	Number of Children				
	0—2	7% (147)	0% (82)	12% (52)	4% (25)
	3+	3% (93)	1% (95)	4% (24)	0% (43)

compared to a wider variety of kin for Blacks. This is consistent with the findings of Hays and Mindel (1972) and suggests more kin involvement on the part of these Black respondents as compared to their more nuclear family orientated white counterparts.

Summary and Conclusions

Although Black respondents are more likely to approve of family violence and to report that they actually slapped a spouse within the last year, when class and social network embeddedness are controlled, most of these differences disappear. In fact, in many cases, after controlling for class-related variables like income and husband's occupation, Black respondents are *less* violent than their White counterparts.

Overall Black respondents are *less* likely to report slapping or spanking a child within the last year. This is directly contrary to much of the literature which suggest that Blacks, as compared to Whites, are more likely to condone and use physical punishment of children. When income and husband's occupation are controlled, Blacks are also *less* likely to engage in child abuse, sibling abuse, and parent abuse at the higher income levels than is the case for their white counterparts. These findings are consistent with the idea that there may exist unique Black values and child-rearing norms and practices (Aschenbrenner, 1975; Herkovits, 1958; Shimkin, Louie, and Frate, 1973; Staples, 1976a). It is possible that such cultural mechanisms work best when the effects of poverty and low income are overcome. And as we shall discuss later the key here may be in the nature of different social relationships rather than simply the independent effect of the attitudinal components of culture.

When income is controlled, Black respondents are *less* likely to report instances of spousal slapping at every income range except the $6–11,999 level. Black respondents at the lowest and higher income levels are *less* likely to report engaging in such behavior than their white counterparts.

The persistence of higher rates of spousal violence for the large income group containing the Black working class, and for Blacks in both occupational groups, suggests that even aside from income differentials Black spousal violence is notably high. There may be some effects of racial oppression which are independent of income and which may cause marital stress and tensions that may erupt in violence. Also, as mentioned previously such behavior may be more normatively accepted among certain segments of Blacks. Some researchers would simply attribute such findings to what they refer to as a "culture of violence" (Wolfgang and Ferracuti, 1967; Hepburn, 1971; Curtis, 1975). They would assume that violent attitudes lead to violent behavior when, in fact, it is just as plausible to suggest that persons who because of social structural (e.g., discrimination and under-employment) or situational conditions (e.g., lack of adequate privacy and/or the carry home effects of social deprivations and extra-familial indignities) may find it necessary to justify their violent behavior in the home by reporting that such behavior is necessary or normal. In this case the social structure may have effected violent family behavior which in turn may lead to violent attitudes rather than violent cultural attitudes *causing* violent behavior.

If we were simply to assume a simple direct causal relationship between attitudes and behavior, we would explain the low rates of reported corporal punishment, sibling violence, and parent abuse for our Black respondents by a "culture of nonviolence." Such an analysis would obviously be overly simplistic considering that Black respondents are no less likely to approve of the use of corporal punishment than are white respondent parents. In brief, although we cannot resolve this issue in any definitive fashion in the present analysis, our findings do suggest the possibility of a more complex interactive process between social relationships, behavior, and attitudes, than is generally acknowledged to be the case.

Robert Staples (1976b) states that since Blacks are not inherently more violent than whites, and in other countries may be less violent than either Black or White Americans, the explanation for high rates of Black family violence (where they do exist) must lie in the particular social predicament in which Blacks find themselves in American society.

The subjugation of Blacks then can take many forms, some involving economic exploitation, and others where racism and its consequences are manifested in other ways, regardless of income. Much of the Black family violence in this country may simply be a reflection of the internalization and amplification of systemic violitions (violence) against Blacks in American society-at-large.

The data presented in this paper suggest that there are also family, kin, and neighborhood networks which may serve as social support systems and family violence control mechanisms. Social network embeddedness is closely related to fewer instances of family violence for both Black and White respondents. Although network embeddedness is related to both attitudes and behavior, it appears to have its clearest impact on behavior, per se. This suggests that social network embeddedness has some independent effect on violence control aside from the institutionalization of family violence norms.

There is much more consistency in the relation of social networks to spousal than to parent-child violence norms and behavior. Norms toward traditional corporal discipline of children may create an ideology supportive of discipline at the same time that network involvements act to reduce parent-child violence and abuse. This may be particularly true among working class families categorized by "close knit" social networks and traditional familial roles (Bott, 1971).

One hypothesis implicit in the literature on the Black extended family is that family-kin-neighborhood social networks are particularly salient for Black Americans and serve as potent support systems and buffers against the socio-economic forces which might cause a variety of pathological disorders in more isolated nuclear families. Overall, the Black respondents in this study appear to be more embedded in family-kin networks than their white counterparts, and these networks appear to be more operative in reducing family violence as compared to whites at similar socio-economic levels.[4] This is especially true for the reduction of spousal violence.

In brief, the relatively high degree of embeddedness of Blacks and other minority group peoples in primary social networks may serve as buffers against the even higher rates of family violence which might ordinarily be expected of persons in their social predicament. Such networks seem to offer some ameliorative relief while the ultimate solution—the elimination of social inequality—is being addressed.

Notes

1. A subsample of white respondents was used (1) because of complications and costs involved in working with the entire sample on the computer which was available, (2) because a sample of 427 whites is large enough for any differences to be worth commenting on to be statistically significant, and (3) because the N of 147 Black couples imposed a limit on the number of variables which could be included in a cross tabulation, irrespective of the size of the white sample.

   To check on the representativeness of the white subsample, it was compared with the full sample of whites, and no important differences were found. For example, percent with no relatives of the husband living within an hour's travel time: 25.5% for the full sample and 27.6% for the sample: percent with no relatives of the wife living within an hour's distance: 24.5% versus 25.1%: percent of respondents who reported slapping a child in the past year: 58.4% versus 59.1%: percent of husbands who reported slapping their wife in the past year: 4.3% versus 4.5%: percent of wives who reported slapping their husband in the past year: 4.3% versus 3.3%.

2. The Conflict Resolution Technique (CRT) operationalizes violence into 18 items in reference to how respondents resolved intrafamily conflict within the last year. Items range from discussing the issue calmly, to verbal insults, to the actual using of various gradients of physical force. The indexes of severe violence consisted of those five items judged to be most severe in terms of the possible injury they could inflict on their victims.

3. The authors recognize the limitations involved in using only structural measures of network embeddedness, but it is felt that while they are limited they do provide useful data which may have important implications for future research. In addition to focusing on structural variables, future research should stress the interactive and more dynamic aspects of primary networks. Variables like the intensity, nature, quality, and meaning of relationships should be important in further delineating differential rates and outcomes of family violence.

4. Social network embeddedness implies a high degree of social and geographical stability: The rates of family violence (especially marital violence) were particularly high for young, low income, Blacks who constituted a particularly "high risk" group. In addition to the advantages of income; middle-class, residentially mobile individuals generally have greater access to more open-ended and diverse networks to help them obtain professional and other types of help as needed. It

is at least possible that given the present opportunity structure for young low-income Blacks that geographical mobility, combined with the American values of upward mobility, materialism, competition, and individualism may have a deleterious effect on family violence rates.

20

Violence in Hispanic Families in the United States: Incidence Rates and Structural Interpretations

Murray A. Straus and Christine Smith

The purpose of this chapter is to (1) provide a more accurate national estimate of the incidence of violence among Hispanic families; (2) examine the incidence of family violence through an ecological perspective, taking into account the many demographic characteristics of Hispanic families that may explain the violence occurring within them; and (3) explore the dynamics of learning violence within Hispanic families.

The Perils and Potential of a Study of Violence in Hispanic Families

The findings presented have the potential for greatly increasing our understanding of the extent and causes of physical violence in Hispanic families because they have several important assets. First, they use a relatively large and representative sample from the 1985 Resurvey of families who identify themselves as Hispanic (N = 711). Second, they contain unique data on physical abuse of children and of spouses as measured by the Conflict Tactics Scales (CTS). Third, a considerable amount of demographic information is also available about these families, including region and urbanicity of residence, age, employment status, socioeconomic status, and household composition. Nevertheless, this chapter is presented with some trepidation and caution, because of specific limitations of the 1985 survey and because of the controversial nature of the topic.

The first specific limitation in using this data to study Hispanic families is its lack of a measure of national origin. The validity of combining the diversity of peoples identified in the census as "Hispanic" into a single ethnic category is questionable at best (Moore and Pachon, 1985). Second, although Chapters 3 and 4 demonstrate that the CTS is a reliable and valid instrument, the validity of this measure for use with Hispanic families is not known. Further grounds for caution are found in the data collection methods of the 1985 survey. The interviews were conducted only in English and by telephone. This obviously excludes a distinct segment of the Hispanic community, the monolingual Spanish-speaking population, as well as the more transient migrant workers who are less likely to have telephones.

Finally, we have misgivings about presenting this study because of the inevitable controversy that will arise from the high rate of violence in Hispanic families reported here. These findings are likely to be used by bigoted and prejudiced persons for their own ends. We hope to avert such reactions by studying Hispanic families in their social-structural context in order to discern the underlying causes of the violence occurring within them. Despite the perils of presenting such findings, we believe policymakers and Hispanic leaders need to know the extent of the problem as a first step in the process of reducing the level of family violence within the Hispanic community.

Hispanic Family Research and Its Critics

Previous sociological depictions of Hispanic families have been met with ardent criticism in the past fifteen years by many Hispanic scholars (Baca Zinn, 1979; Mirande, 1977 and 1979; Montiel, 1973; Romano, 1973; Staples and Mirande, 1980). Critics of this literature point to two prominent features in the "traditional" sociological view of the Hispanic family: close-knit kin networks and the so-called "cult of machismo." Baca Zinn calls this social science perspective ethnocentric, claiming that sociology has a long-standing preoccupation with (and bias in favor of) the "modern" family (1979:64). This ideal type from the dominant American culture includes an autonomous "nuclear" family unit with an egalitarian power structure between husband and wife (Reiss, 1980:19–20). In comparing Hispanic families to this Anglo standard, social science has portrayed them as "pathological." Mexican-American cultural values of family ties and masculinity are said to impede Hispanics' individual success and personality development and to propagate women's dependence and subordination (see Mirande, 1977, for a summary of this literature). Based on the established relationship of male dominance to family violence (Chapter

16; Dobash and Dobash, 1979; Star et al., 1979; Straus, 1973), the theorized high level of male dominance among Hispanic couples is also expected to lead to high levels of family violence (Carroll, 1980).

Mirande (1977) calls these social scientific depictions "pejorative," pointing to the lack of empirical support for the claimed preeminence of the macho patriarch in Hispanic family life. Indeed, many contemporary empirical investigations find that Hispanic families are less rigid and male-dominant than traditional sociological works once proposed. With regard to sex-typed household labor, Grebler et al. (1970) found a "conspicuous presence of a basically *egalitarian* division of household tasks" (1970:362–363) in a Los Angeles sample of Mexican-American couples. In a comparison of Anglo, Black, and Hispanic couples, Cromwell and Cromwell found egalitarian decision making to be the norm across all three ethnic groups as perceived by both husband and wife (1978:755). Hawkes and Taylor (1975) also found shared marital power structures, both in terms of decision making and action taking, in most of the Mexican and Mexican-American couples they surveyed. While Ybarra (1982) reports similar findings among a majority of her sample of one hundred Mexican-American couples, she further finds that an egalitarian role structure is most likely when the wife works outside the home.

The Ecological Model of Family Violence

If male dominance is not the norm in Hispanic families, what else might predict the occurrence of family violence within them? Another perspective, termed *the ecological approach,* stresses the importance of viewing the family as but one in "an interactive set of systems" (Garbarino, 1977:722). Baca Zinn argues that Hispanic family systems can be best understood in view of the *structural conditions* with which they must cope rather than in terms of *cultural values* (1979:67). This is consistent with much family violence research that has found that family violence is influenced by such structural factors as husband's and wife's employment status and income and educational levels (Chapters 8, 15, 17, 19, and 21 of this book; Allen and Straus, 1980; Blood and Wolfe, 1960; Brown, 1980; Smith, 1988). If these factors influence family dynamics in general, Baca Zinn argues, why not also Hispanic families in particular?

Garbarino and Ebata (1983) review the evidence on ethnic differences in rates of child maltreatment, concluding that "almost none of the existing data present ethnic and cultural groups unconfounded by class" (1983:774). They warn that to confound ethnicity with social class is to risk confusing actual cultural differences with the harmful effects of socioeconomic deprivation. In their "ecological approach," social stress is one sufficient condition for child abuse. In addition, two necessary conditions are identified: cultural legitimation of violence against children and isolation from buffering support systems (Garbarino, 1977).

This approach is in substantial agreement with other studies on family violence reported in this volume (see Chapter 11 on social stress, chapters 8 and 28 on legitimation of violence, and Chapter 19 on social networks). Its relevance to the study of violence in Hispanic families lies in the fact that Hispanic families have substantially lower income levels on average than non-Hispanic White families (Staples and Mirande, 1980). As an ethnic minority, they may also have less access to external social supports such as welfare or other human services (Mirande, 1977:751). Thus Hispanic families may incur more social stress. Viewed in this structural context, Hispanics might be expected to exhibit high rates of violence, particularly among low income families. This suggests that if the stresses associated with poverty and discrimination are controlled, Hispanic families would not have high rates of family violence. However, a study by Bergdorf (1981, as summarized in Garbarino and Ebata, 1983) compared "Black" versus "White" (combining Anglo, Hispanic, and others) child abuse rates. Bergdorf found that low income Whites in the National Incidence Study had significantly *higher* rates of child maltreatment than low income Blacks. Garbarino and Ebata suggests this finding may indicate that Blacks have better informal social networks to help them cope with socioeconomic stress in ways that protect children (1983:775).

Empirical Evidence on Violence in Hispanic Families

Before turning to the literature on child and spouse abuse, data on the incidence of intrafamily homicide are presented below. Intrafamily homicide is, of course, the most severe outcome of family violence. Because nearly all homicides become part of the public record, this information is the most objective source of data available. Since they do not depend on self-reports, homicide studies can be considered the most accurate of all available sources of data on family violence.

Homicide Studies

In the United States, about one-quarter of all murders are of other members of the same family (Straus, 1986). In other countries the percentage is much higher. In Canada, for example, 48% of all homicides are within-family, and in Denmark it is 67% (Straus, 1987). These percentages can be misleading. Canada and Denmark actually have *low* homicide rates: the real meaning of the Danish percentage is that when homicide has been almost eliminated in a society, the setting in which it is most likely to remain is within the family.

The incidence of intrafamily homicide within the Hispanic population for the city of Los Angeles for 1970–1979 is reported by Loya, Mercy, and Associates (1985). These data, which are summarized in Table 20.1, permit a comparison of the Hispanic rate of intrafamily homicide with the overall Hispanic homicide rate and with the rates for other ethnic groups. Three of the most important findings given in Table 20.1 are

- The *intrafamily* homicide rate for Hispanics, although low relative to the rate in the Black community, is 1.3 times greater than the Anglo rate (3.1 / 2.3 = 1.34). See Row 1.
- The *overall* homicide rate for Hispanics is 2.3 times greater than the Anglo rate. See Row 2.
- Hispanic *intrafamily* homicides were only 8.4% of the overall Hispanic homicide rate in Los Angeles. This relates not so much to a low rate of

TABLE 20.1

Intrafamily Homicide, by Race of Victim, Los Angeles (from Loya, Mercy, and Associates, 1985, Tables 4, 13, 17, and 21

Homicide Measure*	Hispanic	Black	Anglo
A. Total			
Intra-Family Rate	3.1	17.9	2.3
Overall Homicide Rate	36.7	94.5	16.3
% Intra-Family	8.4%	18.9%	14.1%
B. Male			
Intra-Family Rate	1.7	11.7	1.0
Overall Homicide Rate	32.3	76.6	11.3
% Intra-Family	5.2%	15.2%	8.8%
C. Female			
Intra-Family Rate	1.4	6.2	1.3
Overall Homicide Rate	4.4	17.9	5.0
% Intra-Family	31.8%	34.6%	26.0%

* The rates in the first two rows of each section of the table are per 100,000 of each ethnic group.

homicide within Hispanic families as to an even higher non-family homicide rate.[1] (See Row 3.)

The homicide rate of 3.1 per 100,000 families found in Los Angeles, if supported by other studies,[2] indicates that intrafamily violence is a major threat to Hispanic families.

Child Abuse

Hispanic children were 12% of all reported cases of physically abused children in 1984 (American Association for Protecting Children, 1986, Figures 5 and 6). According to data from the U.S. Census, Hispanic children were 9.7% of the total number of children in the United States in 1985 (*Statistical Abstract of the United States, 1986,* Table 38). Thus Hispanic children are over-represented by about a fifth in the official child abuse statistics.

The overrepresentation of Hispanic children needs to be interpreted with caution, first because census figures may not include all Hispanics in the United States. More important, some studies indicate that professionals are more likely to recognize and report abuse involving ethnic minority and/or lower income families (Gelles, 1982; Hampton and Newberger, 1985; Newberger et al., 1977). Findings from the National Incidence Study (NIS) of child abuse are consistent with this. The NIS counted all child abuse cases known to a sample of service providers and thus went beyond officially reported cases. Hampton (1987) found that Hispanic cases in the NIS comprise only 4.2% of all *substantiated* cases of child maltreatment.

Hampton (1987) also compared Hispanic, Black, and White cases of child maltreatment using the same NIS data and found important demographic differences by race: maltreated Hispanic children and their mothers tended to be younger than their White counterparts; Hispanic mothers had less formal education and less participation in the paid labor force and were more likely to live in an urban area than Black mothers of maltreated children.

Spouse Abuse

Unfortunately, no "official" data on spouse abuse currently exist. The most widely used data on crime in the United States are the "crimes known to the police" given in an annual FBI publication, *Crime in the United States.* These data do not provide information on wife beating because assaults between spouses are not reported separately from other assaults. The National Crime Survey is also not useful because it does not provide separate data for Hispanic victims.

In a clinical sample of 358 battered women from California, Mirande and Perez (1987) found no significant differences between Whites, Blacks, and Hispanics in the frequency or severity of abuse. Since Hispanics are known to have close-knit kin networks, it was expected that Hispanic battered women would be more likely to have been referred for services by family members. They found no difference in sources of referral for services by ethnicity, suggesting that Black, White, or Hispanic women do not rely on different social networks for help. Torres reports similar findings between clinical samples of 25 Hispanic and 25 White women residing in battered women's shelters.

The same problem that hampered interpretation of the NIS data by Hampton is also at work in clinical samples of battered women. We do not know if ethnic differences are masked by selection into these service organizations. Perhaps women who are beaten repeatedly and severely enough to lead them to seek shelter from their husbands are a relatively homogenous group, in contrast to the larger group of women who are assaulted but never seek help. Only community samples can address the question of ethnic differences among the latter.

Sorenson and Telles (1987) report on one such community survey of 2,391 Los Angeles residents that measured ethnicity in three categories: Mexican-born Hispanics, U.S.-born Hispanics, and non-Hispanic Whites born in the U.S. The measure of spouse abuse was a simple question asking if the respondent had ever hit or thrown things at his/her partner. The child abuse measure asked if the respondent had ever hit the child so hard that bruises were inflicted or the child had to stay in bed or be taken to the doctor. Sorenson and Telles found the highest lifetime prevalence rates for spouse assault by U.S.-born Hispanics (30.3%), followed by non-Hispanic Whites (21.5%), with Mexican-born Hispanics exhibiting the lowest rates (12.1%). No significant differences were found in the child abuse rates of the three ethnic groups, which ranged from 1.1 to 2%.

Methods

Sample and Violence Measures

The sample used in this chapter was based on the 1985 National Family Violence Resurvey. Hispanic and non-Hispanic White cases were drawn from the national probability sample and the Hispanic oversample.[3] A total of 721 Hispanic families were available in the Resurvey, in addition to the

4,052 non-Hispanic Whites who are also analyzed here for purposes of comparison.

The *Conflict Tactics Scales* or CTS (described briefly in Chapter 1 and in full detail in Chapters 3 and 4) was used to measure the incidence of parent-to-child and marital violence. The Overall Violence index was used to measure the percent of spouses who used *any* of the violent acts included in the CTS during the year covered by the study. The Severe Violence index measures those acts that have a relatively high probability of causing an injury. Thus kicking is classified as severe violence because kicking a child or a spouse has a much greater potential for producing an injury than an act of "minor violence" such as spanking or slapping.[4]

Child Abuse.   What constitutes "abuse" is, to a considerable extent, a matter of social norms. Spanking or slapping a child or even hitting a child with an object such as stick, hairbrush, or belt is not "abuse" according to either the legal or informal norms of American society, although it is in Sweden and several other countries (Haeuser, 1985). The operationalization of child abuse attempts to take such normative factors into consideration by computing two child abuse rates: *Child Abuse 1* is the use by a parent of any of the acts of violence in the Severe Violence index, except that, to be consistent with current legal and informal norms, hitting or trying to hit with an object such as a stick or belt is *not* included. *Child Abuse 2* adds hitting with an object such as a belt or paddle (even though many people do not consider that to be abusive), because such acts carry a greater risk of causing an injury.[5]

Spousal violence.   The problem of terminology and norms is even greater for violence between spouses than for violence by parents. Although spanking or occasionally slapping a child is not usually considered abuse (or even "violence"), the same act is often considered abusive if done to a spouse. Thus in the case of violence between spouses, the occurrence of *any* violence, measured by the Overall Violence index, is emphasized.

Wife beating.   Because of the greater average size and strength of men, the acts in the Severe Violence list are likely to be more damaging when the assailant is the husband. Consequently, to facilitate focusing on the rate of severe violence by husbands, the term *wife beating* will be used to refer to that rate.

Demographic Measures

Several demographic measures were included in the analysis, because of their association with both ethnicity and family violence. Measures of socioeconomic status included family income and husband's and wife's occupational status. Annual family income was measured in six intervals, ranging from a low of none to ten thousand dollars to the highest of fifty thousand dollars and over. Occupational status was dichotomized as either "blue collar" or "white collar" using the Bureau of Labor Statistics revised Occupational Classification System following a procedure developed by Rice (as given in Robinson, Athanasiou, and Head, 1969). Husband's and wife's employment status were measured in four categories: full-time, part-time, unemployed (including students and homemakers), and retired.

Region and urbanicity of residence were also included. Region was measured by the four major census categories of Northeast, North Central, South, and West. Urbanicity was trichotomized into central cities with populations of one hundred thousand or more, suburban areas with populations between twenty-five hundred and one hundred thousand, and rural areas with fewer than twenty-five hundred residents.

Data Analysis

The incidence rates of parent-to-child and marital violence were calculated by ethnicity and the other demographic variables (listed above) using cross-tabulation and chi-square tests of significance. Because cross-tabulations revealed important demographic differences between the Hispanic and non-Hispanic White samples, ethnic differences in the incidence of family violence had to be examined more closely. Logistic regression was therefore used to determine if ethnic differences in the incidence of family violence were primarily due to socioeconomic deprivation. The independent variables were a dichotomous measure for ethnicity (Hispanic vs. non-Hispanic), region and urbanicity of residence, family income, husband's and wife's occupational and employment status, and the age and gender of the respondent. For the analysis of child abuse, age and gender of child and the number of children in the family were also included.

In the logistic regression analysis, ethnicity and the other demographic measures were conceived as competing with one another to explain family violence. The dependent measures were first regressed against all the demographic measures listed above; then the equations were reduced via backward elimination until only those variables significantly related (p < .1) remained. Thus ethnic differences in the incidence of family violence were tested for spuriousness with the other demographic variables in the model.

Violence Rates in Hispanic Families

Incidence of Marital Violence[6]

Couple Rates.   The first row of Part A of Table 20.2 shows an extremely high rate of violence between Hispanic couples. This conclusion is based on the absolute rate—the fact that almost one out of four (23.1%) of the Hispanic families in this sample experienced one or more assaults against a spouse during the year of this survey—and on a comparison with the non-Hispanic White part of the sample the Hispanic rate is 54% greater (Table 20.2, first row: 23.1 divided by 15.4 = 1.54).

Applying this rate to the approximately 2.8 million Hispanic couples in the United States in 1985, results in an estimate of about 693,000 Hispanic couples who experienced at least one violent incident during the year (see last column of Table 20.2).

Most of those violent incidents were relatively minor—pushing, slapping, shoving, or throwing things. However, the Severe Violence rate of 11.0 (see second row of Table 20.2) indicates that almost half of the assaults were acts that carried a high risk of producing an injury, such as kicking, punching, biting, or choking. Thus the figure in the column headed "Number Assaulted" indicates that about 330,000 Hispanic households experienced one or more assaults that had a relatively high risk of causing injury.

Husband-to-wife violence.[7]   The middle two rows of Part A of Table 20.2 focus on assaults by husbands. The rate of 17.3 per 1,000 couples shows that almost 1 out of 8 Hispanic husbands physically assaulted their partner during the year of this study. The most important statistic, however, is in the row for severe violence by the husband. This is the measure used as the indicator of "wife beating." It shows that more than 7 out of every 100 women were severely assaulted by their partner in 1985. If this rate is correct, it means that about 219,000 Hispanic women were beaten by their partner that year.

As high as these rates are, it is important to note that all the rates shown in Table 20.2, including the rate of wife beating, must be regarded as an underestimate. There are a number of reasons for this (see Straus, Gelles, and Steinmetz, 1980: 35), including the virtual certainty that not every respondent was completely frank in describing violent incidents. The true rates could be as much as double those shown in Table 20.2.

Wife to husband violence.   The last two rows of Part A show the rates for violence *by wives* are remarkably similar to the rates for violence by husbands for both the Hispanic and White samples. This applies to both the overall rate, which is 16.8 for assaults by wives as compared to 17.3

TABLE 20.2

Annual Incidence Rate of Violence in Hispanic and Non-Hispanic White Families and Estimated Number of Hispanic Cases Based on These Rates. Data from 1985 National Family Violence Resurvey.

Type of Intra-Family Violence[1]	Rate per 100 Couples or Children Non-Hisp White	Hispan	Estimated Number of Hispanics Assaulted Per Year[2]
A. VIOLENCE BETWEEN HUSBAND AND WIFE			
ANY violence during the yr (slap, push, etc)	15.0	23.1	693,000**
SEVERE violence (kick, punch, stab, etc)	5.4	11.0	330,000**
ANY violence by the HUSBAND	10.8	17.3	519,000**
SEVERE violence by HUSBAND ("wife beating")	3.0	7.3	219,000**
ANY violence by the WIFE	11.5	16.8	504,000**
SEVERE violence by the WIFE	4.0	7.8	234,000**
B. VIOLENCE BY PARENTS - CHILD AGE 0-17			
ANY hitting of child during the year	Near 100% for young children		
VERY SEVERE violence ("Child Abuse 1")[3]	1.8	4.8	288,000*
SEVERE violence ("Child Abuse 2")	9.8	13.4	804,000*

    * = Significant difference between Hispanic and Non-Hispanic at p ≤ .05
   ** = Significant at p ≤ .01

    1.   The   rates   in   the   first   column   differ   from   those   in   previous
publications for two reasons.   First, the rates in Straus and Gelles (1986)
were computed in a way which enabled the 1985 rates to be compared with the
more restricted sample and more restricted version of the Conflict Tactics
Scale used in the 1975 study.   Second, the other previously published rates
(e.g. Straus and Gelles, 1988) are based on the entire sample of 6,002
families, whereas the rates in the first column exclude all minority groups.
The N's for section A of this table are 3,690 Non-Hispanic White families and
602 Hispanic families.   Section B N's are the number of families with a
child aged 0-17 at home. These are 2,104 for the Non-Hispanic White families
and 499 for the Hispanic families.

    2. The column giving the "Number Assaulted" was computed by multiplying
the rates in this table by the 1984 population figures as given in the 1986
Statistical Abstract of the United States. The population figures (rounded to
millions) are 2.8 million Hispanic couples, and 6.1 million Hispanic children
age 0-17.   The number of children 3-4 and 15-17 was estimated as a
proportionate fraction of the total number of children, e.g. 2/18ths and
3/18ths of the number of children age 0-17.

    3. See "Definition and Measurement" section for an explanation of the
difference between "Child Abuse 1" and "Child Abuse 2."

for assaults by husbands, and to the severe violence rate (7.8 for assaults by wives versus 7.3 for assaults by husbands). The many controversial issues involved in findings on violence *by wives* are discussed in Chapters 1, 4, 5, and 9 of this volume.

Incidence of Violence against Children

Overall violence rate. No rates or numbers are shown for "any hitting" of children (first row of Part B, Table 20.2) because that statistic is almost meaningless unless one takes into account the age of the child. For children age four and under, the true figure is close to 100%. For example, 97% of the parents of three-year-olds in the 1975 national survey and 90% of the parents in the 1985 study reported one or more times during the year when they had hit the child (Chapter 8, Figure 8.1; Chapter 23, Figure 23.4). The rate drops rapidly from age six on.

Child abuse 1 rate. This measure of child abuse is confined to acts by parents that are almost universally regarded as abusive: kicking, biting, punching, beating up, scalding, and attacks with weapons. The second row of Table 20.2, Part B, shows that the rate of such indubitably abusive violence was 4.8 per 100 Hispanic children in 1985. This is almost certainly an underestimate, because not all parents were willing to tell us about instances in which they kicked or punched a child. If we nevertheless apply this rate to the 6.1 million Hispanic children living in the U.S. in 1985, it results in an estimate of about 288,000 severely assaulted Hispanic children per year.

Child abuse 2 rate. This measure of child abuse (as noted earlier) adds hitting the child with an object such as a stick or belt. Hitting with an object was omitted from the Child Abuse 1 rate because neither legal nor informal norms presume that as "abuse." However, since hitting a child with an object involves a greater risk of injury than spanking or slapping with the hand, the best measure of physical abuse of children may be the Child Abuse 2 rate. The second row of Part B shows that, in 1985, 13.4 out of every 100 Hispanic children were assaulted by a parent severely enough to be classified as "abuse." When this rate is applied to the number of Hispanic children living in the U.S. in 1985, it results in an estimate of 804,000 abused children per year.

How Violent Are Hispanic Families?

As indicated earlier, the rates and numbers just presented are almost certain to be underestimates. But even at face value, the statistics indicate violence is a major problem in Hispanic families, as it is in non-Hispanic families. However, since we are trained to see the loving and supportive side of the family and to discount the "dark side" of the family, these figures are sometimes dismissed. For example, it can be noted that there was severe violence between the spouses in "only" 11% of the Hispanic couples, i.e., 89% were *not* seriously violent.

Suppose, however, that this was a study of universities rather than families. It seems unlikely that the findings would be dismissed by saying that 89% of the faculty did not severely assault a student in 1987. A one out of ten rate of severe assault in a university or in any other civilian setting except the family would not be tolerated for an instant. This of course raises the question of why there is so much violence in families, both Hispanic and other. This book details many investigations into the causes of violence among non-Hispanic families conducted over the past fifteen years. The next section of this chapter will examine some of the demographic characteristics of Hispanics in the United States that may explain the higher incidence of assaults within the Hispanic families in this study.

Structural Factors and Violence in Hispanic and White Families

Table 20.3 compares the Hispanic and non-Hispanic White families on key demographic variables. The first panel in Table 20.3 shows that 41.5% of the Hispanics in our sample lived in the Western region of the United States, compared to only 19.2% of the Whites. The second panel of Table 20.3 shows that Hispanics are also more likely to live in an urban area. Table 20.3 also shows that Hispanic men tend to work in blue collar occupations while their wives are more likely not to work outside the home and Hispanic families are more likely to earn less than ten thousand dollars a year.[8]

Demographic Controls by Cross-Tabulation

None of the findings in Table 20.3 is particularly surprising given the position of ethnic minority groups within the status hierarchy in American society. The demographic differences are discussed here because they point to the possibility that the higher rate of family violence among Hispanics (shown in Table 20.2) may be spuriously confounded with these demographic characteristics. As a first step in exploring this possibility, Table 20.4 presents the incidence rates for three forms of family violence by ethnicity within categories of the demographic measures.[9] For example, the first two columns of Row 1 show little difference in the rates of parent-to-child severe violence for Hispanic and White families living in the

TABLE 20.3

Demographic Differences between Hispanics and Non-Hispanic Whites, 1985 Family Violence Resurvey

| Demographics | Percentage of: | |
	Hispanics	Whites
Region***		
Northeast	15.4	18.8
North Central	5.1	27.3
South	38.0	34.7
West	41.5	19.2
Urbanicity***		
City	55.5	23.9
Suburb	31.1	46.8
Rural	13.5	29.2
Family Annual Income***		
none - $10,000	25.8	9.4
$10,000 - $20,000	31.6	21.3
$20,000 - $40,000	21.5	24.7
$40,000 and over	21.1	44.6
Husband's Occup. Status***		
Blue Collar	72.8	49.3
White Collar	27.2	50.7
Wife's Occup. Status***		
Blue Collar	56.0	66.5
White Collar	44.0	33.5
Husband's Employment**		
Full Time	77.2	75.1
Part Time	5.9	3.4
Unemployed, other	9.5	6.1
Retired	7.4	14.8
Wife's Employment***		
Full Time	38.1	40.8
Part Time	9.5	13.6
Unemployed, other	50.1	36.9
Retired	2.3	8.8

Chi-square test of significance: **p < .01, ***p<.001

TABLE 20.4

Violence Rates by Demographics and Ethnicity

	Type of Violence					
	Parent-to-Child (Child Abuse 1)		Husband-to-Wife (Any Violence)		Wife-to-Husband (Any Violence)	
Demographics	Hispanics (N=436)	Whites (N=1973)	Hispanics (N=582)	Whites (N=3463)	Hispanics (N=582)	Whites (N=3467)
Region						
Northeast	15.5	12.9	21.9	9.8***	21.9	11.2**
North Central	22.6	9.2*	15.1	11.4	12.1	11.5
South	12.0	9.0	13.0	9.0*	16.4	9.3***
West	12.6	9.1	16.4	10.2**	12.7	11.4
Urbanicity						
City	12.2	8.7	17.9	12.1*	18.8	12.9**
Suburb	12.7	9.6	12.5	10.3	10.4	10.2
Rural	19.4	10.8*	14.6	7.9*	13.4	9.6
Family Annual Income						
none - $20,000	13.2	12.6	18.9	11.7**	16.9	12.0*
$20,000 - $40,000	14.3	18.7*	14.2	10.2	16.2	11.7
$40,000 and over	16.3	8.6	10.0	9.1	5.0	8.8
Husband's Occup. Status						
Blue Collar	14.3	12.1	16.1	11.7*	15.8	12.5
White Collar	13.6	7.6*	15.1	9.0*	14.5	9.5*
Wife's Occup. Status						
Blue Collar	12.6	10.7	15.5	11.2	14.0	11.2
White Collar	15.1	9.6*	15.2	9.6**	15.7	10.3*
Husband's Employment						
Full Time	13.1	9.3	15.4	10.8**	15.5	11.9*
Part Time	15.4	7.1	22.9	12.0	25.7	8.0*
Unemployed, other	10.8	7.4	20.7	13.2	17.2	13.2
Wife's Employment						
Full Time	12.2	8.1	15.1	11.9	14.7	11.7
Part Time	20.0	9.6*	20.0	10.1*	11.7	10.7
Unemployed, other	13.3	11.0	16.2	9.5**	17.2	11.4**

--

Chi-Square tests for Hispanic-White comparisons: *p < .05, **p < .01, ***p < .001

Northeast. The next two columns in Row 1 do indicate, however, that 21.9% of Hispanic husbands (compared to 9.8% of Whites) in the Northeast used some form of violence against their wives in the year prior to the survey.

Turning to the socioeconomic controls, the Hispanic sample exhibits generally higher violence rates across nearly all income, occupational, and employment status levels. Note that Row 8 shows that among those earning less than twenty thousand dollars, Hispanics have similar parent-to-child rates as White families but greater rates of husband-to-wife and wife-to-husband violence.[10] Row 17 also shows higher rates of violence among Hispanics when the husband is unemployed (10.8% for the child abuse measure, 20.7% for husband-to-wife violence, and 17.2% for wife-to-husband violence).

Figure 20.1 displays the relationship of husband's unemployment to husband's and wife's violence among the Hispanic families in the 1985 sample. For greater clarity, the rates of minor and severe violence are graphed separately. The top line in the figure represents minor violence by Hispanic husbands. It shows that 15% of full-time employed husbands carried out an act of minor violence, while the rate doubles for unemployed Hispanic men to one out of three. The third line from the top in Figure 20.1 plots the rate of severe assaults by Hispanic husbands. It shows that the severe violence rate among unemployed Hispanic husbands was two and a half times greater than among men with full-time jobs (16.1% to 6.5%).

Simultaneous Controls via Logistic Regression

The finding from Table 20.4 that differences in the rates of family violence between the Hispanic and White samples remain within many categories of the demographic variables indicate that they are not simply spurious to any one of them. These findings do not entirely rule out the possibility that ethnic differences are due to differentials in the social environment, however. Hispanic families may exhibit higher rates of violence due to the combined effect of several structural factors. To test this possibility, these three forms of family violence were each analyzed by all the demographic measures concurrently using logistic regression. The first logistic regression equation included all the demographic measures (including a dummy variable for Hispanic) regressed against the family violence measure. The equation was then simplified by eliminating, one by one, those measures that were not significantly related to family

FIGURE 20.1

Marital Violence by Employment of Husband, Hispanic Sample

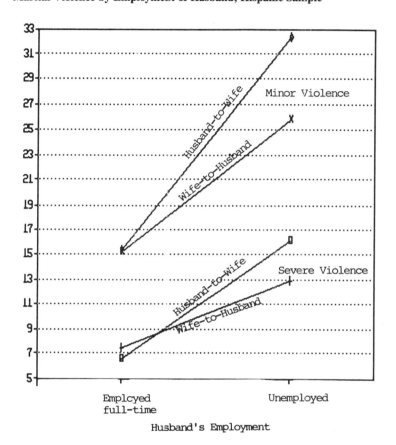

violence (p > .1). The results after this backward elimination procedure are given in Table 20.5.

Section A of Table 20.5 shows that the Hispanic sample had a higher probability of exhibiting severe parent-to-child violence, even when all other significant variables were held constant (p < .05). Other factors significantly related to parent-to-child violence were the number of children in the home, the age of respondent, the urbanicity of residence, and living in the Northeast. In a multivariate analysis such as this, the number

TABLE 20.5

Family Violence by Ethnicity and Other Demographic Measures, Logistic Regression Results after Backward Elimination

Demographic Variable	Regression Coefficient	Standard Error	t	Level of Significance
A. Parent-to-Child Severe Violence				
intercept	-1.990292	.3597251	-5.533	0.000
Hispanic	.3683517	.1610541	2.287	0.022
Number of Children	.2544956	.058194	4.373	0.000
Age of Respondent	-.0146155	.0082999	-1.761	0.078
urbanicity	-.162862	.0907062	-1.795	0.073
Northeast	.4357909	.1578924	2.760	0.006

N of Cases - 2598, chi-square - 35.28, d.f.-5, p < .0001

B. Husband-to-Wife Any Violence				
intercept	-.2211164	.2351924	-0.940	0.347
Hispanic	.158825	.1399747	1.135	0.257
Urbanicity	.1956515	.0710459	2.754	0.006
Family Income	-.0915721	.0368518	-2.485	0.013
Age of Respondent	-.0546981	.0048057	-11.382	0.000

N of Cases - 4016, chi-square - 203.68, d.f.-4, p <.0001

C. Wife-to-Husband Any Violence				
intercept	.1574334	.2334105	0.674	0.500
hispanic	.0042086	.1421076	0.030	0.976
Urbanicity	.1785339	.070024	2.550	0.011
Family Income	-.0925591	.036595	-2.529	0.011
Age of Respondent	-.0624862	.0049689	-12.575	0.000

N of cases - 4020, chi-square - 244.66, d.f.-4, p <.0001

of cases available for analysis is important to consider. This analysis is based on a relatively small number of Hispanic families (N = 436) and an even smaller number of Hispanic families exhibiting parent-to-child violence (N = 67). These findings might not be replicated with a larger sample.

Sections B and C of Table 20.5 show that in sharp contrast to the findings on parent-to-child violence, Hispanic couples do not have a higher probability of marital violence when structural factors are held constant. The three key factors explaining higher rates of marital violence among Hispanics are urbanicity of residence, family income, and age of respondent. Thus the *combined* effects of the concentration of the Hispanic population in urban areas and the low income and the youthfulness of the Hispanic population account for the differences in rates of marital violence between Hispanic and non-Hispanic White couples.

Poverty and Violence

The evidence just presented indicates that the strong linkage of violence to low income, urbanization, and youthfulness explains much of the higher rates of violence in Hispanic families. At least part of the reason is the greater number of stressors that low SES families experience (Chapter 11).[11] This suggests that steps to raise the socioeconomic level of Hispanic families and improve the quality of life in urban areas are more than a matter of equity and social justice. This is also one of the most fundamental ways of reducing the high level of intrafamily violence in the Hispanic community.

Dynamics of Violence within Hispanic Families

Equality with the non-Hispanic White community in respect to violence is hardly a worthy target to seek. Although the rates are lower than in Hispanic families, non-Hispanic White families have an intolerably high rate of intrafamily violence. Thus much more needs to be included in an adequate theory explaining why families are so violent and to provide a sound basis for primary prevention. In previous papers and books a more comprehensive theory has been developed (Gelles and Straus, 1979; Straus, 1973; Straus and Hotaling, 1980; Straus, Gelles, and Steinmetz, 1980). Chapters in this book point to many of the factors involved, such as alcohol and drug use (Chapter 12: Coleman and Straus, 1983), male dominance in the family and society (Chapters 7 and 22; Straus, 1976), and social stress and social networks (Chapters 11 and 19). Unfortunately, the 1985 Resurvey does not include measures of social support networks that are key components of the ecological model of child abuse (Garbarino, 1977). The higher probability of parent-to-child violence in Hispanic families may well be due to a lack of social support for many of these families.

Another factor in understanding parent-to-child violence lies in its link to the use of physical punishment, discussed with regard to the total 1985 Resurvey sample in Chapter 8. The remaining section of this chapter will examine the link between physical punishment and severe violence within the sample of Hispanic families.

Does Physical Punishment Lead to Physical Abuse?

A previous section presented data on the near universality of physical punishment of young children and also indicated that as children grew older, parents on the average used less physical punishment. However, even in the late teens—ages 15, 16, and 17 to be exact—1 out of 5 Hispanic children in this sample were still being hit by parents. Elsewhere in the interview, respondents were asked if they themselves had been hit by a parent when they were about 13. Forty percent reported physical punishment by their mother when they were about 13 years old, and 28% reported having been hit by their father at that age. This indicates a continuity between generations in the use of physical punishment.

The data on use of physical punishment by the respondents in this study and the data on the use of physical punishment by their parents refer to what can be called "legitimate violence" (Baron and Straus, 1987; Straus, 1985). This is in contrast to violence by parents that goes beyond the culturally permissible level of severity and is therefore labeled as "physical abuse" rather than "physical punishment." These data can be analyzed to provide information on the question of whether parents who experienced "physical *punishment*" as a 13 year old have a higher rate of "physical *abuse*" of their own children than parents who were not physically punished at that age. Since it was shown previously that severe assaults on children occur more often in blue collar than in white collar familes, the occupational status of the husband was controlled in this analysis.

Each row of Table 20.6 compares respondents who were physically punished at age 13 with those who were not. Age 13 was chosen because it seemed to be the youngest age at which this information could be remembered and reported in an interview, and because it is past the age at which physical punishment is nearly universal. It was further assumed that children who were physically punished at age 13 were likely to have been physically punished since infancy. The first row of Table 20.6 indicates that 2.3% of the respondents who were not physically punished at age 13 severely assaulted one of their children during the year of this survey. This, of course, is an extremely high rate for such serious and dangerous acts as kicking or punching a child. However, the next figure to the right indicates that the rate for respondents who were physically punished as a teenager is even higher—9.8%. The right-hand column indicates that the rate of severe assaults on children by parents who were physically punished at age 13 is 4.3 times greater than the rate of those who did not experience physical punishment at that age.

Twenty-three out of the 24 comparisons in Table 20.6 show that parents who were physically punished at age 13 engaged in assaultive behavior more often than parents who were not hit at that age.[12] There are also some potentially important differences within Table 20.6. Specifically, the pattern is somewhat different for child abuse as compared to spouse abuse.

TABLE 20.6

Intrafamily Violence Rate by Physical Punishment Experienced by the Perpetrator and Occupational Class of Husband

Type of Violence	Husband's Occ. Class	Physical Punishment At Age 13			Ratio of Yes/No
		Parent	No	Yes	
Child Abuse 1	Manual	Mother	2.3	9.8	4.3**
	Non-Manual		0.0	11.4	@ **
	Manual	Father	4.0	8.7	2.8
	Non-Manual		1.4	12.1	8.6*
Child Abuse 2	Manual	Mother	8.5	23.3	2.7**
	Non-Manual		6.0	25.0	4.2**
	Manual	Father	12.9	16.3	1.3
	Non-Manual		10.8	21.2	2.0
Husband-to-Wife Any Violence	Manual	Mother	8.1	27.8	3.4**
	Non-Manual		8.8	29.4	3.3**
	Manual	Father	10.8	27.8	2.6**
	Non-Manual		16.8	12.5	.7
Husband-to-Wife Severe Violence	Manual	Mother	4.3	15.4	3.6**
	Non-Manual		0.0	9.8	@ **
	Manual	Father	6.2	13.9	2.2*
	Non-Manual		2.8	5.0	1.8
Wife-to-Husband Any Violence	Manual	Mother	8.5	26.6	3.1**
	Non-Manual		10.8	23.5	2.2**
	Manual	Father	10.8	28.7	2.7**
	Non-Manual		15.0	17.5	1.2
Wife-to-Husband Severe Violence	Manual	Mother	5.2	15.4	3.0**
	Non-Manual		0.0	13.7	@ **
	Manual	Father	5.8	17.6	3.0**
	Non-Manual		3.7	7.5	2.1**

Footnotes For Table 6

* - Chi-square significant at the .05 level, ** - significant at .01 level

The N's for the cells in this table are:

	Child Abuse	Spouse Abuse
Manual worker, Not Physically punished by mother at age 13	173	234
Manual Worker, Physically punished by mother at age 13	163	169
Non-manual Worker, Not physically punished by mother at age 13	66	102
Non-manual Worker, Physically punished by mother at age 13	44	51
Manual worker, Not Physically punished by father at age 13	198	277
Manual Worker, Physically punished by father at age 13	92	108
Non-manual Worker, Not physically punished by father at age 13	73	107
Non-manual Worker, Physically punished by father at age 13	33	40

Class Differences in the Effects of Physical Punishment

Child abuse.   The relation between experiencing physical punishment as a child and severely assaulting one's own child is greater for non-manual (i.e., white collar or middle-class) workers than for manual workers. This is puzzling at first because the overall child abuse rate is lower in middle-class Hispanic families than in working-class Hispanic families. Consequently, it is important to understand what produces the stronger relationship between physical punishment and physical abuse in white collar Hispanic families.

Statistically, the stronger relationship between experiencing violence and child abuse among middle-class parents occurs because the middle-class respondents who were not hit have a lower rate of physically abusing their own children than blue collar parents who were not hit. In addition, middle-class parents who were hit at age 13 have a higher rate of physically abusing children than blue collar parents who were hit at age 13. Consequently the difference between those who were hit and those who were not hit is very large for the white collar parents.

A theoretical explanation for the greater effect of being hit as a teenager on middle-class parents is more difficult. One possibility is based on studies that find that working-class norms permit or require use of physical punishment to a greater extent than is true in the middle class (Bronfenbrenner, 1958; Kohn, 1969; Kohn and Schooler, 1983). Consequently, if a middle-class teenager is hit by his or her parents, it may be a more dramatic event because it also tends to be a norm violation and as a result makes a deeper impression and therefore increases the probability of relying on physical force as a mode of child rearing.

Spouse abuse.   Each of the eight possible comparisons in Table 20.6 show that the effect of being hit as a child is greatest in the families of manual workers. This is the reverse of the class difference for child abuse. No plausible explanation has as yet been formulated to explain why physical punishment is more closely related to spouse abuse in blue collar Hispanic families.

How Physical Punishment Teaches Family Violence

The importance of physical punishment is that in addition to teaching the child to do or not do whatever led to the punishment, it also teaches violence. The process takes place in several ways.

The first way in which physical punishment trains people in violence, and intrafamily violence in particular, is that it sets up an association between love and violence. Studies in England (Newson, 1963:204) and the U.S. (Chapters 8 and 23) show that physical punishment typically begins in infancy with parental slaps to correct and teach. Parents are the first and usually the only ones to hit an infant. For most children this continues throughout childhood. Children therefore learn that those who love them the most are also those who hit.

The second process by which physical punishment trains people in intrafamily violence occurs because physical punishment is used to train the child in morally correct behavior or to teach about danger to be avoided. Ironically, since this is a very desirable objective, it also teaches the moral rightness of hitting other family members.

A third process stems from the fact that parents often refrain from hitting until the anger or frustration reaches a certain point. Consequently, the child learns that anger and frustration justify the use of physical force. Children are therefore trained to be violent when they are out of control.

We believe that these indirect lessons become a fundamental part of the child's personality and are later generalized to other social relationships, especially to such intimate relationships as those of husband and wife and of parent and child. This is confirmed by the findings just presented and by other studies that show that the more physical punishment experienced as a child, the higher the rate of hitting a spouse (Chapter 23; Straus, Gelles, and Steinmetz, 1980).[13]

Summary and Conclusions

This paper presented preliminary findings from a study of violence in a nationally representative sample of 721 Hispanic families. Since these are preliminary findings and since the study has a number of limitations (see introduction), the conclusions must be regarded as tentative.[14]

Incidence of Violence in Hispanic Families

The first part of the paper focused on estimating the incidence rate of intrafamily violence, including physical abuse of children and of spouses. Extremely high rates were found:

- Almost one out of four Hispanic households were the scene of an assault between the married or cohabiting partners during the year of the survey. About half of these incidents involved acts that carried a substantial risk of injury, such as kicking, punching, biting, and choking.
- Hispanic women, like non-Hispanic women, have about the same rate of assaults on husbands as husbands have of assaults on wives.

- About one out of seven Hispanic children were severely assaulted by their parents during the year of this survey.
- The violence rate in Hispanic families is much greater than the rate in non-Hispanic White families. For example, the rate of severe assaults on wives, which can be considered a measure of wife beating, is more than double that of non-Hispanic White families.
- The rates presented in this paper, although extremely high, are probably underestimates of the true incidence.
- The higher rate of spouse abuse in Hispanic families reflects the economic deprivation, youthfulness, and urban residence of Hispanics. When these factors are controlled, there is no statistically significant difference between Hispanics and non-Hispanic Whites.
- Hispanic parents have a higher rate of child abuse even with statistical controls for poverty, youthfulness, urbanization, and other demographic factors.

Etiology of Family Violence

We also found a number of important relationships between characteristics of the families and the incidence of violence:

- Hispanic families in the North Central States had the highest rate of *child* abuse, whereas families in the Northeast had the highest rate of *spouse* abuse.
- Hispanic families living in small towns or rural areas had the highest rate of *child* abuse, whereas those living in the central cities of large metropolitan areas had the highest rate of *spouse* abuse.
- Families with low-income, low-status occupation of the husband and unemployment had child abuse and spouse abuse rates that are considerably higher (in some cases two to four times greater) than the rates of better-off families.
- Respondents who experienced more than average amounts of physical punishment as children had a much higher rate of child abuse and spouse abuse.

Although this study identified certain factors that probably contribute to the high rate of violence in Hispanic families, it is important to realize that none of these factors is deterministic. For example, the rate of wife beating by unemployed Hispanic men is about two and a half times greater than the rate in families where the husband has a full-time job (16.1% versus 6.5%). This is an astoundingly and intolerably high rate of wife beating. On the other hand, the same statistics show that 84% of unemployed

Hispanic men in this sample did *not* assault their wife during the year of the survey. Moreover, the fact that 6.5% of the men with a full-time job *did* assault their wives also needs to be kept in mind. In short, with or without unemployment, wife beating and child abuse are major problems in the Hispanic community. Nevertheless, it is important not to let these statistics be converted to a stereotype in which all Hispanic men or all unemployed or poor Hispanic men are wife beaters or child abusers.

Programmatic and Policy Implications

Even at this stage in the analysis of the data from the 1985 Resurvey, some programmatic and policy implications are clear.

- Since the rates from this survey and the homicide rates indicate that family violence is a major threat to the integrity and well-being of Hispanic families, efforts to change that situation need high priority. This means services to aid and protect victims, treatment programs for offenders, and primary prevention.
- Although the high intrafamily assault and homicide rates are likely to be an embarrassment to the Hispanic community, the reality of the problem needs to be acknowledged so that the Hispanic community itself can control the remedial steps.
- The close link of violence to low income and unemployment is one more reason to close the economic gap between Hispanics and the majority of Americans.
- The high rate of assault by women on their husbands (both Hispanic women and other women) and the finding that physical punishment is part of the etiology of both child abuse and spouse abuse suggest that family violence is not just a problem of "macho" males. It is built into the family system and the society as it is presently constituted. Consequently, programs to aid victims and treat aggressors, important as they are, will not be sufficient.
- Primary prevention programs are needed to address the fundamental causes of the overall high level of violence in families and in society generally. Examples include ending physical punishment of children, eliminating poverty and discrimination, and improving the quality of life in urban areas. Perhaps even more fundamental is eliminating the widespread violence committed by public officials, ranging from police who beat up a bicyclist for going against traffic (*New York Times*, 6 September 1987:42) to capital punishment and presidents who authorize bombing ships of tiny nations whose political system we dislike. Research by Archer and Gartner (1984), Baron and Straus (1987, 1988, 1989), and

Levinson (1989) shows that the more these types of "legitimate violence" characterize a society, the higher the rate of criminal violence, including child abuse and spouse abuse. These are examples of the way violence is deeply embedded in the fabric of society. As will be argued in Chapter 28, primary prevention must seek to remove each of the violent threads in the fabric until a new design ultimately emerges.

Notes

1. In fact, Block (1987) found in an analysis of Chicago police data that Hispanics were at greatest risk of homicide outside the home as a result of an altercation between groups of teenage or adult men.
2. It is not at all certain that other studies will produce similar findings. For example, the rates may be higher than elsewhere because of the huge size of the Hispanic population of Los Angeles and the history of violent youth gangs.
3. See Appendix 1 for a complete description of the sampling techniques used in the 1985 Resurvey. The specific question on ethnic identity was "In which of the following categories do you feel you belong? Pacific Islander, American Indian or Alaskan Native, Asian (Oriental), Hispanic, Hispanic/Black, White but not Hispanic, Black but not Hispanic, Not sure, Refused." For purposes of this chapter, the Hispanic and Hispanic/Black groups were combined.
4. It should be recognized that in most instances, the outcome of being kicked, although painful, does *not* result in an injury. However, absence of injury does not remove it from the category of an abusive act. Our distinction between minor and severe violence parallels the legal distinction between a "simple assault" and an "aggravated assault." For a more in-depth discussion, see the section on violence, abuse, and assault in Chapter 5.
5. From a scientific perspective it would be preferable to avoid the term *abuse* because of the definitional problems just mentioned and because it is more a political and administrative term than a scientific term. Despite this, we will use *abuse* for two reasons. First, it is less awkward than *Very Severe Violence index*. Second, it is such a widely used term that avoiding it creates communication difficulties.
6. These statistics and the analysis that follows are not confined to women who are legally married to their male partners. Unmarried cohabiting women and women who are divorced or separated are at least as likely to be victims of assault by their partner or former partner as are married women (Gaquin, 1977–1978; Yllo and Straus, 1981). Such assaults tend to be ignored by the public and the criminal justice system in essentially the same way as assaults on married women.
7. For convenience and economy of wording, terms such as *marital, spouse, wife,* and *husband* are used to refer to couples, irrespective of whether they are a married or a non-married cohabiting couple. For an analysis of differences and similarities between married and cohabiting couples in the 1975–1976 survey, see Yllo 1978; Yllo and Straus, 1981.
8. T-tests for difference of means verify that the Hispanic sample earn less, are younger, and have larger families than the non-Hispanic White sample (all significant at the $p < .001$ level).

9. These three forms of violence were selected for discussion because they had the least skewed distributions, allowing a maximal number of cases in each cell. The analysis of parent-to-child violence was replicated using the Child Abuse #2 measure (which excludes the "hitting with an object" item), with the same results.

10. This relationship is the same when income is divided into "less than $10,000" and "$10,000 to $20,000" categories.

11. It is possible that the lower violence rates for men who are white collar, high income, or employed represents less willingness to report such incidents rather than fewer such incidents. However, that could not explain the many studies showing an association of poverty with the most severe form of violence of all—homicide. Moreover, research on "self-disclosure" has found that higher SES people are much more willing to reveal themselves to others than low SES persons.

12. Analyses were also run taking into account *how often* the respondent was hit at age 13. That information was not included in Table 20.6 because it would make the table large and complicated. In addition, the increase in degrees of freedom and the drop in the number of cases per cell results in few statistically significant relationships. If, however, one is willing to ignore the lack of statistical significance, these analyses show that the *more often* a respondent was hit, the higher the assault rate during the year of this survey.

13. A dramatic portrayal of the expression of intimacy by violence in a Hispanic family is in the film *La Bamba*.

14. Perhaps the fact that the survey was carried out by phone rather than personal interview produced an artificially high Hispanic rate, but there do not seem to be any obvious reasons why such an effect would occur more for Hispanics than for others. See Straus and Gelles (1986) for a discussion of the possible effects of conducting the survey by telephone. Another possible artifact that might cause an overestimate of the extent of violence in Hispanic families could occur if some respondents perceived the interviewer as expecting there to be violence. If so, the tradition of cordiality to strangers may have led some Hispanic respondents to agree to having carried out acts that they did not actually do. Although this and other methodological artifacts cannot be ruled out, the correspondence between the ethnic group differences in assaults as measured by this survey and the ethnic group differences in homicides makes it more likely that the assault rates are actually higher in Hispanic families.

21

Wife's Marital Dependency and Wife Abuse

Debra S. Kalmuss and Murray A. Straus

Systems of sex stratification typically foster women's economic and psychological dependency on marriage. Women's social status as well as their access to various systems of resources are determined largely by their relationships with men through marriage. Within this overall pattern of subordination, however, there are individual differences in the level of women's marital dependency. Some women are less dependent on their husbands for financial support, status, and self-esteem than are other women. These individual differences in marital dependency are relevant to the study of wife abuse. This study focuses on the relationship between women's dependency on marriage and violent abuse from their husbands.

The literature on marital violence suggests a relationship between women's marital dependency and wife abuse, but this relationship has not been demonstrated empirically. Some work in the area provides a basis for expecting dependency to be associated with high levels of abuse (Dobash and Dobash, 1979; Marsden, 1978; Straus, 1976; Truninger, 1971; Walker, 1978), while other work yields the opposite expectation (Allen and Straus, 1980; Brown, 1980; Goode, 1971; Whitehurst, 1974).

Those who suggest a positive relationship do not argue that women's marital dependency directly causes wife abuse. They suggest, rather, that the relationship is mediated by women's tolerance for physical abuse from their husbands. Women high in marital dependency have (or perceive) few viable alternatives to marriage, which forces them to be more tolerant of negative treatment from their husbands, including physical abuse. Women who have children and rely on their husbands for financial support cannot easily leave abusive marriages, nor do they possess sufficient resources to negotiate changes in their husbands' behavior. In a sense, marital dependency traps women in abusive marriages.

Indirect empirical support exists for the positive relationship between dependency and abuse. Gelles (1976) found that women who were unemployed and those who had a relatively low educational level were less likely to seek outside intervention (police, social service agency, divorce, or separation) than were women who were employed or had completed more schooling. Roy (1977) reported that women's explanations for staying in abusive marriages included economic dependency, presence of young children, fear of living alone, and perceived stigma of divorce. Although these studies did not directly examine the relationship between dependency and abuse, they indicate that factors reflecting high marital dependency among women are related to those reflecting a high tolerance for wife abuse.

As previously mentioned, some studies suggest the opposite: that high levels of women's marital dependency are associated with low levels of wife abuse.[1] The apparent contradiction between the two groups of studies may be best explained by distinguishing between short-term and long-term effects. Family theorists generally agree that, in the long run, equality for women will yield a decline in the rate of wife abuse by decreasing (a) men's perceived right to abuse their wives, (b) women's lack of alternatives to the victim's role, and (c) the unresponsiveness of social institutions to the problem of wife abuse. On the other hand, many of these same theorists have suggested that, in the short run, equality between the sexes may increase wife abuse.

Given that men benefit from the current system of sex stratification, it is unlikely that they will voluntarily give up their dominant positions. Husbands, in fact, may resort to violence if the struggle for sexual equality increases their wives' resource base and encourages women to question the power relationships. (Marsden, 1978; Whitehurst, 1974). Violence may be used as the ultimate resource by husbands to keep wives in their place (Allen and Straus, 1980; Brown, 1980; Goode, 1971). Thus, in the short run, equality for women may increase rather than decrease conflict and violence within the family.

This leads to the prediction that wife abuse is negatively related to marital dependency. Husbands of dependent wives can maintain their dominant positions without resorting to violence because their wives are in no position to question their dominance. However, an independent woman is in a better position to challenge her husband's right to dominate. The relative equality of resources between an independent wife and her husband undermines his use of resource superiority as a defense against such a challenge. Instead, he may use force to assert and maintain his dominance.

Indirect support for this relationship is found in the work of Allen and Straus (1980). Their study of the relationship between the distribution of power and resources between spouses and wife abuse indicated that in blue collar families, husbands who did not possess clear resource superiority over their wives tended to use violence to maintain their power in the family more than husbands who possessed such resource superiority. Since husbands' resource superiority should be related to high marital dependency in wives, their findings support a negative relationship between the women's marital dependency and wife abuse.

Although these two competing hypotheses are suggested by the literature, they have not been examined empirically. Both hypotheses are rooted in speculation as well as in studies of the relationship between wife abuse and variables associated with women's dependence on marriage.

The Concept of Marital Dependency

Perhaps because of the lack of research, marital dependency has not been clearly defined in family or wife-abuse literature. The most common conception of marital dependency is economic. In fact, some theorists use the two terms interchangeably. The following statement by Kinsley is representative:

> At the core of a wife's dependence on her husband is her inferior earning power. As long as she is not able to get a job with pay and prestige at least equivalent to that of her husband, she must rely upon him to maintain her standard of living and social status (1977:80).

Many theorists add the presence of young children to their economic-based conceptions of marital dependency (Gelles, 1976; Prescott and Letko, 1977; Truninger, 1971). Young children make it difficult for women to hold jobs outside of the home, thus reinforcing their dependency on husbands and marriage.

Finally, some theorists refer to women's psychological or emotional dependency on marriage. However, this type of dependency is illusive and typically serves as a residual category for women's intangible ties to marriage. Marsden (1978) defined such ties as a woman's investment in the ideals of marriage and motherhood contrasted with the alternative identities she has available to her as lone mother or worker. Similarly, Straus (1976) emphasized forced dependence on the role of the wife as the basis for a respected position in society. While their definitions are vague, these theorists at least have approached the definitional problem. Many theorists use the notion of emotional or psychological dependency on marriage without any attempts at definition. Still others ignore the existence of noneconomic marital dependency altogether.

This study examines the relationship between two dimensions of women's marital dependency (objective and subjective) and violence toward wives. Objective dependency is characterized by conditions that tie a woman to marriage, whether or not she is aware of the ties. The key situational factors associated with objective marital dependency are economic in nature. Married women who do not work and thus have no potential for economic self-sufficiency are objectively dependent on their husbands, even if they are not aware of that dependency.

Wives' objective marital dependency is reinforced by factors that limit women's participation in the labor force (e.g., presence of young children, occupational discrimination, traditional husbands who do not permit their wives to work). However, given the wage differential between men and women, being employed does not necessarily make a woman economically self-sufficient. Employed wives whose husbands earn considerably more than they do remain dependent on their spouses' incomes for their current standard of living. Thus, a woman's contribution to the total family income is a necessary adjunct to her employment status and potential in determining her objective dependency on marriage.[2]

Women's subjective dependency on marriage refers to how tied to the marital relationship a woman perceives herself to be. At this level, dependency is a psychological state that may or may not reflect objective conditions. Operationally, it is defined as wives' perceptions about whether they or their husbands would be hurt more (financially, interpersonally, emotionally) if there marriages were to break up. Only those women who consistently indicated that they would be hurt more were considered subjectively dependent.[3]

Since perceived ties to marriage are not necessarily congruent with actual ties, we do not expect a perfect correlation between wives' objective and subjective marital dependency. While for some women, subjective dependency may be a direct function of objective dependency, for others it may not be. Some women may feel strongly dependent on their marriages even though situational factors do not make them particularly dependent. Others who are structurally bound to the relationship because of economic ties may not perceive themselves to be dependent. As such, we expect the two dimensions of marital dependency to be related but nonetheless empirically distinguishable.

In short, this study explores the relationship between women's objective and subjective dependency on marriage, as well as the relationship between these two dimensions of dependency and the extent to which husbands abuse their wives. It examines whether women's marital dependency is positively or negatively related to wife abuse. Finally, it explores whether objective and subjective dependency are differentially related to abuse.

Methods

Measures

Objective marital dependency. The index of wives' objective dependency is the sum of scores on three dichotomous variables: whether the woman worked, whether she had children age five or younger at home, and whether her husband earned 75% or more of the couple's income.[4] The value of the index ranged from 0 (low objective dependency) to 3 (high dependency) and the internal consistency of the index, measured by Cronbach's *alpha* coefficient of reliability, was .59 (Cronbach, 1970).

Subjective marital dependency. The subjective dependency index is the sum of scores on five variables assessing perceptions about whether the respondent or her husband would be hurt more in each of five areas if their marriage were to break up. The specific areas were financial, sexual, loss of friends, angry relatives, and loneliness. The response categories included respondent would be hurt more, husband would be hurt more, both would be hurt equally, and neither would be hurt. Dummy variables were constructed with 1 equal to "respondent would be hurt more" and 0 equal to any other response. The range of the index was 0 to 5; however, since only 6% of all female respondents scored 4 or higher, scores of 3 and above were combined. The *alpha* coefficient of reliability was .35.[5]

Violence toward wives. Violence toward wives was assessed using the Conflict Tactics Scales. Given the range of items included in the physical violence scale, we developed two violence measures: minor and severe. The measure of minor violence contained those items that did not carry a high risk of serious injury ("threw something at wife" to "slapped wife") and the measure of severe violence contained the remaining items, all of which carried the risk of serious injury. The two scales were constructed as dichotomous variables with 1 indicating the presence of one or more acts of violence and 0 indicating the absence of violence. Eleven percent of the women interviewed reported experiencing at least some minor violence, and 4% reported severe violence.[6]

Sample and Data Analysis

The analysis is based on the data from the 1975 survey. Log-linear techniques were used to examine the patterns suggested in the contingency tables. The approach was selected over regression because the dependent variables were dichotomous. Goodman's ECTA program (Goodman, 1978) was used to identify the model which best fit the data (i.e., the model with expected cell frequencies closest to those obtained in the data.) (See Table 21.1 for the cell frequencies that were the input for the ECTA program.)

Results of Bivariate Analyses

Objective and Subjective Marital Dependency

The correlation of .147 between wives' subjective and objective marital dependency indicates a weak but significant relationship ($p = .001$). This provides the first empirical indication of the importance of distinguishing between the two dimensions of marital dependency. While the two are positively related, it appears that women are able to perceive themselves as tied to their marriages in the absence of situational factors that objectively create such ties. Similarly, they may not recognize marital dependency that exists at the objective level. The weak relationship between objective and subjective marital dependency suggests that they, in fact, may be differentially related to wife abuse.

The Bivariate Relationships between Minor Violence and Marital Dependency

The bivariate relationships between minor violence toward wives and the two dimensions of marital dependency are presented in Part A of Table 21.2. Both relationships are positive: the rate of minor violence increases as wives' marital dependency increases. This suggests that both objectively and subjectively dependent wives tolerate more minor abuse than "non-dependent" wives, perhaps because they have (or perceive) fewer

TABLE 21.1
Observed Cell Frequencies: Cross-Tabulations with Minor and Severe Violence

Experienced Violence	Level of Subjective Dependence	Level of Objective Dependency			
		Low		High	
No	Very low	114	(118)	63	(63)
Yes	Very low	6	(2)	4	(4)
No	Low	144	(163)	130	(139)
Yes	Low	21	(1)	21	(10)
No	High	107	(116)	105	(116)
Yes	High	17	(6)	21	(9)
No	Very high	59	(63)	81	(91)
Yes	Very high	8	(3)	16	(6)

Note: Severe violence in parentheses.

TABLE 21.2

Marital Violence Rates by Wives' Objective and Subjective Marital Dependency

Type of Dependency	Level of Marital Dependency			
	Very Low	Low	High	Very High
	A. Minor Violence			
Objective Dependency[a]	10.5%	10.6%	12.0%	17.5%
Subjective Dependency[b]	5.3	12.3	13.6	13.5
	B. Severe Violence			
Objective Dependency[c]	2.4	2.5	6.7	6.5
Subjective Dependency[d]	3.1	3.3	5.9	4.7

[a] $x^2 = 5.39, p = .146, N = 973.$
[b] $x^2 = 12.17, p = .03, N = 1081.$
[c] $x^2 = 10.08, p = .018, N = 966.$
[d] $x^2 = 4.59, p = .468, N = 1072.$

viable alternatives to marriage. This interpretation does not assume that violence against wives is directly "caused" by dependency. Our position is that such violence is rooted in many factors, including male-dominant family relationships, the level of conflict between the spouses, role models for marital violence provided by the husband having observed his father hit his mother, implicit cultural norms tolerating such violence, etc. (Straus et al., 1980:Chapter 9). Whatever the causal matrix, women in unbalanced relationships are more likely to tolerate wife abuse than women in relationships where the resources and outside options are more equally balanced between husband and wife.

While both objective and subjective dependency are positively related to minor violence, the strength of the relationship differs. Subjective dependency appears to have a stronger relationship to minor violence than does objective dependency. The former relationship is statistically significant, while the latter is not. Moreover, the rate of minor violence among women who score very high in subjective dependency is almost triple that of women who score very low on that dependency dimension; whereas, the difference in minor violence between the extreme categories of objective dependency is less than twofold.

The Bivariate Relationships between Severe Violence and Marital Dependency

Part B of Table 21.2 shows that the bivariate relationships between severe violence toward wives and the two dependency dimensions are positive. The rate of severe violence increases as wives' marital dependency increases.

Once again, the magnitude of the two relationships differ. Subjective dependency appears to have little effect on the rate of severe violence, while the relationship between such violence and wives' objective marital dependency is strong. The rate of severe violence is almost three times higher among women high than among those very low in objective dependency. The increment in severe violence between the parallel levels of subjective dependency is only twofold.

In summary, subjective but not objective marital dependency is significantly related to minor violence toward wives, while the reverse is true for severe violence. To explore these differential patterns further, we examined the multivariate relationships between the two dependency dimensions and the measures of violence toward wives.

Results of Multivariate Analyses

The Multivariate Relationships between Minor
Violence and Marital Dependency

The multivariate relationships between *minor* violence and the two dependency dimensions are presented in Table 21.3. The figures in that table are within-cell percentages, so that among women very low on both dependency dimensions, 5% experienced minor violence.

These data support the conclusions drawn from the bivariate relationships. Subjective dependency has a stronger relationship to minor violence than does objective dependency. Within categories of subjective dependency, the rates of minor violence are similar whether a woman is high or low in objective marital dependency. At no point is the rate of minor violence among women high in objective dependency twice that of women low in objective dependency. On the other hand, within categories of objective dependency, the rate of minor violence almost triples as subjective dependency increases (5% vs. 14%). Moreover, the rate of minor violence is higher among women high in subjective but low in objective dependency (14%) than among those high on both dimensions (10%). Finally, although the rate of minor violence is highest (16%) among women

TABLE 21.3

Minor Violence Rate at Different Levels of Objective and Subjective Marital Dependency

	Subjective Dependency			
Objective Dependency	Very Low	Low	High	Very High
Low	5%[a]	13%	14%	12%
High	6%	14%	10%	16%

[a]The percentage in each cell is the rate of severe violence for that particular combination of objective and subjective marital dependency.

high on objective and very high on subjective dependency, those low on objective and high on subjective dependency report a minor violence rate almost as high (14%). In summary, once subjective dependency is taken into account, objective dependency does not add much to the prediction of minor violence against wives.

The Multivariate Relationships between Severe Violence and Marital Dependency

The multivariate relationships between the dependency dimensions and *severe* violence against wives follow the opposite pattern. The relationship between severe violence and objective dependency is stronger than that between such violence and subjective dependency. These relationships are presented in Table 21.4.

Among women low in objective dependency, the rate of severe violence increases as subjective dependency increases. However, once objective dependency is high, subjective dependency has virtually no effect on the violence rate. When objective dependency is high, the rate of severe violence is relatively high at all levels of subjective dependency. On the other hand, within categories of subjective dependency, the rate of severe violence tends to increase as objective dependency increases. Thus, unlike minor violence, knowledge of a wife's level of objective dependency on her marriage appears to be a better predictor of whether her husband severely abuses her than is knowledge of the level of her subjective dependency.

Log-Linear Analysis of the Dependency-Violence Relationships

The final stage of analysis involved the use of log-linear techniques to test the differential relationships between the dependency dimensions and the violence measures suggested by the raw data. The procedure for selecting a model began with the saturated or perfect-fit model and,

TABLE 21.4
Severe Violence Rate at Different Levels of Objective and Subjective Marital Dependency

	Subjective Dependency			
Objective Dependency	Very Low	Low	High	Very High
Low	2%[a]	6%	5%	5%
High	6%	7%	8%	7%

[a]The percentage in each cell is the rate of severe violence for that particular combination of objective and subjective marital dependency.

through systematic elimination of individual terms (effects), tested progressively simpler models. The optimal model was one that was most parsimonious and could not be rejected statistically at the .10 level.[7]

A procedure suggested by Davis (1974) was used to test the significance of individual effects in the models selected. We assessed the fit of the model that contained all effects in the selected model other than the one being tested. If the simpler model had a significant *chi*-square, we concluded that removal of the effect in question left us with a poorly fitting model which, therefore, was rejected. On the other hand, if the simpler model had a nonsignificant *chi*-square, then we concluded that the simpler model could be retained.

Minor violence. Results of the log-linear analysis presented in Table 21.5 support patterns of association suggested by the contingency tables. The optimal model includes two-way effects between minor violence and subjective dependency (AB) and between subjective and objective dependency (BC). This model fits the observed frequencies with a likelihood *chi*-square ratio of 1.23 ($df = 4$, $p = .5$). Tests of the individual terms showed them to be significant.

In short, subjective dependency is significantly related to minor violence while objective dependency is not. Moreover, there is no significant interaction between the dependency dimensions and minor violence toward wives. Thus, the relationship between subjective dependency and minor violence is essentially the same among women high and those low in objective dependency. Finally, there is a significant positive relationship between wives' objective and subjective marital dependency.

Severe violence. The log-linear results for severe violence also support our previous findings. Table 21.6 indicates that for severe violence the best-fitting model contains two-way effects between violence and objective

TABLE 21.5

Log-Linear Models for Minor Violence

Model	*Chi*-square Statistic	Degrees of Freedom	Significance Level	Effect Tested
ABC	0.00	0		
AB AC BC	.20	3	> .5	
AB BC	1.23	4	> .5[a]	
AC BC	11.67	6	.070	
AB AC	19.02	6	.004	
AB C	21.06	7	.004	BC[b]
BC A	13.71	7	.056	AB[b]
AC B	31.49	9	.000	

Note: A = minor violence toward wives; B = wives' subjective marital dependency; C = wives' objective marital dependency.
[a]This is the optimal (best-fitting model).
[b]These effects (from the optimal model) are statistically significant.

TABLE 21.6

Log-Linear Models for Severe Violence

Model	Chi-square Statistic	Degrees of Freedom	Significance Level	Effect Tested
ABC	0.00	0		
AB AC BC	4.39	3	.221	
AB BC	11.15	4	.018	
AC BC	6.63	6	.356a	
AB AC	23.96	6	.001	
AB C	32.27	7	.000	BCb
BC A	14.93	7	.037	ABb
AC B	27.04	9	.002	

Note: A = severe violence; B = subjective dependency; C = objective dependency.
aThis is the optimal.(best-fitting model).
bThese effects (from the optimal model) are statistically significant.

marital dependency and between the two dependency dimensions (AC, BC). Once again, the tests of these two individual effects show them to be significant. Thus, wives' objective but not subjective marital dependency is significantly related to severe violence and there is no significant interaction between the dependency dimensions and violence.

Discussion

The results of this study indicate that women whose dependency on marriage is high tend to experience more physical abuse from their husbands than women whose dependency is low. Although the causal dynamic between wives' marital dependency and abuse is not addressed by our data, we can indicate at least a plausible scenario. We suggest that dependency is a mediating rather than a direct causal variable. As noted earlier in the paper, violence by husbands arises out of multiple causes, including the use of force as a means of maintaining a dominant power position. Whatever the specific causes of the violence, we suggest that wives who are highly dependent on marriage are less able to discourage, avoid, or put an end to abuse than are women in marriages where the balance of resources between husbands and wives is more nearly equal. Dependent wives have fewer alternatives to marriage and fewer resources within marriage with which to negotiate changes in their husbands' behavior. Thus, marital dependency reinforces the likelihood that women will tolerate physical abuse from their husbands.

The results also indicate that while the marriage license may be considered a license for husbands to abuse their wives, there are limits on that license. The wives in our sample reported far more minor than severe abuse. While some of this differential may be due to respondents' greater willingness to report minor than severe acts of violence, it also is possible that women's tolerance of violence by their husbands decreases with its severity. The literature on wife abuse has documented the pervasive economic, legal, social, and psychological obstacles that women face in attempting to terminate abusive relationships. Perhaps the threat or experience of violent acts carrying a high risk of serious injury (severe violence) provides an impetus for confronting those obstacles that is absent when the violence does not carry such a risk (minor violence). Wives' greater tolerance for minor than for severe violence is consistent with previous research which shows that severity of the abuse is one of the primary factors associated with whether women seek outside intervention (and thus exhibit low tolerance) for physical violence from their husbands (Bowker and MacCallum, 1980; Gelles, 1976).

The tendency to tolerate violence up to, but not beyond, a certain point is supported by our findings that subjective but not objective dependency is significantly related to minor violence and that the reverse is true for severe violence. Subjectively dependent women, like women in general, tend to tolerate minor but not severe violence. The primary group of women who tolerate severe violence are those highest in objective dependency. For such women it is not a question of necessary motivation to overcome the obstacles keeping them in abusive marriages, because, in a sense, the obstacles for them are insurmountable. They have virtually no alternatives to their marriages and, therefore, "must" tolerate the conditions of those marriages.

These findings suggest that reducing subjective dependency will only affect the level of mild violence toward wives. When wife abuse is severe, it does not matter how dependent on marriage a woman perceives herself to be. As long as situational factors keep her objectively tied to marriage, she is almost as likely to be a victim of severe abuse if she is high than if she is low in subjective dependency. Thus, decreasing women's tolerance for severe violence requires a change in the structural conditions that tie them to marriage. This may be partially accomplished by fundamental changes such as universal child care services, reduced occpational discrimination against women, and an end to sex-based wage differentials. Therapeutic, educational, and support services designed to deal with wife abuse by building women's self-confidence, independence, and belief that they can survive outside of marriage will not be successful unless supplemented by programs and policies that reduce women's objective dependency on marriage.

A final contribution of this research is the evidence that both marital dependency and violence are multidimensional concepts. Specifically, the results suggest that it is important to distinguish between subjective and objective dependency, and between minor and severe violence. If these distinctions are incorporated into future theoretical and empirical analyses, it is likely that we will achieve a better understanding of the system of sexual stratification which keeps women dependent on their male partners and of the system of violence which is an integral part of the male-dominant family system.

Notes

1. The negative relationship between marital dependency and wife abuse is not portrayed as mediated through women's tolerance of abuse. Instead, low levels of marital dependency are said to directly cause relatively high levels of physical abuse toward wives because "independent" wives are threatening to their husbands and challenge their power within the family.
2. Many theorists have ignored employed women's contribution to the family income as a factor contributing to their economic dependency. They implicitly assume that employment yields independent economic resources and thus economic independence for women. See for example Brown (1980).
3. The measure of wives' subjective marital dependency actually assessed their dependency relative to that of their husbands. Women who felt that they would experience more hurt than their husbands by the breakup of their marriage, were coded as highly subjectively dependent even if their absolute level of hurt was low. This questions the meaning of high subjective dependency. However, in the aggregate, we expect a strong correlation between relative and absolute marital dependency. Moreover, as is common in secondary analysis, this was the best available measure of subjective dependency.
4. Missing values on variables included in both dependency scales were replaced by the mean scores on those variables. However, to be conservative, substitution only occurred if there were missing data on no more than one of the variables in the index. Using this substitution procedure, the sample size was 993 women for the objective dependency scale and 1,101 for the subjective dependency scale. The results of the analyses were the same with and without substitution of missing data.
5. The relatively low interitem reliability is not uncommon with social psychological scales. Moreover, factor analysis of all the dependency items produced two dimensions corresponding to our subjective and objective dependency scales. The only exception was that the financial item in the subjective dependency scale loaded on the objective dependency dimension. However, on a conceptual level, the item measured perceived rather than actual economic dependency. Moreover, analyses comparing the subjective dependency scale with and without the financial item showed minimal differences.
6. While these percentages may seem low, when projected to population figures they take on more meaning. They indicate that in 1975, 3,590,000 or one out of every nine married women in the United States experienced some minor acts of violence by her husband and 940,000 women experienced abuse carrying a high risk of physical injury. Given the sensitive nature of violence within the family it is highly probable that these rates of wife abuse are underestimates. In addition, it is possible that women who experienced high rates of physical violence from their husbands were systematically excluded from the sample because they were separated or divorced. For a more complete discussion of under-reporting in the data, see Straus et al. (1980).

7. The *chi*-square test typically assesses the probability of making an error by rejecting the simple hypothesis of no association between two variables (and thus accepting the alternate hypothesis that the two variables are related). Generally, low significance levels (e.g., .05) are selected to make rejection of the simple and acceptance of the research hypothesis difficult. In log-linear analysis, *chi*-square tests assess the fit of various models, of which the model of no association is just one (see Table 21.2). In such analyses the simple hypothesis also is the research hypothesis (i.e., that a set of parameters specified by a particular model accurately predicts the obtained cell frequencies). As such, a low significance level would not have a conservative effect, but would make it relatively difficult to reject the alternate hypothesis. A higher level reduces the probability of accepting a false alternate hypothesis and, thus, is desirable in log-linear analysis.

22

Patriarchy and Violence against Wives: The Impact of Structural and Normative Factors

Kersti A. Yllo and Murray A. Straus

Over the last decade our awareness of the relationship between wife beating and the sexist social structure and patriarchal norms has grown enormously. Studies of this relationship can be grouped into two broad categories. Feminists have used historical and case study data to analyze the link between patriarchy as a social system and wife abuse (Dobash and Dobash, 1980; Martin, 1976). Other researchers have assessed the relationship between the balance of power within marriages and spousal violence (Allen and Straus, 1980; Straus, Gelles, and Steinmetz, 1980). While both approaches have made important contributions to understanding violence against wives, each is also limited. The feminist expositions generally lack empirical evidence regarding the impact of sexual inequality. In particular, quantitative data have not been brought to bear on this issue. The interpersonal power researchers, on the other hand, have been myopic in perspective. Husband dominance has been studied empirically, but in isolation from the patriarchal system of which it is a part.

The purpose of this paper is to begin to bridge the gap between these two approaches. We take up the interrelationship between the patriarchal social structure, norms, and violence against wives using quantitative data. Specifically, we examine the relationship between wife beating and (1) the status of women in the economy, education, politics, and law, and (2) sexist social norms about who should dominate within the family.

Defining Patriarchy and Violence

The discussion of patriarchy by the Dobashes in *Violence Against Wives* (1980) is pertinent. They write:

> The patriarchy is comprised of two elements: its structure and its ideology. The structural aspect of the patriarchy is manifest in the hierarchical organization of social institutions and social relations . . . The maintenance of such a hierarchical order and the continuation of the authority and advantage of the few is to some extent dependent upon its 'acceptance' by the many. It is the patriarchal ideology that serves to reinforce this acceptance [1980:43].

The structural element of patriarchy can be seen in the low status women generally hold relative to men in the family and in economic, educational, political, and legal institutions. The ideological element is reflected in the values, beliefs, and norms regarding the "legitimacy" of male dominance in all social spheres. The degree to which these two elements of patriarchy affect the level of violence against wives in American states is the central concern of this paper.

The concept of violence can be broadly defined to include a wide range of abuses. It is possible to conceive of verbal aggression and psychological torment as types of "violence" women suffer. For the purposes of this analysis, however, the term *violence* will refer only to severe PHYSICAL aggression. This restriction is not meant to imply that non-physical abuse is unimportant. Nevertheless, it is physical violence that presents the greatest danger to life and health and it is physical violence to which women are particularly vulnerable, given the difference in size and strength between the sexes.

Violence is defined here as an act carried out with the knowledge that the likely consequence of it will be physical injury or pain to another person. The terms *wife beating* and *wife abuse* are used interchangeably with *violence against wives*.

Patriarchy and Wife Beating: The Feminist Analysis

The feminist analysis of wife beating is, at heart, a critique of patriarchy. The central argument is that the brutalization of an individual wife by an individual husband is not an individual or "family" problem. It is simply one manifestation of the system of male domination of women that has existed historically and cross-culturally. Societal tolerance of wife beating is a reflection of patriarchal norms that, more generally, support male dominance in marriage. Traditional marriage, in turn, is a central element of patriarchal society.

Del Martin, a noted feminist analyst of wife beating, writes in *Battered Wives* (1976):

> The historical roots of our patriarchal family models are ancient and deep. . . . New norms for marriage and family must be created, since the battering of wives grows naturally out of ancient and time-honored traditions [1976:26].

Martin provides an overview of the cruelty directed at women, and wives in particular, throughout history. For centuries, husbands have tortured and killed disobedient wives with the support of the state and the church. Physical violence against wives in the name of "chastisement" was legal in the United States until the mid-1800's, provided that the husband used a switch no bigger than his thumb—a "rule of thumb," so to speak. Though wife beating is no longer legal (in the U.S.), it is condoned because society and the law are still geared toward husband dominance in marriage. Martin illustrates this point with reference to the economic entrapment of battered wives and the reactions of law enforcement and social service agencies to them. She concludes "marriage is the mechanism by which the patriarchy is maintained" (1976:37).

A more scholarly volume on wife beating that follows along the lines of Martin's work is the Dobashes' *Violence Against Wives* (1980). The authors set wife abuse in historical and social context through comprehensive analysis of its legacy in the past and its perpetuation in the present. Using a wealth of international data and their own interviews with battered women, the authors illustrate how being a wife makes a woman an "appropriate victim" of assault. They assert that

> . . . men who assault their wives are actually living up to cultural prescriptions that are cherished in Western society—aggressiveness, male dominance, and female subordination—and they are using physical force as a means to enforce that dominance [1980:24].

Their book concludes with the statement that "the problem lies in the domination of women. The answer lies in the struggle against it" (p. 243).

The works of Martin and the Dobashes (emphasized here because they are two of the best and best-known feminist analyses of this issue) are powerful. They and other explicitly feminist analyses reveal the connection between societal patriarchy and the abuse of individual wives by building a strong case from many historical examples and contemporary illustrations.

What the feminist approach has not included is any quantitative analysis. In part, this may be true because reliable statistics on violence against wives have generally been unavailable. But it is also a consequence of a distrust of quantitative methodology as a whole. The Dobashes, for example, maintain that in such analysis

> the goal of understanding society is forgotten and ignored: the major preoccupation . . . is the development of standardized measuring techniques to test hypothetical statements, an activity unlikely to lead to an understanding and explanation of social problems . . . [1980:25]

This sweeping indictment of quantitative sociology is neither justified nor necessary for their pruposes, one of which is to show the value of a "context specific" approach.

The feminist focus on the social context of violence against wives, which emphasizes that wife abuse is neither deviant nor pathological, is not *inherently* linked to a particular type of methodology. More important than the particular research tool are the theoretical questions asked. The questions raised by feminist theory can be answered most fully through the use of a range of research designs by many researchers working in a cooperative atmosphere. Any single research method has its limitations. Feminist analyses of wife beating relying on qualitative data have been rich in detail regarding particular incidents and cases. However, they have lacked generalizability. The issue of how the current context of patriarchy affects the level of violence against wives throughout American society has not yet been adequately addressed.

Marital Power and Wife Beating: The Interpersonal Power Research

Researchers studying marital power and violence against wives came to the issue because of an academic interest in marital relationships and interaction. While some have feminist sympathies, they regard their purpose as doing research to explain social behavior rather than to formulate a critique of patriarchy.

This body of research has focused not on structured inequality at the societal level, but on inequality and the balance of power within the family. In the 1975 survey, Straus, Gelles, and Steinmetz (1980) found the level of violence against wives is lowest among couples who followed a pattern of egalitarian decision making. Fewer than 3% of these wives had suffered a severe violent attack within the previous year. In contrast, more than double that percent (7.1%) of wife-dominant couples reported such violence. The rate of wife beating in couples where the husband dominates is 10.7%: that is, 50% higher than for wife-dominant couples and more than 300% greater than for egalitarian couples. Chapter 16 further explores this connection between power and violence at the individual level of analysis.

Clearly, husband violence is associated with non-egalitarian decision making. It may be that among couples where the wife tends to make the final decisions, for whatever reasons, some husbands lash out violently because their masculinity is threatened. In male-dominant relationships, a sizeable number of husbands may turn to violence to maintain the subordination of their wives.

Empirical research has also been conducted to test the "Ultimate Resource Theory" of family violence. This theory holds that violence may be used by husbands as a final resource to maintain control when other resources are insufficient or lacking (Goode, 1971). The underlying assumption of this theory is that in achievement-oriented, industrialized countries, such as the U.S., the traditional norms legitimizing male superiority are inadequate as a sole basis of power. The premise is that under egalitarian norms, husbands dominate family decision making because they possess certain material goods or personal attributes that legitimize their power in the eyes of their wives. It is postulated that when husbands feel entitled to dominate yet lack the resources to do so "legitimately," they will turn to violence as the ultimate resource.

Allen and Straus (1980) have tested the propositions of the Ultimate Resource Theory and found limited support for it. They found that male power was associated with violence only when the husband lacked other validating resources. This finding held only for working-class families, however. They suggest that this relationship does not hold in middle-class families because the use of instrumental violence is less legitimate and therefore more costly in the middle class and that this may restrict its use.

While the empirical research discussed above provides valuable evidence on the relationship between husband dominance and violence, it is too narrowly focused. Its major shortcoming is common to all analyses that consider male-female power and inequality within the confines of the family unit. The patriarchal social and cultural context, within which the family is enmeshed and marital power relations are played out, is overlooked. The notion that patriarchal norms have, to a large degree, been replaced by egalitarian ones is accepted too readily. The inequitable social structure from which husbands derive legitimizing resources is not taken into account, as Del Martin argues:

> . . . wife-beating . . . is a complex problem that involves much more than the act itself or the personal interaction between a husband and a wife. It has its roots in historical attitudes toward women, the institution of marriage, the economy, the intricacies of criminal and civil law, and the delivery system of social service agencies (1976:xvi]

It follows that research concentrated on the interpersonal relationship between spouses is too restricted. However, this limitation is more a consequence of the theoretical orientation of the researchers, rather than the quantitative methodology they use. The patriarchal social context (including institutional structure and norms) can be examined using a quantiative methodology, as the remainder of this chapter will show.

Methodology

States as Social Context Units

This research, with its emphasis on macro sociological context, focuses on the American states as the contextual unit of analysis for a number of reasons. First, the states are theoretically appropriate units for the comparative study of the status of women. Despite the sense that America is becoming increasingly "nationalized" through centrally controlled media, corporations, and the federal government, states are still more than different colored areas on the map. Not only were states founded by peoples of diverse national backgrounds and values, but the timing of their settlement and development have influenced their individual characteristics and the position of women within them. Further, states are often the initiators of legislation and programs and are frequently the unit of implementation of federal policies, all of which can affect women.

The second reason that this research focuses on states is a practical one. Many of the variables of interest here are gathered by the census bureau on a state-by-state basis. In addition, a number of other agencies gather state-level data (for example, N.O.W.'s information on women and education). The uniformity of data from state to state makes it most useful for comparative purposes. Variables from different sources can easily be related to one another.

Violence against Wives: The Dependent Variable

As we indicated earlier, the term *violence,* as used here, refers to *Physical* aggression. The data on rates of violence were obtained from the 1975 national survey. Although the violence rates are based on data gathered from a national area-probability sample, only 36 states were included in this sample. In addition, since only certain areas of states were included after the first stage of sampling, these areas might not be representative of the whole state, particularly in those states in which only one or two areas were selected.

Rather than proceed on the assumption that the state samples are representative, this was investigated by comparing key variables from the survey data with parallel variables from census data, which we know to be representative. The variables that were considered were men's/husband's income; men's/husband's employment rate; men's/husband's education; women's/wives' education.

Generally, the sets of variables paralleled in value. States with high income, education, and employment levels according to the census ranked similarly on the survey data, in most cases. However, all but 2 of the states (Oregon with 14 cases and Mississippi with 13) having sample sizes 20 or fewer cases appeared to be unrepresentative. These 6 states were dropped from the analysis, leaving a final sample size of 30 states.

In most of the analyses, states are grouped into quartiles or quintiles by degree of patriarchal structure or norms. The mean violence rate for a group of states is more reliable than individual state rates because it is based on a larger number of cases.

Measurement of Wife Beating

Wife beating was measured through the use of Conflict Tactics Scales (CTS). The rate of wife beating is the proportion of couples who indicated that the husband had used any of the following tactics against his wife in the year prior to the interview: kicked, bit, or hit with a fist; hit or tried to hit with something; beat up; threatened with a knife or gun; used a knife or gun. A state violence rate of 10%, for example, indicates that 10% of the husbands perpetrated serious acts of violence against their wives within the past year. Note that more "minor" forms of violence, such as pushing, shoving, or slapping, are not included in the calculation of the rate. This is true not because such acts are condoned here, but that they are so common an element of family conflict that they would weaken the discriminating power of the index.

Patriarchal Structure and Patriarchal Norms: The Independent Variables

As the Dobashes (1980) indicated, the patriarchy is composed of two key elements: hierarchical organization of institutions and ideology. In this research, measures of both of these elements for American states are utilized.

Patriarchal Structure

Patriarchal structure is defined here as the status of women as a group, compared with the status of men as a group, in key societal institutions. The status of women relative to men in these institution spheres is assessed through a Status of Women index (Yllo, 1980).[1] Each sphere is considered a distinct dimension of women's status and makes up a separate part of the index. The specific dimensions that are included are the economic, educational, political, and legal. The particular items making up each dimension are listed below. The sources for the data are listed in Appendix B.

Economic Dimension

EC1, of women in the labor force
EC2, female in professional and technical occupations
EC3, female in managerial, administrative occupations
EC4, Unemployment: male rate as percent of female rate
EC5, Median income: female as percent of male, for full-time workers
ECX, Economic status of women index

Educational Dimension

ED1, High school graduation: female rate as percent of male rate
ED2, Post-secondary enrollment: percent female
ED3, High school interscholastic athletes: percent female
ED4, High school administrators: percent female
EDX, Educational status of women index

Political Dimension

POL1, Members in U.S. Congress: percent female
POL2, Members of state senate: percent female
POL3, Members of state house: percent female
POL4, Judges on major appellate and trial courts: percent female
POLX, Political status of women index

Legal Dimension

L1, No occupations barred to women
L2, Equal pay laws
L3, Fair employment practices act
L4, No maximum hours restrictions for females
L5, Proof of resistance not required for rape conviction
L6, Corroborating testimony not required for rape conviction
L7, Husband and wife jointly responsible for family support
L8, Husband and wife have equal right to sue for personal injury
L9, Husband and wife have equal right to sue for loss of consortium
L10, Wife's property rights unrestricted
L11, Wife's right to use maiden name unrestricted

L12, Wife's right to maintain separate domicile unrestricted
L13, Ratified federal Equal Rights Amendment
L14, Passed a state Equal Rights Amendment
LEGX, Legal status of women index

The individual items were standardized so that they could be combined into indexes for each of the four dimensions and a total index. Table 22.1 gives the rank order of the state from most to least egalitarian. Clearly,

TABLE 22.1

State Rankings on the Dimensions and on the Overall Status of Women Index

Economic Status of Women		Educational Status of Women		Political Status of Women		Legal Status of Women		Status of Women Index (SWX)	
D.C.	89	VT	77	ARIZ	79	ALAS	100	ALAS	70
N.C.	68	ALAS	74	MD	71	N.J.	89	CONN	62
VT	67	Wash	67	N.H.	69	DEL	78	MD	61
ALAS	64	CONN	66	WASH	67	WIS	78	VT	61
ARK	64	MINN	64	COLO	66	CONN	73	COLO	61
HAWA	63	MICH	63	CONN	66	COLO	65	N.J.	60
S.C.	63	IOWA	62	OREG	65	WASH	65	N.H.	60
N.Y.	63	MD	62	R.I.	61	N.H.	65	WASH	59
TENN	60	KANS	61	N.J.	60	CAL	65	WIS	57
MD	58	N.D.	60	N.C.	58	S.D.	65	NEBR	57
NEBR	58	MONT	59	HAWA	56	HAWA	66	HAWA	55
NEV	57	WYO	58	FLA	55	INDI	66	OREG	55
GA	57	S.D.	57	DEL	53	MASS	66	ARIZ	55
CAL	56	COLO	57	NEBR	52	NEBR	66	MASS	55
COLO	55	ME	56	MASS	52	WYO	62	N.Y.	55
MISS	54	OREG	55	KANS	52	N.Y	55	D.C.	55
WIS	54	N.M.	54	NEV	52	MD	55	CAL	54
N.H.	53	N.Y.	53	VT	52	ARIZ	55	S.D.	54
KY	62	N.H.	52	ME	51	IOWA	55	IOWA	53
MINN	62	VA	51	IOWA	50	MINN	55	MINN	53
FLA	52	NEBR	51	N.D.	50	OREG	55	KANS	53
MASS	51	WIS	50	D.C.	49	PA	55	FLA	53
PA	51	MASS	50	ILL	49	FLA	55	MICH	52
MO	50	FLA	49	S.D.	49	KANS	55	WYO	51
VA	49	KY	49	TENN	48	R.I.	55	DEL	50
MICH	49	CAL	48	ARK	48	MICH	50	ME	50
ME	48	D.C.	48	INDI	48	VT	50	TENN	49
N.J.	48	IDA	48	N.Y.	48	ARK	44	R.I.	49
ALA	47	TEX	47	OHIO	48	KY	44	ARK	49
IOWA	46	MISS	47	CAL	47	TENN	44	INDI	49
OREG	45	NEV	47	WIS	46	N.D.	44	PA	49
KANS	44	N.C.	45	IDA	46	IDA	44	N.D.	48
R.I.	43	TENN	45	PA	46	OHIO	44	N.C.	48
TEX	43	OKLA	45	MICH	45	GA	44	MONT	47
S.D.	43	N.J.	44	MONT	44	MONT	44	KY	46
N.M.	43	ILL	44	MO	43	MO	44	GA	45
WYO	42	ARIZ	44	TEX	42	TEX	44	MO	45
ARIZ	41	OHIO	43	MINN	42	ME	44	NEV	44
CONN	41	PA	43	WYO	41	UTAH	33	TEX	44
OKLA	40	INDI	42	ALAS	41	ILL	33	OHIO	44
N.D.	40	GA	42	LA	41	MISS	33	IDA	43
OHIO	39	MO	42	KY	41	D.C.	33	MISS	43
ILL	39	ARK	39	OKLA	40	VA	33	VA	42
MONT	39	DEL	39	W.VA	40	N.M.	33	N.M.	41
W.VA	39	W.VA	38	UTAH	39	NEV	21	ILL	41
INDI	38	R.I.	37	GA	39	N.C.	21	S.C.	41
WASH	36	UTAH	36	VA	37	OKLA	21	OKLA	36
IDA	36	HAWA	36	N.M.	37	W.VA	21	W.VA	34
DEL	32	LA	34	S.C.	36	S.C.	21	UTAH	34
UTAH	29	S.C.	34	MISS	36	LA	10	ALA	28
LA	27	ALA	24	ALA	33	ALAS	10	LA	28

this is a just relative ranking since no state was truly egalitarian on any index.

Patriarchal Norms

The ideological component of patriarchy is quite complex. It includes the values taught in the schools, preached in the churches, and perpetrated by the media. It is beyond the scope of this study to fully assess these interrelated elements. Our measure of patriarchal norms taps only one aspect of this complex pattern, but it is an aspect that is central for this analysis. Specifically, we measured the degree to which state residents believe that husbands *should* dominate family decision making using the modified Decision Power index described in Chapter 17. Their answers to the index were aggregated by state, and the states were then ranked from least to most patriarchal in terms of family norms.

Patriarchal Structure, Patriarchal Norms, and Violence against Wives

The purpose of this empirical analysis is to examine the interrelationship between the dimensions of patriarchy and the level of violence against wives in the U.S. We recognize that there is less variance in degree of patriarchy among American states than between the U.S. and many other cultures. Nevertheless, as shown in Table 22.1, American states do vary in the extent to which sexual inequality is structurally and normatively embedded (Yllo:1980). Our aim is to assess the degree to which differences in institutional inequality and sexist family norms are associated with varying amounts of wife beating.

Structural Inequality and Wife Beating

There is good reason to expect that there is a positive linear relationship between structural inequality and level of wife beating. As economic, educational, and political opportunities for women improve, there are more alternatives to violent marriage. Where structural inequality is great, women are more likely to be trapped in abusive marriages. Further, more violence may be used to keep women "in their place."

However, there is another possibility. In states where women's status is highest, there may be increased violence against wives. As the patriarchal structure and traditional male-female roles break down, some husbands may be more likely to resort to violence in an attempt to retain control and bolster threatened masculinity. Martin writes that in areas where traditional modes of life are changing, both men and women are having difficulty with the contradiction between traditional expectations and emerging possibilities.

In this light, it is not difficult to see how serious conflict between social expectation and personal preference might tear a marriage apart. If that conflict expresses itself violently, as it very well may, the woman as the physically weaker partner is most apt to bear the physical brunt of the ordeal (1976:44).

Turning to Figure 22.1, we find that the rate of violence against wives is highest in those states where structural inequality is greatest. As the status

FIGURE 22.1

Structural Status of Women and Violence against Wives

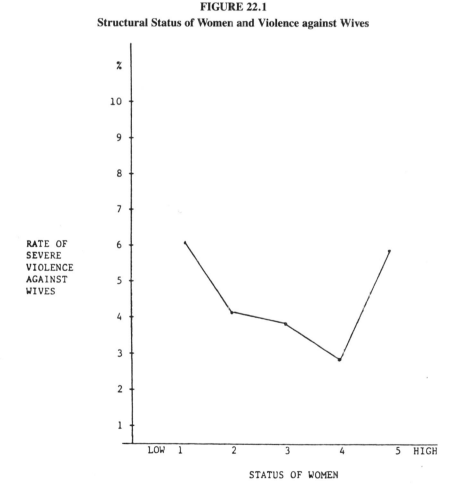

of women improves, violence declines—to a point. In those states where economic, educational, political, and legal inequality is relatively low, wife beating is quite high. In other words, a curvilinear relationship between the structural status of women and violence against wives emerges here (Eta = .46).

The fact that violence against wives is greatest in states that fall at the two extremes of women's status requires us to consider both explanations discussed above. It was suggested that low-status states might have the most wife beating because greater force may be necessary to keep women "in their place" and because women in these states have fewer alternatives to violent marriages. On the other hand, violence may be greater in high-status states because these are the states in which the patriarchal structure is breaking down and in which husbands may feel most threatened. Domestic conflict may increase in those areas where women are achieving equality most quickly. While the traditional formula and norms for the relationship between husbands and wives disappear, new patterns or guidelines are not yet institutionalized. As Moore states in *Social Change,* the probability of conflict is related to rapid social change (even if it is favorable change) and to the decreased predictability of interpersonal relations (1974:68). It seems likely that changes of this sort would also result in increased conflict in marriages.

The empirical evidence suggests that both of these processes may be at work. Women in states where their economic, educational, political, and legal status is low are the victims of the greatest violence at the hands of their husbands, and the rate declines steadily as the status of women increases. Yet at the same time, wives in the top fifth of states, where women have achieved the greatest equality, also suffer high levels of physical aggression from their husbands. Note, however, that even these states are far from true equality and that this analysis does not (and cannot) deal with the long-range consequences of real equality between the sexes.

Structural Inequality and Patriarchal Norms

Structural inequality and male-dominant ideology are both elements of a patriarchal system. Our analysis focuses on one specific part of the ideological element: sexist norms regarding the balance of power in the family. Before considering the impact of such norms on the level of wife abuse, it is important for us to look at the connection between these norms and structural inequality. To what extent is the structural status of women outside the family related to norms about their subordination within the family?

The correlation between the status of women and patriarchal norms is near zero. That is, we find no significant association between women's status in non-family institutions and social support for the notion that husbands should be the final authority within the family.

It is important to note that our data are cross-sectional and reflect differences between states. The data show that there is no correlation between the degree of institutional sexual inequality in a state and the patriarchal family norms held by state residents. We do not take this finding to mean that historically or in the long run structural inequality and male-dominant norms are unrelated. The data do indicate that currently there is often an inconsistency between the opportunities available to women outside the family and social norms regarding their position within the family. The meaning of such inconsistency for the rate of violence against wives will be taken up in a later section. However, an analysis of the factors that might account for these inconsistencies (such as the general economic or religious climate of a state) is beyond the scope of this paper.

Patriarchal Norms and Violence against Wives

Figure 22.2 shows a linear relationship between patriarchal norms and violence against wives. The more patriarchal the norms about marital power, the more wife abuse. In fact, the rate of wife beating in states with the most male-dominant norms (6.2%) is *double* that in states with more egalitarian norms (3.1%).

These results regarding the normative *context* parallel the findings of previous research on the actual decision-making patterns *within* families that we discussed earlier. At both levels equalitarian patterns are the least violent, whereas husband-dominant patterns are the most violent. This parallel reveals the connection between patriarchy as it operates in the societal context and in the micro-sociological interaction within the family.

Whether we are dealing with actual husband dominance within the marriage or with general societal support of such domination, we find an association between dominance and violence against wives. In areas where there is general ideological support for the patriarchal family we might have expected that there would be less wife abuse because the norms could ensure husband dominance without a battle. The findings indicate the contrary. Even where patriarchal norms are strong, it appears that there are important issues on which wives do not acquiesce to the norms. It appears that husbands are more prone to use violence in a context that is generally supportive of their "right" to dominate marriages.

The relationship between patriarchal norms and wife beating is under-

FIGURE 22.2
Patriarchal Norms and Violence against Wives

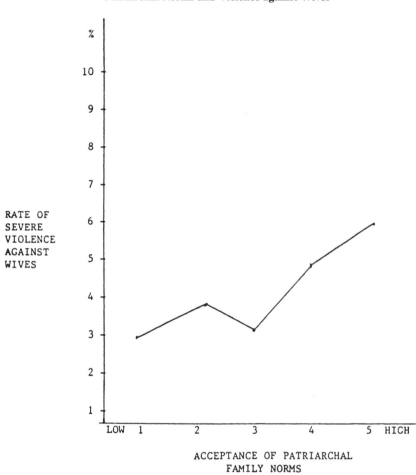

ACCEPTANCE OF PATRIARCHAL
FAMILY NORMS

standable. The incongruity between this relation and the structural ine-
quality-violence connection requires further explanation, however. The
more egalitarian the normative climate, the less wife beating. Yet the
relationship between structural equality and wife abuse is curvilinear.
True, violence against wives is most common where the societal status of
women is lowest. However, the rate of violence is almost as high in states
where women's status is (relatively) the highest.

Multivariate Analysis

To better interpret these results, we turned to multivariate analysis. The relationship between patriarchal norms and wife abuse was controlled for the structural status of women. In other words, we examined the norm-violence relationship within categories of women's status.

In states where the status of women in economic, educational, political, and legal spheres is low or moderate, there is little consistent relationship between patriarchal norms and violence. However, in the quartile of states where the status of women is highest, there is an association between patriarchal norms and the rate of violence against wives. The highest rate of violence occurs when normative support for husband dominance is high, even though the structural status of women is relatively high.

Wife beating is most common where there is an *inconsistency* between women's status in economic, educational, political, and legal institutions and social norms that hold that their status within marriage should be subordinate. In such a context, social changes may be occurring quite rapidly. Social values, for whatever reason, have not kept up with the realities of structural changes. The conflict between norms and structural opportunities may well be being waged within the home. And that battle appears to include physical violence for a sizable proportion of couples.

Summary and Conclusions

This paper examined the relationship between the rates of wife beating in American states and the degree to which each state is characterized by (1) a patriarchal social structure and (2) patriarchal family norms. The findings reveal that

1. There is a curvilinear relationship between patriarchal structure and the rate of wife beating. Wife beating is highest in those states where structural inequality in economic, educational, political, and legal institutions is greatest. As the status of women improves, violence declines—to a point. In the quintiles of states where the status of women is highest the rate of wife beating is also quite high. We suggest that the different parts of the curve represent the operation of two different processes. The downward slope on the left side of the curve reflects the principle that the greater the degree of social inequality, the more coercion is needed to maintain such a system. Thus the greatest force is needed to keep wives "in their place" in states where women have the lowest status. The increase in the rate of wife beating at the right side of the curve may reflect increased marital conflict growing out of a

rapid social change in sex roles and in the balance of power between the sexes.

2. There is a linear association between patriarchal family norms and wife beating. States with male-dominant norms have *twice* as much wife beating as states with more egalitarian norms.

3. A multivariate analysis was used to analyze the interaction of structural and normative factors in their impact on rates of wife beating. This analysis revealed that in states where the structural status of women is low or moderate, patriarchal family norms have no clear relationship to rates of wife beating. Only in the quintile of states where the status of women is highest is there an association between patriarchal norms and violence. Thus wife beating is most common in a context where women's status in economic, educational, legal, and political institutions is relatively high but where prevailing norms favor their subordination within marriage. We suggest that this is true because of the conflicts inherent in the *inconsistency* between the relatively equal structural status of women and the attempt to maintain a traditional patriarchal power structure within the family.

The findings reported in this paper represent an effort to bridge the gap between the feminist and marital power research approaches to understanding the causes of wife beating. It addresses the questions raised by feminists using quantitative data, a method favored by the marital power researchers. In a fundamental way, this paper has more in common with previous feminist research, and this is a central contribution of this paper. The triangulation of research methods is central to the development of a better understanding of any research issue, and feminist issues are no exception. Since each method has particular strengths and weaknesses, there is always a danger that a finding will reflect, in part, the method of inquiry. This paper provides a balance to the qualitative analyses that have been predominantly feminist research. In doing so, it has expanded our understanding of the relationship between patriarchal society and the violence that individual wives endure.

Notes

An abridged version of this chapter was published in the *Journal of International and Comparative Social Welfare*, 1 (1) (Fall, 1984), under the title "The Impact of Structural Inequality and Sexist Family Norms on Rates of Wife-Beating."

1. A revised version of this index was constructed by Sugarman and Straus (1988) and used in a study of state-to-state differences in rape (Baron and Straus, 1989 & 1989).

Appendix A. Sources of Data for the Status of Women Index

Items from source are listed in parentheses.

Alexander, Shana. 1975. *Women's Legal Rights*. Los Angeles: Wollenstonecraft, Inc. (L1–L14)

Council of State Governments. 1975. Book of the States. Lexington, KY: Council of State Governments. (POL1–POL4)

Johnson, Marilyn, and Kathy Stanwick. 1978. Profile of Women Holding Office. New Brunswick, NJ: Eagleton Institute of Politics. (POL1–POL4)

Project on Equal Education Rights. 1979. "Back to School Lineup: Where Girls and Women Stand in Education Today." Washington, DC: National Organization for Women. (ED3–ED4)

U.S. Bureau of the Census. 1977. Statistical Abstract of the U.S. Washington, DC (ED1–ED2)

U.S. Department of Labor. 1978. *Survey of Income and Education*, Spring 1976. Washington, DC: Bureau of Labor Statistics, Report 536. (EC1–EC5)

Part VI
THE AFTERMATH OF FAMILY VIOLENCE: COPING AND CONSEQUENCES OF VIOLENCE

23

Ordinary Violence, Child Abuse, and Wife Beating: What Do They Have in Common?

Murray A. Straus

From its beginning, the Family Violence Research Program at the University of New Hampshire has operated on the assumption that there are common elements underlying the occurrence of all types of physical violence. This does not deny the importance of the difference between, for example, physical punishment and child abuse, or between throwing something at a husband or wife versus the brutal and often life-threatening assaults that go under the name "wife beating." Indeed, a major part of an earlier theoretical work on family violence (Gelles & Straus, 1979) is devoted to specifying a number of dimensions on which violence must be classified to avoid confusion and make family violence research cumulative.

There is no contradiction between the idea that all violence has something in common and the idea that there are important differences between various types of violence. Both approaches are necessary to understand this complex phenomenon fully. Whether one focuses on the common elements in all violence or on the unique aspects of a certain type of violence depends on the purpose. For purposes of emergency intervention services, it makes sense to have a special category of "battered women" or "abused children" so that such cases can be given immediate assistance. Or, to take another example, Chapter 20 reveals that the more a wife subjectively perceived herself as dependent on her husband, the greater the rate of *minor* violence. However, mere subjective dependency apparently is not enough in respect to *severe* violence. Economic dependency much more than psychological dependency keeps a woman in a severely abusive marriage.

On the other hand, as I will try to show in this chapter, there are common elements underlying physical punishment, child abuse, throwing things at a spouse, and wife beating. This information throws light on the causes of family violence and is information that may also be extremely important for primary prevention.

Theoretical and Practical Importance of the Issue

The theoretical issue of this chapter is whether child abuse and wife beatings are unique types of violence that require a separate explanatory theory. Or are they simply more extreme aspects of the everyday violence that goes almost unnoticed in American families? More specifically, I have argued that physical punishment trains children in the use of violence— that is, that this most ordinary of ordinary types of family violence is one of the root causes of child abuse and wife beating (Straus, 1979a; Straus, Gelles, & Steinmetz, 1980, chap. 5; and chapters 8 and 20 of this volume). This idea is supported by Frude and Goss (1979), who showed that the more the parents in their sample used ordinary physical punishment, the greater the percentage who were worried that they might get carried away to the point of child abuse. The analyses to be reported are intended to determine whether there is more direct empirical support for this theory.

Issues of considerable practical importance are at stake. If ordinary physical punishment is, in fact, related to child abuse and wife beating, it means that to break the cycle of violence from generation to generation more attention must be paid to helping parents find alternatives to the use of physical punishment.

Of course, many other factors seem to be part of the etiology of child abuse and wife beating, including, for example, a male-dominant balance of power in the family, the level of stress experienced by the family, and the larger pattern of intrafamily violence, such as violence between siblings and violence by women toward their children and their husbands. These are pervasive types of violence. In fact, children are the most violent members of American families. In early childhood, practically all children hit their brothers or sisters. Even among the 15- to 17-year-olds in this study, two thirds had hit a sibling during a one-year period, and in about a third of the cases this was a severe assault. In the case of women, well over 50% of mothers use physical punishment; child abuse rates are at least as high as those for men; and assaults on husbands are almost as high as assaults by husbands on wives (Straus, 1980). It seems reasonable to assume that these are also factors which must be included in any consideration of what is necessary to reduce the level of wife beating.

But what do they have to do with the question of whether ordinary violence has anything in common with child abuse and wife beating? The link is indirect but important: If the variables listed above are part of an interrelated system of social relationships that includes ordinary physical punishment, violence between siblings, and ordinary marital violence as key elements, then primary prevention efforts aimed at child abuse and wife beating will probably be ineffective unless all the component elements are addressed.

Method

Research Design

The strategy used to investigate whether ordinary physical punishment and child abuse share the same etiology, and whether the ordinary pushes, slaps, and shoves which occur between spouses have the same origins as wife beating, is to compare the correlates of "abusive" violence with the correlates of ordinary violence. If the same set of variables that statistically explain child abuse and wife beating also explain ordinary physical punishment and minor acts of violence between spouses (such as pushing, shoving, slapping, or throwing things), this will be taken as support for the idea that ordinary violence has much in common with child abuse and wife beating.

Sample and Violence Measures

The sample used to test these relationships was the 1975 National Family Violence Survey. Husband-to-wife violence, parent-to-child violence, and sibling violence were all measured using the Conflict Tactics Scales (described briefly in Chapter 1 and fully in Chapters 3 and 4). Both the minor violence index (referred to as "ordinary violence" in this chapter) and the severe violence index (referred to as "wife beating" and "child abuse" in this chapter) are examined in this study. Using these two measures, support was claimed for the idea that the same set of etiological variables that were found to statistically explain child abuse and wife beating also account for family-to-family differences in ordinary violence (Straus et al., 1980: p. 208). Due to a methodological error (described below), that claim was unwarranted.

A new measure: the "ordinary violence" rate.   The error just mentioned occurred because we overlooked the fact that the Overall Violence rate is just that—it includes *all* the violent acts in the CTS, whereas for the purposes of comparing ordinary violence and severe violence a different measure is needed. What is needed is a measure that is restricted to the minor acts of violence so common in American families. Consequently, an "Ordinary Violence" index was computed for this study (called the "Minor Violence" index elsewhere in this book). It identifies respondents who engaged in pushing, slapping, shoving, and throwing things (items k, l, and m of the CTS) and did *not* engage in any of the more serious acts of violence listed in the CTS. In addition, when parent-to-child violence is being measured, respondents were classified as having used ordinary violence if they reported using physical punishment during the year.[1]

Frequency of assault. In addition to distinguishing between ordinary violence and severe violence, another refinement is necessary. Most abused children and most of the women who seek assistance at shelters have been *repeatedly* beaten. It is possible that what distinguishes child abuse and wife beating from ordinary violence is not just the severity of the assault, but the fact that it is a continuing pattern. Consequently, in relation to husband-to-wife violence, I will distinguish between four groups of husbands: (1) those who seriously assaulted their wife three or more times during the year of the survey, 2) those who engaged in such attacks once or twice that year, (3) those who used only ordinary violence as defined above, and (4) the nonviolent. In the case of parent-to-child violence, the same procedure was followed except that for group 3 the classification is based on both the Ordinary Violence index of the CTS described above and on questions which asked how often the respondent and his or her spouse had used physical punishment during the year covered by this survey. Parents who indicated either some act of minor violence in response to the CTS questions or who reported using physical punishment were classified in group 3, provided they did not report any instance of severe violence.

The "Violence Begets Violence" Theory

The idea that child-abusing parents were themselves victims of abuse, and that wife beating husbands come from violent families, is now widely accepted. Consequently, that is not the main purpose of this section. Rather, the objective is to determine whether the links are confined to violence at an equivalent level: Is it only victims or observers of *severe* violence who have elevated rates of child abuse and wife beating? Or is merely being subjected to ordinary physical punishment or ordinary minor violence between spouses also associated with a greater probability of being a child abuser or wife beater?

Physical Punishment and Violence by Children

The point plotted in the lower left of Figure 23.1 shows that "only" 15% of children whose parents used no physical punishment or other violence during the year covered by this survey repeatedly and severely assaulted a sibling. By contrast, the point plotted at the upper right corner shows that 76% of the children who were repeatedly abused by their parents repeatedly and severely assaulted a sibling.[2] In general, the more violence experienced by the child, the higher the rate at which such children are violent toward a sibling. It does not take being a victim of child abuse to produce an elevated rate of being violent to others. Ordinary physical punishment also "works." In fact, children who experienced only culturally permissible physical punishment frequently and severely assaulted a sibling at almost three times the rate of children who were not physically punished during the year (42 versus 15).

There are, of course, many problems with these data. By itself, Figure 23.1 cannot be taken as strong evidence. For example, the causal direction may be the reverse of that implied above. That is, children who engage in repeated serious assaults on a sibling may evoke repeated extreme measures on the part of parents who have tried everything else to no avail. Whether this is the case or not is best established by detailed case studies.

Another problem is that the association between the self-reported parental violence and the violence reported for their child may reflect a common tendency to view the world in violent terms, rather than a real causal linkage. Detailed cases studies, and especially observational studies, could help settle this issue. More can also be done using the data for this sample. For example, an analysis that uses independent variables which do not involve the possibility of reciprocal violence provide a better test of the common etiology theory. Such analyses will be reported later.

Wife Beating and Child Abuse

Readers who are not familiar with the base rates for child abuse in previous reports on this research may be startled at the rates in the lower left of Figure 23.2. These show that 7% to 10% of parents who reported *no* instances of marital violence frequently abused their children. However, the issue that figure 23.2 is designed to investigate is whether the rate of child abuse is even higher in families with ordianry marital violence as well as in families where there was wife beating.

The answer is "no" for fathers and "yes" for mothers. The data for abuse by fathers (the line of Fs) is contrary to the idea that ordinary violence has the same effect (even though less strongly) as severe violence.

FIGURE 23.1

Child-to-Child Violence by Parent-to-Child Violence

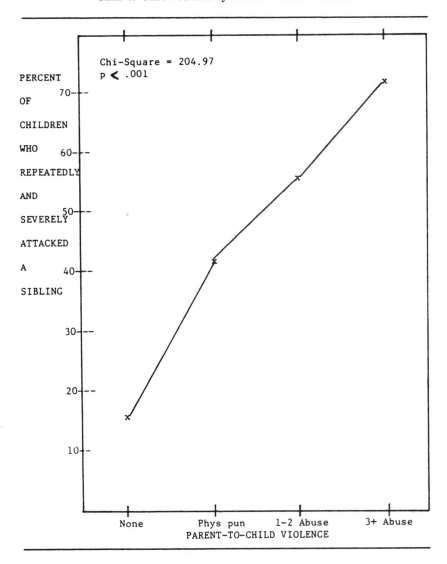

FIGURE 23.2

Frequent Child Abuse by Husband-to-Wife Violence

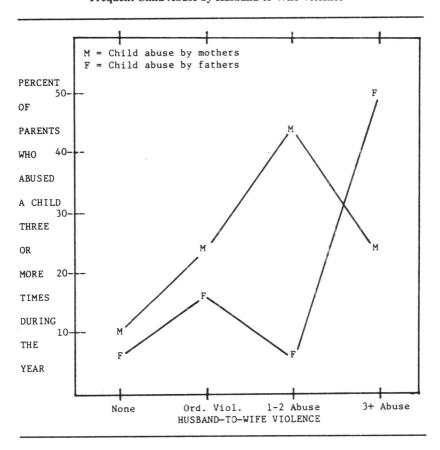

Only fathers who frequently abused their wives have elevated rates of frequently abusing their children. For mothers, however, Figure 23.2 shows that the rate of child abuse by those who have been beaten is at least double that of mothers whose husbands did not assault them. Moreover, this is true irrespective of whether the wives were the victims of many severe assaults or only one or two such assaults, or had only been pushed, slapped, or shoved by their husbands.

Antecedents of Physical Punishment and Child Abuse

The findings to this point are consistent with the theory that violence in one role is associated with violence in other roles. Furthermore, and most important for the issue of this study, this is true irrespective of whether the violence is within the normal range typical of American society or is more severe. In this section the focus shifts to a more detailed analysis of the etiology of child abuse. Two overlapping analyses will be presented. The first is concerned with whether parents who themselves experienced ordinary nonabusive physical punishment when they were children are more likely to *abuse* a child than others. The second issue is whether the other factors that previous studies have found to be related to child abuse are also related to the use of ordinary physical punishment.

Experience with Physical Punishment and Child Abuse

It is often asserted that abusing parents tend to be people who were themselves abused as children. For the most part, quantitative data demonstrating such an association are lacking. This study also lacks data on whether the parents we interviewed were abused as children. However, we do have data on the extent to which they experienced ordinary physical punishment. Fortunately, this is the critical variable as far as the issue of this chapter is concerned.

The top line of Figure 23.3 shows little or no relationship between the amount of physical punishment experienced by the parents in this sample and using physical punishment on their own children. However, the line labeled A shows that the more parents in this sample were physically punished, the greater the rate of frequently abusing their own child.

These findings seem somewhat odd. Why should experiencing ordinary physical punishment be related to child abuse but not to using ordinary physical punishment? One possibility has to do with the age at which the punishment occurred. Recall data over such a long period are hazardous at best. To minimize this hazard, the physical punishment questions asked how often this happened when the respondent was about 13. However, experiencing physical punishment at age 13 and later might also be an atypical experience, if that is after most parents cease to use this form of discipline. To check on this (at least indirectly), Figure 23.4 indicates the extent to which physical punishment was used by these parents on their own children. It shows that 13 happens to be the age at which a majority (though only a bare majority) stop using physical punishment.

On the other hand, very close to half (49.4%) of children *are* physically punished at age 13. Moreover, a generation or more ago, when these parents were children, physical punishment was probably more widely used than it is today (Bronfenbrenner, 1958; Miller & Swanson, 1958). So they might actually have been part of the majority at that time. Given these pros and cons, it is obvious that additional research will be needed

FIGURE 23.3

Parental Violence by Amount of Physical Punishment Eexperienced at about Age 13

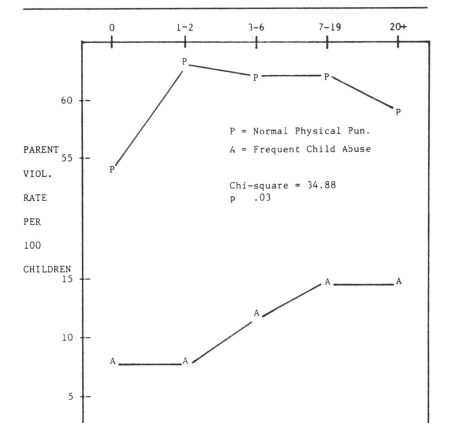

to determine whether experiencing physical punishment does increase the probability of abusing one's own children, and if so, what the thresholds are in respect to the amount of physical punishment and whether this applies to children of all ages. Unfortunately, that research will be a long time in coming because a longitudinal study is needed to even approach a reasonably firm answer to these important questions.

FIGURE 23.4

Percentage of Children Physically Punished, by Age of Child and Sex of Parent

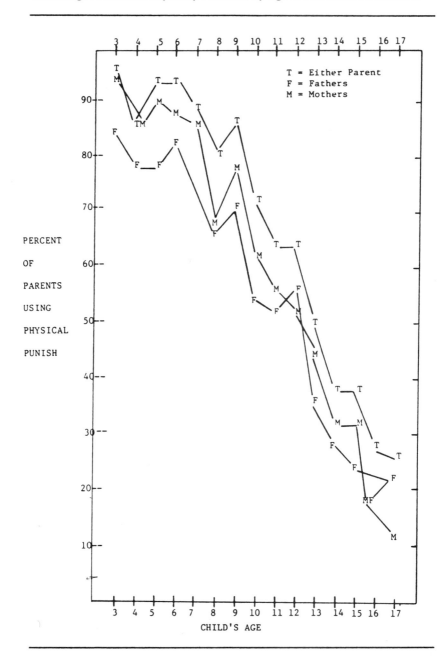

Other Factors Associated with Child Abuse

Previous analyses of these data identified a large number of individual and family characteristics that are associated with child abuse. Physical punishment as a child was one of these. The data on that variable were described in detail in the previous section. Within the limited space of this chapter it is not practical to do this for each of the other variables separately. Instead, a "Child Abuse Checklist" was used to summarize the combined effect of these variables. It consists of 16 variables found to have a statistically significant and nonoverlapping relationship to child abuse.[3] Since these variables were selected long before this study was written, and solely using the criterion of their association with child abuse, they can be considered a reasonable sample of factors associated with child abuse. The question is, do these same factors also account for a significant part of the variance in ordinary physical punishment?

For purposes of this index, the variables were first dichotomized. Families were given one point for each variable that applied. A family with none of these characteristics was scored zero, a family with 6 of them received a score of 6, and so on.

Figure 23.5 shows the relationship of the checklist score to three measures of violence by the parents in this study. The line labeled with A's gives the rate of child abuse. There were no instances of child abuse among the families with checklist scores of 2 or less. Thereafter, the higher the checklist score, the higher the rate of child abuse. A third of the children from families with a score of 10 or more were abused.

The new findings are those represented by the other two lines in Figure 23.5. The line marked by threes gives the percentage of parents who used physical punishment three or more times during the year but who did *not* engage in any of the acts included in the measure of child abuse. It can be seen that the Child Abuse Checklist is as highly associated with this measure of ordinary violence as is child abuse itself. That is, the same factors which (at least in the statistical sense) explain child abuse also explain the normal violence employed in child rearing.

On the other hand, the middle line in Figure 23.5, which gives the rate of using physical punishment once or twice, can be interpreted as showing either a curvilinear relationship or essentially no relationship between the checklist score and the rate of using physical punishment once or twice. This can be taken as evidence against the theory that physical punishment and child abuse share a similar etiology. An alternative interpretation, however, is that in the context of a society where the use of physical punishment is both typical and frequent, parents who have done so only

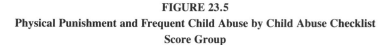

FIGURE 23.5
Physical Punishment and Frequent Child Abuse by Child Abuse Checklist Score Group

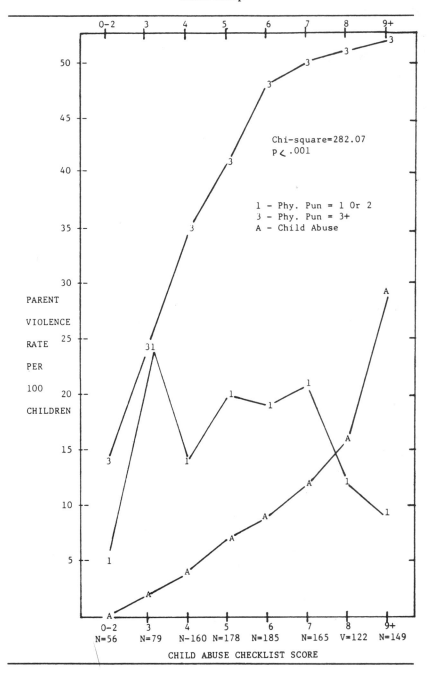

once or twice during an entire year are likely to be parents who are, in effect, committed to nonviolence in child rearing.

The individual items. Although the checklist provides a compact method of summarizing and estimating the combined effect of a large number of etiological factors, there are hazards in using this method. Perhaps the effects are really the result of only some of the items included in the checklist. Or it could be that one subset of items is related to abuse and another subset is related to use of ordinary physical punishment. To check this possibility, the cross-tabulations were repeated separately for each of the 16 items in the Child Abuse Checklist. All but three of the individual items were found to be associated with ordinary physical punishment as well as with child abuse. The three that are associated with child abuse but not with ordinary physical punishment are husband dissatisfied with his standard of living, blue-collar occupation, and two or more children.

Controls for age of child and sex of parent. The checklist analysis findings were replicated with controls for the source of the data (fathers reporting on their own behavior toward the child and on the mother's behavior; mothers reporting on their own behavior and that of the father). Essentially the same relationship was found within each of the four categories. However, the link between the checklist score and both child abuse and physical punishment is somewhat greater for mothers than for fathers. Two possible reasons for this come to mind. First, mothers are the primary caretakers (often the almost exclusive caretakers); therefore, the impact of factors associated with child abuse may show up more clearly for mothers. Second, when the items included in the checklist are examined (see note 4), they include variables that can be taken as indicators of the extent to which wives are victimized—for example, a husband who verbally and/or physically abused the wife. Since previous research indicates that victims of violence tend to victimize others more than do nonvictims (Owens & Straus, 1975), this might account for the closer correlation of the index with violence by mothers.

Frequency of punishment. Before leaving the issue of the common ties between ordinary physical punishment and child abuse, one additional set of findings may help round out the picture. This is the average number of times parents reported using physical punishment (Figure 23.6). Since child-abusing families also engage in less severe violence, Figure 23.6 is restricted to families in which the parents did *not* engage in any of the acts in the child abuse measure. It can be seen that irrespective of the age of the child, the higher the Child Abuse Checklist score, the more often parents use ordinary physical punishment.[4]

FIGURE 23.6
Mean Number of Times Nonabusing Parents Used Physical Punishment

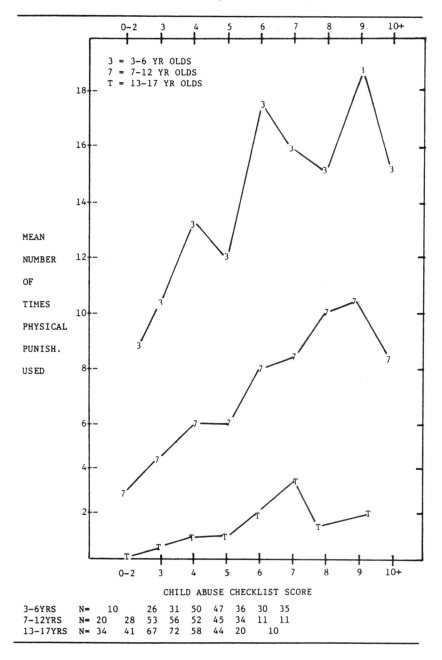

Factors Associated with Wife Beating

The same questions that were examined in relation to child abuse will be examined in this section in relation to wife beating, specifically: Do husbands who experienced physical punishment as a teenager have a higher rate of wife beating than other husbands? Are the other factors that previous research indicated are associated with wife beating also associated with minor violence by husbands?

Physical Punishment and Marital Violence

Figure 23.7 shows that the more physical punishment was experienced by the husbands in this sample, the higher was the rate of violence against wives. Moreover, this applies not only to frequent and severe attacks (the line of threes) but also to relatively infrequent severe attacks, and to the ordinary violence that is so frequent in American marriages.[6] Finally, Figure 23.8 shows the same results for violence by wives. That is, the more the wives in this sample were physically punished, the greater was the rate at which they attacked their husbands, and this applies to measures of all three levels of severity of attack.

Other Factors Associated with Wife Beating

Space limitations again rule out presenting the findings on each of the other variables found to be associated with wife beating. Instead, the variables associated with wife beating will be summarized using a Wife Beating Checklist. This consists of 26 items and is similar to the Child Abuse Checklist. Indeed, the two indexes share a number of variables. Among the characteristics which were scored in this index are a male-dominant balance of power in the family and a high score on an index to measure stresses experienced during the survey year (see note 6).

Examination of Figure 23.9 leads to roughly the same conclusions as emerged from the other analyses. It shows that the rate of frequent wife-beating (the line of threes) starts at zero for those with checklist scores of 4 or under, then climbs gradually, and finally jumps to one out of five among the husbands with checklist scores of 20 or higher. Thus, the findings reported previously (Straus et al., 1980: Chapter 9) for *any* severe assault on wives also apply when the more stringent criterion of frequent assaults is used. For purposes of this chapter, however, the most relevant data plotted in Figure 23.9 is the line of zeros. This shows that the rate for the ordinary minor violence of American marriages also increases as the checklist score increases.

FIGURE 23.7

**Husband-to-Wife Violence by Physical Punishment Experienced by Husband
at about Age 13**

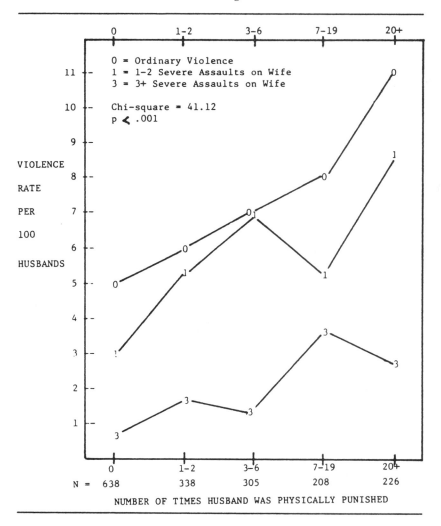

FIGURE 23.8
**Wife-to-Husband Violence by Physical Punishment Experienced by Wife
at about Age 13**

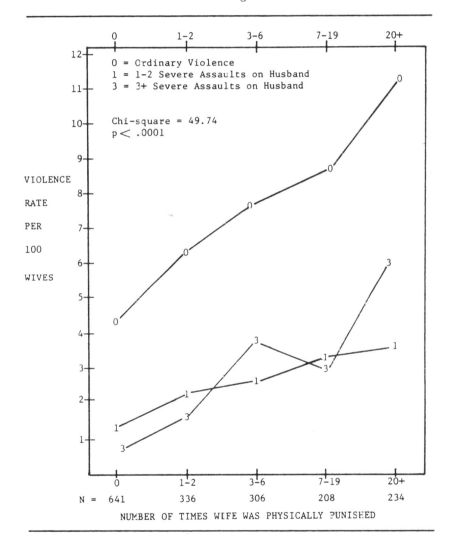

FIGURE 23.9

Ordinary Violence and Wife-Beating by Spouse Abuse Checklist Score

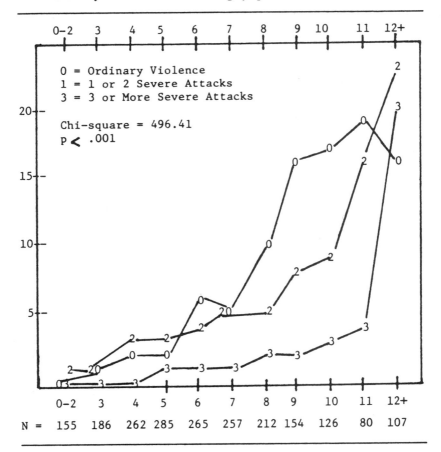

Since the checklist is a composite of 26 variables, the similar association of the checklist score with both minor violence and severe violence might not reflect a real similarity in etiological factors. It could be that one subset of the 26 is associated with minor violence and another subset is associated with wife beating. To check whether this is the case, each of the 26 items in the checklist was examined separately. This revealed that 24 of the 26 items were related to ordinary violence as well as to wife beating.[7] Thus, the same factors that are associated with frequent and severe assaults on wives also explain such minor violence as pushing, slapping, and throwing things.

Summary and Conclusions

This analysis of the 1975 survey shows how pervasive and interconnected violence is in the lives of these families.

(1) Over 97% of American children experience physical punishment. The data presented in this chapter show that the rate of physical punishment decreases rapidly as the child matures. However, data from another study indicate that for half of all American children, it does not end until the child leaves the parental home (Straus, 1971). Here I argue that such widespread use of ordinary physical punishment is one of the factors accounting for the high rate of child abuse and wife beating.

(2) The more parents are violent toward their children, the more violent these children are to their siblings. This relationship applies to parents' use of ordinary physical punishment as well as to child abuse. The relationship is particularly dramatic for the 100 children in this sample who were frequently abused by their parents. Seventy-six percent of them repeatedly and severely assaulted a sibling during the year studied.

(3) The more violent husbands are toward their wife, the more violent the wife is toward her children. Wives who were victims of violence that is sufficiently severe to meet the popular conception of wife beating had the highest rate of child abuse. Even those who were subjected to minor violence such as pushes and slaps had more than double the rate of frequent severe assaults on their children than did wives whose husbands did not hit them.

(4) The experience of violence as a child in the form of presumably benign physical punishment shows up a generation later in the form of equally benign physical punishment of the respondent's own children *and also* in the form of elevated rates of child abuse and spouse abuse. In general, the more the parents in this study were physically punished, the higher was the rate of both ordinary physical punishment and child abuse.

These findings are consistent with other research in showing that being a victim of violence is strongly related to engaging in violence oneself. This does not mean that everyone who has been a victim is violent. That probably depends in part on the intensity and length of victimization. To the extent that this is the case, the unintended training in violence that takes place in the family is particularly effective. Victimization in the family starts in infancy and, for half of all American children, continues until they leave home. Moreover, for one out of every seven children the violence is severe enough to be classified as child abuse. In addition, millions of American children have the opportunity to observe violent role models in the form of violence between their parents.

(5) Important as intrafamily experience with violence may be, one can overstate the case. Far from all husbands who experienced violence at the hands of their parents grow up to hit their wives. Not all abused children or abused wives abuse others. Conversely, there are violent people among those who grew up in nonviolent families. Clearly, many other variables are needed to fully account for both individual differences in violence and for the high overall incidence rate.

A number of these other variables were investigated as part of the larger study. Because of space limitations, two summary measures were used in this chapter to study the link between these variables and violence by parents and spouses. A Child Abuse Checklist was used to summarize the combined effect of 16 variables that previous analysis had shown to have a statistically significant and nonoverlapping relationship to child abuse. Similarly, a Spouse Abuse Checklist was used to summarize the combined effect of 26 variables known to be related to wife beating.

Previous reports show that these checklist scores are highly related to the incidence of child abuse and wife beating. The issue under study here is whether these same factors are also related to ordinary physical punishment and the minor violence which occurs between so many couples.

The results show that the same factors which explain child abuse and wife-beating also explain ordinary physical punishment and minor violence between spouses. Thus, in respect to at least the etiological variables investigated in this study, it seems that violence is violence—irrespective of the severity of the attack and irrespective of whether the violence is normatively legitimate (as in the case of physical punishment) or illegitimate (as in the case of child abuse and wife beating). These findings have a number of implications and also raise questions which cannot be answered with these data.

One of the most important of these questions concerns the process which accounts for the link between ordinary violence and "abuse." The explanation which is implicit throughout this chapter is that even though ordinary violence provides a role model that limits the severity of violence, for a considerable number of people the limits are not learned as well as is the principle that violence can and should be used when necessary, when under stress, when frustrated, and so on.

Another, and probably complementary, intervening process hinges on the distinction between "expressive" or "hostile" aggression versus instrumental aggression (Gelles & Straus, 1978). Physical punishment is a clear example of instrumental aggression—that is, where the primary goal is not to hurt the other person but to use hurting to achieve some other end. However, cases of pure instrumental aggression are probably rare. Parents are usually also frustrated and angry when they physically punish.

Consequently, they are modeling both instrumental and expressive aggression. It is likely that some children who experience physical punishment attend to the instrumental part of the parents' behavior and others attend more to the expressive or hostile part. It is the latter group which may account for the link between physical punishment and child abuse and wife-beating. These and other processes that might account for the link between ordinary violence and abuse need to be investigated. But even the findings reported here have important theoretical and practical implications.

The theoretical implication is that some reconsideration must be given to conceptual distinctions between different types or aspects of violence, such as instrumental versus expressive violence, minor versus severe violence, or socially approved versus illegitimate violence. Each of these has different antecedents, intervening processes, and reinforcers. At the same time, the findings I report suggest that each of these types of violence may also have more in common than is generally thought to be the case.

The practical implication of these findings concerns primary prevention (as contrasted with intervention to help victims of child abuse and wife-beating). To the extent that ordinary violence is linked to child abuse and wife beating, efforts to reduce the incidence of child abuse and wife beating must include attention to the ordinary violence typical of American families, including (and perhaps especially) ordinary physical punishment.

Notes

I am indebted to Susan Frankel for the computer analysis, and to the members of the Family Violence Research Program 1981 Seminar for comments and suggestions on an earlier draft.
1. Physical punishment was measured by four questions which asked "How often would you say that (your mother, stepmother, father, stepfather, you, your husband, your wife) used physical punishment, like slapping or hitting." The response categories were for the number of times during a one-year period, as follows: never, once or twice, 3–5 times, 6–10 times, 11–20 times, more than 20 times.
2. For purposes of this study, child abuse was measured by whether the parent did any of the following during the year: punching, kicking, biting, hitting with an object, beating up, threatening with a knife or gun, or actually using a knife or gun.
3. The items included are belong to no organization; 2 or more children; respondent physically punished 2+ times by mother; respondent physically punished 2+ times by father, respondent age 30 or under; husband slightly or not satisfied with standard of living; respondent's mother hit father; married less than 10 years; lived in neighborhood 0–1 years; above average conflict with spouse; verbal aggression to child; verbal aggression to wife; husband violent to wife; blue-collar husband; blue-collar wife; wife not employed outside the home.

Further information on the checklist is given in Straus et al. (1980: Chap. 9). The special questions from which these items were scored is available in the codebook for this study (Straus & Gelles, 1980).

4. The line for abuse of teenagers appears to indicate a less pronounced relationship. This is a function of the fact that teenagers are physically punished much less often than younger children. To adequately portray the findings for teenagers, the vertical axis scale would have to be set to a scale that would run the much higher figures for the younger children off the graph. For all three age groups, parents in families with checklist scores of 7 or more use physical punishment at least twice as often as is the case in families with scores of 0 to 2.

5. The items included in this index are 2 or more children; respondent physically punished 2+ times by father; respondent age 30 or under; respondent non-White; family income under $6,000; agreed about children never or only sometimes; part-time employed husband; unemployed husband; husband quite or extremely worried about economic future; respondent's father hit mother; respondent's mother hit father; wife slightly or not at all satisfied with standard of living; wife extremely worried about economic future; married less than 10 years; lived in neighborhood 0–1 years; above-average conflict with spouse; stress index 70 or more; verbal aggression to wife; wife verbally aggressive to husband; blue-collar husband; blue-collar wife; wife not employed outside home; no religious participation; couple get drunk rarely or more often; wife-dominant couple; husband-dominant couple.

6. The prevalence of violence in American marriages is much greater than one might surmise from Figure 23.7. This is true partly because the data in that figure are annual incidence rates—that is, whether these events occurred during the year of the survey. The prevalence rates—whether an assault had ever occurred—are much higher. For this survey sample, the prevalence rate is 28%. But for reasons stated elsewhere (Straus et al., 1980: 34–36), the probable true prevalence rate is well over 50%; in other words, more than half of all American couples have engaged in physical violence at some point in the marriage.

7. The two items found to be related to wife beating, but not to ordinary marital violence, are a wife who is not employed outside the home and respondents who are non-White.

24

The Medical and Psychological Costs
of Family Violence

Richard J. Gelles and Murray A. Straus

The relatively few attempts to estimate the degree of injury and the monetary cost of family violence (Bureau of Justice Statistics, 1980; Schulman, 1979; Stark, 1981; Straus, 1986) are based on limited or questionable data and undemonstrated assumptions. Estimates based on the National Crime Survey (Bureau of Justice Statistics, 1980), for example, are meaningless because of severe under-reporting of intrafamily assaults (see Chapter 6).

The data on intrafamily homicides, however, are much more complete and are probably the most accurate figures on family violence. Intrafamily homicides reached a peak in 1980 (approximately 5,800 cases) and declined steadily to approximately 4,400 cases in 1984. Inclusion of spouse-like relationships (nonmarried cohabiting couples, boyfriend-girlfriend) could increase the number substantially. One estimate put the 1984 cost of intrafamily homicides at $1.7 billion (Straus, 1986). This estimate, however, can be highly misleading.

First, although the incidence rate data may be accurate, the cost estimates are necessarily based on a series of questionable assumptions. An even more important problem comes from taking the death and the incidents immediately surrounding the death as the starting point for the cost analysis. It is important to know the economic cost of the long period of nonlethal family violence that typically precedes the lethal violence.

The true accounting of the cost of family violence must also include the cost of providing mental health and social services to victims and the cost of treating aggressors. This chapter and chapters 9 and 25 begin the process of estimating the true cost. All three chapters use data from the 1985 survey. They report rough estimates of the increased risk of medical and psychological problems, and of violence and other anti-social behavior by victims. The data in this chapter supplement Chapter 9 by giving the incidence of specific medical and psychological problems experienced by women victims (in contrast to the summary indexes used in that chapter) and supplement the data in Chapter 25 by reporting the incidence of additional behavior problems experienced by child victims of parental assaults.

Spouse Violence and Its Consequences

As indicated in Chapter 6, the estimated annual incidence rate of spouse violence (defined as any physical assault on a spouse) for the 5,349 survey couples was 161 victims per 1,000 couples. Most of these incidents involved minor assaults, such as slapping and throwing something at the spouse.

The rate of wife beating, defined as one or more violent acts that pose a serious risk of injury (for example, kicking, biting, punching, choking, beating, and use of weapons) was 34 victims per 1,000 couples, or an estimated 1.8 million seriously assaulted wives per year in the United States. Although these are extremely high figures, they are almost certain to be an underestimate because not all respondents are willing to reveal such incidents; nonreporting is especially likely in the cases of the most serious violence. Under-reporting of the most serious cases of violence may be one reason why medical intervention was reported for only 3 percent of the wife-beating incidents.

Although immediate medical intervention for acute conditions was rare, survey findings suggest that wife beating has important adverse effects on the mental and physical health of women who experience severe violence by their partner. For instance, severely assaulted women averaged almost double the days in bed due to illness than did other women (fig. 24.1); a third fewer severely assaulted wives reported being in excellent health than other women, and three times as many severely assaulted wives reported being in poor health (fig. 24.2). Severely assaulted women had much higher rates of psychological distress than other women, including double the incidence of headaches, four times the rate of feeling depressed, and five-and-a-half times more suicide attempts (fig. 24.3).

FIGURE 24.1

Relationship Between Women Who Experienced Violence In Last Year and Mean Number of Days In Bed Due to Illness In Last Month

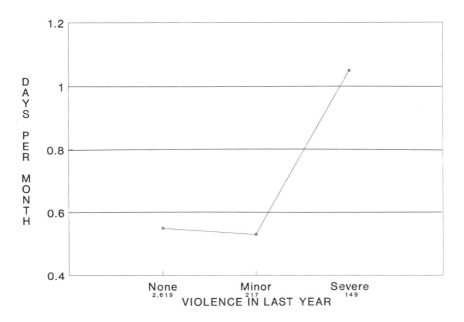

Child Abuse and Its Consequences

If the same criteria were used for child abuse as were used for wife beating, the rate (based on the 3,334 children in the survey) is 110 incidents per 1,000 children, which is an estimated 6.9 million children severely assaulted each year in the United States. If "hitting with an object" is dropped from the list of physically abusive acts (because many people do not consider that as necessarily abusive with children), the estimated rate is 23 incidents per 1,000 children, or 1.5 million children seriously assaulted each year in the United States. As with spouse violence, these child-abuse rates are almost certainly underestimates; they are based on reports by parents, not all of whom are willing to reveal incidents in which they severely assaulted their children. In addition, physical abuse of

FIGURE 24.2

Relationship Between Women's Health and Experience with Violence in the Last Year

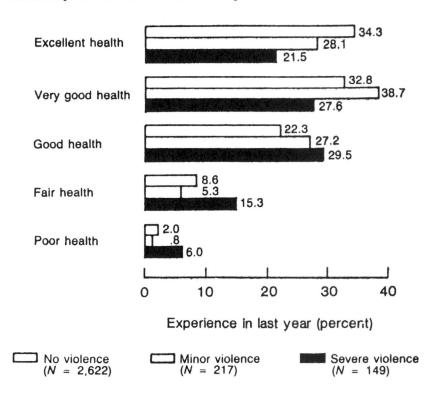

Experience in last year (percent)

☐ No violence
(*N* = 2,622)

☐ Minor violence
(*N* = 217)

■ Severe violence
(*N* = 149)

children often starts before birth because assaults on wives continue unabated during pregnancy (Chapter 16: Gelles, 1975).

For each of the 3,334 survey children, researchers asked the parent whether there were any "special difficulties" with the child during the past 12 months. Figure 24.4 shows that abused children consistently experienced more of these difficulties than did other children. For example, the child victims of severe violence had two to three times higher rates of trouble-making friends, temper tantrums, failing grades in school, disciplinary problems in school and at home, physically assaultive behavior at home and outside the home, vandalism and theft, and drinking and drug use.

The last bar of Figure 24.4 shows that these misbehaviors are part of a cumulative pattern more often than is the case for nonabused children. Moreover, the next-to-the-last bar shows that abused children were ar-

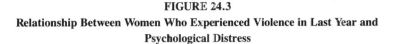

FIGURE 24.3

Relationship Between Women Who Experienced Violence in Last Year and Psychological Distress

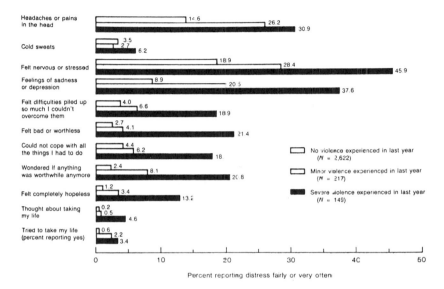

rested four times more often than other children. Because it is well established that it typically takes many repetitions of a criminal behavior for an arrest to be likely, this is further evidence of the much more serious behavior problems characteristic of children who are victims of severe violence. A multivariate analysis shows that the differences between abused and other children reported in this section hold regardless of socioeconomic status.

The Costs

Methods are currently being developed for using these incidence rates as the basis for rough estimates of the dollar costs of the medical and nonmedical expenses of intrafamily violence. Some of the findings presented in Figures 24.3 and 24.4 suggest that mental health (Carmen, 1984) and nonmedical costs may be much greater than the cost of treating physical injuries. Examples of other costs are psychiatric and other psychological services; police services; social services, including the cost of child-abuse investigations and remedial actions; legal costs, including divorce; and the cost of the violence and other crimes committed by those

FIGURE 24.4

**Relationship Between Experiencing Severe Violence and Special Difficulties
of the Child**

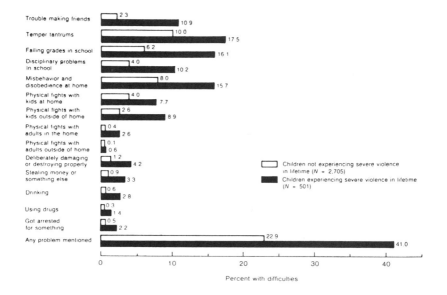

Percent with difficulties

abused in childhood (Chapter 25; Straus, 1985). There is also the cost of imprisonment or other institutionalization that occurs at a much higher rate for victims of intrafamily violence than for the general population.

Although the cost estimates being developed will be subject to a wide margin of error, even the minimum estimate will show that the United States is paying a huge price for the violence that occurs in so many American families. The tragedy is compounded by the fact that these are preventable costs.

There has now been enough research on the etiology of intrafamily violence to suggest plausible programs of primary prevention (Chapter 28; Gelles and Straus, 1988; Straus, Gelles, and Steinmetz, 1980). Such programs are likely to reduce the costs of violence to society by many times the cost of the program—to say nothing of their effect on reducing human suffering and enhancing the quality of family life.

25

Intrafamily Violence and Crime and Violence Outside the Family

Gerald T. Hotaling and Murray A. Straus with
Alan J. Lincoln

This chapter has three major purposes. We consider in Section I why family violence research and criminological research have not taken full account of one another in their work on violent behavior. In Sections II–VIII we review research on the link between family and nonfamily violence and present, for the first time, epidemiological data on the relations between violence in the family and crime and violence "in the streets." We evaluate our current state of knowledge in this area and suggest key issues for future research in Section IX.

Criminology and Family Violence Research

Over the past ten years there have been sporadic reports of family violence researchers attending the meetings of criminological research societies. Likewise, there have been rumors of criminologists sighted at conferences on family violence research. Some people say they have actually witnessed family violence researchers and criminologists talking with one another, but there is no hard evidence that these events actually have taken place. The data are not based on a systematic sample and most probably inflate the amount of interaction between these two groups.

Violence between family members has been studied quite separately from the general study of criminal violence. A recent review article on the link between family and stranger violence reported the results of a computer search of professional journals in five data bases and found not a single entry on the relation between family and stranger violence (Fagan and Wexler 1987).

How can this be? Criminologists and family violence researchers have similar academic training, and both are concerned with uncovering risk factors of violent behavior and with the development and testing of theories to explain violent behavior. They use similar measures, and both collect data through surveys, experiments, and case studies in order to understand violent behavior. Even if they never directly interact, these researchers have such common concerns that the intersection of family and nonfamily criminal violence should be an extremely well-researched area. It may be, however, that violence in families is so fundamentally different from violence between strangers that distinctive approaches to separate subjects are necessary and quite appropriate.

Reasons for Separate Approaches to the Study of Violence in Families

There has been some merging of criminological and family violence research. There has, for example, been research on the response of the criminal justice system to family violence (Bard 1971; Parnas 1972; Lerman and Livingston 1983; Buzawa 1984; Sherman and Berk 1984; Carmody and Williams 1987; Elliott, in this volume). Some family violence researchers have worked from a criminological perspective, and criminologists have incorporated family violence topics into their studies of criminal violence, especially research on family homicide (e.g., Wolfgang 1958; Palmer 1972; Walker 1979, 1984; Straus, 1986, 1987; Browne 1987). The nonintegration of these two literatures is most prominent in etiological research and theory development on nonlethal violent behavior.

Gelles (1982) attributes the nonintegration of criminological and family violence to the lack of interest of criminologists in family violence. This may result from a general cultural reluctance to recognize family violence as a problem of significant magnitude or consequence. Only in the mid-1960s did child welfare groups begin to focus on physical abuse, and only in the mid-1970s did the women's movement begin to focus on wife beating. Before that time, neither social institutions, including the academic community, nor the general public paid much attention to assaults on women and children in the home. In short, criminological researchers did not investigate family violence because the prevalent cultural norms and practices did not define it as a problem.

Even in the middle and late 1970s, as evidence accumulated about the high prevalence of family violence (Gil 1970; Straus 1973; Gelles 1974; Steinmetz and Straus 1974; Martin 1976; Gaquin 1977; Dobash and Dobash

1979; Straus, Gelles, and Steinmetz 1980), family violence was still commonly viewed as something different from "real" violence and "real" crime.

The criminal justice system during this time was especially resistant to responding to family violence as criminal violence. Police, prosecutors, and courts regarded violence in the home as a private matter, subject to sanction as a crime only when it resulted in death or serious injury (Fagan and Wexler 1987). The training manual published by the International Association of Chiefs of Police recommended a policy of noninterference, and some cities had an informal "stitch rule" that required a wound needing more than a certain number of stitches to justify an arrest (Straus 1976). Both Straus (1976) and Gelles (1982) view the general cultural tolerance of family violence as authority for the criminal justice system to regard it as something different from criminal violence. The lack of response of the legal system, in turn, reinforced the view that family violence is not a crime. Since family violence was not criminal behavior, no official records needed to be kept about its occurrence, and no criminological research was needed to understand it (Gelles 1982, pp. 202–3).

This explanation is probably largely correct but does not fully account for why little attention is now paid to the criminological aspects of violence in the family. Throughout the 1970s, there was a more general absence of theoretical activity to incorporate knowledge about family violence into existing paradigms. Practitioners and researchers from a number of fields declined to claim family violence as an area of their concern. Thus, child abuse and wife abuse were equally ignored by medicine (Rounsaville 1978; Stark, Flitcraft, and Frazier 1979; Gelles 1982), public health (Bowen et al. 1984), mental health and social services (Martin 1976), religion (Dobash and Dobash 1979), and sociology (Steinmetz and Straus 1974). None of the corresponding research arms of these disciplines rushed to integrate knowledge of family violence into their existing theoretical and methodological work (with the exception of psychiatry; see Gelles [1973] for a review of the psychiatric model of family violence). Not until 1979 was any attempt made to explore the relevance of a number of sociological and psychological theories of violence and aggression to the understanding of family violence (Gelles and Straus 1979).

Development of Family Violence Research as a Separate Research Area

Because no one field or academic discipline claimed family violence as a primary focus of research interest, the interdisciplinary area of "family violence research" began to take shape in the late 1970s. Today, this is an area composed of a broad array of researchers and practitioners from sociology, women's studies, psychology, psychiatry, social work, anthropology, medicine, law, human and child development, public health, biology, and other disciplines. Current definitions, concepts, and theories used in family violence research reflect the diverse research traditions of this group. This diversity is one of the primary obstacles to incorporating research on family violence into the study of criminal violence. Paradoxically, family violence research has constructed a knowledge base that depicts violence in families in such a way that criminological methods and theories do not easily apply. In a sense, we have come full circle. At first, criminologists treated family violence as something different than criminal violence; now family violence researchers approach family violence as something different than criminal violence. In the meantime, however, very little empirical evidence has been generated to determine just how different violence in families is from violence "in the streets." We now turn to a discussion of how definitions, knowledge of risk factors, typologies, and theories used to understand family violence can no longer be easily reconciled with the general study of criminal violence.

Expansion of the Definition of Family Violence

The greatest convergence between family violence research and criminology occurs in the study of murder (Wolfgang 1958; Palmer 1960; Straus 1986, 1987; Browne 1987; Flewelling and Browne 1987). A major reason is that both fields use the same definition of homicide.

Criminologists adopt a fairly consistent research definition of assault, one that is codified in law and generally agreed on. The same cannot be said for those who study intrafamily assault. The conceptual and definitional development of family violence research has produced a wide array of operational definitions of violent behavior in families. Family violence, such as physical abuse of children and wife beating, has been operationally defined through violent *acts* (Chapter 3; Schulman 1979; Straus, Gelles, and Steinmetz 1980), *injuries* (Kempe et al. 1962; Washburn and Frieze 1981; Bark et al. 1983), both violent *acts and injuries* (McLeod 1983; Pagelow 1984), and through a *"battering syndrome"* involving repetitive acts of physical violence and psychological harm (Walker 1979, 1984).

This diversity accurately reflects a complex reality but is one of the reasons for difficulty in comparing incidence rates and correlates of family violence with knowledge on general criminal violence. More generally, there seem to be three main factors that make it difficult for criminologists to work with the conceptual and operational definitions used in family violence research: normative ambiguity concerning what acts of intrafamily violence are criminal, a tendency for family violence researchers to use injuries rather than acts to conceptualize and measure family violence, and expansion of the terms "abuse" and "violence" to cover many behaviors in addition to assault.

Normative ambiguity.   Violence in families that has a high probability of producing an injury is typically seen as comparable to criminal violence, but there is a lack of consensus as to whether "minor" violence in families should be similarly conceptualized. Pushing, shoving, or slapping one's spouse or one's child is clearly violent behavior, but is it criminal to the same degree as pushing or slapping the spouse or child of a neighbor would be? The reluctance to view "minor" violence in families as assaults has inhibited research on the links between family and nonfamily violence. Gelles (1982) argues that the lack of a criminological perspective on family violence is partly due to normative confusion over behavior in families that is clearly violent but not viewed as criminal because of the implicit cultural support that exists for this kind of behavior. In addition, there are important ethical and practical problems connected with "criminalizing" all behavior in the family that would be a crime if the same act took place between strangers (Straus and Lincoln 1985).

Acts versus injuries.   The legal definition of assault (see page 76) focuses on acts rather than on injuries. As Marcus (1983, p. 89) puts it: "Physical contact is not an element of the crime." As the Uniform Crime Reports puts it: "Attempts are included [in the tabulation of aggravated assault] because it is not necessary that an injury result" (Federal Bureau of Investigation, 1985, p. 21). However, many (or most) family violence researchers believe that the criterion should be injury, and this is part of the reason why the inclusion of "minor" violence is seen as expanding the notion of violence beyond criminal assault. Since minor violence is unlikely to cause an injury that needs medical attention, those who incorrectly define assault and violence by an outcome such as physical injury have difficulty including so-called minor violence within the family as a criminal assault.

Expansion to cover many types of maltreatment.   As indicated in Chapter 5, family violence research has come to include work on psychological abuse of children and spouses; child sexual abuse; marital rape; physical, emotional, and educational neglect of children; and other forms of interpersonal maltreatment. Subsuming all of this under the general heading of "family violence" has created conceptual confusion and probably inhibited the application of criminological theory to family violence research.

Belief in Need for Special Theories of Family Violence

Just as definitions of family violence have expanded to incorporate notions of harmful behaviors against family members, so have calls for the development of concepts and theories that are different from those used to interpret criminal violence. Are unique or special theories necessary to understand family violence? Gelles and Straus (1979) have argued that physical violence against children and spouses are "special" cases of violence that require family-based theories to explain them. Hotaling and Straus (1980) list a number of aspects of family structure and dynamics to justify the need for special theories of family violence, and Dobash and Dobash (1979) have argued that violence against wives is a special and unique type of violence and should not be approached as a subset of general violent behavior.

Criminologists have generally agreed with this point of view. Megargee (1982) sees intimacy as a key variable in necessitating a separate theoretical approach to the study of violent families: "Given the long-standing and intimate nature of the relations between offenders and victims, it is natural to suppose that to some degree the familial violence stems from these relationships and constitutes an episode in a continuing pattern of interactions. This sets familial violence apart from most other violent offenses and makes it worthy of study in its own right" (p. 101).

All of these authors make persuasive arguments, but they represent a decision made within the research community that has discouraged the application of criminological theory to the study of family violence. Since "special" theories are needed, it may seem as though there is no reason to explore theories of general criminal violence. Unfortunately, assertions about the need for unique theories have never been tested by empirical evidence. The etiology of violent behavior may be very similar whether it is used against a family member or nonfamily member. Notions of intimacy and the primary group nature of the family are very important for understanding the dynamics of violence in families, but not necessarily for understanding the motivations of offenders. Similarly, patriarchal norms may be very important for understanding the motivation of violent husbands but may also be very important for understanding violence outside of family relationships (Toby 1966).

The belief in the need for special theories may stem from the fact that data on violence in families come largely from victims, while data on nonfamily violence come largely from offenders. Criminology has recognized the need for a victim's perspective as the growing field of victimology and increased use of victimization surveys attests, but in family violence research, the victim's perspective is often used to gauge the offender's motivation. Consequently, criminological theories may appear inappropriate. The need for presumed special theories may mask the need for more direct study of violent offenders in families.

Risk Factors in Use of Violence in Families

The violent spouse and violent parent are often seen as different from the violent street criminal in terms of basic demographic and social correlates. How different are adults who are violent in the family from those who are violent outside of it?

The study of criminal violence has produced a number of risk factors that differentiate the criminally violent from the nonviolent. These include being male (Mednick et al. 1982; Elliott and Huizinga 1983, 1984); low socioeconomic status (Elliott and Ageton 1980; Braithwaite 1981); being non-White (Hindelang 1981; Weiner and Wolfgang 1985); school adjustment problems (Fagan, Piper, and Moore 1986); disruption in family of orientation (Strasburg 1978); aggressive parental figures (McCord 1984); and a history of juvenile crime involvement (Farrington 1982).

The family violence literature produces a very different image of the abusive spouse and abusive parent. Abusive spouses are also believed to more likely be male but, beyond that, are indistinguishable on the basis of other social and demographic characteristics. Violent males in families are depicted as coming from all socioeconomic backgrounds, races, religions, occupations, and walks of life (Star et al. 1979; Walker 1979, 1984; Giles-Sims 1983; Pagelow 1984; Sonkin, Martin, and Walker 1985). The exposure to violent role models in childhood is also seen as failing to discriminate the violent from the nonviolent (Pagelow 1984).

The image of the "batterer as everyone" is typically based on clinical samples and the reports of victims. Since comparison groups of nonviolent men are not used, there is no way to calculate the risk-to-violence of any social or demographic variable. A recent review of comparison group studies of men violent toward wives (Hotaling and Sugarman 1986) revealed a set of risk factors that are very similar to risk factors of men who are criminally violent. These men report, or are reported to have, lower occupational status, lower income, and lower educational attainment than nonviolent male comparison groups. Violent husbands are also more likely to have had aggressive role models for parents and to be more generally violent (to children and nonfamily members) than comparison group males.

Physical child abusers are also dipicted in the family violence literature as coming from all social classes, educational backgrounds and as no more likely than anyone else to have a history of abuse (Pagelow 1984). But again, comparison group evidence tends to depict physical child abusers as somewhat similar to the criminally violent, at least on the basis of some risk factors. For example, parents who severely assault children do seem more likely than nonchild abusers to have a history of physical abuse (Mclnick and Hurley 1969; Conger, Burgess, and Barrett 1979; Hunter and Kilstrom 1979; Straus, Gelles, and Steinmetz 1980), lower educational attainment (Hunter et al. 1978; Gelles 1980), and lower socioeconomic status (Giovannoni and Billingsley 1970; Smith, Hanson, and Noble 1973; Gelles 1980).

Violent criminals are portrayed as inhabiting a different sociodemographic space than violent family members. While a profile of the street criminal begins to emerge through the discovery of risk factors, the violent family member remains invisible. He is depicted as being anyone. He could possess some of the characteristics of the street criminal, but that is not seen in the research literature as setting him apart. His distinctiveness resides in his ability to avoid sociological labels. If those who assault other family members are depicted as otherwise law-abiding citizens, there is no compelling reason to apply notions of criminality to explain their behavior.

A Separate Typology of Offenders

If the violent family members cannot be identified sociologically, then perhaps they can be distinguished psychologically. Specifically, what is the motivational basis for violence against family members? The depiction of violent family members in the research literature tells us that special theories that take into account primary group dynamics are necessary to understand this violence and that we cannot rely on risk factors that apply to general criminal violence.

The motivators for violence against family members are depicted as very different from those influencing violent criminals. One way to examine these depictions or images is to compare typologies or profiles of violent family members to those of general violent criminals. Some common depictions of the reasons for criminal violence are "normal" (Bromberg 1961), "culturally appropriate" (Glaser, Kenefick, and O'Leary 1968), "environmental" (Revitch and Schlesinger 1978), "avenging" (Guttmacher 1960), "instrumental" (Williams 1972; Ochberg 1980), "reputation defending," "norm enforcing," "defending," and "pressure removing" (Toch 1969) (see Megargee [1982] for a complete listing). Nonfamily violent offenders are portrayed in these depictions as rational, instrumental, and goal seeking. Based on known risk factors of criminal violence, the use of physical force is seen as a largely rational response to powerlessness and deprivation. Violence is interpreted as being used to deal with threats posed by the immediate social environment or by an unjust and racist society.

Violent criminal offenders also are studied in terms of personal history. They have been conditioned to violence by growing up in a violent family and neighborhood and have a history of violent behavior starting in adolescence. Again, this violent history underscores the rationality of their adult violence.

There are some depictions of violent family members as instrumental (Straus, 1973, 1977; Browne, 1987), but the general image of the violent spouse and parent in the family violence literature is quite different from the depiction of violent criminal offender. Profiles and typologies depict violent family members as "overcontrolled loners," "cowards" (Caesar 1985), "approval seeking" (Elbow 1977), "extremely jealous" (Faulk 1974; Pagelow 1984; Walker 1984), "dependent and passive" (Faulk 1974; Sonkin, Martin, and Walker 1985), "fearing abandonment" (Dutton and Browning 1984), "lacking in assertiveness" (Rosenbaum and O'Leary 1981; Pagelow 1984), "having low self-esteem" (Rouse 1984; Telch and Lindquist 1984), "having no impulse control" (Sonkin, Martin, and Walker 1985), "neurotic" (Symonds 1979), "frustration displacing" (Walters 1975; Pagelow 1984), "moody" (Pagelow 1984), "immature and hysterical" (Brandon 1976), "angry" (Walker 1984), and "having feelings of incompetence, inadequacy, and worthlessness" (Kent et al. 1978).

Wife beaters are depicted as psychologically distressed, and their violence as irrational. Wife beating is seen as a response to the husband's dependency, jealousy, and anger. Rather than being depicted as rational and unemotional, violent husbands are characterized as extremely emotional and highly sensitive to situational stress, and their violence is primarily expressive rather than instrumental. The personal inadequacies and frustrations of these people motivate them to victimize the weak and powerless (Finkelhor 1983; Pagelow 1984).

Child abusers are also seen as incompetent and immature. They are unable to cope with the responsibilities of parenting and hold unrealistic expectations of children. They are seen as overwhelmed by the demands of situtational stress (see review by Wolfe [1985]).

Current conceptions of the violent offender and of the violent family member are at considerable odds. Street violence is seen as a "deliberate, rational activity to further instrumental goals" (Megargee 1982: 106), while family violence is an angry response triggered by psychological flaws and situational stressors.

Megargee (1982, p. 106) has suggested that this conceptual difference may reflect "a real difference between 'street crimes' and 'family crimes,' but it seems equally likely that it is due to the facts that 1) family violence occurs in the home, where the influence of these environmental variables is more readily apparent, and 2) those who have written about family violence have often been more interested in marital dynamics than in criminal behaviors per se." It may be that family violence researchers and criminologists are both correct. The motivations and risk factors associated with why someone is violent toward a relative rather than an acquaintance or stranger may, in fact, be very dissimilar. Unfortunately, the answer will not be known until more direct comparisons can be made between violence in family and nonfamily contexts.

Lack of Attention to the Link between Forms of Family Violence

The lack of an examination of the relations between violence across social contexts is also true of types of violence within the family. Family violence research has not explicitly examined the links between violence against children, violence against spouses, sibling violence, or child-parent violence. There is even a lack of epidemiological data on what proportion of families are multiviolent, that is, in what proportion of American families do assaults against children and wife beating co-exist?

Within the family violence research area, separate traditions have evolved for the study of physical violence against children and violence against adult partners (Finkelhor 1983). Family violence research is composed of several individual research tracks that have not been linked in any systematic manner. Each area has invested in particular theories and research strategies that do not necessarily lend themselves to a search for common features of violent behavior. This compartmentalization of family violence research may also be another factor that impedes the application of a criminological perspective on family violence.

In summary, current definitions, appraisals of risk factors, and theoretical conceptions of the use of violence in families construe it as something different from criminal violence "in the streets." However, the empirical evidence for this view is weak, relying on clinical accounts and single group studies. In fact, some evidence suggests that violence against family members may be very similar in important respects to violence against nonfamily persons. The important issue, however, is that the possible linkages between family and nonfamily violence have rarely been systematically studied. Before examining the evidence for these linkages in more detail, we turn to a discussion of a major source of conceptual confusion: the terms "violence," "abuse," and "assault."

Violence, Abuse, and Assault

The terms "violence" and "abuse" are a source of considerable difficulty and confusion because they cover many types of events, not just acts of physical assault. These issues are discussed in chapter 5. "Assault" is the term we prefer to use in this chapter, rather than "violence," because the focus here is on illegal violence. Moreover, even though there are now statutes that define "child abuse" as a crime, physical assaults on children make up only about one-quarter of the cases identified under these statutes. The remainder are cases of neglect, psychological abuse, or sexual abuse. In view of these considerations, from this point on we try to avoid the term "abuse" in favor of more specific terms such as "child assault" and "spouse assault."

Social Learning Theory and the Linkage Issue

Social learning theory would seem to be an excellent starting point for examining the links between assaults in and outside of families. Early studies on social learning suggest that aggressive behavior is learned and is acquired through direct experience (trial and error), by observing the behavior of others (modeling), or in both ways (Singer 1971; Bandura 1973). The learning theory approach to family violence contends that the family serves as a training ground for violence. In terms of modeling, the family provides examples for imitation that can be adopted in later life as the individual draws from childhood experiences to structure appropriate parent or conjugal roles. The family can also encourage and reinforce assaultive behavior in children by rewarding aggressive behavior (e.g., sibling violence). This process is often unintentional but quite effective (Patterson, Cobb, and Roy 1973).

A key issue in the social learning view of assaultive behavior is generalizability. Is learning specific to particular targets, certain contexts, and limited temporally, or do learned responses become a more general mode of behavior? There is some experimental evidence that aggressive models transmit general lessons as well as specific ones and that observers learn general aggressive strategies that go well beyond the specific modeled examples (Bandura 1971, 1973). In Chapter 23, Straus presents evidence that also supports the "generalization" hypotheses in that abusive husbands are more likely to have both witnessed and experienced parental assaults as children (see Hotaling and Sugarman [1986] for a complete review of these studies). How generalizable, then, is assaultive behavior in families, particularly across targets within families, across generations, and across contexts?

Generalizability of Violence across Targets within Families

Two questions are examined in this essay in relation to the generalizability of assaults across targets. The first, a descriptive issue, is What proportion of American families during any given year experience both child assault and spouse assault? Families that report *both* child and spouse assault can be called assaultive families. Existing data on this question are based on clinical samples, and there has been no attempt, using epidemiological methods, to estimate the incidence of multiassaultive families. Data from three general population surveys are analyzed later in this essay to examine the extent of multiassaultive families in American society.

The second question about the use of violence across targets within families concerns children. In multiassaultive families, children both experience and observe parental assaults. What short-term effects result from this intensive modeling? Given the power of the models in these roles and the intensity of the modeling, these children may be more likely to learn assaultive responses. But whether they engage in violence in the family is the issue of interest here. The key question is Are children in multiassaultive families more likely to use violence against siblings and parents than children from families with different assault constellations?

Other factors also effect modeling outcomes. For example, boys seem to be more influenced than girls by the modeling of parental violence (Bandura 1973; Pagelow 1984). The severity of the observed assault may also affect the strength of modeling as may the social class of the family. Consequently, children's violence in families is examined below in terms of its link to intensity of modeling, sex of child, severity of violence observed, and social class.

Generalizability of Violence across Contexts

The generalizability of assaultive behavior in families to other contexts remains largely unexplored. This issue must be considered for both children and spouses.

Children. If children who are exposed to assaultive models are more likely to initiate violence against family members, will they also be more likely to engage in violence against persons outside of the family? The observation and direct experience of assault in the home could spill over into relationships with nonfamily persons. This would be predicted by social learning theory. What about other nonviolent forms of behavior, such as property offenses? Are children from multiassaultive families also more likely to engage in these behaviors? Assaultive behavior is a form of deviant behavior, and the lesson it teaches may also be generalizable. The modeling of violent behavior in the family may weaken one's allegiance to social norms in general and facilitate a more general antisocial response. A third issue to be examined is Are children exposed to multiassaultive parental models more likely than other children to be violent outside of the family? Are they also more likely to engage in nonviolent delinquent behavior outside the family? Again, the issue of how modeling in this regard is affected by sex of child, severity of violence, and social class is also be examined.

Spouses. Using the notion of multiassaultive families, we examine whether adults in these family contexts are more likely to engage in violence and other antisocial behaviors outside of the family. A major issue here is whether husbands are assaultive only toward their female partners or whether they are more generally assaultive in social relations. Even though assaultive behavior is rare among women (Saunders, 1986), we also examine whether the link between assaults inside and outside the home holds for both men and women.

Sample and Methods

The issues introduced in the preceding sections are examined through an analysis of data from three studies, each of which contains information on both family and nonfamily violence and crime. The aspects of these issues on which empirical data are presented stem from the contention that assault in interpersonal relationships is a learned response and is generalizable across both targets and contexts. Further, the greater an individual's exposure to assaults in the family, the higher the likelihood of assaultive behavior in both family and nonfamily realms.

The Three Surveys

The analyses in this chapter are based on a third source of data in addition to the 1975 and 1985 National Family Violence Surveys.[2] The additional study describes the families of orientation of a sample of university students. Because some of the crime data are unique to the student survey, they enable the theory to be tested on a wider range of criminal acts. The third data set also provides an opportunity to replicate the findings from the two national samples using a different type of sample and different data gathering methods.

Student survey. The first of the three surveys examined here is variously identified as the "student sample," the "student study," or the "1972 student study." The data were obtained through questionnaires distributed in introductory sociology and anthropology classes at a state university in New England during 1971, 1972, and 1973. The questionnaire asked about family characteristics and about conflict in the family that occurred during the senior year in high school (which in many cases was only two months earlier). The questionnaire was anonymous and voluntary (although completed during the class period). Of the 583 questionnaires distributed, 95.2 percent, or 555, were completed. However, the number of cases for the analyses in this essay, which require data on both parents, is 334 because the remaining students were not living with both parents that year. Data are available for this sample on intrafamily violence by both the parents and the respondents (see Straus 1974), but the crime data are restricted to the respondents.

An obvious limitation of the student sample is that it describes only families with a child in college. Such families and their children are far from representative. For example, since all are attending college, they may be more adequately functioning individuals and families than would be a representative cross-section of the general population. Consequently, descriptive statistics on intrafamily violence and on crime by these students are likely to be underestimates. Nevertheless, a great deal of family violence and nonfamily crime was reported. Moreover, the central issue of this essay is not the amount of family violence or the amount of crime, but whether these are correlated. Consequently, since a correlation is not affected by the absolute level of the two variables, valid results are possible, even if the two variables are each severely underestimated (Straus 1970: 572–73), provided there is no "interaction" between the reasons for the underestimate and either the independent or dependent variable.

The two national surveys.   The second study is the 1975 "National Family Violence Survey." At various places in this chapter the 1975 survey will be referred to as the "National Survey." The cases for the analyses in this chapter are those 1,092 families with a minor child living at home. Comparison with census data on husband-wife families shows a close correspondence on such variables as income, percent of women in the paid labor force, and racial or ethnic background.

The third source of data for this analysis is the "National Family Violence Resurvey" conducted in the summer of 1986, which for brevity will be referred to as the "National Resurvey" or simply the "Resurvey." The analyses reported in this chapter use only the cross-sectional national sample (i.e. the state and ethnic over-samples were excluded), and only those cases in which both parents and at least one child were household members (N = 2,688).

Measures

The Conflict Tactics Scales (described briefly in Chapter 1 and fully in Chapters 3 and 4) was used to measure the incidence of intrafamily assault in all three studies. The methods used to obtain data on non-family assault and other crime varied across the three studies. If these different methods were to be described at this point, readers might find these details difficult to recall when the results are presented. Consequently, measures of nonfamily assault and other crime will be described in the sections of the chapter where the data on these variables are presented.

Measure of child assault. Two criteria were used to identify families in which child assault occurred. The first criterion is whether the parent engaged in any assaultive act in the CTS list that is more severe than pushing, grabbing, slapping, shoving, spanking, or throwing things at the child. Thus, the assaultive acts are kicked, bit, hit with fist, hit with an object, beat up, threatened with a knife or gun, and used a knife or gun. If the parent engaged in one or more of the assaultive acts, it was counted as a case of child assault.

The second criterion was high frequency of violence, irrespective of whether it was severe enough to fall into our assault category. If a parent engaged in any of the violent acts more often than 90 percent of the parents in the sample, we classified the family as a case involving child assault. The number of assaults during the year which put a family in the top 10 percent varied from sample to sample: twenty-eight or more for the Student Sample, twenty-five or more for the National Survey, and twenty-three or more for the National Resurvey.

Measure of spouse assault. The procedure for determining whether spouse assault had occurred was simpler since the legal right to hit a child is not paralleled by the legal right to hit a spouse.[3] Consequently, we classified a family as one in which spouse assault was present if any one or more of the CTS violence acts were reported for the year of the study, regardless of whether they were acts of minor violence (such as slapping or throwing things at the spouse) or acts with a higher risk of injury that we classified as "severe violence," such as kicking, biting, punching, and choking.

Family assault type. A basic issue addressed in this essay is the extent to which intrafamily violence pervades all family roles or is specific to one role such as that of parent or husband. To answer this question, and to provide a basis for investigating the links between intrafamily violence and violence and other crime outside the family, we created a typology by cross-classifying the child-assault and spouse-assault measures, as shown in figure 25.1. Four types of family assault are created. They include Type I, nonassaultive; Type II, child assault only; Type III, spouse assault only; and Type IV, both child and spouse assault. It should be noted that, although Type I families are non*assaultive* (as we operationally defined assault), this does not mean that every family in that category is non*violent* because almost all American parents use physical punishment. For the

FIGURE 25.1
Family Assault Types

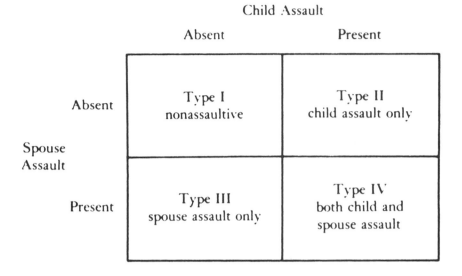

National Survey sample, this ranged from 97 percent of the parents of three-year-olds to 28 percent of parents of seventeen-year-olds (Chapter 23). Nevertheless, for stylistic variation we sometimes refer to violent and nonviolent families.

Data Analysis

The data analysis began with the incidence rates for each family assault type derived from each of the three surveys. With this foundation in place, the following dependent variables were then examined in relation to the typology illustrated in Figure 25.1: Violence committed *by children* against siblings, parents, and persons outside the family; several measures of juvenile delinquency; and physical and verbal assault *by adults* against persons outside the family. Many of these relationships were further tested while introducing controls for gender of parent, victim, and offender; and for the family's socioeconomic status.

The multivariate analyses were performed using Analysis of Variance (ANOVA). We chose ANOVA in order to test the effects of child abuse and spouse abuse when they occur alone and in possible interaction with each other. The interaction effects provide a test of whether this most violent group are at additional risk, beyond the simple additive effect of child and spouse abuse, on the dependent measures. The limitation of such an approach lies in the assumption within ANOVA of normality of the residuals, which is violated here by the skewness of many of the dependent measures. While the rates shown in the ANOVA tables are unbiased estimates, the F tests of significance may be erroneous (Iversen and Norpoth, 1976:23). These significance tests should therefore be interpreted with caution.

Rates of Assault in American Families

The first question to be answered on the basis of these three surveys is the extent to which a general pattern of family assault cuts across child assault, spouse assault, and assaults by children within the family.

Assault in Multiple Relationships in the Family

Research is accumulating that shows a link between wife assault and child assault. The extent and nature of this link is difficult to determine since the data on this issue come largely from clinical samples. Studies of wife assault among shelter residents consistently find between 25–45 percent of battered women reporting violence against one or more of the children in the family (Hilberman and Munson 1978; Roy 1982; Fagan, Stewart, and Hansen 1983; Stacey and Shupe 1983). Studies of abusive parents also indicate a higher likelihood of spouse assault in families where a child or children are at risk of physical injury. Case comparison studies have found abusive parents to be more abusive toward spouses and generally to exhibit more aversive and less prosocial behavior than nonassaultive parents (reviewed in Wolfe [1985]).

It cannot be determined from these studies what proportion of families in the general population are multiassaultive because data are based on clinical samples, and measures of violence and assault are not always standardized. The exact nature of the link between wife assault and child assault is also a matter of some controversy. Is it the assaulter who is generally violent toward wife and children or is it the victim who strikes out against other family members? The existing literature seems to support the idea that violent husbands are also more likely to be violent fathers. Washburn and Frieze (1981) found that 25 percent of the battered women they interviewed reported that their husbands were violent toward their children "several times" or "often" during the last year compared with 4 percent of the nonbattered women they interviewed. Telch and Lindquist (1984) also report that violent husbands are significantly more likely to be violent fathers when compared with nonviolent husbands. Chapter 23 reports that, in the 1975 survey, men who frequently and severely assault their wives are significantly more likely than nonviolent husbands to assault their children. This study also found that the more violent a husband is toward his wife, the more violent she is toward her children. Even women who were subjected to "minor" violence such as pushes and slaps had more than double the rate of frequent, severe assaults on their children than wives who were not subjected to assaults by their partners.

The literature does indicate a link between assaults on wives and on children in the family. However, the extent and nature of this link is not well understood. The application of the typology in figure 25.1 to the three samples in this research provides more definitive information on the extent to which intrafamily violence pervades all family roles or is role specific.

Prevalence of Four Patterns of Family Assault

The first column of table 25.1 shows that almost three-quarters of the families in these three samples were nonassaultive. However, that same column of data shows that some form of assault took place in over one out of four American families during the years of these surveys. The uniformity of results across the three studies is remarkable. As with most findings, one can choose to interpret these results as either "fully" 25% or "only" 25% (Hirschi and Selvin, 1967).

Of particular interest is the uniformity in rates of multiassaultive families, as shown in column 4—between 5.6 and 6.9 percent of all intact families with children report both forms of assault. According to the U.S. Bureau of the Census (1986), in 1984 there were 24,700,000 two-parent families with at least one child in the household. Based on this number, the percentages in table 25.1 indicate that from 1.4 to 1.7 million children live with parents who assault each other *and* their children. The actual number of children who experience parental assault and who witness assaults between their parents is surely much higher than the 1.4 to 1.7 million estimate because under-reporting of assaults is almost inevitable and because many of these families contain more than one child.

Column 5 in table 25.1 give the number of multiassaultive families (Type IV) as a percentage of all assaultive families (sum of Types II, III, and IV). Again, there is a good deal of consistency across data sets. These rates indicate that "fully" a fifth of all abusive families are generally assaultive, or that both types of assault occur in "only" a fifth of violent families.

TABLE 25.1

Distribution of Family Assault Types in Three Samples (%)

| Study | Family Assault Type | | | | Percentage of Assaultive Families That Are Type IV V |
	Non-abusive I	Child Assault Only II	Spouse Assault Only III	Both Child Assault and Spouse Assault IV	
1972 Student Survey (N = 334)	73.1	11.1	10.1	5.7	21.1
1975 National Survey (N = 1,092)	68.1	15.8	9.2	6.9	21.6
1985 National Resurvey (N = 2,688)	69.6	12.4	12.4	5.6	18.4

Gender Differences in the Relation between Spouse and Child Assault

The first column of table 25.2 shows that, even in the absence of spouse assault, the rate of assaults on children in families is high: about one out of six American children was severely assaulted by a parent in the year of this survey. Moreover, as previously suggested, not all parents who kicked or bit a child will describe such events in interview, so the actual rate is probably much higher.

The second and third columns of table 25.2 show that, when either spouse assaults the other, the rate of assaults on children increases, especially assaults by mothers. The last column of the table shows that when both parents physically assault each other, children are at the highest risk of also being assaulted, especially by fathers.

Assaultive Families and Violence by Children in the Family

Violence by children in the family can occur against siblings or against parents. Each form is described below.

Sibling Violence

Are children who experience physical assault from parents, witness assaults between their mothers and fathers, or both more likely than other

TABLE 25.2

Child Assault Rate for Each Spouse Assault Type by Gender of Parent
(1985 National Resurvey)

	No Spouse Assault (N)	Wife Only Is Assaultive (N)	Husband Only Is Assaultive (N)	Both Husband and Wife Are Assaultive (N)
A. By mothers	15.5	28.6	28.9	36.1
	(1,213)	(63)	(76)	(138)
B. By fathers	14.7	19.2	15.7	41.1
	(992)	(62)	(41)	(103)

NOTE.—For rate of assault on children by mothers and by fathers: $\chi^2 = 45.81$; df = 3; $p < .001$; $N = 1,198$. Rates are per 100 and are therefore equal to percentages.

children to engage in violence toward family and nonfamily members? Table 25.3 shows sibling violence rates for children six years of age and older clustered[4] in the four family assault types. The results are very consistent across all three data sets. The rate of sibling violence is higher among children in families in which child assault and spouse assault are present and, in two of the three samples, highest of all when both child assault and spouse assault are present. However, the analysis of variance shows that sibling violence is more strongly associated with child assault than with spouse assault.

Several points must be noted about data in table 25.3. First, the rates that appear in cells for the 1985 survey data are much lower than those in both the 1972 and 1975 surveys. This is true because, unlike the two earlier surveys, the 1985 survey did not measure sibling violence through the CTS. Instead of asking whether a variety of forms of physical violence occurred between children, as is done in the CTS, the 1985 survey asked only whether the respondent considered "fights with children in the family" to be a problem. The discrepancy between the CTS rates and the percent of parents who regard violence between siblings as a problem is a reflection of the acceptance of this type of violence in American families. This issue is discussed further in Chapter 23. The important issue for this essay, however, is the pattern of sibling assault in relation to other forms of family violence. All three data sets are in accord on this issue.

Second, these data *cannot* be used to posit a causal relation between sibling assault and other forms of family violence. All three surveys are cross-sectional and can demonstrate only that sibling violence and other forms of intrafamily assault co-occur.

TABLE 25.3

Rate of Sibling Violence by Parent-to-Child Assault and Spouse Assault
(Three Samples)

| | Child Assault | | | ANOVA | |
	Absent (N)	Present (N)	Total (N)	Effect	F
Spouse Assault					
A. 1972 student survey (CTS scores):					
Absent	54.5	78.5	66.6	child assault	7.65**
	(189)	(29)	(218)	spouse assault	6.04*
Present	75.9	93.8	84.9	child assault x spouse assault	.12
	(28)	(16)	(44)	df = 3,262	
Total	65.2	86.2	75.7		
	(217)	(45)	(262)		
B. 1975 National Survey (CTS scores):					
Absent	67.5	93.4	80.5	child assault	17.11***
	(452)	(76)	(528)	spouse assault	4.98*
Present	85.7	91.7	88.7	child assault x spouse assault	3.24
	(56)	(36)	(92)	df = 3.620	
Total	76.6	92.6	84.6		
	(508)	(112)	(620)		
C. 1985 National Resurvey ("fights with children in the family"):					
Absent	3.6	8.5	6.0	child assault	10.77***
	(1,289)	(141)	(1,430)	spouse assault	2.99
Present	6.0	11.5	8.8	child assault x spouse assault	.37
	(168)	(84)	(252)	df = 3,1680	
Total	4.8	10.0	7.4		
	(1,457)	(225)	(1,682)		

NOTE.—Rates are per 100 and are therefore equal to percentages. Numbers in parentheses are sample sizes.
$*p < .05.$ $**p < .01.$ $***p < .001.$

Third, while boys are more likely than girls to engage in sibling violence, separate analysis of the data in table 25.3 for boys and girls revealed no major differences in main or interaction effects of child and spouse assault on rates of sibling assault. Thus, the pattern of relationships between sibling violence and violence in other family relationships for both boys and girls is very similar, although boys display more assaultive behavior toward siblings.

Fourth, the effect of child assault and spouse assault is more strongly related to rates of sibling violence when severity of sibling assault is taken into account. The version of the CTS used in the 1975 National Survey enables a "severe violence" or "sibling assault" index to be computed on the basis of the occurrence of items such as punching, kicking, biting, and attacking with weapons. Use of that measure reveals a similar but stronger relation of child and spouse assault to sibling violence than is shown in table 25.3. For example, 37 percent of the 498 children from otherwise nonassaultive families severely assaulted a sibling during the survey year. For children from families in which both child and spouse assault are present, 100 percent of the twelve children in this type of family severely assaulted a brother or sister during the survey year. These results suggest that perhaps not only minor violence, but violence that is severe enough to be classified as a criminal assault, is a learned family behavior.[5]

Part A of table 25.4 examines the rate of sibling violence controlling for family socioeconomic status.[6] There are no significant differences in rates of sibling violence for children from blue or white collar families. Child assault victimization is significantly related to sibling violence for both socioeconomic status groups, and the highest rates of sibling violence occur among children from multiassaultive families regardless of social class.

Child-to-Parent Violence[7]

Table 25.5 indicates that siblings are not the only targets of assault by children from multiassaultive families. Parents are more likely to experience violence from their children when children have been assaulted by their parents or observe assaults between the parents. The results from both the surveys that included the necessary data show that the rate of child-to-parent violence among children six years of age and older is higher for children living in households where both child assault and spouse assault occurred. In the 1975 National Survey there is a very strong main effect for child assault. While the effect for child assault is also strong in the 1985 survey, the interaction between child assault and spouse assault is even stronger. It seems that child-to-parent violence cannot be explained

TABLE 25.4

Violence Rates of Children by Family Assault Type, Controlling for Socioeconomic Status (1985 National Resurvey)

	A. Family Assault Type							
	Blue Collar				White Collar			
Dependent Variable*	Non-assaultive (N = 631)	Child Assault Only (N = 84)	Spouse Assault Only (N = 93)	Child Assault and Spouse Assault (N = 54)	Non-assaultive (N = 611)	Child Assault Only (N = 54)	Spouse Assault Only (N = 73)	Child Assault and Spouse Assault (N = 28)
A. Sibling violence	3.6	10.1	6.2	13.1	3.1	6.5	5.8	9.1
B. Child-to-parent violence	.2	.4	.6	6.6	.0	.0	.7	.0
C. Nonfamily violence	2.9	10.7	3.4	17.0	1.2	4.9	2.5	3.5

B. ANOVA F-Values			
	Sibling Assault	Child-Parent Assault	Nonfamily Violence
Child assault	11.89***	8.17**	28.83***
Spouse assault	3.47	7.81**	1.67
Socioeconomic status	.70	2.60	8.13**
Child × spouse	.01	13.66***	.86
Child × Socioeconomic Status	1.02	4.91*	6.22*
Spouse × Socioeconomic Status	.00	4.77*	.27
Child × Spouse × Socio-economic Status	.01	8.07**	2.14

*The dependent variables in this table were measured by a question that asked the respondent if any of a list of social psychological problems caused "any special difficulties" for the child within the past year. Thus, the data reflect a combination of whether the acts occurred and, if they did, whether the parent considered them to be a problem for the child. For this reason, the rates are lower than the rates of violent acts by children obtained using the CTS, which requires only that the act occurred. The three items from the list used to obtain the data in this table are: "physical fights with kids who live in your house," "physical fights with adults who live in your house," and "physical fights with adults who don't live in your house."
NOTE.—Rates are per 100 and are therefore equal to percentages.
*p < .05.   **p < .01.   ***p < .001.

TABLE 25.5

Rate of Child-to-Parent Violence by Parent-to-Child and Spouse Assault (1975 and 1985 National Surveys)

| | Child Assault | | | ANOVA | |
	Absent (N)	Present (N)	Total (N)	Effect	F
Spouse Assault					
A. 1975 National Survey (CTS scores):					
Absent	7.9	27.6	17.8	child assault	26.40***
	(570)	(87)	(657)	spouse assault	2.45
Present	12.9	37.8	25.4	child assault × spouse assault	.27
	(62)	(37)	(99)	df = 3,756	
Total	10.4	32.7	21.6		
	(632)	(124)	(756)		
B. 1985 National Resurvey "fights with adults at home"):					
Absent	.1	.3	.2	child assault	12.46***
	(1,289)	(141)	(1,430)	spouse assault	11.30***
Present	.3	5.5	2.9	child assault × spouse assault	23.79***
	(168)	(84)	(252)	df = 3,1680	
Total	.2	2.9	1.6		
	(1,457)	(225)	(1,682)		

NOTE.—Rates are per 100 and are therefore equal to percentages. Numbers in parentheses are sample sizes.
***$p < .001$.

simply in terms of retaliation for child assault. The rate of child violence against parents is eighteen times higher in multiassaultive families than in families in which only one form of assault occurs.

There are no significant differences between boys and girls on this measure, but there are differences due to family socioeconomic status. Part B of table 25.4 indicates that the rate of child-to-parent violence is higher among blue-collar families. Furthermore, children from blue-collar, multiassaultive families have rates of violence toward parents that are nine times higher than any other type of family constellation.

Assaultive Families and Violence and Crime[8] by Children Outside the Family

A consistent theme in the criminology and family violence literatures is the relation between experiencing violence as part of one's family socialization and later antisocial behavior. Both the experience of parental violence and witnessing spousal violence while growing up have been found in the childhood backgrounds of wife assaulters (see Hotaling and Sugarman [1986] for a review), child assaulters (Alfaro 1978; Potts, Herzberger, and Holland 1979; Gelles 1980), violent criminals (McCord 1979; Sedgely and Lund 1979), and persons who approve of the use of violence (Owens and Straus 1975).

While the *long-term* effects of exposure to family violence are clear-cut, the results of studies of the *short-term* effects are mixed and conceptually confusing. Some research has found a strong link between child assault and adolescent aggression or delinquency (Glueck and Glueck 1950; Strasberg 1978; Conger 1984; Straus 1985), while other research finds little relationship (Morse, Sahler, and Friedman 1970; Elmer, Evans, and Reinhart 1977). Other research suggests that some assaulted children become withdrawn rather than aggressive (Martin and Beezley 1974; George and Main 1979), and still other research suggests that the role of family violence in promoting delinquency is exaggerated relative to the influence of peers, schools, and a host of other socializing influences (Bolton, Reich, and Gutierres 1977; Hawkins and Weis 1980; Fagan and Wexler 1987).

To complicate the issue further, several dimensions of harmful family behaviors are often lumped together as "child abuse" and examined for their effect on children's antisocial behavior, thereby making it difficult to determine whether assault in the family is a true risk factor of adolescent difficulties (Loeber and Dishion 1983; Loeber and Stouthamer-Loeber 1986). Studies have used a variety of measures of "parental lack of affection," "lack of supervision," "excessive discipline," "rejection," "neglect," and "abuse" but have rarely directly measured the effects on children of parental assaultive behavior (Lane and Davis 1987).

Many of the problems involved in establishing a link between childhood exposure to assaultive behavior in the family and juvenile delinquency arise from the use in most studies of samples of children who have come to the attention of agencies for their delinquency, rather than general population surveys. Without appropriate control groups, the proportion of children exposed to violence in their family who do *not* become delinquent cannot be determined. It is almost certainly a large proportion; over one out of four children grow up in violent families (see table 25.1).

The data used for the analyses in this essay avoid that problem because they do not derive from clinical samples. This alleviates one of the major obstacles to answering the question of whether children who have been the victim of parental assault, have witnessed spouse assault, or both are more likely to be violent toward persons outside the family and to engage in acts of delinquency. Furthermore, the sample for the 1985 National Resurvey contains enough cases to permit use of controls for the separate effects of sex of child, severity of spouse violence witnessed by the child, and family socioeconomic status.

Nonfamily Violence by Children

Part A of table 25.6 shows that, in the 1972 student survey, there were no significant main or interaction effects associated with being the victim of child assault or witnessing spouse assault on assaultive behavior outside

TABLE 25.6

Nonfamily Assault Rates of Children by Parent-to-Child and Spouse Assault

(Two Samples)

| | Child Assault | | | ANOVA | |
| | Absent | Present | Total | | |
Spouse Assault	(N)	(N)	(N)	Effect	F
A. 1972 student survey ("child used violence against nonfamily person"):					
Absent	34.3	3?.1	35.7	child assault	1.41
	(239)	(35)	(274)	spouse assault	2.29
Present	39.4	63.2	51.3	child assault x spouse assault	1.64
	(33)	(19)	(52)	df = 3,326	
Total	36.9	50.2	36.8		
	(272)	(54)	(326)		
B. 1985 National Resurvey "fights with nonfamily children"):					
Absent	2.1	8.2	5.2	child assault	15.59***
	(1,281)	(141)	(1.422)	spouse assault	.58
Present	3.0	12.1	7.6	child assault x spouse assault	2.75
	(168)	(84)	(252)	df = 3,1674	
Total	2.6	10.2	6.4		
	(1,449)	(225)	(1,674)		

NOTE.—Rates are per 100 and are therefore equal to percentages.
*** p < .001.

of the family. Nevertheless, the differences are large. The nineteen students who were exposed to *both* forms of assault in the family have double the high rate of nonfamily assault compared to students from nonassaultive families (63.2 percent vs. 34.3 percent).

The 1985 National Resurvey (part B of table 25.6) found a strong relation between parental assault and assaults by children outside the home. Children who are *both* the victims of parental assaults and who witness spouse assault have a rate of assault against nonfamily children six times higher than children from nonassaultive families (12.1 percent vs. 2.1 percent).[9]

Separate analyses of the 1985 data for boys and girls indicate that the rate of assault outside the family by boys is much higher than the rate for girls. Despite this, the pattern of findings is very similar for each sex. For boys, a significant main effect was found for child assault victimization, while for girls there was both a significant main effect on child assault and a significant interaction effect between child assault and witnessing spouse assault on out-of-home assault rates.

The findings did not vary when controlling for the severity of spouse assault witnessed by the child. Again, whether children viewed minor or severe acts of violence between their parents, their assault rate outside the family was equally high.

Control for Socioeconomic Status

Part C of table 25.4 shows the relation between family assault type, assaults by children outside the home, and family socioeconomic status using the 1985 Resurvey data. The results show a significant main effect for both child assault and socioeconomic status and a significant interaction effect between child assault and socioeconomic status on outside-family assault by children. The rate of outside assault is significantly higher for children from blue-collar families compared with the rate for children from white-collar families, but for blue-collar and white-collar children, the rate of extrafamily assault is three times higher for victims of child assault compared with rates for children from nonassaultive families. Children from multiassaultive blue-collar families have an inordinately high rate of assault against nonfamily members.

These results suggest that one of the short-term effects of child exposure to family violence is an increase in assaults by children outside the family. The effect of experiencing assaults by parents is stronger than the modeling effect of observing assaults between parents for children from both blue- and white-collar families. An important conclusion of these analyses is that, while children from white-collar families are less violent than lower socioeconomic status children, there are important within-group differences. Specifically, assaults within the family are related to assaults by children outside the family to the same extent, regardless of social class.

Nonviolent Crime by Children

Although social learning theory provides a perspective for understanding the ways in which violence can be learned through direct experience and modeling processes, explanation of nonviolent antisocial acts that focus on these same processes are not plausible. However, it can be argued that being assaulted by a parent weakens the bonds between child and parent and that witnessing physical assaults between parents weakens one's allegiance to societal norms. While the data do not allow for an investigation of the mediating processes, the analyses presented in table 25.7 do indicate a link between family assaults and nonviolent antisocial acts on the part of children.

Table 25.7 presents nineteen tests of the hypothesis that nonviolent delinquent acts are related to intrafamily violence. Overall, the highest rates of delinquent behaviors occur in "child-assault only" families (thirteen of nineteen comparisons). This pattern is most prominent for stealing. Three items measuring this behavior—"taking things worth less than $2.00," "taking things worth more than $50.00," and "child steals"—are consistently related to the presence of child assault. Two items measuring property destruction show an inconsistent relation to child assault. A measure of "vandalism" in the 1985 resurvey is strongly related to child assault, while in the 1972 student study, "destroyed property" occurred

TABLE 25.7

Juvenile Delinquency Rates by Parent-to-Child and Spouse Assault (Three Samples)

Data Sets and Indicators	Nonassaultive (N)	Child Assault Only (N)	Spouse Assault Only (N)	Both Child Assault and Spouse Assault (N)	ANOVA Effect	F
A. 1972 student survey:						
Nye-Short Delinquency Scale	85.3	100.0	93.1	100.0	child assault	13.82***
(one or more items)	(224)	(36)	(29)	(14)	spouse assault	1.20
					child assault × spouse assault	1.26
Drove with no license	20.3	40.5	35.3	26.3	child assault	7.88**
	(237)	(37)	(34)	(19)	spouse assault	.28
					child assault × spouse assault	4.59*
Took things worth less	35.1	59.5	29.4	47.4	child assault	8.16**
than $2.00	(239)	(37)	(34)	(19)	spouse assault	1.52
					child assault × spouse assault	1.27
Destroyed property	23.8	29.7	32.4	31.6	child assault	2.00
	(239)	(37)	(34)	(19)	spouse assault	.19
					child assault × spouse assault	1.84
Took things worth more than	2.1	13.5	3.0	.0	child assault	10.59***
$50.00	(237)	(37)	(33)	(18)	spouse assault	1.83
					child assault × spouse assault	6.15*
Defied parents	57.6	80.6	76.5	94.4	child assault	11.46***
	(238)	(36)	(34)	(18)	spouse assault	11.69***
					child assault × spouse assault	.88
Used drugs	36.5	32.4	31.3	33.3	child assault	.53
	(230)	(37)	(32)	(15)	spouse assault	1.37
					child assault × spouse assault	.93
Questioned by police	21.3	29.7	17.6	36.8	child assault	1.94
	(239)	(37)	(34)	(19)	spouse assault	.57
					child assault × spouse assault	7.47**
Disciplining problem in school	11.7	29.7	20.6	21.1	child assault	6.54**
	(239)	(37)	(34)	(19)	spouse assault	1.26
					child assault × spouse assault	.12
Kicked out of school	2.9	2.7	.0	15.8	child assault	1.94
	(239)	(37)	(34)	(19)	spouse assault	.57
					child assault × spouse assault	7.47**
B. 1975 National Survey:						
Child caught doing something	4.3	5.0	11.3	4.3	child assault	.14
illegal	(599)	(100)	(71)	(47)	spouse assault	3.16
					child assault × spouse assault	1.87
Kicked out of school/suspended	2.2	4.0	5.6	4.3	child assault	1.06
	(602)	(100)	(71)	(47)	spouse assault	2.63
					child assault × spouse assault	1.84
C. 1985 National Resurvey:						
Vandalism	.9	7.1	.8	3.6	child assault	31.09***
	(1,289)	(141)	(168)	(84)	spouse assault	.96
					child assault × spouse assault	3.59
Stealing	.7	6.7	.7	4.6	child assault	34.05***
	(1,289)	(141)	(168)	(84)	spouse assault	.50
					child assault × spouse assault	4.37*
Drinking	.9	2.9	1.4	1.7	child assault	7.85**
	(1,289)	(141)	(168)	(84)	spouse assault	.44
					child assault × spouse assault	6.14*
Used drugs	.2	1.1	.5	1.7	child assault	8.59**
	(1,289)	(141)	(168)	(84)	spouse assault	5.23*
					child assault × spouse assault	22.99***
Got arrested	.6	3.5	.0	.0	child assault	11.22***
	(1,289)	(141)	(168)	(84)	spouse assault	1.05
					child assault × spouse assault	.95
Disciplining problem in school	4.1	14.7	4.5	16.2	child assault	32.61***
	(1,289)	(141)	(168)	(84)	spouse assault	.83
					child assault × spouse assault	.26
Failing in school	9.1	19.3	17.3	17.6	child assault	15.68***
	(1,289)	(141)	(168)	(84)	spouse assault	2.02
					child assault × spouse assault	.97

NOTE.—Rates are per 100 and are therefore equal to percentages.
*$p < .05$.   **$p < .01$.   ***$p < .001$.

about equally often among children in nonassaultive and assaultive families. The same inconsistent pattern is evident on items concerning the use of alcohol and drugs.

Perhaps the most sensitive indicator of child problems in the community concerns involvement with police. Two data sets contain items concerning contact with the police. The 1972 student survey asked whether respondents were "questioned by police." Children from families in which multiple assaults occur are significantly more likely to report police involvement. The 1985 National Resurvey asked parents whether the referent child "got arrested" in the last year and found that child assault victims are significantly more likely to have been arrested than are children from other family types.

As is true for other rates of child antisocial behavior, the rate of nonviolent delinquency for boys is significantly higher than the rate for girls. Once again, however, the pattern of findings linking family violence type to delinquency is similar for both sexes, at least for minor acts of delinquency. For more serious problems such as stealing and contact with police, the female offense rate is very low and follows no pattern in terms of exposure to assault in the family.

Control for Socioeconomic Status

Data from the 1985 National Resurvey in table 25.8 examines the link between exposure to family violence and conduct problems, controlling for social class. The most important finding is that socioeconomic status exerts no significant main effects on conduct problems of any kind. Even for property offenses such as vandalism and stealing and for arrest rates, there are no significant differences between children from blue or white collar families in rates of conduct disorders. In six of seven separate analyses, there is a significant effect due to child assault victimization on conduct problems outside the family but little evidence for an association between growing up in a multiassaultive family and conduct problems.

Summary

It appears that children assaulted by parents are more violent toward brothers, sisters, parents, and persons outside the family. They are also more likely to be involved in property crime, to have adjustment difficulties in school, and to be involved with the police. It is not possible to determine the causal direction of this relation with the data used in these analyses, but family assault victimization is clearly linked to antisocial behavior.

Assault by children and other conduct problems are more strongly

TABLE 25.8

Delinquency Rate by Family Assault Type and Socioeconomic Status

(1985 National Resurvey)

	A. Family Assault Type							
	Blue Collar				White Collar			
Dependent Variable	Non-assaultive (N = 631)	Child Assault Only (N = 84)	Spouse Assault Only (N = 93)	Child Assault and Spouse Assault (N = 54)	Non-assaultive (N = 611)	Child Assault Only (N = 54)	Spouse Assault Only (N = 73)	Child Assault and Spouse Assault (N = 28)
Vandalism	1.1	7.0	.8	2.8	.5	7.7	.9	.0
Stealing	.5	6.0	1.2	2.8	.9	8.1	.0	8.4
Child drinking	1.0	4.8	2.0	2.7	.7	.0	.7	.0
Child drug use	.2	1.8	.3	2.7	.3	.0	.7	.0
Child arrested	.5	4.1	0	.0	.8	2.7	.0	.0
Failing in school	10.1	18.1	12.9	19.1	8.2	21.7	11.9	15.9
School discipline problem	4.6	16.3	5.2	19.1	3.8	12.6	3.6	8.2

B. ANOVA F-Values

	Vandalism	Stealing	Child Drinking	Child Drug Use	Child Arrested	Failing in School	School Discipline Problem
Child assault	35.14***	40.51***	3.18	3.97*	9.39**	14.35***	38.04***
Spouse assault	1.19	.41	.01	.55	4.88*	.83	.04
Socioeconomic status	.15	1.17	2.56	.26	.04	.84	1.91
Child × spouse	3.08	1.12	1.18	.12	4.25	.46	.01
Child × socioeconomic status	.74	3.27	4.80*	5.15*	.78	.88	1.88
Spouse × socioeconomic status	.29	.04	.02	.03	.01	.05	.53
Child × spouse × socioeconomic status	.10	1.75	.74	.38	.33	.56	.67

NOTE.—Rates are per 100 and are therefore equal to percentages.

$*p < .05.$

$**p < .01.$

$***p < .001.$

related to being assaulted by parents than to witnessing assaults between parents. However, children from multiassaultive families have higher rates of child-to-parent violence and violence toward persons outside the family. These two variables are also related to family socioeconomic status, with blue-collar children having higher rates of assaulting parents and nonfamily members. No social class differences occur in rates of sibling violence or rates of conduct problems among children.

These results support and specify the theory that family assault trains children in the use of violent behavior. Children who are exposed to multiple forms of assault in the family are more likely to be violent themselves, especially toward parents and peers. These types of assault are also more likely to be committed by boys and children from blue-collar families.

Victimization Effects

The process linking victimization to aggression is not well understood. After all, why would victims of assault be more likely to be violent themselves and more likely to experience a variety of conduct problems? Straus (1985) suggested that victims of violence tend to lose faith in the efficacy and fairness of the world, a belief that is conducive to conforming behavior. Another interpretation may be that victims of violence often see firsthand that violence is effective and that offenders are not often sanctioned for their behavior. The victim may generalize this to other forms of deviant behavior and feel freer to engage in antisocial behavior.

We have no data to address these speculations. The cross-sectional data presented in this essay cannot demonstrate whether persons are victimized *before* or *after* they become victimizers. But it is clear from previous analyses that there is a strong link between being the victim of assault within the family and assault and other conduct problems on the part of children outside of the family. This section examines whether victimization effects exist among adults who are the targets of assaults within families.

Assaults by Assaulted Husbands

Part A of table 25.9 indicates that husbands who have been assaulted by their wives, and are in a family in which child assault occurs, are more likely to engage in verbal aggression and physical assault outside the family than are men who are not assaulted, and they are also more likely to have been arrested in the previous twelve months. A significant main effect for assault by wives was found for each indicator of the husband's nonfamily aggression and violent behavior. Although the highest rates of nonfamily aggression and assault by husbands occurs when there are both assaults by the wife and assaults on children, the results show a stronger main effect of assault by wives.

This pattern of results is very similar for both blue-collar and white-collar males. Among both groups of men, the rate of nonfamily verbal aggression and assault and the arrest rate is highest for men in multi-assaultive families. However, blue-collar males who are victims of family assaults commit higher rates of outside family assaults.

Assaults by Assaulted Wives

The analyses of variance reported in part B of table 25.9 show that being assaulted by husbands is significantly related to the probability of verbal aggression, assault, and arrest of female victims. Thus, the analysis in part B reveals the same pattern of nonfamily assault and arrest of wives who are the victims of assaults by their husbands as was shown in part A for husbands who have been assaulted by their wives.

TABLE 25.9

Rates of Nonfamily Verbal and Physical Assault by Family Assault Type and Gender of Adult Victims (1985 National Resurvey)

Dependent Variable	Family Assault Type				ANOVA	
	Non-violent (N)	Wife-to-Husband Assault, No Child Assault (N)	No Wife-to-Husband Assault, Child Assault (N)	Both Child and Wife-to-Husband Assault (N)	Effect	F
A. For husbands who are victims of assault by wives:						
Husband got angry at non-family person and yelled at him/her	49.8 (1,922)	57.9 (359)	58.6 (243)	81.1 (122)	child assault	12.28***
					assault by wife	51.19***
					child assault × wife assault	.36
Husband got angry at non-family person and smashed something	5.9 (1,953)	11.2 (360)	20.6 (241)	25.8 (120)	child assault	11.77***
					assault by wife	88.28***
					child assault × wife assault	.95
Husband got into fight with nonfamily member and hit him/her	2.3 (1,954)	4.3 (362)	9.1 (242)	9.5 (122)	child assault	3.69
					assault by wife	34.36***
					child assault × wife assault	.27
Husband got into fight with nonfamily member and injured him/her	.7 (1,959)	.6 (362)	1.7 (242)	5.6 (121)	child assault	2.49
					assault by wife	16.53***
					child assault × wife assault	11.33***
Husband got arrested in last twelve months	1.4 (881)	.0 (152)	2.9 (110)	6.5 (54)	child assault	.13
					assault by wife	7.39**
					child assault × wife assault	4.43*
B. For wives who are victims of assault by husbands:						
Wife got angry at nonfamily person and yelled at him/her	42.1 (1,945)	47.9 (360)	54.2 (234)	69.2 (118)	child assault	11.14***
					assault by husband	28.22***
					child assault × husband assault	2.59
Wife got angry at nonfamily person and smashed something	4.0 (1,955)	5.7 (358)	9.7 (233)	18.3 (119)	child assault	7.16**
					assault by husband	35.82***
					child assault × husband assault	5.22*
Wife got in fight with nonfamily person and hit him/her	.7 (1,960)	1.0 (364)	1.8 (237)	3.7 (121)	child assault	1.55
					assault by husband	17.42***
					child assault × husband assault	1.45
Wife got in fight with nonfamily person and injured him/her	.2 (1,965)	.0 (364)	.7 (237)	.0 (121)	child assault	1.34
					assault by husband	4.27*
					child assault × husband assault	1.80
Wife got arrested in last twelve months	.3 (1,067)	.8 (206)	2.3 (142)	1.9 (72)	child assault	.17
					assault by husband	11.84**
					child assault × husband assault	1.23

NOTE.—Rates are per 100 and are therefore equal to percentages.
*$p < .05$.
**$p < .01$.
***$p < .001$.

Rates of assault outside the family by victims of wife assault show an identical relation to social class as was the case for males. Both blue-collar and white-collar women in families where multiple assault occurs have the highest rate of outside family aggression.

The uniformity in findings for victims of adult family assault is striking. Whether male or female, blue- or white-collar, the presence of spouse assault appears to be strongly related to aggression against nonfamily persons.

Offender Effects

The preceding sections reported a strong victimization effect: victims of intrafamily assault are more likely to engage in assault and verbal aggression outside the family. What of offender effects? Are assaultive husbands and assaultive fathers also violent men outside the family? There are suggestions in the literature that family and nonfamily assault is related among adult men, but this literature is difficult to interpret because only one existing study (an analysis by Straus [1985] of the 1975 National Survey sample) has examined this issue using data from general populations. All the other reports are based on studies of men identified as batterers to determine the proportion who have histories of assault toward nonfamily members, other criminal offenses, and arrest records. These proportions are listed in Table 25.10

Although the figures strongly suggest that men who assault their wives also engage in nonfamily criminal activities, one cannot be certain because of the absence of comparison groups. However, there have been some case comparison studies of violent and nonviolent husbands. These studies found violent husbands to be significantly more likely than nonviolent husbands to be violent toward nonfamily members (Graff 1979) and significantly more likely to have arrest records for criminal offenses (Hofeller 1980; Dvoskin 1981; Straus 1985).

Two studies examined whether violent family members can be differen-

TABLE 25.10

Proportion of Male Batterers Who Have Histories of Other Antisocial Behaviors

Study	Antisocial Behavior	Proportion (%)
Faulk 1974	previous criminal assault	12
Flynn 1977	nonfamily criminal assault	33
Gayford 1975	previously incarcerated (one-third of above for violent offenses)	50
Stacey and Shupe 1983	arrest record (one-third of above for violent offenses)	80
Walker 1979	previous arrest	71
	violent to nonfamily members	20
Rounsaville 1978	arrest record	35
	previous incarceration	35
	nonfamily violence	51
Fagan, Stewart, and Hansen 1983	previous arrests for other violence	46
Browne 1984 (batterers who were killed by their wives)	previous arrest	92

tiated on the basis of their psychiatric, social, and demographic profile from violent "street criminals." Daniel and Holcomb (1985) compared 213 men who were charged with domestic or nondomestic homicide and given pretrial psychiatric evaluations. Using institutional records, they found that family murder defendants were significantly different from the nondomestic defendants in that they were older, had a more stable adjustment in the community, a prior violent criminal record, to have killed females, had a history of juvenile conduct problems including delinquency and school problems, and were more likely to receive psychotic diagnoses as a result of pretrial psychiatric evaluations.

In another study of this type, Shields and Hanneke (1981) examined the characteristics of three types of violent men: those violent only toward wives, those violent only toward persons outside the family, and "generally violent" men whose violence was indiscriminate. Their results indicate that generally violent men and men violent only toward nonfamily members are virtually indistinguishable, but wife assaulters were better educated, more law-abiding, and more loyal and concerned about their marital relationships. The authors note that many of the variables suggested by the literature did not differentiate the "family-only" violence group from the "generally violent." However, it is difficult to interpret the applicability of these findings (and those of Daniel and Holcomb [1985]) to more general populations.

Child Assault

The child assaulter has typically been depicted as nonaggresive in social relationships and posing no threat to the society at large. Steele and Pollack (1974) describe the abusing parent as not generally violent: "The abusing parents we have seen do not show evidence of an unusually strong basic aggressive drive. They are not fundamentally 'mean' people . . . although their release of aggression is overt and intense, they usually show significant inhibition of aggression in many areas of their lives" (p. 107).

Some evidence, however, shows that fathers of assaulted children have criminal records (Skinner and Castle 1969; Gil 1970; Smith, Hanson, and Noble 1973). Smith, Hanson, and Noble (1973), in a comparison study, found that 29 percent of fathers had a criminal record and Gil (1970) reported that 15.6 percent of abusive fathers had criminal records. By contrast, Steele and Pollack (1974) and Straus (1985) found little relation between child assault and involvement in crime for either mothers or fathers. Gil (1970), however, found that one-tenth of the abusive mothers in his national sample had criminal records. None of this research specifically examines nonfamily assault as an indicator of criminal behavior.

Assaultive Families and Outside Family Conflict and Violence

To determine whether adults in assaultive families are also more likely to assault persons outside the family, rates of verbal aggression and assault against nonfamily persons and arrest rates were examined for the four family assault types. Table 25.11 shows that the relation between assaults in the family and crime outside of the family is as strong for adults as it is for children.

Husbands. Part A of table 25.11 examines male rates of aggression outside the home in the four family assault types. In every comparison, the analysis of variance shows that there is a significant main effect of

TABLE 25.11

Rates of Nonfamily Verbal and Physical Assault by Family Assault Type and Gender of Adult *Offender* (1985 National Resurvey)

	Family Assault Type				ANOVA	
Indicator of Nonfamily Aggression	Non-violent (N)	Child Assault, No Assault by Husband (N)	Assault by Husband, No Child Assault (N)	Both Child Assault and Husband Assault (N)	Effect	F
A. For husbands who assault wives:						
Husband got angry at nonfamily person and yelled at him/her	49.8 (1,931)	59.3 (158)	69.2 (234)	77.3 (120)	child assault	12.84***
					assault by husband	44.46***
					child assault × husband assault	.79
Husband got angry at nonfamily person and smashed something	6.1 (1,960)	11.8 (363)	19.4 (235)	25.7 (118)	child assault	13.03***
					assault by husband	72.03***
					child assault × husband assault	.27
Husband got into fight with nonfamily member and hit him/her	2.3 (1,960)	3.7 (364)	9.0 (236)	11.4 (120)	child assault	3.30
					assault by husband	41.76***
					child assault × husband assault	.49
Husband got into fight with nonfamily member and injured him/her	.8 (1,964)	.2 (364)	.9 (236)	6.6 (120)	child assault	2.60
					assault by husband	14.02***
					child assault × husband assault	26.31***
Husband got arrested in last twelve months	1.4 (896)	.6 (158)	3.2 (95)	5.1 (49)	child assault	.82
					assault by husband	5.18*
					child assault × husband assault	1.23
B. For wives who assault husbands:						
Wife got angry at nonfamily person and yelled at him/her	41.9 (1,937)	46.4 (358)	55.5 (242)	73.7 (120)	child assault	10.40***
					assault by wife	39.73***
					child assault × wife assault	5.18***
Wife got angry at nonfamily person and smashed something	3.8 (1,948)	5.1 (356)	10.7 (240)	20.0 (121)	child assault	6.20*
					assault by wife	53.60***
					child assault × wife assault	8.49**
Wife got in fight with nonfamily person and hit him/her	.6 (1,954)	.9 (362)	2.4 (242)	4.1 (122)	child assault	1.55
					assault by wife	17.42***
					child assault × wife assault	1.45
Wife got in fight with nonfamily person and injured him/her	.2 (1,960)	.0 (362)	.7 (242)	.0 (127)	child assault	1.34
					assault by wife	4.27*
					child assault × wife assault	1.80
Wife got arrested in last twelve months	.3 (1,077)	1.3 (210)	3.0 (132)	.5 (68)	child assault	.29
					assault by wife	7.29**
					child assault × wife assault	6.62**

NOTE.—Rates are per 100 and are therefore equal to percentages.
*$p < .05$.
**$p < .01$.
***$p < .001$.

assault by husband on the rate of nonfamily verbal aggression, assault, and arrest. For example, the third row of table 25.11 shows that the rate of hitting a nonfamily member during the study year was four times higher for husbands who had been violent toward their wives than in nonviolent families (2.3 vs. 9.0) and five times higher when there was both wife assault and child assault (2.3 vs. 11.4). In short, men who assault their wives are significantly more likely to have engaged in verbal and physical assault outside the family, and to have been arrested, than men who have not assaulted their wives.

Data in table 25.12 examine the same issue separately for blue- and white-collar men. In every comparison, the multiassaultive group has the highest rates of verbal aggression and physical assault outside the family, regardless of social class. However, as the outside aggression becomes more serious ("hitting," and "hitting and injuring"), social class differences become more pronounced, with blue-collar men having significantly higher rates of assault against nonfamily persons. Even though social class differences exist in rates of "street violence," we cannot overlook the fact that among white-collar men, the rate of "hitting a nonfamily person" is over five times higher for men in families where there is child assault and wife assault than in families where neither type of assault occurs, while the rate of "hitting and injuring a nonfamily person" is also nine times higher.

Wives.   Part B of table 25.11 indicates that the same relation between in-family assault and out-of-family aggression holds for women. In all comparisons, there is a significant connection between intrafamily assault by women and nonfamily assault, verbal aggression, and arrest of women. Although the rate of nonfamily crime committed by women is much lower than for men, women who are assaultive within their family are much more likely to engage in assaultive and other aggressive behavior with nonfamily members.

The analysis shown in table 25.12 was replicated for women. The findings parallel the pattern for men. For example, as in the analysis of men, "yelling at a nonfamily member" and "getting angry at a nonfamily person and smashing something" was not significantly different for blue and white collar women, whereas the rate for assaults against persons outside the family is significantly higher for blue-collar women.

In summary, the results shown in tables 25.11 and 25.12 provide substantial support for an association between assaults in the home and assaults and other antisocial behavior outside the family. Those who assault a spouse are more likely to engage in verbally and physically assaultive behavior outside the family and are more likely to have been

TABLE 25.12

Rates of Nonfamily Verbal and Physical Assault for Men by Family Assault Type and Socioeconomic Status (1985 National Resurvey)

Dependent Variable	Blue Collar				White Collar			
	Non-assaultive (N)	Child Assault Only (N)	Spouse Assault Only (N)	Child Assault and Spouse Assault (N)	Non-assaultive (N)	Child Assault Only (N)	Spouse Assault Only (N)	Child Assault and Spouse Assault (N)
Yelled at nonfamily member	51.7 (916)	58.6 (204)	70.4 (137)	73.6 (73)	48.6 (930)	60.2 (147)	65.4 (101)	85.8 (43)
Angry at nonfamily and smashed something	6.3 (940)	11.3 (207)	24.6 (128)	31.6 (70)	5.8 (942)	10.2 (147)	18.4 (102)	15.2 (46)
Hit nonfamily member	3.4 (941)	6.2 (208)	12.8 (130)	13.1 (72)	1.4 (942)	.4 (147)	2.0 (102)	7.6 (44)
Injured nonfamily member	1.3 (943)	.4 (208)	1.7 (129)	9.4 (73)	.3 (942)	.0 (147)	.0 (103)	2.6 (44)
Arrested in last year*	2.1 (402)	.0 (83)	6.1 (50)	7.0 (27)	1.0 (459)	1.4 (72)	.0 (43)	2.7 (21)

B. ANOVA F-Values

	Yelled	Smashed	Hit	Injured	Arrested
Child assault	12.08***	8.70**	2.51	1.58	.17
Wife assault	42.27***	71.47***	30.71***	11.78***	4.73*
Socioeconomic status	.69	4.12*	23.56***	10.22***	2.94
Child × wife	.02	.87	.31	24.65***	1.14
Child × socioeconomic status	1.88	.00***	1.13	.23	1.37
Wife × socioeconomic status	.17	14.92***	7.59**	3.80*	4.90*
Child × wife × socioeconomic status	1.60	.28	3.54	4.79*	.02

*The N for this row is low because the question was asked only about the respondent. For other questions in this table, respondents were asked parallel questions about themselves and their spouse.
NOTE.—Rates are per 100 and are therefore equal to percentages.
*$p < .05$.
**$p < .01$.
***$p < .001$.

arrested for some nonfamily crime than are others, and this finding applies to both men and women, and to blue and white collar persons.

Summary and Conclusions

There are at least two important and related reasons for a dual focus on violence in the family and violence and other crime "in the streets." The first reason is often overlooked: so much crime takes place in families (Lincoln and Straus 1985). Many of the studies of physical violence within the family discussed in this essay show that the average citizen is much more likely to be assaulted in his or her own home than on the streets of the most dangerous city in the United States (Straus, Gelles, and Steinmetz 1980: 49). Likewise, family members commit a high rate of nonviolent crime against each other, including larceny, robbery, and forgery (Straus and Lincoln 1985). If the violent crime and property crime that occurs within the family were aggregated, it would suggest that crime in the family is pervasive, more common than crime in any other setting.

Second, violence in the family and assaults and other crime outside the family are linked in important ways. Evidence was presented in this essay for the existence of both victimization and offender effects. Both offenders and victims of assault in the family have elevated rates of violent and nonviolent crime outside the family.

Victimization Effects

Data from three general population surveys found that an assault against a spouse or child takes place in over one out of four American families each year and that in one out of five of these families both spouses *and* children are assaulted. The actual figures are probably much higher because of under-reporting. This high incidence of assaults by spouses and by parents constitutes a serious problem in itself, but members of these same families also have higher rates of sibling violence, child-parent violence, and assaults and other crime outside the family.

Children who are assaulted in the family are more likely to assault and commit property crimes outside the family. The relation applies to both genders and cuts across socioeconomic groups but is stronger for males and children from blue-collar families.

Neither previous research nor the current study provide information on why family victimization is linked to outside the family offending behavior. It is not simply the direct experience of being assaulted by a parent that is associated with assaults and other behavioral problems of children outside the family, but the experience of being in a multiassaultive family. Children with the highest rates of outside-family violence are from families in which they were not only assaulted by a parent but also witnessed assaults between parents as well.

This pattern also occurs among adults, both male and female and both blue collar and white collar. The highest rates of assault and other crime outside the family occurs among persons in multiassaultive families.

Offender Effects

The findings support the notion that assault is a generalized pattern in interpersonal relations that crosses settings and is used across targets. Men in families in which children and wives are assaulted are five times more likely to have also assaulted a nonfamily person than are men in nonassaultive families. These same men are also more severely violent toward fellow citizens, being eight times more likely to have assaulted and injured someone outside the family. Men from multiassaultive families also come to the attention of police more often than others, having an arrest rate that is 3.6 times higher than their less violent counterparts.

This same pattern occurs among women offenders in multiassaultive families although not as strongly as it does for men. These women do have higher rates of assault and other crime against outside-family persons, even though severe assaults are very infrequent among all women.

The link between family and nonfamily assault also holds across social class although blue-collar persons report higher rates, especially of more severe assaults outside the family.

Research Implications

There are literally hundreds of research questions that spring from these findings, and there would be hundreds more if criminologists and family violence researchers jointly sought a full accounting of the links between crime in the family and crime "in the streets." The first part of this essay explored the problems that might explain why there has been little collaborative work between these two fields. There are no serious structural barriers to discourage joint work, but there is a set of beliefs that continues to define "family violence" as unique and requiring a separate body of theory and separate research approaches.

There is no contradiction between the idea that all violence has something in common and the idea that there are important differences between various types of violence. Both approaches are necessary to understand this complex phenomenon fully. Whether the focus is on the common elements in all violence or on the unique aspects of a certain type of violence depends on the purpose. For purposes of emergency intervention services, it makes sense to have special categories of "battered women" or "abused children" so that such cases can be given appropriate assistance. For some research purposes, it may also be appropriate to examine each of these separately. However, for other research purposes, it may be more important to explore the common elements of etiology and consequences of violent behavior.

Research should be undertaken to specify the conditions under which victimization effects develop. To explain fully the high rate of assault by victims, multivariate analyses must be conducted that simultaneously examine not only childhood exposure to violence but also parental neglect (Loeber and Stouthamer-Loeber 1986), gender sex role socialization (Fagan and Wexler 1987), and social class-related variables. Ideally, this work would be conducted on general population surveys.

There is a need to develop concepts and theories about victimization effects. Aspects of social learning theory may be helpful in this regard (modeling of victim behavior), but other theories and concepts should be explored including work on attribution theory, culture of violence theory, control theory, and feminist theories of patriarchal social structure.

Research is needed to specify the effects of particular types of exposure to family assault on outside family violence and crime. For example, the differential influences of experiencing assault from one's mother or father are not well understood. There is some evidence that fathers' behavior in the family exerts a stronger effect than mothers' on children's antisocial behavior outside the family (Loeber and Stouthamer-Loeber 1986). Information is also needed on whether observing assaultive behavior of father against mother or mother against father or both has a differential impact on children's behavior.

The influence of assaults between siblings on assaults against non-family members is rarely studied in terms of victimization effects. Are victims of sibling violence more likely to aggress against peers? Does the effect of sibling victimization vary for boys and girls?

Much needs to be known about the out-of-home assault and other crimes of adults who assault others in their family. A typology of offenders, including "family assault only," "outside assault only," and "generally assaultive" (Shields and Hanneke 1981) needs to be tested on samples from general populations in order to determine the risk factors associated with each type.

Much research is needed on the links between family and nonfamily violence. This essay is a step in that direction. Further steps would be facilitated by the realization on the part of criminologists and family violence researchers that each contributes to the other in understanding crime and in understanding the family.

Notes

1. We pointed out in a previous theoretical article (Gelles and Straus 1979) that a physical assault has taken place is not sufficient for understanding violence. Other dimensions also need to be considered. Each of these other dimensions should be measured separately so that their causes and consequences and joint effects can be investigated. Among the other dimensions are the seriousness of the assault (which can range from a slap to stabbing and shooting); whether a physical injury was produced (which can range from none to death); the motivation (which might range from a concern for a person's safety, as when a child is spanked for going into the street, to hostility so intense that the death of the person is desired), and whether the act of violence is normatively legitimate (as in the case of slapping a child) or illegitimate (as in the case of slapping a spouse), and what norms are applicable (legal, ethnic or class norms, couple norms, etc.).

2. The two National Surveys were the source of the data used in a previous analysis of the link between intrafamily assault and crime (Straus 1985). The

work reported in this chapter refines and extends that work by using a more adequate measure of the independent variable—the "family assault types" given in figure 25.1—and by a better specified statistical analysis that includes a control for the socioeconomic status of the father.

3. Under common law, husbands had the right to "physically chastise an errant wife" (see Calvert, 1974). Although the courts ceased to recognize this right by the late nineteenth century de facto norms that tolerate such behavior continue to exist (Straus, 1976, 1980).

4. The measure of sibling violence in this table includes all of the violent acts in the CTS, not just those with a high potential for injury. For the 1975 survey it was also possible to do the analysis using a measure of "severe violence," the results of which are presented below.

5. Whether it is sound social policy to invoke the criminal justice process in such cases is another matter, and one that is fraught with dilemmas, some of which are discussed in Straus and Lincoln (1985).

6. For this analysis, each spouses's occupation was classified as "manual" or "non-manual" (alternative terms are blue collar and white collar, and working class and middle class) using the Bureau of Labor Statistics, revised Occupational Classification system. Each Bureau of Labor Statistics occupation code was classified as either manual or nonmanual using the list of occupations falling into these categories by Rice (see Robinson et al. 1969). All analyses were run separately using wife's occupational ranking and husband's occupational ranking. Results were not significantly different. The analyses presented in this essay were done controlling for husband's occupational ranking.

7. The measure of child-to-parent violence, like the measure of sibling violence in the previous section, uses all the violent acts in the CTS; i.e., it is not restricted to the acts of "severe" violence.

8. Although the term "crime" is used here and in the title of the essay, some items to be analyzed are not criminal but could best be called conduct problems. Nevertheless, the majority of issues addressed in this section concern illegal behavior by children and adolescents.

9. The first point in the discussion of table 25.3 also explains why the rates in part B of table 25.6 are so much lower than the rates in part A. In addition, part A is based on self-reports, and part B is based on those incidents that were known to the parent who was interviewed.

Part VII
STOPPING FAMILY VIOLENCE

26

Response of Victims and the Police to Assaults on Wives

Glenda Kaufman Kantor and Murray A. Straus

Although there has been a growing awareness of the prevalence and criminality of assaults on women by their male partners, there is little evidence concerning the extent to which the actual behavior of victims and police reflects these changes. Victims may still be reluctant to use the criminal justice system, and police may still resist arresting men who assault their wives. This would not be surprising given the long historical traditions of gender inequality and the belief that the intact family is sacrosanct. These traditions have obscured public and private perception of the prevalence and criminality of wife assault. Changes in law, policy, and attitudes have occurred only through strenuous efforts by feminists and battered women's advocates (Kaufman Kantor et al., 1985; Kaufman Kantor and OBrien Stevens, 1986; Lerman, 1982; Schechter, 1982), through research that identified a "battered woman's syndrome" (Walker, 1979), through survey research that documented the high incidence rates of wife assault (Chapter 6), and through research that provides evidence that a policy of arresting assailants reduces recidivism (Sherman and Berk, 1984; Sherman and Cohen, 1989).

Although public attitudes and police policy may be changing, the extent to which this has affected their actual response to assaults on women by their male partners is unknown. This chapter provides some of the needed information, using data from the 1985 Family Violence Resurvey. These data provide information on the following questions: (1) How often were police involved in instances of wife beating? (2) In what proportion of cases was an arrest made? (3) Are the characteristics of the family and the severity of the assault related to whether the police are called and whether an arrest is made? (4) What strategies, other than calls to police, are used by victims to stop the assaults? (5) What strategies, other than arrest, are used by police in cases of wife assault?

Theoretical Issues

Two major theoretical perspectives need to be considered in understanding battered women's reluctance to seek criminal justice support and police failure to intervene vigorously in wife assault cases. Both of these perspectives will be examined as they relate to definitions of criminality. The feminist point of view articulated by Dobash and Dobash (1979) and Martin (1976) emphasizes the historical role of patriarchy in controlling and subordinating women. The other view is concerned not only with wife assault but with *all* crimes occurring in the family and the normative ambiguity surrounding them. This ambiguity stems from the state's need and desire to protect the privacy and integrity of the family as a social institution.

Feminist Theory

A feminist analysis of wife beating views the inadequate responses of the criminal justice system, such as police failure to arrest batterers, as evidence of the legitimation of coercive control of women (Kaufman Kantor and OBrien Stevens, 1986). It can also be argued that historical definitions of the criminality of assaults on wives, implying official tolerance of *some violence* against women, were shaped by patriarchal interests. Eighteenth- and nineteenth-century legal definitions viewed wife assaults as non-criminal as long as they left no visible marks (Dobash and Dobash, 1977) or were inflicted by a stick no thicker than a man's thumb (Davidson, 1977). Modern-day vestiges prescribing the legal limits of wife assault are seen in the "stitch rule" used until recently by some police departments to determine the seriousness of wife assault (Straus, 1976). Moreover, criminal justice categorizations of assaults on wives as "family disputes" and as "domestic disturbances" have contributed to the ambiguity shared by battered women and police about when, short of homicide, a beating is "serious enough" to call for police protection (Reed et al., 1983).

Normative Ambiguity Theory

The second theoretical approach explains the differential treatment of wife beating, compared to other assaults, as but one manifestation of a separate set of norms governing all types of crime occurring within the family. These norms reflect the value society places on preserving the family's privacy and integrity (Gordon, 1988). This value can also be seen as serving patriarchal interests. Moreover, these values and norms have grown beyond their patriarchal roots to become an autonomous part of our culture.

As with many other aspects of social structure, there are conflicting rules and principles governing the family (Ryan and Straus, 1954; Straus and Straus, 1953) so that the situation regarding differential treatment of within-family crime is more adequately described as one of normative ambiguity. The norms concerning the family enjoin us to have a special concern for the well-being of other family members. At the same time, because of the social and legal connections that bind family members together, there are other norms that tolerate a certain level of mistreatment of family members. These norms include, for example, the social expectation that parents use physical punishment in controlling their children's behavior and that family members express their feelings (even of hostility) rather than "holding them in." These family norms legitimating violence are also discussed in Chapter 11 and elsewhere (Hotaling and Straus, 1980; Straus, 1974).

Such normative ambiguity exists toward all criminal acts within the family (Straus and Lincoln, 1985). It is part of the reason for the difficulty in distinguishing child abuse from "normal" physical discipline of children (Giovannoni and Becerra, 1979), "minor" husband-to-wife violence from "serious" wife assault, and in identifying who are the "real" battered women (see Chapter 5). As Straus and Lincoln (1985) point out, we also tolerate intrafamily property crimes, such as children stealing from parents or siblings, that would be prosecuted if the victim and offender were strangers. This is true for property crimes within families and for crimes of violence.

In addition to the historically derived interest of the state in non-interference in family matters (and also the conflicting interest of the state in regulating the family) and with preserving the family as a social institution, there are other reasons for the different standards regarding family crime. These reasons are located in the characteristics of families and the needs of its individual members. For example, the family meets important personal needs and there is therefore a reluctance to dissolve a family even when there are serious abuses. As the quintessential "primary group," the family is concerned with the "whole person" and his or her welfare, not just with one aspect of the member's behavior, such as whether he or she hit or steals. These broader concerns make it possible to minimize or deny behaviors when needs such as intimacy, affection, and economic survival are also being met by the "family offender."

Method

This study uses data from the 1985 survey. The forms of husband-to-wife violence analyzed in this paper include both the Minor Violence and Severe Violence indexes. The percent of victims of minor or severe assaults who reported the violence to the police were then cross-tabulated by race, income, employment status, urbanicity, and alcohol use during the violent incident. Women's other responses to the minor or severe violence were also investigated. Finally, police response to the violent incident is discussed, again separately for minor and severe violence cases.

Prevalence of Wife Assault and Reporting Effects

Prevalence Estimates

Estimates of the number of domestic assault victims (largely women) have been placed at 420,000 per year for the years 1978–1982 based on *National Crime Survey* (Langan and Innes, 1986). These figures are considerably less than those of the 1975 National Family Violence Survey (NFVS), which estimated wife assault victims to number about 1.8 million *per year* (Straus, Gelles, and Steinmetz, 1980). The incidence rate from the 1985 data on wife beating (reported in Chapter 6) shows some reductions in both minor and severe violence rates compared to the 1975 survey. Gelles and Straus point out in that chapter, however, that the apparent reduction may be due, at least in part, to a greater reluctance by men in 1985 to admit to wife assaults. Evidence of such reporting effects are found in the fact that women respondents in the 1985 survey reported more incidents of violence than did men. Gender bias in reporting by male partners has also been found by other researchers (Edleson and Brygger, 1986; Szinovacz, 1983).

Police Involvement

The NFVS data revealed that only 6.7% of all husband-to-wife assaults are reported to police. This rate is similar to that of a Kentucky survey of one thousand women. (Harris and Associates, 1979) that found that only 9% of the beatings by husbands were reported to the police. On the other hand, the National Crime Survey (NCS) findings are very different. NCS analysts estimate that 52% of domestic violence victims reported crimes

(Langan and Innes, 1986). What are the reasons for these greatly varying estimates?

We suggest that the large differences in the prevalence rates and in police reporting rates from the National Crime Survey (NCS) and the National Family Violence Survey (NFVS) are a function of differences in the context and nature of the two surveys. Although the NCS and NFVS are similar in that they both use large random samples, their differing approaches to the study of family violence are revealed in the wording and context of their questions (Straus and Lincoln, 1985). Respondents participating in the NCS are informed that they are part of the National *Crime* Survey and asked if they have been victimized by *crime* in the previous six months. If NCS respondents answer "yes," they are then asked a series of questions regarding the criminal incidents. In contrast, the major focus of the NFVS is *families* and things that family members do. This study is introduced to respondents as a study "for the National Institute of Health about family life, American couples and their children. . . ." Questions about family violence are thus embedded in a series of questions about family characteristics.

These contextual differences between the two surveys appear to lead to the NCS's underestimating the prevalence of family violence and overestimating the incidence of reports of family violence to the police. In order for victims to report crimes to either or both the NCS interviewers and the police, they must perceive their assaults as criminal in the legal sense as opposed to "just wrong or bad things done by someone in their family" (Straus and Lincoln, 1985). Congruent with this belief is the NCS finding that the most frequent reason women give for not calling police is that they consider the violent assault a "private or personal matter." The next most frequent reason for non-reporting is fear of reprisal (Langan and Innes, 1986).[1]

Factors Affecting Reports to the Police

Because most research on the police and wife assault has examined cases in which the police were involved, little is known about the characteristics of families and violent events when the police are not called (Dutton, 1988; Loving, 1980; Parnas, 1971; Stephens, 1977). Because our data come from a random national sample, they can provide information on those violent families who do report to the police, as well as those who do not. First, we examine how the severity of the assaults and characteristics of the family are related to reports of husband-to-wife violence to the police.

Severity of Assault

When assaults are categorized according to the degree of severity, we found that only 3.2% of minor violence cases and 14.4% of instances of severe violence are reported to police (p <.001). Although assaults categorized as minor by the CTS have the potential (albeit less so than severe violence) to result in major injuries, more than 96% of minor assault victims did not call the police. Even if only those cases where the type of severe violence often characterized as "wife beating" is examined, the vast majority (86%) of violence by husbands remains unreported.

Despite the low rate of reporting instances of assaults to the police, the fact that the police were involved four times more often in cases of severe assault than in cases of minor assault is an important finding. It contradicts long-standing police claims that domestics are "social work" (Reed et al., 1983) and official categorizations of wife assaults as domestic "disputes." These stereotypical conceptions of wife assaults are paradoxical since they co-exist with police beliefs that "domestic" calls are among the most dangerous to police. However, recent research reveals little risk of death or injury to police during responses to domestic calls (Garner and Clemmer, 1986).

Social Characteristics

Race. Table 26.1 shows that there are no significant differences by race in reporting violent incidents to the police, whether the incident involved minor or severe violence. Again, our findings differ from those of the National Crime Survey, which found greater reporting to police by Black women (Langan and Innes, 1986), but in this case we do not have an explanation for the difference between the surveys. Comparing the figures in the two columns of Table 26.1 shows that severity of assault is associated with the use of the police regardless of the race of respondent.

Income. No statistically significant differences were found in respect to income. These results are not only non-significant, but also inconsistent: families with incomes below the poverty threshold called the police three times more often in cases of minor violence than did financially better-off families. This is consistent with previous research on socioeconomic status and calls to police. However, low-income families reported severe violence only half as often as families above the poverty line. One explanation of these findings is that impoverished women's reluctance to report severe violence to the police is related to their fears that their spouse may be incarcerated.

Husband's unemployment. For minor violence there is no difference

TABLE 26.1

Percent Reporting to Police by Violence Type and Social Characteristics

	Minor Violence		Severe Violence	
	Percent	N	Percent	N
Race				
White	3.3%	346	14.3%	122
Black	3.7%	32	14.4%	20
Hispanic	3.4%	22	15.6%	16
Other	4.0%	30	19.3%	6
	x^2, N.S.		x^2, N.S.	
Income				
Poverty < $10,000	9.5%	37	7.5%	32
> $10,000	2.6%	381	16.7%	130
	p = .07*		p = .30	
Husb. Employment				
Unemployed	2.1%	17	34.8%	13
Employed	2.9%	373	13.2%	131
	x^2, N.S.		x^2,p =.10	
Wife Employment				
Housewife	6.0%	109	9.8%	46
Employed	1.7%	264	16.2%	89
	p = .06*		x^2, N.S.	
Urbanness				
Central City	3.3%	135	8.5%	60
Suburb	4.1%	213	20.1%	77
Small City	.7%	86	11.5%	32
	x^2, N.S.		x^2, N.S.	
Drinking at Time				
of Violence				
No Drinking	3.5%	318	10.7%	115
Drinking by one				
of the parties	2.6%	105	22.9%	52
	x^2, N.S.		p = .07*	

in the rate at which the assaults of employed and unemployed husbands are reported to the police. For severe violence, assaults by unemployed husbands are much more likely to be reported. It may be that women find it easier to label an unemployed husband's status as "criminal." Another possibility is that unemployment is associated more with severe rather than minor violence, meaning that the relationship of unemployment to police reporting is a spurious one. Unfortunately, too few cases are available in these data to test this possibility.

Housewives. Although the differences are not statistically significant, the percentages in Table 26.1 suggest that housewives are more likely to report in cases of minor violence, but less likely to report in cases of severe violence.

Despite the fact that the differences are not statistically significant, the findings for both husband's unemployment and housewives are worth discussing, in part because they seem to be consistent with each other and also theoretically meaningful. Both refer to families with limitations based on the number of wage-earners. It appears that situations that limit the economic resources of a family—unemployment, poverty, and one–wage-earner families—diminish the likelihood of severely battered women calling police. Economically dependent women may fear the consequences if police are called. At the same time, husbands with greater economic resources are less likely to receive official sanctions.

Size of city.   This was examined as a potential factor in police reporting because perceptions of police, police effectiveness, and police-community cohesiveness can vary by community size and geography. However, no significant differences were found.

Drinking and drunkenness.   This is commonly associated with wife assaults and other crimes of violence, though these relationships can be spurious (see Chapter 12 in this volume and Pernanen, 1981) and alcohol may be more an excuse for than a cause of violence (Coleman and Straus, 1983). Nevertheless, in the instance of severe violence, police were twice as likely to be called when one or both partners had been drinking. Further, drinking-related severe violence was ten times more likely to be reported to the police than drinking-linked minor assaults.

Women's Immediate Response to Violence

Table 26.2 presents data on women's responses to their husband's violence. If, as was usually the case, there was more than one incident during the year, we asked about the most recent occurrence of the most severe violence in the past year.[2] The table classifies women's responses by two other factors: whether they reported the violence and the severity of the assault. Not surprisingly, the most frequent response by non-reporting women, regardless how severe the violence, was to cry. It is also not surprising that yelling and cursing was the second most frequent response to the humiliation and pain of a spousal assault. Taken together, passive strategies account for almost half of unreported minor and severe violence. Active strategies such as hitting back, fleeing the batterer by running out of the room or leaving the house, or calling someone rarely occurred. Considered collectively, they account for a quarter of unreported minor and severe violence victim behavior. Victims of both types

TABLE 26.2

Women's Responses to Violence by Violence Type and Reports to Police

| | Non-Reporters | | Reporters | |
	Minor (N = 209)	Severe (N = 122)	Minor (N = 6)	Severe (N = 18)
Hit Back	12.1%	12.5%	--	7.8%
Cried	27.7%	33.2%	--	37.5%
Yelled, cursed	18.6%	25.0%	7.1%	37.1%
Ran to other room	13.7%	17.8%	--	26.6%
Left house	6.1%	7.0%	--	34.4%
Called someone	3.0%	8.5%	7.1%	20.2%
Other	2.7%	9.9%	7.1%	2.0%

of violence respond in similar ways, though women experiencing the worst assaults more often escape to another room and are two and a half times more likely to call someone.

As noted above, minor assault victims rarely call police. Table 26.2 also demonstrates that victims who call the police are less likely to have retaliated than have non-reporting women. Perhaps this is due to guilt experienced by women socialized into non-aggressiveness. Women violating traditional sex-role norms, though few in number, may feel that because they have fought back they are equally guilty and therefore less deserving of police assistance. On the other hand, when victim-aggressor roles are clearly differentiated, women can feel more justified in getting help. Police also need victim-aggressor roles to be clearly defined, and they are less likely to arrest when they believe the violence has been mutual (Reed et al., 1983). Women reporting to police are much more likely to react in *some way* than non-reporters, though three-quarters simply cry, yell, or curse.

In contrast to the small proportion (a quarter) of non-reporting women using active strategies, 81% of reporting women actively tried to escape. This means that the minority of women who report to police also are more likely to try other active strategies. These differences between reporting and non-reporting women lend support to patterns of learned helplessness handicapping a majority of women. It is also possible that husbands physically stopped women from leaving as well as from contacting the police or that women were too stunned or injured to react in any active manner (Reed et al., 1983).

Police Responses to Wife-Assault Calls

A large body of research for the past twenty years has documented the rarity of arrest of men who have assaulted their wives (Berk and Loseke, 1980–1981; Berk et al., 1983; Black, 1980; Ford, 1983; Loving, 1980; Parnas, 1967; Reed et al., 1983; Straus, 1974). Consistently, researchers have documented other problems in police behavior, including siding with the batterer, patriarchal and patronizing attitudes, infrequent referrals of battered women to services, failure to file reports, and failure to adhere to prescribed policies and laws. Some of these actions or failures to act have been attributed to police fear of the dangerousness of these calls to their own lives, frustration with battered women's failure to sign complaints, lenient or unsympathetic prosecutors and judges, and police training practices stressing crisis intervention and mediation strategies (Bard, 1970; Liebman and Schwartz, 1973; Loving, 1980; Reed et al., 1983).

The recent improvement in police response (Crime Control Institute, 1987; Kaufman Kantor et al., 1985) can be attributed to concerted efforts by battered women advocates and new laws making explicit the criminality of domestic violence. Additionally, researchers have exerted influence by directing criminal justice attention to the association between inadequate police response, family violence and family homicides (Wilt et al., 1977), and the deterrent effects of police arrest on misdemeanor assaults (Sherman and Berk, 1984). Sherman and Berk's notable Minneapolis experiment found a lower rate of repeat assaults when police made an arrest. Langan and Innes's (1986) analysis of NCS data revealed that just calling the police decreased the likelihood and severity of subsequent assaults. However, both the Minneapolis experiment and the National Crime Survey reports are relatively recent. Diffusion of these results, consensus on the need for change, and efforts to enforce change may be slow in coming.

The results of this study show just how slow that process is. In fact, reports to police of assaults on wives are so rare that when one seeks to analyze what the police actually did in those few cases where police intervention occurred, the number of cases becomes extremely small. Nevertheless, because the data are based on a representative sample of couples and because of the importance of this issue, even these few cases need to be analyzed. Table 26.3 therefore shows the distribution of police actions in the 14 cases where the police intervened in assaults that were restricted to minor violence and in the 24 cases of severe violence.

It is apparent from Table 26.3 that arrest is far from typical. An arrest

TABLE 26.3
Police Responses by Violence Type

Police Response	Minor N = 14	Severe N = 24
Broke up fight	27.9%	31.7%
Hit or pushed someone	--	4.6%
Tried to calm everyone	32.5%	74.8%
Listened to response's story	30.1%	55.9%
Gave warning	10.1%	49.3%
Took info; filed report	35.9%	37.3%
Ordered husb. out of house	13.0%	33.5%
Threatened arrest, now	--	10.6%
Threatened arrest, next time	--	27.9%
Arrested husband	7.0% (1)	20.8% (5)
Arrested wife	--	4.2% (1)

was made in only one (7%) of the minor violence police calls, and this may not be surprising. However, it is remarkable that, despite the alleged improvements, these national survey findings show arrests occurred in response to only five (21%) of severe wife assaults. Furthermore, in the majority of cases police do not file reports or, at least, victims are not aware that they have. With regard to instances of minor violence, even threats of arrest or other warnings are rare.

Comparison of the minor and severe violence columns of Table 26.3 shows that just as battered women use more strategies in severe violence, so do police. However, these are predominantly mediation or "cooling out" strategies. The most frequently used police techniques are calming the participants, listening to the partners' stories, warning the parties, ordering husbands out, and breaking up the fight. Arrest or threat of arrest is rare. The practice of police favoring arrest for assaults on wives may be spreading, but the experience of the 504 battered women in this 1985 national sample suggests that little has actually changed.

Impediments to Change

Despite extensive efforts over the past decade, battered women still rarely call police and, when called, police rarely arrest or threaten to arrest assailants. Why has change been so slow? The reasons are numerous and complex. For example, patriarchal attitudes and behaviors are difficult to change because they are entrenched in the economic and political organization of society. In addition, most wife beating occurs in isolation, inducing passivity and maintaining the isolation of battered women. Moreover, as we suggested, defining family violence as criminal poses important contradictions and moral dilemmas.

Although we do not pretend to have a full understanding of the impediments to change, the following sections are intended to provide a better understanding by looking at the issue from the perspectives of the batterers, the battered women, and the law enforcement agents involved.

Batterers

An analysis of the extent to which legal and other sanctions might deter potential batterers was carried out by Carmody and Williams (1987) using other data from the NFVS. This analysis sheds some light on the assailants' perspective. They examined the relationship between perceptions of possible sanctions for wife assault and actual incidence, i.e., deterrent effects. The formal and informal sanctions they considered were retaliatory violence, police intervention, separation and divorce, and social condemnation (loss of respect or disapproval of friends and relatives). Two perceptual components of sanctions were considered: *certainty* (the respondent's estimate of the chances that the sanction would be imposed) and *severity* (how bad it would be if it happens). One of the main findings is that although arrest was viewed as a severe sanction, the subjectively experienced deterrence of this sanction may be almost zero because batterers believe that arrest is very unlikely. Our finding of a police intervention rate of only 6.7% and an arrest rate of about 1% indicates that batterers are correct in this belief. Carmody and Williams also examined the perceived deterrent effect of the spouse leaving. The results were similar to the analysis of arrest and for the same reason: few assailants think their wives would leave them. These findings suggest that part of the reason men beat their wives is that they believe they can get away with it.

Battered Women

Our survey did not ask women specifically about why they did not call the police, but inferences are possible based on the relationships examined. For example, the predominance of passive strategies in coping with violence suggests that learned helplessness (Walker, 1979) may play an important role. It also appears that economic dependency undermines decisions to call police, as it does in determining whether the woman stays or leaves (see Chapter 20). Women's helplessness is not just learned or psychological but real in economic terms.

Other research findings indicate that perceptions of assaults as personal and private matters, fear of reprisals (Langan and Innes, 1986), physical inability to call the police, and difficulty in defining themselves as "sufficiently battered" are all factors in decisions not to report (Reed et al., 1983). The following comment by a woman who did not call police (from Reed et al., 1983:29) is an example of women's difficulty in defining themselves as battered: "He didn't really beat me. He just grabbed me, turned me upside down and banged my head on the floor." Reed et al. give several examples of the most frequent reason they found for lack of police contact, the physical inability to call the police: phones were often destroyed by batterers or the household simply did not receive telephone service, victims were sometimes too injured to place a phone call or were held captive by their husbands. Thus many victims might seek help from the police if they had the opportunity to do so.

Furthermore, the same dynamics that maintain women in abusive relationships such as "the battered women's syndrome" (Walker, 1979) deter women from calling the police. Erratic, unpredictable, uncontrollable violence induces helplessness, passivity, and despair. Because the violence is inconsistent with the partner's loving behavior, the spouse expresses remorse or assures his wife it won't recur, so she remains silent. Moreover, calling the police on one's spouse is a flagrant violation of family norms.

Police

Why do our data show such a low arrest or even warning of arrest? Part of the answer probably lies in the general reluctance of police to arrest for any type of civil disturbance crime. However, police are also greatly influenced by prosecutorial and judicial decisions. Another part of the answer is that police have gone to the same cultural school as women. Women have been "trained" to be dependent on men and to preserve family relationships. The police equivalent of this is the formal and informal injunction to tread carefully in family situations. Both battered women and police are likely to experience the same ambiguity about whether a family assault is truly "criminal," even though the same standards for misdemeanor and felony assaults should apply regardless of the victim-perpetrator relationship. Another factor may be that police are responding to some women's wishes that the violence just stop or that the assailant be simply removed (Ford, 1983; Reed, et al., 1983; Straus, 1976).

The data from the 1985 Resurvey provides some evidence indicating that this is still the case. We found that despite the rarity of arrest, 77% of severely assaulted women and 92% of victims of less serious assaults were satisfied with police response. Perhaps women feel that the symbolic threat posed by police presence is a sufficient deterrent.

Summary and Conclusions

This chapter, based on data from the 1985 Resurvey, found that reports to police were the exception rather than the rule. Only 6.7% of all husband-to-wife assaults are reported to police. When severity of violence is considered, 3.2% of minor violence and 14.4% of severe violence is reported. In contrast, the NCS found that 52% of domestic violence victims reported crimes to police. We suggested that the reason for the difference is that respondents in the NCS did not define most assaults by husbands as a "crime." Rather, NCS respondents may have limited their reports to only those assaults that were perceived as criminal, such as those resulting in serious injury. This explains why the NCS finds a much lower incidence rate of wife assault and a much higher rate of reporting assaults to the police. Normative ambiguity about when violent acts by family members can be considered criminal appears lessened only when the assaults fall at the extreme end of the violence continuum. However, even when physical violence is extreme or brutal, reasons other than ambiguity can interefere with actual reports to the criminal justice system.

Examination of characteristics associated with reports to police revealed that severity of violence is the most important correlate. Factors promoting economic dependency such as husband's unemployment, housewife status, and poverty deter victims of severe violence from calling police. On the other hand, women were significantly more likely to call police when drinking had occurred at the time of violence. This may be related to women's disgust with the husband's drunkenness or greater feelings of justification when a spouse is drunk, regardless of how severe the assault. Additionally, they may fear more extreme violence because of past experiences with their husband's drunken rages.

Calling the police and arrests by police remain rare strategies of last resort. Mediation still dominates as the typical means of police intervention. While mediation may be appropriate under certain circumstances, recent research has shown that the strongest deterrent effects occur when police arrest. It is clear that a double standard for criminal justice processing of extra-family and intrafamily crime remains. This is part of the reason why wife beating persists despite almost universal condemnation of this type of assault and despite recent legislation that more clearly defines it as criminal. Until the probability of arrest increases, assailants will continue to receive a de facto message that they can assault their wives with impunity. Nevertheless, important as legal sanctions may be from the police through the judiciary, formal sanctions alone will not make the problem of wife beating disappear. Many other aspects of our culture also underlie the high rate of assault on wives in the United States and are discussed in Chapters 23 and 28. These include the high level of "legitimate violence" in American society (Baron and Straus, 1987) and gender-based inequality under which women are socialized for dependent roles and denied the economic resources to leave violent marriages.

Notes

1. This explanation also helps us to understand the huge differences in injury rates from the two surveys. Approximately half of all spouse assaults in the NCS involved injury, compared to only 2.5% of the assaults in the NFVS. We suggest that the difference exists because the occurrence of an injury is one of the factors that leads a woman to redefine the assault from a "family problem" to a "crime" and therefore to describe it to the NCS interviewer.
2. The question posed to women about their immediate responses to the violence was of a forced choice type: "Which of the following describes what you did as a result?" Therefore, the responses discussed here may not be representative of the creativity of women's reactions and strategies in eluding or deterring the violence. See Bowker, 1983, for a discussion of women's strategies in coping with violence.

27

Escalation and Desistance from Wife Assault in Marriage

Scott L. Feld and Murray A. Straus

Over half of American couples experience one or more incidents of assault between the partners during the course of a marriage (Straus, Gelles, and Steinmetz, 1980:35–36). Since there are implicit norms tolerating a certain amount of violence in families (Straus, 1976), not much importance is typically attached to this statistic. The relevance of these assaults for criminology also tends to be minimized because most of the incidents are "simple assaults" such as slapping, shoving, or throwing something at a spouse, rather than "aggravated asssaults." Moreover, in any one year most couples do not experience violence at any level. For the sample described in this chapter, the 1985 rate was 16.1%, and it has been argued that this shows a relatively low assault rate (Scanzoni, 1978). However, there are grounds for regarding even these levels of minor violence as an important social problem and as central to understanding severely assaultive behavior.

First, over a third of these incidents *do* involve severe assaults such as punching, kicking, and attacks with objects or weapons (Straus and Gelles, 1988).

Second, the "true" annual incidence rate is probably much greater than 16%, because it is almost certain that there was under-reporting. Moreover, when an assault occurred, it was typically part of a repeated pattern. Two-thirds of the couples who experienced an assault reported more than one incident during the base year of this study.[1]

Third, even if one regards 16.1% as a low rate, a large number of people are involved. If this rate is applied to the 54 million cohabiting couples in the United States in 1984, it yields an estimated 8.7 million assault victims (Straus and Gelles, 1988).

Fourth, violence between spouses tends to be transmitted from generation to generation (Hotaling and Sugarman, 1986; Straus, 1983) and also is related to assaults and other crime outside the family (Hotaling and Straus, 1988).

Finally, even though the bulk of the assaults that occur in marriage are minor, they could continue indefinitely and escalate into more severe assaults. A number of studies report such a pattern (Giles-Sims, 1983; Pagelow, 1981; Walker, 1979).

Violence and Assault

The definition of violence used here is "an act carried out with the intention or perceived intention of causing physical pain or injury to another person" (see Gelles and Straus, 1979, for an explication of this definition and an analysis of alternative definitions). *Violence* and *assault* are used interchangeably since there is no "marital exemption" from prosecution for assault analogous to the exemption from prosecution for rape that still exists in five states.[2]

Careers of Wife Assault

The defining characteristic of the "criminal career" perspective is its emphasis on examining the pattern of criminal activity of individuals over time (see Blumstein et al., 1985, 1986, 1988; Gottfredson and Hirshi, 1988). The value of the approach depends on the nature of the empirical phenomena being considered. At one extreme, if criminal events are independent of one another, then there can be nothing that can be learned from examining a "criminal career," because knowing about one event indicates nothing about the likelihood of another. At the other extreme, if criminal events strictly follow one of a few patterns of succession, then the way to determine whether an individual will perpetrate a crime would be to determine that individual's current position in a particular pattern (succession) of events. The dual problems of the criminal career paradigm are to identify patterns of criminal careers and to identify the position of each individual within a particular pattern.

The most common approach to the application of the "criminal career" perspective is for researchers to try to identify a small number of career patterns and then determine which applies to a particular individual. Researchers often identify patterns that involve engaging in criminal activity on a regular basis from a point of onset until a point of termination; such patterns differ from one another in their points of onset and termination. A further simplification in the set of patterns is to consider only three "ideal type" patterns: (1) No criminal activity, (2) One criminal event followed by termination, and (3) Regular criminal activity without termination. Such a simplification obviously cannot account for all cases, but if it could account for almost all of the cases it would be very parsimonious.

This typology has been suggested in the research on wife beating (see Pagelow, 1981:43). The most significant substantive assumption of this typology is that wife assault that occurs more than once persists until the termination of the relationship (by separation or death). This assumption is widely accepted both by researchers and the general public. Pagelow (1981:45) says: "One of the few things about which almost all researchers agree is that batterings escalate in frequency and intensity over time." The New Jersey Public Opinion Survey Regarding Domestic Violence (Irving Crespi and Associates, 1987) asked: "Which do you think is more likely to be the case with domestic violence—that it is something that repeatedly happens between two people, or, that it is an isolated incident that will pass over?" Eighty-three % said that it "repeatedly happens."

However, the perception of continued violence by both researchers and the general public is based primarily on experience with "treatment" group samples such as clients of shelters for battered women and the sensational cases that appear in the news media. Those women who experience violence that subsides might not go to shelters or receive treatment, even if the assaults are severe. Thus "treatment" samples and news stories do not necessarily indicate the experience of most victims of violence. See Chapter 5 for a discussion of how victims from clinical samples differ from victims in the general population.

Despite the well-entrenched beliefs about the persistence of wife assault, the available evidence suggests that most wife assault subsides. Sherman and Berk (1984) followed up men who had been reported to the police for wife assault; among those men who received the least intervention by police ("mediation"), 37% assaulted their wives again within six months; i.e., 63% did not. This low recidivism rate excludes many cases that were not available for follow-up and does not take account of recidivism after the six months. Furthermore, the low recidivism rate may reflect both the initial intervention by police and the ongoing interview process by the researchers. Nevertheless, the low rate of recidivism stands in marked contrast to entrenched beliefs of researchers and the public in the inevitable persistence of violence. Dutton's (1986a) follow-up of arrested wife assaulters showed that 60% of the untreated men did not generate new police reports within three years after their arrest. Here the low rate of recidivism may be deflated by the exclusion of assaults that did not come to the attention of police, and the actual recidivism rate may have been lowered as a consequence of the initial arrest. Finally, Fagan et al. (1984), summarized in Fagan (1988), found that 55% of men with whom police used the minimal intervention ("informal" mediation and separation) reported no subsequent assaults (Carmody and Williams, 1987). Again, the mere involvement of the police could have lowered recidivism. Nevertheless, the low recidivism rates in all of these studies contradict the conventional wisdom that wife assault does not cease.

Desistance, Persistence, and Escalation

Desistance refers to cessation of a pattern of criminal behavior. It is used in contrast with *recidivism* or *persistence*, which refer to continuing a pattern of criminal behavior, and to *escalation*, which specifically refers to continuing the criminal behavior at a higher level. In the article in which he introduced *desistance* to research on intrafamily violence, Fagan (1988) uses the term in two different ways: (1) In the broad sense, *desistance* refers to the termination of criminal behavior for any reason except incapacitation. (2) In the narrow sense, *desistance* refers to termination in the absence of any effects of others.[3] For purposes of this article, we use the term in the broader sense. We believe that most desistance results from actions taken by the husband, wife, family, neighbors, and associates without any formal outside intervention. However, this is an empirical issue that should be addressed in further research.

Another problematic aspect of the definition of desistance is its permanence. If a husband assaults his wife and then does not do so again for a year, we consider that he has desisted, even if he were to assault her again at some later time. From a longer-term perspective, desistance that is later followed by violence might be considered "false" (Blumstein et al., 1985:217). However, we believe that a year of peace is important enough to be considered true desistance even if new violence is initiated later. Furthermore, these data indicate that the rate of initiation of severe violence (following a year with no severe assaults) is low, as will be shown later in Table 27.2. For these reasons, we believe that a year without violence is appropriately considered "desistance," even while recognizing that violence that recurs after long intervals is another important subject for further research.

The data used for this chapter are from both the 1985 Resurvey and a follow-up study, termed the 1985–86 panel study, of the 1985 Resurvey respondents described below. These data are used to determine the desistance of wife assault among those couples in which the husband was reported to have severely assaulted the wife in 1985. We hypothesize that there will be a high rate of desistance among all couples, including those with the highest rate of assault, although we expect that the highest rates of desistance will be among those who begin with lower frequencies of assault. We separate those couples in which one or two instances were reported from those in which more instances were reported in 1985 and examine their desistance in 1986.

Minor/Severe Violence

The link between "minor" violence and "severe" violence is a controversial aspect of research on family violence. The public and many researchers emphasize the distinction between "innocuous" violence ("minor" violence and violence by women) and "real" violence (severe assaults, especially by husbands toward wives), as exemplified in the comments of U.S. Representative Scheuer in congressional hearings on family violence, as reported in the *Congressional Record* and reprinted in Straus (1979). Feminist scholars such as Breines and Gordon (1983) emphasize the unique nature of assaults by husbands on wives. Such distinctions lead to the expectation that the different types of violence have different causes and that understanding one does not help to understand the other.

On the other hand, the "continuum of violence" and "cultural spillover" approaches (Archer and Gartner, 1984; Baron and Straus, 1987; Straus, 1983) suggest that although there are important differences between types of violence, all violence has certain common elements and there is a spillover effect in which the existence of one type of violence tends to legitimate and increase the likelihood of other types. From these perspectives, understanding severe violence is helped by simultaneously understanding violence in its more innocuous forms.

To the extent that violence by the wife is thought to affect the violence of a husband, it is often assumed to deter the continuation of wife assault (see Pagelow, 1984). Bowker (1983) reports that some formerly assaulted wives believe that "aggressive defense" was effective for stopping the assaults; however, he also reports that other formerly assaulted wives believed that such tactics had only exacerbated their victimization. At this point, there is no systematic evidence of either the deterrent or escalatory effect of violence by wives on the behavior of their husbands.

Using the 1985–1986 panel data, we investigate whether the occurrence of minor assaults by either the husband or the wife and/or severe violence by the wife increase the likelihood of severe assaults by the husband in the following year. The occurrence of *any* assaults can be viewed both as an indicator of the presence of certain underlying causes of severe violence and as a cause of escalation of violence. Consequently, we hypothesize that the occurrence of *any* assaults in Year 1 will be associated with presence of *severe* assaults by the husband in Year 2.

Causes of Escalation and Desistance

We suggest that there are four reasons why minor assaults indicate the likelihood of subsequent more severe assaults. These reasons are similar to reasons one might expect that other minor forms of deviance (e.g., use of marijuana) could indicate a risk of more major forms of deviance (e.g., use of heroin). (1) The presence of minor violence may indicate that the counter-normative aspect of violence has been "neutralized" (see Sykes and Matza, 1957) for this couple; i.e. the presence of minor violence may indicate that violence is permissible or tolerable and therefore severe violence is more likely to occur. (2) Although the motivation toward violence varies from time to time and situation to situation, the presence of any violence at one time indicates a greater likelihood of violence-motivating factors (e.g. stress, power struggles, etc.) at other times; some of those factors could motivate severe as well as minor assaults. (3) Violence could be an effective way for a husband to achieve his ends; consequently, he might be motivated to continue and even escalate its use when minor violence is no longer effective. (4) Finally, assaults of any level by one partner increase the likelihood of violent response by the other partner, which in turn may provoke response from the first partner, etc. Such interchanges could continue over a long time and sometimes escalate.

The relevance of these four reasons for escalation of other forms of deviance is easily recognized if the reasons are only slightly generalized: (1) Neutralization of the countervailing norms (e.g., drugs are okay because no one is hurt.). (2) Some stability in the external factors causing deviance (e.g., young people who are not successful by conventional means may search for alternatives). (3) The effectiveness of deviance for meeting the goals of the individual (e.g., selling drugs may bring money and prestige). (4) Minor deviance may provoke negative responses from others (authorities, friends, relatives) that provoke further deliberate acts of rebellion or spite.

At any given time there are countervailing pressures toward desistance corresponding to each of the reasons for persistence and escalation. (1) Norms are rarely completely neutralized; consequently, individuals may stop their deviance in response to the continued normative pressures. (2) Although the motivation for deviance has some stability, it also changes.

For example, financial stresses may be overcome, one spouse may give up the power struggle, etc. (3) The deviant behavior may not accomplish the ends of the individual and may lead to undesired consequences. (4) The responses of others (whether punitive or permissive) may deter or discourage further deviance.

Each of the above reasons may cause the violence and accompanying intimidation to stop. It is also important to recognize that assaults may cease temporarily or permanently even as the threat of violence continues to intimidate. The husband may accomplish his goals of getting his own way and/or punishing his wife using verbal assaults and other punitive behaviors accompanied by the threat of violence. If the wife is effectively intimidated, she may be able to avoid assaults by her husband for long periods of time by doing what her husband wants, avoiding situations that she knows to start him off, etc. (see Walker, 1979). Under such conditions, the threat of violence is ever present and the wife remains its victim. Such "desistance" fits the letter of the definition without fitting its spirit. In the present study, there is no way to distinguish this form of desistance from others.

Sample and Method

To summarize, our purpose in this chapter is to determine if intrafamily assaults are similar to other forms of deviance in two ways: (1) Desistance is high, and (2) Minor forms are a risk factor for major forms. More formally, our two hypotheses are:

(1) There will be a high rate of desistance among all couples, including those with the highest rate of assault.

(2) The occurrence of *any* assaults in Year 1 will be associated with presence of *severe* assaults by the husband in Year 2.

If these hypotheses are supported, further research should investigate the specific characteristics and circumstances of individuals and couples that encourage desistance and discourage escalation of wife assault.

Rates of persistence and escalation of spouse assault cannot be estimated from cross-sectional survey data. Both the 1975 and the 1985 National Family Violence Surveys (Straus, Gelles, and Steinmetz, 1980; Gelles and Straus, 1988) find a steady decrease with age in the rate and severity of assaults between partners. However, since violence frequently precipitates divorce, this could be the result of selective attrition of marriages rather than desistance of violence within marriages. Also, the selective attrition of marriages could obscure the fact that violence escalates within the violent marriages that remain. A panel analysis is necessary to test the hypotheses.

Many of the respondents in the cross-sectional surveys who report no recent assaults nevertheless report that they have experienced violence within this relationship in the past. However, this information is insufficient to determine the nature, extent, or duration of the previous experience with violence, and no information was obtained on assaults in relationships that eventually fell apart. A panel study over a relatively short time period allows us to investigate changes that take place within relationships.

Wife assault was measured using the Conflict Tactics Scales (CTS), which is described briefly in Chapter 1 and fully in Chapters 3 and 4. Both the minor and severe CTS indexes were used. Almost everyone who engages in a severe assault also commits less violent acts; our prior cross-sectional analyses show that husbands who punch or kick their wives almost always also slap and throw things. However, this does not indicate whether there were periods involving only minor assaults prior to incidents of severe assault. A panel study provides a way to determine if, at some prior time, there was minor violence but no severe assaults.

The National Family Violence Surveys

The 1985 resurvey sample. The Year 1 data to be reported in this chapter are from the 1985 Resurvey. When more than one eligible adult was in the household, a random procedure was used to select one respondent according to gender and marital status. Thus one member of each household, either the husband/male partner or the wife/female partner, was interviewed. Although a husband and wife from the same couple may not report identical information, analyses presented in Chapter 9 have indicated that substantive results are generally similar, whether they are based upon reports from the husbands or wives (see also Szinovacz, 1983, for similar findings). In the present context, the small numbers of cases involving severe assaults make separate analyses too unreliable to report, but the general patterns for each are similar to the combined analyses that are reported.

For the purposes of the current chapter, the weights designed to compensate for the Black, Hispanic, and state oversamples make no substantive difference. We therefore present the raw numbers because they better represent the data to the reader and avoid the statistical ambiguities of weighting. See Appendix 1 for details on the 1985 sample and weighting procedures.

The median age for male respondents was 40 years and 38 years for females. The median duration that couples were married was 14 years. The median years of education were 12. Fifty-four % had at least one child less than 18 years old at home. The median family income was in the $25–30,000 range. Eight-two % of respondents designated themselves as married and 4% as cohabiting, and 10% were single parent families or persons who were separated or divorced during the two years prior to the interview.

1986 reinterviews. Eight hundred and thirty-five of the 1985 married respondents reported one or more assaults in their marriage in the previous year; attempts were made to reinterview all of these respondents. In addition, respondents who reported no violence in the past year were asked whether they had ever experienced violence in their relationship, and attempts were made to reinterview all 560 of those who reported some previous violence. For the 2,801 respondents who reported no previous violence at all, attempts were made to reinterview only a random sample of 1,528.

Panel studies have often been hailed as the best approach to studies of causal and time-ordered processes. Unfortunately, the reality of panel studies presents new and different problems from cross-sectional studies. Specifically, many individuals who were initially interviewed will not be reinterviewed. The attrition is multifaceted and has both substantive and methodological implications.

First, divorce and separation are important causes of sample attrition, and divorce and separation are known to be associated with marital violence. The interviewers found non-working or wrong numbers for 157 (17%) of the 835 subjects who reported one or more assaults in Year 1.[4] Most of these are probably people who moved, including many broken households. In another 59 cases (7%), the respondent was reported to have moved; these are cases that are most likely to be separations. In addition, there were 9 "no-answer," 33 "respondent not available," and 8 "respondent incapacitated" cases. These numbers suggest that many of the "lost" subjects could have terminated their violence through separation.

At the same time, the couples who engage in continued violence might be difficult to reinterview. Seventy-two respondents refused (and two were refused by the spouse), and four terminated the interview. Another seventy respondents were reached at a time when the interviewers could not complete the interview and were not successfully reached again. These respondents could have been disproportionately violent couples.

Overall, about half (420) of the relevant respondents were successfully reinterviewed. Analysis of the panel sample indicates that it is comparable to the entire sample with respect to major demographic variables (see

Louis Harris and Associates, 1987); however, the reinterviewed subsample had reported somewhat less violence in Year 1 than those who were lost. Table 27.1 shows that there was a greater loss of violent couples; this loss could reflect both a disproportionate breakup of violent marriages and relative inaccessibility of violent couples. Thus the sample could over-represent the continued violence (to the extent that the violent couples that were lost had separated) or underrepresent the continued violence (to the extent that the violent couples that were lost disproportionately continued their violence). No definitive conclusions can be drawn, because the information about subsequent violence is obviously lacking for those who were not reinterviewed. Also, sample attrition might have complex effects on the associations that are observed (e.g. Berk and Ray, 1982), and one must consider the possibility that the sample results might reflect an attrition bias. However, these data are more complete than any others that have been collected.

TABLE 27.1

Success of Reinterview by Frequency of Husband's Assaults in Year 1

Success of Reinterview	Husband's Assault Frequency At Time 1		
	1-2	3+	Total
Reinterviewed	55.6%	44.4%	49.6%
Lost	44.4	55.6	51.4
	100%	100%	100%
	(350)	(416)	(766)

Chi-Square = 0.43, d.f.=1,   p <.51

Note: This table indicates a bias in the panel sample, even though the lack of statistical significance indicates that we cannot be confident that such biases will generally be found.

Violence over Time

Persistence of and Desistance from Severe Violence by Husbands as a
Function of Frequency of Severe Violence by Husbands

Couples were classified by the most severe husband-to-wife assault in Year 2 as "None," "Minor," or "Severe." This is the dependent variable for our analyses of desistance and persistence over the year of the study. Table 27.2 shows how the frequency of severe assaults by the husband in Year 1 is related to the level of husband-to-wife violence in Year 2. (Note that one cannot reconstruct the entire non-panel sample in Year 1 from this table without weighting, because the reinterviewed sample deliberately overrepresented respondents who had experienced violence.) The table clearly indicates that the level and persistence of wife assault are related to the frequency of the initial assaults. The left-hand column of Table 27.2 shows that when the husband had committed no severe assaults in Year 1, 3% committed a severe assault in Year 2; the middle column shows that 20% of the husbands who committed one or two severe assaults in Year 1 severely assaulted their wives in Year 2; and the right-hand column shows that 57% of the husbands who committed "3+" assaults severely assaulted their wives in Year 2. If the percentages for minor and severe assaults in each column of Table 27.2 are added, it shows that assaults by the husband (either minor or severe) followed in 11% of the cases when there were no assaults in Year 1, in 43% of the cases of husbands who had engaged in one or two severe assaults in Year 1, and in 67% of the cases where the husband had severely assaulted three or more times in Year 1.

For the present purposes, the most important implication of Table 27.2 is the high rate of desistance even among the most frequent perpetrators of severe assaults. The right-hand column of Table 27.2 shows that 33% of the most frequent perpetrators did not assault their wives in Year 2, and an additional 10% (making a total of 43%) used no severe violence. A 57% severe assault rate obviously constitutes a serious social problem, but the other 43% hold out the possibility of desistance. Other evidence in the study suggests that outside intervention of any sort (e.g., by police or counselors) was rare (Kaufman Kantor and Straus, 1989) and probably cannot account for the desistance. Thus the possibility of desistance holds out some hope, and as Fagan (1988) suggests, researchers and policy-makers might try to encourage and build upon the situational tendencies toward desistance that are already present to encourage desistance in more cases.

We should make it clear that however important this "high" rate of desistance is, it leaves a high rate of recidivism. Desistance itself may be

TABLE 27.2
Severity of Husband's Assaults in Year 2 by Frequency of His Severe
Assaults in Year 1

Husband's Severity in Year 2	Husband's Severe Assault Frequency In Year 1		
	0*	1-2	3+
None	90%	58%	33%
Minor	7	23	10
Severe	3	19	57
	100%	100%*	100%
	(1270)	(54)	(22)

Chi-Square=195.5, d.f.=4, p <.001

* This column underrepresents couples with no previous history of assault because attempts were only made to interview a random half of such couples. Thus, this column overstates these assault rates. This does not affect the desistance rates -- the substantive issue of this table.

part of the solution and lessons learned from desistance may be another part, but neither obviates the need for intervention to further reduce the continuing levels of wife assault.

Another implication of Table 27.2 is that severe assaults by husbands occurred in Year 2 in a small but significant proportion of cases (3%) where the husband had engaged in no severe assaults in Year 1. In the next section, we examine the significance of minor assaults and assaults by wives for indicating the likelihood of escalation to severe violence by husbands over time.

Persistence of and Desistance from Severe Violence by Husbands as a Function of Minor Violence and Violence by Wives

The analysis up to this point used frequency of *severe* assaults by the husband as the independent variable. For the analysis in this section, we classified couples by the maximum severity of the assaults that *each* employed in Year 1. The dependent variable is the presence of a severe assault by husbands in Year 2. Table 27.3 shows the percentage of husbands who severely assaulted their wives in Year 2 for couples having each combination of severity of assaults by husbands and wives in Year 1. The percentages in Table 27.3 should be interpreted tentatively because of the small numbers of cases in most cells. Nevertheless, there is a clear pattern whereby minor assaults by either spouse increases the likelihood of severe assaults by the husband and minor assaults by both husband and wife triples the probability of subsequent severe assaults by the husband (6% compared with 2%). Even so, minor assaults escalate infrequently.

Another important finding concerns "severe" violence by the wife. It is generally accepted that "severe" violence by the wife does not usually indicate a high risk of injury (Breines and Gordon, 1983; Straus and Gelles, 1986:410), but researchers have not determined whether violence by the wife puts *her* at risk of injury because it increases the probability of violence by the husband. Table 27.3 shows that when a husband does not severely assault but his wife does, there is a one in seven chance (13% or 15%) that he will severely assault her in the following year. That is a substantial increase in risk compared with the risk of escalation associated with minor assaults by the wife.

Furthermore, minor assaults by the wife are associated with a substantial increase in the probability of continued severe assaults by the husband. When the wife abstained from violence, only 6% of the husbands continued. When the wives used minor violence, 23% of the husbands continued. And when the wife severely assaulted her husband, then 42% of the husbands continued. These findings suggest that assaults by the wife increase the probability of severe assaults by the husband.

Although this is one plausible interpretation of the findings, an alternative possibility could be that the assaultive behavior of wives is in response to assaults by husbands that occurred before the one-year referent period of the Year 1 study. To the extent that occurred, the wives who assaulted are those who were already confronted by abusive husbands and one might expect those husbands to continue or escalate apart from the behavior of the wives.[5] Only experimental intervention (e.g., by encouraging either retaliatory violence or non-retaliation) could distinguish between the

TABLE 27.3

Percent of Couples Reporting Severe Husband-to-Wife Assault in Year 2, by Severity of Assaults by Husbands and Wives in Year 1

Wife's Severity in Year 1	Husband's Severity In Year 1[*]			p[#]
	None	Minor	Severe	
None	2%@ (942)	3% (63)	6% (16)	.001
Minor	4% (72)	6% (87)	23% (13)	.089
Severe	15% (34)	13% (23)	42% (40)	.012
p[#]	.001	.029	.026	

[*] Percents in the body of the table are the percent of couples reporting severe violence by husbands in Year 2.

[#] These are the significance levels for Chi-square with four degrees of freedom, based upon each partial table, with dependent variable "Husband Severity in Year 2" in three categories (None, Minor, Severe).

@ This cell includes those who reported no assaults in Year 1 but had experienced an assault in some previous year, and those who reported no assaults in Year 1 or ever. When both husbands and wives reported no assaults in Year 1, they were asked whether either had ever assaulted the other; for those who had never assaulted, 1% (613) of husbands severely assaulted in Year 2; for those who had assaulted before but not in Year 1, 3% (321) of husbands severely assaulted in the Year 2. The panel sample overweighted the latter group; thus, the best estimate for the "none-none" group in the population is less than 2%.

causal processes. In any case, assaults by wives are indicative of the future violence by husbands.

Bowker (1983) and Gelles and Straus (1988) find that there are several strategies wives use that have been somewhat effective in discouraging subsequent violence (e.g., threatening to leave and/or leaving the situation). The findings presented here are consistent with findings in these other analyses that hitting was the least effective strategy for discouraging subsequent assaults.

Summary and Conclusions

This chapter analyzes follow-up interviews conducted in 1986 with respondents from the 1985 Resurvey. It examines the extent to which a pattern of assaults persisted or desisted from Year 1 of the study to Year 2 and the extent to which "minor" assaults (pushing, shoving, slapping, throwing things at the spouse) escalated into "severe" assaults (e.g., punching, kicking, attacks with objects and weapons).

The findings confirmed the hypothesis, which specified a high rate of desistance, even for husbands who had frequently used severe violence. The reported rates of desistance could be somewhat inflated by the methodological artifacts of selective attrition of the panel and reactive effects of the Year 1 interview, but these high rates of desistance are the best estimates available for the general population of the U.S.

The findings also confirmed the hypothesis that minor assaults and assaults by wives are associated with subsequent severe assaults by husbands.[6] These findings may indicate that minor assaults tend to encourage major assaults. However, there are two important alternative possibilities. (1) Couples with severely assaultive husbands typically also exhibit lesser forms of violence by both husbands and wives; if the severe assaults by husbands are intermittent, then the survey might only pick up the less serious assaults in the first year. The minor assaults might not cause the severe assaults, but only indicate their presence in the behavioral repertory. (2) Both minor assaults and severe assaults might result from the same precipitating factors (e.g. unemployment, stress, youth, male dominance) and not be causing one another, in which case frequent minor assaults might indicate the underlying precipitating factors that cause severe assaults.

Although it is difficult to disentangle these different types of causal processes, the extent to which minor assaults "cause" subsequent severe assaults is not crucial for our purposes. Our purpose has been to investigate an aspect of the natural history of violence by testing the hypothesis that minor and severe assaults are related. Since this hypothesis was supported, one implication is that steps to reduce severe assaults of wives should pay attention to minor violence as well. Even if frequent minor assaults are only a minimal cause of subsequent severe assaults, they are an indication of the increased risk of more severe violence.

It would be useful to specifically know whether reducing minor assaults could reduce the likelihood of major violence. Experiments could be done involving intervention with couples reporting minor violence. Intervention might involve reduction of stress, provision of social and material support, and efforts to increase equality between spouses and change values that tolerate minor violence. The rates of desistance and escalation among these couples can be compared with the rates among couples without intervention.

We have only begun to describe careers of wife assault. It is clear that the simple conceptions of the process that are commonly held by the public and many researchers are insufficient, particularly the ideas that minor violence is irrelevant to major violence and that major violence by husbands almost always continues or escalates. Further research must elaborate the processes of desistance and escalation to determine the other factors (especially age, life circumstances, etc.) that affect the likelihood of desistance or escalation over the life courses of marriages.

Notes

We appreciate the comments and suggestions of Kirk Williams and the members of the Family Violence Research Seminar at the University of New Hampshire.

1. As discussed in Chapter 24, the NCS *domestic* assault rate is much lower than the rate from our 1975 national survey and from Time 1 of the 1985 survey reported in this article. The extremely low NCS rate occurs because although most people can be presumed to consider such assaults to be wrong, even horrible, they do not experience them as a "crime" in the legal sense and do not report such assaults to the NCS. However, two circumstances do lead to reporting such assaults in the NCS: if an injury occurs or if the assault is by a former spouse or separated spouse. This causes the NCS injury rate from domestic assaults to be extremely high. It also produces statistics that appear to indicate that women are more vulnerable to assault by a former than a current spouse. Both of these "findings" are erroneous.

2. There are a number of other conceptual issues that are discussed in other chapters of this book. First, we avoid the term *abuse* because of the ambiguity and inconsistency associated with this term (Chapter 5; Gelles, 1985; Gelles and Straus, 1979). Second, there are dilemmas connected with "criminalization" of acts within the family (Chapter 25). Third, some feminist scholars criticize the use of *acts* as the criterion for defining and measuring violence, favoring a definition that uses *injuries* as the criterion (e.g., Breines and Gordon, 1983; reviewed in Chapter 5). However, there are important reasons for defining and

measuring injury separately. One of the most important is consistency with the legal concept of assault, for which, as Marcus (1983:89) puts it: "Physical contact is not an element of the crime [of assault]"; or as the United States Department of Justice (1975–1984:21) puts it: "Attempts are included [in the tabulation of aggravated assault] because it is not necessary that an injury result." Five other reasons for measuring assaults and injuries separately are discussed in Chapter 5.

3. Fagan (1988) concludes: "There are no studies which document natural or spontaneous desistance without intervention by the victim or as a result of some form of sanction or treatment." However, this statement implies an unusual limitation on the definition of natural desistance, by treating actions of the wife as apart from the natural desistance of violence in relationships. Bowker (1983) shows that successful "intervention by the victim" can include a wife talking to friends or relatives, making non-violent threats, and taking other actions within the context of ongoing relationships. Presumably these types of behaviors of a wife are among the factors that encourage "natural" desistance in many other types of deviant behavior, including alcoholism, drug abuse, and property crimes. (see Fagan, 1988; Gottfredson and Hirshi, 1986). The common difficulty in distinguishing "desistance" from the results of intervention is exaggerated with regard to "wife abuse" because the wife is both part of the "natural" process of desistance and the victim.

4. The description of the sample attrition is based upon the report from the interviewing organization (Louis Harris and Associates, 1987). The specific information applies to the complete sample of "coupled" respondents. The present analysis excludes the respondents who were not married or who separated during the intervening year, 1985–1986. The information available does not allow separate analysis of the sources of attrition of the married couples alone.

5. Respondents who reported no violence in the past year were asked whether they had ever experienced violence in their relationship. This information did not distinguish whether husband or wife used the violence. Nevertheless, those who had experienced previous violence reported higher subsequent husband violence (5% minor and 3% severe) compared with those who had never experienced violence (3% minor and 1% severe). These findings indicate that prior violence (more than a year ago) is obviously a risk factor for subsequent violence (compared with no prior violence), but much less so than violence within the past year (19% minor and 11% severe).

6. As previously mentioned, sample attrition could bias associations. In this case, the evidence suggests that the perpetrators of more severe violence (presumably including those who escalate to severe violence) are disproportionately part of the attrition. If that is so, our results would only underestimate the association between minor violence and subsequent major violence.

28

Family Patterns and Primary Prevention of Family Violence

Murray A. Straus and Christine Smith

The concept of primary prevention is borrowed from the fields of public health and mental health. To paraphrase a definition from Caplan (1964, quoted in Cowen, 1978:8) primary prevention of family violence involves lowering its incidence by counteracting harmful circumstances *before they have had a chance to produce violence*. It does not seek to prevent a specific person from committing a violent act; instead, primary prevention seeks to reduce the risk for a whole population. The outcome envisioned as a result of primary prevention is that, although some individuals may continue to be violent, their number will be reduced.

Cowen suggests two broad areas of interest to primary prevention: personal-adaptational and social-environmental. The first area of personal adaptation argues that "the best possible defense against problems is to build resources and adaptive strengths in people from the start" (Cowen, 1978:17). As indicated in Chapter 3 (see also Hotaling and Straus, 1980), conflict is, for a variety of reasons, an inherent feature of family life. Power differences between young and old, women and men, often induce family members to use physical force in order to prevail in these inevitable conflicts. Primary prevention in the personal adaptational domain will involve teaching families how to deal with conflicts without resorting to the use of physical force. Primary prevention at the societal level will involve changes in the structure of the society and of the family system that reduces family conflict and stress. At both levels, the primary prevention approach implies an effort on a mass scale, moving beyond restorative efforts targeted at those families already plagued with violence from within.

The research reported in this book, since it identified many social factors that have an impact on the incidence and prevalence of family violence, speaks more directly to the area of social-environmental primary prevention. While the evidence is not incontrovertible, this research points to many aspects of the social environment that can be changed to reduce the incidence of family violence. Some may believe that such changes are unattainable or ought not be undertaken unless they are scientifically *proven* to be necessary and effective. We believe that, having located many of the causes of the problem, it is our obligation as members of society as well as of the scientific community to advocate such changes, even without incontrovertible proof, provided that the changes are desirable for other reasons as well.

Much of the research on intrafamily violence reported in this volume is particularly relevant for primary prevention because these studies are drawn from community rather than clinical populations. A clinical population is obviously essential for research intended to evaluate the effects of various treatment modalities (see Chapter 5). However, for interventions to prevent such cases from arising in the first place, the most appropriate research is that based on a broad cross-section of the community in which the prevention steps are to take place.

One advantage to community studies is that they provide estimates of the incidence or prevalence of intrafamily violence in the United States—data that are particularly important in determining the need for prevention programs. Findings based on a community rather than a clinical sample describe processes associated with violence in a broader cross-section of American families. Such findings therefore identify family characteristics that might be appropriate targets for interventions to prevent physical violence.

With these considerations in mind, this chapter has two main objectives: first, to discuss the limitations of individual-level treatment strategies in dealing with intrafamily violence and its consequences; and second, to identify some of the characteristics of the family that are associated with violence and from which primary prevention steps can be deduced.[2]

The Extent of Family Violence

Incidence rates given in Chapters 6, 7, and 8 are relevant to primary prevention because they indicate that physical violence between family members occurs so frequently that it will be almost impossible to reduce the incidence of family violence through clinical intervention alone—

important as that is for the specific families receiving such treatment. Specifically, the 1985 National Family Violence Resurvey revealed that one out of six American couples (16.1%) experienced one or more incidents of physical violence during the year of the survey. Over the course of the marriage the figure is much higher—28% of the 1975 sample and 30% of the 1985 sample. Moreover, there are several reasons to think that these are underestimates and that the true rates may be twice as high (Straus, Gelles, and Steinmetz, 1980: 34–36). If so, the majority of American couples have experienced at least one violent incident.

The majority of these incidents involved "minor" assaults such as slapping and throwing things at the partner. However, in 39% of these incidents, the assault went beyond slapping or throwing things to serious violence such as punching, kicking, biting, beating, and attacks with knives and guns. Moreover, the minor violence is important in its own right, both in human terms and in terms of its adverse effect on mental health (see Chapters 9 and 24) and as a precursor of more severe violence (see Chapter 27).

Some of the rates of greatest importance for primary prevention are those that show that physical punishment is used by almost all parents of young children. The specific figure for the parents of three-year-olds in the 1975 survey was 97% (Chapter 23) and 90% among the 1985 sample (Chapter 8). Moreover, Chapter 8 reports that about one out of four parents start hitting children in infancy, i.e., before one year of age. Rates of more severe forms of parent-to-child violence are alarmingly high, indicating *a minimum* of one in ten children are victims of severe violence each year. We say "a minimum" because these rates are based on parents' own admissions, and it is almost certain that not everyone divulged such abusive behavior, even to an anonymous interviewer.

Consequences of Family Violence

Several chapters demonstrate that these enormous rates of violence have profound negative consequences for the stability and quality of family life and for the mental and physical health of family members.

Effects on Spouses

Chapter 9 compares spouses who experienced relatively minor violence, those who experienced severe violence in 1985, and those who had not been attacked by their partners. Since Chapter 9 reports that women victims were even more likely to suffer these consequences than men victims (illustrated in Figures 1–4 in that chapter), the findings regarding women victims are highlighted here. These comparisons reveal that:

- Seriously assaulted women averaged almost double the days in bed due to illness than did other women.
- Women who were victims of minor violence were almost one and a half times more likely to report experiencing stress, and severely assaulted women were two and a half times more likely to feel stress than non-victims.
- Seriously assaulted women had much higher rates of psychological distress, including:
  —Double the incidence of headaches
  —Four times the rate of depression
  —Five and a half times more suicide attempts

Chapter 25 also reports the association of spouse abuse with violence outside the family. All of these findings hold regardless of the gender or social class of the victim or the offender.

- Victims of assault by a spouse are more likely to themselves engage in verbal aggression and physical assault against non-family members than are non-victims.
- Compared to non-offenders, those who assault their spouse are four times more likely to have also assaulted someone outside the family.

Effects on Children

Chapter 24 compared children who had been severely assaulted by a parent with the other children in the 1985 Resurvey and found that the abused children consistently experienced more behavior problems. For example, the child victims of severe violence had two to four times higher rates of:

- Trouble making friends
- Temper tantrums
- Failing grades in school
- Disciplinary problems in school and at home

Chapter 25 also reveals that family violence has a profound effect on extra-family violence and other crimes committed by children.

- Children who are both victims of parental assault and who witness assault between their parents are ten times more likely to assault a non-family member than are children from non-assaultive families.
- Assaulted children, especially boys, are more likely than non-victims to commit "property crimes" (such as vandalism and theft) against non-family members.
- All of these findings hold true regardless of the victim's or offender's gender or of the family's social class.

Practical Limitations of Treatment

The most obvious limitations of the treatment approach to family violence stem from the extent of the problem and the many serious consequences described above. There is a huge imbalance between the resources available to organizations treating violent families—child welfare and law enforcement agenices, mental health programs, battered women's shelters—on the one hand and the number of families suffering from such violence on the other.

Child Protective Services

The most direct outgrowth of the child abuse reporting laws enacted in the 1970's was the expansion of child welfare agencies responsible for handling child abuse reports. As public awareness has grown, official reports of child abuse have risen each year. In an era of restrictions on spending for social services, child protective service agencies have been doubly burdened with more child abuse cases on the one hand and fewer resources to draw upon in treating them on the other. Moreover, the tremendous discrepancy between the rate of officially reported child abuse cases and the rates from the National Family Violence Surveys (cf. Chapter 6) casts serious doubt as to the ability of the child welfare system to deal with the scope of the problem if all cases of child abuse *were* reported. Even with the present level of reporting, state Child Protective Services do not have the resources to investigate a large proportion of the reports they do receive. For example, over a third of child abuse reports in Massachusetts and about half of those in New Hampshire were not investigated in 1985.

Spouse Abuse

The recent trend toward recognizing that an assault against a spouse is a criminal act (Sherman and Cohen, 1989) poses a similar dilemma.

Chapter 26 reports that only about 7% of assaults between spouses are reported to the police and even these few rarely result in arrest. Consequently, there is formal legal intervention in the form of arrest in less than one in a hundred marital assaults. Straus and others advocate a public policy which declares that assault on one's spouse is as much a criminal act as an assault against a stranger, combined with a policy of arresting violators (Straus, 1977, 1983). Nevertheless, there are reasons for caution regarding use of the criminal justice system as a means of preventing family violence. First, there are not enough police or courts to deal with the actual number of cases. Second, there are dangers in expanding the role of the police in American life. Third is the risk that a criminal sanctions approach will undermine family commitment, loyalty, and privacy and thus result in negative consequences. Finally, the ineffectiveness of incarceration as a method of preventing other types of crimes raises questions about how effective such sanctions will be for preventing intrafamily assaults. These problems with a criminal sanctions approach to intrafamily crime are discussed more fully elsewhere (Straus and Lincoln, 1985).

Mental Health Treatment Response

The mental health services system is also not likely to be able to provide help to more than a minute fraction of those in need. The figures summarized above show that violence between spouses occurs in a minimum of one-third of all American families. Consequently, we lack the resources, now or in the foreseeable future, to make available sufficient mental health treatment services for all but a small fraction of those who experience this damaging family problem. Thus, as with many other aspects of mental health, the approach must be through prevention.

Five Causes of Intrafamily Violence

Thus far, this chapter has established two grounds for primary prevention: first, the impossibility of providing services for the multitude of victims of family violence, and second, the tragic effects of such victimization. A third basis for primary prevention is the social roots of the problem, to be discussed below. If the nature of society puts people at risk of violence, only primary prevention can address those risk factors.

A great many social factors converge to cause the high rates of intrafamily violence—many more than can be discussed in this chapter. Consequently, discussion is restricted to five of these factors: (1) the high level of conflict characteristic of family life, (2) male dominance in the family and in society at large, (3) cultural norms that permit family violence, (4) the inadvertent training in violence that goes on in most families, and (5) use of violence for socially legitimate purposes. Of these five factors, the first and fourth can be classified as what Cowen (1978) calls personal-adaptational prevention strategies, while the other three suggest his category of social-environmental strategies.

These five factors were selected because each meets the following criteria:

1. The target factor is characteristic of a large proportion of the population. Therefore, remedial steps will be an advantage to a correspondingly large group of families.
2. The factor focuses on prevention efforts that are desirable even if they have no preventative effect on intrafamily violence.
3. The goal of the prevention effort is, in our opinion, attainable.

Intrafamily Conflict

One of the distinctive characteristics of the family is a high level of conflict—probably higher than most other groups. The high level of conflict inherent in family life is difficult to perceive because the family is simultaneously the locus of deep love and support. As Hotaling and Straus (1980:15) point out, one of the ironies of family life is that many of the same characteristics that contribute to family intimacy and love also contribute to family conflict. For example, because the family is concerned with "the whole person" rather than just specific role performance, disagreements are possible over almost anything.

Differences in generational and gender cultures. The fact that the family typically includes both males and females exacerbates the probability of conflict because men and women tend to have different perceptions, interests, and attitudes. Consequently, the so-called battle of the sexes is built into the basic structure of the family. Similarly, because family typically includes two generations—parents and children—there is still another inherent basis for disagreement: the so-called generation gap. In addition, as will be discussed below, the difference in power ascribed to male and female and to young and old is also a source of conflict.

Prevention strategies. Not all intrafamily violence involves conflict, but a great deal of it does (Straus, Gelles, and Steinmetz, 1980: 115). Since that is the case, and as noted above, a high level of conflict is inherent in the very nature of the family, this combination explains a great deal of intrafamily violence. The prevention strategy that follows from these facts is that many families need help in dealing with the inevitable conflicts of family life. Among adequately functioning families, these conflicts are resolved by negotiation and compromise and by an implicit system of reciprocity that allows each person to make concessions to the other, knowing that things will balance out in the long run. In contrast, distressed families tend to lack these skills. Consequently an important method of preventing family violence is to teach these skills. This in fact is the approach of certain family therapists (e.g., Blechman, 1980; Blechman, Kotanchik, and Taylor, 1981; Patterson, 1982; Turkewitz and O'Leary, 1981).

However, professional therapists can reach only the most troubled families and far from all of those. A true primary prevention approach would make courses and workshops in family problem-solving skills available through a wide variety of channels, such as sponsorship by churches, schools, and other community groups. It would include the teaching of such skills as part of the high school curriculum. Still another possibility is a videocassette tape on resolving family conflicts, and possibly subsidized distribution of this tape, so that it could be sold at a relatively low price.

Male Dominance in the Family and in Society

Another characteristic of the family that engenders violence is the concept of the husband as the head of the family. Each of the studies on this issue that have been conducted at the Family Research Laboratory find that male-dominant marriages have the highest level of violence (see for example Chapters 17, 21, and 22 and Straus, 1973). Despite the greater acceptance of an equalitarian rhetoric and despite some progress toward gender equality in the last decade, the husband as head of the family conception of family organization remains the mode.

Force as a resource in resolving conflict.   The problem with this conception is that many, if not most, husbands implicitly presume, because of being the husband, they have the right to have the final say in decisions affecting the family. If agreement cannot be reached and they have "tried everything"—persuasion, yelling, reasoning, sulking, pleading, etc.— there is an almost overwhelming temptation to use physical force as a resource to maintain their power within the family (Allen and Straus, 1980). That often assures the man does have the final say. As one husband put it after an incident in which he slapped his wife, "And we haven't had any trouble since" (LaRossa, 1980).

Just as violence in the family both reflects and perpetuates violence outside the family, male dominance in the family is part of a larger system of gender inequality. Chapter 21 reflects one of the ways that gender inequality in the society supports inequality and violence in the family: the economic dependence of women on men, which leads them to remain in violent marriages. Half of all married women with children do not work outside the home and therefore have no separate income. Even those women who are employed full-time earn only two-thirds the income of their male counterparts. If the marriage is terminated, a drastic reduction in economic status is a typical consequence for women (Blechman, 1982). Moreover, the fact that in more than 90% of divorce cases the wife will have custody of the children means even more pressure to tolerate violence. The alternative, all too often, is bringing up children in poverty.

Prevention strategies.   One cannot emphasize too strongly the preventive value of sexual equality, both within and outside the family. Moreover, since we found that child abuse is also more frequent in male-dominant families (Straus, Gelles, and Steinmetz, 1980), sexual equality has prophylactic potential for child abuse as well as spouse abuse. Many specific policy implications follow from the fact that sexual inequality engenders family violence. Family therapists should as a matter of routine intake information, determine the power structure of the family, because inequality is a risk factor for violence as well as for other social-psychological problems. When the therapist has done that, part of the therapeutic effort can be devoted to achieving a more egalitarian relationship. Parents and schools can also take important preventive steps by training boys to expect equality in power with girls and later in life with their wives, and girls should be taught that it is not unfeminine to claim equal personal power.

On a societal level, women should not be discouraged from participation in the paid labor force, either logistically by the lack of adequate child care in this country or philosophically on the grounds that it is stressful to themselves and harmful to their children. On the contrary, the available evidence indicates that employment is associated with *enhanced* mental health for both mothers and children (Hotaling, 1984). Moreover, employment is associated with greater equality in marriage and lower rates of spouse abuse and child abuse. Finally, one of the most important steps toward reducing intrafamily violence lies in eliminating the disparity in pay between men and women. If equity in pay could be achieved, equality in many other spheres of life would not trail far behind, and this would bring with it a reduction in family violence.

Cultural Norms Permitting Family Violence

So far we have attributed the high rates of intrafamily violence to the high level of conflict inherent in the family and to the sexual inequality characteristic of the American family. However, important as these are in suggesting prevention strategies, they are not sufficient. Other groups have a high level of conflict, even if it is not quite as high. Academic departments are notorious for their conflicts. Moreover, sexual equality, including equality in pay, had not yet arrived on the American academic scene. Yet university departments are not violent. In Straus's 39 years of teaching at 6 universities, despite some horrendous conflicts, the closest thing to violence occurred at a contentious department meeting at a famous American university. Insults were being traded and voices were rising when the chairman sensibly adjourned the meeting. At this point a colleague jumped up in anger, grabbed an eraser, and threw it *at the wall*.

Why didn't this colleague throw the eraser at the man he had just insulted? Had that dispute taken place in a family rather than in a sociology department, the chances are it would have been thrown at an individual, rather than at the wall. The answer probably lies in the fact that, as with many other types of behavior, the family operates on the basis of different rules than those that apply outside the family. The rule outside the family is that, with the exception of self-defense, you cannot hit anyone, even if he or she behaves terribly.

Family norms and violence. The rule within the family is almost the opposite. This is most clear in the case of parents. They have the legal right, and in the view of 80 to 90% of the population, the moral *obligation* to spank or slap (Carson, 1987), and Chapters 8 and 23 show that well over 90% do use physical punishment. In the case of spouses, the situation is less clear but similar. At one time the common law gave husbands the right to "physically chastise an errant wife" (Calvert, 1974). The courts ceased to enforce this aspect of the common law by the mid-1800's, but it remains a de facto principle. In short, just as parents have the right to hit, the marriage license is an implicit hitting license, provided one does not "go too far" (Straus, 1980:39; see also Chapter 13).

Prevention strategies. The preventative implications of the cultural norm that makes the marriage license a hitting license lies in the fact that it is largely an implicit norm, whose existence is not realized and which, in fact, is usually denied. Furthermore, this norm embodies a principle that is contrary to the conception of marriage as a loving, supportive, personally fulfilling experience. To the extent that this is the case, there might be important preventive effects from simply bringing the implicit norm to the fore. Discussions of marital violence, for example, should be part of the social science and family life education curriculum. This is the appropriate place to begin, because the studies reviewed in Chapter 13 show that couple violence is widespread among unmarried dating couples. Churches have an important stake in the enhancement and stability of the family, and the family curriculum for Sunday schools can bring this issue to the surface and be explicit in declaring that the sacrament of marriage does not include the right to hit. This applies even more to pre-marital classes conducted by many churches, which do not even bring up the issue, much less encourage a pledge to never hit one's spouse.

Some states have increased the marriage license fee as a means of obtaining funds to support shelters for battered wives. However, marriage license applicants are not informed of this, and an important preventive opportunity is lost. An additional step might be to indicate this fact at a promiment place on the marriage license application. It could serve as a means of calling attention to the problem and as a means of making shelters known to the population that will shortly be needing the service. It might be even better to go one step further and include a warning notice: "Marriage may be dangerous to your physical and mental health if steps are not taken to avoid violence. The Surgeon General urges you to discuss this with your prospective spouse before signing this application."

Family Socialization in Violence

The etiological theory that is the basis for the preventative steps put forward up to this point is based on the idea that conflict is inherent in all human associations, but especially the family, that sexual inequality leads many men to feel that they have the right, after all else has been tried, to use physical force to have the final say in family matters, and that there are implicit cultural norms that tolerate intrafamily violence. Each of these elements is a part of the causal sequence, but they are not sufficient. In a certain sense, this theory begs the question because it does not explain why the family has norms that tolerate violence—just the opposite of the norms for other groups.

Broadly speaking, the norms are different because they reflect the pattern of socialization that typically occurs in the family—a pattern of socialization that includes violence in the form of physical punishment in over 90% of American families (cf. Chapters 8 and 23). In the course of historical development, these typical family experiences become embedded as cultural norms.

Physical punishment. In our view, this plays a crucial role in training people to accept violence in family relationships. There are a number of reasons for this. First, physical punishment begins in infancy, before even speech is established. Thus what is learned is built into the deepest layers of the child's emerging personality. Let us examine what is learned.

Take the case of an eight-month-old child crawling on the ground. The child puts something in his or her mouth. The parent removes it and says, "No, no, you'll get sick." But a few minutes later the child puts something else in his or her mouth. This time the parent removes the object, repeats the admonition, *and* slaps the child gently on the hand. That is obviously an act of love and concern on the part of the parent and one that will presumably teach the child to avoid a certain danger. But it also teaches some unintended lessons about violence.

First is the association between love and violence. Mommy and Daddy are usually the first and the only ones to hit an infant. For most children, being hit by parents continues throughout childhood. The child therefore learns that those who love him the most are also those who hit.

Second, since this occurs when the earliest and deepest layers of the personality are being formed, it establishes a fusion or a link between love and violence that is so deeply embedded that it is easily mistaken for a biologically determined linkage. Love and violence become fused. Those you love are those you can hit.

Third, and ironically, since physical punishment is most often an act of love and concern, carried out for the child's own good, the problem is made worse. Under these circumstances physical punishment teaches not only the empirical fact that love and violence go together, but also that it is morally right to hit other members of the family.

The above suggests that early and continuing experience with physical punishment lays the groundwork for the norms legitimizing violence of all types, but especially intrafamily violence. It provides a role model—a specific "script" (Gagnon and Simon, 1973) for violence. Indeed, for many children, there is not even the need to generalize from the parent-child relationship to other family relationships. The National Family Violence Survey shows that millions of children can directly observe and role model violence between husbands and wives.

Although some researchers and child development specialists do not agree that physical punishment has negative consequences, findings reported in Chapter 23 (and several other studies summarized by Hotaling and Sugarman, 1986) suggest a link between physical punishment and violence by the child. Figure 28.1 (from Straus, Gelles, and Steinmetz, 1980) shows that the more physical punishment the respondent experienced as a child, the greater the rate of violence against his or her spouse. Similarly, the more these respondents used violence, including ordinary physical punishment, in dealing with their children, the greater the risk that the child will repeatedly and severely assault a sibling (Chapter 23). Thus each generation is training the next generation to replicate the pattern shown by the incidence rates presented above.

Prevention strategies.   Given the importance of physical punishment in the etiology of less socially approved types of intrafamily violence, elimination (or at least reduction) of physical punishment is a crucial step

FIGURE 28.1

Marital Violence in Survey Year by Amount of Family Violence Experienced as a Teenager

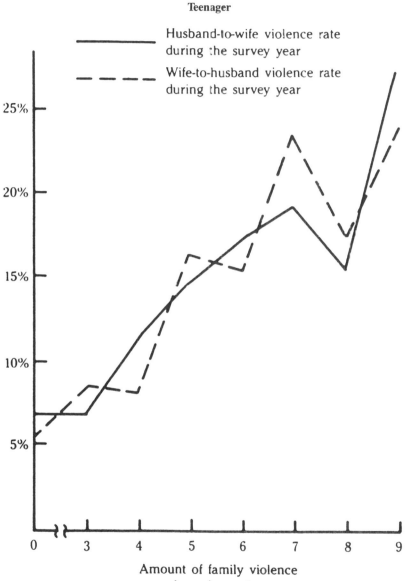

Husband-to-wife violence rate during the survey year

Wife-to-husband violence rate during the survey year

Amount of family violence experienced as a teenager

toward prevention of family violence. It also involves an activity—parent education and advice—that, unlike some of the other prevention steps mentioned in this chapter, is within the traditional purview of mental health professionals. Unfortunately, a clear anti–physical punishment stance seems to have been avoided by mental health professionals and writers of books on child rearing (Carson, 1987).

Parent education programs such as STEP and PET go part of the way by providing parents with alternatives to hitting. But they fail to *explicitly* take an anti–physical punishment stance. Perhaps these authors avoided the issue because of their own ambivalance concerning physical punishment. Perhaps it is because these authors fear that telling parents not to use physical punishment will raise the anxiety level of their readers and in the process cause loss of rapport and sales. Whatever the reason, leading experts on child rearing can make an important contribution to preventing family violence by clearly opposing use of physical punishment, and by providing alternatives through training that will enable parents to exercise discipline and to meet their responsibilities as parents without resorting to hitting their children.

A primary prevention approach also calls for training in alternative discipline techniques *early,* before individuals become spouses or parents. Re-learning new approaches to conflict and discipline are probably more difficult when people are in the midst of intense life changes (e.g. getting married, undergoing marital problems or having a baby). Although empirical support is not yet available, it follows logically that early family education programs, within the public schools and before participants have begun a family of their own, could go far in preventing family violence.

Pervasiveness of Violence in American Society

Violence, usually for socially desirable purposes, is woven into the fabric of American society. Socially legitimate violence includes physical punishment by teachers as well as parents, unnecessary use of force by the police, the death penalty, and the use of terrorism and military force against governments that are based on a different political philosophy. In addition to a high level of "legitimate violence," the United States has an extremely high rate of criminal violence such as assault and murder. The U.S. murder rate, for example, is 5 times greater than that of Canada, 8.8 times greater than that of Italy, and 13 times greater than that of England and Wales. Taken together, the high rates of legitimate violence and criminal violence make violence an everyday part of American life, as it has been since colonial times.

Violence permeates American society in more subtle ways as well. The frequency with which violent acts are portrayed on television and in the movies creates a social climate that views violence as a natural part of everyday life (Rothenberg, 1975). The fact that guns are present in at least half of all American homes undoubtedly contributes to another fact: the majority of family homicides involve the use of a gun (Godwin, 1978). The more insidious forms of institutional violence—manifested in the poverty, homelessness, and unemployment suffered by so many Americans—also contribute to the incidence of family violence in this society.

A critical point for prevention of family violence is the evidence that shows that violence in one sphere of life tends to spill over into other spheres of life. Baron and Straus, for example, created a measure of "legitimate violence" for each of the fifty states of the United States. They found that the higher the level of legitimate violence, the higher the rate of criminal violence, including rape and murder (Baron and Straus, 1988, 1989). Violence in the society at large is one of the factors producing intrafamily violence such as child abuse and wife beating.

Implications for prevention. Societal level prevention of family violence ultimately involves reduction of the violence that permeates our society. Primary prevention in this area would include enacting gun control legislation, regulating violence in the media, and abolishing institutional violence such as executions and armed intervention in the affairs of other nations.

Fortunately, it is not necessary to wait until the level of violence in the society declines. This is true because, as indicated above, intrafamily violence has many other causes. Significant reductions can be achieved by attending to those causes. Even more fortunate is the fact that the level of violence in a society is partly influenced by the level of violence within families. Consequently, steps to reduce intrafamily violence will ultimately help reduce the level of violence outside the family. This can create a feedback cycle that will further reduce intrafamily violence.

Theoretical Basis of the Primary Prevention Approach

The previous sections indicate that primary prevention of family violence is needed, not merely because of the sheer magnitude of the problem (and the accompanying lack of resources to treat all the families involved), but because characteristics *of society* put families at risk of violence. To the extent that this is correct, the solution must also be located in the same sphere as the cause—society. But as will be indicated below, that has not typically been the approach.

Medical Model of Child Abuse

When Kempe (1962) identified the "Battered Child Syndrome," he did so within the professional paradigm of medicine. From this perspective, the problem of child abuse was an *illness* located *within the individual*. Kempe's pioneering article on this aspect of family violence was an important step in garnering public attention to the problem of child abuse, which in turn prompted states to enact child abuse reporting laws (Nelson, 1984).

Public response was relatively swift, probably due in part to the way the problem was conceived. In locating the problem within the individual, the new legislation enabled the government to attempt to protect children in a way that offered no real threat to the social order. However, the conception of family violence as a problem of medical or psychological illness of the abusing parent limits response to the individual, treatment level. In so doing, the root causes of child abuse, such as the heavy reliance on physical punishment, were safely left unaddressed. Ironically, the campaign against child abuse may have reinforced the old system, because many of the new child abuse laws declared that the legislation does not deny the right of parents to use physical punishment. The new child abuse laws therefore had the effect of converting what was a common law right of parents into a statutory right.

Feminist Model of Wife Abuse

In sharp contrast to the response to child abuse, the problem of wife abuse came to public attention within a distinctly political context. In the first book published in the U.S. on the topic, feminist activist Del Martin (1976) clearly portrayed wife abuse as an outcome of the fundamental framework of American society—patriarchy. Of course, this perspective is more of a challenge to the prevailing family system (and to society) than Kempe's medical model of child abuse.

Probably due in part to its political tone, the call for protection for battered women was met with much greater skepticism and slower public response than the earlier issue of child abuse had received. There are no federal programs to deal with wife abuse, and state programs are minuscule compared to even the inadequately funded child abuse programs.

Government officials and the public at large preferred to think of wife abuse as a problem faced mainly by lower-class women at the hands of "sick" husbands (Pagelow, 1984:263). In keeping with the American ethic of individualism, this public conception of family violence again located the source of the problem within the individual. Thus remedial action was sought in the treatment of individual families, ignoring such risk factors as male dominance in the family, implicit cultural norms that permit family members to hit each other under certain circumstances, and the wide use of violence for socially legitimate purposes.

Summary

The vital importance of treating victims and perpetrators of family violence is not to be denied. Clearly, the personal safety of victims of family violence must be assured, through law enforcement intervention, battered women's shelters, child protective services, and other intervention strategies. Further, victims need and deserve help in dealing with the emotional trauma of the abuse; and perpetrators need help to learn to change their violent behaviors.

We as a society must also move beyond treating the wounded to preventing the conditions that bring about violence in so many American families. This involves changing features of American society, such as the five described in this chapter, that put people at high risk of family violence. Moreover, a prevention approach is both more humanitarian and more efficient. It is humanitarian because of the suffering of victims of violence that is avoided. It is efficient because (as shown in Chapters 9, 24, and 25) reduction in family violence is likely to make a major contribution to the amelioration of many other social and psychological problems. These include reduced rates of depression and suicide, and violent and anti-social behavior outside the family, such as homicide.

Putting the Pieces Together

Although the five causes of family violence that were selected for inclusion in this chapter are among the most important, each by itself accounts for no more than 5 to 10% of the variance. However, a wide range of risk factors have been identified, and a number of them have been confirmed across two or more studies (Hotaling and Sugarman, 1987). Thus there is a knowledge base that meets minimal scientific standards on which to build prevention work. The possibilities are illustrated by the 1975 national survey, which identified 25 risk factors for spouse abuse, including those described in this chapter (the complete list is in Straus, Gelles, and Steinmetz, 1980:203).

Figure 28.2 shows that with each additional risk factor, the probability of spouse abuse increased at an accelerating rate:

- Couples with none, one, or two of these risk factors have a near zero probability of violence during a one-year period. From there the chance

FIGURE 28.2
Couple Violence Rate by Checklist Score

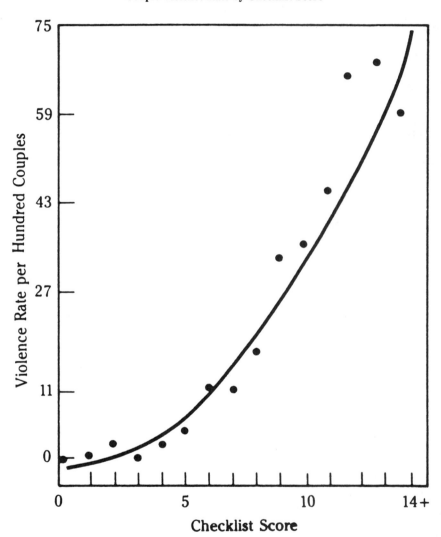

of a violent incident occurring gradually increases with each additional risk factor up to eight risk factors.

- Couples with six to eight of the risk factors have about one in ten chance of violence.
- The probability of violence then climbs precipitously with each additional risk factor until those with 12 or more have about a 2 out of 3 chance of experiencing violence during the year.

These findings are based on a large and nationally representative sample of American families, but they are retrospective rather than prospective. A prospective study is needed to determine whether the risk factors have temporal predictive validity. Even more crucial are intervention experiments focused on bringing about community change in one or more of the manipulable risk factors in the checklist. A high priority example would be programs to provide parents with alternatives to physical punishment. This topic is ignored or treated minimally in almost all American child rearing manuals, including those by Dr. Spock (Carson, 1987).

The use of correlational evidence as the basis for primary prevention programs would ordinarily call for extreme caution and skepticism. However, in this instance it would be a mistake to wait the many years before the results of prospective and experimental studies become available. This is true because the risk factors described in this chapter are aspects of the family and society that need to be changed even if they have no impact on intrafamily violence.[3] The same applies to a number of other risk factors, such as early marriage, unwanted children, lack of skills in child management, and the stress, anger, and frustration associated with racism, poverty, and unemployment. Moreover, Chapter 7 presents indirect evidence that changes in some of these aspects of the family and society have already contributed to a reduction in family violence. The decade from 1975 to 1985 was also a period characterized by campaigns to educate the public about child abuse and spouse abuse. In this context, it is probably no accident that we also found a significant reduction in both child abuse and spouse abuse over the course of that decade. Thus there are grounds for optimism that primary prevention can achieve a significant reduction in family violence.

Notes

1. Because the terms *violence* and *abuse* are used in so many ways in the literature, it is essential to clearly define those terms. In Chapters 1 and 3, we define violence as an act carried out with the *intention* of causing physical pain or injury to another person, deliberately leaving unspecified the amount of pain

actually inflicted or the legitimacy of the act. This definition was carefully chosen for reasons explained in those chapters.
2. Additional discussion of primary prevention of family violence can be found in Straus, Gelles, and Steinmetz (1980), Chapter 10; and Gelles and Straus (1988), Chapter 9.
3. In addition, a number of the interventions are consistent with the type of interventions suggested by studies of the etiology of criminal behavior in general. Although the book by Wilson and Herrnstein (1985) emphasizes the biological determinants of criminal behavior, most of the *interventions* that they suggest on the basis of an extremely comprehensive review of the research are similar to those mentioned in this paper: head start, more attention to public health, and reducing family violence, including removing children from violent families.

METHODOLOGICAL APPENDIXES

Appendix A.

Sample Design and Comparability of the Two National Surveys

Richard J. Gelles and Murray A. Straus

Sample and Administration of the 1975 Study

Data for the 1975 National Family Violence Survey were gathered via face-to-face interviews of a national probability sample of 2,143 currently married or cohabiting persons ages 18 through 70. Participating households were drawn from a sample of interviewing locations that had been stratified by geographic region, type of community, and other population characteristics. The sampling design and interviewing for this study was carried out for us by Response Analysis Corporation of Princeton, New Jersey. The sequence of steps used in sample selection included:

Selection of a national sample of 103 primary areas (counties or groups of counties) stratified by geographic region, type of community, and other population characteristics.

Selection of three hundred interviewing locations or secondary areas (census enumeration districts or block groups) from the national sample for use in this study.

Field counts by trained interviewers to divide interviewing locations into sample segments of 10 to 25 housing units.

Selection of specific sample segments in each interviewing location for field administration of the survey.

Random selection of the eligible person to be interviewed using a specific scheme assigned for each sample household.

More detailed information on each of these steps is available in the methodological report prepared by Response Analysis Corporation (Weisbrod, 1976). This will be supplied at cost (write to Response Analysis Corporation, Research Park, Route 206, Princeton, NJ 08540). The data tape and code for the 1975 survey are available from the Inter-University Consortium for Political and Social Research, University of Michigan, as ICPSR study number 7733.

A random half of the respondents were women and the other half men. If the household included a child or children between the ages of 3 and 17 years of age, a "referent child" was selected using a random procedure. The restriction to children 3 through 17 was made because one aim of the study was to obtain meaningful data on sibling violence and we erroneously believed that the data on younger children would not be meaningful for this purpose. Interviews lasted approximately one hour. The completion rate of the entire sample was 65%.

The 1985 National Family Violence Resurvey

Data for the 1985 Resurvey were obtained by telephone interviews of a national probability sample of 4,032 U.S. households conducted for us by Louis Harris and Associates. Telephone numbers were selected using random digit dialing, which stratifies the United States into four regions (East, South, Midwest, and West) and three community types (urban areas with populations greater than one hundred thousand, suburban areas with populations of less than one hundred thousand, and rural areas with populations of less than twenty-five hundred). This cross-sectional national sample was augmented by three oversamples. First, 958 households were randomly selected from 25 states in order to assure that the total sample would include at least 100 completed interviews per state from 36 of the 50 states. Second, over-samples of 508 Black and 516 Hispanic households were also added to the total sample to assure enough Black and Hispanic families to provide reliable data on these two groups. The data from this total sample of 6,002 households were then weighted to adjust for the state, Black, and Hispanic over-samples, thus making the total weighted sample representative of the U.S. population. However, comparisons with the 1975 study use only the unweighted national sample and only the comparable age and marital status parts of that sample.

To be eligible for inclusion, a household had to include two adults, a male and female 18 years of age or older who were (1) presently married, or (2) presently living as a male-female couple. Also eligible for inclusion were households with one adult 18 years of age or older who was either (3) divorced or separated within the last two years or (4) a single parent living with a child under the age of 18. When more than one eligible adult was in the household, a random procedure was used to select the gender and marital status of the respondent. When more than one child under the age of 18 was in the household, a random procedure was used to select the "referent child" as the focus of the parent-to-child violence questions. Interviews lasted an average of 35 minutes. The response rate, calculated as "completes as a proportion of eligibles," was 84%. A detailed report on the methodology of the study is available from the authors for the cost of reproduction (five dollars as of this writing). The data tape and codebook are available from the Inter-University Consortium for Political and Social Research at the University of Michigan.

Methodological Differences between the Two Surveys

Data collection for the two surveys differ in two important respects. First, data for the 1975 survey were collected by in-person interview, while the 1985 survey was conducted over the telephone. Research has shown no major differences between results from telephone and face-to-face interviews (Groves and Kahn, 1979; Marcus and Crane, 1986), and the telephone is now the most widely used method of interviewing. The telephone survey offers a greater sense of anonymity for the respondent, and trained telephone interviewers have been able to increase response rate by converting many would-be refusals into completed interviews. The 1985 survey had an 85% completion rate, compared to the 65% completion rate of the 1975–1976 survey. The second major difference in the data collection methods of the two surveys is that the 1975 survey was limited to married and cohabiting couples, while the 1985 survey also included recently separated or divorced individuals and/or single parents. This inclusion, combined with the higher completion rate, presumably means that the 1985 survey is a more representative sample of the U.S. and the anonymity of the telephone interviews may have led to more truthful responses to sensitive questions.

Another methodological difference is that in the 1975–1976 survey, respondents were handed a card listing the response categories for the Conflict Tactics Scales (CTS). All possible answers, including "never," were on the card. For the 1985 telephone interviews, interviewers read the response categories, beginning with "once" and continuing to "more than 20 times." Respondents had to volunteer "never" or "don't know" responses. Experience has shown that rates of reported sensitive or deviant behavior are higher if the subject has to volunteer the "no" or "never" response (see for example Kinsey *et al.*, 1948).

Strengths and Limitations of the Two Surveys

While questionnaires and interviews allow us to obtain data rapidly from a large number of people, the amount of information obtainable is small compared to data derived from clinical studies of intimate violence. Our 1976 survey lasted sixty minutes (which is probably maximum length of time for a structured in-person interview), and we were able to ask about two hundred questions. Our 1985 telephone survey included about 125 questions and lasted, on the average, 35 minutes (the outer limit of time one can expect to keep a respondent on the telephone).

Large national surveys allow one to develop a portrait of behavior that can be generalized to families throughout the United States. But such a portrait is little more than a snapshot of families at a particular point in time. Obtaining more data requires additional interview sessions, which raises the cost of such research into the millions of dollars.

A second limitation of this research is that we learn only what people are willing to reveal. Survey research provides information on what people say about their behavior. The most bizarre and humiliating events experienced by the most victimized individuals are typically not accessible in surveys. For this type of information, clinical studies or in-depth interviews with a limited number of individuals offer the most detailed and useful data.

Finally, there are biases of inclusion and exclusion in surveys. In the 1975 survey, our face-to-face interviewers had the most difficulty conducting interviews in dangerous as well as in the most affluent neighborhoods. The 1985 telephone survey fails to include transients and all those without telephones. Fortunately, there is no evidence that the 1985 survey is more or less biased in this respect than the 1975 survey.

Ninety-three percent of the households in the United States have telephones. Thus a telephone survey will theoretically cover a less representative sample than an in-person survey. Since homes without telephones are more likely to be low income or minority households, telephone sampling is systematically biased.

However, this problem also applies to in-person interviews. Anyone who has attempted to interview low income inner city residents knows that the completion rate for face-to-face interviews is low. Our colleagues at survey research organizations inform us that for all intents and purposes, sampling coverage is the same with in-person and telephone interviewing. This occurs because in-person interviewers are frequently unable (or unwilling—see Roth, 1966) to secure complete interviews from the lower income and minority households that do not have telephones. Thus, there is little practical evidence that the sampling frames in the two surveys were different. The category of households excluded from the second survey were in all likelihood not reached in the first survey either—even though they were theoretically available in the sampling frame.

Direct evidence of equality of coverage in the two surveys is presented in Table A.1. The first two rows show a high degree of consistency between the two surveys. Both produced samples with almost the same average age of respondent and average length of marriage. The unemployment rate for men in the 1985 study, however, was lower than in 1975. Rather than being evidence of sampling bias, the lower rate is consistent with the lower actual national unemployment rate in 1985. It is also consistent with the section of Chapter 7 which suggested that a reduced level of unemployment was one of the reasons for the decrease in the rates of family violence.

TABLE A.1

Socioeconomic Characteristics of 1975 and 1985 Samples

| | | Study | |
Characteristic	Measure	1975	1985
Age of respondent	Mean	41.4	42.0
Race			
Black	Percent	7.1	7.2
Hispanic	Percent	3.2	4.7
Years married or together	Mean	17.5	17.8
Husband unemployed	Percent	4.8	3.0
Education[a]			
Husband	Mean	4.7	4.7
Wife	Mean	4.4	4.5

[a]Scale ranges from 0 (no formal schooling) to 8 (advanced degree).

The row showing the average education indicates little difference in the educational level of the two samples. The racial composition of the sample shows changes that are consistent with the growth of the Black and Hispanic populations during this decade. Taken as a whole, the findings in Table A.1 are consistent with the methodological research on telephone versus in-person interviews in showing no important difference (see references in Chapter 7 and Groves and Kahn, 1979; Marcus and Crane, 1986; and Smith, 1986).

Appendix B

New Scoring Methods for Violence and New Norms for the Conflict Tactics Scales

Murray A. Straus

In the ten years between the writing of Chapter 3 and the writing of this appendix, a great deal has been learned about the psychometric characteristics of the CTS and about the limitations of the original methods of scoring the violence items of the CTS. In response to these limitations, alternative methods of using the violence items to create measures of intrafamily violence were developed. The first part of this appendix describes the different versions of the CTS and gives the rationale for these new measures and also scoring instructions.

Within that same time span, a second and much larger nationally representative sample of families was tested. These new data make possible more current and more reliable norms. The last section of this appendix therefore provides new normative data and also presents this data in a form that better fits the needs of both researchers and clinicians than the norms in Chapter 3.

Forms A, N, and R

The three versions of the CTS, Forms A, N, and R, are fundamentally the same, but differ in respect to the number of items for each scale and the response categories presented to the subjects. Form A was administered as a written questionnaire, Form R as an in-person interview, and Form N as part of a telephone interview. However, any of these forms can be administered by using any of these three methods.

Form A.   The first version of the CTS was administered in questionnaire format to college student subjects (this version was sometimes referred to as form S). The subjects were asked to respond by indicating what happened in their family of orientation during the last year they lived at home. In most cases this was when they were seniors in high school (Straus, 1973, 1974). This version of the CTS was also used for the validity study in which the responses of students concerning the conflict tactics used by their parents and the response of the parents themselves were compared. The results are summarized in Chapter 3 and presented in detail in Bulcroft and Straus (1975).

Form N.   Form N was developed for use in the 1975–1976 National Family Violence Survey, as reported in the book *Behind Closed Doors: Violence in the American Family* (Straus, Gelles, and Steinmetz, 1980) and in many of the chapters in this book. Form N differs from Form A in having additional violence items and fewer reasoning items, and the response categories were expanded from 0 to 5 to 0 to 6.

Form R.   Form R is the version used in the 1985 National Family Violence Resurvey, as reported in the book *Intimate Violence* (Gelles and Straus, 1988), in several chapters in this book, and in the panel study that reinterviewed a subsample in 1986 and 1987. The difference between Forms N and R is that Form R has an additional parent-child item, "Burned or scalded him/her," inserted after "Beat him/her up," and an additional spouse item, "Choked him/her/you," inserted after "Beat him/her/you up." In addition, with Form R the interviewer read the response categories, starting with "once" and continuing to "more than 20 times." Using this format, respondents must volunteer "never" or "don't know." This change was made because it tends to increase the rate of reporting sensitive or deviant behavior (see for example Kinsey, Pomeroy, and Martin, 1948).

Role Relationships Measured by the CTS

Form R as reprinted in Chapter 3 shows the headings for conflict tactics used in the husband-to-wife and wife-to-husband role relationships. Other role relationships were measured by substituting different headings and introductory statements, as follows:

To measure *parent-to-child* tactics, the following wording was used:

> Parents and children use many different ways of trying to settle differences between them. I'm going to read a list of some things that you and your spouse/ partner might have done *when you had a problem with this child.* I would like

you to tell me how often you did it with (him/her) in the last year. READ CATEGORIES

To measure tactics used in the *child-to-child* relationship, the 1975 survey asked:

> In some families where there are children, they always seem to be having spats, fights, disagreements, or whatever you want to call them; and they use many different ways of trying to settle differences between themselves. I'm going to read you a list of some things that (REFERENT CHILD) might have done when (he/she) had a disagreement with the other (child/children) in the family. For each one, I would like to know how often (REFERENT CHILD) did it in the past year.

To measure *child-to-parent* tactics, the 1975 survey first asked about parent-to-child tactics and then:

> Now, let's talk about (child's name). Tell me how often in the past year when you had a disagreement (he/she):

Student Questionnaire (Form A)

The original version of the CTS (Form A) was administered to college students who described the tactics they and their siblings used with each other and the tactics used by the parents with each other and with them.

To measure *child-to-child* tactics, there were two columns of response numbers, one headed "The brother or sister in Question 27" (which identified the sibling closest in age) and a column headed "Me." The introductory wording was

> Here is a list of things that you and the brother or sister named in Question 27 might have done when you had a conflict. Now, taking all disagreements into account [a preceding question asked what the worst conflicts were], we would like you to say how often you had done the things listed below during your last year in high school. Answer by circling one of the numbers for the brother or sister and one for yourself.

To measure *parent-to-child* and *child-to-parent* tactics in the student study, there were four columns headed Father, Me, Mother, Me. The introductory wording was

> Here is the same list of things that you and your father and mother might have done when you had a conflict. Now, taking into account *all* disagreements (not just the most serious one), we would like you to say how often you had done the

things listed at any time during your last year in high school. Answer by circling one of these numbers for each person.

Finally, to measure conflict tactics in *spouse roles,* the student question-naire contained columns headed Father and Mother, preceded by the following:

> Finally, we have the same list of things your father and mother might have done when they had a conflict. Now, taking *all* disagreements into account (not just the most serious one), how often did they do the things listed at any time during your last year in high school?

Terminology

The three basic summative scales (for Reasoning, Verbal Aggression, and Violence) are described in Chapter 3. This appendix focuses on the additional ways to measure violence, including more sophisticated sum-mative scales, rates, and typologies. Before describing each of these, the terminology to be used needs to be defined.

Indexes

For purposes of this appendix, the term *index* is a general term that is used to refer to a variable created by combining two or more of the "items" ("indicators") in the CTS. The index can be in the form of a summative scale, a Guttman Scale, a rate, or a typology. There are summative scale indexes to measure Reasoning, Verbal Aggression, and Physical Aggression or Violence.

Scales Versus Rates

The Violence indexes can be expressed as either scales or rates. The difference between the CTS Violence scales and CTS Violence rates is that the *scales* are continuous variables and the *rates* are binary variables, usually coded 0 versus 1. Thus an ANOVA using the *scale* version of the Husband-to-Wife Violence index will give the mean number of assaults that occurred during the year. If the analysis is repeated using logistic regression and the *rate* version of the Husband-to-Wife Violence index, the results will show the predicted proportion of couples who experienced one or more violent incidents during the year.

Types of Scales

Several different methods have been used to compute Violence Index scales, including scales weighted by the frequency of occurrence of each violent act in the index, scales weighted by the product of the frequency times a weight for the severity (injury producing potential) of each violent act, and Guttman scales.

The original CTS indexes described in Chapter 3 are frequency-weighted scales because each consists of the sum of the number of times each act occurred. Thus if a respondent indicated that pushing or shoving occurred once, throwing things occurred four times, and slapping occurred once, the scale on Overall Violence index scale would be six.

Violence Types

Several different typologies have been developed to classify families according to the severity of the violence and according to which member of the couple engaged in assaults against the other.

New Violence Measures

Chapter 3 provides the conceptual and theoretical rationale for the CTS and information on how to score the items dealing with physical violence to obtain an "Overall Violence index." It also suggests but does not detail methods of creating what we have come to call "Severe Violence" indexes, which can be used to measure the occurrence of child abuse and wife beating.

Most of the analyses in this book and most research by others using the CTS make use of the Overall Violence and Severe Violence indexes, either in the form of a frequency weighted scale or (more usually) in the form of a rate (see above for the difference between the terms *scale* and *rate* for purposes of this appendix). However, as noted in Chapter 4, reliance on these two indexes has certain drawbacks. They do not fully reflect the differences in severity of violence inherent in the hierarchical structure of the violent acts. Moreover, the somewhat arbitrary distinction between "minor" and "severe" violence can, under some circumstances, distort the data. In addition, measuring the assaultive behavior of one person in the family, without taking into account whether that person was also victimized, may also be misleading. For these and other reasons, additional methods of scoring the CTS violence items were developed. These additional measures may be more appropriate for certain purposes. This section describes the rationale and scoring method for several of these alternative violence measures.

Rates

An annual incidence rate has the advantages of unambiguous meaning and ease of understanding by the general public. In addition, since incidence rates are so frequently used in criminology and epidemiology, expressing family violence as incidence rates permits comparisons with other related phenomena. For this reason almost all the statistics we report are in the form of rates.

There are also certain statistical advantages to using rates rather than scales. This is true because the distribution of the violence scores is extremely skewed (85 versus 16% at best for spouses). This causes problems when violence is used as the dependent variable. The skewed distribution problem becomes even worse if the measure is in the form of a *score* that indicates how much violence occurs, i.e., if the violent 15% of the distribution is further extended by weighting those cases according to how often the violence occurred. Regression parameters can be seriously distorted by such a skewed distribution. Ironically, the situation is improved slightly if the score is transformed into a *rate* by dichotomizing it into 1 = any violence of the type measured (e.g., parent-child, husband-wife, minor, severe, etc.) versus 0 = no violence.[1]

Because rates do not exacerbate the skewness problem and also because rates are a statistic that more people can understand, they are used in most analyses of the CTS Violence indexes. There are circumstances where use of the continuous CTS scores may be preferable, however.

To transform a Violence index scale into a rate, it is only necessary to dichotomize the violence items or any of the Violence indexes as 0 versus 1. Users of SPSS can do this with a simple recode command, for example to record the eight CTS violence items (items k through s):

RECODE   Q78K TO Q78S (1 thru 6 = 1)

Chronicity

In one situation in which scale scores rather than rates are needed is when the analysis focuses on a group of persons who are known to have been violent. The issue in this instance is not whether there is violence, but how much violence has occurred. The "how much" issue is relevant to clinical samples such as abusive family members in treatment programs and also to analyses of violent groups identified by the CTS itself (as in Chapter 8). Both of these are examples of populations where the issue is not *whether* but *how often* a family member has been assaulted. Norms for chronicity are given in Tables B.4 through B.7.

Minor and Severe Violence Scales and Rates

It is often important to distinguish between assaults that are "minor" (in the sense that they are less dangerous and less the focus of moral condemnation) and "severe" violence, which are acts that have a greater likelihood of causing an injury and which make up what the public thinks of as "child abuse" and "wife beating."

Severe violence.   The severe violence scales are computed by summing items N through R in Form N and N through S in Form R. If the items are first recoded from the 0 to 6 format to the midpoints of the approximate frequency designated by each response category (0, 1, 2, 4, 8, 15, and 25), the resulting scale scores will be a measure of the number of assaults that occurred. The following SPSS commands can be used to create the Severe Violence scale:

```
COMPUTE   SEVERV = ITEMN + ITEMO + ITEMP +ITEMQ +
          ITEMR + ITEMS
```

The rate version of this index (see above for the way in which the term rate is used here) can be created with the following SPSS commands:

```
COMPUTE   SEVEREVR = SEVEREV
RECODE    SEVEREVR (1 THRU HI = 1)
```

Very severe violence.   When the CTS is used to measure physical abuse of children older than infants, there is widespread reluctance to including hitting a child with an object (such as a hairbrush or belt) as necessarily abusive. To meet this criticism, we developed a measure of physical abuse for children, the Very Severe Violence index, which omits item O (hit with something) and is therefore restricted to items N, P. Q, R, and S, all of which are almost universally accepted as "abusive" acts. This measure and the rationale behind it are described in more detail in Chapter 7.

Minor violence.   For some purposes it may also be desirable to have a separate measure of "minor violence" that measures how often assaults of this type occurred (see for example Chapters 7, 9, 10, 13, 19, and 21). Since the minor violence acts are items K, L, and M, the following SPSS commands can be used to compute this scale:

```
COMPUTE   MINORV = ITEMK + ITEML = ITEMM
```

The rate version of this index (see above for the way in which the term *rate* is used here) can be created with the following SPSS commands:

```
COMPUTE   MINORVR = MINORV
RECODE    MINORVR (1 THRU HI = 1)
```

A difficulty with this measure of minor violence is that, since most persons who have committed severe assaults also engaged in minor violence, this measure mixes people who have committed only minor violence with those who have also severely assaulted. At first glance one might think that this problem can be avoided by a "conditional transformation," i.e., one that computes the Minor Violence index only if the scale on the Severe Violence index is zero. However, this is not satisfactory because it does not deal with the cases where there was both severe and minor violence. If they are scored as zero on minor violence, this is misleading in the extreme, since they would be mixed in with those who had used no violence. If they are assigned the "missing value" code, then these critically important cases are lost from the analysis. One solution is to create a typology or nominal variable to identify the "level" of violence, as explained below in the section on violence types.

Wife beating.   Users of the severe or very severe violence rates as measures of "wife beating" must be alert to the fact that these rates reflect *one or more* violent incidents, while the public's perception of wife beating tends to entail *repeated* severe beatings. Indeed, as noted in the section on clinically meaningful populations in Chapter 5, victims seeking help from battered women's shelters incur many more beatings on average than those from community samples.

Severity Weighted Scale

The Overall Violence index, the Severe Violence index, and the Minor Violence index reflect differences in how often (1) *any* acts of violence, (2) *severe* acts of violence, or (3) acts of *minor* violence occurred. One then has to choose between these three indexes. If it is desirable to take into account different degrees of severity of violence as well as the frequency of violence, two sets of statistics must be computed and presented. A less cumbersome method of taking into account both the severity and the frequency of violence is possible with a "Severity Weighted scale." This multiplies the frequency of each violent act by the following weights (chosen on the basis of consultation with colleagues concerning the injury producing potential of each act): Items K, L, and M (the minor violence acts) are unweighted, i.e., they have a weight of 1. The weights for the other items are: kick, bit, punch = 2; hit with object = 3; beat up, choked, burned, scalded = 5; threatened with a knife or gun = 6, used knife or gun = 8. The response categories must first be recoded from the codes of 1 through 6 (Form N) or 0 through 5 (Form R) to the approximate midpoints of these categories: 0, 1, 2, 4, 8, 15, and 25.

Although the Severity Weighted scale results in a continuous variable, it has the same problems with extreme skewness as the other violence scales. The skewness problem is actually worsened because the severity weighting creates even more extreme outliers than occur when the items are weighted only by their frequency of occurrence. Consequently, as with the frequency weighted scales, the severity weighted index should not be used with statistical techniques (such as ordinary least square regression) that assume at least a moderately normal distribution. However, the severity weighted scores can be used in several ways. First, non-parametric regression techniques, such as TOBIT, can be used. Second, the severity weighted scale values can be used to divide the sample into nominal categories for use in cross-tabular analysis, discriminant analysis, or ANOVA. Third, the severity weighted scores can be a useful indicator of *how much* violence occurred within a group known to be violent. This can be either a treatment group or the part of a community sample in which at least some violence occurred. Tables B.4 through B.7 provide normative data for evaluating the Severity Weighted Scale scores in this way.

Wife beating.   The problem of terminology and norms is even greater for violence between spouses than for violence by parents. Although occasionally slapping a child is not usually considered abuse (or even "violence"), the same act is typically considered to be violent if done to a spouse. Thus since any assault on a spouse tends to be considered as abusive, in the case of violence between spouses, the "Overall Violence" index is important. This is in contrast to the situation for parent-to-child violence, where (as noted in Chapter 4) the Overall Violence index is not a meaningful measure because the acts of minor violence included in the Overall Violence index are common occurrences and rarely considered to be abusive.

Although I consider any hitting of a spouse, including "only" slapping or throwing something at wife, to be abusive, such acts of minor violence are not "wife beating" as the public understands that term. For the public at large, wife-beating means *severe* assaults and probably also *repeated* severe assaults. Violence of less severity or less frequency may be considered abusive, but the public does not think of it as "wife beating." Consequently, if the purpose at hand requires a measure that approximates the public conception of wife beating, the Severe Violence index should be used. If one wants to measure the level of violence that approximates the level that tends to prevail among women who seek refuge in a "safe house" for battered women, then Chapter 5 suggests that it is also necessary to require that such acts have occurred repeatedly, for example, four or more times during the past year.

Guttman Scales

The CTS items were selected and arranged in what was believed to be a hierarchical ordering. The main reason for this sequence was to increase the willingness of respondents to report acts of violence. The hierarchial sequence may reduce the refusal rate because it takes into account the covert norms regarding the use of physical violence in the family. These norms justify violence if the parent or spouse has "tried everything"—reasoned, pleaded, gotten help, gotten angry—and, despite this, the conflict is still not resolved. This sequence is also what is required to make it possible to compute Guttman scales for violence.

To the extent that the items form a perfect hierarchy, Guttman scale versions of the Violence indexes have the advantage of producing scales that indicate the specific degree of severity of the violence used. For example, a score of three means that the respondent used the three least severe acts but *not* any of the five more severe acts of violence included in the CTS. By contrast, an Overall Violence index score of three can result from engaging in any one of the violent acts three times, from any three of them once, etc. Guttman scales avoid this problem, but at the price of having to dichotomize each item, i.e., of ignoring how often each act of violence occurred.

When computing the Guttman scales for violence, the "division point" for all items is 0 versus 1 or more occurrences of the act. However, since the marginals are so skewed for the most extreme items (beating up, threatening with a knife or gun, using a knife or gun), Straus (1980c) found that these items must be combined. This produces a composite item in which 0 is scored if the respondent did none of these and 1 is scored if any one or more of them were done. In SPSS this can be done using: COUNT Q78PQR = Q78P, Q78Q, Q78R (1).

Highest of Either

Szinovacz (1983) administered the CTS to both partners and found that when the Violence index is based on events reported by either spouse, the rate is about 50% higher than the rate based on the report of only one spouse. This suggests that where data from both partners are available, the most complete measurement will be obtained by using the response of the spouse who reports the most violence on the grounds that the spouse reporting less violence has forgotten or is concealing violent incidents.

Ever Rates and Scales

Rates. The CTS items in Forms N and R are followed by a question for each item that asks whether that act had ever occurred. This supplemental question is asked only for those who indicated that the act did not occur during the one-year referent period. By combining the main item and the "ever" question, one can determine a prevalence rate over the course of a marriage or since the birth of a child. However, these rates must be used with considerable caution, because recall errors are almost certain to be large.

Scale.   It is also possible to create a continuous scale, starting with 0 for no violence ever, 1 for no violence in the referent year of the study but violence occurred at some point prior to that, and then scores of 2, 3, 4, etc., for varying amounts of violence during the referent year. However, as noted in the earlier section on rates, the distribution of violence is skewed so extremely that it is probably best to recode this scale into a trichotomy by recoding scores of 2 or more into two or three nominal categories.

Violence Types

Violence level.   If, as will often be the case, the objective is to identify people who used *only* minor violence, a typology rather than an index must be constructed. This is necessary because, as explained above, most people who severely assault also engage in minor violence. One method is to create a three-category typology: the non-violent, those who used only minor violence, and those who severely assaulted.[2] This type of variable can be computed for child-to-child, parent-to-child, child-to-parent, husband-to-wife, and wife-to-husband violence. The percentage distributions of the latter two are given in Chapter 9, Table 2.

Since the procedure to create these types is not entirely obvious, the SPSS commands used to create them for the National Family Violence Resurvey are given below. The first three commands are to create the type we labeled as "Husband Violence Level" and for which the SPSS variable name XC12L was used; the second three are for "Wife Violence Level" (XC15L), followed by "Couple Violence Level" (XC21L), and "Parental Violence Level" (XC6L). In the case of the Parent Violence Level, the Severe Violence category is divided into "Severe" and "Very Severe" (for reasons explained in Chapters 6 and 8).

```
IF (XC12W EQ 0) XC12L = 0
IF (XC12N GE 1 AND XC12WS EQ 0) XC12L = 1
IF (XC12WS GE 1) XC12L = 2
VARIABLE LABELS   XC11L 'HUSBAND VIOLENCE LEVEL'

IF (XC15W EQ 0) XC15L = 0
IF (XC15N GE 1 AND XC15WS EQ 0) XC15L = 1
```

```
IF (XC15WS GE 1) XC15L = 2
VARIABLE LABELS   XC15L 'WIFE VIOLENCE LEVEL'

IF (XC21W EQ 0) XC21L = 0
IF(XC21N GE 1 AND XC21WS EQ 0) XC21L = 1
IF (XC21WS GE 1) XC21L = 2
VARIABLE LABELS   XC21L 'COUPLE VIOLENCE LEVEL'

IF   (XC6W EQ 0) XC6L = 0
IF   (XC6N GE 1 AND XC6WS EQ 0 AND XC6AB EQ 0) XC6L = 1
IF   (XC6WS GE 1 AND XC6AB EQ 0) XC6L = 2
IF   (XC6AB GE 1) XC6L = 3
VARIABLE LABELS   XC6L 'PARENT VIOLENCE LEVEL'

RECODE XC12L TO XC6L (SYSMIS = -999)
MISSING VALUES XC121 TO XC6L (-999)
```

Couple violence types. The label "Couple Violence" applied to the CTS scales, rates, and types described up to this point is somewhat misleading. A more accurate label would be Couple Violence *Sum* because these variables are created by adding the score for husband-to-wife violence to the score for wife-to-husband violence. The misleading aspect occurs because a score of 6 can occur when the husband has a score of 3 and the wife a score of 3, when the husband has a score of 6 and the wife a score of zero, and when the husband has a score of zero and the wife a score of 6. In the second and third of these possibilities, only one person is violent, not both members of the couple as implied by the term *couple violence*. This is not to say that the couple violence sums are invalid measures. They are valid when one wants to know the total amount of violence that occurred, regardless of the identity of the perpetrator or victim. But when the issue is whether one or the other or both are violent, then the Couple Violence Types (CPLV) described in this section and in Chapter 13, Tables 1 and 2) are more appropriate.

To create the CPLV, let us assume that XC12HR is the Overall Violence Index of the husband, and that a score of 0 is assigned to non-violent husbands and a score of 1 is assigned to husbands who carried out one or more assaults on the wife. The variable XC15WR gives the same information for wife-to-husband violence.

```
IF (XC12WR EQ 0 AND XC15WR EQ 0) CPLV = 0
IF (XC12WR EQ 0 AND XC15WR EQ 1) CPLV = 1
IF (XC12WR EQ 1 AND XC15WR EQ 0) CPLV = 2
IF (XC12WR EQ 1 AND XC15WR EQ 1) CPLV = 3
```

VALUE LABELS CPLV 0 'NEITHER SPOUSE VIOLENT'
                1 'WIFE ONLY VIOLENT'
                2 'HUSBAND ONLY VIOLENT'
                3 'HUSB AND WIFE VIOLENT

The Couple Violence types described above do not distinguish between minor and severe violence. Consequently, type 3 (both violent) does not identify couples where one partner uses minor violence and the other engages in more severe assaults, as was done in chapter 9. The typology used for that analysis used another computed variable called "Couple Violence 2" (CPLV2), created using the "Violence Level" variables (XC12L and XC15L) described in a previous section.

IF (XC12L EQ 0 AND XC15L EQ 0) CPLV2 = 0
IF (XC12L EQ 1 AND XC15L EQ 0) CPLV2 = 1
IF (XC12L EQ 0 AND XC15L EQ 1) CPLV2 = 2
IF (XC12L EQ 1 AND XC15L EQ 1) CPLV2 = 3
IF (XC12L EQ 2 AND XC15L EQ 0) CPLV2 = 4
IF (XC12L EQ 0 AND XC15L EQ 2) CPLV2 = 5
IF (XC12L EQ 2 AND XC15L EQ 1) CPLV2 = 6
IF (XC12L EQ 1 AND XC15L EQ 2) CPLV2 = 7
IF (XC12L EQ 2 AND XC15L EQ 2) CPLV2 = 8

VARIABLE LABELS   CPLV2 'COUPLE VIOLENCE TYPES 2'
VALUE LABELS CPLV2 0 'NEITHER VIOLENT'
                1 'H-MINOR, W-NONE'
                2 'H-NONE, W-MINOR'
                3 'BOTH MINOR'
                4 'H-SEVERE, W-NONE'
                5 'H-NONE, W-SEVERE'
                6 'H-SEVERE, W-MINOR'
                7 'H-MINOR, W-SEVERE'
                8 'BOTH SEVERE'

Steinmetz types. Suzanne Steinmetz (1977) developed a typology based on a cross-classification of the Verbal and Physical Aggression indexes. This typology includes four types of problem solving: 1) the pacifists, who had not used either verbal or physical aggression; 2) the threateners, who had used verbal but not physical aggression; 3) the silent attackers, who were not verbally aggressive but had used physical aggression; and 4) the screaming sluggers, those who used both verbal and physical aggression. This typology has the advantage of permitting investigation of the interaction of these two forms of conflict tactics.

Which Violence Measure?

This appendix adds several new methods of indexing violence to the methods originally described. Which method to use depends mainly on the theoretical purpose and intended readership and only secondarily—because of the "robustness" of composite indexes (Straus and Kumagai, 1980)—on statistical criteria.

A Guttman scale would be the choice only if the hierarchy of acts is central to the issue being investigated (as in Straus, 1980c). This is because Guttman scales are, in other respects, typically less adequate instruments than ordinary linear additive indexes (Straus and Kumagai, 1980). Moreover, since the Guttman scales for violence, like almost all Guttman scales, have less than perfect coefficients of reproducibility, even the theoretical advantage of scores with a precise hierarchical meaning is only partly attained.

Scales. The Minor Violence scale is obviously appropriate in research that focuses on the "ordinary" violence in American families and the Severe Violence scale for research on "child abuse" or "spouse abuse." The Severity Weighted index is the most comprehensive because it takes into account both the frequency and the severity of violence. However, as explained above, this advantage creates a statistical difficulty because it exacerbates the problem of skewness and outliers. Consequently, the most appropriate use of the Severity Weighted Violence Index is probably to differentiate severity of violence within a violent group.

Rates and types. Expressing intrafamily violence in the form of a rate or a percentage who fall into each type has a number of advantages that make it the preferred measure in most instances. First, percentages and rates are the most widely understood method of presenting statistics, and this is important to the extent that the intended readership is not statistically oriented. Second, an annual incidence rate allows for comparison with annual incidence rates from other data sources and with rates for other behaviors (especially crime and mental illness). Finally, the Couple Violence Types allow for a key aspects of the context to be built into the measure of violence, specifically whether one or both are violent. The disadvantage of rates and of the first of the couple violence types is that they do not measure the frequency of violence within a given family. However, when this is desired, it can be done by applying the violence scales to those cases in which one of more acts of violence have occurred (see Chapter 8 for an example).

Recoding Respondent-Spouse Items into Husband-Wife Format

This transformation is needed if only one member of a couple is interviewed and is asked to respond to each CTS item twice: once for what the respondent did and then for what the spouse did. Unless this is done, SELECT IF specifications must be included as part of the commands for each statistical analysis. To avoid this the respondent/spouse items can be transformed into husband/wife items, as illustrated below. In this example:

Q35A TO Q35S are the CTS items for the respondent
Q36A to Q36S are the CTS items for the spouse
SEXR = 1 for male respondents, SEXR = 2 for female respondents

Only the SPSS commands to transform Q35A and Q36A into CTAH and CTAW are shown since the identical procedures are used to transform Q35B and Q36B into CTBH and CTBW, to transform Q35C and Q36C into CTDH and CTDW, etc.

```
IF   (SEXR EQ 1) CTAH = Q35A
IF   (SEXR EQ 1) CTAW = Q36A
IF   (SEXR EQ 2) CTAH = Q36A
IF   (SEXR EQ 2) CTAW = Q35A
VAR LABELS   CTAH 'CTS ITEM A: DISCUSSED ISSUE—HUS-
             BAND'
             /CTAW 'CTS ITEM A: DISCUSSED ISSUE—
             WIFE'
```

Norms

The norms presented in this section differ from those in Chapter 3 in several ways.

New Normative Sample

First and most obviously, the norms presented below are based on a sample interviewed in 1985 rather than 1975–1976. Up-to-date norms are important because of the changes that are occurring in the incidence of child abuse and wife beating shown in Chapter 7. In addition, the 1985 sample of 6,002 families is almost three times larger than the 1975 sample. Finally, in contrast to the 1975 sample, the 1985 sample includes children under three and single parent families.

Improved Method of Presentation

The original normative table for the Violence index was not as useful as it could be because it combined in a single percentile distribution whether violence occurred at all and how often it occurred. The problem with that method of norming the scales is that the distribution is so highly skewed that variation within the violent group is obscured. In the present version, this is replaced by two tables: one giving the violence rate per one thousand and the other giving percentiles for chronicity occurrence.

The violence *rate* can be used to compare the rate for a particular study population (for example, a particular community or occupational group) with the national rate. It is therefore primarily useful for epidemiological or sociological research.

The *percentiles,* on the other hand, are particularly useful with a clinical sample of either victims or offenders. Since, by definition, all have experienced violence, the issue is how does the amount of violence experienced by a given person or clinical group compare with the national norms for violent (but mostly not in-treatment) couples?

New Violence Indexes and Typologies

Since Chapter 3 was written in 1978, the importance of differentiating various aspects of intrafamily violence has become more apparent. Consequently, rather than presenting only norms for whether any assaults took place and how many such incidents occurred, separate norms are now presented for "Minor Violence" (pushed, grabbed, shoved, threw objects at other, slapped or spanked), "Severe Violence" (kicked, bit, punched, hit with object, choked, beat up, burned or scalded (in parent-to-child version), choked (in spouse versions), threatened with a knife or gun, used a knife or gun), and "Overall Violence" (i.e., whether any acts of violence occurred, regardless of severity). Finally, for parent-to-child violence, there are norms for "Very Severe Violence." This is the measure that comes closest to measuring clinical child abuse (see Chapters 6, 7, and 8).

In addition to these normative tables, the percentage distributions given for each of the typologies described in the section on methods of scoring the violence items are the norms for each of those types.

Gender and Age-specific Norms

Gender-specific norms. To our surprise, the 1975 National Family Violence Survey did not find important "gender of respondent" differences in the reporting of violence by either partner (Straus, Gelles, and Steinmetz, 1980: Appendix). In the 1985 survey this pattern was repeated for "minor violence." However, for "severe violence" Chapter 9 shows that women reported substantially higher rates of husband-to-wife assault than did male respondents. Consequently, this section includes separate norms for the CTS as reported by male and female respondents.

Age-specific norms for parent-to-child violence. Minor violence by parents toward children, which is essentially a measure of use of physical punishment, is highly related to the age of the child. The Child Abuse 2 measure is also age-related, but not as clearly. The most severe types of assaults against children, the Child Abuse 1 measure, occurs about equally often at all ages from birth through 17 (see Chapter 8). Consequently, separate norms for parent-to-child violence are given for ages 0–2, 3–6, 7–14, and 15–17, with the exception of Child Abuse 1, which was not found to be age-related.

Violence by the child is also linked to the age of the child. Consequently, age-specific norms are also presented for child-to-child and child-to-parent violence. These data are from the 1975 National Survey because, due to the shorter interview time available in the 1985 study, the CTS "cycle" for tactics used by the child had to be omitted.

Age-specific norms for spousal violence. The much higher incidence of violence among young people (see Chapters 13 and 17) indicates a need for age-specific couple violence norms. Consequently, the appendix tables for spousal violence present normative data separately for respondents ages 18 to 24 years and those 25 years and older.

Notes

1. Previous reports on the 1975 study (and some reports on the 1985 study) expressed the violence rate as a *percentage* of husbands, wives, or children. However, it is often preferable to use a rate per one thousand couples or children. There are three reasons for this. (1) *Comparability with other crime and child abuse rates*. The National Crime Survey (NCS), which has become the *de facto* standard for survey research on the incidence of crime and victimization, and the annual rates of child abuse cases reported to child protective services in the United States both use rate per thousand. Adopting that standard facilitates comparison of rates from this survey with the rates for reported cases of child abuse and with NCS rates for assault and other crime. Another alternative is the Uniform Crime Reports system of rates per one hundred thousand. However, a rate per hundred thousand is not appropriate, since our survey samples were in the thousands, not hundred thousands. (2) *Results are presented as integers*. It is customary in demography, criminology, and medical sociology to use a rate that enables the data to be presented in integers. For example, the 1981 cancer death rate is given in the *Vital Statistics*

as 184 per 100,000 population rather than 0.00184 per capita or 0.184%, because most people find it easier to conceptualize integers. Thus the difference between the cancer rate and the suicide rate is more easily perceived when presented as 184 versus 12 per 100,000 than as 0.184% versus 0.012%. (3) *Avoids confusion with percent change*. In the context of this paper, using "x per thousand" instead of "x percent" avoids confusion with "x percent change" or the awkwardness in spelling out the letter as "x percent change in the percent violent."

2. In principle, one could add a category for those who used severe violence and no minor violence. However, there is little point to this, because almost everyone who severely assaults also engages in minor violence. In addition, there is no obvious conceptual reason for identifying those few people who seriously assault, but do not also slap or shove.

TABLE B.1

Annual Incidence Rates for Assaults Against Spouses 1985 Resurvey*

Severity of Assault	Rate Per 1,000 Couples or As Reported by:		
	Total	Husbands	Wives

A. For Respondents 18 to 24 years old

MINOR assaults by the HUSBAND	263	226	287
SEVERE assaults by the HUSBAND ("wife beating")	90	13	139
ANY assaults by the HUSBAND	271	226	299
MINOR assaults by the WIFE	322	261	361
SEVERE assaults by the WIFE	133	80	167
ANY assaults by the WIFE	329	266	370
MINOR assaults by EITHER husband OR wife	369	307	409
SEVERE assaults by EITHER husband OR wife	155	86	199
ANY assaults by EITHER husband OR wife	377	313	418

B. For Respondents 25 years or older

MINOR assaults by the HUSBAND	97	97	97
SEVERE assaults by the HUSBAND ("wife beating")	30	14	42
ANY assaults by the HUSBAND	104	100	108
MINOR assaults by the WIFE	100	104	97
SEVERE assaults by the WIFE	41	48	35
ANY assaults by the WIFE	108	116	102
MINOR assaults by EITHER husband OR wife	133	133	132
SEVERE assaults by EITHER husband OR wife	55	51	59
ANY assaults by EITHER husband OR wife	144	145	144

* Rates are based on the 1985 sample of 6,002 households. The rates given in other chapters may differ because they are based on portions of this sample selected for the specific purpose of that chapter.

TABLE B.2

Annual Incidence Rates for Assaults Against Children*

Severity of Assault	Rate Per 1,000 Families As Reported by:		
	Total	Fathers	Mothers
ANY assaults against 0-2 year olds	575	575	574
ANY assaults against 3-6 year olds	894	863	916
ANY assaults against 7-10 year olds	777	728	804
ANY assaults against 11-14 year olds	539	488	571
ANY assaults against 15-17 year olds	287	209	329
SEVERE assaults against 0-2 year olds	79	61	93
SEVERE assaults against 3-6 year olds	143	135	148
SEVERE assaults against 7-10 year olds	143	154	136
SEVERE assaults against 11-14 year olds	107	89	118
SEVERE assaults against 15-17 year olds	70	64	74
VERY SEVERE assaults against 0-2 year olds	22	6	34
VERY SEVERE assaults against 3-6 year olds	26	20	30
VERY SEVERE assaults against 7-10 year olds	24	20	26
VERY SEVERE assaults against 11-14 year olds	25	30	21
VERY SEVERE assaults against 15-17 year olds	21	34	14

*   Rates are based on the 1985 sample of 3,232 households with a child age 17 and under. The rates given in other chapters may differ because they are based on portions of this sample selected for the specific purpose of that chapter.

TABLE B.3

Annual Incidence Rates for Assaults by Children Against Siblings and Parents, 1975*

Severity of Assault	Rate Per 1,000 Children As Reported by:		
	Total	Fathers	Mothers

A. ASSAULTS AGAINST SIBLINGS

Severity of Assault	Total	Fathers	Mothers
ANY assaults on sibling by child 3-6	823	780	857
ANY assaults on sibling by child 7-10	829	735	900
ANY assaults on sibling by child 11-14	741	745	738
ANY assaults on sibling by child 15-17	557	494	613
SEVERE assaults on sibling by child 3-7	592	551	624
SEVERE assaults on sibling by child 7-10	553	471	616
SEVERE assaults on sibling by child 11-14	442	450	435
SEVERE assaults on sibling by child 15-17	309	253	358

B. ASSAULTS AGAINST PARENTS

Severity of Assault	Total	Fathers	Mothers
ANY assaults on parent by child 3-6	327	301	349
ANY assaults on parent by child 7-10	136	67	183
ANY assaults on parent by child 11-14	92	73	110
ANY assaults on parent by child 15-19	90	7C	107
SEVERE assaults on parent by child 3-6	213	205	219
SEVERE assaults on parent by child 7-10	66	32	89
SEVERE assaults on parent by child 11-14	28	21	35
SEVERE assaults on parent by child 15-17	35	10	56

* The rates in this table are based on the 1975-76 study because data on violence by children was not collected in the 1985 survey.

TABLE B.4
Chronicity Norms for 18 to 24 year olds, National Family Violence Resurvey, 1985

A. RAW SCORES AS REPORTED BY HUSBANDS

Centile	Husband-to-Wife RS	VB	MV*	SV*	WV*	AV*	Wife-to-Husband RS	VB	MV*	SV*	WV*	AV*	Couple Sum Index RS	VB	MV*	SV*	WV*	AV*	Centile
1	1	1			1	1	1	1					2	2	0				1
5	2	2	1		1	1	2	1	1		1	1	4	2	1		1	1	5
10	3	2	1		1	1	4	2	1	1	1	1	7	3	1	1	1	1	10
15	6	2	1		1	1	5	2	1	1	1	1	10	4	1	1	2	1	15
20	6	3	1		1	1	6	3	1	1	1	1	14	6	1	1	2	2	20
25	7	4	1		1	1	8	4	1	1	1	1	16	9	2	1	2	2	25
30	8	4	1		1	1	8	5	1	1	2	1	16	9	2	1	2	2	30
35	9	6	1	1	1	1	9	6	1	1	2	2	18	13	2	1	3	2	35
40	12	8	1	1	1	1	10	8	2	1	2	2	23	18	2	1	3	2	40
45	12	9	2	2	2	2	12	8	2	1	2	2	25	19	3	1	4	3	45
50	15	10	2	2	2	2	15	10	2	1	3	2	28	21	3	1	4	3	50
55	16	10	2	2	2	2	16	12	2	2	4	2	32	24	4	1	4	4	55
60	17	12	3	2	3	3	17	14	2	2	4	3	34	26	5	2	5	5	60
65	19	15	3	3	3	3	23	16	4	2	4	4	42	31	5	2	5	5	65
70	25	16	4		4	4	25	19	4	2	5	4	50	38	5	2	6	5	70
75	25	18	4		4	4	25	24	5	2	8	5	50	42	6	2	7	6	75
80	26	22	4		4	4	27	26	6	2	8	7	53	47	6	2	10	7	80
85	30	25	4		4	4	30	38	8	2	9	8	60	59	8	3	13	11	85
90	33	33	4		8	6	33	40	8	4	12	9	67	64	11	5	16	13	90
95	50	43	7		9	8	40	54	9		13	10	80	77	15		16	15	95
99	50	130					50	100					100	230					99

RS = Reasoning, VB = Verbal Aggression, MV = Minor Violence, SV = Severe Violence, WV = Severity Weighted Violence AV = Any Violence. The norms for Reasoning and Verbal aggression cover all cases. *The norms for the four violence indexes are for cases in which at least one violence incident occurred (See text). N of cases for each column are: RS = 148, VB = 133, MV = 35, SV = 12, WV = 41, AV 41.

Appendix Table 4 (Continued).

B. RAW SCORES AS REPORTED BY WIVES

Centile	Husband-to-Wife RS	VB	MV*	SV*	WV*	AV*	Wife-to-Husband RS	VB	MV*	SV*	WV*	AV*	Couple Sum Index RS	VB	MV*	SV*	WV*	AV*	Centile
1	1	1					1	1	1				2	1			1	1	1
5	2	1	1	1	1	1	2	1	1	1	1	1	4	2	1	1	1	1	5
10	3	2	1	1	1	1	4	2	1	1	1	1	7	4	1	1	1	1	10
15	4	2	1	1	1	1	4	3	1	1	1	1	9	4	1	1	1	1	15
20	4	4	1	1	1	1	5	4	1	1	1	1	10	7	1	1	1	1	20
25	6	4	1	1	2	2	6	5	1	1	1	1	13	10	2	2	2	2	25
30	8	5	2	1	2	2	8	6	1	1	2	2	16	12	2	2	3	2	30
35	8	7	2	1	3	2	9	8	2	1	2	2	20	16	2	2	4	3	35
40	10	8	2	1	4	3	12	10	2	2	3	2	24	18	3	2	4	3	40
45	12	10	2	2	4	3	12	12	2	2	4	2	27	21	3	3	5	4	45
50	16	12	3	2	4	3	16	13	2	2	4	3	33	24	4	3	8	4	50
55	16	14	3	2	5	4	19	15	3	2	5	4	37	29	4	4	8	6	55
60	19	16	4	2	5	4	25	17	4	3	7	5	40	33	6	4	9	8	60
65	25	19	4	2	7	5	25	20	4	4	8	6	46	42	6	5	11	8	65
70	25	23	4	3	8	5	27	25	4	4	10	7	50	48	8	6	14	10	70
75	26	27	4	4	11	6	29	29	6	4	11	8	52	57	8	7	18	12	75
80	29	35	6	4	13	8	30	38	7	5	14	8	58	70	9	8	22	14	80
85	31	41	7	7	14	8	39	46	8	5	17	11	66	87	12	12	30	17	85
90	33	53	11	17	27	14	40	57	12	12	19	14	72	104	21	18	49	26	90
95	40	68	26	33	63	43	46	67	38	16	71	45	81	130	44	33	100	71	95
99	54	94					52	108					100	193			254	126	99

RS = Reasoning, VB = Verbal Aggression, MV = Minor Violence, SV = Severe Violence, WV = Severity Weighted Violence AV = Any Violence. The norms for Reasoning and Verbal aggression cover all cases. *The norms for the four violence indexes are for cases in which at least one violence incident occurred (See text). N of cases for each column are: RS = 235, VB = 212, MV = 69, SV = 34, WV = 72, AV = 72.

TABLE B.5

Chronicity Norms for Subjects 25 Years and Older, Based on National Family Violence Resurvey, 1985

A. RAW SCORES AS REPORTED BY HUSBANDS

Centile	Husband-to-Wife						Wife-to-Husband						Couple Sum Index						Centile
	RS	VB	MV*	SV*	WV*	AV*	RS	VB	MV*	SV*	WV*	AV*	RS	VB	MV*	SV*	WV*	AV*	
1	1	1	1		1	1	1	1	1	1	1	1	2	1	1	1	1	1	1
5	1	1	1	1	1	1	2	1	1	1	1	1	4	2	1	1	1	1	5
10	2	1	1	1	1	1	2	1	1	1	1	1	5	2	1	1	1	1	10
15	4	2	1	1	1	1	4	2	1	1	1	1	8	3	1	1	1	1	15
20	4	2	1	1	1	1	4	2	1	1	1	1	8	4	1	1	1	1	20
25	5	3	1	1	1	1	5	2	1	1	2	1	10	4	1	1	2	2	25
30	6	4	1	1	1	1	6	4	1	1	2	2	13	6	2	2	2	2	30
35	8	4	1	1	1	1	8	4	2	2	2	2	16	7	2	2	2	2	35
40	8	4	1	1	1	1	8	4	2	2	2	2	16	8	2	2	3	2	40
45	9	5	1	2	2	1	9	5	2	2	3	2	20	9	2	2	3	3	45
50	12	6	2	2	2	2	12	6	2	2	4	2	24	12	3	2	4	3	50
55	12	8	2	2	2	2	12	8	3	2	4	3	27	14	3	3	4	4	55
60	16	8	2	2	2	2	16	8	3	4	5	4	31	16	4	4	6	4	60
65	17	9	2	2	2	2	19	10	4	4	6	4	35	19	4	5	7	5	65
70	23	12	2	2	4	3	23	12	4	6	7	5	45	22	6	6	8	6	70
75	25	14	3	3	4	3	25	14	5	7	9	6	50	26	6	8	10	8	75
80	26	16	4	8	4	4	27	18	6	8	12	8	52	32	8	8	14	9	80
85	29	20	4	9	6	4	29	23	8	12	22	10	58	39	9	12	18	12	85
90	33	25	6	25	8	8	33	31	10	21	33	17	66	50	14	20	30	18	90
95	41	37	8	25	15	11	49	48	12	36	70	26	82	75	16	50	64	26	95
99	51	76	16		200	25	50	81	58	75	212	83	101	151	47	75	410	83	99

RS = Reasoning, VB = Verbal Aggression, MV = Minor Violence, SV = Severe Violence, WV = Severity Weighted Violence AV = Any Violence. The norms for Reasoning and Verbal aggression cover all cases. *The norms for the four violence indexes are for cases in which at least one violence incident occurred (See text).
N of cases for each column are: RS = 1991, VB = 1586, MV = 213, SV = 30, WV = 220, AV = 220.

Appendix Table 5 (Continued).

B. RAW SCORES AS REPORTED BY WIVES

Centile	Husband-to-Wife						Wife-to-Husband						Couple Sum Index						Centil
	RS	VB	MV*	SV*	WV*	AV*	RS	VB	MV*	SV*	WV*	AV*	RS	VB	MV*	SV*	WV*	AV*	
1	1	1	1	1	1	1	1	1	1	1	1		2	1	1	1	1	1	1
5	2	1	1	1	1	1	2	1	1	1	1	1	4	2	1	1	1	1	5
10	2	2	1	1	1	1	3	2	1	1	1	1	6	2	1	1	1	1	10
15	4	2	1	1	1	1	4	2	1	1	1	1	8	4	1	1	1	1	15
20	4	2	1	1	1	1	4	3	1	1	1	1	8	4	1	1	2	1	20
25	5	4	1	1	2	1	5	4	1	1	1	1	10	6	2	1	2	2	25
30	6	4	2	1	2	2	6	4	1	1	1	1	12	7	2	1	2	2	30
35	8	4	2	2	2	2	8	4	1	1	2	1	16	8	2	2	2	2	35
40	8	6	2	2	2	2	8	6	2	1	2	2	16	10	2	2	3	2	40
45	9	7	2	2	2	2	10	7	2	1	2	2	20	12	2	2	4	2	45
50	12	8	2	2	4	2	12	8	2	2	2	2	24	15	3	2	4	3	50
55	15	9	2	2	4	2	15	9	2	2	3	2	30	16	3	2	5	4	55
60	16	10	3	3	4	3	17	10	2	2	4	3	34	20	4	3	6	4	60
65	19	12	4	4	5	4	23	12	3	2	4	4	41	23	4	3	8	5	65
70	25	15	4	5	7	4	25	14	4	2	4	4	50	27	6	4	9	6	70
75	25	18	4	6	9	5	25	17	4	4	7	5	50	33	7	8	12	8	75
80	27	23	6	8	12	7	29	21	5	4	8	6	54	41	8	10	15	9	80
85	29	29	8	12	20	9	30	27	6	6	11	8	58	53	10	12	19	13	85
90	33	38	9	14	34	18	33	35	9	8	17	12	66	70	17	15	37	21	90
95	40	55	24	22	62	35	46	49	14	32	30	17	80	96	30	36	75	39	95
99	50	90	57	80	298	108	51	83	39		142	70	100	150	79	80	295	124	99

RS = Reasoning, VB = Verbal Aggression, MV = Minor Violence, SV = Severe Violence, WV = Severity Weighted Violence AV = Any Violence. The norms for Reasoning and Verbal aggression cover all cases. *The norms for the four violence indexes are for cases in which at least one violence incident occurred (See text).
N of cases for each column are: RS = 2426, VB = 2037, MV = 266, SV = 115, AV = 295.

TABLE B.6
Chronicity Norms for Parent-to-Child Conflict Tactics As Reported by Mothers, National Family Violence Resurvey, 1985

Age of Child

Centile	0 to 2 years RS	VB	MV*	SV*	AB*	3 to 6 years RS	VB*	MV*	SV*	AB*	7 to 10 years RS	VB	MV*	SV*	AB*	11 to 14 years RS	VB*	MV*	SV*	AB*	15 to 17 years RS	VB	MV*	SV*	AB*	Centile
1	1	1	1	1		1	1	1	1		1	1	1	1		1	1	1	1		1	1	1	1		1
5	1	1	1	1		4	1	1	1		2	1	1	1		2	1	1	1		2	1	1	1		5
10	5	2	1	1	1	4	2	2	2	1	4	1	1	1	1	3	2	1	1	1	3	1	1	1		10
15	3	2	2	1	2	6	2	4	4	1	5	1	2	1		3	2	1	1	1	4	2	1	1	1	15
20	4	2	3	2	2	8	3	4	4	1	8	3	2	2	1	6	3	2	2	1	5	2	1	1	1	20
25	4	2	4	2	2	8	4	4	4		8	4	2	2	1	8	4	2	2	2	6	3	1	1	1	25
30	5	3	4	2	2	9	4	4	4	1	9	4	3	2	2	8	4	2	3	2	8	4	1	1		30
35	6	4	4	4	2	12	5	4	5	2	10	5	4	4	2	9	5	3	4	2	8	4	1	2	2	35
40	8	4	4	4	2	16	7	6	8	2	12	6	4	4	2	12	6	4	4	2	10	5	2	2	3	40
45	8	4	8	4	2	20	8	8	8	2	16	7	4	4	2	15	8	4	4	2	12	6	2	2	3	45
50	12	7	8	4	4	25	9	8	8	2	19	8	5	5	3	17	8	4	5	2	13	6	2	2	4	50
55	16	8	8	4	4	25	10	8	12	2	23	9	6	6	4	20	9	4	6	2	16	8	2	4	4	55
60	25	11	12	6	5	26	14	12	15	2	25	9	8	8	4	25	12	5	8	2	19	8	3	4	4	60
65	25	15	15	8	5	27	16	15	17	3	26	12	8	8	4	25	13	6	8	3	25	10	4	4	6	65
70	25	20	16	13	7	29	20	16	23	4	29	14	8	9	4	27	16	8	8	4	26	12	4	4	7	70
75	27	23	25	15	15	31	23	19	25	4	33	17	8	13	5	30	18	8	10		29	13	5	5	8	75
80	29	25	25	25	17	33	26	25	25	4	34	20	12	16	5	33	25	8	15		31	16	6	6	8	80
85	33	27	25	25	23	40	30	25	27	10	40	27	16	21	13	35	32	15	20		33	22	8	8		85
90	40	30	25	25	25	41	33	26	32	15	50	33	23	25		42	42	19	32		40	28	8	17		90
95	50	50	29	40		50	40	29	51		50	46	29	37		50	75	33	85		50	35	16	27		95
99	75	63	46			65	59	50	104		75	67	47	73		61					65	57	33	73		99
N –	218	137	180	29	11	390	312	388	64	13	367	289	315	54	10	374	300	233	49	9	377	279	131	30	6	N –

RS – Reasoning, VB – Verbal Aggression, MV – Minor Violence, SV – Severe Violence, AV – Any Violence. The norms for the three violence indexes are for cases in which at least one violence incident occurred (See text). *The norms for Reasoning and Verbal aggression cover all cases.

TABLE B.7
Chronicity Norms for Parent-to-Child Conflict Tactics As Reported by Fathers, National Family Violence Resurvey, 1985

Age of Child

Centile	0 to 2 years RS	VB	MV*	SV*	AB*	3 to 6 years RS	VB*	MV*	SV*	AB*	7 to 10 years RS	VB	MV*	SV*	AB*	11 to 14 years RS	VB*	MV*	SV*	AB*	15 to 17 years RS	VB	MV*	SV*	AB*	Centile
1	1		1			1	1	1			2	1	1			1	1	1			1	1				1
5	1	1	1	1		3	1	1	1		2	2	1	1	1	2	1	1	1		2	1	1	1		5
10	2	1	2	1		4	2	1	1		4	2	1	1	1	3	1	1	1		3	1	1	1		10
15	3	2	2	1		5	2	2	1		6	2	2	2	1	4	2	1	1	2	4	1	1	1	1	15
20	4	2	4	2		8	3	2	2	1	8	4	2	2	1	5	2	1	1	2	4	2	1	1	1	20
25	4	3	4	2		8	4	2	2	1	8	4	2	3	1	6	2	2	2	2	5	2	1	2	1	25
30	6	4	4	3		10	4	4	2	1	10	5	3	4	1	8	3	2	2	2	7	2	1	2	1	30
35	8	4	4	4	3	15	5	5	2	1	12	6	4	4	1	8	4	2	2	2	8	2	2	2	1	35
40	10	6	8	4	4	16	6	8	4	2	16	8	4	4	2	12	4	2	4	2	8	3	2	3	2	40
45	12	8	8	5	5	23	8	8	4	2	23	8	4	4	3	15	6	4	4	2	10	4	2	4	2	45
50	15	10	8	7	6	25	8	8	4	2	25	8	5	6	4	16	8	4	4	2	12	4	2	4	2	50
55	16	12	10	8	6	25	8	8	4	2	27	10	6	8	4	19	10	4	4	3	16	6	3	4	2	55
60	25	14	15	11		25	10	12	8	11	30	12	8	8	4	24	11	4	5	3	19	7	3	5	2	60
65	25	15	15	15		28	12	15	8	19	30	14	8	12	4	25	13	6	8	3	23	8	4	5	3	65
70	25	17	17	15		30	15	17	8	25	33	16	11	14		29	15	6	8	3	25	10	4	6	3	70
75	29	19	25	23		33	17	25	15	25	40	19	12	17		30	18	8	13	4	28	13	6	7	4	75
80	30	25	25	25		40	24	25	19		40	24	16	23		33	24	12	20		33	16	6	10	4	80
85	33	26	25	25		50	28	25	23		50	31	22	27		41	27	17	26		37	25	8	15		85
90	40	29	25	25		50	37	29	34		54	51	30	34		50	41	29	36		42	30	8	19		90
95	50	36	33			54	53	39			54					54	64	40	91							95
99	55		50			75	83	50		123	75	65	50	57							51	62				99
N =	152	95	143	15	2	287	214	264	42	6	200	155	159	34	4	244	167	130	24	8	190	124	45	14	7	N =

RS = Reasoning, VB = Verbal Aggression, MV = Minor Violence, SV = Severe Violence, AV = Any Violence. The norms for Reasoning and Verbal aggression cover all cases. *The norms for the three violence indexes are for cases in which at least one violence incident occurred (See text).

About the Authors

NOEL A. CAZENAVE is associate professor of sociology at Temple University in Philadelphia. His Ph.D in sociology is from Tulane University (1977). He is the author of "Family Violence and Aging Blacks: Theoretical Perspectives and Research Possibilities" in the *Journal of Minority Aging* (1979) and "Elder Abuse and Black Americans," published in a collection on abuse of the elderly in 1983. He is co-author with Margaret Zahn of the forthcoming (1987) article, "Women, Murder and Male Domination: A Research Note on Domestic Homicide in Chicago and Philadelphia," which will appear in *Victimology*. Cazenave is currently doing a historical sociological study of applied social science researchers involved in the "Great Society" and "War on Poverty" program initiatives.

DIANE H. COLEMAN is deputy director of Southeastern Vermont Community Action. Her Ph.D. in sociology is from the University of New Hampshire (1985). She oversees a number of projects that are designed to empower individuals and challenge the social structural causes of inequality. Action for Children is a child sexual abuse prevention program carried out in conjunction with educators throughout the state of Vermont. The Young Women's Empowerment Program is designed to help female high school students avoid traps that make women vulnerable to violence. Futures Unlimited assists single parents, usually women, in recognizing and overcoming the barriers to educational and career achievement. She is the co-author of "Alcohol Abuse and Family Violence" in *Substance Abuse and Aggression* (1983), which showed that the relationship between alcohol abuse and family violence is not as linear as many have thought. It is one of the few empirical research reports on alcohol and family violence. She is also the co-author of "Sociological Antecedents to Structural Family Therapy," presented to the American Association of Marriage and Family Therapy.

URSULA G. DIBBLE works for the city of Hartford, Connecticut, study-ing educational and municipal problems. Her Ph.D. in sociology is from the University of Connecticut (1978). She has done research on violence in protest situations, for which she won the Candace Rogers Award of the Eastern Sociological Association. She has done research on marital insta-bility and family violence in second marriages and presented a paper at the American Sociological Association annual meeting on stepchildren, remarriage, and marital instability and published a review essay of books on child abuse in *Contemporary Sociology*.

SCOTT L. FELD is associate professor of sociology at the State Univer-sity of New York at Stony Brook. His Ph.D. in sociology is from Johns Hopkins University. He is a national expert on the study of social net-works. In addition to articles on social networks in sociological journals, he is the author of many articles on individual and collective decision making, several aspects of applied sociology. As a post-doctoral research fellow at the University of New Hampshire, he applied social network analysis to the field of family violence in a study of how networks influence parental practices in the disciplining of young children. He is also the author of a theoretical paper on the role of weaker partners (wives, younger siblings) in family violence episodes.

RICHARD J. GELLES is dean of the College of Arts and Sciences and professor of sociology and anthropology at the University of Rhode Island. He received his Ph.D. in sociology at the University of New Hampshire (1973). His publications include 14 books, more than 50 articles, and many papers presented at scientific meetings. His first book, *The Violent Home* (1974) was the first systematic investigation of family violence and contin-ues to be highly influential. He is also the author of *Family Violence* (1979; revised, 1987), and co-author of *Behind Closed Doors: Violence in the American Family* (1980). He co-edited *The Dark Side of the Family: Current Family Violence Research* (1983), *International Perspectives on Family Violence* (1983), *Child Abuse and Neglect: Biosocial Dimensions* (1987), and *Intimate Violence* (1988). He has consulted for numerous groups including Louis Harris and Associates, the National Center on Child Abuse and Neglect, and Children's Hospital of Boston. He served on the NIMH research grant study section on violent and anti-social behavior and has served on the editorial boards of thirteen professional journals and helped found (and for nine years edited) the journal *Teaching Sociology*. He received the American Sociological Association, Section on Undergraduate Education, Outstanding Contributions to Teaching Award in 1979 and was named by *Esquire* magazine one of the "Men and Women Under Forty Who Are Changing America" in 1984.

EILEEN F. HARGREAVES received her B.A. in sociology from the University of Rhode Island in 1977. She is a research analyst who has worked with Richard Gelles.

GERALD T. HOTALING is research associate professor in the Family Research Laboratory at the University of New Hampshire and assistant professor of criminal justice studies at the University of Lowell. His Ph.D. in sociology is from the University of New Hampshire (1984). He is the author of over a dozen papers on family violence, and co-editor of four books, *The Social Causes of Husband-Wife Violence* (1980), *The Dark Side of Families* (1983), *Family Abuse and Its Consequences* (1988), *Coping With Family Violence*. He was the chief organizer of the first and second National Family Violence Research conferences (1981 and 1984). His current research includes national studies of the problem of sexual abuse in day care and of missing children. He is a consultant for the Center for Disease Control and the National Institute of Justice.

DEBRA S. KALMUSS is associate professor of public health at Columbia University. Her Ph.D. in sociology is from the University of Michigan (1980). Her published research on family violence includes an experimental study on family violence, "The Attribution of Responsibility in a Wife Abuse Context," in *Victimology* (1979); a study of factors that affect the level of services to battered women in each of the fifty states, published as "Feminist, Political and Economic Determinants of Wife Abuse Services" in *The Dark Side of Families* (1983); "The Intergenerational Transmission of Marital Aggression" (1985) and "Continuity of Marital Behavior in Remarriage: The Case of Spouse Abuse" (1986), both in the *Journal of Marriage and the Family*.

GLENDA KAUFMAN KANTOR is research director of an AIDS-intravenous-drug user study affiliated with the Department of Psychiatry, Harvard Medical School at Cambridge Hospital. Her Ph.D. in sociology is from the University of Illinois (1984) and she also holds an M.S. in nursing from the University of Pennsylvania. She was formerly assistant professor at De Paul University in Chicago and director of the Centralized Domestic Violence Court Evaluation Project for the Chicago Battered Women's Network and the Chicago Law Enforcement Study Group. In addition to the two chapters in this book, Dr. Kantor's published work on family violence includes a paper, "Substance Abuse as a Precipitant of Wife Abuse Victimizations," to be published in the *American Journal of Drug and Alcohol Abuse*, a paper, "Stress and Child Abuse," in the fourth edition of *The Battered Child* edited by Ray Helfer and Henry Kempe, and two co-authored monographs, *You Have to Be Strong: An Evaluation of the Centralized Domestic Violence Court of Cook County, Illinois* and *All They Can Do: Police Response to Battered Women's Complaints*, both published by The Chicago Law Enforcement Study Group.

ALAN J. LINCOLN is professor of criminal justice studies and director of graduate studies at the University of Lowell. His M.S. (1969) in social psychology and Ph.D. in sociology (1973) are from the University of Massachusetts. He has served on the faculty of Virginia Polytechnic Institute, American University, and the University of New Hampshire, and as a Fulbright Hays Professor in the Netherlands. In 1984, he held a research position with the Centre for Library and Information Management at the University of Loughborough, England, and conducted national studies of library crime and security in Great Britain. His recent books include *Crime in the Library* (1984) and *Library Crime and Security: An International Perspective* (1987). He is the co-author of *Crime and the Family* (1985) and editor of the journal, *Library and Archival Security*. He has also served as Guest Editor for a *Library Trends* issue on "Protecting the Library." His many articles in psychological and sociological journals include "Justification for Violence and Genocide" (1978), "Crowds, Leisure, and Conflict" (1978), "School Crime, Power and the Student Subculture" (1978), "Observers' Evaluations of the Victim and the Attacker in an Aggressive Incident" (1972), and "Justifying and Condemning Violence: A Research Review and a Look in New Directions" (1973).

KARL PILLEMER is assistant professor of sociology and a research associate of the Family Research Laboratory at the University of New Hampshire. His Ph.D. in sociology is from Brandeis University (1985). He is co-editor of *Elder Abuse: Conflict in the Family* (1986) and co-author of *Helping Elderly Victims* (in press). His articles on conflict and abuse of the elderly within families have appeared in the *Journal of Marriage and the Family*, *Social Problems*, *The Gerontologist*, the *Handbook of Family Violence*, and elsewhere. He is currently conducting research on maltreatment of patients in nursing homes and is also the co-principal investigator of a study on social relations of Alzheimer's caregivers across time (with Jill Suitor), funded by the National Institute of Mental Health.

CHRISTINE SMITH is a research scientist with Abt Associates, Cambridge, Massachusetts. She received her M.A. in sociology from the University of New Hampshire in 1987. Her paper, "Status Discrepancies and Husband-to-Wife Violence," won the Candace Rogers Award from the Eastern Sociological Society for best graduate student paper submitted in 1987–1988. She is also co-author of "Cohabitation, Commitment, And Control," which was presented at the 1988 meeting of the Eastern Sociological Society.

JAN. E. STETS is assistant professor of sociology at Washington State University. Her Ph.D. in sociology is from Indiana University (1987). She is the author of *Domestic Violence and Control* (1988), a ground-breaking interactionist perspective on domestic violence. She has also examined dating violence. Her work includes "Violence in Dating Relationships" (1987), "Gender Identity, Self-Esteem and Physical and Sexual Abuse in Dating Relationships" (1988), and *Violence in Dating Relationships: Emerging Social Issues* (1989, co-edited with Maureen A. Pirog-Good). This work established her as one of the leading scholars nationwide on dating violence.

MURRAY A. STRAUS is professor of sociology and co-director of the Family Research Laboratory at the University of New Hampshire. His Ph.D. in sociology is from the University of Wisconsin (1956). He has also taught at Minnesota, Cornell, Wisconsin, Washington State, York (England), Bombay (India), and Ceylon (Sri Lanka). He is a former president of the National Council on Family Relations, vice president of the Eastern Sociological Society, and member of the Council, American Association for the Advancement of Science, and president-elect of the Society for the Study of Social Problems. In 1977 he was given the Ernest W. Burgess Award of the National Council of Family Relations for outstanding research on the family. His publications include over 125 articles on the family, research methods, and South Asia and ten books, including *Intimate Violence*, (1988), *Social Stress in the United States* (1986), *Crime and the Family* (1985), *The Dark Side of Families* (1983), *The Social Causes of Husband-Wife Violence* (1980), *Behind Closed Doors: Violence in the American Family* (1980). *Family Measurement Techniques* (1978), *Sociological Analysis* (1968).

J. JILL SUITOR is assistant professor of sociology at Fordham University. Her Ph.D. in sociology is from the State University of New York at Stony Brook (1985). She is the co-author of a comprehensive review article on elder abuse in the *Handbook of Family Violence*, which integrates literature on the family relations of the elderly with the literature on elder abuse, and the author or co-author of numerous recent articles on family sociology, including "Mother-Daughter Relations When Married Daughters Return to School" in *Journal of Marriage and the Family* (1987), "Husband's Support for Wives' Return to School" in *Gender and Society* (1988), and "The Presence of Adult Children: A Source of Stress for Elderly Couples' Marriages?" in *Journal of Marriage and the Family* (1987). She is also co-principal investigator of a study on social relations of Alzheimer's caregivers across time, funded by the National Institutes of Health. This study follows up on some of the questions concerning social support and maltreatment that were raised in her previous research on elder abuse.

BARBARA A. WAUCHOPE is a researcher at the Family Research Laboratory and doctoral student in the sociology department of the University of New Hampshire. Her research interests include causes of violent behavior in the family, service utilization and social support of victims of violence, and the elderly. She presented a paper, "Help-Seeking Decisions of Battered Women: A Test of Learned Helplessness and Two Stress Theories, at the 1988 meeting of the Eastern Sociological Society.

KERSTI A. YLLO is associate professor of sociology at Wheaton College in Norton, Massachusetts, where she is also the coordinator of the Gender-Balanced Curriculum Project. Her Ph.D. in sociology is from the University of New Hampshire (1980). She is the co-author of *License to Rape: Sexual Abuse of Wives* (1985), co-editor of *Feminist Perspectives on Wife Abuse* (1988), and author of articles on topics such as cohabitation and the status of women, including "Nonmarital Cohabitation: Beyond the College Campus" (1978), "Sexual Equality and Violence Against Wives in American States" (1983), and "The Status of Women, Marital Equality, and Violence Against Wives: A Contextual Analysis" (1984).

References

ADAMHA 1980. National Data Book. Rockville, MD: Alcohol, Drug Abuse and Mental Health Administration, DHEW Publication No. (ADM) 80–938.

Adams, Bert N. 1965. "Coercion and Consensus Theories: Some Unresolved Issues." *American Journal of Sociology* 71(May):714–716.

———. 1971. "Isolation, Function, and Beyond; American Kinship in the 1960's." Pp. 163–185 in *A Decade of Family Research and Action*, edited by Carlfred B. Broderick. Minneapolis: National Council on Family Relations.

———. 1975. *The Family: A Sociological Interpretation*. Chicago: Rand McNally.

Adler, Emily Stier. 1981. "The Underside of Married Life: Power, Influence, and Violence." Pp. 300–319 in *Women and Crime in America*, edited by Lee H. Bowker. New York: Macmillan.

Alfaro, J. 1978. *Child Abuse and Subsequent Delinquent Behavior*. New York: Select Committee on Child Abuse.

Alford, Richard D. 1982. "Intimacy and Disputing Styles Within Kin and Nonkin Relationships." *Journal of Family Issues* 3(September):361–374.

Allen, C. 1984. "On the Validity of Relative Validity Studies of 'Final Say' Decision Measures of Marital Power." *Journal of Marriage and the Family* 46.

Allen, Craig M., and Murray A. Straus. 1980. "Resources, Power, and Husband-Wife Violence." Chapter 12 in *The Social Causes of Husband-Wife Violence*, edited by Murray A. Straus and Gerald T. Hotaling. Minneapolis: University of Minnesota Press.

———. 1985. "Final Say Measures of Marital Power: Theoretical Critique and Empirical Findings from Five Studies in the U.S. and India. *Journal of Comparative Family Studies* 15:329–344.

American Association for Protecting Children. 1985. *Highlights of Official*

Child Neglect and Abuse Reporting, 1983. Denver: American Association for Protecting Children.

————. 1986. *Highlights of Official Child Neglect and Abuse Reporting, 1984*. Denver: American Association for Protecting Children.

American Humane Association. 1982. *National Analysis of Office Child Neglect and Abuse Reporting, 1980*. Denver: American Humane Association.

————. 1983. *Highlights of Official Child Neglect and Abuse Reporting*. Denver, CO: American Humane Association.

————. 1986. *Highlights of Official Child Neglect and Abuse Reporting, 1984*. Denver: Author.

Amir, Menachem. 1971. *Patterns in Forcible Rape*. Chicago: University of Chicago Press.

Anderson, J. E. 1972. *The Young Child in the Home*. NY: Arno. (Original work published 1936).

Archer, Dane, and Marjorie R. Garter. 1984. *Violence and Crime in Cross-National Perspective*. New Haven, CT: Yale University Press.

Arias, Ileana, and Steven R. H. Beach. 1987. "Validity of Self-Reports of Marital Violence." *Journal of Family Violence* 2(2):139–149.

Arias, Ileana, Mary Samios, and K. Daniel O'Leary. 1987. "Prevalence and Correlates of Physical Aggression During Courtship." *Journal of Interpersonal Violence* 2:82–90.

Aschenbrenner, J. 1973. "Extended Families Among Black Americans." *Journal of Comparative Family Studies* 4:257–268.

————. 1975. *Life-Lines: Black Families in Chicago*. New York: Holt, Rinehart and Winston.

Atkinson, Maxine, and Becky Glass. 1985. "Marital Age Heterogamy and Homogamy, 1900 to 1980." *Journal of Marriage and the Family* 47:685–691.

Ausubel, D. P. 1958. *Theory and Problems in Child Development*. New York: Grune and Stratton.

Babbie, Earle R. 1983. *The Practice of Social Research*. 2/E. Belmont, CA: Wadsworth.

Baca Zinn, Maxine. 1979. "Chicano Family Research: Conceptual Distortions and Alternative Directions." *Journal of Ethnic Studies* 7:59–71.

————. 1982. "Chicano Men and Masculinity." *Journal of Ethnic Studies* 10:29–43.

Bach, George R., and Peter Wyden. 1968. *The Intimate Enemy*. New York: Avon Books (William Morrow and Co.).

Back, Susan M., Judith Blum, Ellen Nakhnikian, and Susan Stark, 1980. *Spouse Abuse Yellow Pages*. Denver, CO: Denver Research Institute, University of Denver.

Bahr, Stephen J. 1973. "The Internal Consistency of Blood and Wolfe's Measure of Conjugal Power: A Research Note." *Journal of Marriage and the Family* 52:293–295.

Bakan, D. 1971. *Slaughter of the Innocents: A Study of the Battered Child Phenomenon*. Boston: Beacon Press.

Baldwin, J., and J. Oliver. 1975. "Epidemiology and Family Characteristics of Severely Abused Children." *British Journal of Preventive Social Medicine* 29:202–221.

Ball-Rokeach, Sandra J. 1973. "Values and Violence: A Test of the Subculture of Violence Thesis." *American Sociological Review* 38:736–749.

Bandura, Albert. 1971. *Psychological Modeling*. Chicago: Aldine-Atherton.

———. 1973. *Aggression: A Social Learning Analysis*. Englewood Cliffs, NJ: Prentice-Hall.

Bard, Morton. 1970. "Training Police as Specialists in Family Crisis Intervention." U.S. Department of Justice.

———. 1971. "The Study and Modification of Intra-Familial Violence." In *The Control of Aggression and Violence: Cognitive and Physiological Factors*, edited by J. L. Singer. New York: Academic Press.

Bard, Morton, and J. Zacker. 1974. "Assaultiveness and Alcohol Use in Family Disputes: Police Perceptions." *Criminology* 12:281–292.

Barling, J., K. D. O'Leary, E. N. Jouriles, D. Vivian, and K. E. MacEwen. 1987. "Factor Similarity of the Conflict Tactics Scales Across Samples, Spouses, and Sites: Issues and Implications." *Journal of Family Violence* 2(1):37–55.

Baron, Larry, and Murray A. Straus. 1988. "Cultural and Economic Sources of Homicide in the United States." *Sociological Quarterly* 29:371–390.

———. 1987. "Four Theories of Rape: A Macrosociological Analysis." *Social Problems* 34:467–489.

———. 1989. *Four Theories Of Rape In American Society: A State-Level Analysis*. New Haven, CT: Yale University Press.

Baron, Larry, Murray A. Straus, and David Jaffee. 1988. "Legitimate Violence, Violent Attitudes, and Rape: A Test of the Cultural Spillover Theory." *Annals of the New York Academy of Sciences*, Vol. 528:79–110.

Baumrind, Diana. 1973. "The Development of Instrumental Competence Through Socialization." Pp. 3–46 in *Minnesota Symposia on Child Psychology*. Vol. 7, edited by A. D. Pick. Minneapolis: University of Minnesota.

Bavolek, Stephen J. 1984. *Handbook for the Adult-Adolescent Parenting Inventory (AAPI)*. Schaumburg, IL: Family Development Associates, Inc.

Benedetti, J. K., and M. B. Brown. 1978. "Strategies for the Selection of Log-Linear Models." *Biometrics* 34:680–686.

Bengtson, Vern L., Neal E. Cutler, David J. Mangen, and Victor W. Marshall. 1985. "Generations, Cohorts, and Relations Between Age

Groups." Pp. 304–338 in *Handbook of Aging and the Social Sciences*, edited by R. H. Binstock and E. Shanas. New York: Van Nostrand Reinhold.

Bennie, E. H., and A. B. Sclare. 1969. "The Battered Child Syndrome." *American Journal of Psychiatry* 125:975–979.

Berger, Dale E., and John R. Snortum. 1986. "A Structural Model of Drinking and Driving: Alcohol Consumption, Social Norms, and Moral Commitments." *Criminology* 24:139–154.

Berk, Richard A., Donileen R. Loseke, Sara Fenstermaker Berk, and David Rauma. 1980. "Bringing the Cops Back In: A Study of Efforts to Make the Criminal Justice System More Responsive to Incidents of Family Violence." *Social Science Research* 9:193–215.

Berk, Richard A., Sarah Fenstermaker Berk, Donileen R. Loseke, and David Rauma. 1983. "Mutual Combat and Other Family Violence Myths." Pp. 197–212 in *The Dark Side of Families: Current Family Violence Research*, edited by D. Finkelhor, R. Gelles, G. Hotaling, and M. A. Straus. Newbury Park, CA: Sage Publications.

Berk, Richard A., and Subhash C. Ray. 1982. "Selection Biases in Sociological Data." *Social Science Research* 11:352–398.

Berk, Sarah F., and Donileen R. Loseke. 1980–1981. "Handling 'Family Violence': Situational Determinants of Police Arrest in Domestic Disturbances." *Law and Society Review* 15:316–346.

Berkowitz, Leonard. 1962. *Aggression: A Social-Psychological Analysis*. New York: McGraw-Hill.

Berkowitz, Leonard. 1973. "The Case For Bottling Up Rage." *Psychology Today* 7 (July):24–31.

Bernard, Jessie L. 1982. *The Future of Marriage*. New Haven, CT: Yale University Press.

Bernard, Jessie L., S. L. Bernard, and M. L. Bernard. 1985. "Courtship Violence and Sex Typing." *Family Relations* 34:573–576.

Billings, Andrew G., Marc Kessler, Christopher A. Gomberg, and Sheldon Weiner. 1979. "Marital Conflict Resolution of Alcoholic and Nonalcoholic Couples During Drinking and Nondrinking Sessions." *Journal of Studies on Alcohol* 40:183–195.

Billingsley, Andrew. 1969. "Family Functioning in the Low-Income Black Community." *Casework* 50:563–572.

Black, D. 1980. *The Manners and Customs of Police*. New York: Academic Press.

Blau, Peter. 1964. *Exchange and Power in Social Life*. New York: John Wiley and Sons.

Blechman, Elaine A. 1980. "Family Problem-Solving Training." *American Journal of Family Therapy* 8(Fall):3–21.

———. 1982. "Are Children with One Parent at Psychological Risk? A Methodological Review." *Journal of Marriage and the Family* 44:179–196.

Blechman, Elaine A., Nancy L. Kotanchik, and Cynthia J. Taylor. 1981. "Families and Schools Together: Early Behavioral Intervention with High Risk Children." *Behavior Therapy* 12(June):308–319.

Block, Carolyn. 1987. "Lethal Violence in the Chicago Latino Community: 1965–1981. Paper presented at the Research Conference on Violence and Homicide in the Hispanic Community, September 14–15, Los Angeles.

Blood, Robert O., and Donald M. Wolfe. 1960. *Husbands and Wives*. Glencoe, IL: Free Press.

Blum, Richard H. 1981. "Violence, Alcohol, and Setting: An Unexplored Nexus." In *Drinking and Crime: Perspectives on the Relationships Between Alcohol Consumption and Criminal Behavior*, edited by James J. Collins, Jr. New York: Guilford Press.

Blumberg, Rae Lesser. 1978. *Stratification: Socioeconomic and Sexual Inequality*. Dubuque, IA: Wm. C. Brown.

Blumstein, Alfred, Jacqueline Cohen, and David P. Farrington. 1988. "Criminal Career Research: Its Value for Criminology." *Criminology* 26:1–35.

Blumstein, Alfred, Jacqueline Cohen, Jeffrey Roth, and Christy A. Visher (eds.). 1986. *Criminal Careers and "Career Criminals,"* vol 1. Report of the Panel on Research on Criminal Careers, National Research Council. Washington, DC: National Academy Press.

Blumstein, Alfred, David P. Farrington, and Soumyo D. Moitra. 1985. "Delinquency Careers: Innocents, Desisters, and Persisters." In *Crime and Justice*, vol. 6, edited by M. Tonry and N. Morris. Chicago: University of Chicago Press.

Bogal-Allbritten, R. B., and W. Allbritten. 1985. "The Hidden Victims: Courtship Violence Among College Students." *Journal of Student Personnel* 19:201–04.

Bolton, R. G., J. W. Reich, and S. E. Gutierres. 1977. "Delinquency Patterns in Maltreated Children and Siblings." *Victimology* 2:349–357.

Bordin, Ruth. 1981. *Woman and Temperance: A Quest for Power and Liberty, 1873–1900*. Philadelphia: Temple University Press.

Bott, Elizabeth. 1971. *Family and Social Network*. New York: Free Press.

Bousha, D. M., and C. T. Twentyman. 1984. "Mother-Child Interactional Style in Abuse, Neglect, and Control Groups: Naturalistic Observations in the Home." *Journal of Abnormal Psychology* 93:106–114.

Bowen, Garry L., Murray A. Straus, Andrea J. Sedlak, Gerald T. Hotaling, and David B. Sugarman. 1984. *Domestic Violence Surveillance System Feasibility Study: Phase I Report, An Identification of Outcomes and Risk Factors*. Rockville, MD: Westat, Inc.

Bowker, Lee H. 1983. *Beating Wife-Beating*. Lexington, MA: Lexington Books, D. C. Heath and Company.

Bowker, Lee H., and K. MacCallum. 1980. "Women Who Have Beaten Wife-Beating." Unpublished manuscript, School of Social Welfare, University of Wisconsin-Milwaukee.

Boyatzis, Richard E. 1983. "Who Should Drink What, When, and Where if Looking For a Fight." In *Drug Abuse and Aggression*, edited by E. Gottheil, K. A. Druley, T. E. Skoloda, and H. W. Waxman. Springfield, IL: Charles C. Thomas.

Bradburn, Sudman, and Associates. 1979. *Improving Interview Method and Questionnaire Design*. San Francisco: Jossey-Bass.

Braithwaite, J. 1981. "The Myth of Social Class and Criminality Reconsidered." *American Sociological Review* 46:36–57.

Brandon, S. 1976. "Physical Violence in the Family: An Overview." In *Violence in the Family*, edited by M. Borland. Atlantic Highlands, NJ: Humanities Press.

Breines, Wini, and Linda Gordon. 1983. "Review Essay: The New Scholarship on Family Violence." *Signs: Journal of Women in Culture and Society* 8:490–531.

Brenner, Harvey M. 1976. "Estimating the Social Costs of National Economic Policy: Implications for Mental and Physical Health, and Criminal Aggression." Paper presented to the Joint Economic Committee, U.S. Congress, 1976; revised version to be published as "The Impact of Social and Industrial Changes on Psychopathology, A View of Stress from the Standpoint of Macrosocietal Trends." In *Society, Stress and Disease*, edited by L. Levi. 1979. Oxford University Press.

Brinberg, David, and Louise H. Kidder (eds.). 1982. *New Directions for Methodology of Social and Behavioral Science: Forms of Validity in Research*. San Francisco, CA: Jossey-Bass.

Bromberg, W. 1961. *The Mold of Murder*. New York: Grune and Stratton.

Bronfenbrenner, Urie. 1958. "Socialization and Social Class Through Time and Space." Pp. 400–425 in *Readings in Social Psychology*, edited by E. E. Maccoby, T. Newcomb, and E. Hartley. New York: Holt.

Brown, Bruce W. 1980. "Wife Employment, Marital Equality and Husband-Wife Violence." Pp. 176–187 in *The Social Causes of Husband-Wife Violence*, edited by M. A. Straus and G. Hotaling. Minneapolis: University of Minnesota Press.

Brown, G. W., and T. Harris. 1978. *Social Origins of Depression: A Study of Psychiatric Disorder in Women*. London: Tavistock Publications.

Brown, Sandra A., Mark S. Goldman, Andres Inn, and Lynn R. Anderson. 1980. "Expectations of Reinforcement from Alcohol: Their Domain and Relation to Drinking Patterns." *Journal of Consulting and Clinical Psychology* 48:419–426.

Browne, Angela. 1984. "Assault and Homicide at Home: When Battered Women Kill." Paper presented at the Second National Conference for Family Violence Researchers, Durham, NH.

Browne, Angela. 1987. *When Battered Women Kill*. New York: Free Press.

Browning, James, and Donald Dutton. 1986. "Assessment of Wife Assault with the Conflict Tactics Scale: Using Couple Data to Quantify the

Differential Reporting Effect." *Journal of Marriage and the Family* 48(May):375–379.

Brutz, Judith L., and Craig M. Allen. 1986. "Religious Commitment, Peace Activism, and Marital Violence in Quaker Families." *Journal of Marriage and the Family* 48:491–502.

Brutz, Judith L., and Bron B. Ingoldsby. 1984. "Conflict Resolution in Quaker Families." *Journal of Marriage and the Family* 46:21–26.

Bryan, J. W., and F. W. Freed. 1982. "Corporal Punishment: Normative Data and Sociological and Psychological Correlates in a Community College Population." *Journal of Youth and Adolescence* 11:77–87.

Buckley, Walter. 1967. *Sociology and Modern Systems Theory*. Englewood Cliffs, NJ: Prentice-Hall.

Bulcroft, Richard A., and Murray A. Straus. 1975. "Validity of Husband, Wife, and Child Reports of Conjugal Violence and Power." University of New Hampshire, Family Research Laboratory, mimeographed paper.

Bureau of Justice Statistics. 1980. *Intimate Victims*. Washington, DC: United States Department of Justice.

———. 1985. *Criminal Victimization in the United States, 1985*. Washington, DC: U.S. Department of Justice.

Bureau of the Census. 1986. *Statistical Abstract of the United States, 106th ed.* Washington, DC: U.S. Government Printing Office.

Burgdorf, K. 1980. *Recognition and Reporting of Child Maltreatment*. Rockville, MD: Westat.

Buzawa, Eve. 1984. "Patrol Officers' Response to Domestic Violence Calls in Massachusetts." Paper presented at the Second National Conference for Family Violence Researchers, Durham, NH.

Byles, John A. 1978. "Violence, Alcohol Problems and Other Problems in Disintegrating Families." *Journal of Studies on Alcohol* 39:551–553.

Caesar, Patti Lynn. 1985. "The Wife Beater: Personality and Psychosocial Characteristics." Paper presented at the annual American Psychological Association Convention, Los Angeles, CA.

Cahalan, Don. 1970. *Problem Drinkers: A National Survey*. San Francisco: Jossey-Bass.

Cahalan, Don, Ira H. Cisin, and Helen M. Crossley. 1969. *American Drinking Practices: A National Study of Drinking Behavior and Attitudes*. New Brunswick, NJ: Rutgers Center for Alcohol Studies.

Cahalan, Don, and Robin Room. 1974. *Problem Drinking Among American Men*. New Brunswick, NJ: Rutgers Center for Alcohol Studies.

Calvert, Robert. 1974. "Criminal and Civil Liability in Husband-Wife Assaults." Chapter 9 in *Violence in the Family*, edited by Suzanne K. Steinmetz and Murray A. Straus. New York: Harper and Row.

Campbell, Angus, Phillip E. Converse, and Willard Rodgers. 1976. *The Quality of American Life*. New York: Russell Sage.

Campbell, Donald T., and Donald W. Fiske. 1959. "Convergent and

Discriminant Validation by the Multitrait-Multimethod Matrix.'' *Psychological Bulletin* 56:81–105.

Caplan, Gerald. 1974. *Support Systems and Community Mental Health.* New York: Behavioral Publications.

Carlson, Bonnie. 1977. ''Battered Women and Their Assailants.'' *Social Work* 22:455–460.

Carmody, Diane Cyr, and Kirk R. Williams. 1987. ''Wife Assault and Perceptions of Sanctions.'' *Violence and Victims* 2(1):25–38.

Carr, A. 1979. *Reported Child Maltreatment in Florida: The Operation of Public Child Protective Service Systems.* A report submitted to the Administration on Children, Youth and Families, National Center on Child Abuse and Neglect, Department of Health, Education, and Welfare, Kingston, Rhode Island, mimeographed.

Carroll, J. C. 1980. ''A Cultural Consistency Theory of Family Violence in Mexican-American and Jewish-Ethnic Groups.'' Ch.5 in *The Social Causes of Husband-Wife Violence*, edited by G. T. Hotaling and M. S. Straus. Minneapolis: University of Minnesota Press.

Carroll, Joseph C. 1977. ''The Intergenerational Transmission of Family Violence: The Long Term Effects of Aggressive Behavior.'' *Aggressive Behavior* 3(Fall):289–299.

Carson, Barbara A. 1986. ''Parents Who Don't Spank: Deviation in the Legitimation of Physical Force.'' Doctoral Dissertation, University of New Hampshire.

———. 1987. ''Content Analysis of Childrearing Manuals' Advice About Spanking.'' Paper presented at the Third National Family Violence Research Conference, University of New Hampshire, Durham, July 6–9.

Cate, Rodney M., June M. Henton, James Koval, F. Scott Christopher, and Sally Lloyd. 1982. ''Premarital Abuse: A Social Psychological Perspective.'' *Journal of Family Issues* 3:79–90.

Cazenave, Noel A., and Murray A. Straus. 1979. ''Race, Class, Network Embeddedness and Family Violence: A Search for Potent Support Systems.'' *Journal of Comparative Family Studies* 10:280–299.

Chafetz, Janet Saltzman. 1984. *Sex and Advantage: A Comparative Macro-Structural Theory of Sex Stratification.* Totowa, NJ: Bowman and Allanheld.

Chapa, D., P. Smith, F. Rindon, R. Valdez, M. Yost, and T. Cripps. 1978. ''The Relationship Between Child Abuse and Neglect and Substance Abuse in a Predominantly Mexican-American Population.'' Pp. 116–125 in *Child Abuse and Neglect: Issues on Innovation and Implementation*, vol. 1, edited by M. Lauderdale et al. Proceedings of the Second Annual Conference on Child Abuse and Neglect, 1977. Washington, DC: Department of Health, Education and Welfare.

Chodorow, Nancy. 1978. *The Reproduction of Mothering: Psychoanalysis and the Sociology of Gender.* Berkeley: University of California Press.

Clarke, C. 1987. "Domestic Violence: A Community Survey." Unpublished manuscript, Department of Psychology, University of Illinois.

Cohen, S., and A. Sussman. 1975. "The Incidence of Child Abuse in the United States." Unpublished manuscript.

Cohen, Sheldon, Tom Kamarck, and Robin Mermelstein. 1983. "A Global Measure of Perceived Stress." *Journal of Health and Social Behavior* 24:385–396.

Cohn, D. A., C. Christopoulos, and R. Emery. 1984. "The Psychological Adjustment of School-Aged Children of Battered Women: A Preliminary Look." Paper presented at the Second National Conference for Family Violence Researchers, University of New Hampshire, Durham.

Cole, C. 1977. "Cohabitation in Social Context." In *Marriage and Alternatives: Exploring Intimate Relationships*, edited by R. Libby and R. Whitehurst. Glenview, IL: Scott Foresman.

Coleman, Diane H. 1985. *Marital Power, Conflict and Violence.* Unpublished doctoral dissertation, University of New Hampshire.

Coleman, Diane H., and Murray A. Straus. 1983. "Alcohol Abuse and Family Violence." Pp. 104–124 in *Alcohol, Drug Abuse and Aggression*, edited by E. Gottheil, K. A. Druley, T. E. Skoloda, and H. M. Waxman. Springfield, IL: Charles C. Thomas.

———. 1986. "Marital Power, Conflict, and Violence in a Nationally Representative Sample of American Couples." *Violence and Victims* 1:141–157.

Coleman, K. H., M. L. Weinmen, and B. P. Hsi. 1980. "Factors Affecting Conjugal Violence." *Journal of Psychology* 105:197–202.

Coleman, Karen Howes. 1980. "Conjugal Violence: What 33 Men Report." *Journal of Marital and Family Therapy* 6:207–13.

Collins, A., and D. L. Pancoast. 1976. *National Helping Networks: A Strategy for Prevention.* Washington, DC: National Association of Social Workers.

Collins, James J., Jr. 1981. "Alcohol Use and Criminal Behavior: An Empirical Theoretical and Methodological Overview." Pp. 288–316 in *Drinking and Crime: Perspectives on the Relationships Between Alcohol Consumption and Criminal Behavior*, edited by James J. Collins, Jr. New York: Guilford Press.

Collins, Randal. 1975. *Conflict Sociology: Toward an Explanatory Science.* New York: Academic Press.

Condran, John C., and Jerry G. Bode. 1982. "Rashomon, Working Wives, and Family Division of Labor: Middletown, 1980." *Journal of Marriage and the Family* 421–426.

Conger, Rand D. 1984. "Family Profiles of Serious Juvenile Offenders." Paper presented at the Second National Conference for Family Violence Researchers, Durham, NH.

Conger, Rand. D. 1978. "Family Change and Child Abuse." Pp. 74–79 in *Child Abuse and Neglect: Issues on Innovation and Implementation*, vol. 1, edited by M. Lauderdale et al. Proceedings of the Second Annual Conference on Child Abuse and Neglect, 1977. Washington, DC: Department of Health, Education and Welfare.

Conger, Rand D., Robert L. Burgess, and C. Barrett. 1979. "Child Abuse Related to Life Change and Perceptions of Illness: Some Preliminary Findings." *Family Coordinator* 28:73–78.

Coser, Louis. 1956. *The Functions of Social Conflict*. New York: Free Press.

Cowen, Emory. 1978. "Demystifying Primary Prevention." Chapter 2 in *Primary Prevention of Psychopathology*, edited by Donald G. Forgays. Hanover, NH: University of New England Press.

Crime Control Institute. 1987. "176 Cities Surveyed on Policing Violence." *USA Today* (February 18): 13A.

Critchlow, Barbara. 1983. "Blaming the Booze: The Attribution of Responsibility for Drunken Behavior." *Personality and Social Psychology Bulletin* 9:451–473.

Cromwell, Robert E., and David H. Olson. 1975. *Power in Families*. New York: Wiley.

Cromwell, Vicky L., and Ronald E. Cromwell. 1978. "Perceived Dominance in Decision-Making and Conflict Resolution among Anglo, Black and Chicano Couples." *Journal of Marriage and the Family* 40:749–759.

Cronbach, Lee J. 1970. *Essentials of Psychological Testing*, edited by Gardner Murphy and Wayne H. Holtzman. New York: Harper and Row, Publishers.

Crouter, A. C., M. Perry-Jenkins, T. L. Huston, and S. M. McHale. 1987. "Processes Underlying Father Involvement in Dual-Earner and Single-Earner Families." *Developmental Psychology* 23:431–440.

Curtis, Lynn. 1975. *Violence, Race, and Culture*. Lexington, MA: Heath.

Dahrendorf, Ralf. 1959. *Class and Class Conflict in Industrial Society*. London: Routledge and Kegan Paul.

Daniel, A. E., and W. R. Holcomb. 1985. "A Comparison Between Men Charged with Domestic and Non-Domestic Homicide." *Bulletin of the American Academy of Psychiatry and the Law* 13(3):233–241.

Davidson, Terry. 1977. "Wife Beating: A Recurring Phenomenon Throughout History." In *Battered Women*, edited by M. Roy. New York: Van Nostrand-Reinhold Company.

Davis, Elizabeth Gould. 1971. *The First Sex*. New York: Putnam.

Davis, James A. 1973–1974. "The Goodman System for Significance Tests in Multivariate Contingency Tables." Pp. 189–231 in *Sociological Methodology*, edited by Herbert L. Costner. San Francisco: Jossey-Bass.

Davis, James A. 1974. "Hierarchical Models for Significance Tests in Multivariate Contingency Tables." Pp. 189–231 in *Sociological Methodology 1973–1974*, edited by H. L. Costner. San Francisco: Jossey-Bass.

de Lissovoy, V. 1980. "The Behavioral and Ecological Syndrome of the High-Risk Child." Pp. 11–17 in *The Maltreatment of the School-Aged Child*, edited by R. Volpe, M. Breton, and J. Mitton. Lexington, MA: Lexington Books.

De Mause, L. (ed.). 1974. *The History of Childhood*. New York: Psychohistory Press.

De Mause, L. 1975. "Our Forbearers Made Childhood a Nightmare." *Psychology Today* 8(April): 85–87.

Deal, James E., and Karen Smith Wampler. 1986. "Dating Violence: The Primacy of Previous Experience." *Journal of Social and Personal Relationships* 3:457–471.

DeFrancis, V. 1973. "Testimony at the Hearing Before the Subcommittee on Children and Youth of the Committee on Labor and Public Welfare." United States Senate, 93rd Congress, First Session. On S.1191 Child Abuse Prevention and Treatment Act, 1973. U.S. Government Printing Office.

Delli, Quadri, T. C. 1978. "Changing Family Roles and Structures: Impact on Child Abuse and Neglect." Pp. 70–73 in *Child Abuse and Neglect: Issues on Innovation and Implementation*, vol. 1, edited by M. Lauderdale et al. Proceedings of the Second Annual Conference on Child Abuse and Neglect, 1977. Washington, DC: Department of Health, Education and Welfare.

Dembo, R., M. Dertke, L. La Voie, S. Borders, M. Washburn, and J. Schmeidler. 1987. "Physical Abuse, Sexual Victimization and Illicit Drug Use: A Structural Analysis Among High Risk Adolescents." *Journal of Adolescence*.

Devereux, Edward C., Urie Bronfenbrenner, and R. R. Rogers. 1969. "Child-Rearing in England and the United States: A Cross-Cultural Comparison." *Journal of Marriage and the Family* 31:257–270.

Dibble, Ursula G., and Murray A. Straus. 1980. "Some Social Structure Determinants of Inconsistency Between Attitudes and Behavior: The Case of Family Violence." *Journal of Marriage and the Family* 42(February):71–80.

Dobash, R. Emerson, and Russell P. Dobash. 1978. "Wives: The 'Appropriate' Victims of Marital Violence." *Victimology* 1:416–441.

———. 1979. *Violence Against Wives: A Case Against the Patriarchy*. New York: Free Press.

———. 1988. "Research as Social Action: The Struggle for Battered Women." Chapter 2 in *Feminist Perspectives on Wife Abuse*, edited by Kersti Yllo and Michele Bograd. Newbury Park: Sage Publications.

Dobash, Rebecca E., and Russell P. Dobash. 1984. "The Nature and Antecedents of Violent Events." *British Journal of Criminology* 24:269–288.

Dobash, Russell P., and R. Emerson Dobash. 1983. "Do We Need New Methods for Studying Wife Abuse?: The Context-Specific Approach."

Chapter 15 in *The Dark Side of Families: Current Family Violence Research*, edited by David Finkelhor, Richard J. Gelles, Gerald T. Hotaling, and Murray A. Straus. Newbury Park, CA: Sage Publications.

Dohrenwend, Bruce P., Patrick E. Shrout, Gladys Egri, and Frederick S. Mendelsohn. 1980. "Nonspecific Psychological Distress and Other Dimensions of Psychopathology." *Archives of General Psychiatry* 37:1229–1236.

Durkeim, Emile. 1951. *Suicide*. New York: Free Press.

Dutton, Donald G. 1986. "The Outcome of Court-Mandated Treatment for Wife Assault: A Quasi-Experimental Evaluation." *Violence and Victims* 1:163–175.————VF1

————. 1988. *The Domestic Assault Of Women: Psychological and Criminal Justice Perspective*. Boston: Allyn and Bacon.

Dutton, Donald G., and J. J. Browning. 1984. "Power Struggles and Intimacy Anxieties as Causative Factors of Wife Assault." In *Violence in Intimate Adult Relationships*, edited by G. Russell. New York: Spectrum Press.

————. 1988. "Concern for Power, Fear of Intimacy and Aversive Stimuli for Wife Abuse." Chapter 11 in this volume.

Dvoskin, J. A. 1981. "Battered Women—An Epidemiological Study of Spousal Violence." Unpublished doctoral dissertation, University of Arizona.

Eberle, Patricia A. 1980. "Alcohol Abusers and Non-users: A Discriminant Analysis of Differences Between Two Sub-Groups of Batterers." Paper presented at the annual meeting of the Society for the Study of Social Problems, Toronto, Canada.

Eblen, Cristobal Neal. 1987. *The Influence of Stress and Social Support Upon Child Abuse*. Ph.D. dissertation, Arizona State University.

Edleson, Jeffrey L., and Mary Pat Brygger. 1986. "Gender Differences in Reporting of Battering Incidences." *Family Relations* 35:377–382.

Edleson, Jeffrey L., Zvi Eisikovits, and Edna Guttmann. 1985. "Men Who Batter Women: A Critical Review of the Evidence." *Journal of Family Issues* 6:229–247.

Edmunds, Vernon H. 1967. "Marital Conventionalization: Definitions and Measurement." *Journal of Marriage and the Family* 29:681–688.

Egeland, B., M. Breitenbucher, and D. Rosenberg. 1980. "Prospective Study of the Significance of Life Stress in the Etiology of Child Abuse." *Journal of Consulting and Clinical Psychology* 48(2):195–205.

Egeland, B., D. Jacobvitz, and K. Papatola. 1987. "Intergenerational Continuity of Abuse." In *Child Abuse and Neglect: Biosocial Dimensions*, edited by R. Gelles and Lancaster. Hawthorne, NY: Aldine deGruyter, in press.

Egeland, B., and L. A. Sroufe, 1981. "Development Sequelae of Maltreatment in Infancy." In *New Directions of Child Development: Developmental Perspectives in Child Maltreatment*, edited by R. Rizley and D. Cicchetti. San Francisco, CA: Jossey Bass, Inc.

Egley, Lance C. 1988. "What do the Conflict Tactics Scales Measure?" Unpublished paper, Department of Sociology, University of Minnesota.

Eisenberg, Susan, and Patricia Micklow. 1977. "The Assaulted Wife: 'Catch 22' Revisited." *Women's Rights Law Reporter* 3–4:138–161.

Elbow, M. 1977. "Theoretical Considerations of Violent Marriages." *Social Casework* 58:515–526.

Elliott, Delbert S., and S. S. Ageton. 1980. "Reconciling Race and Class Differences in Self-Reported and Official Estimates of Delinquency." *American Sociological Review* 45:95–110.

Elliott, Delbert, and D. Huizinga. 1983. "Social Class and Delinquent Behavior in a National Youth Panel: 1976–1980." *Criminology* 21:149–177.

———. 1984. "The Relationship Between Delinquent Behavior and ADM Problems." *The National Youth Survey* (Project Report No. 28). Boulder, CO: Behavioral Research Institute.

Elmer, E., S. Evans, and J. Reinhart. 1977. *Fragile Families, Troubled Children*. Pittsburgh, PA: Pittsburgh University Press.

Erlanger, Howard S. 1974. "Social Class Differences in Parents' Use of Physical Punishment." Pp. 150–158 in *Violence in the Family*, edited by S. K. Steinmetz and M. A. Straus. New York: Harper and Row.

Fagan, Jeffrey A. 1988. "Cessation of Family Violence: Deterrence and Dissuasion. In *Crime and Justice, An Annual Review of Research*, edited by M. Tonry and L. Ohlin. Chicago: University of Chicago Press.

Fagan, Jeffrey A., Elizabeth Friedman, Sandra Wexler, and Virginia S. Lewis. 1984. *National Family Violence Evaluation: Final Report*, vol. 1: *Analytic Findings*. San Francisco: URSA Institute.

Fagan, Jeffrey A., E. S. Piper, and M. Moore. 1986. "Violent Delinquents and Urban Youth." *Criminology* 23:439–472.

Fagan, Jeffry A., D. K. Stewart, and K. V. Hansen. 1983. "Violent Men or Violent Husbands? Background Factors and Situational Correlates." In *The Dark Side of Families: Current Family Violence Research*, edited by D. Finkelhor, R. Gelles, G. Hotaling, and M. A. Straus. Newbury Park, CA: Sage Publications.

Fagan, Jeffry A., and S. Wexler. 1987. "Crime at Home and in the Streets: The Relationship Between Family and Stranger Violence." *Violence and Victims* 2(1):5–24.

Farrington, David P. 1982. "Longitudinal Analyses of Criminal Violence." In *Criminal Violence*, edited by M. E. Wolfgang and N. A. Weiner. Newbury Park, CA: Sage.

Farrington, Keith. 1980. "Stress and Family Violence." Chapter 7 in *The Social Causes of Husband-Wife Violence*, edited by M. A. Straus and G. T. Hotaling. Minneapolis: University of Minnesota Press.

Faulk, M. 1974. "Men Who Assault Their Wives." *Medicine, Science and the Law* 14(18):1–183.

Fergusson, D. M., L. J. Horwood, K. L. Kershaw, and F. T. Shannon.

1986. "Factors Associated with Reports of Wife Assault in New Zealand." *Journal of Marriage and the Family* 48:407–412.

Ferraro, Kathleen J., and John M. Johnson. 1983. "How Women Experience Battering: The Process of Victimization." *Social Problems* 30:325–338.

Field, Martha H., and H. F. Field. 1973. "Marital Violence and the Criminal Process: Neither Justice nor Peace." *Social Service Review* 47:221–240.

Finkelhor, David. 1977. "Education and Marital Violence." Family Research Laboratory, University of New Hampshire. Mimeographed paper.

———. 1979. *Sexually Victimized Children*. New York: Free Press.

———. 1983. "Common Features of Family Abuse." In *The Dark Side of Families: Current Family Violence Research*, edited by D. Finkelhor, R. J. Gelles, G. T. Hotaling, and M. A. Straus. Newbury Park, CA: Sage Publications.

Finkelhor, David, and Gerald Hotaling. 1984. "Sexual Abuse in the National Incidence Study of Child Abuse and Neglect: An Appraisal." *Child Abuse Neglect International Journal* 8:23–33.

Finkelhor, David, and I. A. Lewis. 1987. "Identifying Child Molesters in Social Surveys Using the Randomized Response Technique." Draft paper, University of New Hampshire, Durham.

———. 1988. "An Epidemiologic Approach to the Study of Child Molestation." In *Human Sexual Aggression: Current Perspectives*, edited by Robert Prentky and Vernon Quinsey. New York: Annals of the New York Academy of Sciences.

Finkelhor, David, and Karl Pillemer. 1986. "Understanding Conflict in Marriages of the Elderly." Paper presented at the annual meeting of the Gerontological Society of America, Chicago, November.

Finley, Jno P. 1884. "Tornado Predictions." *American Meteorological Journal* 1:85–88.

Fischer, Claude S., R. M. Jackson, C. A. Stueve, K. Gerson, L. M. Jones, and M. Boldassare. 1977. *Networks and Places: Social Relations in the Urban Setting*. New York: Free Press.

Flanzer, Jerry. 1982. "Alcohol and Family Violence: Double Trouble." Pp. 136–142 in *The Abusive Partner*, edited by M. Roy. New York: Van Nostrand Reinhold.

Flewelling, Robert, and Angela Browne. 1987. "Female Perpetrated Homicide Within American Families." Paper presented at the Third National Family Violence Research Conference, July 1987, University of New Hampshire, Durham.

Flitcraft, Anne. 1977. "Battered Women: An Emergency Room Epidemiology and Description of a Clinical Syndrome and Critique of Present Therapeutics." Yale Medical School thesis, unpublished.

Flynn, J. D. 1977. "Recent Findings Related to Wife Abuse." *Social Case Work* 58:17–18.

Fontana, Vincent. 1973. *Somewhere a Child Is Crying: Maltreatment—Causes and Prevention*. New York: Macmillan.

Ford, David A. 1983. "Wife Battery and Criminal Justice: A Study of Victim Decision-Making." *Family Relations* 32:463–475.

Foss, Joyce E. 1980. "The Paradoxical Nature of Family Relationships and Family Conflict." In *The Social Causes of Husband-Wife Violence*, edited by M. A. Straus and G. Hotaling. Minneapolis: University of Minnesota Press.

Fox, J., and P. Tracy. 1986. *Randomized Response: A Method for Sensitive Surveys*. Newbury Park, CA: Sage Publications.

Frankenstein, William, William M. Hay, and Peter E. Nathan. 1985. "Effects of Intoxication on Alcoholics' Marital Communication and Problem Solving." *Journal of Studies on Alcohol* 46:1–6.

French, J. R. P., W. Rodgers, and S. Cobb. 1974. "Adjustment As Person-Environment Fit." Pp. 316–333 in *Coping and Adaptation*, edited by G. Coelho et al. New York: Basic Books.

Frude, N., and A. Goss. 1979. "Parental Anger: A General Population Survey." *Child Abuse and Neglect* 3:331–333.

Gagnon, John H., and Cathy Stein Greenblatt. 1978. *Life Designs*. Glenview, IL: Scott, Foresman.

Gagnon, John H., and William Simon. 1973. *Sexual Conduct: The Sources of Sexuality*. Chicago: Aldine.

Galdston, R. 1965. "Observations of Children Who Have Been Physically Abused by Their Parents." *American Journal of Psychiatry* 122(4):440–443.

Gallup, George. 1978. "More Americans Drink and They're Drinking More." *Boston Globe*, July 2:C1–C3.

Gann, L. H., and P. J. Duignan. 1986. *The Hispanics in the United States: A History*. Boulder, CO: Westview Press.

Gans, Herbert. 1962. *The Urban Villagers*. New York: Free Press.

Gaquin, D. A. 1977–1978. "Spouse Abuse: Data from the National Crime Survey." *Victimology* 2:632–643.

Garbarino, James. 1976. "A Preliminary Study of Some Ecological Correlates of Child Abuse: The Impact of Socioeconomic Stress on Mothers." *Child Development* 47:178–185.

———. 1977. "The Human Ecology of Child Maltreatment: A Conceptual Model for Research." *Journal of Marriage and the Family* 39:721–735.

———. 1986. "Can We Measure Success in Preventing Child Abuse? Issues in Policy, Programming and Research." *Child Abuse and Neglect* 10:143–156.

Garbarino, James, and Aaron Ebata. 1983. "The Significance of Ethnic and Cultural Differences in Child Maltreatment." *Journal of Marriage and the Family* 45:773–783.

Garbarino, James, and G. Gilliam. 1980. *Understanding Abusive Families*. Lexington, MA: Lexington Books.

Garfinkel, Harold. 1964. "Studies of the Routine Grounds of Everyday Activities." *Social Problems* 11(Winter):225–250.

Garner, Joel H. and Elizabeth Clemmer. 1986. *Danger to Police In Domestic Disturbances—A New Look*. Washington, D.C. Research In Brief. National Institute of Justice.

Garofalo, James, and Michael J. Hindelang. 1977. *An Introduction to the National Crime Survey*. Albany, NY: Criminal Justice Research Center.

Gayford, J. J. 1975. "Ten Types of Battered Wives." *Welfare Officer* 25:5–9.

———. 1975. "Wife Battering: A Preliminary Study of 100 Cases." *British Medical Journal* 1:194–197.

Gecas, Victor. 1976. "The Socialization and Child Care Roles." Pp. 33–59 in *Role Structure and Analysis of the Family*, edited by F. I. Nye. Newbury Park, CA: Sage Publications.

Gelles, Richard J. 1974. "Child Abuse as Psychopathology: A Sociological Critique and Reformulation." Pp. 190–204 in *Violence in the Family*, edited by S. K. Steinmetz and M. A. Straus. New York: Harper and Row.

———. 1974. *The Violent Home: A Study of Physical Aggression Between Husbands and Wives*. Newbury Park, CA: Sage Publications.

———. 1975. "The Social Construction of Child Abuse." *American Journal of Orthopsychiatry* 45(April):363–371.

———. 1975. "Violence and Pregnancy: A Note on the Extent of the Problem and Needed Services." *Family Coordinator* 24:81–86.

———. 1976. "Abused Wives: Why Do They Stay?" *Journal of Marriage and the Family* 38:659–668.

———. 1978a. "Violence Towards Children in the United States." *American Journal of Orthopsychiatry* 48(October):580–592.

———. 1978b. "A Profile of Violence Towards Children in the United States." Paper presented at the Annenberg School of Communications Conference on Child Abuse: Cultural Roots and Public Policy, Philadelphia.

———. 1979. "Etiology of Violence: Overcoming Fallacious Reasoning in Understanding Family Violence and Child Abuse." Pp. 169–178 in *Family Violence*, edited by R. Gelles. Newbury Park, CA: Sage Publications.

———. 1980. "Violence in the Family: A Review of Research in the Seventies." *Journal of Marriage and the Family* 42:873–885.

———. 1982. "Child Abuse and Family Violence: Implications for Medical Professionals." In *Child Abuse*, edited by Eli H. Newberger. Boston: Little Brown.

———. 1982. "Domestic Criminal Violence." In *Criminal Violence*, edited by M. E. Wolfgang and N. A. Weinger. Newbury Park, CA: Sage Publications.

———. 1983. "An Exchange/Social Control Theory." In *The Dark Side of Families: Current Family Violence Research*, edited by Finkelhor et al. Newbury Park, CA: Sage Publications.

————. 1983. "Parental Child Snatching: The Use of Telephone Survey Techniques to Study a Hidden Family Problem." Paper presented at the National Council on Family Relations Theory, Construction and Research Methods Workshop, Minneapolis.

————. 1985. "Family Violence." *Annual Review of Sociology* 11:347–367.

Gelles, Richard J., and Clair P. Cornell (eds.). 1983. *International Perspectives on Family Violence*. Lexington, MA: Lexington Books.

Gelles, Richard J., and Murray A. Straus. 1975. "Family Experience and Public Support of the Death Penalty." *American Journal of Orthopsychiatry* 44(July):596–613.

————. 1979. "Determinants of Violence in the Family: Towards a Theoretical Integration." Chapter 21 in *Contemporary Theories About the Family*, edited by Wesley R. Burr, Rueben Hill, F. Ivan Nye, and Ira L. Reiss. Vol. 1. New York: Free Press.

————. 1986. "Societal Change and Change in Family Violence from 1975 to 1985 as Revealed by Two National Surveys." *Journal of Marriage and the Family* 48(August):465–479.

————. 1987. "The Cost of Family Violence." *Public Health Reports* 102:638–641.

————. 1987. "Is Violence Toward Children Increasing? A Comparison of 1975 and 1985 National Survey Rates." *Journal of Interpersonal Violence* 2:212–222.

————. 1988. *Intimate Violence*. New York: Simon and Schuster.

George, C., and M. Main. 1979. "Social Interactions of Young Abused Children: Approach, Avoidance, and Aggression." *Child Development* 50:306–318.

Gersten, J. C., T. S. Langner, J. G. Eisenberg, and L. Orzek. 1974. "Child Behavior and Life Events: Undesirable Change or Change Per Se." Pp. 159–170 in *Stressful Life Events: Their Nature and Effects*, edited by B. S. Dohrenwend and B. P. Dohrenwend. New York: Wiley.

Gil, David. G. 1970. *Violence Against Children: Physical Child Abuse in the United States*. Cambridge, MA: Harvard University Press.

————. 1975. "Unraveling Child Abuse." *American Journal of Orthopsychiatry* 45:346–356.

Giles-Sims, Jean. 1983. *Wife Battering: A Systems Theory Approach*. New York: Guilford Press.

————. 1985. "A Longitudinal Study of Battered Children of Battered Wives." *Family Relations* 34:205–210.

Gillespie, D. L. 1971. "Who Has the Power? The Marital Struggle." *Journal of Marriage and the Family* 33:445–458.

Giovannoni, Jeanne M., and Rosina M. Becerra. 1979. *Defining Child Abuse*. New York: Free Press.

Giovannoni, Jeanne M., and A. Billingsley. 1970. "Child Neglect Among the Poor: A Study of Parental Adequacy in Families of Three Ethnic Groups." *Child Welfare* 49:196–204.

Glaser, D., D. Kenefick, and V. O'Leary. 1968. *The Violent Offender*. Washington, DC: U.S. Department of Health, Education and Welfare, Office of Juvenile Delinquency and Youth Development.

Glick, Paul C. 1984. "Marriage, Divorce and Living Arrangements: Prospective Changes." *Journal of Family Issues* 5:7–26.

Glick, Paul C., and A. J. Norton. 1977. *Marrying, Divorcing, and Living Together in the U.S. Today*. Washington, DC: Population Reference Bureau.

Glick, Paul C., and Graham B. Spanier. 1980. "Married and Unmarried Cohabitation in the United States." *Journal of Marriage and the Family* 42:19–30.

Glueck, Sheldon, and Eleanor Glueck. 1950. *Unraveling Juvenile Delinquency*. Cambridge, MA: Harvard University Press.

Godwin, John. 1978. *Murder U.S.A.* New York: Ballantine.

Goode, William J. 1960. "A Theory of Role Strain." *American Sociological Review* 25:483–496.

———. 1971. "Force and Violence in the Family." *Journal of Marriage and the Family* 33(November):624–636.

———. 1974. "Force and Violence in the Family." In *Violence in the Family*, edited by S. K. Steinmetz and M. A. Straus. New York: Harper and Row.

Goodman, Leo A. 1970. "The Multivariate Analysis of Qualitative Data: Interaction Among Multiple Classifications." *Journal of the American Statistical Association* 65:226–256.

———. 1971. "The Analysis of Multidimensional Contingency Tables: Stepwise Procedures and Direct Estimation Methods for Building Models for Multiple Classifications." *Technometrics** 13:33–61.

———. 1972. "A General Model for the Analysis of Surveys." *American Journal of Sociology* 77:1035–1086.

———. 1978. *Analyzing Qualitative/Categorical Data*. Cambridge, MA: Abt Associates.

Goodman, Leo A., and William H. Kruskal. 1959. "Measures of Association for Cross Classifications. II: Further Discussion and References." *Journal of the American Statistical Association* 54:123–163.

Gorad, Stephen L. 1971. "Communicational Styles and Interaction of Alcoholics and Their Wives." *Family Process* 10:475–489.

Gordon, Linda. 1988. *Heroes of Their Own Lives: The Politics and History of Family Violence*. New York: Viking.

Gottfredson, Michael R., and Travis Hirschi. 1986. "The True Value of Lambda Would Appear to Be Zero: An Essay on Career Criminals, Criminal Careers, Selective Incapacitation, Cohort Studies, and Related Topics." *Criminology* 24:213–233.

———. 1988. "Science, Public Policy, and the Career Paradigm." *Criminology* 26:37–55.

Gottheil, Edward, Keith A. Druley, Thomas E. Skoloda, and Howard M. Waxman. 1983. "Aggression and Addiction: Summary and Overview." *In Drug Abuse and Aggression*, edited by E. Gottheil, K. A. Druley, T. E. Skoloda, and H. W. Waxman. Springfield, IL: Charles C. Thomas.

Gove, Walter R., and Michael R. Geerken. 1977. "Response Bias in Surveys of Mental Health: An Empirical Investigation." *American Journal of Sociology* 82:1289–1317.

Graff, T. T. 1979. "Personality Characteristics of Battered Women." Unpublished doctoral dissertation, Brigham Young University.

Grebler, Leo, Joan W. Moore, and R. C. Guzman. 1970. *The Mexican American People*. New York: Emerson Hall.

Greenberg, David F. 1977. "Delinquency and the Age Structure of Society." *Contemporary Crisis: Crime, Law and Social Policy* 1:189–223.

———. 1985. "Age, Crime, and Social Explanations." *American Journal of Sociology* 91:1–21.

Greenberg, Stephanie W. 1981. "Alcohol and Crime: A Methodological Critique of the Literature." In *Drinking and Crime: Perspectives on the Relationships Between Alcohol Consumption and Criminal Behavior*, edited by James J. Collins, Jr. New York: Guilford Press.

Greenblat, Cathy S. 1983. "A Hit Is a Hit Is a Hit . . . or Is It? Approval and Tolerance of the Use of Physical Force by Spouses." Pp. 235–260 in *The Dark Side of Families*, edited by David Finkelhor, R. J. Gelles, G. T. Hotaling, and M. A. Straus. Newbury Park, CA: Sage Publications.

Griswald, Barbara, and Andrew Billingsley. 1967. "Personality and Social Characteristics of Low-Income Mothers Who Neglect or Abuse Their Children." Unpublished manuscript.

Groves, R. M., and R. L. Kahn. 1979. *Surveys by Telephone: A National Comparison with Personal Interviews*. New York: Academic Press.

Gully, Kevin J., Harold A. Dengerink, Mary Pepping, and Douglas Bergstrom. 1981. "Research Note: Sibling Contribution to Violence Behavior." *Journal of Marriage and the Family* 43:333–337.

Gusfield, Joseph. 1963. *Symbolic Crusade: Status Politics and the American Temperance Movement*. Urbana: University of Illinois Press.

Guttmacher, M. S. 1960. *The Mind of the Murderer*. New York: Farrar.

Haeuser, A. A. June 1985. "Social Control over Parents' Use of Physical Punishment: Issues for Cross-National Child Abuse Research." Paper presented at the United States-Sweden Joint Seminary on Physical and Sexual Abuse of Children, Satra Bruck, Sweden.

Haeuser, A. A. 1985. "Social Control over Parents' Use of Physical Punishment: Issues for Cross-National Child Abuse Research." Paper presented at the United States-Sweden Joint Seminary on Physical and Sexual Abuse of Children, Satra Bruck, Sweden.

Hampton, Robert. 1987. "Race, Class, and Child Maltreatment." *Journal of Comparative Family Studies* 18:113–126.

Hampton, Robert, and Richard J. Gelles. 1988. "Is Violence In Black Families Increasing? A Comparison of 1975 and 1985 National Survey Rates." Paper presented at the 1988 meeting of the American Sociological Association.

Hampton, Robert, and Eli H. Newberger. 1985. "Child Abuse Incidence and Reporting by Hospitals: The Significance of Severity, Class, and Race." *American Journal of Public Health* 75:56–69.

Harris, Louis, and Associates, 1979. *A Survey of Spousal Abuse Against Women in Kentucky*. New York: Harris and Associates.

Hawkes, Glenn R., and Minna Taylor. "Power Structure in Mexican and Mexican-American Farm Labor Families." *Journal of Marriage and the Family* 37:807–811.

Hawkins, J. D., and J. G. Weiss. 1980. *The Social Development Model: An Integrated Approach to Delinquency Prevention*. Seattle: Center for Law and Justice, University of Washington.

Hays, William, and Charles H. Mendel. 1973. "Extended Kinship Relations in Black and White Families." *Journal of Marriage and the Family* 35:51–57.

Helfer, R., and C. H. Kempe. 1976. *Child Abuse and Neglect: The Family and the Community*. Cambridge, MA: Ballinger.

Helton, Anne. 1986. "Battering During Pregnancy." *American Journal of Nursing* 86:910–913.

Henry, Jules. 1974. "Making Pete Tough." Pp. 238–240 in *Violence in the Family*, edited by S. K. Steinmetz and M. A. Straus. New York: Harper and Row.

Henton, J., R. Cate, J. Koval, S. Lloyd, and S. Christopher. 1983. "Romance and Violence in Dating Relationships." *Journal of Family Issues* 4:467–482.

Henton, June, Rodney Cate, James Koval, Sally Lloyd, and Scott Christopher. 1983. "Romance and Violence in Dating Relationships." *Journal of Family Issues* 4:467–482.

Henze, L., and J. Hudson. 1974. "Personal and Family Characteristics of Cohabiting and Non-Cohabiting Students." *Journal of Marriage and the Family* 36:722–727.

Hepburn, John R. 1971. "Subcultures, Violence, and the Subculture of Violence." *Criminology* 9:87–98.

Herrenkohl, R. C., E. C. Herrenkohl, B. Egolf, and M. Seech. 1980. "The Repetition of Child Abuse: How Frequently Does It Occur?" In *The Abused Child in the Family and in the Community: Selected Papers from the Second International Congress on Child Abuse and Neglect, London 1978*, vol. 1, edited by C. H. Kempe, A. W. Franklin, and C. Cooper. Oxford: Pergamon Press.

Herrenkohl, E. C., R. C. Herrenkohl, L. J. Toedler, and A. M. Yanushefski. 1984. "Parent-Child Interactions in Abusive and Non-Abusive Families." *Journal of the American Academy of Child Psychiatry* 23:641–648.

Herskovits, Melville. 1958. *The Myth of the Negro Past*. Boston: Beacon Press.

Hess, Robert D. 1970. "Social Class and Ethnic Influences upon Socialization." Chapter 25 in *Manual of Child Psychology*, vol. 2, edited by Paul Mussen. New York: John Wiley and Sons, Inc.

Hesselbrock, Michie, Thomas F. Babor, Victor Hesselbrock, Roger E. Meyer, and Cathy Workman. 1983. "Never Believe an Alcoholic? On the Validity of Self-Report Measures of Alcohol Dependence and Related Constructs." *International Journal of the Addictions* 18:593–609.

Hilberman, Elaine, and K. Munson. 1977–1978. "Sixty Battered Women." *Victimology: An International Journal* 2:460–471.

Hill, Reuben, and Howard P. Becker (eds.). 1955. "Plans for Strengthening Family Life." Pp. 773–806 in *Family, Marriage and Parenthood*, edited by R. Hill. Boston: D. C. Heath.

Hill, Robert B., and Lawrence Shakleford. 1978. "The Black Extended Family Revisited." Pp. 201–206 in *The Black Family: Essays and Studies*, 2d ed. edited by Robert Staples. Belmont, CA: Wadsworth.

Hindelang, M. J. 1981. "Variations in Sex-Race-Age Specific Incidence Rates of Offending." *American Sociological Review* 46:461–474.

Hirschi, Travis, and Michael Gottfredson. 1983. "Age and the Explanation of Crime." *American Journal of Sociology* 89:552–584.

Hirschi, Travis, and Hanon C. Selvin. 1967. *Delinquency Research: An Appraisal of Analytic Methods*. New York: Free Press.

Hochstim, J. R. 1977. "A Critical Comparison of Three Strategies of Collecting Data from Households." *Journal of the American Statistical Association* 62:976–989.

Hofeller, K. H. 1980. "Social, Psychological, and Situational Factors in Wife Abuse." Unpublished doctoral dissertation, Claremont Graduate School.

Hoffman Lois W. 1961. "Effects of Maternal Employment on the Child." *Child Development* 32:187–197.

———. 1974. "Effects of Maternal Employment on the Child—A Review of the Research." *Developmental Psychology* 10:204–228.

Holmes, Thomas H., and Richard H. Rahe. 1967. "The Social Readjustment Rating Scale." *Journal of Psychosomatic Research* 11:213–218.

Hornung, Carlton, B. Claire McCullough, and Taichi Sugimoto. 1981. "Status Relationships in Marriage: Risk Factors in Spouse Abuse." *Journal of Marriage and the Family* 43:675–692.

Hotaling, Gerald T. 1984. "Gender and Mental Health: An Analysis and Reinterpretation." Unpublished dissertation, University of New Hampshire.

Hotaling, Gerald T., Saundra G. Atwell, and Arnold S. Linsky. 1979.

"Adolescent Life Changes and Illness: A Comparison of Three Models." *Journal of Youth and Adolescence* 7:393–403.

Hotaling, Gerald T., and Murray A. Straus. 1980. "Culture, Social Organization, and Irony in the Study of Family Violence." In *The Social Causes of Husband-Wife Violence*, edited by Murray A. Straus and Gerald T. Hotaling. Minneapolis MN: University of Minnesota Press.

Hotaling, Gerald T., and Murray A. Straus with Alan J. Lincoln. 1988. "Violence in the Family and Violence and other Crime Outside the Family." To appear in *Crime and Justice: An Annual Review of Research*, edited by M. Tonry and L. Ohlin. Chicago: University of Chicago Press.

Hotaling, Gerald T., and David B. Sugarman. 1986. "An Analysis of Risk Markers in Husband to Wife Violence: The Current State of Knowledge." *Violence and Victims* 1:101–124.

Howard, Jane. 1970. *Please Touch*. New York: Delta.

Hudson, Walter W., and Sally Rau McIntosh. 1981. "The Assessment of Spouse Abuse: Two Quantifiable Dimensions." *Journal of Marriage and the Family* 43(November):873–885.

Hunter, R. S., and N. Kilstrom. 1979. "Breaking the Cycle in Abusive Families." *American Journal of Psychiatry* 136:1320–1322.

Hunter, R. S., N. Kilstrom, E. Kraybill, and F. Loda. 1978. "Antecedents of Child Abuse and Neglect in Premature Infants: A Prospective Study in a Newborn Intensive Care Unit." *Pediatrics* 61:629–635.

International Association of Chiefs of Police. 1976. *Wife Beating*. Training Key 245.

Irving Crespi and Associates. 1987. New Jersey Public Opinion Survey Regarding Domestic Violence. New Jersey Department of Community Affairs.

Iversen, Gudmond, and Helmut Norpoth. 1976. *Analysis of Variance*. Newbury Park, CA: Sage Publications.

Jack, Lenus, Jr. 1979. *Kinship and Residential Propinquity: A Study of the Black Extended Family in New Orleans*. Ph.D. dissertation. University of Pittsburgh.

James, H. 1975. *The Little Victims: How America Treats Its Children*. New York: David McKay.

Jameson, P. A., and C. J. Schellenbach. 1977. "Sociological and Psychological Factors in the Background of Male and Female Perpetrators of Child Abuse." *Child Abuse and Neglect: The International Journal* 1:77–83.

Johnson, B., and H. Morse. 1968. "Injured Children and Their Parents." *Children* 15:147–152.

Jorgensen, Stephen R. 1977. "Societal Class Heterogamy, Status Striving, and Perception of Marital Conflict: A Partial Replication and Revision of Pearlin's Contingency Hypothesis." *Journal of Marriage and the Family* 39:653–689.

Jouriles, E. N., and K. D. O'Leary. 1985. "Interspousal Reliability of Reports of Marital Violence." *Journal of Consulting and Clinical Psychology* 53:419–421.

Justice, Blair, and D. F. Duncan. 1975. "Child Abuse as a Work-Related Problem." Presented at Child Abuse Session, A.P.H.A., Mental Health Section.

———. 1976. "Life Crisis as a Precursor to Child Abuse." *Public Health Reports* 91:110–115.

Justice, Blair, and Rita Justice. 1976. *The Abusing Family*. New York: Human Services Press.

Kadushin, Alfred, and Judith A. Martin. 1981. *Child Abuse: An Interactional Event*. New York: Columbia University Press.

Kagan, J. 1964. "Acquisition and Significance of Sex Typing and Sex Role Identity." Pp. 137–167 in *Review of Child Development Research*, vol. 1, edited by M. L. Hoffman and L. W. Hoffman. New York: Russell Sage Foundation.

Kalmuss, Debra, and Judith A. Seltzer. 1986. "Continuity of Marital Behavior in Remarriage: The Case of Spouse Abuse." *Journal of Marriage and the Family* 48:113–120.

Kalmuss, Debra S., and Murray A. Straus. 1982. "Wives' Marital Dependency and Wife Abuse." *Journal of Marriage and the Family* 44:277–286. Also reprinted in *Framing the Family: Contemporary Portraits*, edited by Bert N. Adams and John L. Campbell. Prospect Heights, IL: Waveland Press, 1985.

Kaplan, Abraham. 1964. *The Conduct of Inquiry*. San Francisco: Chandler.

Kaplan, H. B. 1970. "Self-Deregation and Adjustment to Recent Life Experiences." *Archives of General Psychiatry* 22:324–331.

Kaufman, Edward. 1985. *Substance Abuse and Family Therapy*. New York: Grune and Stratton.

Kaufman Kantor, Glenda, L. Landis, M. Luft, W. OBrien, A. OBrien Stevens. 1985. *You've Got to Be Strong: Evaluation of the Centralized Domestic Violence Misdemeanor Court Project of the Circuit Court of Cook County*. Chicago: Chicago Law Enforcement Study Group and Chicago Battered Women's Network.

Kaufman Kantor, Glenda and Anne OBrien Stevens. 1986. "Reflections on the Social Control of Women and Social Change Processes: An Evaluation of the Centralized Domestic Violence Court in Chicago, Illinois." Paper presented at the American Society of Criminology Meeting, Atlanta, GA, November, 1986.

Kaufman Kantor, Glenda, and Murray A. Straus. 1987. "The 'Drunken Bum' Theory of Wife Beating." *Social Problems* 34:213–230.

———. 1989. "Response of Victims and the Police to Assaults on Wives." Chapter 26 in this book.

Kempe, C. Henry. 1971. "Pediatric Implications of the Battered Baby Syndrome." *Archives of Disease in Children* 46:28–37.

Kempe, C. Henry, Frederic Silverman, Brandt Steele, William Droege-mueller, and Henry Silver. 1962. "The Battered Child Syndrome." *Journal of the American Medical Association* 181:17–24.

Kennedy, L. W., and D. G. Dutton. 1987. Edmonton Area Series Report No. 53: *The Incidence of Wife Assault in Alberta*. University of Alberta, Edmonton, Alberta, Canada: Population Research Laboratory.

Kent, J., H. Weisbar, B. Lamar, and T. Marx. 1978. "Physical Abuse of Young Children: A Preliminary Typology of Cases." In *House Committee on Science and Technology, Research into Violent Behavior: Domestic Violence*. Washington, DC: U.S. Congress.

Kinard, E. M. 1980. "Emotional Development in Physically Abused Children." *American Journal of Orthopsychiatry* 50:606–696.

Kinsey, A. C., W. B. Pomeroy, and C. E. Martin. 1948. *Sexual Behavior in the Human Male*. Philadelphia: W. B. Saunders.

Kinsley, S. 1977. "Women's Dependency and Federal Programs." Pp. 79–191 in *Women into Wives: The Legal and Economic Impact of Marriages*, edited by J. R. Chapman and M. Gates. Newbury Park, CA: Sage Publications.

Klecka, W. R., and A. J. Tuchfarber. 1978. "Random Digit Dialing: A Comparison to Personal Surveys." *Public Opinion Quarterly* 42:105–114.

Klein, Dorie. 1981. "Drinking and Battering: Some Preliminary Considerations on Alcohol, Gender Domination, and Marital Violence." Paper presented at the Society for the Study of Social Problems Meeting, Toronto, Ontario, August.

Knoke, David, and Peter J. Burke. 1980. *Log-Linear Models*. Newbury Park, CA: Sage Publications.

Kohn, Melvin L. 1969. *Class and Conformity: A Study in Values*. Homewood, IL: Dorsey Press.

Kohn, Melvin L., and C. Schooler. 1983. *Work and Personality: An Inquiry into the Impact of Social Stratification*. Norwood, NJ: Ablex Publishing Corporation.

Kolb, Trudie M., and Murray A. Straus. 1974. "Marital Power and Marital Happiness in Relation to Problem Solving Ability." *Journal of Marriage and the Family* 36:756–766.

Komarovsky, Mirra. 1967. *Blue-Collar Marriage*. New York: Random House.

Korbin, Jill E. 1978. "Changing Family Roles and Structures: Impact on Child Abuse and Neglect? A Cross Cultural Perspective." Pp. 98–107 in *Child Abuse and Neglect: Issues on Innovation and Implementation*, vol. 1, edited by M. Lauderdale et al. Proceedings of the Second Annual Conference on Child Abuse and Neglect, 1977. Washington, DC: Department of Health, Education and Welfare.

———. 1981. *Child Abuse and Neglect: Cross-Cultural Perspectives*. Berkeley: University of California Press.

Labell, Linda S. 1977. "Wife Abuse: A Sociological Study of Battered Women and Their Mates." *Victimology* 4:258–267.

Lane, Katherine E., and Patricia Gwartney-Gibbs. 1985. "Violence in the Context of Dating and Sex." *Journal of Family Issues* 6:45–59.

Lane, T. W., and G. E. Davis. 1987. "Child Maltreatment and Juvenile Delinquency: Does a Relationship Exist?" In *Prevention of Delinquent Behavior*, edited by J. D. Burchard and S. N. Burchard. Newbury Park, CA: Sage Publications.

Laner, Mary R. 1983. "Courtship Abuse and Aggression: Contextual Aspects." *Sociological Spectrum* 3:69–83.

Laner, Mary R., and Jeanine Thompson. 1982. "Abuse and Aggression in Courting Couples." *Deviant Behavior: An Interdisciplinary Journal* 3:229–244.

Langan, Patrick A., and Christopher A. Innes. 1986. "Preventing Domestic Violence Against Women: Discussion Paper." In BJS Special Report *Preventing Domestic Violence Against Women* (August 1986, NCJ-102037).

LaPiere, Richard T. 1934. "Attitudes vs. Actions." *Social Forces* 13:230–237.

LaRossa, Ralph. 1980. " 'And We Haven't Had Any Problems Since': Conjugal Violence and the Politics of Marriage." In *The Social Causes of Husband-Wife Violence*, edited by Murray A. Straus and Gerald T. Hotaling. Minneapolis: University of Minnesota Press.

Larzelere, Robert E. 1986. "Moderate Spanking: Model or Deterrent of Children's Aggression in the Family?" *Journal of Family Violence* 1:27–36.

Lazarus, Richard S. 1966. *Psychological Stress and the Coping Process.* New York: McGraw-Hill.

Legg, J., D. E. Olday, and B. Wesley. 1984. "Why Do Females Remain in Violent Dating Relationships?" Paper presented at the Second National Family Violence Research Conference, University of New Hampshire.

Leonard, Kenneth E. 1984. "Alcohol Consumption and Escalatory Aggression in Intoxicated and Sober Dyads." *Journal of Studies on Alcohol* 45:75–80.

Lerman, Lisa G. 1981. *Prosecution of Spouse Abuse: Innovations in Criminal Justice Response.* Washington, DC: Center for Women Policy Studies.

———. 1982. "Court Decisions on Wife Abuse Laws: Recent Developments." *Response* 3:21–22.

Lerman, Lisa G., Leslie Landis, and Sharon Goldzweig. 1981. "State Legislation on Domestic Violence." *Response* 4:1–18.

Lerman, Lisa G., and F. Livingston. 1983. "State Legislation on Domestic Violence." *Response to Violence in the Family and Sexual Assault* 6:1–28.

Levine, Sol, and Norman A. Scotch. 1967. "Toward the Development of

Theoretical Models: II." *Milbank Memorial Fund Quarterly* 45:163–174.

Levinger, George. 1965. "Marital Cohesiveness and Dissolution: An Integrative Review." *Journal of Marriage and the Family* 27:19–28.

———. 1974. "Physical Abuse Among Applicants for Divorce." Pp. 85–97 in *Violence in the Family*, edited by Suzanne K. Steinmetz and Murray A. Straus. New York: Harper and Row.

Levinson, David. 1983. "Social Setting, Cultural Factors and Alcohol-Related Aggression." In *Drug Abuse and Aggression*, edited by E. Gottheil, K. A. Druley, T. E. Skoloda, and H. W. Waxman. Springfield, IL: Charles C. Thomas.

Levinson, David. 1989. *Family Violence in Cross-Cultural Perspective*. Newbury Park, CA: Sage.

Liebman, Donald A., and J. A. Schwartz. 1973. "Police Programs in Domestic Crisis Intervention: A Review." In *The Urban Policeman in Transition*, edited by J. R. Snibbe and H. M. Snibbe. Springfield, IL: Charles C. Thomas.

Light, R. J. 1973. "Abused and Neglected Children in America: A Study of Alternative Policies." *Harvard Educational Review* 43(November): 556–598.

Lincoln, Alan J., and Murray A. Straus. 1985. *Crime and the Family*. Springfield, IL: C. C. Thomas.

Linsky, Arnold S., and Murray A. Straus. 1986. *Social Stress in the United States: Clues to Regional Patterns of Crime and Illness*. Dover, MA: Auburn House.

Linsky, Arnold S., Murray A. Straus, and John P. Colby. 1985. "Stressful Events, Stressful Conditions and Alcohol Problems in the United States: A Partial Test of Bales' Theory of Alcoholism." *Journal of Studies on Alcohol* 46:72–80.

Linton, Ralph. 1936. *The Study of Man: An Introduction*. New York: Appleton-Century-Crofts.

Liska, A. E. 1974. "Emergent Issues in the Attitude-Behavior Consistency Controversy." *American Sociological Review* 39:261–272.

———. 1975. *The Consistency Controversy: Readings on the Impact of Attitude on Behavior*. New York: John Wiley and Sons.

Lockhart, L. L. 1987. "A Reexamination of the Effects of Race and Social Class on the Incidence of Marital Violence: A Search for Reliable Differences." *Journal of Marriage and the Family* 49:603–610.

Loeber, R., and M. Stouthamer-Loeber. 1986. "Models and Meta-Analysis of the Relationship Between Family Variables and Juvenile Conduct Problems and Delinquency." In *Crime and Justice: An Annual Review of Research*. vol. 7, edited by N. Morris and M. Tonry. Chicago: University of Chicago Press.

Loeber, R., and T. J. "Dishion." 1983. "Early Predictors of Male Delinquency: A Review." *Psychological Bulletin* 94:68–99.

Loftin, Colin, and Robert H. Hill. 1974. "Regional Subculture and Homicide: An Examination of the Castil-Hackney Thesis." *American Sociological Review* 39:714–724.

London, J. 1978. "Images of Violence Against Women." *Victimology* 2:510–524.

Louis Harris and Associates. 1987. Family Violence Follow-up Survey. Survey Methodology. New York: Louis Harris and Associates.

Loving, Nancy. 1980. *Responding to Spouse Abuse and Wife Beating: A Guide for Police*. Washington, DC: Police Executive Research Forum.

Loya, F., J. A. Mercy, and Associates. 1985. *The Epidemiology of Homicide in the City of Los Angeles, 1970–79*. University of California at Los Angeles and Centers for Disease Control, Department of Health and Human Services, Public Health Service, Centers for Disease Control.

MacAndrew, Craig, and Robert B. Edgerton. 1969. *Drunken Comportment*. Chicago: Aldine.

Maccoby, Eleanor E. 1980. *Social Development: Psychological Growth and the Parent-Child Relationship*. San Diego: Harcourt Brace Jovanovich.

Maccoby, Eleanor E., and Carol Nagy Jacklin. 1974. *The Psychology of Sex Differences*. Stanford, CA: Stanford University Press.

Macklin, E. D. 1972. "Heterosexual Cohabitation Among Unmarried College Students." *Family Coordinator* 21:463–472.

Maden, Marc F., and David F. Wrench. 1977. "Significant Findings in Child Abuse Research." *Victimology* 2:196–224.

Magnuson, E. 1983. "Child Abuse: The Ultimate Betrayal." *Time* 122:20–22.

Mahmood, T. 1978. "Child Abuse in Arabia, India and the West—Comparative Legal Aspects." Pp. 281–289 in *Family Violence: An International and Interdisciplinary Study*, edited by J. Eekelaar and S. Katz. Toronto: Butterworth and Co.

Maisto, S. A., L. C. Sobell, and M. B. Sobell. 1979. "Comparison of Alcoholics' Self-Reports of Drinking Behavior with Reports of Collateral Informants." *Journal of Consulting and Clinical Psychology* 47:106–112.

Makepeace, James M. 1981. "Courtship Violence Among College Students." *Family Relations* 30:97–102.

———. 1983. "Life Events Stress and Courtship Violence." *Family Relations* 32:101–109.

———. 1986. "Gender Differences in Courtship Violence Victimization." *Family Relations* 35:383–388.

———. 1988. "The Severity of Courtship Violence and the Effectiveness of Individual Precautions." Chapter 21 in this volume.

Marcus, Alfred C., and Lori A. Crane. 1986. "Telephone Surveys in Public Health Research." *Medical Care* 24:97–112.

Marcus, Alfred C., and Judith M. Siegel. 1982. "Sex Differences in the Use of Physician Services: A Preliminary Test of the Fixed Role Hypothesis." *Journal of Health and Social Behavior* 23:186–197.

Marcus, Paul. 1983. "Assault and Battery." *Encyclopedia of Crime and Justice*, vol. 1, edited by Sanford H. Kadish. New York: Free Press.

Margolin, Gayla. 1988. "Interpersonal and Intrapersonal Factors Associated with Marital Violence." Chapter 14 in this volume.

Margolin, Gayla, Linda Gorin Sibner, and Lisa Gleberman. 1988. "Wife Battering." Pp. 89–117 in *Handbook of Family Violence*, edited by V. B. Van Hasselt, R. L. Morrison, A. S. Bellack, and M. Hersen. New York: Plenum.

Marlatt, G. Allan, and Damaris J. Rohsenow. 1980. "Cognitive Processes in Alcohol Use: Expectancy and the Balanced Placebo Design." Pp. 159–199 in *Advances in Substance Abuse: Behavioral and Biological Research*, a research annual, vol. 1, edited by N. K. Mello. Greenwich, CT: JAI Press.

Marsden, D. 1978. "Sociological Perspectives on Family Violence." In *Violence and the Family*, edited by J. P. Martin. New York: Wiley.

Martin, D. 1976. *Battered Wives*. San Francisco: Glide.

Martin, H. L. 1970. "Antecedents of Burns and Scalds in Children." *British Journal of Medical Psychology* 43:39–47.

Martin, H. P., and P. Beezley. 1974. "Prevention and the Consequences of Abuse." *Journal of Operational Psychiatry* 6:68–77.

Mayfield, Demmie. 1983. "Substance Abuse and Aggression: A Psychopharmacological Perspective." In *Drug Abuse and Aggression*, edited by E. Gottheil, K. A. Druley, T. E. Skoloda, and H. W. Waxman. Springfield, IL: Charles C. Thomas.

McAdoo, Harriette P. 1978. "Role of the Extended Family Support Network in the Maintenance of Stability and Mobility of Single and Married Black Mothers." Paper presented at the Conference on Support for Single-Parent Families through Extended Family Networks, University of Notre Dame, May 26–27.

McClelland, David C., William N. Davis, Rudolph Kalin, and Eric Wanner. 1972. *The Drinking Man*. New York: Free Press.

McCord, Joan. 1979. "Some Child-Rearing Antecedents of Criminal Behavior in Adult Men." *Journal of Personality and Social Psychology* 37:1477–1486.

———. 1984. "Parental Aggressiveness and Physical Punishment in Long-Term Perspective." Paper presented at the Second National Conference for Family Violence Researchers, Durham, NH.

McGrath, Joseph E. 1970. "A Conceptual Formulation for Research on Stress." Pp. 10–21 in *Social and Psychological Factors in Stress*, edited by J. E. McGrath. New York: Holt, Rinehart and Winston.

McGrath, Patricia E. with Phyllis Stine Schultz and P. O'Dea Culhane. 1980. *The Development and Implementation of a Hospital Protocol for the Identification and Treatment of Battered Women.* Monograph series. Rockville, MD: National Clearinghouse on Domestic Violence.

McKinley, D. G. 1964. *Social Class and Family Life.* London: Collier-Macmillan Limited.

McLeod, M. 1983. "Victim Non-Cooperation in the Prosecution of Domestic Assault." *Criminology* 21:395–416.

Mechanic, David. 1962. *Students Under Stress: A Study in the Social Psychology of Adaptation.* New York: Free Press.

Mednick, S. A., V. Pollock, J. Volavka, and W. Gabrielli, Jr. 1982. "Biology and Violence." In *Criminal Violence*, edited by M. E. Wolfgang and N. E. Weiner. Newbury Park, CA: Sage Publications.

Megargee, E. I. 1982. "Psychological Determinants and Correlates of Criminal Violence." In *Criminal Violence*, edited by M. E. Wolfgang and N. A. Weiner. Newbury Park, CA: Sage Publications.

Melnick, B., and J. R. Hurley. 1969. "Distinctive Personalilty Attributes of Child-Abusing Mothers." *Journal of Consulting and Clinical Psychology* 33:746–749.

Meredith, W. H., D. A. Abbott, and S. L. Adams. 1986. "Family Violence: Its Relation to Marital and Parental Satisfaction and Family Strengths." *Journal of Family Violence* 1:299–305.

Merton, Robert K. 1938. "Social Structure and Anomie." *American Sociological Review* 3:672–682.

Merton, Robert K., and Robert Nisbet. 1976. *Contemporary Social Problems.* 4th ed. New York: Harcourt Brace Jovanovich.

Miller, A. 1983. *For Your Own Good: Hidden Cruelty in Child-Rearing and the Roots of Violence.* New York: Farrar, Straus and Giroux.

Miller, B., B. Rollins, and D. L. Thomas. 1982. "On Methods of Studying Marriages and Families." *Journal of Marriage and the Family* 44:851–873.

Miller, D. R., and G. E. Swanson. 1958. *The Changing American Parent: A Study in the Detroit Area.* New York: John Wiley.

Milner, Joel S. 1986. *The Child Abuse Potential Inventory: Manual.* 2d ed. Webster, NC: Psytec Corporation.

Mirande, Alfredo, 1977. "The Chicano Family: A Reanalysis of Conflicting Views." *Journal of Marriage and the Family* 39:747–756.

———. 1979. "A Reinterpretation of Male Dominance in the Chicano Family." *Family Coordinator* 28:473–479.

Mirande, Alfredo, and Patricia Perez. 1987. "Ethnic and Cultural Differences in Domestic Violence: A Test of Conflicting Models of the Chicano Family." Paper presented at the Research Conference on Violence and Homicide in the Hispanic Community, September 14–15, Los Angeles.

Montiel, Miguel. 1973. "The Social Science Myth of the Mexican-Americans." Pp. 57–64 in *Voices: Readings from El Grito*, edited by Octavio Romano. 1967–1973. Berkeley, CA: Quinto Sol.

Moore, David, and Murray A. Straus. 1987. *Violence of Parents Toward Their Children, New Hampshire, 1987.* Report submitted to the New Hampshire Task Force on Child Abuse and Neglect, P.O. Box 607, Concord, NH 03301.

Moore, Joan, and Harry Pachon. 1985. *Hispanic Families in the United States.* Englewood Cliffs, NJ: Prentice-Hall.

Morgan, Patricia. 1982. "Alcohol and Family Violence: A Review of the Literature." Pp. 223–259 in *Alcohol Consumption and Related Problems, Alcohol and Health Monograph 1*, DHHS Publication (ADM) 82–1190. Washington, DC: U.S.G.P.O.

———. 1983. "Alcohol, Disinhibition, and Domination: A Conceptual Analysis." Pp. 405–420 in *Alcohol and Disinhibition: Nature and Meaning of the Link*, edited by Robin Room and Gary Collins. Washington, DC: U.S.G.P.O., NIAAA.

Morse, A., J. N. Hyde, Jr., E. H. Newberger, and R. B. Reed. 1977. "Environmental Correlates of Pediatric Social Illness: Preventive Implications of an Advocacy Approach." *American Journal of Public Health* 67:612–615.

Morse, C. W., O. J. Sahler, and S. B. Friedman. 1970. "A Three-Year Follow-Up Study of Abused and Neglected Children." *American Journal of Diseases of Children* 120:439–446.

Mulligan, Martha A. 1977. "An Investigation of Factors Associated with Violent Modes of Conflict Resolution in the Family." Unpublished M. A. thesis, University of Rhode Island.

Murphy, Christopher M. 1987. "Verbal Aggression As a Predictor of Aggression in Early Marriage." Paper presented at the Third National Family Violence Research Conference, Durham, NH, July.

Murphy, John E. 1988. "Date Abuse and Forced Intercourse Among College Students." Chapter 20 in *Violence in Dating Relationships: Emerging Social Issues*, by Maureen A. Pirog-Goode and Jan E. Stets. New York: Springer-Verlag, forthcoming.

Nagi, Saad Z. 1975. "Child Abuse and Neglect Programs: A National Overview." *Children Today* 4:13–17.

———. 1976. *Child Maltreatment in the United States: A Challenge to Social Institutions.* New York: Columbia University Press.

National Center on Child Abuse and Neglect (NCCAN). 1981. *Study Findings: National Study of Incidence and Severity of Child Abuse and Neglect.* Washington, DC: Department of Health, Education and Welfare.

Neff, James A., and Baqar A. Husaini. 1985. "Stress-Buffer Properties of Alcohol Consumption: The Role of Urbanicity and Religious Identification." *Journal of Health and Social Behavior* 26:207–222.

Nelson, Barbara. 1984. *Making an Issue of Child Abuse: Political Agenda Setting for Social Problems.* Chicago: University of Chicago Press.

Neidig, Peter H., Dale H. Friedman, and Barbara S. Collins. 1986. "Attitudinal Characteristics of Males Who Have Engaged in Spouse Abuse." *Journal of Family Violence* 1:223–233.

Newberger, Eli H. 1978. "Treatment of Abused Children: Search for a More Adequate Foundation for Clinical Practice." Testimony presented before the subcommittee on Domestic and International Scientific Planning, Analysis, and Cooperation, Committee on Science and Technology, U.S. House of Representatives.

Newberger, Eli H., et al. 1977. "Pediatric Social Illness: Toward an Etiologic Classification." *Pediatrics* 60:178–185.

Newberger, Eli H., and James N. Hyde, Jr. 1975. "Child Abuse: Principles and Implications of Current Pediatric Practice." *Pediatric Clinics of North America* 22:695–715.

Newson, J., and E. Newson. 1963. *Patterns of Infant Care in an Urban Community.* Baltimore: Penguin Books.

Nie, Norman H., C. Hadlai Hull, Jean G. Jenkins, Karen Steinbrenner, and Dale H. Bent. 1975. *SPSS Statistical Package for the Social Sciences.* 2d ed. New York: McGraw-Hill.

Nisonoff, Linda, and Irving Bitman. 1979. "Spouse Abuse: Incidence and Relationship to Selected Demographic Variables." *Victimology* 4:131–140.

Nunnally, J. C. 1978. *Psychometric Theory.* 2d ed. New York: McGraw-Hill.

O'Leary, K. Daniel, and Ileana Arias. 1988. "Assessing Agreement of Reports of Spouse Abuse." Chapter 15 in *Family Abuse and Its Consequences: New Directions In Research,* edited by Geralt T. Hotaling, David Finkehor, John T. Kirkpatrick, and Murray A. Straus. Newbury Park, CA: Page.

Oakland, L., and R. L. Kane. 1973. "The Working Mother and Child Neglect on the Navajo Reservation." *Pediatrics* 51:849–853.

Ochberg, F. M. 1980. "On Preventing Aggression and Violence." *Police Chief* 67:52–56.

Office of Human Development Services. 1981. *Study Findings: National Study of the Incidence and Severity of Child Abuse and Neglect.* U.S. Department of Health and Human Services.

Okun, Lewis. 1986. *Women Abuse: Facts Replacing Myths.* Albany: State University of New York Press.

Olsen, L. J., and W. M. Holmes. 1986. "Youth at Risk: Adolescents and Maltreatment." *Children and Youth Services Review* 8:13–35.

Osgood, Charles, George Suci, and Perry Tannenbaum. 1957. *The Measurement of Meaning.* Urbana: University of Illinois Press.

Owens, David, and Murray A. Straus. 1975. "The Social Structure of Violence in Childhood and Approval of Violence as an Adult." *Aggressive Behavior* 1:193–211. Also in *Corporal Punishment in American Education: Readings in History, Practice, and Alternatives,* edited by I. H. Hyman and J. H. Wise. Philadelphia: Temple University Press, 1979.

Pagelow, Mildred D. 1981. *Woman-Battering: Victims and Their Experiences*. Newbury Park, CA: Sage Publications.

———. 1984. *Family Violence*. New York: Praeger.

Palmer, Stuart. 1960. *A Study of Murder*. New York: Crowell.

———. 1972. *The Violent Society*. New Haven, CT: College and University Press.

Parke, R. D., and C. W. Collmer. 1975. "Child Abuse: An Interdisciplinary Analysis. Pp. 509–590 in *Review of Child Development Research*, vol. 5, edited by E. M. Hetherington. Chicago: University of Chicago Press.

Parnas, Raymond I. 1970. "The Judicial Response to Intra-Family Violence." *Minnesota Law Review* 54:585–645.

———. 1971. "The Police Response to the Domestic Disturbance." In *The Criminal in the Arms of the Law*, edited by L. Radzinowicz and M. E. Wolfgang. New York: Basic Books.

Parsons, Talcott. 1942. "Age and Sex in the Social Structure of the United States." *American Sociological Review* 7:604–616.

Parsons, Talcott, and Robert F. Bales. 1955. *Family Socialization and Interaction Process*. New York: Free Press.

Patterson, Gerald R. 1982. *A Social Learning Approach*. Vol. 3: *Coercive Family Process*. Eugene, OR: Castalia.

Patterson, Gerald R., J. A. Cobb, and R. S. Ray. 1973. "A Social Engineering Technology for Retraining the Families of Aggressive Boys." In *Issues and Trends in Behavior Therapy*, edited by H. E. Adams and I. P. Unkel. Springfield, IL: Charles C. Thomas, Publishers.

Paykel, E. S. 1974. "Life Stress and Psychiatric Disorder: Applications of the Clinical Approach." Pp. 135–149 in *Stressful Life Events: Their Nature and Effects*, edited by B. S. Dohrenwend and B. P. Dohrenwend. New York: John Wiley.

Pearlin, L. I., and C. Schooler. 1982. "The Structure of Coping." Pp. 109–135 in *Family Stress, Coping, and Social Support*, edited by H. I. McCubbin, A. E. Cauble, and J. M. Patterson. Springfield, IL: Charles C. Thomas.

Pelton, L. G. 1979. "Interpreting Family Violence Data." *American Journal of Orthopsychiatry* 49:194.

Pelton, L. H. (ed.). 1981. Introduction. *The Social Context of Child Abuse and Neglect*. New York: Human Sciences Press.

Pernanen, Kai. 1976. "Alcohol and Crimes of Violence." In *The Biology of Alcoholism*, vol. 4: *Social Aspects of Alcoholism*, edited by B. Kissin and H. Begleiter. New York: Plenum.

———. 1981. "Theoretical Aspects of the Relationship Between Alcohol Use and Crime." In *Drinking and Crime: Perspectives on the Relationships Between Alcohol Consumption and Criminal Behavior*, edited by James J. Collins, Jr. New York: Guilford Press.

Peterman, D., C. Ridley, and S. Anderson. 1974. "Comparison of Cohabiting and Non-Cohabiting Students." *Journal of Marriage and the Family* 36:344–354.

Pillemer, Karl. 1985. "The Dangers of Dependency: New Findings on Domestic Violence against the Elderly." *Social Problems* 33:146–158.

Pillemer, Karl, and J. Jill Suitor. 1988. "Elder Abuse." Pp. 247–270 in *Handbook of Family Violence*, edited by V. Van Hasselt, H. Bellack, R. Morrison, and M. Hersen. New York: Plenum.

Pirog-Good, Maureen, and Jan Stets-Kealey. 1985. "Domestic Violence Victimization: A Multiyear Perspective." Paper presented at the 1985 Annual Meeting of the American Society of Criminology, San Diego, CA.

Plass, Margaret S. 1986. "Patterns in Spousal Homicide: An Analysis of Racial, Regional, and Gender Variations." Durham: University of New Hampshire, Family Research Laboratory.

Plass, Margaret S., and J. C. Gessner. 1983. "Violence in Courtship Relations: A Southern Example." *Free Inquiry in Creative Sociology* 11:198–202.

Plass, Margaret S., and M. A. Straus. 1987. "Intra-Family Homicide in the United States: Incidence Rates, Trends, and Differences by Region, Race and Gender." Paper presented at the Third National Family Violence Research Conference, University of New Hampshire, Family Research Laboratory, Durham.

Pleck, Elizabeth, Joseph H. Pleck, Marlyn Grossman, and Pauline B. Bart. 1977. "The Battered Data Syndrome: A Comment on Steinmetz' Article." *Victimology: An International Journal* 2:680–683.

Pleck, Joseph H. 1977. "The Work-Family Role System." *Social Problems* 24:417–427.

———. 1979. "Men's Family Work: Three Perspectives and Some New Data." *Family Coordinator* 28:481–495.

Polich, J. Michael. 1982. "The Validity of Self-Reports in Alcoholism Research." *Addictive Behaviors* 7:123–132.

Portes, A., and C. Truelove. 1987. "Making Sense of Diversity: Recent Research on Hispanic Minorities in the United States." *Annual Review of Sociology* 13:359–385.

Potts, D. A., S. D. Herzberger, and A. E. Holland. 1979. "Child Abuse: A Cross-Generational Pattern of Child Rearing." Paper presented at the Midwestern Psychological Association Convention.

Powers, Robert J., and Irwin L. Kutash. 1982. "Alcohol, Drugs, and Partner Abuse." Pp. 39–75 in *The Abusive Partner: An Analysis of Domestic Battering*, edited by M. Roy. New York: Van Nostrand Reinhold.

Prescott, S., and C. Letko. 1977. "Battered Women: A Social Psychological Perspective." Pp. 71–96 in *Battered Women: A Social Psychological Study of Domestic Violence*, edited by M. Roy. New York: Van Nostrand Reinhold.

Price-Bonham, S. 1976. "A Comparison of Weighted and Unweighted Decision-Making Scores." *Journal of Marriage and the Family* 38:629–640.

Rada, Richard T. 1978. *Clinical Aspects of the Rapist.* New York: Grune and Stratton.

Radbill, S. 1974. "A History of Child Abuse and Infanticide." Pp. 3–21 in *The Battered Child*, 2d ed., edited by R. Helfer and C. Kempe. Chicago: University of Chicago Press.

Radbill, Samuel X. 1980. "Children in a World of Violence: A History of Child Abuse." Chapter 1 in *The Battered Child*, 3d ed., edited by C. Henry Kempe and Ray E. Helfer. Chicago: University of Chicago Press.

Radloff, Lenore. 1975. "Sex Differences in Depression: The Effects of Occupation and Marital Status." *Sex Roles* 1:249–265.

Reed, D., S. Fischer, G. Kaufman Kantor, and K. Karales. 1983. *All They Can Do . . . Police Response to Battered Women's Complaints.* Chicago, IL: Chicago Law Enforcement Study Group.

Reidel, Mark, and Margaret A. Zahn. 1985. *The Nature and Pattern of American Homicide.* Washington, DC: National Institute of Justice.

Reiss, Ira. 1980. *Family Systems in America.* New York: Holt, Rinehart and Winston.

Resick, Patricia A., and Donnis Reese. 1986. "Perception of Family Social Climate and Physical Aggression in the Home." *Journal of Family Violence* 1:71–83.

Resnick, P. J. 1969. "Child Murder by Parents: A Psychiatric Review of Filicide." *American Journal of Psychiatry* 126:325–334.

Revitch, E., and L. B. Schlesinger. 1978. "Murder: Evaluation, Classification and Prediction." In *Violence: Perspectives on Murder and Aggression*, edited by I. L. Kutash, S. B. Kutash, and L. B. Schlesinger and Associates. San Francisco: Jossey-Bass.

Riley, Matilda White. 1973. "Aging and Cohort Succession: Interpretations and Misinterpretations." *Public Opinion* Quarterly 37:35–49.

———. 1985. "Age Strata in Social Systems." Pp. 369–411 in *Handbook of Aging and the Social Sciences*, edited by R. H. Binstock and E. Shanas. New York: Van Nostrand Reinhold.

———. 1987. "On the Significance of Age in Sociology." *American Sociological Review* 52:1–14.

Roberts, Robert E., and Sally W. Vernon. 1981. "Usefulness of the PERI Demoralization Scale to Screen For Psychiatric Disorder in a Community Sample." *Psychiatry Research* 5:183–193.

Robinson, J. P., R. Athanasiou, and K. B. Head. 1969. *Measures of Occupational Attitudes and Occupational Characteristics.* Ann Arbor: University of Michigan, Survey Research Center of the Institute for Social Research.

Rodman, Hyman. 1968. "Family and Social Pathology in the Ghetto." *Science* 161:756–762.

Rohner, R. P. 1975. *They Love Me, They Love Me Not. A Worldwide Study of the Effects of Parental Acceptance and Rejection.* New Haven, CT: HRAF Press.

Roizen, Judy. 1981. "Alcohol and Criminal Behavior Among Blacks: The Case for Research on Special Populations." In *Drinking and Crime: Perspectives on the Relationships Between Alcohol Consumption and Criminal Behavior*, edited by James J. Collins, Jr. New York: Guilford Press.

Roizen, Judy, and D. Schneberk. 1977. "Alcohol and Crime." In *Alcohol Casualties and Crime*, edited by M. Aarens, T. Cameron, J. Roizen, R. Roizen, R. Room, D. Schneberk, and D. Wingard. Berkeley, CA: Social Research Group.

Romano, Octavio. 1973. "The Anthropology and Sociology of the Mexican-Americans: The Distortion of Mexican-American History." Pp. 43–56 in *Voices: Readings from El Grito, 1967–1973*, edited by Octavio Romano. Berkeley, CA: Quinto Sol.

Room, Robin. 1980. "Alcohol as an Instrument of Intimate Domination." Paper presented at the Society for the Study of Social Problems Annual Meeting, New York, August.

———. 1980. "Treatment Sampling Populations and Larger Realities." Pp. 205–224 in *Alcoholism Treatment and Transition*, edited by Griffith Edwards and Marcus Grant. London: Croom Helm.

Room, Robin, and Gary Collins (eds.). 1983. *Alcohol and Disinhibition: Nature and Meaning of the Link*. Washington, DC: U.S.G.P.O., NIAAA.

Roscoe, B., and N. Benaske. 1985. "Courtship Violence Experienced by Abused Wives: Similarities in Patterns of Abuse." *Family Relations* 34:419–424.

Rosenbaum, Alan, and K. Daniel O'Leary. 1981. "Marital Violence: Characteristics of Abusive Couples." *Journal of Consulting and Clinical Psychology* 49:63–71.

Rothenberg, M. B. 1975. "Effects of Television Violence on Children and Youth." *Journal of the American Medical Association* 234:1043–1046.

Rounsaville, B. J. 1978. "Theories in Marital Violence: Evidence from a Study of Battered Women." *Victimology* 3:11–31.

Rouse, Linda P. 1984. "Conflict Tactics Used by Men in Marital Disputes." Paper presented at the Second National Conference for Family Violence Researchers, Durham, NH.

Rowe, Alan R., and Charles R. Tittle. 1977. "Life-cycle Changes and Criminal Propensity." *Sociological Quarterly* 18:223–236.

Roy, Maria. 1977. "A Current Study of 150 Cases." Pp. 25–44 in *Battered Women: A Psychosocial Study of Domestic Violence*, edited by Maria Roy. New York: Van Nostrand Reinhold.

———. 1982. "Four Thousand Partners in Violence: A Trend Analysis." In *The Abusive Partner*, edited by M. Roy. New York: Van Nostrand Reinhold.

Rubin, L. B. 1976. *Worlds of Pain: Life in the Working-Class Family*. New York: Basic Books.

Runyon, Desmond. 1986. *Computer Output Provided in Personal Communication.* Chappel Hill: University of North Carolina.

Ryan, Bryce F. & Murray A. Straus. 1954. *A report from the Center for Comparative Studies in Technological Development and Social Change: The Integration Of Sinhalese Society.* Minneapolis, MN: Office of International Programs, University of Minnesota.

Ryder, Norman. 1965. "The Cohort as a Concept in the Study of Social Change." *American Sociological Review* 30:843–861.

Sack, A. R., J. F. Keller, and R. D. Howard. 1982. "Conflict Tactics and Violence in Dating Situations." *International Journal of Sociology of the Family* 12:89–100.

Safilios-Rothschild, Constantina. 1970. "The Study of Family Power Structure: A Review of 1960–69." *Journal of Marriage and the Family* 32:539–552.

Sammons, Lucy N. 1981. "Battered and Pregnant." *MCN: American Journal of Maternal Child Nursing* 6:246–250.

Sampson, R. J. 1987. "Urban Black Violence: The Effect of Male Joblessness and Family Disruption." *American Journal of Sociology* 93:348–382.

Saunders, Daniel G. 1986. "When Battered Women Use Violence: Husband-Abuse or Self-Defense?" *Violence and Victims* 1:47–60.

Saunders, Daniel G., and Darald Hanusa. 1986. "Cognitive-Behavioral Treatment of Men Who Batter: The Short-Term Effects of Group Therapy." *Journal of Family Violence* 1:357–372.

Saunders, Daniel G., Ann B. Lynch, Marcia Grayson, and Daniel Linz. 1987. "The Inventory of Beliefs About Wife Beating: The Construction and Initial Validation of a Measure of Beliefs and Attitudes." *Violence and Victims* 2:39–57.

Scanzoni, John. 1970. *Opportunity and the Family.* New York: Free Press.

———. 1972. "Marital Conflict as a Positive Force." In *Sexual Bargaining*, edited by John Scanzoni. Englewood Cliffs, NJ: Prentice-Hall.

———. 1975. *Sex Roles, Life Styles and Childbearing: Changing Patterns in Marriage and Family.* New York: Free Press.

———. 1978. *Sex Roles, Women's Work, and Marital Conflict.* Lexington, MA: Lexington Books.

Schaie, Warner K., and Sherry L. Willis. 1986. *Adult Development and Aging.* Boston: Little Brown.

Schechter, Susan. 1982. *Women and Male Violence.* Boston, MA: South End Press.

Schulman, Mark. A. 1979. *A Survey of Spousal Violence Against Women in Kentucky.* Washington, DC: Law Enforcement Assistance Administration, U.S. Government Printing Office, Study No. 792701.

Schuman, Howard, and Michael P. Johnson. 1976. "Attitudes and Behavior." Pp. 161–207 in *Annual Review of Sociology* 2, edited by Alex Inkeles. Palo Alto: Annual Review, Inc.

Schumm, Walter R., Stephen R. Bollman, Anthony P. Jurich and Michael J. Martin. 1982. "Adolescent Perspectives on Family Violence." *Journal of Social Psychology* 117:153–154.

Schumm, Walter R., and Margaret A. Bugaighis. 1986. "Marital Quality over the Marital Career: Alternative Explanations." *Journal of Marriage and the Family* 48:165–168.

Schumm, Walter R., Anthony P. Jurich, Stephan R. Bollman, and Margaret A. Bugaighis. 1985. "His and Her Marriage Revisited." *Journal of Family Issues* 6:221–227.

Schumm, Walter R., Michael J. Martin, Stephan R. Bollman, and Anthony P. Jurich. 1982. "Classifying Family Violence: Whither the Woozle?" *Journal of Family Issues* 3:319–340.

Scott, Robert, and Alan Howard. 1970. "Models of Stress." Pp. 259–278 in *Social Stress*, edited by Sol Levine and Norman A. Scotch. Chicago: Aldine.

Sears, Robert R., Eleanor E. Maccoby, and Harry Levin. 1957. *Patterns of Child Bearing*. Evanston, IL: Row, Peterson and Co.

Sedgeley, J., and D. Lund. 1979. "Self-Reported Beatings and Subsequent Tolerance for Violence." *Public Date Use* 7:30–38.

Selye, Hans. 1966. *The Stress of Life*. New York: McGraw-Hill.

Sher, Kenneth J. 1985. "Subjective Effects of Alcohol: The Influence of Setting and Individual Differences in Alcohol Expectancies." *Journal of Studies on Alcohol* 46:137–146.

Sherman, Lawrence W., and Richard A. Berk. 1984. "The Minneapolis Domestic Violence Experiment." *Police Foundation Reports* April:1.

———. 1984. "The Specific Deterrent Effects of Arrest for Domestic Violence." *American Sociological Review* 49:261–272.

Sherman, Lawrence W. and Ellen G. Cohn. 1989. "The Impact Of Research On Legal Policy: The Minneapolis Domestic Violence Experiment." *Law and Society Review.* 23 (1):117–144.

Shields, Nancy M., and Christine R. Hanneke. 1981. "Patterns of Family and Non-Family Violence: An Approach to the Study of Violent Husbands." Paper presented at the National Conference for Family Violence Researchers, Durham, NH.

Shorter, Edward. 1975. *The Making of the Modern Family*. New York: Basic Books.

Shostrom, Everett L., and James Kavanaugh. 1971. *Between Man and Woman*. Los Angeles: Nash Publishing Co.

Shupe, L. M. 1954. "Alcohol and Crime." *Journal of Criminal Law, Criminology and Police Science* 44:661–664.

Sigelman, Carol K., Carol J. Berry, and Katharine A. Wiles. 1984. "Violence in College Students' Dating Relationships." *Journal of Applied Social Psychology* 5,6:530–548.

Silver, L., C. Dublin, and R. Lourie. 1971. "Agency Action and Interaction in Cases of Child Abuse." *Casework* 52:164–171.

Simmel, Georg. 1955. *Conflict and the Web of Group Affiliations*. Glencoe, IL: Free Press.

Simmons, B., E. Downs, M. Hurster, and M. Archer. 1969. "Child Abuse: Epidemiologic Study of Medically Reported Cases." *New York State Journal of Medicine* 66:2738–2788.

Singer, J. L. 1971. "The Influence of Violence Portrayed in Television or Motion Pictures upon Overt Aggressive Behavior." In *The Control of Aggression and Violence: Cognitive and Physiological Factors*, edited by J. L. Singer. New York: Academic Press.

Skimkin, D. B., G. J. Louie, and D. Frate. 1973. "The Black Extended Family: A Basic Rural Institution and a Mechanism of Urban Adaptation." Paper presented at the International Congress of Anthropological and Ethological Sciences, Chicago.

Skinner, A. E., and R. L. Castle. 1969. *Seventy-eight Battered Children: A Retrospective Study*. London: National Society for the Prevention of Cruelty to Children.

Smith, Christine & Murray A. Straus. 1988. *Cohabiting, Commitment And Social Control*. Unpublished manuscript.

Smith, Christine. 1988. "Status Discrepancies and Husband-to-Wife Violence." Paper presented at the 1988 meeting of the Eastern Sociological Society.

Smith, Michael D. 1986. "Effects of Question Format on the Reporting of Woman Abuse: A Telephone Survey Experiment." *Victimology*, Vol. 11.

———. 1985. "Woman Abuse: The Case for Surveys by Telephone." Toronto: York University. La Marsh Research Program on Violence. Report 12.

Smith, S. M. 1975. *The Battered Child Syndrome*. London: Butterworths.

Smith, S. M., R. Hanson, and S. Noble. 1973. "Parents of Battered Children: A Controlled Study." *British Medical Journal* 4:388–391.

Sobell, L. C., and M. B. Sobell. 1978. "Validity of Self-Reports in Three Populations of Alcoholics." *Journal of Consulting and Clinical Psychology* 46:901–907.

Sonkin, D. J., D. Martin, and L. E. Walker. 1985. *The Male Batterer: A Treatment Approach*. New York: Springer.

Sorenson, Susan, and Cynthia Telles. 1987. "Violence in Hispanic Families: Immigration Issues." Paper presented at the Research Conference on Violence and Homicide in the Hispanic Community, September 14–15, Los Angeles.

Spanier, Graham B. 1983. "Married and Unmarried Cohabitation in the United States: 1980." *Journal of Marriage and the Family* 45:277–288.

Sprey, Jetse 1969. "The Family as a System in Conflict." *Journal of Marriage and the Family* 31:699–706.

———. 1971. "On the Management of Conflict in Families." *Journal of Marriage and the Family* 33:722–732.

―――. 1972. "Family Power Structure: A Critical Comment." *Journal of Marriage and the Family* 34:235–238.

Stack, Carol B. 1970. "The Kindred of Viola Jackson: Residence and Family Organization of an Urban Black American Family." Pp. 203–312 in *Afro-American Anthropology: Contemporary Perspectives*, edited by Norman E. Whitten Jr., and John F. Szwed. New York: Free Press.

―――. 1974. *All Our Kin: Strategies for Survival in a Black Community.* New York: Harper and Row.

Stacy, W. A., and Anson Shupe. 1983. *The Family Secret: Domestic Violence in America.* Boston: Beacon Press.

Stafford, R., B. Backman, and P. Dibona. 1977. "Division of Labor Among Cohabiting and Married Couples." *Journal of Marriage and the Family* 39:43–57.

Staples, Robert. 1976a. *Introduction to Black Sociology.* New York: McGraw-Hill.

Staples, Robert. 1976b. "Race and Family Violence: The Internal Colonialism Perspective." Pp. 85–96 in *Crime and Its Impact on the Black Community*, edited by Lawrence E. Gary and Lee P. Brown. Washington, DC: Howard University, Institute for Urban Affairs and Development Center.

Staples, Robert, and Alfredo Mirande. 1980. "Racial and Cultural Variations among American Families: A Decennial Review of the Literature on Minority Families." *Journal of Marriage and the Family* 42:887–903.

Star, Barbara, Carol Clark, Karen Goetz, and Linda O'Malia. 1979. "Psychosocial Aspects of Wife Beating." *Social Casework* 37:479–487.

Stark, Evan. 1986. "Service Encounters of Victims and Perpetrators: A Conceptual Overview." Paper presented at the American Society of Criminology, Atlanta, GA.

Stark, Evan, and Anne Flitcraft. 1983. "What Factors Shape Professional and Social Responses?: Social Knowledge, Social Policy, and the Abuse of Women: The Case Against Patriarchal Benevolence." In *The Dark Side of Families: Current Family Violence Research*, edited by David Finkelhor, Richard J. Gelles, Gerald T. Hotaling, and Murray A. Straus. Newbury Park, CA: Sage Publications.

Stark, Evan, Anne Flitcraft, and W. Frazier. 1979. "Medicine and Patriarchal Violence: The Social Construction of a 'Private' Event." *International Journal of Health Services* 9:461–493.

Stark, Evan, Anne Flitcraft, D. Zuckerman, A. Grey, J. Robison, and W. Frazier. 1981. *Wife Abuse in the Medical Setting: An Introduction for Health Personnel.* Domestic Violence Monograph Series. No. 7. Rockville, MD: National Clearinghouse on Domestic Violence.

Stark, Rodney, and James McEvoy III. 1970. "Middle Class Violence." *Psychology Today* 4:52–65.

Starr, R. H., S. J. Ceresnie, and B. Steinlauf. 1978. "Social and Psychological Characteristics of Abusive Mothers.'' Paper presented at the meeting of the Eastern Psychological Association, Washington, DC.

Statistical Abstract of the United States. 1985. Washington, DC: U.S. Government Printing Office.

Steele, B. F., and C. B. Pollack. 1974. ''A Psychiatric Study of Parents Who Abuse Infants and Small Children.'' In *The Battered Child*, 2d ed., edited by R. E. Helfer and C. H. Kempe, Chicago: University of Chicago Press.

Steinglass, Peter, Donald I. Davis, and David Berenson. 1977. ''Observations of Conjointly Hospitalized 'Alcoholic Couples' During Sobriety and Intoxication: Implications for Theory and Therapy.'' *Family Process* 16:1–16.

Steinmetz, Suzanne K. 1971. ''Occupation and Physical Punishment: A Response to Straus.'' *Journal of Marriage and the Family* 33:664–666.

———. 1974. ''The Sexual Context of Social Research.'' *American Sociologist* 9:111–1116.

———. 1977. *The Cycle of Violence: Assertive, Aggressive, and Abusive Family Interaction.* New York: Praeger.

———. 1977. ''The Use of Force for Resolving Family Conflict: The Training Ground for Abuse.'' *Family Coordinator* 26:19–26.

———. 1977–1978. ''The Battered Husband Syndrome.'' *Victimology: An International Journal* 2:499–509.

———. 1978. ''Services to Battered Women: Our Greatest Need. A Reply to Field and Kirchner.'' *Victimology: An International Journal* 3:222–226.

Steinmetz, Suzanne K., and Murray A. Straus. 1974. ''General Introduction: Social Myth and Social System in the Study of Intra-Family Violence.'' Pp. 3–25 in *Violence in the Family*, edited by Suzanne K. Steinmetz and M. A. Straus. New York: Harper and Row.

———. 1974. *Violence in the Family.* New York: Harper and Row. (Originally published by Dodd, Mead, and Co.)

Stephens, Darrel W. 1977. ''Domestic Assault: The Police Response.'' In *Battered Women*, edited by M. Roy. New York: Van Nostrand-Reinhold Co.

Stets, Jan E. 1988. *Domestic Violence and Control.* New York: Springer-Verlag.

Stets, Jan E., and Maureen A. Pirog-Good. 1987. ''Violence in Dating Relationships.'' *Social Psychology Quarterly* 50:237–246.

———. 1988. ''Violence and Control in Dating Relationships.'' Unpublished manuscript.

Stets, Jan. E., and Murray A. Straus. 1989. ''Gender Differences in Reporting Marital Violence and Its Medical and Psychological Consequences.'' Chapter 9 in this book.

———. 1989. ''The Marriage License as a Hitting License: A Comparison of Assaults in Dating, Cohabiting, and Married Couples.'' Chapter 13 in this book.

Stolz, Lois M. 1967. *Influences on Parent Behavior*. Stanford: Stanford University Press.

Strasburg, P. A. 1978. *Violent Delinquents: A Report to the Ford Foundation from the Vera Institute of Justice*. New York: Monarch.

Straus, Jacqueline H., and Murray A. Straus. 1953. "Suicide, Homicide, and Social Structure in Ceylon." *American Journal of Sociology* 63:461–469.

Straus, Murray A. 1964. "Measuring Families." Chapter 10 in *Handbook of Marriage and the Family*, edited by Harold T. Christensen. Chicago: Rand McNally.

———. 1969. "Social Class and Farm-City Differences in Interaction with Kin in Relation to Societal Modernization." *Rural Sociology* 34:476–495.

———. 1970. "Methodology of a Laboratory Experimental Study of Families in Three Societies." In *Families in East and West*, edited by R. Hill and R. Konig. Paris: Mouton.

———. 1971. "Some Social Antecedents of Physical Punishment: A Linkage Theory Interpretation." *Journal of Marriage and the Family* 33:658–663. Also reprinted in *Violence in the Family*, edited by Suzanne K. Steinmetz, and M. A. Straus. 1974. New York: Harper and Row.

———. 1973. "A General Systems Theory Approach to a Theory of Violence Between Family Members." *Social Science Information* 12 (June): 105–125.

———. 1974. "Cultural and Social Organizational Influence on Violence Between Family Members." Pp. 53–69 in *Configurations: Biological and Cultural Factors in Sexuality and Family Life*, edited by Raymond Prince and Dorothy Barrier. Lexington, MA: Lexington Books—D.C. Heath.

———. 1974. "Leveling, Civility, and Violence in the Family." *Journal of Marriage and the Family* 36:13–29. Plus addendum in August 1974 issue.

———. 1976. "Sexual Inequality, Cultural Norms, and Wife-Beating." In *Victims and Society*, edited by Emilio C. Viano. Washington, DC: Visage Press. Also in *Victimology* 1 (Spring 1976): 54–76, and in *Women into Wives: The Legal and Economic Impact of Marriage*, edited by Jane Roberts Chapman and Margaret Gates. Sage Yearbooks in Women Policy Studies, vol. 2. Newbury Park, CA: Sage Publications, 1977.

———. 1977. "Normative and Behavioral Aspects of Violence Between Spouses: Preliminary Data on a Nationally Representative USA Sample." Paper presented at the Symposium on Violence in Canadian Society, Simon Fraser University (March).

———. 1977. "Societal Morphogenesis and Family Violence in Cross-Cultural Perspectives." In *Issues in Cross-Cultural Research*, edited by Leonore Loeb Adler, *Annals of the New York Academy of Sciences* 285:717–730.

————. 1977. "A Sociological Perspective on the Prevention and Treatment of Wifebeating." Pp. 194–238 in *Battered Women: A Psycho-Sociological Study of Domestic Violence*, edited by M. Roy. New York: Van Nostrand Reinhold.

————. 1977. "Wife-Beating: How Common, and Why?" *Victimology* 2:443–458. Also reprinted in Straus and Hotaling, 1980.

————. 1979. "Family Patterns and Child Abuse in a Nationally Representative American Sample." *Child Abuse and Neglect* 3:213–225.

————. 1979. "Measuring Intrafamily Conflict and Violence: The Conflict Tactics (CT) Scales." *Journal of Marriage and the Family* 41:75–88; and revised or in Chapter 3 in this book.

————. 1979. *Socioeconomic Status, Aggression, and Violence*. Durham: Family Research Laboratory, University of New Hampshire.

————. 1980a. "The Marriage License As a Hitting License: Evidence from Popular Culture, Law and Social Science." Chapter 3 in *The Social Causes of Husband-Wife Violence*, edited by Murray A. Straus and Gerald T. Hotaling. Minneapolis: University of Minnesota Press.

————. 1980b. "Social Stress and Marital Violence in a National Sample of American Families." Pp. 229–250 in *Forensic Psychology and Psychiatry*, edited by F. Wright, C. Bahn, and R. Rieber, *Annals of the New York Academy of Sciences* 347(1979):119–150.

————. 1980c. "Victims and Aggressors in Marital Violence." *American Behavioral Scientist* 23:681–704.

————. 1981. "Re-Evaluation of the Conflict Tactics Scale." Paper presented at the Second National Conference for Family Violence Researchers, Durham, NH, July. A revised and expanded version of this paper is Chapter 4 of this book.

————. 1981. "Societal Change and Change in Family Violence." Paper presented at the National Conference for Family Violence Researchers, University of New Hampshire, July 21–24.

————. 1983. "Ordinary Violence, Child Abuse, and Wife-Beating: What Do They Have in Common?" Pp. 213–234 in *The Dark Side of Families: Current Family Violence Research*, edited by D. Finkelhor, R. J. Gelles, G. T. Hotaling, and M. A. Straus. Newbury Park, CA: Sage Publications; and Chapter 23 in this book.

————. 1983. "Violence in the Family: 2. Wife Beating." Pp. 1629–1634 in *Encyclopedia of Crime and Justice*, edited by Sanford H. Kadish. New York: Free Press.

————. 1985. "Family Training in Crime and Violence." Chapter 10 in *Crime and the Family*, edited by Alan J. Lincoln and Murray A. Straus. Springfield, IL: Charles C. Thomas.

————. 1985. "The Index of Legitimate Violence." Durham: Family Research Laboratory, University of New Hampshire.

————. 1986a. "Domestic Violence and Homicide Antecedents." *Bulletin of the New York Academy of Medicine* 62:446–465.

———. 1986b. "Medical Care Costs of Intrafamily Assault and Homicide." *Bulletin of the New York Academy of Medicine* 62, 5:556–561.

———. 1987. "Primary Group Characteristics and Intra-family Homicide." Paper presented at the Third National Family Violence Research Conference, Durham, University of New Hampshire.

———. 1988. "Exchange and Power in Marriage in Cultural Context: Bombay and Minneapolis Comparisons." In *Family and Support Systems Across the Life Span*, edited by Suzanne K. Steinmetz. New York: Plenum.

———. 1988. "Measuring Psychological and Physical Abuse of Children with the Conflict Tactics Scales." Durham: Family Research Laboratory, University of New Hampshire.

———. 1989. "The Conflict Tactics Scales and Its Critics: An Evaluation and New Data on Validity and Reliability." Chapter 4 in this book.

Straus, Murray A., and Bruce W. Brown. 1978. *Family Measurement Techniques: Abstracts of Published Instruments, 1935–1974* (rev. ed.). Minneapolis: University of Minnesota Press.

Straus, Murray A., and Richard J. Gelles. 1980. *Physical Violence in American Families*. Interuniversity Consortium for Political and Social Research, Codebook 7733. Ann Arbor: Institute for Social Research, University of Michigan.

———. 1986. "Societal Change and Change in Family Violence from 1975 to 1985 as Revealed by Two National Surveys." *Journal of Marriage and the Family* 48:465–479.

———. 1988. "How Violent Are American Families? Estimates from the National Family Violence Resurvey and Other Studies." In *New Directions in Family Violence Research*, edited by Gerald T. Hotaling et al. Newbury Park, CA: Sage Publications; and Chapter 6 in this book.

———. 1988. "Violence in American Families: How Much is There and Why Does It Occur?" In *Families in Trouble*, edited by C. C. Chilman, F. Cox, and E. Nunnally. Newbury Park, CA: Sage Publications.

Straus, Murray A., Richard J. Gelles, and Suzanne K. Steinmetz. 1980. *Behind Closed Doors: Violence in the American Family*. New York: Doubleday/Anchor.

Straus, Murray A., and Gerald T. Hotaling. 1980. "Culture, Social Organization, and Irony in the Study of Family Violence." Pp. 3–22 in *The Social Causes of Husband-Wife Violence*, edited by Murray A. Straus and Gerald T. Hotaling. Minneapolis: University of Minnesota Press.

Straus, Murray A., and Gerald T. Hotaling (eds.). 1980. *The Social Causes of Husband-Wife Violence*. Minneapolis: University of Minnesota Press.

Straus, Murray A., and Glenda Kaufman Kantor. 1987. "Stress and Physical Child Abuse." In *The Battered Child*, 4th ed., edited by Ray E. Helfer and C. Henry Kempe. Chicago: University of Chicago Press.

Straus, Murray A., and Fumie Kumagai. 1980. "An Empirical Comparison of Eleven Methods of Constructing Indexes.'' Chapter 2 in *Indexing and Scaling for Social Science Research with SPSS*, book in preparation. A copy of this chapter available on request.

Straus, Murray A., and Alan J. Lincoln. 1985. ''A Conceptual Framework for Understanding Crime and the Family.'' In *Crime and the Family*, edited by A. J. Lindon and M. A. Straus. Springfield, IL: Charles C. Thomas, Publishers.

Strube, Michael J., and Linda S. Barbour. 1984. ''Factors Related to the Decision to Leave an Abusive Relationship.'' *Journal of Marriage and the Family* 46:837–844.

Sturgess, T., and K. Heal. 1967. ''Non-Accidental Injury to Children Under the Age of 17 (Res 663/2/25): A Study to Assess Current Probation Service Involvement with Cases of Non-Accidental Injury.'' London: Home Office Research Unit, House of Commons Select Committee on Violence in the Family, Session #350.

Suitor, J. Jill, and Karl Pillemer. 1987. ''The Presence of Adult Children: A Source of Stress for Elderly Couples' Marriages?'' *Journal of Marriage and the Family* 49:717–725.

———. 1988. ''Declining Health: A Factor in the Negative Relationship between Age and Domestic Violence?'' Durham: Family Research Laboratory, University of New Hampshire, mimeographed.

Sullivan, Lee. 1988. *Gender Differences in Physical and Psychological Injury from Spouse Assault*. Durham: University of New Hampshire. M.A. thesis.

Sussman, Marvin B. 1959. ''The Isolated Nuclear Family: Fact or Fiction?'' *Social Problems* 6:333–339.

Sykes, Gresham M., and David Matza. 1957. ''Techniques of Neutralization: A Theory of Delinquency.'' *American Sociological Review* 22:664–670.

Symonds, A. 1979. ''Violence Against Women: The Myth of Masochism.'' *American Journal of Psychotherapy* 33:161–173.

Szinovacz, Maximiliane E. 1983. ''Using Couple Data as a Methodological Tool: The Case of Marital Violence.'' *Journal of Marriage and the Family* 45:633–644.

Tavis, Carol, and Carole Offir. 1977. *The Longest War: Sex Differences in Perspective*. New York: Harcourt Brace Jovanovich.

Taylor, L., and E. H. Newberger. 1979. ''Child Abuse in the International Year of the Child.'' *New England Journal of Medicine* 301:1205–1212.

Taylor, Stuart P., and Kenneth E. Leonard. 1983. ''Alcohol and Human Physical Aggression.'' In *Aggression: Theoretical and Empirical Reviews*, vol. 2, edited by Russell G. Geen and Edward I. Donnerstein. New York: Academic Press.

Telch, C. F., and C. U. Lindquist. 1984. ''Violent Versus Non-Violent Couples: A Comparison of Patterns.'' *Psychotherapy* 21:242–248.

Thompson, L., and A. J. Walker. 1982. ''The Dyad as the Unit of Analysis:

Conceptual and Methodological Issues." *Journal of Marriage and the Family* 44:889–900.

Thorton, Arland, Duane F. Alwin, and Donald Camburn. 1983. "Causes and Consequences of Sex-Role Attitudes and Attitude Change." *American Sociology Review* 48:211–227.

Toby, Jackson. 1974. "Violence and the Masculine Ideal: Some Qualitative Data." Pp. 58–65 in *Violence in the Family*, edited by Suzanne Steinmetz and Murray A. Straus. New York: Harper and Row.

Toch, Hans. 1969. *Violent Men*. Chicago: Aldine.

Torres, Sara. 1987. "Hispanic-American Battered Women: Why Consider Cultural Differences?" *Response* 10:20–21.

Truninger, E. 1971. "Marital Violence: The Legal Solutions." *Hastings Law Review* 13:159–176.

Turbett, J. P., and R. O'Toole. 1980. "Physician's Recognition of Child Abuse." Paper presented at the annual meeting of the American Sociological Association, New York.

Turkewitz, H., and K. D. O'Leary. 1981. "A Comparative Outcome Study of Behavioral Marital Therapy and Communication Therapy." *Journal of Marital and Family Therapy* (April):159–169.

U.S. Bureau of Justice. 1974. *National Crime Survey Report* NCJ-96459. Washington, DC: U.S. Government Printing Office.

U.S. Department of Commerce. 1986. *Statistical Abstract of the United States, 106th ed.*, Washington, DC: U.S. Government Printing Office.

U.S. Department of Justice. 1975–1984. *FBI Uniform Crime Reports 1975–1984*. Washington, DC: U.S. Government Printing Office.

U.S. Department of Justice. 1980. *Intimate Victims: A Study of Violence Among Friends and Relatives*. Washington, DC: U.S. Government Printing Office.

U.S. Department of Justice. 1984. *Family Violence*. Washington, DC: Bureau of Justice Statistics.

U.S. Department of Justice. 1985. *Uniform Crime Reports: Crime in the United States, 1984*. Washington, DC: U.S. Government Printing Office.

U.S. Senate. 1973. Hearing Before the Subcommittee on Children and Youth of the Committee on Labor and Public Welfare. United States Senate, 93rd Congress, First Session on S.1191 Child Abuse Prevention Act. Washington, DC: U.S. Government Printing Office.

Van Hasselt, Vincent B., Randall L. Morrison, and Alan S. Bellock. 1985. "Alcohol Use in Wife Abusers and Their Spouses." *Addictive Behaviors* 10:127–135.

Verbrugge, Lois M. 1985. "Gender and Health: An Update on Hypotheses and Evidence." *Journal of Health and Social Behavior* 26:156–182.

Verhoff, J., and S. Feld. 1970. *Marriage and Work in America: A Study of Motives and Roles*. New York: Van Nostrand Reinhold.

Vernis, J. S. 1983. "Agreement Between Alcoholics and Relatives When

Reporting Follow-Up States." *International Journal of the Addictions* 18:891–894.

Walker, Lenore E. 1977–1978. "Battered Women and Learned Helplessness." *Victimology* 2:525–534.

———. 1978. "Treatment Alternatives for Battered Women." Pp. 143–174 in *The Victimization of Women*, edited by J. R. Chapman and M. Gates. Newbury Park, CA: Sage Publications.

———. 1979. *The Battered Woman*. New York: Harper and Row.

———. 1984. *The Battered Woman Syndrome*. New York: Springer Publishing Company.

Walters, D. R. 1975. *Physical and Sexual Abuse of Children*. Bloomington: Indiana University Press.

Warner, S. 1965. "Randomized Response: A Survey Technique for Eliminating Evasive Answer Bias." *Journal of the American Statistical Association* 60:63–69.

Warrior, Besty. 1982. *Battered Women's Directory*. 8th ed. Cambridge, MA: Betsy Warner, 46 Pleasant Street (privately published).

Washburn, C., and I. H. Frieze. 1981. "Methodological Issues in Studying Battered Women." Paper presented at the First National Conference for Family Violence Researchers, Durham, NH.

Wauchope, Barbara A., and Murray A. Straus. 1987. "Age, Class, and Gender Differences in Physical Punishment and Physical Abuse of American Children." Paper presented at the Third National Conference on Family Violence Research, University of New Hampshire, Durham, July 6–9.

Weber, Max. 1947. *The Theory of Social and Economic Organization*. New York: Oxford University Press.

Weiner, N. A., and M. E. Wolfgang. 1985. "The Extent and Character of Violent Crime in America, 1969 to 1982." In *American Violence and Public Policy*, edited by L. Curtis. New Haven, CT: Yale University Press.

Weis, Joseph G. 1989. "Issues in Family Violence Research Methodology and Design." In *Crime and Justice: An Annual Review of Research*, in press.

Weissman, M., and G. L. Klerman. 1977. "Sex Differences and the Epidemiology of Depression." *Archives of General Psychiatry* 34:98–111.

———. 1985. "Gender and Depression." *Trends in Neurosciences* 9:416–420.

Whitehurst, Robert N. 1974. "Violence in Husband-Wife Interaction." Pp. 75–81 in *Violence in the Family*, edited by S. Steinmetz and M. A. Straus. New York: Harper and Row.

Whiting, Bertrice. 1972. "Work and the Family: Cross-Cultural Perspectives." Proceedings of the Conference on Women, Resource for a Changing World, Cambridge, England.

Williams, J. E. 1972. "Treatment of Violence." *Medicine, Science and the Law* 12:269–274.

Williams, Kirk R., and Richard Hawkins. 1985. "Perceptual Research on General Deterrence: A Critical Review." *Law Society*, in press.

Wilson, James Q., and Richard J. Hernstein. 1985. *Crime and Human Nature*. New York: Simon and Schuster.

Wilt, G. M., J. D. Bannon, and R. K. Breedlove. 1977. *Domestic Violence and the Police: Studies in Detroit and Kansas City*. Washington, DC: Police Foundation.

Winkler, Iris, and William J. Doherty. 1983. "Communication Styles and Marital Satisfaction in Israeli and American Couples." *Family Process* 22:221–228.

Wolfe, D. A. 1985. "Child-Abusive Parents: An Empirical Review and Analysis." *Psychological Bulletin* 97:462–482.

Wolfe, Donald M. 1959. "Power and Authority in the Family." Pp. 75–81 in *Studies in Social Power*, edited by D. Cartwright. Ann Arbor: University of Michigan.

Wolfgang, Marvin E. 1956. "Husband-Wife Homicides." *Corrective Psychiatry and Journal of Social Therapy* 2:263–271. Reprinted in *Deviancy and the Family*, edited by C. D. Bryand. Philadelphia: F. A. Davis.

———. 1958. *Patterns of Criminal Homicide*. Philadelphia: University of Pennsylvania Press.

Wolfgang, Marvin E., and F. Ferracutti. 1967. *The Subculture of Violence: Towards an Integrated Theory in Criminology*. London: Tavistock.

Yarrow, M., P. Scott, L. DeLeeuw, and C. Heinig. 1962. "Child-Rearing in Families of Working and Non-Working Mothers." *Sociometry* 25:122–140.

Ybarra, Lea. 1982. "When Wives Work: The Impact on the Chicano Family." *Journal of Marriage and the Family* 44:169–178.

Yllo, Kersti A. 1978. "Nonmarital Cohabitation: Beyond the College Campus." *Alternative Lifestyles* 1:37–54.

———. 1980. "The Status of Women and Wife-Beating in the U.S." Unpublished dissertation, Department of Sociology, University of New Hampshire.

Yllo, Kersti A., and Murray A. Straus. 1981. "Interpersonal Violence Among Married and Cohabiting Couples." *Family Relations* 30:339–347.

———. 1983. "Physical Force by Any Other Name . . .: Quantitative Data, Qualitative Data, and the Politics of Family Violence Research." Pp. 277–288 in *The Dark Side of Families: Current Family Violence Research*, edited by David Finkelhor, Richard Gelles, Gerald Hotaling, and Murray Straus. Newbury Park, CA: Sage Publications.

———. 1984. "Patriarchy and Violence Against Wives: The Impact of Structural and Normative Factors." *Journal of International and Comparative Social Welfare* 1:16–29.

Young, D. M., E. G. Beier, P. Beier, and C. Barton. 1975. "Is Chivalry Dead?" *Journal of Communication* 28:57–64.

Young, Leontine R. 1963. *The Behavior Syndromes of Parents Who Neglect and Abuse Their Children*. Doctoral dissertation, Columbia University School of Social Work.

———. 1964. *Wednesday's Children: A Study of Child Neglect and Abuse*. New York: McGraw-Hill.

Zdep, S. M., and Isabelle N. Rhodes. 1976. "Making the Randomized Response Technique Work." *Public Opinion Quarterly* 40:531–537.

Ziegler, Edward. 1976. "Controlling Child Abuse in America: An Effort Doomed to Failure." Paper presented at the First National Conference on Child Abuse and Neglect, Atlanta, GA, January.

Index